PHYSICAL EDUCATION METHODS

Creating a quality lesson plan

W9-CFJ-465

KEEP IN MIND!

When developing and teaching a quality physical education program, the goal is to enhance the students' lives beyond just the physical fitness level. Your lesson plans should incorporate all eight of these elements to help students in the classroom and beyond.

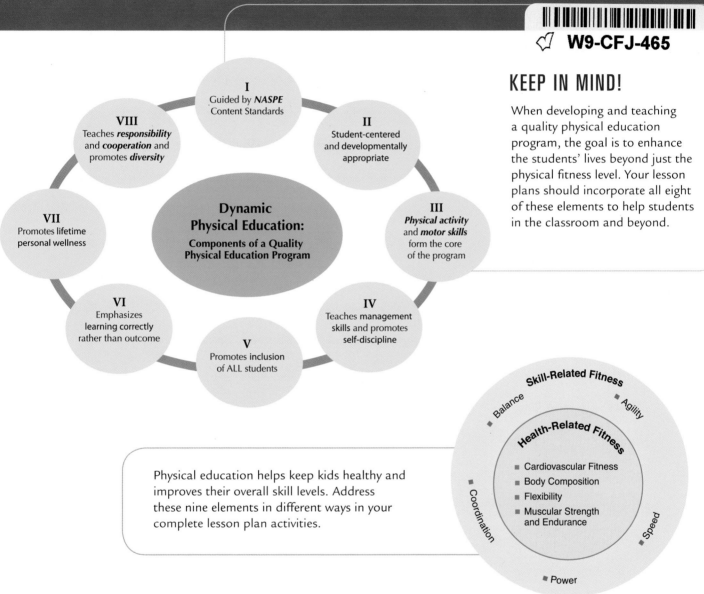

I Guided by *NASPE* Content Standards

II Student-centered and developmentally appropriate

III *Physical activity* and *motor skills* form the core of the program

IV Teaches management skills and promotes self-discipline

V Promotes inclusion of ALL students

VI Emphasizes learning correctly rather than outcome

VII Promotes lifetime personal wellness

VIII Teaches *responsibility* and *cooperation* and promotes *diversity*

Dynamic Physical Education: Components of a Quality Physical Education Program

Skill-Related Fitness
- Balance
- Agility
- Coordination
- Speed
- Power

Health-Related Fitness
- Cardiovascular Fitness
- Body Composition
- Flexibility
- Muscular Strength and Endurance

Physical education helps keep kids healthy and improves their overall skill levels. Address these nine elements in different ways in your complete lesson plan activities.

DON'T FORGET!

Have you met the National Standards for Physical Education? In creating a lesson plan, remember to focus on these six national standards. They are a necessary element of any physical education program.

A physically educated person:

Standard 1: Demonstrates competency in motor skills and movement patterns needed to perform a variety of physical activities.

Standard 2: Demonstrates understanding of movement concepts, principles, strategies, and tactics as they apply to the learning and performance of physical activities.

Standard 3: Participates regularly in physical activity.

Standard 4: Achieves and maintains a health-enhancing level of physical fitness.

Standard 5: Exhibits responsible personal and social behavior that respects self and others in physical activity settings.

Standard 6: Values physical activity for health, enjoyment, challenge, self-expression, and/or social interaction.

*Source: National Association for Sport and Physical Education (NASPE), Association of AAHPERD (www.aahperd.org/NASPE)

SAMPLE LESSON PLAN

1 OBJECTIVES
The specific instructional outcomes teachers expect students to accomplish as a product of their teaching. The objectives give direction to instructional goals for each individual lesson.

2 NASPE NATIONAL STANDARDS
The NASPE National Standards are the expected outcomes that school leaders and parents expect physical education to contribute to the school.

3 EQUIPMENT REQUIRED
Specific equipment needed for each lesson is listed.

Manipulative Skills Using Playground Balls
Level I – Week 5

① Instructional Objectives:
To perform combinations of locomotor and non-locomotor movements
To bounce, toss, and catch a ball in a stationary position
To roll, bounce, and throw a ball to a partner.

② NASPE National Standards:
Introductory Activity: 1
Fitness Activity: 1, 4, 6
Lesson Focus: 2, 3, 5
Game: 1, 2, 5

③ Equipment Required:
Tom-tom
Music for Fitness Challenges
One 8½" playground or vinyl covered foam ball for each student

④ Instructional Activities   **⑤ Teaching Hints**

Introductory Activity -- Combination Movements

1. Hop, turn around, and shake.
2. Jump, make a shape in the air, balance.
3. Skip, collapse, and roll.
4. Curl, roll, jump with a half turn.
5. Whirl, skip, sink slowly.
6. Hop, collapse, creep.
7. Kneel, sway, jump to feet.
8. Lift, grin, and roll.

Use the tom-tom to signal movement changes.

Challenge students to develop their personal combinations.

Create different movements using the same words.

Fitness Development Activity -- Fitness Challenges

Alternate locomotor movements with strength and flexibility challenges. Repeat the challenges as necessary.

Locomotor Movement: Walk for 30 seconds.

Flexibility and Trunk Development Challenges
1. Bend in different directions.
2. Stretch slowly and return quickly.
3. Combine bending and stretching movements.
4. Sway back and forth.
5. Twist one body part; add body parts.
6. Make your body move in a large circle.
7. In a sitting position, wave your legs at a friend; make circles with your legs.

Locomotor Movement: Skip for 30 seconds.

Upper Body Strength Challenges
In a push-up position, do the following challenges:
1. Lift one foot; the other foot.
2. Wave at a friend; wave with the other arm.
3. Scratch your back with one hand; use the other hand.
4. Walk your feet to your hands.
5. Turn over and face the ceiling; shake a leg; Crab Walk.
Locomotor Movement: Jog for 30 seconds.

Abdominal Development
From a supine position:
1. Lift your head and look at your toes.
2. Lift your knees to your chest.
3. Wave your legs at a friend.
From a sitting position:
1. Slowly lay down with hands on tummy.
2. Lift legs and touch toes.

Locomotor Movement: Run and leap for 30 seconds.

Tape alternating segments (30 seconds in length) of silence and music to signal duration of exercise. Music segments indicate doing the locomotor movements while intervals of silence announce performing the strength and flexibility challenges

Students select the fitness challenge they feel capable of performing. This implies that not all youngsters are required to do the same workload. Children differ and their ability to perform fitness workloads differs. Make fitness a personal challenge.

Since the range of activities is from easy to challenging, all youngsters can be successful. All youngsters should be able to do one of the fitness challenges.

Vary the locomotor movements as desired. Another alternative is to allow students to select the locomotor movement they would like to do.

1. Controlled Rolling and Handling in Place
   a. In a wide straddle position (other possible positions are seated with legs crossed or outstretched, and push-up position), place the ball on the floor, and roll it with constant finger guidance between and around the legs.
   b. Roll the ball in a figure-eight path in and out of the legs.
   c. Reach as far to the left as possible with the ball and roll it in front of you to the other side. Catch it as far to the right of the body as possible.
   d. Turn in place and roll the ball around with one hand in a large circle.
   e. Roll the ball around while lying on top of it. Roll the ball around the floor while on all fours, guiding it with the nose and forehead.
   f. With the back moderately bent, release the ball behind the head, let it roll down the back, and catch it with both hands.
   g. Make different kinds of bridges over the ball while using the ball as partial support for the bridge.
2. Bounce and Catch
   a. Two hands, one hand.
   b. Bounce at different levels.
   c. Bounce between legs.
   d. Close eyes and bounce.
   e. Dribble ball in a stationary and/or moving position.
   f. Dribble and follow the commands, such as move forward, backward, in a circle, or sideways, while walking, galloping, trotting, etc.
3. Toss and Catch
   a. Toss and catch, vary height.
   b. Add various challenges while tossing (i.e., touch floor, clap hands, turn, sit down, lie down).
   c. Toss and let bounce. Also add some challenges as above.
   d. Toss up and catch behind back--toss from behind back and catch in front of body.
   e. Create moving challenges (i.e., toss, run five steps and catch, toss and back up five hops and catch.)
4. Foot Skills
   a. Lift the ball up with both feet and catch. Both front and rear of body catch.
   b. From a sitting position with the ball between feet, toss it up, and catch with hands.
   c. Keep the ball in the air with feet and different body parts.

Give students two or three activities to practice so you have time to move and help youngsters. Alternate activities from each of the categories so students receive a variety of activities for practice.

Place emphasis on control of the ball. Students should be challenged to have "their ball under control."

An effective approach is to tell students to assume their feet are "glued to the floor." Tosses must be made directly overhead and caught without moving.

Tosses must begin at a low level and gradually be raised as students gain control of the ball. Little is gained by tossing the ball to a height where it can't be caught.

Game Activity

Teacher Ball
Supplies: A gray foam ball or rubber playground ball
Skills: Throwing, catching
One child is the teacher or leader and stands about 10 ft in front of three other students, who are lined up facing him. The object of the game is to move up to the teacher's spot by avoiding making bad throws or missing catches. The teacher throws to each child in turn, beginning with the child on the left, who must catch and return the ball. Any child making a throwing or catching error goes to the end of the line, on the teacher's right. Those in the line move up, filling the vacated space. If the teacher makes a mistake, he must go to the end of the line and the child at the head of the line becomes the new teacher. The teacher scores a point by remaining in position for three rounds (three throws to each child). After scoring a point, the teacher takes a position at the end of the line and another child becomes the teacher.

Scarecrow and the Crows
Supplies: None
Skills: Dodging, running
Children form a large circle representing the garden that is guarded by two or three players who are designated as scarecrows. Six to eight crows scatter on the outside of the circle, and the scarecrows assume a characteristic pose inside the circle. Players in the circle raise their joined hands and let the crows run through, into the garden, where they pretend to eat. The scarecrows try to tag the crows. The circle children help the crows by raising their joined hands and allowing them to leave the circle, but they try to hinder the scarecrows. If the scarecrows run out of the circle, all the crows immediately run into the garden and start to nibble at the vegetables while the circle children hinder the reentry of the scarecrows. After 15-20 seconds, new players are selected for the roles. If, after a reasonable period of time, the scarecrows have failed to catch any crows, change players.

4

INSTRUCTIONAL ACTIVITIES
Instructional activities and skill experiences to be taught in the lesson are delineated in proper developmental sequence. Four parts of instructional activities (Introductory Activity, Fitness Development Activity, Lesson Focus Activities, Closing Activity) are integral to a successful plan. See next page for more details.

5

TEACHING HINTS
Organization tips and important learning cues. How equipment is arranged, how students are grouped, and proper technique cues are examples of information placed in this column.

INSTRUCTIONAL PARTS OF THE LESSON PLANS

The four instructional parts of the lesson plan and major purposes of each are as follows:

Introductory Activity: Introductory activities change weekly and are used to physiologically prepare children for activity when entering the gymnasium or activity area. Activities used in this section demand little instruction and allow time to practice class management skills.

Fitness Development Activity: The fitness development section usually utilizes 7 to 8 minutes of a 30-minute lesson. The purpose of this section is to try to familiarize children with many different types of physical fitness activities. A second major focus for this part of the lesson is to develop positive attitudes toward physical activity. Discussion about the values of physical activity for a healthy lifestyle should be included here also.

Lesson Focus Activities: The purpose of the lesson focus is to teach toward global NASPE Physical Education Standards and specific lesson instructional objectives such as the development of eye-hand coordination, body management competency, and fundamental and specialized skills (e.g., folk dancing, shooting a basket, and catching an object). The lesson focus usually takes 15–20 minutes of the daily lesson depending on the length of the teaching period. Lesson focus activities are organized into units and vary in length depending on the developmental level of children. Lesson focus activities change weekly except when continuity of instruction demands longer units.

Content in each lesson is organized in a developmentally appropriate sequence, with the first activity being the easiest and the last activity the most difficult. This progression assures each student will begin with success, since all children are capable of performing the beginning activities. It offers a proper and safe sequence of activities for instruction.

Closing Activity: This part of the lesson plan takes place at the end of the lesson and utilizes the last 5–7 minutes of the period. The closing activity should help children feel positive about activity so they look forward to the next lesson. If a lesson has been physically demanding, a less active game or cooperative activity can be played and vice versa. When appropriate, a low key, relaxing activity can be used to help children unwind before returning to the classroom. At the end of the closing activity, it is appropriate to review and bring closure to what has been practiced and learned throughout the entire lesson.

OTHER RESOURCES:

FITNESS TESTS
www.cooperinst.org

STRENGTH TRAINING AND CHILDREN
www.acsm.org

YOUTH SPORTS
www.nays.org

PHYSICAL EDUCATION TEACHING AND CURRICULUM INFORMATION
www.pecentral.com,
www.pelinks4u.org,
www.pe4life.com,
www.masterteacher.com

ACTIVITY CUES
www.pecentral.org/climate/monicaparsonarticle.html

CLASSROOM MANAGEMENT
www.honorlevel.com/x47.xml

CHILDREN'S DISABILITIES INFORMATION
www.childrensdisabilities.info

NATIONAL STANDARDS
www.apens.org

EQUIPMENT
www.gophersport.com

PLAYGROUND SAFETY
www.playgroundsafety.org

Dynamic Physical Education Curriculum Guide:

Lesson Plans for Implementation

Seventeenth Edition

Robert P. Pangrazi
Arizona State University

PEARSON

Boston   Columbus   Indianapolis   New York   San Francisco   Upper Saddle River

Amsterdam   Cape Town   Dubai   London   Madrid   Milan   Munich   Paris   Montréal   Toronto

Delhi   Mexico City   São Paulo   Sydney   Hong Kong   Seoul   Singapore   Taipei   Tokyo

Executive Editor: Sandra Lindelof

Project Editor: Emily Portwood

Development Director: Barbara Yien

Editorial Assistant: Briana Verdugo

Managing Editor: Deborah Cogan

Associate Production Project Manager: Megan Power

Production Management and Composition: Integra

Main Text Cover Design: Derek Bacchus

Supplement Cover Design: 17th Street Studios

Manufacturing Buyer: Stacey Weinberger

Executive Marketing Manager: Neena Bali

Cover Photo Credit: Digital Vision/Getty Images

ISBN 10: 0-321-79355-2
ISBN 13: 978-0-321-79355-3

1 2 3 4 5 6 7 8 9 10 11—**BRR**—15 14 13 12 11

www.pearsonhighered.com

CONTENTS

DYNAMIC PHYSICAL EDUCATION CURRICULUM GUIDE
Lesson Plans for Implementation, 17th Edition

The *Dynamic Physical Education Curriculum Guide* is designed to complement the text *Dynamic Physical Education for Elementary School Children*, 17th Edition (*DPE*).[1] Information and activities presented in the *Curriculum Guide* are covered in greater detail in the text. The *DPE* curriculum guide forms a foundation for developing a program that is both personal and broad in scope. The curriculum can be personalized for each school by adding lessons that meet local needs and interests.

The NASPE *National Standards for Physical Education*[2] are listed for each of the four parts of the lesson. This helps teachers and administrators understand which national (institutional) standards the lesson is designed to facilitate and meet. Academic Integration Activities in each lesson plan help teachers integrate academic concepts into their instruction. Teaching such concepts in the physical education environment offers students a different mode for learning and supports the efforts of classroom teachers. It also creates goodwill when physical education teachers support the academic outcomes of the school.

Using the Lesson Plans

The lesson plans provide a guide for presenting movement experiences in a sequential and well-ordered manner. The lesson plans should be regarded as a roadmap for planning the physical education curriculum. The lessons can be modified and shaped into a personalized curriculum that meets the needs of individual teachers. Many teachers find it useful to write activity sequences and teaching hints on 4" by 6" note cards. The note cards relieve the burden of trying to remember the proper sequence of activities and the worry of forgetting key points of instruction.

Three complete sets of lesson plans are included to cover three major developmental levels. Yearly plans for each of the three developmental levels are listed at the start of each set of lessons. The following is a brief description of the curriculum by developmental level:

- *Developmental Level I.* For the majority of children, activities placed in Developmental Level I are appropriate for *kindergarten through second grade* children. Learner characteristics in Developmental Level I make it necessary to create a positive instructional learning environment. By stressing the joy and rewards of physical activity, behaviors can be developed that last a lifetime. The majority of activities for younger children are individual in nature and center on learning movement concepts through theme development. Children learn movement principles and body management skills at this level.
- *Developmental Level II.* Developmental Level II activities are appropriate for the majority of *third and fourth grade* children. However, because of ability and maturity

---

[1] Pangrazi, R. P. (2013). *Dynamic physical education for elementary school children* (17th ed.). San Francisco: Pearson.
[2] National Association for Sport and Physical Education. (2004). *Moving into the future: National standards for physical education* (2nd ed.). Reston, VA: Author.

differences, it is common to find youngsters who are performing at Level I or Level III. During Developmental Level II, refinement of fundamental skills and initial specialized skills is emphasized. Practicing a variety of manipulative skills enhances visual-tactile coordination. Children are given the opportunity to explore, experiment, and create activities without fear. Students are taught the how and why of activity patterns. Cooperation with peers is encouraged with more emphasis placed on group and team play. Initial instruction in sport skills begins in Developmental Level II. Sport lead-up activities are utilized so youngsters can apply newly learned skills in a small-group setting.

- *Developmental Level III.* Developmental Level III activities shift toward specialized skills and sport activities. The majority of activities at this level are used with *fifth and sixth grade* students. Football, basketball, softball, track and field, volleyball, and hockey are added to the sport offerings. Students continue learning and improving sport skills while participating in cooperative sport lead-up games. Less emphasis is placed on movement concept activities and a larger percentage of instructional time is devoted to manipulative activity. Adequate time is set aside for the rhythmic program, body management skills, and gymnastics. Fitness routines are offered with instruction focused on helping students make decisions about personal approaches to maintaining fitness levels.

The number references included with the dance activities are for music from Wagon Wheel Records, a company the authors have recommended as a reliable source for music accompaniment:

Wagon Wheel Records
16812 Pembrook Lane
Huntington Beach, CA 92649
Phone/Fax: (714) 846-8169
Website: www.wagonwheelrecords.net
E-mail: info@wagonwheelrecords.net

The music sets they have available are created specifically for physical education movement patterns and dance. The code included with each dance indicates if the music is on CD (WWCD) or cassette tape (WWC). The catalogue number (such as -572) can help identify the music when ordering from the company.

Instructional Elements of the Lesson Plans

Each lesson plan is divided into four instructional elements as described in Chapter 3 of *DPE*. Each weekly lesson plan offers enough activities for about one week of instruction when classes meet four to five times per week. Since few schools have physical education on a daily basis, each lesson contains more content than necessary for most situations. **It is better to teach a few things well than to try and cover all the activities listed in the lesson plans.** Many factors dictate how many activities can be covered and it was never the intent to include exactly the right number of activities for all situations. When more activities are needed, refer to *DPE*. Briefly, the four instructional parts of the lesson plan and major purposes for each are as follows:

1. **Introductory Activity**: Introductory activities change weekly and are used to physiologically prepare children for activity when entering the gymnasium or activity area. Activities used in this section demand little instruction and allow time to practice class management skills. (Descriptions of introductory activities can be found in *DPE*, Chapter 16.)

2. **Fitness Development Activity**: The Fitness Development section usually utilizes 7 to 8 minutes of a 30-minute lesson. The purpose of this section is not to try to "whip children into shape," but rather to familiarize them with many different types of physical fitness activities. A second major focus for this part of the lesson is to develop positive attitudes toward physical activity. Discussions about the values of physical activity for a healthy life style should be included here also. (Comprehensive coverage of physical activity and fitness is found in *DPE*, Chapters 12, 13, and 14.)

3. **Lesson Focus Activities**: The purpose of the lesson focus is to teach toward global NASPE Physical Education Standards and specific lesson instructional objectives such as the development of eye-hand coordination, body management competency, and fundamental and specialized skills (e.g., folk dancing, shooting a basket, and catching an object). The lesson focus usually takes 15–20 minutes of the daily lesson depending on the length of the teaching period. Lesson focus activities are organized into units and vary in length depending on the developmental level of children. Lesson focus activities change weekly except when continuity of instruction demands longer units.

    Content in each lesson is organized in a developmentally appropriate sequence, with the first activity being the easiest and the last activity the most difficult. Instruction starts with the first activity. This progression assures each student will begin with success, since all children are capable of performing the beginning activities. It offers a proper and safe sequence of activities for instruction. Developmentally mature children are allowed to progress farther along the continuum of activities than less capable children.

4. **Closing Activity**: This part of the lesson plan takes place at the end of the lesson and utilizes the last 5–7 minutes of the period. The closing activity includes low organization games, sport lead-up activities, and cooperative activities. The closing activity should help children feel positive about activity so they look forward to the next lesson. If a lesson has been physically demanding, a less active game or cooperative activity can be played and vice versa. When appropriate, a low-key, relaxing activity can be used to help children unwind before returning to the classroom. At the end of the closing activity, it is appropriate to review and bring closure to what has been practiced and learned throughout the entire lesson.

Components of the Lesson Plans

Each lesson plan includes the following components:

1. **Objectives**: This category lists the specific instructional outcomes teachers expect students to accomplish as a product of their teaching. The objectives give direction to instructional goals for each individual lesson.
2. **NASPE National Standards:** The NASPE national standards are the expected outcomes that school leaders and parents expect physical education to contribute to the school.
3. **Equipment Required:** Specific equipment needed for each lesson is listed.
4. **Instructional Activities:** Instructional activities and skill experiences to be taught in the lesson are delineated in proper developmental sequence.
5. **Teaching Hints:** This section includes organization tips and important learning cues. How equipment is arranged, how students are grouped, and proper technique cues are examples of information placed in this column.

In addition to these standard components, this edition of the *Curriculum Guide* also includes lesson plan numbers that look like this **LP 12**, numbered 1–119. These numbers are included so that activities listed in the *DPE* book can be easily found and identified within the lesson plans in this *Curriculum Guide*.

A Note of Appreciation

Deb Pangrazi, Elementary Physical Education Supervisor for the Mesa (Arizona) Public Schools, gave much direction and feedback about proper instructional sequences and the addition of academic integration. A warm note of thanks goes to Connie Orlowicz, Arizona State University; Don Hicks, St. Francis Episcopal Day School (Houston); Nicki Rippee, Abilene Christian University; and Carole Casten, CSU–Dominguez Hills for their contributions. The professionalism of all these individuals is unparalleled.

SELF-EVALUATION GUIDE

The following points can be used to evaluate your instructional effectiveness.

1. Did you prepare ahead of time? Mental preparation prior to a lesson assures that flow and continuity occur in a lesson.

2. Did you understand the "whys" of your lesson? Knowing why you are teaching something. will give you greater strength and conviction in your presentation.

3. Was equipment arranged prior to your class? Proper equipment placement reduces management time and allows more time for instruction and practice.

4. Did you constantly move and reposition yourself during the lesson? Moving allows you to be close to more students so you can reinforce and help them. It usually reduces behavior problems.

5. Did you keep alert for children who are having trouble performing the activities? Youngsters want to receive relevant but subtle help.

6. Did you tell your class what your instructional goals were for the lesson? Students will be more focused when they know what they are supposed to learn.

7. Did you teach with enthusiasm and energy? Your energy and zest will rub off on students.

8. Did you use praise when youngsters made an effort or improved? Saying something positive to children increases their desire to perform at a higher level.

9. Did you give sufficient attention to the development of personalization and creativity?

10. Did you teach students to be responsible for learning? Students need to learn self-direction skills. Take time for such learning.

11. Did you teach for quality of movement or just offer a large quantity of activities in an attempt to keep students motivated? Repetition is an important part of skill learning and a component of quality instruction.

12. Did you bring closure to your lesson? This gives you feedback about the effectiveness of your instruction. Use methods of closure that give you information about all students.

13. Did you evaluate the utility of activities you presented? Try to find ways to modify activities to better contribute to educational outcomes.

14. Did you evaluate how you handled discipline problems? What are some ways you could handle situations differently or better in the future?

Try keeping a portfolio related to your instruction. Write down personal growth indicators and situations that make you feel your students are learning. Evaluation is a dynamic and ongoing process.

DPE CURRICULUM GUIDE – LESSON PLANS
Developmental Level I
With Instructional and Academic Integration Concepts

WEEK	INTRODUCTORY ACTIVITY	FITNESS DEVELOPMENT ACTIVITY	LESSON FOCUS ACTIVITY	CLOSING ACTIVITY	PAGE
1	Move & Freeze on Signal	Fitness Challenges	Orientation and Class Management Activities	Toe to Toe Whistle Mixer	8
	Estimation of time *Spatial awareness*	*Body part identification* *Counting patterns* *Contrasting terms*	*Grouping*	*Body part identification* *Grouping* *Center of area* *Counting*	LP 1
2	Following Activity	Four Corners Movement	Manipulative Skills Using Hoops	Animal Tag Bottle Bat Ball Pigs Fly	10
	Categorization *Grouping*	*Reading signs* *Geometric shape recognition* *Patterning* *Short/long side of rectangle* *Recognizing order of sequence*	*Jumping & hopping patterns* *Vocabulary (inside/outside, in front of/ behind)* *Prediction* *Skip counting*	*Categorization* *Parallel lines* *Estimation*	LP 2
3	Group Over & Around	Astronaut Exercises	Throwing Skills (1)	Aviator Sneak Attack	12
	Ratio (50% = ½) *Estimation (how many times)*	*Perimeter* *CW & CCW* *Geometric shape recognition*	*Sequence of steps* *Vocabulary (velocity/accuracy)* *Letter recognition* *Following a checklist*	*Parallel lines* *Weather disturbances* *Listening skills*	LP 3
4	Bend, Stretch, Shake	Fitness Games & Challenges	Manipulative Skills Using Beanbags	Midnight Leap the Brook	14
	Body part identification *Right & left concepts* *Upper & lower* *Number recognition*	*Counting patterns* *Sorting* *Body part identification*	*Body part identification* *Right & left* *Directional cues* *Sequencing patterns* *¼, ½, ¾ and full turns*	*Time recognition* *Prediction* *Parallel lines*	LP 4
5	Combination Movements	Fitness Challenges	Manipulative Skills Using Playground Balls	Teacher Ball Scarecrow & Crows	16
	Patterns *Action verbs*	*Sorting exercises* *Body part identification* *Counting patterns* *Contrasting terms*	*Spatial awareness* *Sequencing of steps* *Midpoint* *Right & left concepts* *¼, ½, ¾, & full turns* *Degrees (90˚, 180˚)*	*Right & left concepts* *Ordinal numbers* *Circumference*	LP 5

WEEK	INTRODUCTORY ACTIVITY	FITNESS DEVELOPMENT ACTIVITY	LESSON FOCUS ACTIVITY	CLOSING ACTIVITY	PAGE
6	European Running	Jump Rope Exercises	Movement Skills (1) Walking, Body ID and Personal Space	Change Sides Where's My Partner? Colors/Numbers/ Shapes/Coins	18
	Geometric shapes *Letter recognition* *CW & CCW* *Steady beat* *Count every 4th beat* *Patterns*	*Vocabulary (isometrics – names and muscles)* *Number & shape recognition*	*Geometric shape recognition* *Contrasting terms* *Body part identification* *Spatial awareness*	*Parallel lines* *Spatial awareness* *Match color name with color, number name with ordinal number, geometric shape name with shape, coin name with coin equivalent*	LP 6
7	Countdown	Animal Movements & Fitness Challenges	Gymnastics Skills (1)	Circle Straddle Ball Statues Soap Bubbles	21
	Skip counting *Counting forward & backward* *Odds & evens*	*Reading signs* *Patterns (a/b, hands/feet)* *Animal recognition* *Skip counting*	*Unilateral movements* *Directions (N/S/E/W)* *Shape recognition* *Momentum*	*Shape recognition* *Less than (space)* *Cause & effect* *Diameter/radius/ circumference* *Wide/narrow*	LP 7
8	Run, Stop, Pivot	Astronaut Exercises	Movement Skills (2) Jumping, Tossing, & Moving in Space	Fire Fighter Animal Tag Sneak Attack	24
	Spatial awareness *¼ & ½ turns* *Degrees (90° & 180°)* *CW & CCW*	*Grouping* *Perimeter* *CW & CCW* *Geometric shapes*	*Spatial awareness* *Directional cues* *Right/left concepts* *Opposites* *Geometric shapes* *Letter recognition*	*Circumference* *CW & CCW* *Habitat of animal* *Animal recognition* *Beginning letter sounds* *Counting*	LP 8
9	Tag Games	Fitness Challenges	Kicking, Trapping, Bowling, & Rolling	Change Sides Musical Ball Pass	27
	Grouping *Body part identification* *Skip counting* *Quadrants* *Color recognition* *Shape recognition*	*Sorting exercises* *Body part identification* *Counting patterns* *Contrasting terms*	*45° angle* *Contrasting/Opposition* *Body part identification* *Prediction* *Grouping* *Shape recognition* *Vocabulary*	*Parallel lines* *Spatial awareness* *Shape recognition* *Passing patterns*	LP 9
10	Magic Number Challenges	Mini-Challenge Course	Fundamental Skills Using Parachute Activities	May I Chase You? Tommy Tuckers Land Colors/Numbers/ Shapes/Coins	29
	Number patterns *Missing numbers* *Factors* *Sequencing*	*Over/under/around* *Reading signs* *CW & CCW* *Number patterns* *Following a course*	*Contrasting terms* *Counting steps* *Circumference/diameter/ radius* *Segments*	*Match color name with color, number name with ordinal number, geometric shape name with shape*	LP 10

WEEK	INTRODUCTORY ACTIVITY	FITNESS DEVELOPMENT ACTIVITY	LESSON FOCUS ACTIVITY	CLOSING ACTIVITY	PAGE
11	Ponies in the Stable	Astronaut Exercises	Recreational Activities	Recreational Activities	31
	Speed variations *Shape recognition* *Skip counting*	*Perimeter* *CW & CCW* *Geometric shape recognition*	*Reading signs* *Quadrants* *Addition (scoring)*	*Reading signs* *Quadrants* *Addition (scoring)*	LP 11
12	Run & Assume Shape	Walk, Trot, Jog	Walking/Jogging Skills	Low Organization Games	32
	Shape recognition *Antonyms (opposites)* *Patterns* *Skip counting*	*Accelerate/decelerate* *Stop light application* *CW & CCW* *Geometric shape recognition*	*Perimeter* *Vocabulary* *Counting steps (w/ pedometer)*		LP 12
13	Simple Games	Parachute Fitness	Rhythmic Movement Skills (1)	Squirrel in the Trees Stop Ball	34
	Body part identification *Spatial awareness* *Grouping*	*CW & CCW* *Skip counting* *Segments* *Level identification (high, medium, low)*	*Cultural awareness* *Sequence & patterns* *Body part identification* *Directional movements* *Listening comprehension* *Grouping*	*Grouping* *CW & CCW*	LP 13
14	Crossing the River	Circuit Training	Fundamental Skills Using Long Jump Ropes	Ball Passing Hot Potatoes Aviator	38
	Spatial awareness *Parallel lines*	*CW & CCW* *Reading signs* *Counting (w/ flexibility ex.)* *Grouping* *Choral rhyming*	*Grouping* *Horizontal & vertical* *Pendulum swing* *360°* *Rhythmic turning* *Choral response* *Time concepts*	*Grouping* *Circumference of circle* *CW & CCW* *Adding of scores* *Weather disturbances* *Parallel lines*	LP 14
15	Popcorn	Mini-Challenge Course	Gymnastics Skills (2)	Where's My Partner? Up Periscope Change Sides	40
	Opposites *Spatial awareness*	*Over, under & around concepts* *Reading signs* *CW & CCW* *Counting (w/ flex ex)* *Following a course*	*Patterning (animal walks)* *Sequencing movements* *Balance* *Body part identification*	*Matching number name with ordinal number, coin with value, color with name* *Parallel lines*	LP 15
16	Drill Sergeant	Mini-Challenge Course	Rhythmic Movement Skills (2)	Skunk Tag Aviator Right Angle	43
	Grouping *Ordinal numbers* *Reading instructional card*	*Over, under & around concepts* *Reading signs* *CW & CCW* *Following a course*	*Cultural awareness* *Sequence & patterns* *Right & left movements* *Listening comprehension* *Rhythmic counting*	*Sorting* *Weather terminology* *Parallel lines* *90° angle* *Directions (N/S/E/W)*	LP 16

WEEK	INTRODUCTORY ACTIVITY	FITNESS DEVELOPMENT ACTIVITY	LESSON FOCUS ACTIVITY	CLOSING ACTIVITY	PAGE
17	Move & Perform Task on Signal	Four Corners Fitness	Throwing Skills (2)	Charlie Over the Water Circle Straddle Ball Flowers and Wind	47
	Skip counting *Discriminating sounds*	*Reading signs* *Geometric shape recognition* *Patterning* *Short/long side of a rectangle* *Recognizing order of sequence*	*Sequencing of steps* *Velocity vs. Accuracy* *Letter recognition* *Following a checklist*	*Recognition of flowers* *Distance recognition* *Wide/narrow* *Geometric shape recognition* *Grouping* *Parallel lines*	LP 17
18	Activity with Playground Balls	Fitness Games & Challenges	Manipulative Skills - Basketball Related	Blindfolded Duck Cat & Mice Freeze	49
	Patterns	*Counting (w/ flex ex)* *Sorting* *Body part identification*	*Sequencing of steps* *Midpoint* *Right & left concepts*	*Listening & comprehension skills* *CW & CCW* *Geometric shape recognition* *Perimeter* *Moving inside area of a shape*	LP 18
19	Marking	Parachute Fitness	Movement Skills (3) Sliding, Galloping, Hoops, & Movement Combinations	Corner Spry Hot Potato Popcorn	51
	Body part identification *Spatial awareness*	*CW & CCW* *Skip counting* *Segments of a circle* *Level identification (high, medium, low)*	*Movement patterns* *Combinations* *Right & left* *Body part identification*	*Quadrants* *Listening skills* *Predicting numbers* *CW & CCW* *Temperature* *Acceleration*	LP 19
20	New Leader Warm-up	Jump Rope Exercises	Fundamental Skills Using Benches	Bottle Kick Ball Hill Dill Pigs Fly	54
	Grouping *Ordinal numbers* *Shape recognition*	*Vocabulary* *Isometrics (names of muscles)* *Number & shape recognition*	*Reading signs* *Dismounts (degrees & fractions of turns)* *Sequencing and patterns* *Ordinal numbers*	*Choral response* *Parallel lines* *Circumference of a circle* *45˚angle of kick*	LP 20
21	Countdown	Walk, Trot, Jog	Movement Skills (4) Skipping, Scoops, Leading & Body Support	Flowers and Wind Mousetrap	56
	Skip counting *Counting forward & backward* *Odds & evens*	*Stop lights* *Acceleration/deceleration* *CW & CCW* *Geometric shapes* *Factors (walk 5, trot 10, jog 15)*	*Number recognition* *CW & CCW* *Patterns* *Prediction* *Body part identification*	*Parallel lines* *Grouping* *Syllable (2-lips = tulips)*	LP 21

WEEK	INTRODUCTORY ACTIVITY	FITNESS DEVELOPMENT ACTIVITY	LESSON FOCUS ACTIVITY	CLOSING ACTIVITY	PAGE
22	Tag Games	Fitness Challenges	Movement Skills (5) Hopping, Hoops, & Body Shapes	Rollee Pollee Stop Ball	58
📖	*Grouping Sorting Spatial awareness Quadrants Color & shape recognition*	*Sorting exercises Body part identification Counting patterns Contrasting terms*	*Number sequence Shape recognition Opposites Letter recognition*	*Circumference Distinguishing between rolling throwing bouncing Dodging CW & CCW*	LP 22
23	Movement Varieties	Circuit Training	Movement Skills (6) and Concepts Using Jump Rope Patterns	Change Sides Where's My Partner? Colors	61
📖	*Shape Recognition Vocabulary (high, medium, low)*	*CW & CCW Reading signs Counting (w/ flexibility ex.) Grouping Choral rhyming*	*Geometric shapes Letter recognition Small word recognition Number recognition Math problems (with rope patterns)*	*Color recognition Coin value recognition Parallel lines Spatial awareness*	LP 23
24	Airplanes	Astronaut Exercises	Partner Manipulative Activities Using Balls	Animal Tag Aviator Toe to Toe	63
📖	*CW & CCW Listening skills*	*Grouping Perimeter CW & CCW Geometric shapes*	*Grouping Sequencing steps Midpoint Right & left*	*Body part identification Weather disturbances Parallel lines Animal recognition*	LP 24
25	Secret Movement	Fitness Games and Challenges	Fundamental Skills Using Jumping Boxes	Squirrel in the Trees Stop Ball	65
📖	*Logical thinking Prediction Reading signs*	*Counting (w/ flexibility ex.) Sorting Body part identification*	*Dismounts (degrees & fraction) Reading signs*	*Grouping CW & CCW*	LP 25
26	Creative and Exploratory Opportunities	Animal Movements & Fitness Challenges	Movement Skills (7) Twisting, Turning, Stretching/Relaxing	Midnight Twins (Triplets) Up Periscope	67
📖	*Quadrants*	*Reading signs Patterns (a/b, hand/feet) Animal recognition Skip counting*	*Opposites CW & CCW*	*Time recognition Number patterns Sequencing*	LP 26
27	New Leader Warm-up	Jump Rope Exercises	Rhythmic Movement Skills (3)	Jack Frost & Jane Thaw Marching Ponies Tag Games	70
📖	*Grouping Ordinal numbers Shape recognition*	*Isometrics exercises (names of muscles) Number & shape recognition*	*Cultural awareness Sequencing patterns Body part identification Grouping Rhythmic counting*	*Cause & effect Body part identification Counting Prediction Adjectives*	LP 27

WEEK	INTRODUCTORY ACTIVITY	FITNESS DEVELOPMENT ACTIVITY	LESSON FOCUS ACTIVITY	CLOSING ACTIVITY	PAGE
28	Body Part Identification	Parachute Fitness	Gymnastics Skills (3)	Charlie Over the Water Circle Straddle Ball Flowers and Wind	73
	Body part identification *Sorting*	*CW & CCW* *Skip counting* *Segments of a circle* *Level identification (high, medium, low)*	*Grouping* *Time recognition (set mats up like a clock)*	*Flower recognition* *Distance recognition* *Wide/narrow* *Geometric shape recognition* *Grouping* *Parallel lines*	LP 28
29	Locomotor Movements with Equipment	Four Corners Fitness	Individual Rope Jumping Skills	Tommy Tucker's Land Change Sides	76
	Directional cues *Spatial awareness* *Number patterns*	*Reading signs* *Geometric shape recognition* *Patterns* *Short/long side of a rectangle* *Sequencing patterns*	*Skip counting* *Slow time/fast time* *Patterns (jump/bounce, jump/bounce = slow time)*	*Choral rhyme response* *Parallel lines* *Scoring with bean bags each color has a different value* *Spatial awareness*	LP 29
30	Activity Using Hoops	Walk, Trot, & Jog	Movement Skills (8) Bending, Stretching, & Weight Transfer	Marching Ponies Cat & Mice	78
	Sequencing patterns *Prediction*	*Traffic light recognition* *Acceleration & deceleration* *CW & CCW* *Geometric shape recognition* *Factors (walk 5, trot 10, jog 15)*	*CW & CCW* *Skip counting* *Segments* *Level identification (high, medium, low)* *Contrasting terms*	*Counting* *Prediction* *Adjectives* *Geometric shapes* *Perimeter*	LP 30
31	Locomotor Movement Variations	Animal Movements & Fitness Challenges	Movement Skills (9) Leaping, Levels, and Speed	Mix & Match Colors	80
	Body part identification *Accelerate & decelerate* *Shape recognition*	*Reading signs* *Patterns* *Animal recognition* *Skip counting*	*Spatial awareness* *Height vs. Distance* *Accelerate & decelerate* *Geometric shapes* *Opposite movements* *Letter recognition*	*Matching number name with ordinal number* *Coin recognition* *Number recognition* *Color recognition* *Geometric shapes* *Spatial awareness*	LP 31
32	Ponies in the Stable	Parachute Fitness	Rhythmic Movement Skills (4)	Circle Stoop Blindfolded Duck	82
	Speed variations *Shape recognition* *Skip counting*	*CW & CCW* *Skip counting* *Segments of a circle* *Level identification (high, medium, low)*	*Cultural awareness* *Sequence & patterns* *Body part identification* *Listening comprehension* *Grouping* *Rhythmic counting*	*Listening skills* *CW & CCW* *Perimeter* *Moving inside the area of a shape*	LP 32

WEEK	INTRODUCTORY ACTIVITY	FITNESS DEVELOPMENT ACTIVITY	LESSON FOCUS ACTIVITY	CLOSING ACTIVITY	PAGE
33	Locomotor Movements & Freeze	Fitness Challenges	Fundamental Skills Using Individual Mats	Sneak Attack Mat Games	86
📖	*Spatial awareness*	*Sorting exercises* *Body part identification* *Counting patterns* *Contrasting terms*	*Action verbs* *Perimeter* *Patterning on & off the mat activities* *Letter recognition*	*Listening skills* *Counting* *Spatial awareness*	LP 33
34	Airplanes	Astronaut Exercises	Fundamental Skills Using Balance Beams	Toe to Toe Mousetrap Aviator	89
📖	*CW & CCW* *Listening skills*	*Grouping* *Perimeter* *CW & CCW* *Geometric shapes*	*Grouping* *Sequencing* *Dismounts (degrees & fractions)*	*Body part identification* *Circumference of a circle* *Weather disturbances* *Parallel lines*	LP 34
35	Movement Varieties	Circuit Training	Movement Skills (10) Running and Racquet Skills	Rollee Pollee Mix & Match	91
📖	*Shape recognition* *Vocabulary (low, medium, high)*	*CW & CCW* *Reading signs* *Grouping* *Choral rhyming*	*Contrasting terms* *Sequencing patterns*	*Circumference* *Dodging* *Matching number name with ordinal number, coin with value*	LP 35
36	Run & Assume Shape	Walk, Trot, & Jog	Movement Skills (11) Pushing Pulling, & Rope Jumping	Change Sides Bottle Bat Ball	94
📖	*Opposites & antonyms* *Shape recognition* *Skip counting* *Patterns*	*Stop lights* *Acceleration/deceleration* *CW & CCW* *Geometric shape recognition*	*Opposites* *Degrees (angles)* *Sequencing* *Vertical/horizontal*	*Parallel lines*	LP 36
Alternate Lesson 1	Use the introductory activity from the lesson that was replaced.	Use the fitness activity from the lesson that was replaced.	Fundamental Skills Using Climbing Ropes	Skunk Tag Aviator	97
📖			*Patterns (hands/legs)* *Hanging with leg parallel to ground* *Legs perpendicular to rope* *Moving in a vertical plane*	*Weather terminology* *Parallel lines* *90°angle* *Directions (N/S/E/W)*	LP 37
Alternate Lesson 2	Use the introductory activity from the lesson that was replaced.	Use the fitness activity from the lesson that was replaced.	Fundamental Skills using Climbing Walls	Who's Leading Is it Raining?	99
📖			*Moving in different planes* *Climbing terminology* *Vertical/transverse*	*Cooperative problem solving* *Weather terminology* *Learning body parts*	LP 38

DPE Curriculum Guide – Lesson Plans
Orientation and Class Management Activities
Level I – Week 1

Instructional Objectives:
To learn and follow basic management activities necessary for participation in physical education classes

NASPE National Standards:
Introductory Activity: 1
Fitness Activity: 1, 4, 6
Lesson Focus: 2, 5
Game: 2, 5

Equipment Required:
Music for Fitness Challenges
Tom-tom

Instructional Activities	Teaching Hints

Orientation Instructional Procedures

The first week of school should be used to teach students the system you are going to use throughout the year. The following are reminders you might find useful in establishing your expectations and routines.

1. Establish rules and expectations. Discuss your expectations with the class to assure students understand reasons for your guidelines. Explain what the consequences are when rules are not followed. Show where time-out boxes are located and how they will be used.

2. Explain to the class the method you will use to learn names. It might be helpful to ask classroom teachers to have students put their name on a piece of masking tape (nametag). Tell students that you will ask their name on a regular basis until it is learned.

3. Practice entry and exit behaviors for students coming and leaving physical education classes. Have students enter the activity area on the move and continue moving until signaled to stop. Teach students not to touch any equipment that is placed in the teaching area.

4. Decide how excuses for nonparticipation will be handled. If possible, set up a routine where the school nurse determines which students are excused for health reasons.

5. Safety is important. Children should receive instruction on safety rules for apparatus and playground equipment. Safety procedures to be followed in physical education classes should be discussed.

6. Illustrate how you like to stop and start the class. In general, a whistle (or similar loud signal) and a raised hand is effective for stopping the class. A voice command should be used to start the class. Telling the class when before what (Chapter 6) will assure they do not begin before instructions are finished.

7. Discuss the issue, distribution, and care of equipment. Make students responsible for acquiring a piece of equipment and returning it at the end of the lesson. Place your teaching equipment around the perimeter of the area to avoid the rush of students vying to get a ball or beanbag located in one central area.

8. Explain to the class that the format of the daily lesson will include an introductory activity, fitness development, lesson focus, and finish with a game activity. Briefly explain why each part of the lesson is included.

9. Manage students on the move. Have them move throughout the area, freeze, and quickly find a partner. Practice various teaching formations such as open-squad formation and closed-squad formation. Practice moving into a circle while moving (fall-in). Transitions between formations should be done while moving, i.e., jogging from scatter formation into a circular formation.

10. Refer to Chapters 3, 5, and 6 in the text for detailed information about planning, enhancing instructional effectiveness, and class management and discipline strategies.

Introductory Activity — Move and Freeze on Signal

Have students move throughout the area using a variety of locomotor movements. On signal (whistle), they quickly freeze. Try to reduce the response latency by reinforcing students who stop quickly on signal.

The primary objective is to teach students the importance of moving under control (without bumping others or falling down) and quickly freezing.

Fitness Development Activity — Fitness Challenges

1. Locomotor Movement: Walk for 30 seconds.

2. Flexibility and Trunk Development Challenges
   a. Bend in different directions.
   b. Stretch slowly and return quickly.
   c. Combine bending and stretching movements.
   d. Sway back and forth.
   e. Twist one body part; add body parts.

3. Locomotor Movement: Skip for 30 seconds.

4. Upper Body Strength Challenges
   In a push-up position, do the following challenges:
   a. Lift one foot; the other foot.
   b. Wave at a friend; wave with the other arm.
   c. Scratch your back with one hand; use the other hand.
   d. Walk your feet to your hands.

5. Locomotor Movement: Jog for 30 seconds.

6. Abdominal Development Challenges
   From a supine position:
   1. Lift your head and look at your toes.
   2. Lift your knees to your chest.
   3. Wave your legs at a friend.
   From a sitting position;
   1. Slowly lie down with hands on tummy.
   2. Lift legs and touch toes.

7. Locomotor Movement: Run and leap for 30 seconds.

The goal should be to move students through a number of movement challenges. Emphasis should be placed on starting the fitness activities at a level where all students can feel successful.

Alternate the locomotor movements with the strength and flexibility challenges. Repeat the challenges as necessary.

Tape alternating segments (30 seconds in length) of silence and music to signal duration of exercise. Music segments indicate locomotor movements while intervals of silence announce doing the movement challenges.

Teach youngsters the different challenges and then allow them to select a challenge they can successfully perform.

The challenges should be enjoyable to perform.

Encourage students to focus on effort and feeling successful.

Workloads should be moderate with emphasis on success for all youngsters.

Lesson Focus — Orientation

Since much time during the first week is used for orientation procedures and management, no lesson focus activity is scheduled.

Game Activity — Management Games

Play one or two management games to teach students how to move into partner and small-group formation

Toe to Toe
   Supplies: None
   Skills: Fundamental locomotor movements
   Youngsters perform a locomotor movement around the area. On signal, each child must find a partner and stand toe to toe (one foot only) with that person. An important skill is to take the nearest person for a partner without searching for a friend. Youngsters who can't find a partner within their immediate area must run quickly to the center of the area (use a marking spot or cone) to find a partner. The goal is to find a nearby partner as quickly as possible and avoid being the last pair formed. If the number of youngsters playing is uneven, the teacher can join in and play. Change locomotor movements often.

Whistle Mixer
   Supplies: None
   Skills: All basic locomotor movements
   Children are scattered throughout the area. To begin, they walk around in any direction they wish. A whistle is blown a number of times in succession with short, sharp blasts. Children then form small groups with the number in each group equal to the number of whistle blasts. If there are four blasts, children form groups of four—no more, no less. When players have the correct number, they sit down immediately to signal that no one may leave the group and no one may enter the group. The goal is not to be left out or caught in a circle with the incorrect number of students. Encourage players to move toward the center of the area and raise their hands to facilitate finding others without a group. After the circles are formed, the teacher calls "Walk," and the game continues. In walking, children should move in different directions.

DPE Curriculum Guide – Lesson Plans
Manipulative Skills Using Hoops
Level I – Week 2

Instructional Objectives:
To learn to move in an evasive fashion
To manipulate the hoop in a variety of challenges
To strike a ball with a bat

NASPE National Standards:
Introductory Activity: 1, 3, 5
Fitness Activity: 1, 4, 6
Lesson Focus: 2, 3, 5
Game: 1, 2, 5

Equipment Required:
Music for Four Corners Movement
One hoop per child
Plastic bottle bat and ball
Batting tee (optional)

Instructional Activities	Teaching Hints

Introductory Activity — Following Activity

One partner leads and performs various kinds of movements. The other partner must follow in a similar fashion. This can also be used with squads or small groups, allowing the captain to lead.

Student demonstration can be used to stimulate new ideas among students.

Fitness Development Activity — Four Corners Movement

Outline a large rectangle with a cone at each corner. Place signs with movement tasks on both sides of the cones. Youngsters move around the outside of the rectangle and change movements as they pass each sign. The following movement activities are suggested:

Corner 1. Skipping/Jumping/Hopping
Corner 2. Sliding/Galloping
Corner 3. Various animal movements
Corner 4. Sport imitation movements

Stop the class after 30 seconds of movement and perform fitness challenges (see Week 1).

Tape alternating segments of silence and music to signal duration of exercise. Music segments (30 seconds) indicate Four Corner aerobic activity while intervals of silence (45 seconds) announce performance of flexibility and strength development activities.

Faster-moving students should pass on the outside of the area.

If signs are not used at the corners, teachers can specify by voice what movements are to be performed.

Lesson Focus — Manipulative Skills Using Hoops

1. Hula-hoop using various body parts such as waist, neck, knees, arms and fingers.
   a. While hula-hooping on the arms, try to change the hoop from one arm to the other.
   b. Change hoop from one partner to another while hula-hooping around the waist.
   c. Try leg skippers--hula-hoop with one leg and jump the hoop with the other leg.
   d. Hula-hoop around waist while on knees. While hooping, try to stand up and go back to knees.
   e. Exploratory activity.
2. Place the hoops on the floor to create various patterns. Have the children perform various fundamental locomotor movements and animal walks in, out of, and between the hoops. Create different challenges by having students go in and out of various color hoops and specify a certain number of hoops they must enter.
3. Jump rope with the hoop--forward and backward. Begin with a back-and-forth pendulum swing. Try sideways jumping.
4. Thread the needle. Balance the hoop on head and try to step through the hoop. Do it forward, backward and sideways.
5. Roll hoop and run alongside it. Run ahead of it. Cross in front of it. Go through the hoop.
6. Spin the hoop like a top. How many times can you make it spin? How many times can you run around the spinning hoop before it falls?
7. Balance the hoop and then go through it before it falls.

Place the hoops around the perimeter of the area. Students move and pick up a hoop and begin practicing the assigned activity.

Encourage youngsters to find their personal space.

When learning to hula-hoop, teach youngsters to move the body part back and forth rather than in a circle. The natural tendency is to move the body part in a circle, making it impossible to keep the hoop circling.

Place the hoops on the floor when calling the class to attention. If students don't put the hoop on the floor, they will drop and disrupt the class.

The reverse spin can be taught by telling students to pull back and down toward the floor just prior to releasing the hoop.

8. For a change-of-pace activity, put hoops on floor. Perform various locomotor movements around many hoops. On signal, curl up inside a hoop. For challenge, have fewer hoops than students.
9. Roll hoop with a reverse spin to make it return to the thrower.
10. Reverse spin, catch on arm, and hula-hoop it. Try catching on foot.

Offer students a chance to perform their favorite activities.

Game Activity

Animal Tag

Supplies: None

Skills: Imagery, running, dodging

Two parallel lines are drawn about 40 ft apart. Children are divided into two groups, each of which takes a position on one of the lines. Children in one group get together with their leader and decide what animal they wish to imitate. Having selected the animal, they move over to within 5 ft or so of the other line. There they imitate the animal, and the other group tries to guess the animal correctly. If the guess is correct, they chase the first group back to its line, trying to tag as many as possible. Those caught must go over to the other team. The second group then selects an animal, and the roles are reversed. If the guessing team cannot guess the animal, however, the performing team gets another try. To avoid confusion, children must raise their hands to take turns at naming the animal. Otherwise, many false chases will occur. If children have trouble guessing, the leader of the performing team can give the initial of the animal.

Bottle Bat Ball

Supplies: A plastic bottle bat, whiffle ball, batting tee (optional), home plate, base marker

Skills: Batting, retrieving balls

Formation: Scattered

A home plate is needed, and a batting tee can be used. Foul lines should be marked wide enough so as not to be restrictive. The batter gets three pitches (or swings) to hit a fair ball, or she is out. The pitches are easy (as in slow-pitch softball), so that the batter has a good chance to hit the ball. The batter hits the ball and runs around the base marker and back to home. If the ball is returned to the pitcher's mound before the batter reaches home, she is out. (A marker should designate the pitcher's mound.) Otherwise, the batter has a home run and bats again. One fielder other than the pitcher is needed, but another can be used. The running distance to first base is critical. It can remain fixed or can be made progressively (one step) longer, until it reaches such a point that the fielders are heavily favored.

Teaching suggestion: The game should make use of a plastic bottle bat and fun (whiffle) ball. A rotation system should be established when an out is made.

Variation: A batting tee can be used.

Pigs Fly

Supplies: None/Photos or drawings of animals if desired

Skills: Locomotor movements

The leader stands at the front of the room and calls out the name of a mammal, bird, fish, or reptile, and a movement. For instance, the leader might call out, "Rabbits swim. Pigs Fly. Bears Crawl." When the leader states a correct relationship, the class must move accordingly. In this example, they would begin a bear crawl on their hands and feet. Games should be kept short so that all children have a chance to lead and no one has to sit out too long.

DPE Curriculum Guide – Lesson Plans
Throwing Skills (1)
Level I – Week 3

Instructional Objectives:
To throw a ball using the overhand
  technique
To throw with velocity using side
  orientation and opposition
To learn the basic rules of simple game
  activities

NASPE National Standards:
Introductory Activity: 1, 5
Fitness Activity: 1, 4, 6
Lesson Focus: 2, 3, 5
Game: 1, 2, 5

Equipment Required:
Music and tape for Astronaut Exercises
Beanbags, whiffle balls, fleece balls, rag
  balls, and tennis balls
Hoops and/or mats for targets

Instructional Activities	Teaching Hints

Introductory Activity — Group Over and Around

One half of the class is scattered and is in a curled position. The other half of the class leaps or moves around the down children. On signal, reverse the groups quickly. In place of a curl, the down children can bridge as others go around. The down children can also alternate between curl and bridge, as well as move around the area while in bridge position.

Remind students not to touch the students who are in bridge or curl position.

Use different locomotor movements.

Fitness Development Activity — Astronaut Exercises

Walk, do arm circles	30 seconds	Tape alternating segments of silence and music to signal duration of exercise. Music segments (30 seconds) indicate aerobic activity while intervals of silence (30 seconds) signal flexibility and strength development activities.
Flexibility and trunk development challenges	30 seconds	
Skip forward, backwards, and sideways	30 seconds	
Upper body strength challenges	30 seconds	
Slide; change lead leg	30 seconds	
Abdominal development challenges	30 seconds	
Jump like a pogo stick	30 seconds	
Upper body strength challenges	30 seconds	See Chapter 13 for a description of how to perform challenge activities.
Trot lightly in different directions	30 seconds	
Flexibility and trunk development challenges	30 seconds	
Gallop backwards	30 seconds	Allow students to adjust the workload to an intensity that is consistent with their ability level.

Cool down with stretching and walking.

Lesson Focus — Throwing Skills (1)

Mimetics
1. "Pretend you:
    a. have to throw a rock across a big river!"
    b. want to throw a ball over a very tall building!"
    c. are a javelin thrower and you want to make the longest throw ever!"
    d. are a baseball pitcher and you are throwing a fast ball!"

Stand sideways to the target with the nonthrowing side facing the target. Emphasize lifting the throwing arm and pointing at the target with the nonthrowing arm.

Individual Activities
1. Throw beanbag or fleece ball against the wall. Concentrate on the following points:
    a. Feet together
    b. Foot opposite the throwing arm forward
    c. Start with nonthrowing side toward the target area
2. Throw from one side of the gym and try to hit the other wall.

Use instructional cues:

"Raise your elbow to shoulder level."

"Start with your nonthrowing side to the wall."

Mimetics
1. The teacher should cue students and model a good throw.
    a. Teacher should use terms such as "turn your nonthrowing side to the target," "wind-up," "step toward the target," "follow through."
    b. Teacher can also use this time to observe and coach.
    c. *Encourage* students to throw as *hard as you can*.

"Reach up with your throwing arm like you are going to pick an apple"

"Take a step toward the target when you throw."

Individual Activities

1. Throwing yarn balls
   a. Throw against a wall or fence. Throw five balls, retrieve, and repeat.
   b. Teach the proper grip.
2. Throw rag balls or tennis balls against cardboard boxes near a wall or fence.
   a. Throw from 20–25 feet depending on skill level. Student should be able to hit the wall.
   b. Retrieve after all the balls have been thrown.
3. Throw at hoops leaning against a wall or fence.
   Throw from a distance so that children can hit the wall, but only with a forceful throw.

Focus on throwing form rather than accuracy.

Emphasize throwing hard! Proper form can only be learned when students try to throw as hard as possible.

Cue students to move their throwing hand behind their head before the throw.

Give each student 4 or 5 balls to throw. They can be placed in a Frisbee to keep them from rolling around. When all balls have been thrown, students (on signal) retrieve the same number of balls they have thrown.

Game Activity

Aviator

Supplies: None

Skills: Running, locomotor movements, stopping

Players are parked (in push-up position) at one end of the playing area. The air traffic controller (ATC) is in front of the players and calls out, "Aviators aviators, take off!" Youngsters take off and move like airplanes to the opposite side of the area. The first person to move to the other side and land the plane (get into push-up position facing the ATC) is declared the new ATC.

If the ATC yells out some type of stormy weather, all planes must return to the starting line and resume the parked position. Examples of stormy weather commands are lightning, thunder, hurricane, and tornado. Each ATC is allowed to give stormy weather warnings once.

Sneak Attack

Supplies: None

Skills: Marching, running

Two parallel lines are drawn about 60 ft apart. Children are divided into two teams. One team takes a position on one of the lines, with their backs to the area. These are the chasers. The other team is on the other line, facing the area. This is the sneak team. The sneak team moves forward on signal, moving toward the chasers. When they get reasonably close, a whistle or some other signal is given, and the sneak team turns and runs back to their line, chased by the other team. Anyone caught before reaching the line changes to the chase team. The game is repeated, with the roles exchanged.

DPE Curriculum Guide – Lesson Plans
Manipulative Skills Using Beanbags
Level I – Week 4

Instructional Objectives:
To move in a large group without
    bumping into others
To freeze on signal
To learn tossing and catching skills
To cooperate in game activities

NASPE National Standards:
Introductory Activity: 1, 5
Fitness Activity: 1, 4, 5
Lesson Focus: 1, 2, 4, 5
Game: 1, 5

Equipment Required:
Tambourine or tom-tom
Music for Fitness Games & Challenges
One beanbag per student

Instructional Activities	Teaching Hints
Introductory Activity — Bend, Stretch, and Shake	
1. Bend various body parts individually and then bend various combinations of body parts.	Use a tambourine to signal changes between bending, stretching, and shaking.
2. Stretch the body in various levels. Encourage stretching from various positions such as standing, sitting, and prone position.	
3. Practice shaking individual body parts when the tambourine is shaken. Progress to shaking the entire body.	Encourage smooth movements in bending and stretching activities.
4. Bend body parts while doing different locomotor movements. Bend limbs while shaking.	Encourage creative responses.
Fitness Development Activity — Fitness Games and Challenges	
1. Stoop Tag—45 seconds.	Tape alternating segments of silence and music to signal duration of exercise. Music segments indicate fitness game activity while intervals of silence announce flexibility and strength development activities.
2. Freeze; perform stretching activities.	
3. Back-to-Back Tag—45 seconds.	
4. Freeze; perform abdominal challenges using curl-up variations.	
5. Balance Tag—45 seconds.	
6. Freeze; perform arm–upper body strength challenges using push-up variations.	
7. Elbow Swing Tag—45 seconds.	Choose any of the tag games. The names of the tag games indicate a "safe" position when one cannot be tagged, i.e., back to back with a partner or balancing on one foot.
8. Freeze; perform trunk development challenges.	
9. Color Tag—45 seconds.	
	Avoid getting caught up in rule infractions. The purpose of the tag games is to encourage locomotor movement.
Lesson Focus — Manipulative Skills using Beanbags	
Stand in place and practice tossing and catching	
1. Toss and catch with both hands—right hand, left hand	Each student must have a beanbag for practice.
2. Toss and catch with the back of hands. This will encourage children to catch with "soft hands."	
3. Toss the beanbag to an increasingly high level, emphasizing a straight overhead toss. To encourage straight tossing, have the child sit down.	Give students two or three activities to practice so you have time to move and help individuals. Alternate activities from each of the categories so students receive a variety of skills to practice.
Stand in place, toss, and catch while performing stunts	
1. Toss overhead and perform the following stunts and catch the bag.	
a. 1/4 and 1/2 turns, right and left	
b. Full turn	Emphasize tosses that are straight up and about 12 inches above the head.
c. Touch floor	
d. Clap hands	
e. Clap hands around different parts of body, behind back, under legs.	
f. Heel click	
g. Sit down, get up	
h. Look between legs	

Toss, move to a new spot, and catch the beanbag

1. Toss overhead, move to another spot, and catch.
2. Toss, do a locomotor movement, and catch.
3. Toss and move from side to side.
4. Toss overhead behind self, move, and catch.

Balance the beanbag

1. Balance on the following body parts
   a. Head
   b. Back of hand
   c. Shoulder
   d. Knee
   e. Foot
   f. Elbow
   g. Exploratory activity
2. Balance and move as follows:
   a. Walk
   b. Run
   c. Skip
   d. Gallop
   e. Sit down
   f. Lie down
   g. Turn around
   h. Combinations of the above
   i. Exploratory activity

Beanbag challenge activities

1. Hold the beanbag between knees and play tag with a partner or small group.
2. Place the beanbag on tummy and shake it off.
3. Place the beanbag on back and mule kick it off.
4. Push the beanbag across the floor with different body parts.
5. Toss the beanbag up and touch specified body parts.
6. Put beanbags on floor. Rotate various body parts on a beanbag.
7. Beanbag Balance Tag—Balance a beanbag on selected body parts. Announce a color to identify those who are it.

This is an excellent activity for teaching students to track (keep their eyes focused on) the beanbag. Remind them not to look away while tossing and catching.

Students should be encouraged to see how long they can balance the beanbag.

Movements should be controlled with as little bounce as possible.

These are body control activities. Students must be able to concentrate on moving slowly and keeping the beanbag in place.

Use the challenge to motivate students. These activities will be exciting and should be integrated throughout the lesson.

Hand–eye coordination is slowly learned after many repetitions. Encourage students to repeat their attempts.

Game Activities

Midnight

Supplies: None

Skills: Running, dodging

A safety line is established about 40 ft from a den in which two or three players, the foxes, are standing. The others stand behind the safety line and ask, "What time is it, Mr. Fox?" One of the foxes is designated to answer in various fashions, such as "one o' clock," "four o' clock," etc. When the fox says a certain time, the class walks forward that number of steps. For example, if the fox says "six o'clock," the class has to move forward six steps. The fox continues to draw the players toward him. At some point, the fox answers the question by saying "Midnight," and chases the others back to the safety line. Any player who is caught becomes a fox in the den and helps to catch others.

Leap the Brook

Supplies: None

Skills: Leaping, jumping, hopping, turning

A brook is marked off on the floor for a distance of about 30 ft. For the first 10 ft, it is 3 ft wide; for the next 10 ft, it is 4 ft wide; for the last 10 ft, it is 5 ft wide. Children form a single file and jump over the narrowest part of the brook. They should be encouraged to do this several times, using different styles of jumping and leaping. After they have satisfactorily negotiated the narrow part, they move to the next width, and so on. The selection of the distances is arbitrary, and the distances can be changed if they seem unsuitable for any particular group of children.

Variation: Children can use different means of crossing the brook—leaping, jumping, hopping. They also can vary the kinds of turns to be made—right or left; or quarter, half, three-quarter, or full. They should use different body shapes, different arm positions, and so on.

DPE Curriculum Guide – Lesson Plans
Manipulative Skills Using Playground Balls
Level I – Week 5

Instructional Objectives:

To perform combinations of locomotor and nonlocomotor movements

To bounce, toss, and catch a ball in a stationary position

To roll, bounce, and throw a ball to a partner.

NASPE National Standards:

Introductory Activity: 1
Fitness Activity: 1, 4, 6
Lesson Focus: 2, 3, 5
Game: 1, 2, 5

Equipment Required:

Tom-tom
Music for Fitness Challenges
One 8½" playground or vinyl-covered foam ball for each student

Instructional Activities	Teaching Hints
Introductory Activity — Combination Movements	

1. Hop, turn around, and shake.
2. Jump, make a shape in the air, balance.
3. Skip, collapse, and roll.
4. Curl, roll, jump with a half turn.
5. Whirl, skip, sink slowly.
6. Hop, collapse, creep.
7. Kneel, sway, jump to feet.
8. Lift, grin, and roll.

Use the tom-tom to signal movement changes.

Challenge students to develop their personal combinations.

Create different movements using the same words.

Fitness Development Activity — Fitness Challenges

Alternate locomotor movements with strength and flexibility challenges. Repeat the challenges as necessary.

Locomotor Movement: Walk for 30 seconds.

Flexibility and Trunk Development Challenges
1. Bend in different directions.
2. Stretch slowly and return quickly.
3. Combine bending and stretching movements.
4. Sway back and forth.
5. Twist one body part; add body parts.
6. Make your body move in a large circle.
7. In a sitting position, wave your legs at a friend; make circles with your legs.

Locomotor Movement: Skip for 30 seconds.

Upper Body Strength Challenges
In a push-up position, do the following challenges:
1. Lift one foot; the other foot.
2. Wave at a friend; wave with the other arm.
3. Scratch your back with one hand; use the other hand.
4. Walk your feet to your hands.
5. Turn over and face the ceiling; shake a leg; Crab Walk.

Locomotor Movement: Jog for 30 seconds.

Abdominal Development
From a supine position:
1. Lift your head and look at your toes.
2. Lift your knees to your chest.
3. Wave your legs at a friend.
From a sitting position:
1. Slowly lay down with hands on tummy.
2. Lift legs and touch toes.

Locomotor Movement: Run and leap for 30 seconds.

Tape alternating segments (30 seconds in length) of silence and music to signal duration of exercise. Music segments indicate doing the locomotor movements; intervals of silence announce performing the strength and flexibility challenges.

Students select the fitness challenge they feel capable of performing. This implies that not all youngsters are required to do the same workload. Children differ and their ability to perform fitness workloads differs. Make fitness a personal challenge.

Since the activities range from easy to challenging, all youngsters can be successful. All youngsters should be able to do one of the fitness challenges.

Vary the locomotor movements as desired. Another alternative is to allow students to select the locomotor movement they would like to do.

Lesson Focus — Manipulative Skills Using Playground Balls

1. Controlled Rolling and Handling in Place
   a. In a wide straddle position (other possible positions are seated with legs crossed or outstretched, and push-up position), place the ball on the floor, and roll it with constant finger guidance between and around the legs.
   b. Roll the ball in a figure-eight path in and out of the legs.
   c. Reach as far to the left as possible with the ball and roll it in front of you to the other side. Catch it as far to the right of the body as possible.
   d. Turn in place and roll the ball around with one hand in a large circle.
   e. Roll the ball around while lying on top of it. Roll the ball around the floor while on all fours, guiding it with the nose and forehead.
   f. With the back moderately bent, release the ball behind the head, let it roll down the back, and catch it with both hands.
   g. Make different kinds of bridges over the ball while using the ball as partial support for the bridge.

2. Bounce and Catch
   a. Two hands, one hand.
   b. Bounce at different levels.
   c. Bounce between legs.
   d. Close eyes and bounce.
   e. Dribble ball in a stationary and/or moving position.
   f. Dribble and follow the commands, such as move forward, backward, in a circle, or sideways, while walking, galloping, trotting, etc.

3. Toss and Catch
   a. Toss and catch, vary height.
   b. Add various challenges while tossing (i.e., touch floor, clap hands, turn, sit down, lie down).
   c. Toss and let bounce. Also add some challenges as above.
   d. Toss up and catch behind back—toss from behind back and catch in front of body.
   e. Create moving challenges (i.e., toss, run five steps and catch, toss and back up five hops and catch.)

4. Foot Skills
   a. Lift the ball up with both feet and catch. Both front and rear of body catch.
   b. From a sitting position with the ball between feet, toss it up, and catch with hands.
   c. Keep the ball in the air with feet and different body parts.

Give students two or three activities to practice so you have time to move and help youngsters. Alternate activities from each of the categories so students receive a variety of activities for practice.

Place emphasis on control of the ball. Students should be challenged to have "their ball under control."

An effective approach is to tell students to assume their feet are "glued to the floor." Tosses must be made directly overhead and caught without moving.

Tosses must begin at a low level and gradually be raised as students gain control of the ball. Little is gained by tossing the ball to a height where it can't be caught.

Game Activity

Teacher Ball

Supplies: A gray foam ball or rubber playground ball

Skills: Throwing, catching

One child is the teacher or leader and stands about 10 ft in front of three other students, who are lined up facing him. The object of the game is to move up to the teacher's spot by avoiding making bad throws or missing catches. The teacher throws to each child in turn, beginning with the child on the left, who must catch and return the ball. Any child making a throwing or catching error goes to the end of the line, on the teacher's right. Those in the line move up, filling the vacated space. If the teacher makes a mistake, he must go to the end of the line and the child at the head of the line becomes the new teacher. The teacher scores a point by remaining in position for three rounds (three throws to each child). After scoring a point, the teacher takes a position at the end of the line and another child becomes the teacher.

Scarecrow and the Crows

Supplies: None

Skills: Dodging, running

Children form a large circle representing the garden that is guarded by two or three players who are designated as scarecrows. Six to eight crows scatter on the outside of the circle, and the scarecrows assume a characteristic pose inside the circle. Players in the circle raise their joined hands and let the crows run through, into the garden, where they pretend to eat. The scarecrows try to tag the crows. The circle children help the crows by raising their joined hands and allowing them to leave the circle, but they try to hinder the scarecrows. If the scarecrows run out of the circle, all the crows immediately run into the garden and start to nibble at the vegetables while the circle children hinder the reentry of the scarecrows. After 15–20 seconds, new players are selected for the roles. If, after a reasonable period of time, the scarecrows have failed to catch any crows, change players.

DPE Curriculum Guide – Lesson Plans
Movement Skills and Concepts (1)
Walking, Body Part Identification, and Personal Space
Level I – Week 6

Instructional Objectives:
To run rhythmically
To jump a self-turned rope
To perform walking variations
To understand the concept of personal
 space

NASPE National Standards:
Introductory Activity: 1, 5
Fitness Activity: 1, 2, 4, 5, 6
Lesson Focus: 1, 2, 3, 5
Game: 1, 5

Equipment Required:
Tom-tom
One jump rope for each student
One balloon or beach ball for each
 student
Colored paper & shapes for game

Instructional Activities	Teaching Hints

Introductory Activity — European Running

1. Run and stop.
2. Run, and on signal make a full turn; continue in same direction. Turn the other way.
3. Run, and on signal run in general space. On next signal, re-form the original pattern.
4. Run and bend the upper body forward in four counts. Return to the upright position in four counts.
5. Run and clap the rhythm.

Stress personal space and moving without bumping into others.

Use a drum to accentuate the rhythm.

Start the rhythm slowly so students can hear and move easily. Accomplish a walking rhythm before moving to a trotting step.

Fitness Development Activity — Jump Rope Exercises

1. Jump rope—45 seconds. If not able to jump, practice swinging the rope to the side while jumping.
2. Place the rope on the floor and perform locomotor movements around and over the rope. Make different shapes and letters with the rope.
3. Jump rope—45 seconds.
4. Hold the folded rope overhead. Sway from side to side. Twist right and left.
5. Jump rope—45 seconds
6. Lie on back with rope held with outstretched arms toward ceiling. Bring up one leg at a time and touch the rope with toes. Lift both legs together. Sit up and try to hook the rope over the feet. Release and repeat.
7. Jump rope—45 seconds
8. Touch toes with the folded rope.
9. Jump rope—45 seconds.
10. Do push-up variations with the rope folded and held between the hands.
11. Jump rope—45 seconds.

Tape alternating segments (45 seconds in length) of silence and music (30 seconds) to signal duration of exercise. Music segments indicate aerobic activity with the jump ropes; intervals of silence announce using the jump ropes to enhance flexibility and strength development.

Space youngsters so they don't hit others with their rope.

Don't worry about nonjumpers. They will learn sooner or later. Give encouragement and keep them motivated.

Lesson Focus — Movement Skills and Concepts (1)

Fundamental Skill: Walking

1. Walk in different directions, changing direction on signal (90 degrees).
2. While walking, bring up the knees and slap with the hands on each step.
3. Walk on heels, toes, side of the foot, Charlie Chaplin fashion (toes pointed way out).
4. Gradually lower the body while walking; gradually raise body.
5. Walk with a smooth gliding step.
6. Walk with a wide base on tiptoes; rock from side to side.
7. Clap hands alternately front and back. Clap hands under the thighs (slow walk).
8. Walk slowly. Accelerate. Decelerate.
9. Take long strides. Tiny steps.
10. Change levels on signal.
11. Walk quickly and quietly. Slowly and heavily. Quickly and heavily, etc.
12. Change direction on signal while facing the same way.

Select a few activities from each of the categories so students receive a variety of skills to practice. When possible, integrate the manipulative skills activities with fundamental skill activities.

Use the instructional cues to help students walk with proper form.
"Head up; eyes forward. Swing the arms while walking. Keep the shoulders back and the tummy flat."

13. Walk angrily, then happily; add others.
14. Hold arms in different positions. Try different arm movements as you walk.
15. Walk different patterns: circle, square, rectangle, figure-eight, etc.
16. Walk through heavy mud, on ice, on a slick floor, on a rainy day.
17. Walk like a soldier, a giant, a robot; add others.
18. Duck under trees or railings while walking.
19. Point toes out in different directions while walking—in, forward, and out.
20. Walk with high knees, stiff knees, one stiff knee, sore ankle.
21. Walk toward a spot, turn around in four steps. Move in a different direction.
22. Practice changing steps while walking.
23. Walk with a military goose step.

A drumbeat can be used to stimulate different walking speeds.

Skills: Working with Balloons or Beach balls
1. Keep your balloon in the air by rebounding it from the hand, fist, arm, elbow, knee, shoulder, head, and other body parts. Use one finger. Use the feet to keep balloon in the air.
2. Work out combinations of body parts, four different parts in succession.
3. Use contrasting terms while keeping the balloon in the air:
   a. close—far
   b. in front of—behind
   c. near—far
   d. right—left
   e. high—low
   f. sudden—smooth
4. Keep one foot in place, control balloon or beach ball.
5. Play "let's pretend," we are volleyball players. Practice overhand, underhand, dig passes. Show serving.
6. All time for exploratory activity by individuals or partners.

Keep the balloons in control by tapping them into the area rather than striking them.

When first learning the skills, keep the feet in one place rather than moving.

As children master the skills, try performing some of the balloon skills while moving throughout the area.

Movement Concept: Identifying Body Parts
1. Children can be standing or seated. Touch the part of body with both hands without looking at it. Children should repeat out loud the designated part touched by saying, "I am touching _____."
   a. Touch your shoulders
   b. Touch your ankles
   c. Touch your head
   d. Touch your toes
   e. Touch your ears
   f. Touch your knees
   g. Touch your eyes
   h. Touch your hips
   i. Touch your cheeks
   j. Touch your forehead
   k. Touch your thighs
   l. Touch your elbows
2. Thinking Activity
   Teacher touches the incorrect part of the body as commands are given. Students should touch the correct part and not be fooled by the teacher.
3. As a part is named, form a pose and make this part the highest position of your body; the lowest.
4. Move about general space in any manner you wish. When a body part is called, stop and put both hands on the part(s).
5. Select a way you wish to move in general space. The signal to move will be the name of a body part. Move around the room with one hand on the body part. When another body part is called out, change the type of movement and hold the new body part.

Body part identification should be a "snappy" activity. Children should learn to respond quickly without much thought.

Practice combinations of body parts such as shoulders–ankles and knees.

Try the activities with the eyes closed.

Movement Concept: Exploring Personal Space
1. Keeping one foot in place on a spot, make a full arc with the other foot. Keep both one foot and one hand touching the spot, arc again with other foot.

Place emphasis on understanding that most people have a personal space they don't want violated. Encourage

2. Keeping your feet in place sway and reach out without losing balance or moving feet. Try with feet together and feet apart. Which is better for balance? Sit down and repeat movements. Do you need more or less space?

3. Try some different types of movements in your personal space:

   a. Make yourself as wide as possible. Change to narrow. Experiment with narrow, small—large, high—low, etc. Try from other positions—kneeling, sitting balancing on seat, standing on one foot, lying on stomach, and others.

   b. In supine position, move arms and legs in different combinations out and back.

   c. Select one part of the body to keep in place. Make big circles with the rest of the body. Select other parts.

   d. Explore different positions where one foot is higher than any other body part.

   e. Pump yourself up like a balloon. Get bigger and bigger until I say, "Pop!"

   f. Let's pretend you are a snowman melting to the ground under a hot sun.

   g. With your feet in place, twist as far as you can one way and then the other (arms out to sides). Show me how a top spins.

youngsters to stay out of other's personal spaces.

Call out different movements and encourage students to respond quickly.

Offer the activities as challenges and allow students to do their best.

Game Activity

Change Sides

Supplies: None

Skill: Body management

Identify two parallel lines 30 ft apart with half of the class on each line. On signal, all players cross to the other line, face the center, and stand at attention. The first group to do all three things correctly wins a point. Children must be cautioned to use care when passing through the opposite group. They should be spaced well along each line; this allows room for them to move through each group. Vary the locomotor movements used by specifying skipping, hopping, long steps, sliding, and other varieties of movement. The position to be assumed at the finish can be varied also.

Where's My Partner?

Supplies: None

Skills: Fundamental locomotor movements

Children are in a double circle facing a partner. The inside circle has two or three more players than the outside. When the signal is given, the circles skip (or walk, run, hop, or gallop) to the right. This means that they are skipping in opposite directions. On the command "Halt," the circles face each other to find partners. The players left without a partner go to the mush pot (the center area of the circle) for one turn. The circles should be reversed after a time.

Variation: The game can also be played with music or a drumbeat. When the music stops, the players seek partners.

Colors

Supplies: Colored paper (construction paper) cut in circles, squares, or triangles for markers

Skills: Color or other perceptual concepts, running

Five or six different-colored markers should be used, with a number of children having the same color. Children are standing or seated in a circle with a marker in front of each child. The teacher calls out a color, and everyone having that color runs counterclockwise around the circle and back to place. The first one seated upright and motionless is declared the winner. Different kinds of locomotor movement can be specified, such as skipping, galloping, walking, and so on. After a period of play, the children leave the markers on the floor and move one place to the left.

Variation: Shapes (e.g., circles, triangles, squares, rectangles, stars, and diamonds) can be used instead of colors, as can numbers or other articles or categories, such as animals, birds, or fish. This game has value in teaching identification and recognition.

DPE Curriculum Guide – Lesson Plans
Gymnastics Skills (1)
Level I – Week 7

Instructional Objectives:
To be able to perform animal walks
To balance body weight in a variety of positions
To be able to manage body weight in gymnastics activities

NASPE National Standards:
Introductory Activity: 1, 5
Fitness Activity: 1, 2, 5, 6
Lesson Focus: 1, 2, 3, 5
Game: 2, 5

Equipment Required:
Music for Animal Movements
Tumbling mats
8" foam rubber balls (6–8)
Cones

Instructional Activities	Teaching Hints

Introductory Activity — Countdown

Standing with arms stretched overhead, students begin a countdown (10, 9, 8, 7, etc.) and gradually lower themselves into a crouched position with each count. On the words "blast off," they jump upwards and run in different directions. Students can run to a wall and return to their position. After students learn the activity, allow one of them to say, "Blast Off!"

Vary with challenges such as:
1. Different locomotor movements.
2. Various animal walks.
3. Change intervals of counting—slow, fast.

Fitness Development Activity — Animal Movements and Fitness Challenges

1. Puppy Dog Walk—30 seconds.
2. Freeze; perform stretching activities.
3. Measuring Worm Walk—30 seconds.
4. Freeze; perform abdominal development challenges.
5. Frog Jump—30 seconds.
6. Freeze; perform push-up position challenges.
7. Elephant Walk—30 seconds.
8. Freeze; perform stretching activities.
9. Bear Walk—30 seconds.
10. Freeze; perform abdominal challenges.
11. Crab Walk—30 seconds.
12. Freeze; perform stretching and relaxing activities.

Tape alternating segments (30 seconds in length) of silence and music to signal duration of exercise. Music segments indicate performing animal movements; intervals of silence announce doing the fitness challenges.

A variation is to place animal movement signs throughout the area and instruct students to move from sign to sign performing the appropriate animal movement each time they reach a new sign.

Lesson Focus — Gymnastics Skills (1)

Animal Movements
Alligator Crawl
    Lie facedown on the floor with elbows bent. Move along the floor in alligator fashion, keeping the hands close to the body and the feet pointed out. First, use unilateral movements—that is, right arm and leg moving together—then change to cross-lateral movements.

Kangaroo Jump
    Carry the arms close to the chest with the palms facing forward. Place a beanbag or ball between the knees. Move in different directions by taking small jumps without dropping the object.

Puppy Dog Run
    Place the hands on the floor, bending the arms and legs slightly. Walk and run like a happy puppy. Look straight ahead. Keeping the head up, in good position, strengthens the neck muscles. Go sideward, backward, and so on. Turn around in place.

Tumbling and Inverted Balances
Rolling Log
    Lie on the back with arms stretched overhead. Roll sideways the length of the mat. The next time, roll with the hands pointed toward the other side of the mat. To roll in a straight line, keep the feet slightly apart.

Five groups of activities in this lesson ensure that youngsters receive a variety of experiences. Pick a few activities from each group and teach them alternately. For example, teach one or two animal movements, then a tumbling and inverted balance, followed by a balance stunt, etc. Give equal time to each group of activities.

Variations of the Puppy Dog Run
    Cat Walk. Use the same position to imitate a cat. Walk softly. Stretch at times like a cat. Be smooth and deliberate.
    Monkey Run. Turn the hands and feet so that the fingers and toes point in (toward each other).

Place tumbling mats in the area so all youngsters are in view.

Side Roll

Start on the hands and knees, with one side toward the direction of the roll. Drop the shoulder, tuck both the elbow and the knee under, and roll over completely, returning to the hands-and-knees position. Momentum is needed to return to the original position. Practice rolling back and forth from one hand-and-knee position to another.

Forward Roll

Stand facing forward, with the feet apart. Squat and place the hands on the mat, shoulder width apart, with elbows against the insides of the thighs. Tuck the chin to the chest and make a rounded back. A push-off with the hands and feet provides the force for the roll. Carry the weight on the hands, with the elbows bearing the weight of the thighs. If the elbows are kept against the thighs and the weight is assumed there, the force of the roll is transferred easily to the rounded back. Try to roll forward to the feet. Later, try with the knees together and no weight on the elbows.

Balance Stunts

One-Leg Balance

Lift one leg from the floor. Later, bring the knee up. The arms should be free at first and then assume specified positions: folded across the chest, on the hips, on the head, or behind the back.

Double-Knee Balance

Kneel on both knees, with the feet pointed to the rear. Lift the feet from the ground and balance on the knees. Vary the position of the arms. Experiment with different arm positions.

Head Touch

On a mat, kneel on both knees, with feet pointed backward and arms outstretched backward for balance. Lean forward slowly and touch the forehead to the mat. Recover to position. Vary the arm position.

Individual Stunts

Directional Walk

For a left movement, begin in standing position. Do all of the following simultaneously: Take a step to the left, raise the left arm and point left, turn the head to the left, and state crisply "Left." Close with the right foot back to standing position. Take several steps left and then reverse.

Line Walking

Use a line on the floor, a chalked line, or a board. Walk forward and backward on the line as follows. First, take regular steps. Next, try follow steps—the front foot moving forward and the back foot moving up. The same foot always leads. Then do heel-and-toe steps, bringing the back toe up against the front heel on each step. Finally, hop along the line on one foot. Change to the other foot. The eyes should be focused ahead.

Fluttering Leaf

Keeping the feet in place and the body relaxed, flutter to the ground slowly, just as a leaf would do in autumn. Swing the arms back and forth loosely to accentuate the fluttering.

Elevator

With the arms out level at the sides, pretend to be an elevator going down. Lower the body a little at a time by bending the knees, but keep the upper body erect and the eyes forward. Return to position. Add a body twist to the downward movement. (A drum can be used.)

Don't force students to perform tumbling and inverted balances. If youngsters are fearful, gentle encouragement should be used.

The forward roll demands enough arm strength to keep the head off the mat. If youngsters lack strength, substitute the side roll for the forward roll.

Spotting the forward roll should rarely be used. If many children need to be spotted, the activity is probably too advanced. To spot the forward roll, the spotter should kneel alongside the child and place one hand on the back of the child's head and the other under the thigh. As the child moves through the roll, give an upward lift on the back of the neck to assure the neck does not absorb the weight of the body. This technique should be used for all forward roll variations.

Overweight children are at greater risk in stunts and tumbling activities. Allow them to avoid the tumbling activities if they so choose.

The Directional Walk is designed to aid in establishing right–left concepts. Definite and forceful simultaneous movements of the arm, head (turn), and leg (step) coupled with a crisp enunciation of the direction are the ingredients of this stunt.

Individual stunts are enjoyable challenges that all children can do. Place emphasis on form and balance.

Cross-Legged Stand

Sit with the legs crossed and the body bent partially forward. Respond appropriately to these six commands.

"Touch the right foot with the right hand."
"Touch the left foot with the right hand."
"Touch the right foot with the left hand."
"Touch the left foot with the left hand."
"Touch both feet with the hands."
"Touch the feet with crossed hands."

The commands should be given in varied sequences. The child must interpret that his right foot is on the left side, and vice versa. If this seems too difficult, have children start with the feet in normal position (uncrossed). Variation: Do the stunt with a partner, one child giving the commands and the other responding as directed.

Partner and Group Stunts

Bouncing Ball

Toss a lively utility ball into the air and watch how it bounces lower and lower until it finally comes to rest on the floor. From a bent-knee position with the upper body erect, imitate the ball by beginning with a high bounce and gradually lowering the height of the jump to simulate the ball coming to rest. Children should push off from the floor with the hands to gain additional height and should absorb part of the body weight with their hands as well. Toss a real ball into the air and move with the ball.

Try this with a partner, one partner serving as the bouncer and the other as the ball. Reverse positions. Try having one partner dribble the ball in various positions.

Seesaw

Face and join hands with a partner. Move the seesaw up and down, one child stooping while the other rises. Recite the words to this version of "Seesaw, Margery Daw."

Seesaw, Margery Daw,
Maw and Paw, like a saw,
Seesaw, Margery Daw.

Variation: Jump upward at the end of the rise each time.

Game Activity

Circle Straddle Ball

Supplies: Two or more 8-inch foam balls
Skills: Ball rolling, catching

Children are in circle formation, facing in. Each stands in a wide straddle stance with the side of the foot against the neighbor's. The hands are on the knees. Two balls are used. The object of the game is to roll one of the balls between the legs of another player before he can get his hands down to stop the ball. Each time a ball goes between the legs of an individual, a point is scored. The players having the fewest points scored against them are the winners. Keep the circles small so students have more opportunities to handle the ball. Players must catch and roll the ball, rather than batting it. Children must keep their hands on their knees until a ball is rolled at them.

Statues

Supplies: None
Skills: Body management, applying force, balance

Children are scattered in pairs around the area. One partner is the swinger and the other the statue. The teacher voices a directive, such as "Pretty," "Funny," "Happy," "Angry," or "Ugly." The swinger takes the statue by one or both hands, swings it around in a small circle two or three times (the teacher should specify), and releases it. The statue then takes a pose in keeping with the directive, and the swinger sits down on the floor. The statue must hold the position without moving or be disqualified. Reverse positions.

Variation: In the original game, the swinging is done until the directive is called. The swinger then immediately releases the statue, who takes the pose as called. This gives little time for the statue to react. Better and more creative statues are possible if the directive is given earlier.

Soap Bubbles

Supplies: Cones to delineate space, music
Skills: Body management

Each player is a soap bubble floating throughout the area. The teacher calls out the locomotor movement youngsters use to move in the area. The entire area is used to start the game. As the game progresses, the size of the area is decreased by moving the cones. Bubbles freeze on signal. Music can be used to stimulate movement.   The object of the game is not to touch or collide with another bubble. When this occurs, both bubbles burst and sink to the floor and make themselves as small as possible. The space is made smaller until those who have not been touched are declared the winners. Those players who are broken bubbles may move to the unrestricted area and move.

DPE Curriculum Guide – Lesson Plans
Movement Skills and Concepts (2)
Jumping, Tossing and Catching, and Moving in General Space
Level I – Week 8

Instructional Objectives:
To learn to evade or follow a partner while moving under control in general space
To learn a variety of jumping skills
To learn how forceful movements are generated

NASPE National Standards:
Introductory Activity: 1, 5
Fitness Activity: 1, 4, 6
Lesson Focus: 1, 2, 3, 5
Game: 1, 2, 5

Equipment Required:
Music for Astronaut Exercises
One yarn ball for each student

Instructional Activities	Teaching Hints

Introductory Activity — Run, Stop, and Pivot

Have the children run, and on signal, stop and pivot. Begin teaching a 90-degree pivot and move gradually to a 180° pivot. Relate the use of the pivot to various sport activities, such as basketball.

Encourage moving under control.

Bend the knees when stopping and place the weight on the pivot foot.

Fitness Development Activity — Astronaut Exercises

Walk, do arm circles	30 seconds	
Flexibility and trunk development challenges	30 seconds	
Skip forward, backwards, and sideways	30 seconds	
Upper-body strength challenges	30 seconds	
Slide; change lead leg	30 seconds	
Abdominal development challenges	30 seconds	
Jump like a pogo stick	30 seconds	
Upper body strength challenges	30 seconds	
Trot lightly in different directions	30 seconds	
Flexibility and trunk development challenges	30 seconds	
Gallop backwards	30 seconds	

Cool down with stretching and walking.

Tape alternating segments of silence and music to signal duration of exercise. Music segments (30 seconds) indicate aerobic activity; intervals of silence (30 seconds) signal flexibility and strength development activities.

See Chapter 13 for a description of how to perform challenge activities.

Allow students to adjust the workload to an intensity that is consistent with their ability level.

Lesson Focus — Movement Skills and Concepts (2)

Fundamental Skill: Jumping
1. Jump upward, trying for height.
2. Alternate low and high jumps.
3. Jump in various floor patterns--triangle, circle, square, letters, figure-eight, diamond shape.
4. Over a spot, jump forward, backwards, sideways, crisscross.
5. Jump with the body stiff, like a pogo stick. Explore with arms in different positions.
6. Practice jump turns—quarter, half, three-quarter, full. Add heel clicks with turns.
7. Increase and decrease the speed of jumping. Increase the height of jumping.
8. Land with the feet apart sideways and together again. Try it forward and backward (stride).
9. Jump and land as quietly as possible.
10. Jump and crisscross the feet sideways.
11. See how far you can jump in two, three, or four consecutive jumps.
12. Pretend you are a bouncing ball.
13. Clap hands or slap thighs when in the air.
14. Jump so the hands contact the floor.
15. Select a line. Proceed down it by jumping back and forth over the line. Add turns.

Select a few activities from each of the categories so students receive a variety of skills to practice. When possible, integrate the manipulative skill activities with fundamental skill activities. A common error is to teach all the activities from one category. The reason for multiple groups of activities is to provide variety and enhance motivation.

Use instructional cues such as:

"Swing your arms forward as you jump."

"Bend your knees."

"Land lightly by bending your knees."

"Jump as high as you can."

Manipulative Activity: Yarn Balls

Individual Activity

1. Toss and catch to self.
   a. Increase height gradually.
   b. Side to side.
   c. Front to back.
   d. Toss underneath the legs, around the body, etc.
   e. Toss and clap the hands. Clap around the body. Underneath the legs.
   f. Toss and make turns—quarter and half.
   g. Toss, perform the following: catch, heel click, touch elbows, knees, shoulders, and heels.
   h. Use contrasting tosses:
      High and low
      Near and far
      Front and back
2. Bat the ball upward as in volleyball, catch. Bat the ball, run forward and catch.
3. Toss forward, run and catch. Toss sideways and catch. Toss overhead, turn around, run and catch.

Partner Activity

1. Roll the ball back and forth.
2. Toss the ball back and forth, various ways.
3. Throw the ball back and forth.

Movement Concept: Moving in General Space

1. Run lightly in the area, changing direction as you wish without bumping or touching anyone. How many were able to do this? Try running zigzag fashion.
2. Run again in general space. On signal, change direction abruptly. Try again, only this time change both direction and the type of locomotor movement you are doing.
3. Run lightly and pretend you are dodging another runner. Run directly at another runner and dodge him or her.
4. Use a yarn ball to mark your personal space (spot); run in general space until the signal is given; return to your yarn ball and sit down.
5. We are going to do orienteering. Point to a spot on a wall, walk directly to the spot in a straight line. You may have to wait for others so as not to bump them. Pick another spot on a different wall and repeat. Return to home base on signal.
6. What happens when general space is decreased? Walk in general space. Now as space is decreased, walk again. Once more we are decreasing the space.
7. Run around your yarn ball until I say, "Bang." Then explode in a straight direction until the stop signal is sounded. Return.
8. From your spot, take three (four or five) jumps (hops, skips, gallops, slides) in one direction, turn around and do the same back to home base. Try with long steps away and tiny steps back.
9. I am going to challenge you on right and left movements. First, let's walk in general space. When I say "right" (or "left") you change direction abruptly.
10. This time run rapidly toward another child. Stop and bow. Now stop and shake hands.

Movement Concept: Use of Force

1. Show us how you do some forceful movements, such as chopping, batting, hitting with a sledge, punching the punching bag. Try karate chops and kicks, kicking a soccer ball, etc.
2. Show us a light movement you can make with the arm. Repeat the same movement more forcefully.
3. Make some movements that are light and sustained, heavy and sudden, heavy and sustained, light and sudden.
4. Make one part of the body move lightly, while another moves heavily.

Have the yarn balls placed around the perimeter of the area. On signal, ask students to jog to a ball, pick it up, and practice tossing and catching.

Toss the ball to a height where it can be caught. Little is gained by a toss that is too high and out of control.

Encourage a successful toss to be one where the feet do not have to be moved to make a catch.

Partners should start close together and gradually move apart as they become successful.

Place the yarn balls on the floor and use them as objects to move over and around.

Dodging demands running under control. Students should seldom run as fast as possible in physical education classes. Most activities demand controlled movement.

Explain simple orienteering activity.

Help students understand how the amount of force varies.

Sport activities usually demand controlled force rather than doing something "as hard as possible."

Fire Fighter

Supplies: None

Skill: Running

A fire chief runs around the outside of a circle of children and taps a number of them on the back, saying "Firefighter" each time. After making the round of the circle, the chief goes to the center. When she says "Fire," the firefighters run counterclockwise around the circle and back to place. The one who returns first and is able to stand in place motionless is declared the winner and the new chief.

The chief can use other words to fool children, but they run only on the word "Fire." This merely provides some fun, since there is no penalty for a false start. The circle children can sound the siren as the firefighters run.

Animal Tag

Supplies: None

Skills: Imagery, running, dodging

Two parallel lines are drawn about 40 ft apart. Children are divided into two groups, each of which takes a position on one of the lines. Children in one group get together with their leader and decide what animal they wish to imitate. Having selected the animal, they move over to within 5 ft or so of the other line. There they imitate the animal, and the other group tries to guess the animal correctly. If the guess is correct, they chase the first group back to its line, trying to tag as many as possible. Those caught must go over to the other team. The second group then selects an animal, and the roles are reversed. If the guessing team cannot guess the animal, however, the performing team gets another try. To avoid confusion, children must raise their hands to take turns at naming the animal. Otherwise, many false chases will occur. If children have trouble guessing, the leader of the performing team can give the initial of the animal.

Sneak Attack

Supplies: None

Skills: Marching, running

Two parallel lines are drawn about 60 ft apart. Children are divided into two teams. One team takes a position on one of the lines, with their backs to the area. These are the chasers. The other team is on the other line, facing the area. This is the sneak team. The sneak team moves forward on signal, moving toward the chasers. When they get reasonably close, a whistle or some other signal is given, and the sneak team turns and runs back to their line, chased by the other team. Anyone caught before reaching the line changes to the chase team. The game is repeated, with the roles exchanged.

DPE Curriculum Guide – Lesson Plans
Kicking, Trapping, Bowling, and Rolling Skills
Level I – Week 9

Instructional Objectives:
To cooperatively play tag games and maintain body control
To change speeds and directions of movement
To practice kicking, trapping, bowling, and rolling skills
To successfully participate in simple games

NASPE National Standards:
Introductory Activity: 1, 2, 5
Fitness Activity: 1, 4, 5
Lesson Focus: 1, 2, 5
Game: 1, 2, 5

Equipment Required:
Music for Fitness Challenges
8" foam rubber ball (or 8½" partially deflated playground ball) for each student
15 bowling pins

Instructional Activities	Teaching Hints

Introductory Activity — Tag Games

Use a tag game to offer children immediate activity. Many tag games can be found in Chapter 22. Some suggestions are:
1. Skunk
2. Stork
3. Stoop
4. Nose and Toe

Teach moving under control. Students should understand that they should seldom run as fast as possible in order to prevent collisions.

Use different locomotor movements.

Fitness Development Activity — Fitness Challenges

Alternate locomotor movements with strength and flexibility challenges. Repeat the challenges as necessary.

Locomotor Movement: Walk for 30 seconds.

Flexibility and Trunk Development Challenges
1. Bend in different directions.
2. Stretch slowly and return quickly.
3. Combine bending and stretching movements.
4. Sway back and forth.
5. Twist one body part; add body parts.
6. Make your body move in a large circle.
7. In a sitting position, wave your legs at a friend; make circles with your legs.

Locomotor Movement: Skip for 30 seconds.

Upper Body Strength Challenges
In a push-up position, do the following challenges:
1. Lift one foot; the other foot.
2. Wave at a friend; wave with the other arm.
3. Scratch your back with one hand; use the other hand.
4. Walk your feet to your hands.
5. Turn over and face the ceiling; shake a leg; Crab Walk.
Locomotor Movement: Jog for 30 seconds.

Abdominal Development
From a supine position:
1. Lift your head and look at your toes.
2. Lift your knees to your chest.
3. Wave your legs at a friend.
From a sitting position:
1. Slowly lay down with hands on tummy.
2. Lift legs and touch toes.

Locomotor Movement: Run and leap for 30 seconds.

Tape alternating segments (30 seconds in length) of silence and music to signal duration of exercise. Music segments indicate doing the locomotor movements; intervals of silence announce performing the strength and flexibility challenges.

Students select the fitness challenge they feel capable of performing. This implies that not all youngsters are required to do the same workload. Children differ and their ability to perform fitness workloads differs. Make fitness a personal challenge.

Because students can select activities they feel able to do, there is little reason for not trying.

If students do not remember the various challenges, cue them by calling out a number of the activities. They can select one they enjoy.

Use different qualities of movement such as giant skips, quick gallops, tiny jogging steps, etc.

Animal walks can be substituted for locomotor movements.

Lesson Focus — Kicking, Trapping, Rolling, and Bowling Skills

Kicking and Ball Control Skills

1. Inside of Foot Kick. Approach at 45-degree angle; inside of foot meets ball. Place nonkicking foot alongside ball.
2. Outside of Foot Kick. Short distance kick; keep toe down.
3. Long (instep) Pass. Contact the ball with the shoelaces. Not as accurate, but used for distance.
4. Sole of Foot Control. Use sole of foot to stop ball; make sure weight is placed on the nonreceiving foot.
5. Inside of Foot Control. Use inside of foot and learn to "give" with leg so ball doesn't ricochet off foot.
6. The receiver can practice soccer skills. For example, the following skills are suggested:
   a. Toe Trap
   b. The Foot Pickup
   c. Bowl with Your Feet

Give each student a ball. The ball of preference is an 8" foam rubber ball since it will not be painful to kick and trap. Underinflated (they are easier to control) 8½" playground balls can be substituted.

Assign students two or three activities to practice so you have time to move and help youngsters. Alternate activities from each of the categories so students receive a variety of skills to practice.

Rolling and Bowling Skills

1. Two-handed roll; between the legs, with wide straddle stance.
2. Roll the ball with one hand. Use both left and right hands.
3. Roll the ball and put spin on the ball so it will curve to the left and right.
4. Roll the ball through human straddle targets:
   a. Start rolling at moderate stances and gradually increase as bowlers become more proficient.
   b. Use left and right hands.
   c. Scoring can be done giving two points for a ball that goes through the target without touching and one point for a ball going through, but touching a leg.
5. Use objects such as milk cartons, clubs, or bowling pins for targets. Various bowling games can be developed using the targets.
6. Stand with your back facing your partner. Bend over; look through your legs and bowl.

Work with a partner and practice rolling and bowling to each other.

When bowling through the legs of youngsters, students need to take turns. Encourage them to change position after three or four turns.

Game Activity

Change Sides

Supplies: None
Skill: Body management

Identify two parallel lines 30 ft apart with half of the class on each line. On signal, all players cross to the other line, face the center, and stand at attention. The first group to do all three things correctly wins a point. Children must be cautioned to use care when passing through the opposite group. They should be spaced well along each line; this allows room for them to move through each group. Vary the locomotor movements used by specifying skipping, hopping, long steps, sliding, and other varieties of movement. The position to be assumed at the finish can be varied also.

Musical Ball Pass

Supplies: Playground ball per group, music
Skills: Passing and handling

Break the class into a number of small groups (6–7 players) in circle formation facing the center. One ball is given to a player and is passed to the circle players when the music starts. The ball may not be passed to an adjacent person. When the music stops, the player who last passed the ball moves up to another circle. Another alternative is to go into the "well" in the center of the circle for one turn. To avoid arguments, a player must go to the center if the ball is on the way to her. More than one ball may be used.

Instructional Objectives:
To independently identify different locomotor movements
To independently travel the mini-challenge course
To cooperate with peers in parachute activities
To work cooperatively in low-organized game settings

NASPE National Standards:
Introductory Activity: 1, 2
Fitness Activity: 1, 2, 3, 5, 6
Lesson Focus: 2, 3, 5
Game: 1, 5

Equipment Required:
Magic number cards
Music for fitness
Equipment for Mini-Challenge Course
Parachute
Colored paper in shapes for game
10–20 beanbags for game

Instructional Activities	Teaching Hints

Introductory Activity — Magic Number Challenges

Students put together a series of movements based on the magic numbers given. For example, hold up a card with three numbers on it (10, 8, 14). Students respond by performing three different locomotor movements the specified number of times, respectively.	Encourage variety of response. Use movements such as walking, running, jumping, hopping, galloping, sliding, leaping, and skipping.

Fitness Development Activity — Mini-Challenge Course

Arrange four parallel courses with a group at each course. Students perform the challenges from a cone at the start to a finish cone and jog back to continuously repeat the course. On signal, groups rotate to a new course. **Course 1.** Hop in and out of 5 hoops, Puppy Dog Walk around a cone for 5 seconds, and skip to the finish cone. **Course 2.** Weave in and out of four cones, Crab Walk around a cone for 5 seconds, and gallop to finish cone. **Course 3.** Do the Rolling Log the length of mat, do an agility run through 4 hoops, and slide to the finish cone. **Course 4.** Jump over each of 5 cones, jump back and forth over a stretched out jump rope, run backwards around three cones, and hop to a cone.	Tape alternating segments (20 seconds in length) of silence and music to signal duration of exercise. Music segments indicate moving through the mini-challenge course; intervals of silence announce using the chute to enhance flexibility and strength development. Students can set up their own mini-challenges.

Lesson Focus — Fundamental Skills Using Parachute Activity

1. Circular movements.
   Move utilizing locomotor movements and holding the chute at various levels—walk, run, hop, jump, skip, slide, draw steps.
2. Shaking the Rug and Making Waves.
   Shaking the Rug should involve small, rapid movements, whereas Making Waves is large movements.
3. Making a Dome.
   Parachute should be on the floor and held with both hands. Make a dome by standing up and rapidly lifting the chute overhead.
4. Mushroom.
   Similar to the Dome except three or four steps toward the center are taken by each student.
   a. Mushroom Release—all students release the chute at its peak of inflation.
   b. Mushroom Run—Make a mushroom, students move toward center; a few selected students release grip, and run around the inside of the chute back to place.
5. Activities with Balls and Beanbags.
   a. Ball Circle—Use a basketball or cageball and make it circle around the outside of the chute. Add a second ball.
   b. Popcorn—Place 6 to 10 whiffle balls on the chute and shake them into the air.
	When performing locomotor movements with the chute, have students hold the chute with one hand. The direction of the movement can be stated by asking for a "right hand run," or a "left hand skip" etc.
	
	When making a dome, have all students on one knee with both hands on the floor. On signal they make a strong movement upward.
	
	Encourage all students to work together. Discuss how much easier it is when all students pull and lift together.
	
	Try the activities holding the chute with both hands and with one hand.

c. Giant Popcorn—Use beach balls instead of whiffle balls.

d. Poison Snake—Place 6 to 10 jump ropes on the chute. Divide the players in half. Try to shake the ropes so they touch a player on the opposing team.

Play the poison snake activity like a tag game. If the jump rope touches a player, they must release their grip and back away from the chute. Reset the game and start over with all players playing.

6. Kite Run.

Half the class holds the chute on one side. They run in any direction together and as fast as possible. The parachute should trail like a kite.

7. Tug-of-War.

Divide the class into two equal halves. On signal, they pull and try to move each other.

8. Hole in One.

Use 6 or 8 small balls of two different colors. The object is to get the other team's balls to fall through the hole in the center.

Playing hole in one is a challenge. Use many balls so the odds of a ball going into the center are increased.

9. Ocean Walk.

The class is on their knees, making waves with the chute. Three or four youngsters are selected to walk or jog "in the ocean" without falling.

Safety is important when walking on the parachute. The chute must not be lifted.

Game Activity

May I Chase You?

Supplies: None

Skills: Running, dodging

The class stands behind a line long enough to accommodate all. Two or three runners stand about 5 ft in front of the line. The class asks, "May I chase you?" One of the runners (designated by teacher) replies, "Yes, if you are wearing …" and names a color, an article of clothing, or a combination of the two. All who qualify immediately chase the runners until one is tagged. New runners are chosen and the game is repeated. Encourage players to think of other ways to identify those who run.

Tommy Tucker's Land

Supplies: About 10 beanbags for each game

Skills: Dodging, running

Two or three youngsters, Tommy Tuckers (or Tammi Tuckers, if a girl), stand in the center of a 15-ft square where the beanbags are scattered. The Tuckers are guarding their land and treasure (beanbags). The other children chant,

I'm on Tommy Tucker's land,

Picking up gold and silver.

Children attempt to pick up as much of the treasure as they can while avoiding being tagged by the Tuckers. Any child who is tagged must return the treasure and retire from the game. The game is over when only one child is left or when all of the beanbags have been successfully filched. The teacher may wish to call a halt to the game earlier if a stalemate is reached. New Tuckers are selected.

Colors

Supplies: Colored paper (construction paper) cut in circles, squares, or triangles for markers

Skills: Color or other perceptual concepts, running

Five or six different-colored markers should be used, with a number of children having the same color. Children are standing or seated in a circle with a marker in front of each child. The teacher calls out a color, and everyone having that color runs counterclockwise around the circle and back to place. The first one seated upright and motionless is declared the winner. Different kinds of locomotor movement can be specified, such as skipping, galloping, walking, and so on. After a period of play, the children leave the markers on the floor and move one place to the left.

Variation: Shapes (e.g., circles, triangles, squares, rectangles, stars, and diamonds) can be used instead of colors, as can numbers or other articles or categories, such as animals, birds, or fish. This game has value in teaching identification and recognition.

DPE Curriculum Guide – Lesson Plans
Recreational Activities
Level I – Week 11

Instructional Objectives:
To be able to move continuously in
    moderately active activities
To learn the rules of recreational
    activities
To play in recreational activities
    independently without adult
    supervision

NASPE National Standards:
Introductory Activity: 1, 3, 5
Fitness Activity: 1, 4, 6
Lesson Focus: 2, 3, 5, 6
Game: 2, 3, 5, 6

Equipment Required:
One hoop or beanbag per student for
    Ponies in the Stable
Music for Astronaut Exercises
Equipment for desired recreational
    activities

Instructional Activities	Teaching Hints

Introductory Activity — Ponies in the Stable

A beanbag or hoop is used to mark each child's stable. On signal, youngsters gallop around the area and in and out of "stables." On a second signal, students return to the nearest stable.
Variations.
1. Use different locomotor movements.
2. Take different positions in the stable such as seated, balanced, and collapsed.

To introduce excitement into the activity, remove a few stables and encourage students not to be left out.

Teach directions by asking students to move in a certain direction, i.e., north, south, etc.

Fitness Development Activity — Astronaut Exercises

Walk, do arm circles	30 seconds
Flexibility and trunk development challenges	30 seconds
Skip forward, backwards, and sideways	30 seconds
Upper-body strength challenges	30 seconds
Slide; change lead leg	30 seconds
Abdominal development challenges	30 seconds
Jump like a pogo stick	30 seconds
Upper-body strength challenges	30 seconds
Trot lightly in different directions	30 seconds
Flexibility and trunk development challenges	30 seconds
Gallop backwards	30 seconds

Cool down with stretching and walking.

Tape alternating segments of silence and music to signal duration of exercise. Music segments (30 seconds) indicate aerobic activity; intervals of silence (30 seconds) signal flexibility and strength development activities.

See Chapter 13 for a description of how to perform challenge activities.

Allow students to adjust the workload to an intensity that is consistent with their ability level.

Lesson Focus and Game Activity — Recreational Activities

The purpose of this unit is to teach children activities that they can use for recreation outside of school or during recess. Suggested activities are:
1. Shuffleboard
2. Two Square
3. Hopscotch
4. Beanbag Horseshoes
5. Jacks
6. Marbles
7. Sidewalk tennis
8. Quoits
9. Rubber Horseshoes
10. Four Square
11. Basketball, Soccer, and other seasonal sports
12. Any traditional and/or local area games

Teach students the rules of recreational activities so they are able to participate effectively during free time.

Teach any games that are traditional to an area. Older youngsters may be a good source of advice for often-played games.

If desired, set up a number of stations and have youngsters rotate to different stations during the lesson.

DPE Curriculum Guide – Lesson Plans
Walking and Jogging Skills
Level I – Week 12

Instructional Objectives:
To make a variety of shapes with the body
To walk and/or jog at a continuous and personalized pace
To understand the benefits of aerobic activity

NASPE National Standards:
Introductory Activity: 1, 3
Fitness Activity: 1, 4, 6
Lesson Focus: 3, 5, 6
Game: 5

Equipment Required:
Tom-tom or tambourine
Music for Walk, Trot, Jog
Equipment for games

Instructional Activities	Teaching Hints

Introductory Activity — Run and Assume Shape

Place emphasis on making a variety of shapes and balances. Vary the locomotor movements.

1. Run and move to a prone (one drumbeat) or supine (two drumbeats) position on signal.
2. Run and move into a balance position.
3. Run and freeze in various shapes.

Place emphasis on running under control and assuming specified shape quickly.

Have students move into the activity area in scatter formation.

Fitness Development Activity — Walk, Trot, and Jog

Move to the following signals:
1. One drumbeat—walk.
2. Two drumbeats—trot.
3. Three drumbeats—jog.
4. Whistle—freeze and perform exercises.

Use strength and flexibility exercises between bouts of walk, trot, and jog to allow students to recover aerobically. Examples are:
1. Bend and Twist
2. Sitting Stretch
3. Push-up challenges
4. Abdominal challenges
5. Body Twist
6. Standing Hip Bend

Tape alternating segments (20 seconds in length) of silence and music to signal duration of exercise. Music segments indicate walk, trot, and jog activity. Intervals of silence signal performance of the strength and flexibility exercises.

Encourage students to move around the area in the same direction.

See Chapter 13 for a description of how to perform the exercises. Any exercises can be substituted. Try to exercise all body parts.

Lesson Focus — Walking and Jogging

The walking and jogging lesson offers emphasis on developing activity patterns that can be used outside of the school environment. An educational approach to this lesson teaches students that walking and jogging is a personal activity that offers excellent health benefits. It is an activity that can literally be done for a lifetime. The following are suggestions for implementing this unit of instruction:

1. Youngsters should be allowed to find a friend with whom they want to jog or walk. The result is usually a friend of similar ability level. A way to judge correct pace is to be able to talk with a friend without undue stress. If students are too winded to talk, they are probably running too fast. A selected friend will encourage talking and help assure that the experience is positive and within the student's aerobic capacity. *Pace, not race* is the motto.

2. Jogging and walking should be done in any direction so people are unable to keep track of the distance covered. Doing laps on a track can be discouraging for less able youngsters. They usually finish last and are open to chiding by the rest of the class.

3. Jogging and walking should be done for a specified time rather than a specified distance. All youngsters should not have to run the same distance. This goes against the philosophy of accompanying individual differences and varying aerobic capacities. Running or walking for a set amount of time will allow less able students to do the best they can without fear of ridicule.

4. Teachers should not be concerned about foot action, since the child selects naturally the means that is most comfortable. Arm movement should be easy and natural, with elbows bent. The head and upper body should be held up and back. The eyes look ahead. The general body position in walking and jogging should be erect but relaxed. Jogging on the toes should be avoided.

5. Jogging and walking should not be a competitive, timed activity. Each youngster should move at a self-determined pace. Racing belongs in the track program. Another reason to avoid speed is that racing keeps youngsters from learning to

pace their running. For developing endurance and gaining health benefits, teach moving for a longer time at a slower speed rather than run at top speed for a shorter distance.

6. It can be motivating for youngsters if they run with a piece of equipment, i.e., beanbag or jump rope. They can play catch with a beanbag or roll a hoop while walking or jogging.

Game Activity

Low Organization Games

When the jogging activity is finished, students may be somewhat fatigued. Play games that do not place high demand on the cardiovascular system.

DPE Curriculum Guide – Lesson Plans
Rhythmic Movement Skills (1)
Level I – Week 13

Instructional Objectives:
To be able to identify and perform
   animal movements
To march individually and in patterns
To be able to move rhythmically
To perform simple folk dances

NASPE National Standards:
Introductory Activity: 1, 5
Fitness Activity: 1, 2, 4, 5, 6
Lesson Focus: 1, 3, 4, 5, 6
Game: 5

Equipment Required:
Music for Parachute Fitness
Parachute
Music for rhythmic activities
Playground ball for game

Instructional Activities	Teaching Hints

Introductory Activity — Simple Games

Use a game that youngsters learned earlier and contains ample gross motor
activity. The following are suggested:
1. Toe to Toe, see Week 1
2. Sneak Attack, see Week 3
3. Change Sides, see Week 6

Toe to Toe is excellent for teaching
youngsters to find a partner quickly.
Change Sides teaches youngsters to
move across the teaching area without
bumping into others.

Fitness Development Activity — Parachute Fitness

1. Jog while holding the chute in the left hand. (music)
2. Shake the chute. (no music)
3. Slide while holding the chute with both hands. (music)
4. Sit and perform curl-ups. (no music)
5. Skip. (music)
6. Freeze, face the center, and stretch the chute tightly. Repeat five to six times.
   (no music)
7. Run in place while holding the chute taut at different levels. (music)
8. Sit with legs under the chute. Do a seat walk toward the center. Return to the
   perimeter. Repeat four to six times. (no music)
9. Place the chute on the ground. Jog away from the chute and return on signal.
   Repeat. (music)
10. Move into push-up position holding the chute with one hand. Shake the
    chute. (no music)
11. Shake the chute and jump in place. (music)
12. Lie on back with feet under the chute. Shake the chute with the feet. (no music)
13. Hop to the center of the chute and return. (music)
14. Sit with feet under the chute. Stretch by touching the toes with the chute.
    Relax with other stretches while sitting. (no music)

Tape alternating segments (20 seconds
in length) of silence and music to signal
duration of exercise. Music segments
indicate aerobic activity with the
parachute; intervals of silence announce
using the chute to enhance flexibility
and strength development.

Space youngsters evenly around the
chute.

Use different hand grips (palms up,
down, mixed).

All movements should be done under
control. Some of the faster and stronger
students will have to moderate their
performance.

Lesson Focus — Rhythmic Movement Skills (1)

Marching
Try the following sequence:
1. Clap hands while standing in place to the beat of a tom-tom or record.
2. March in place; always start with the left foot.
3. March to the music in scatter formation, adding some of the following
      challenges:
   a. Be as big or small as you can.
   b. Count the rhythm.
   c. Change direction on signal.
   d. March backwards.
   e. March loudly or quietly.
   f. Make up a rhythmic poem like "Sound Off."
   g. Be a drum major leading the band.
   h. Play various instruments in the band while marching.
4. Try some simple patterns such as the following:
   a. Single-line formation.
   b. Double-line formation (with a partner).
   c. Two lines meet and go up the center.

**Include an activity from each area
including marching activities, a
parachute rhythmic routine, and a
rhythmic activity.**

Use scatter formation during early
learning stages.

When marching in line, try to maintain
spacing between individuals.

If desired, teach commands such as
"about face," "forward march," and
"halt."

Parachute Rhythmic Routine

Perform rhythmic activities while holding or manipulating the parachute:

Beats	Movement
1–8	Eight walking steps to the left. Hold chute in both hands.
9–16	Eight backward steps to the right.
17–20	Raise parachute above head (up-2-3-4).
21–24	Lower chute to floor (down-2-3-4).
25–32	Shake the chute (up and down).
33–36	Raise the chute overhead.
37–44	Lower chute quickly to floor and form a dome. Hold the dome for eight beats.

Try saluting each other as they march.

Practice the steps without the parachute when learning the movements.

Instead of holding to a specified number of beats, it might be easier to call out a change. This allows the teacher to continue the movements until most students have learned.

Rhythmic Activities

Make dances easy for students to learn by implementing some of the following techniques:

1. Teach the dances without using partners.
2. Allow youngsters to move in any direction without left-right orientation.
3. Use scattered formation instead of circles.
4. Emphasize strong movements such as clapping and stamping to increase involvement.
5. Play the music at a slower speed when first learning the dance.

Rhythms should be taught like other sport skills. Avoid striving for perfection so students know it is acceptable to make mistakes. Teach a variety of dances rather than one or two in depth in case some students find it difficult to master a specific dance.

Movin' Madness (American)

Music Source: WWCD-1044
Formation: Scattered
Skills: Keeping time, creativity
Directions:
Part I:
The tempo is slow, slow, fast-fast-fast. The children do any series of movements of their choice to fit this pattern, repeated four times. The movements should be large, gross motor movements.
Part II:
During the second part (chorus) of the music, the children do any locomotor movement in keeping with the tempo. The step-hop or a light run can be used with the tempo of Part II.
Teaching suggestions: Have the youngsters clap the rhythm. They should pay particular attention to the tempo in Part I. The music is Bleking, a dance presented later. The music for "I See You" is also suitable, but note that the movements in Part I are repeated twice instead of four times. The Part II music is suitable for skipping, sliding, or galloping.

Did You Ever See a Lassie? (Scottish)

Music Source: WWCD 7054; WWC-7054
Skills: Walking at 3/4 time, creativity
Formation: Single circle, facing halfway left, with hands joined; one child in the center
Verse
Did you ever see a lassie (laddie), a lassie, a lassie?
Did you ever see a lassie go this way and that?
Go this way and that way, and this way and that way?
Did you ever see a lassie go this way and that?
Directions:

Measures	Action
1–8	All walk (one step per measure) to the left in a circle with hands joined. (Walk, 2, 3, 4, 5, 6, 7, 8) The child in the center gets ready to demonstrate some type of movement.
9–16	All stop and copy the movement suggested by the child in the center.

When the verse starts over, the center child selects another to do some action in the center and changes places with her.

Ach Ja (German)

Music Source: WWC-0860
Skills: Walking, sliding
Formation: Double circle, partners facing counterclockwise, partners A on the inside, inside hands joined
Verse
When my father and my mother take the children to the fair,
Ach Ja! Ach Ja! Oh, they haven't any money, but it's little that they care,
Ach Ja! Ach Ja!
Tra la la, tra la la, tra la la la la la la
Tra la la, tra la la, tra la la la la la la
Ach Ja! Ach Ja!
Directions:
Explain that "Ach Ja" means "Oh yes."

Measures	Action
1–2	Partners walk eight steps in the line of direction. (Walk, 2, 3, 4, 5, 6, 7, 8)
3	Partners drop hands and bow to each other. (Bow)
4	Each A then bows to the B on the left, who returns the bow. (Bow)
5–8	Measures 1–4 are repeated.
9–10	Partners face each other, join hands, and take four slides in the line of direction. (Slide, 2, 3, 4)
11–12	Four slides are taken clockwise. (Slide, 2, 3, 4)
13	Partners bow to each other. (Bow)
14	A bows to the B on the left, who returns the bow. (Bow) To start the next dance, A moves quickly toward B, who is the next partner.

Bombay Bounce (American)

Music Source: Any source with a definite and moderately fast beat
Skills: Hesitation step, side step
Formation: Scattered, all facing forward
Directions:

Part I (16 counts): A hesitation step to the left is performed by taking a short step to the left followed by touching the right foot near the left while the weight remains on the left foot. A hesitation step to the right is similar except it begins with a step to the right. To begin the dance, eight hesitation steps are performed in place with a hand clap on each touch. (Left, touch and clap; right, touch and clap). Repeat 4 times.

Part II (16 counts): Take two side steps to the left, then two to the right. Clap on counts 4 and 8. (Left, close; Left, close and clap; Right, close; Right, close and clap). Repeat the pattern.

Part III (16 counts): Take four side steps left and four side steps right. Clap only on count 8. (Left, close, left, close, left, close, left, close and clap). Repeat to the right.

Part IV (16 counts): Take four steps forward and four steps backward, four steps forward, and four steps backward. Clap on counts 4, 8, 12, and 16. (Forward, 2, 3, 4 and clap; Backward, 2, 3, 4 and clap; Forward, 2, 3, 4 and clap; Backward 2, 3, 4 and clap).

Teaching suggestions: Variations are possible (e.g., in Part IV, instead of four steps, use three steps and a kick [swing].)

Circassian Circle (English)

Music Source: WWCD-FDN
Skills: Walking, skipping, promenade
Formation: Large single circle of couples facing center with all hands joined
Directions:

Measures	Action
2	Introduction
1–2	All walk 4 steps toward center and back 4 steps to place (Walk 2, 3, 4; back, 2, 3, 4)
3–4	Repeat measures 1 and 2 (Walk 2, 3, 4; back, 2, 3, 4)
5–6	Girls walk 4 steps toward center and back 4 steps (Girls, 2, 3, 4; back, 2, 3, 4)
7–8	Boys walk 4 steps toward center, then turn a half-turn left and walk diagonally clockwise 4 steps to a new partner. (Boys, 2, 3, 4; move, to, new, partner)
9–10	Using a cross-arm grip, new partners lean away from each other and skip 8 steps clockwise once around each other. (Skip, 2, 3, 4, 5, 6, 7, 8)
11–12	Without dropping hands, couples promenade counterclockwise for 8 steps. Take the last two steps to stop and face the center to do the dance again. (Promenade, 2, 3, 4, 5, 6, face, center)

The dance is performed 4 times.

Danish Dance of Greeting (Danish)

Music Source: WWCD-1041; WWC-07042

Skills: Running or sliding, bowing

Formation: Single circle, all face center. Partner A stands to the left of partner B.

Directions:

Measures	Action
1	All clap twice and bow to partner. (Clap, clap, bow)
2	Repeat but turn back to the partner and bow to the neighbor. (Clap, clap, bow)
3	Stamp right, stamp left. (Stamp, stamp)
4	Turn around in four running steps. (Turn, 2, 3, 4)
5–8	Repeat the action of measures 1–4.
9–12	All join hands and run to the left for four measures. (Run, 2, 3, 4, … 16)
13–16	Repeat the action of measures 9–12, taking light running steps in the opposite direction. (Run, 2, 3, 4, … 16)

Variation: Instead of a running step, use a light slide.

Game Activity

Squirrel in the Trees

Supplies: None

Skills: Fundamental locomotor movements

A number of trees are formed by two players facing each other and holding hands or putting hands on each other's shoulders. A squirrel is in the center of each tree, and one or two extra squirrels are outside. On signal, the trees open up and let the squirrels move around the area. The trees also stay together and move throughout the area. On signal, the trees freeze in place and the squirrels find any available tree. Only one squirrel is allowed in a tree.

Teaching Suggestion: Rotation is necessary so all students get to be a squirrel. Once the squirrels are in a tree, ask them to face one of the tree players. The person they are facing becomes their partner for a tree and the other person becomes a new squirrel.

Stop Ball

Supplies: A ball

Skills: Tossing, catching

The class is divided into small circles with 5 to 7 players. One player, with their hands over their eyes, stands in the center of the circle. A ball is tossed clockwise or counterclockwise from player to player around the circle. Failing to catch the ball or making a bad toss incurs a penalty. That player takes one long step backward and stays out of the game for one turn. At a time of her own selection, the center player calls, "Stop." The player caught with the ball (or the ball coming to her) steps back and stays out for one turn. The center player should be allowed two or three turns and then changed.

DPE Curriculum Guide – Lesson Plans
Fundamental Skills Using Long Jump Ropes
Level I – Week 14

Instructional Objectives:

To perform locomotor movements
  on cue
To perform long rope jumping skills
To know the difference between front
  and back door entry in long rope
  jumping
To pass and catch balls in a game
  setting

NASPE National Standards:

Introductory Activity: 1, 3
Fitness Activity: 1, 3, 4, 6
Lesson Focus: 2, 3, 4, 5
Game: 1, 5

Equipment Required:

Circuit training music, signs, and cones
One long jump rope per 4–6 students
  (12–16 ft in length)
10-ft jump ropes for students who have
  trouble turning the 16-ft ropes
5 or 6 balls for game activities

Instructional Activities	Teaching Hints

Introductory Activity — Crossing the River

Two lines about 40 ft apart designate a river. Each time the youngsters cross the river they must perform a different movement. For example:
  1. Run, walk, hop, skip, leap.
  2. Animal Walks such as bear, crab, and puppy dog.
  3. Partner run, back to back, side by side.

Stress quality of movement rather than speed.

Reinforce creativity and original movements.

Fitness Development Activity — Circuit Training

Make signs, put them on cones and place around the perimeter of the teaching area. Students perform the exercise specified at each station while the music is playing.
  1. Tortoise and Hare
  2. Curl-up variations
  3. Hula-Hooping on arms
  4. Standing Hip Bend
  5. Agility run—run back and forth between two designated lines
  6. Push-up variations
  7. Crab Walk
  8. Bend and Twist

Tape alternating segments of silence and music to signal duration of exercise. Music segments (begin at 30 seconds) indicate activity at each station; intervals of silence (10 seconds) announce it is time to stop and move forward to the next station.

Lesson Focus — Fundamental Skills Using Long Jump Ropes

  1. Jump a stationary rope, gradually raise the rope.
  2. Ocean Waves—Shake the rope with an up-and-down motion. Students try to jump a "low spot."
  3. Snake in the grass—Wiggle the rope back and forth on the grass. Jump without touching the rope.
  4. Pendulum swing—Move the rope back and forth like a pendulum. Jump the rope as it approaches the jumper.
  5. Practice turning the rope with a partner. The skill of turning *must* precede jumping skills. Standard 16-ft-long ropes are difficult for young children to turn. Substitute 8- to 12-ft ropes depending on the maturity of the youngsters.
  6. Practice turning the rope to rhythm. Music with a strong beat or a steady tom-tom beat is useful for developing rhythmic turning. Turning the rope to a steady rhythm *must* precede jumping skills.
  7. Run through a turning rope.
  8. Stand in the center of the turners and jump the rope as it is turned once. Add more jumps.
  9. Run in, jump once, and run out.
  10. Front door—turn the rope toward the jumper.
  11. Try the following variations:
    a. Run in front door and out back door.
    b. Run in back door and out front door.
    c. Run in back door and out back door.

Groups of four students work best because it allows students to rotate easily (two turners and two jumpers) without anyone being left out.

Use shorter jump ropes for students who have trouble learning to turn.

Teach turning by having students hold an end of the rope and standing as far apart as possible. Make small circles with the rope and gradually step toward each other, making large circles.

Rhythmic turning is important! Many students miss the jump because of erratic turning. Practice turning until it becomes a smooth even tempo.

d. Run in front or back door, jump a specified number of times, and out.
e. Run in front or back door, jump, and do a quarter, half, and full turn.
f. Touch the ground while jumping.
g. Turn around while jumping.
12. Recite a chant while jumping.

Allow beginners to tell the turners what activity they want to do. Self-choice helps assure success.

Examples of chants:
Tick tock, tick tock,
What's the time by the clock?
It's one, two, [up to midnight].

I like coffee, I like tea,
How many people can jump like me?
One, two, three, [up to a certain number].

Game Activity

Ball Passing

Supplies: Five or six different kinds of balls for each circle
Skill: Object handling

Divide the class into two or more circles, with no more than 15 children in any one circle. Each circle consists of two or more squads, but squad members need not stand together. A ball is started around the circle and passed from player to player in the same direction. Introduce more balls until 5 or 6 are moving around the circle at the same time and in the same direction. If a child drops a ball, he must retrieve it, and a point is scored against his squad. After a period of time, a whistle is blown, and the points against each squad are totaled. The squad with the lowest score wins. Beanbags, large blocks, or softballs can be substituted for balls.

Hot Potatoes

Supplies: One to three balls or beanbags for each group
Skill: Object handling

Group players in small circles (8 to 12 per circle) so objects can be passed from one to another around the circle. Balls or beanbags or both are passed around the circle. The teacher or a selected student, who is standing with their back to the class randomly shouts, "stop!" The point of the game is to avoid being the person who passes the object to the person who caught it when the signal occurs. If this happens, the player(s) who passed the object gets up and moves to the next circle. Begin the game with one object and gradually add objects if the class is capable. Call out "Reverse" to signal a change in the direction the object is passed.

Aviator

Supplies: None
Skills: Running, locomotor movements, stopping

Players are parked (in push-up position) at one end of the playing area. The air traffic controller (ATC) is in front of the players and calls out, "Aviators aviators, take off!" Youngsters take off and move like airplanes to the opposite side of the area. The first person to move to the other side and land the plane (get into push-up position facing the ATC) is declared the new ATC.

If the ATC yells out some type of stormy weather, all planes must return to the starting line and resume the parked position. Examples of stormy weather commands are lightning, thunder, hurricane, and tornado. Each ATC is allowed to give stormy weather warnings once.

DPE Curriculum Guide – Lesson Plans
Gymnastics Skills (2)
Level I – Week 15

Instructional Objectives:
To sustain moderate physical activity
To absorb the body weight on the hands
To balance the body in a variety of challenges

NASPE National Standards:
Introductory Activity: 1, 3
Fitness Activity: 1, 3, 4, 5, 6
Lesson Focus: 1, 2, 3, 5
Game: 1, 5

Equipment Required:
Music for Mini-Challenge Course
Equipment for Mini-Challenge Course
Tumbling mats
Beanbags for Partner Toe Toucher

Instructional Activities	Teaching Hints

Introductory Activity — Popcorn

Students pair up with one person on the floor in push-up position and the other standing ready to move. On signal, the standing students move over and around the persons on the floor. The person on the floor changes from a raised to a lowered push-up position each time the partner goes over or around her. On signal, reverse positions.

Caution to avoid touching others and respect personal space.

Challenge students to see how many students they can move over and around.

Fitness Development Activity — Mini-Challenge Course

Arrange four parallel courses with a group at each course. Students perform the challenges from a cone at the start to a finish cone and jog back to continuously repeat the course. On signal, groups rotate to a new course.

Course 1. Hop in and out of 5 hoops, Puppy Dog Walk around a cone for 5 seconds and skip to the finish cone.

Course 2. Weave in and out of four cones, Crab Walk around a cone for 5 seconds and gallop to finish cone.

Course 3. Do the Rolling Log the length of mat, do an agility run through 4 hoops, and slide to the finish cone.

Course 4. Jump over each of 5 cones, jump back and forth over a stretched out jump rope, run backwards around three cones; and hop to a cone.

Tape alternating segments of silence and music to signal duration of exercise. Music segments (20 to 30 seconds in length) indicate course activity; intervals of silence (10 to 15 seconds) signal rotating to a new course.

Students can set up their own mini-challenges.

Lesson Focus — Gymnastics Skills (2)

Animal Movements

Bear Walk
    Bend forward and touch the ground with both hands. Travel forward slowly by moving the hand and foot on the same side together (i.e., first the right hand and foot, then the left hand and foot). Make deliberate movements.

Gorilla Walk
    Bend the knees and carry the trunk forward. Let the arms hang at the sides. Touch the fingers to the ground while walking.

Rabbit Jump
    Crouch with knees apart and hands placed on the floor. Move forward by reaching out with both hands and then bringing both feet up to the hands. The eyes look ahead. Emphasize that this is a jump rather than a hop because both feet move at once.

Elephant Walk
    Bend well forward, clasping the hands together to form a trunk. The end of the trunk should swing close to the ground. Walk in a slow, deliberate, dignified manner, keeping the legs straight and swinging the trunk from side to side.

Five groups of activities in this lesson ensure that youngsters receive a variety of experiences. Pick a few activities from each group and teach them alternately. For example, teach one or two animal movements, then a tumbling and inverted balance, followed by a balance stunt, etc. Give equal time to each group of activities.

Scatter tumbling mats throughout the area so that there is little standing in line waiting for a turn.

A major concern for safety is the neck and back region. Overweight children are at greater risk and might be allowed to avoid tumbling and inverted balances.

Tumbling and Inverted Balances
Forward Roll Review (See Week 7)

Backward Curl

Approach this activity in three stages. For the first stage, begin in a sitting position, with the knees drawn up to the chest and the chin tucked. The hands are clasped and placed behind the head with the elbows held out as far as possible. Gently roll backward until the weight is on the elbows. Roll back to starting position.

In stage two, perform the same action as before, but place the hands alongside the head on the mat while rolling back. The fingers are pointed in the direction of the roll, with palms down on the mat. (A good cue is, "Point your thumbs toward your ears and keep your elbows close to your body.")

For stage three, perform the same action as in stage two, but start in a crouched position on the feet with the back facing the direction of the roll. Momentum is secured by sitting down quickly and bringing the knees to the chest. This, like the Back Roller, is a lead-up to the Backward Roll. Teach children to push against the floor to take pressure off the back of the neck.

Climb-Up

Begin on a mat in a kneeling position, with hands placed about shoulder width apart and the fingers spread and pointed forward. Place the head forward of the hands, so that the head and hands form a triangle on the mat. Walk the body weight forward so that most of it rests on the hands and head. Climb the knees to the top of the elbows. (This stunt is a lead-up to the Headstand.)

Balance Stunts
Kimbo Stand

With the left foot kept flat on the ground, cross the right leg over the left to a position in which the right foot is pointed partially down and the toe is touching the ground.

Knee-Lift Stand

From a standing position, lift one knee up so that the thigh is parallel to the ground and the toe is pointed down. Hold. Return to starting position.

Stork Stand

From a standing position, shift all of the weight to one foot. Place the other foot so that the sole is against the inside of the knee and thigh of the standing leg. Hold. Recover to standing position.

Individual Stunts
Rubber Band

Get down in a squat position with the hands and arms clasped around the knees. On the command "Stretch, stretch, stretch," stretch as tall and as wide as possible. On the command "Snap," snap back to original position.

Pumping Up the Balloon

One child, the pumper, is in front of the other children, who are the balloons. The pumper pretends to use a bicycle pump to inflate the balloons. The balloons get larger and larger until the pumper shouts, "Bang," whereupon the balloons collapse to the floor. The pumper should give a "shoosh" sound every time a pumping motion is made.

Rising Sun

Lie on the back. Using the arms for balance only, rise to a standing position. Try with the arms folded over the chest.

Heel Click

Stand with the feet slightly apart, jump up, and click the heels, coming down with the feet apart.

Do not perform many repetitions of tumbling and inverted balances. For most children, limiting the number of forward or backward rolls to 2–3 will prevent fatigue and injury.

The Backward Curl should be used to learn to roll back and forth. No youngster should be expected to roll over if it is difficult for them. In stunts and tumbling, it is important that the student decide if they are capable and confident enough to try the activity.

The Climb-up should only be performed by youngsters who have sufficient strength to support the body weight. Overweight children will find this to be a difficult activity.

Most children can accomplish balance stunts and this should be an area of accomplishment for all students.

Encourage students to hold the balance position for at least five counts.

An added challenge is to see how long the balance can be held with the eyes closed.

Emphasize a quick snapping back to position. Students can change their starting position as they desire.

Allow many children the chance to be a pumper.

Experiment with different positions of the feet. The feet can be crossed, spread wide, both to one side, and so on.

Try with a quarter turn right and left. Try clapping the hands overhead as the heels are clicked.

Partner and Group Stunts

Wring the Dishrag

Face and join hands with a partner. Raise one pair of arms (right for one and left for the other) and turn under, continuing a full turn until back to original position. Try in a reverse direction.

This is an excellent opportunity to talk about cooperation and moving together. Emphasize form rather than doing it as fast as possible.

Partner Toe Toucher

Partners lie on their backs with heads near each other and feet in opposite directions. Join arms with partner using a hand-wrist grip, and bring the legs up so that the toes touch partner's toes. Keep high on the shoulders and touch the feet high. Strive to attain the high shoulder position, as this is the point of most difficulty.

One child carries a beanbag, a ball, or some other article between the feet, and transfers the object to the partner, who lowers it to the floor.

Game Activity

Where's My Partner?

Supplies: None

Skills: Fundamental locomotor movements

Children are in a double circle facing a partner. The inside circle has two or three more players than the outside. When the signal is given, the circles skip (or walk, run, hop, or gallop) to the right. This means that they are skipping in opposite directions. On the command "Halt," the circles face each other to find partners. The players left without a partner go to the mush pot (the center area of the circle) for one turn. The circles should be reversed after a time.

Variation: The game can also be played with music or a drumbeat. When the music stops, the players seek partners.

Change Sides

Supplies: None

Skill: Body management

Identify two parallel lines 30 ft apart with half of the class on each line. On signal, all players cross to the other line, face the center, and stand at attention. The first group to do all three things correctly wins a point. Children must be cautioned to use care when passing through the opposite group. They should be spaced well along each line; this allows room for them to move through each group. Vary the locomotor movements used by specifying skipping, hopping, long steps, sliding, and other varieties of movement. The position to be assumed at the finish can be varied also.

Up Periscope

Supplies: None

Skills: Fundamental locomotor movements

In scattered formation, children move around the area pretending to be ships. Remind the ships to not contact another ship and to keep as much space as possible. When the teacher says "Submarines," players quickly lower their bodies and move at a low level. When the teacher says "Up periscope," students move to their backs and put one leg in the air to imitate a periscope. On "Double periscope," both legs are raised to imitate two periscopes. While the students are in Double periscope position, the teacher can quickly give the previous commands to keep students moving. When the teacher says "Surface," the students resume moving through the area as ships.

Instructional Objectives:
To be able to lead other students in simple locomotor movements
To learn the background of simple folk dances
To move rhythmically

NASPE National Standards:
Introductory Activity: 1, 5
Fitness Activity: 1, 3, 4, 5, 6
Lesson Focus: 1, 2, 3, 5
Game: 1, 3, 5

Equipment Required:
Equipment for Mini-Challenge Course
Music for Mini-Challenge Course
Music for rhythmic activities

Instructional Activities	Teaching Hints

Introductory Activity — Drill Sergeant

Designate a student to be a drill sergeant. The sergeant then gives commands such as:

1. Walk, jog, and halt.
2. March, jump twice, and freeze (pose).
3. March, about face, and halt.
4. March, double time, and march in place.

The teacher can serve as the initial sergeant and then appoint a student to call the group to attention, give directions, and commands to move.

Teach the marching commands of about face, double time, etc.

Fitness Development Activity — Mini-Challenge Course

Arrange four parallel courses with a group at each course. Students perform the challenges from a cone at the start to a finish cone and jog back to continuously repeat the course. On signal, groups rotate to a new course.

Course 1. Hop in and out of 5 hoops, Puppy Dog Walk around a cone for 5 seconds and skip to the finish cone.

Course 2. Weave in and out of 4 cones, Crab Walk around a cone for 5 seconds and gallop to finish cone.

Course 3. Do the Rolling Log the length of mat, do an agility run through 4 hoops, and slide to the finish cone.

Course 4. Jump over each of 5 cones, jump back and forth over a stretched out jump rope, run backwards around 3 cones, and hop to a cone.

Tape alternating segments of silence and music to signal duration of exercise. Music segments (20 to 30 seconds in length) indicate course activity; intervals of silence (10 to 15 seconds) signal rotating to a new course.

Students can set up their own mini-challenges.

Lesson Focus — Rhythmic Movement Skills (2)
Carousel (Swedish)

Music Source: WWCD-1041

Skills: Draw step, sliding

Formation: Double circle, facing center. The inner circle, representing a merry-go-round, joins hands. The outer players, representing the riders, place their hands on the hips of the partner in front.

Verse
Little children, sweet and gay,
Carousel is running; it will run to evening.
Little ones a nickel, big ones a dime.
Hurry up, get a mate, or you'll surely be too late.

Chorus
Ha, ha, ha, happy are we,
Anderson and Peterson and Henderson and me,
Ha, ha, ha, happy are we,
Anderson and Peterson and Henderson and me.

Directions:

Measures	Verse Action
1–16	Moving to the left, children take 12 slow draw steps and stamp on the last three steps. (Step, together, 2, 3, … 12, stamp, stamp, stamp, rest)

Measures	Chorus Action
17–24	Moving left, speed up the draw step until it becomes a slide or gallop. Sing the chorus. (Slide, 2, 3, … 8)
25–32	Repeat measures 17–24 while moving to the right. (Slide, 2, 3, … 8)

During the chorus, the tempo is increased, and the movement is changed to a slide. Children should take short, light slides to prevent the circle from moving out of control.

Variation:

The dance can be done with youngsters holding the perimeter of a parachute.

Jolly Is the Miller (American)

Music Source: WWC-317

Skills: Marching

Formation: Double circle, partners facing counterclockwise with inside hands joined. A Miller is in the center of the circle

Directions:

Verse

Jolly is the Miller who lives by the mill;

The wheel goes round with a right good will;

One hand on the hopper and the other on the sack;

The right steps forward and the left steps back.

Action

All sing. Youngsters march counterclockwise, with inside hands joined. During the second line when "the wheel goes round," the dancers turn their outside arm in a circle to form a wheel. Children change partners at the words "right steps forward and the left steps back." The Miller then has a chance to get a partner. The child left without a partner becomes the next Miller.

Hokey Pokey (American)

Music Source: WWCD-4903; WWC-9126

Skills: Body identification, nonlocomotor movements

Formation: Single circle, facing center

Verse

Line 1: You put your right foot in,

Line 2: You put your right foot out,

Line 3: You put your right foot in

Line 4: And you shake it all about;

Line 5: You do the hokey pokey

Line 6: And you turn yourself around.

Line 7: That's what it's all about.

Directions:

During the first four lines, the children act out the words. During lines 5 and 6, they hold their hands overhead with palms forward and do a kind of hula while turning around in place. During line 7, they stand in place and clap their hands three times.

The basic verse is repeated by substituting, successively, the left foot, right arm, left arm, right elbow, left elbow, head, right hip, left hip, whole self, and backside. The final verse finishes off with the following:

> You do the hokey pokey,
> You do the hokey pokey,
> You do the hokey pokey.
> That's what it's all about.

On each of the first two lines, the children raise their arms overhead and perform a bowing motion with the arms and upper body. On line 3, all kneel and bow forward to touch the hands to the floor. During line 4, they slap the floor five times, alternating their hands in time to the words.

Teaching suggestions:

Encourage the youngsters to make large and vigorous motions during the hokey pokey portions and during the turn around. This adds to the fun. The records all feature singing calls, but the action sequence of the different records varies. The children should sing lightly as they follow the directions given on the record.

Chimes of Dunkirk, Var. 1 (French-Belgian)

Music Source: WWCD-1042; WWC-07042

Skills: Turning in a small circle with a partner, changing partners

Formation: Double circle, partners facing

Directions:

Measures	Action
1–2	Stamp three times in place, right-left-right. (Stamp, 2, 3)
3–4	Clap hands three times above the head (chimes in the steeple). (Clap, 2, 3)
5–8	Partner A places both hands on partner B's hips; B places both hands on A's shoulders. Taking four steps, they turn around in place. (Turn, 2, 3, 4) On the next four counts, partner B (on the outside) moves one person to the left with four steps. (Change, 2, 3, 4) Repeat the sequence from the beginning.

How D'Ye Do, My Partner? (Swedish)

Music Source: WWCD-1041; WWC-07042

Skills: Bowing, curtseying, skipping

Formation: Double circle, partners facing, partner A on inside

Directions:

Measures	Action
1–2	Partners A bow to their partner. (Bow)
3–4	Partners B bow. (Bow)
5–6	A offers the right hand to B, who takes it with the right hand. (Join right hands) Both turn to face counterclockwise.
7–8	Couples join left hands in promenade position in preparation to skip when the music changes. (Join left hands)
9–16	Partners skip counterclockwise in the circle, slowing down on measure 15. (Skip) On measure 16, Bs stop and As move ahead to secure a new partner. (New partner)

The Hitch Hiker (American)

Music Source: WWCD-FDN

Skills: Chug step (a short backward jump with the feet together on the floor), skipping

Formation: Double circle, partners facing each other with boys inside facing out

Directions:

Measures	Action
2	Introduction
1–2	Take two chugs away from partner and clap hands on each step. Jerk right thumb over right shoulder while twisting right foot with heel on the floor. Repeat. (Chug chug, right, right).
3–4	Same as measures 1–2 except use left thumb and foot. (Chug, chug, left, left).
5–6	Same as measures 1–2 except use both thumbs and feet. (Chug, chug, both, both).
7–8	Skip diagonally forward and to the right toward a new partner with 4 skips; continue with four more skips around your new partner with right hands joined and get ready to repeat the dance. (Skip, 2, 3, 4, around, 2, 3, 4).

The sequence repeats eight times.

Looby Loo (English)

Music Source: WWCD-7054; WWC-7054

Skills: Skipping or running, body identification

Formation: Single circle, facing center, hands joined

Directions: The chorus is repeated before each verse. During the chorus, all children skip around the circle to the right. On the verse part of the dance, the children stand still, face the center, and follow the directions of the words. On the words "and turn myself about," they make a complete turn in place and get ready to skip around the circle again. The movements should be definite and vigorous. On the last verse, they jump forward and then backward, shake vigorously, and then turn about. The dance can be made more fun and more vigorous by changing the tasks in the song. Try these tasks: Right side or hip, left side or hip, big belly, backside.

Nixie Polka (Nigarepolska) (Swedish)

Music Source: WWCD-1041; WWC-572

Skills: Bleking step

Formation: Single circle, all facing center, with one or more children scattered inside the circle

Measures	Part I Action
1–4	With hands joined, all spring lightly onto the left foot and extend the right foot forward, heel to ground, toe up. Next, spring lightly onto the right foot and extend the left foot forward. Repeat this action until four slow Bleking steps are completed. (Slow, slow, slow, slow)
5–8	All clap hands once and shout "Hey!" The center child then runs around the inside of the circle, looking for a partner, finally selecting one. They join both hands and run lightly in place until the music is finished. This refrain is repeated, so the children have time to get back to the center of the circle. (Clap, run)
	Part II Action
1–4	The center dancer and partner, with both hands joined, repeat the action of measures 1–4. All dancers in the circle also repeat the action of measures 1–4. (Slow, slow, slow, slow)
5–8	On the first count, all clap hands, shouting "Hey!" The center dancer then about-faces and places both hands on the shoulders of partner, who now becomes the new leader. In this position, both shuffle around the inside of the circle, looking for a third person to dance with. The music is repeated again to allow ample time to return to the center. (Clap, run)

Part III Action

1–4   The action of measures 1–4 is repeated, with the new dancer facing the circle and the two others facing the new dancer. (Slow, slow, slow, slow)

5–8   On the first count, all clap hands, shouting "Hey!" The two people in the center then about-face. All three now face the center to form a line of three dancers with a new leader, who looks for a fourth dancer. The music is repeated. (Clap, run)

The entire dance is thus repeated, accumulating dancers with each repetition. There should be one center dancer for each dozen dancers in the circle.

Game Activity

Skunk Tag

Supplies: None

Skills: Fundamental locomotor movements, dodging

Children are scattered about the area. One child is it and chases the others, trying to tag one of them. When a tag is made, she says, "You're it." The new it chases other children. Children are safe when they move into the skunk position, which is assumed by kneeling and reaching one arm under a knee and holding their nose. The skunk position can only be held for five seconds; students are then eligible to be tagged.

Aviator

Supplies: None

Skills: Running, locomotor movements, stopping

Players are parked (in push-up position) at one end of the playing area. The air traffic controller (ATC) is in front of the players and calls out, "Aviators aviators, take off!" Youngsters take off and move like airplanes to the opposite side of the area. The first person to move to the other side and land the plane (get into push-up position facing the ATC) is declared the new ATC. If the ATC yells out some type of stormy weather, all planes must return to the starting line and resume the parked position. Examples of stormy weather commands are lightning, thunder, hurricane, and tornado. Each ATC is allowed to give stormy weather warnings once.

Right Angle

Supplies: Music

Skills: Rhythmic movement, body management

A tom-tom can be used to provide the rhythm for this activity. Some of the basic rhythm records also have suitable music. Children change direction at right angles on each heavy beat or change of music. The object of the game is to make the right-angle change on signal and not to bump into other players.

Instructional Objectives:
To demonstrate locomotor tasks
To know the cues for correct throwing
To throw a ball using the overhand technique
To throw with velocity using side orientation and opposition

NASPE National Standards:
Introductory Activity: 1, 3, 5
Fitness Activity: 1, 4, 6
Lesson Focus: 2, 3, 5
Game: 2, 5

Equipment Required:
Music and signs for Four Corners Fitness
Yarn balls, whiffle balls, rag balls or tennis balls
Hoops, boxes, pins, and mats for targets
Playground and foam balls for games

Instructional Activities	Teaching Hints

Introductory Activity — Move, Perform Task on Signal

Do a locomotor movement; on signal, stop and perform a task. Suggested tasks are:
1. Seat Circles
2. Balances—foot, seat, and knee
3. Crab Kicks
4. Heel Clicks

Vary the locomotor movements by adding speed and level qualities.

Encourage students to perform their favorite task.

Fitness Development Activity — Four Corners Fitness

Outline a large rectangle with a cone at each corner. Place signs with movement tasks on both sides of the cones. Youngsters move around the outside of the rectangle and change movements as they pass each sign. The following movement activities are suggested for four signs:

Corner 1. Skipping/Jumping/Hopping
Corner 2. Sliding/Galloping
Corner 3. Various animal movements
Corner 4. Sport imitation movements

Stop the class after 30 seconds of movement and perform fitness challenges (see Week 5).

Tape alternating segments of silence and music to signal duration of exercise. Music segments (30 seconds) indicate four corner aerobic activity; intervals of silence (45 seconds) announce performance of flexibility and strength development activities.

Faster-moving students should pass on the outside of the rectangle.

Increasing or decreasing the size of the rectangle can vary the demands of the routine.

Lesson Focus — Throwing Skills (2)

Mimetics
1. Cue students and model a good throw.
   a. Use terms such as "wind-up," "turn your nonthrowing side to the target," "step toward the target, follow through."
   b. *Encourage* children to throw as *hard as possible*.
   c. Use skilled student throwers to model good throws.

Station Format
1. Activities emphasizing form.
   a. Standing on a tumbling mat
      Throwers stand on the edge of the mat and step off the mat (with the foot opposite the throwing arm) as they throw toward the wall. (The other foot remains on the mat.)
   b. Both feet in hoop.
      Throwers begin in a side-facing position to the target, with both feet inside the hoop; they then step outside of the hoop with the foot opposite the throwing arm and throw to the wall.
   c. Cone behind the student.
      The student must touch the cone with the throwing hand on the backswing, and then throw to the wall.

Emphasize lifting the throwing arm and pointing at the target with the nonthrowing arm.

Make a "T" with your arms in preparation to throw (both arms extended to sides at shoulder level).

Focus on throwing form and the velocity of the throw rather than accuracy.

Emphasize throwing hard! Proper form can only be learned when students are encouraged to throw as hard as possible.

Cue students to move their throwing hand behind their head before the throw.

Using large targets (focus on velocity, not accuracy):
1. Throw at a wall or fence.
   a. Throw tennis or rag balls hard from 15–20 ft.
   b. Retrieve the balls after all have been thrown.
2. Throw at cardboard boxes near a fence (the noise from a good hit is reinforcing).
3. Throw at hoops leaning against a wall or fence.
4. Throw at bowling pins that make noise when they fall (audio reinforcement).
5. Throw for distance.
   Encourage students to throw as far as possible. Reinforce distance and throwing hard.

Give each student 4 or 5 balls to throw. They can be placed in a Frisbee to keep them from rolling around. When all the balls have been thrown by all the students, students go retrieve the same number of balls they have thrown. Accuracy of throws should not be reinforced. When students throw for accuracy, they usually regress to an immature form of throwing. Reinforce distance, velocity, and throwing hard.

Game Activity

Charlie Over the Water
Supplies: A volleyball or playground ball
Skills: Skipping, running, stopping, bowling (rolling)
Place the class in circle formation. Two or more children are placed in the center of the circle, holding a ball. One of the center players is designated as Charlie (or Sally). The class skips around the circle to the following chant.

Charlie over the water,
Charlie over the sea,
Charlie caught a bluebird,
But can't catch me!

On the word *me*, the center players toss their balls in the air while the rest of the class runs and scatters throughout the area. When Charlie catches his ball, he shouts "Stop!" All of the children stop immediately and must not move their feet. All of the center players roll their ball in an attempt to hit one of their scattered classmates. If a ball is rolled into a scattered player, that child becomes a new Charlie. If a center player misses, they remain in the center, and the game is repeated. If a center player misses twice, however, he picks another person to replace him.

Circle Straddle Ball
Supplies: Two or more 8" foam balls
Skills: Ball rolling, catching
Children are in circle formation, facing toward the center. Each player stands in a wide straddle stance with the side of their foot against their neighbor's. Their hands are placed on the knees. Two or more balls are used. The object of the game is to roll a ball between the legs of other players before they get their hands down to stop the ball. Keep the circles small so students have more opportunities to handle the ball. Players must catch and roll the ball rather than batting it. Hands must be kept on the knees until a ball is rolled at them. After some practice, the following variation can be played.
Variation: Two or more children are in the center, each with a ball. The other children are in the same formation as before. The center players try to roll the ball through the legs of any child, masking intent by using feints and changes of direction. Any child allowing the ball to go through becomes it.

Flowers and Wind
Supplies: None
Skill: Running
Two parallel lines long enough to accommodate the class are drawn about 30 ft apart. Children are divided into two groups. One group is the flowers and the other the wind. Each of the teams takes a position on one of the lines and faces the other team. The flowers secretly select the name of a common flower. When ready, they walk over to the other line and stand about 3 ft away from the wind. The players on the wind team begin to call out flower names—trying to guess the flower chosen. When the flower has been guessed, the flowers run to their goal line, chased by the players of the other team. Any player caught must join the other side. Reverse the roles and repeat the game. If one side has trouble guessing, give a clue about the color or size of the flower or the first letter of its name.

Instructional Objectives:
To be able to follow simple rules
    fitness games and demonstrate
    cooperative skills
To perform basketball-related skills
    including: Chest and bounce pass,
    dribbling, and shooting

NASPE National Standards:
Introductory Activity: 2, 3
Fitness Activity: 1, 4, 5
Lesson Focus: 2, 3, 5
Game: 1, 3, 5

Equipment Required:
One 8½" playground or foam rubber
    ball for each student
Hoops
Cardboard boxes for ball shooting
    practice
Wand or yardstick and blindfold

Instructional Activities	Teaching Hints
Introductory Activity — Activity with Playground Balls	
Allow students to practice ball control skills. Encourage challenge by allowing them move if they are able to control the ball in place. Activities can range from tossing and catching to dribbling.	Place the balls around the perimeter of the area. On signal, students move throughout the area, acquire a ball and practice doing a favorite activity.
Fitness Development Activity — Fitness Games and Challenges	
1. Stoop Tag.	Alternate simple tag games with fitness challenge activities. Exercise all parts of the body including upper body and abdominal strength and flexibility.
2. Freeze; perform stretching activities.	
3. Back-to-Back Tag.	
4. Freeze; perform abdominal challenges using curl-up variations.	
5. Balance Tag.	
6. Freeze; perform arm–upper-body strength challenges using push-up variations.	
7. Elbow Swing Tag.	Any tag games can be used. Ask students what their favorite tag game is and play it.
8. Freeze; perform trunk development challenges.	
9. Color Tag.	
Lesson Focus — Manipulative Skills (Basketball Related)	
1. Warm-up with informal passing back and forth between partners.	Have students get toe to toe with a partner. One partner gets a ball, returns, and starts passing to their partner.
2. Push (chest) pass—two handed. Emphasize one or two of the following points at a time depending on the skill level of students:	
a. Ball at chest level, face partner.	
b. Fingers spread above center of ball.	Reach for the ball when making the catch. As the ball is caught, bend the arms and bring the ball to the body to absorb the force.
c. Step toward partner and extend arms.	
d. Throw to chest level.	
e. Catch with finger tips.	
f. Thumbs together for high pass.	
g. Little fingers together for low pass.	
h. Hands relaxed, provide a little "give."	
i. Add the bounce pass—same technique.	The ball should be bounced slightly past the midway point nearer the receiver and should bounce to chest level.
3. One-Handed Pass	
a. Side toward catcher.	
b. Ball back with both hands to side of head or above shoulder. Fingers spread, directly behind the ball.	
c. Release the forward hand and throw with a wrist snap.	Foam rubber balls (8") are lighter than playground balls. They are easier to catch and make students more confident and less fearful. Use them if they are available.
d. Practice both right and left.	
4. Birdie in the Cage	
a. Form circles of 7–8 children.	
b. Pass ball among the circle for practice. Be sure everyone handles the ball.	
c. Select "Birdie," put in center until he touches the ball, or there is a loose ball leaving the circle.	
5. Dribbling (each has a ball)	
a. Explain technique: wrist action, finger control, eyes ahead.	Practice dribbling in place before moving and dribbling.
b. Dribble in different directions. Use right and left in turn.	

6. One-Handed Shot
    a. Raise ball up to eye level, sight, and shoot to a partner (demonstrate).
    b. Shoot into cardboard boxes placed around the perimeter of the area.
    c. Shoot at lowered baskets with partners alternating shooting and rebounding.
7. Add a short dribble and a shot.

Lower the baskets so students don't have to fling the ball. The important goal in shooting is correct form. Shooting at boxes and garbage cans allows students to use proper shooting "touch."

Game Activity

Blindfolded Duck
Supplies: A wand and blindfold
Skills: Fundamental locomotor movements

One child, designated the duck (Daisy if a girl, Donald if a boy), stands blindfolded in the center of a circle and holds a wand or similar article. She taps on the floor and tells the class to hop (or perform some other locomotor movement). Children in the circle act accordingly, all moving in the same direction. Daisy then taps the wand twice on the floor, which signals all children to stop. Daisy moves forward with her wand, still blindfolded, to find a child in the circle. She asks, "Who are you?" The child responds, "Quack, quack." Daisy tries to identify this person. If the guess is correct, the identified child becomes the new duck. If the guess is wrong, Daisy must take another turn. After two unsuccessful turns, another child is chosen to be the duck.

Cat and Mice
Supplies: None
Skills: Running, dodging

Form a large circle. One child is the cat and four others are the mice. The cat and mice cannot leave the circle. On signal, the cat chases the mice inside the circle. As they are caught, the mice join the circle. The last mouse caught becomes the cat for the next round. Start at one point in the circle and progress around the circle to select mice so each child gets a chance to be in the center.

Sometimes, one child has difficulty catching the last mouse or any of the mice. The point of the game is for all youngsters to be active. Change mice on a regular time interval rather than waiting until all mice are caught. Another variation is to gradually decrease the size of the circle ("take a step toward the center") so it becomes difficult to evade the cat.

Freeze
Supplies: Music or tom-tom
Skills: Locomotor movements to rhythm

Scatter the class throughout the room. When the music starts, players move throughout the area, guided by the music. They walk, run, jump, or use other locomotor movements, depending on the selected music or beat. When the music is stopped, players freeze and do not move. Players who freeze quickly are reinforced for their excellent work. A tom-tom or a piano is a fine accompaniment for this game, because the rhythmic beat can be varied easily and the rhythm can be stopped at any time. This game is useful for practicing management skills because it reinforces freezing on a stop signal.

Variations:
1. Specify the level at which children must freeze.
2. Have children fall to the ground or balance or go into a different position, such as the Push-Up, Crab, Lame Dog, or some other defined position.

DPE Curriculum Guide – Lesson Plans
Movement Skills and Concepts (3)
Sliding, Galloping, Hoops, and Movement Combinations
Level I – Week 19

Objectives
To learn to move in an evasive fashion

To work cooperatively with others in the parachute activity

To perform a variety of gallop and slide steps

To demonstrate body management skills by performing a variety of movements through hoops

NASPE National Standards:
Introductory Activity: 1, 3, 5

Fitness Activity: 1, 2, 3, 5

Lesson Focus: 1, 2, 3, 5

Game: 1, 3, 5

Equipment Required:
Music for Parachute Fitness

One hoop for each child

Parachute

10–12 beanbags or balls for the game

Instructional Activities	Teaching Hints

Introductory Activity — Marking

To teach marking, start by teaching partner tag. One partner moves while the other partner attempts to tag him. Once tagged, the partners change roles and the other attempts to tag. Progress to marking, which requires one of the partners to move in a desired fashion, while the other attempts to stay near him. On signal, both partners freeze and cannot move their feet. The following partner tries to reach and touch (mark) the partner. If a mark is made, that partner receives a point. Resume the chase with the roles reversed.

The goal is not to play a chase game, but rather to dodge and change directions in order to evade their partner.

Remind students to run under control.

Fitness Development Activity — Parachute Fitness

1. Jog while holding the chute in the left hand. (music)
2. Shake the chute. (no music)
3. Slide while holding the chute with both hands. (music)
4. Sit and perform curl-ups. (no music)
5. Skip. (music)
6. Freeze, face the center, and stretch the chute tightly. Hold for 8–12 seconds. Repeat. (no music)
7. Run in place while holding the chute taut at different levels. (music)
8. Sit with legs under the chute. Do a seat walk toward the center. Return to the perimeter. Repeat four to six times. (no music)
9. Place the chute on the ground. Jog away from the chute and return on signal. Repeat. (music)
10. Move into push-up position holding the chute with one hand. Shake the chute. (no music)
11. Shake the chute and jump in place. (music)
12. Lie on back with feet under the chute. Shake the chute with the feet. (no music)
13. Hop to the center of the chute and return. Repeat. (music)
14. Sit with feet under the chute. Stretch by touching the toes with the chute. Relax with other stretches while sitting. (no music)

Tape alternating segments of silence and music to signal duration of exercise. Music segments indicate aerobic activity with the parachute while intervals of silence announce using the chute to enhance flexibility and strength development.

Space youngsters evenly around the chute.

Use different hand grips (palms up, down, mixed).

All movements should be done under control. Some of the faster and stronger students will have to moderate their performance.

Lesson Focus — Movement Skills and Concepts (3)

Fundamental Skill: Sliding
1. Slide in one direction, stop and slide in another.
2. Begin with short slides increase slide length. Reverse.
3. Do a number of slides (3, 4, 5, 6), do a half turn, continue in the same direction, but leading with the other leg.
4. Slide with a 4-4 pattern.
5. Slide in a figure-eight pattern.
6. Change levels while sliding; touch the floor occasionally while sliding.
7. Slide lightly and noiselessly.
8. Pretend to be a defensive basketball player, sliding.
9. Slide with a partner.

Select a few activities from each of the categories so students receive a variety of skills to practice. When possible, integrate the manipulative skill activities with fundamental skill activities.

Use instructional cues:

"Move sideways; don't cross your feet"

Fundamental Skill: Galloping

1. Form a circle. Slide in one direction (clockwise or counterclockwise). Gradually turn the body to face the line of direction; this is galloping.
2. Practice galloping freely in general space. Gallop backwards.
3. Gallop in a figure-eight and other patterns.
4. Change gallops (leading foot) on 8, 4 and 2 gallops.
5. Gallop with a partner.

Show the relationship between the slide and gallop steps. The gallop is simply a sliding step performed in a forward direction.

Show the uneven rhythm of the gallop.

Manipulative Skills: Hoop Activities

Each group uses 4 or 5 hoops and places them in a line on the floor.

1. Walk, hop, and jump through or on the sides of the hoops.
2. Leap over the hoops from the side.
3. Run around the hoops.
4. Jump astride the hoop and inside it alternately.
5. Jump through each center without touching the hoop.
6. Use different animal walks—Bunny Jump, Frog Jump, Crab Walk.
7. Jump down the line of hoops.
8. Using one hoop, take a push-up position. Keeping the hands on the hoop, circle with the feet. Then put the feet on the hoop and circle with the hands.
9. Jog through with high knees.
10. Do heel clicks in the center of each hoop.
11. Roll a hoop at a partner, who jumps over it as it approaches.

This is an excellent activity to teach cooperative skills. Youngsters should be encouraged to design their hoop patterns and to take turns performing through the hoops.

Near the end of the hoop activities, allow students time to pick up a hoop and perform individual activities.

Movement Concept: Movement Combinations

1. Run, leap, roll.
2. Shake (all over), gallop, freeze.
3. Hop, collapse, explode.
4. Whirl, skip, sink (melt) slowly.
5. Creep, pounce, curl.
6. Begin low, lift, grin, roll.
7. Kneel, sway, jump to feet.
8. Shrink, expand, slide.
9. On all fours, run, roll, jump.
10. Do a jumping jack (two or three times), slide, jump turn.

Encourage individual response. Use student demonstration to illustrate the breadth of responses.

Offer students the opportunity to demonstrate their response to a partner. Each partner then tries to imitate the other's combination.

Game Activity

Corner Spry

Supplies: Blindfold

Skills: Light, silent walking

One person is blindfolded and stands in the center of the square. The other players are scattered in the corner areas. On signal they travel as quietly as possible from corner area to corner area. The blindfolded person, when ready (less than 20 seconds), calls out "Corner Spry!" All players finish their trips to the corner nearest them. The blindfolded person then picks (by pointing) a corner, trying to select the one with the most players. Each time, select a new player to be blindfolded. Variation: Number the corners 1, 2, 3, 4, and have the blindfolded person call out the corner number. The leader can start class movement by naming the locomotor movement to be used.

Hot Potato

Supplies: One to three balls or beanbags for each group

Skill: Object handling

Group players in small circles (8 to 12 per circle) so objects can be passed from one to another around the circle. Balls or beanbags or both are passed around the circle. The teacher or a selected student, who is standing with their back to the class randomly shouts, "stop!" The point of the game is to avoid being the person who passes the object to the person who caught it when the signal occurs. If this happens, the player(s) who passed the object gets up and moves to the next circle. Begin the game with one object and gradually add objects if the class is capable. Call out "Reverse" to signal a change in the direction the object is passed.

Popcorn

Supplies: None

Skills: Curling, stretching, jumping

Half of the class is designated as popcorn; these players crouch down in the center of a circle formed by the rest of the class. The circle children, also crouching, represent the heat. One of them is designated the leader, and his actions serve as a guide to the other children. The circle children gradually rise to a standing position, extend their arms overhead, and shake them vigorously to indicate the intensifying heat. In the meantime, the popcorn in the center starts to pop. This should begin at a slow pace and increase in speed and height as the heat is applied. In the final stages, children are popping up rapidly. After a time, the groups change places and the action is repeated.

DPE Curriculum Guide – Lesson Plans
Fundamental Skills Using Benches
Level I – Week 20

Instructional Objectives:
To be able to lead other students in simple locomotor movements
To learn new exercises utilizing a jump rope
To pull one's body weight across a bench
To balance one's body while moving on a bench

NASPE National Standards:
Introductory Activity: 1, 3, 5
Fitness Activity: 1, 2, 4, 5, 6
Lesson Focus: 1, 2, 3, 5
Game: 1, 3, 4

Equipment Required:
Music for Jump Rope Exercises
One jump rope for each student
6 Benches
Plastic gallon jugs and 8" foam rubber balls

Instructional Activities	Teaching Hints
Introductory Activity — New Leader Warm-Up	
Place students in small groups (3–4). Groups move single file around the area, following a leader in the group. On signal, the last person moves to the head of the squad and becomes the leader. Various types of locomotor movements and exercises can be used by leaders to offer variety and challenge.	If students have trouble working small groups, teach the concept of leading and following by working with a partner. Encourage a variety of responses.
Fitness Development Activity — Jump Rope Exercises	
1. Jump rope—45 seconds. If not able to jump, practice swinging the rope to the side while jumping.	Tape alternating segments (45 seconds in length) of silence and music (30 seconds) to signal duration of exercise. Music segments indicate aerobic activity with the jump ropes; intervals of silence announce using the jump ropes to enhance flexibility and strength development.
2. Place the rope on the floor and perform locomotor movements around and over the rope. Make different shapes and letters with the rope.	
3. Jump rope—45 seconds.	
4. Hold the folded rope overhead. Sway from side to side. Twist right and left.	
5. Jump rope—45 seconds.	
6. Lie on back with rope held with outstretched arms toward ceiling. Bring up one leg at a time and touch the rope with toes. Lift both legs together. Sit up and try to hook the rope over the feet. Release and repeat.	Space youngsters so they don't hit others with their rope.
7. Jump rope—45 seconds.	
8. Touch toes with the folded rope.	
9. Jump rope—45 seconds.	Don't worry about nonjumpers. They will learn sooner or later. Give encouragement and keep them motivated.
10. Do push-up variations with the rope folded and held between the hands.	
11. Jump rope—45 seconds.	
Lesson Focus — Fundamental Skills Using Benches	
Present activities from each of the categories so students receive a variety of skills to practice.	
1. Animal walks on the bench: a. Seal walk b. Cat walk c. Lame dog walk d. Rabbit jump e. Choice activity	Mats should be placed at the ends of the benches to facilitate various rolls and stunts executed after the dismount. Four to five children is the maximum number that should be assigned to one bench.
2. Locomotor movements: a. Skip on the bench. b. Gallop on the bench. c. Step on and off the bench. d. Jump on and off the bench. e. Hop on and off the bench. f. Choice activity	The child next in turn should begin when the performer ahead is about three-quarters of the way across the bench.
3. Pulls—Pull body along the bench in various positions. a. Prone position—head first, feet first. b. Supine position—head first, feet first. c. Side position—head first, feet first.	All activities on the benches should be broken down into three distinct parts: the approach to and mounting of the bench, the actual activity on the bench, and the dismount from the bench.

4. Pushes—same as above activity except push with the arms in all positions.
5. Movements alongside the benches—proceed alongside the bench in the following positions. (Keep the limbs on the floor as far away as possible from the bench to achieve maximum effort.)
   a. Prone position—hands on bench.
   b. Supine position—hands on bench.
   c. Turn over—proceed along bench changing from prone to supine positions with hands on bench.
   d. All of the above positions performed with the feet on the bench.
6. Scooter movements—sit on bench and proceed along bench without using hands.
   a. Regular scooter—feet leading.
   b. Reverse scooter—legs trailing.
   c. Seat walk—walk on the buttocks.

When students have completed their movement across the bench, perform a jump dismount to complete the activity.

Some examples of dismounts are:
a. Single jump—forward or backward.
b. Jump with turns—1/2, 3/4, or full.
c. Jackknife (Pike).
d. Jackknife split (straddle).
e. Jump and follow with a log or forward roll.

Game Activity

Bottle Kick Ball
Supplies: Plastic gallon jugs and 8" foam balls
Skills: Kicking, trapping
Players form a large circle around 10 to 12 plastic gallon jugs (bowling pins) standing in the middle of the circle. Players kick the balls and try to knock over the bottles. Use as many foam balls as necessary to keep all children active. If the group is large, make more than one circle of players.

Hill Dill
Supplies: None
Skills: Running, dodging
Two parallel lines are established 50 ft apart. Two or more players are chosen to be it and stand in the center between the lines. The remainder of the class stands on one of the parallel lines. The center player calls:

> Hill Dill! Come over the hill,
> Or else I'll catch you standing still!

Children run across the open space to the other line, while the one in the center tries to tag them. Anyone caught becomes a tagger. When children cross to the other line, they must wait for the next call. Start a new game when the majority of youngsters have been tagged.

Pigs Fly
Supplies: None/Photos or drawings of animals if desired
Skills: Locomotor movements
The leader stands at the front of the room and calls out the name of a mammal, bird, fish, or reptile, and a movement. For instance, the leader might call out, "Rabbits swim. Pigs Fly. Bears Crawl." When the leader states a correct relationship, the class must move accordingly. In this example, they would begin a bear crawl on their hands and feet. Games should be kept short so that all children have a chance to lead and no one has to sit out too long.

DPE Curriculum Guide – Lesson Plans
Movement Skills and Concepts (4)
Skipping, Catching with Scoops, Leading, and Body Support
Level I – Week 21

Instructional Objectives:
To perform locomotor movements
To be able to support the body weight
　with the arms
To understand the concept of leading
To handle a ball with an implement

NASPE National Standards:
Introductory Activity: 1, 3
Fitness Activity: 1, 4, 6
Lesson Focus: 1, 2, 3, 5
Game: 5

Equipment Required:
Music and tom-tom for Walk, Trot, &
　Jog
Scoops and balls

Instructional Activities	Teaching Hints

Introductory Activity — Countdown

Standing with arms stretched overhead, students begin a countdown (10, 9, 8, 7, etc.) and gradually lower themselves into a crouched position with each count. On the words "blast off," they jump upwards and run in different directions. Students can run to a wall and return to their position. After students learn the activity, allow one of them to say, "Blast Off!"

Vary with challenges such as:
1. Different locomotor movements.
2. Change intervals of counting—slow, fast.

Fitness Development Activity — Walk, Trot, and Jog

Move to the following signals:
1. One drumbeat—walk.
2. Two drumbeats—trot.
3. Three drumbeats—jog.
4. Whistle—freeze and perform exercises.

Use various strength and flexibility exercises between bouts of walk, trot, and jog to allow students to recover aerobically. Examples are:
1. Bend and Twist
2. Sitting Stretch
3. Push-up challenges
4. Abdominal Challenges
5. Body Twist
6. Standing Hip Bend

Tape alternating segments (20 seconds in length) of silence and music to signal duration of exercise. Music segments indicate walk, trot, and jog activity. Intervals of silence signal performance of the strength and flexibility exercises.

Encourage students to move around the area in the same direction.

See Chapter 13 for a description of how to perform the exercises. Any exercises can be substituted. Try to exercise all body parts.

Lesson Focus — Movement Skills and Concepts (4)

Fundamental Skill: Skipping
1. Skip in general space.
2. Vary the skip with exaggerated arm action and lifted knees; side-to-side motion; skip lightly; skip heavily.
3. Skip backward.
4. Clap as you skip.
5. Skip twice on the same side (double skip). Alternate double skips (two on each side).
6. Form a circle. Skip clockwise and counterclockwise.
7. Form by partners or by threes. Skip in general space.

Manipulative Skills: Scoop and Ball Activities
Individual Activities
1. Place the ball on the floor; scoop it up with the scoop.
2. Toss the ball upward and catch it with the scoop. Try with the other hand.
3. Explore various ways of tossing the ball with the hand and catching in the scoop.
4. Throw the ball against a wall and catch with the scoop.
5. Throw the ball against the wall with the scoop and catch with the scoop.
6. Toss either with the hand or with the scoop and do a stunt before catching. Use heel click, quarter turn, touch scoop to floor.

Select a few activities from each of the categories so students receive a variety of skills to practice. When possible, integrate the manipulative skill activities with fundamental skill activities. A common error is to teach all the activities from one category. The reason for multiple groups of activities is to provide variety and enhance motivation.

For students having problems with skipping, be patient. To help them learn, slow down the movement to a step and hop on the same foot. Gradually speed it up to a skip.

Empty and washed plastic gallon jugs make excellent scoops. Cut out half of the bottle opposite the hand and a scoop remains.

Partner Activities
1. Roll the ball and pick up with the scoop.
2. Throw the ball back and forth, catching in the scoop.
3. Toss the ball on first bounce and catch in the scoop.
4. Repeat some of the previous activities and toss with the scoop.
5. Explore from other positions—sitting, kneeling, back to back, prone position.

Yarn balls are excellent with scoops when teaching control skill because they do not travel far when missed. Also, students can apply more force to the racquet, which helps develop proper form.

Movement Concept: Supporting Body Weight with the Hands
1. Begin in all-fours position, practice taking the weight on the hands by kicking up the feet in a one-two fashion.
2. From standing position with the arms overhead, bring the hands to the floor and take the weight on the hands.
3. Take the weight successively on the hands by moving from the side as a preliminary to the cartwheel.
4. Have a partner hold your knees in a wheelbarrow position. Lift the legs as high as possible. May need to shift hands underneath.

If these activities are too difficult for some children, have them start on all fours and gently kick the feet off the floor.

When using partner activities that are weight bearing, match them so they are similar in weight.

Movement Concept: Leading with Different Body Parts
Children move across the space as indicated:
1. Move across with one arm leading.
2. Now a different movement with the other arm leading.
3. Repeat 1 with one foot leading.
4. Repeat 2 with other foot leading.
5. Move so one arm and one foot are leading.
6. Show us a movement where the shoulder leads.
7. How about a movement where one side leads?
8. Show a movement along the floor where the foot is leading.
9. Can you move so your head leads the movement?
10. What other kinds of leading parts can you show?

Use different locomotor movements.

Use different qualities of movement such as speed or force. Encourage use of general and personal space when moving.

Allow students to develop their personal movement and direction.

Movement Concept: Body Support
1. Make a bridge using five, four, three, and two parts of the body.
2. Select the number of body parts you wish to use and see how many different bridges you can make from this base.
3. Select three different bridges and go from one to the next smoothly in sequence (sustained flow).
4. Work with a partner and make different kinds of bridges.
5. Have your partner go under your bridge.

Bridges are an excellent way to begin learning about supporting body weight.

Emphasize creatively changing from one type of bridge to another.

When working with a partner, avoid touching each other.

Game Activity

Flowers and Wind
Supplies: None
Skill: Running

Two parallel lines long enough to accommodate the class are drawn about 30 ft apart. Children are divided into two groups. One group is the flowers and the other the wind. Each of the teams takes a position on one of the lines and faces the other team. The flowers secretly select the name of a common flower. When ready, they walk over to the other line and stand about 3 ft. away from the wind. The players on the wind team begin to call out flower names—trying to guess the flower chosen. When the flower has been guessed, the flowers run to their goal line, chased by the players of the other team. Any player caught must join the other side. Reverse the roles and repeat the game. If one side has trouble guessing, give a clue.

Mousetrap
Supplies: None
Skills: Skipping, running, dodging

Half of the class forms a circle with hands joined, facing the center. This is the trap. The other half of the class is on the outside of the circle. These are the mice. Three signals are given for the game. These can be word cues or other signals. On the first signal, the mice skip around, outside the circle, playing happily. On the second signal, the trap is opened. (The circle players raise their joined hands to form arches.) The mice run in and out of the trap. The third signal signals the trap to snap shut. (The arms come down.) All mice caught in the trap join the circle. The game is repeated until most of the mice are caught. The players exchange places and the game begins anew.

DPE Curriculum Guide – Lesson Plans
Movement Skills and Concepts (5)
Hopping, Hoop Activities, and Body Shapes/Letters
Level I – Week 22

Instructional Objectives:
To cooperatively play tag games and
maintain body control
To hop continuously while performing
a variety of challenges
To be able to recognize different
shapes and make them with their
body

NASPE National Standards:
Introductory Activity: 1, 2, 5
Fitness Activity: 1, 2, 4, 6
Lesson Focus: 1, 2, 4, 6,
Game: 1, 2, 5

Equipment Required:
Tape for Fitness Challenges
One hoop for each child
10–12 foam rubber balls (8")

Instructional Activities	Teaching Hints

Introductory Activity — Tag Games

Use a tag game to offer children immediate activity. Some suggestions are:
1. Skunk
2. Stork
3. Stoop
4. Nose and Toe

Teach moving under control. Students
should understand that they should
seldom run as fast as possible in order to
prevent collisions.

Use different locomotor movements.

Fitness Development Activity — Fitness Challenges

*Alternate locomotor movements with strength and flexibility challenges. Repeat
the challenges as necessary.*

Locomotor Movement: Walk for 30 seconds.

Flexibility and Trunk Development Challenges
1. Bend in different directions.
2. Stretch slowly and return quickly.
3. Combine bending and stretching movements.
4. Sway back and forth.
5. Twist one body part; add body parts.
6. Make your body move in a large circle.
7. In a sitting position, wave your legs at a friend; make circles with your
   legs.

Locomotor Movement: Skip for 30 seconds.

Upper-Body Strength Challenges
In a push-up position, do the following challenges:
1. Lift one foot; the other foot.
2. Wave at a friend; wave with the other arm.
3. Scratch your back with one hand; use the other hand.
4. Walk your feet to your hands.
5. Turn over and face the ceiling; shake a leg; Crab Walk.

Locomotor Movement: Jog for 30 seconds.

Abdominal Development
From a supine position:
1. Lift your head and look at your toes.
2. Lift your knees to your chest.
3. Wave your legs at a friend. From a sitting position:
   a. Slowly lay down with hands on tummy.
   b. Lift legs and touch toes.
Locomotor Movement: Run and leap for 30 seconds.

Tape alternating segments (30 seconds
in length) of silence and music to signal
duration of exercise. Music segments
indicate doing the locomotor
movements; intervals of silence
announce performing the strength and
flexibility challenges

Students select the fitness challenge
they feel capable of performing. This
implies that not all youngsters are
required to do the same workload.
Children differ and their ability to
perform fitness workloads differs. Make
fitness a personal challenge.

Because students can select activities
they feel able to do, there is little reason
for not trying.

If students do not remember the various
challenges, cue them by calling out a
number of the activities. They can select
one they enjoy.

Use different qualities of movement
such as giant skips, quick gallops, tiny
jogging steps, etc.

Animal walks can be substituted for
locomotor movements.

Fundamental Skill: Hopping

1. Hopping (Hopping is done on one foot only.)
   a. Hop in place lightly, changing the feet at will.
   b. Hop numbered sequences, right and left: 1-1, 2-2, 3-3, 4-4, 5-5, 1-2, 2-1, 2-3, 3-2 (hop in place).
   c. Hop, increasing height, reverse.
   d. From your spot, take two, three, or four hops out, turn around and hop back on other foot. How much space can you cover?
   e. Hop on one foot, do a heel-and-toe pattern with the other. Can you change feet each time doing this?
   f. Pick two spots away from you. Hop in place, then move to one spot. Hop in place, then to the other. Return to spot.
   g. Hop forward, backward, sideways.
   h. Hop different patterns—square, triangle, circle, figure-eight, diamond, etc.
   i. Explore different positions in which you can hold the foot while hopping.
   j. Hold the free foot in different positions while hopping.
   k. Hop with the body in different leaning positions—forward, sideways, backward.
   l. Hop lightly, heavily.
   m. While hopping, touch the floor with either or both hands.
   n. Hop back and forth over a board or line, moving down the line.
   o. Trace out letters or numbers. Write your name hopping.
   p. Do quarter or half turns while hopping.

Manipulative Skills: Floor Targets and Hula Hooping

1. Jump in an out of the hoop.
2. Work with a partner and follow the leader through two hoops.
3. Jump in an out of a hoop held by a friend.
4. Hula hoop around the waist.
5. Hula hoop around the hands and arms, the neck, or legs (on back position).
6. Exploratory activity.

Movement Concept: Body Shapes

Possibilities include: Long or short; wide or narrow; straight or twisted; stretched or curled; large or small.

1. Show me a _____ (use terms above) shape.
2. When I say "change," go from a _____ shape to a _____ shape (vary these).
3. Explore symmetrical and asymmetrical. Take one of the above and make it symmetrical. Then change the same to an asymmetrical shape.
4. Explore other kinds of shapes.
5. Contrasting shapes. Do one kind of shape and its contrast. Or name a shape with its contrast or opposite.

Movement Concept: Letters with the Body

1. Make letters standing.
2. Make letters lying on the floor.
3. Divide class into two sets of groups: one group makes a letter and the other names it. Give only one guess. Change groups.
4. Make simple words of two letters or three letters, using one child per letter.
5. Form numbers of two digits.

Select a few activities from each of the categories so students receive a variety of skills to practice. When possible, integrate the manipulative skill activities with fundamental skill activities. A common error is to teach all the activities from one category. The reason for multiple groups of activities is to provide variety and enhance motivation.

Use instructional cues for hopping such as:

"Stay on your toes."

"Swing your arms upward."

"Use your arms for balance."

Change feet regularly so students learn to hop on both. Also, a little hopping goes a long ways. Children fatigue quickly.

Place the hoops around the perimeter of the area. On signal, students move to acquire a hoop and return performing a specified activity.

Teach what the shapes are like to make sure students know what they are. After they have been learned, start to encourage quick response to the shape commands.

Allow students time to think about the shapes of the letters and numbers.

Printing large letters on cards can help youngsters visualize the desired shape.

Game Activity

Rollee Pollee

Supplies: Many 8" foam balls

Skills: Ball rolling, dodging

Half of the class forms a circle; the other half is in the center. Balls are given to circle players. The circle players roll the balls at the feet and shoes of the center players, trying to touch them with a ball. The center players move around to avoid the balls. A center player who is touched leaves the center and joins the circle. After a period of time or when all of the children have been touched with a ball, teams trade places.

If a specified time limit is used, the team having the fewer players hit wins, or the team that puts out all of the opponents in the shorter time wins. Balls that stop in the center are dead and must be taken back to the circle before being put into play again. The preferable procedure is to have the player who recovers a ball roll it to a teammate rather than return to place.

Stop Ball

Supplies: A ball

Skills: Tossing, catching

The class is divided into small circles with 5 to 7 players. One player, with their hands over their eyes, stands in the center of the circle. A ball is tossed clockwise or counterclockwise from player to player around the circle. Failing to catch the ball or making a bad toss incurs a penalty. That player takes one long step backward and stays out of the game for one turn. At a time of her own selection, the center player calls, "Stop." The player caught with the ball (or the ball coming to her) steps back and stays out for one turn. The center player should be allowed two or three turns and then changed.

Instructional Objectives:
To understand and demonstrate the
various factors of movement
To perform locomotor movements
using a rope as a prop
To jump a self-turned rope
To make different letters, numbers,
and shapes with a rope

NASPE National Standards:
Introductory Activity: 1, 3, 5
Fitness Activity: 1, 4, 5, 6
Lesson Focus: 1, 2, 3, 5
Game: 1, 5

Equipment Required:
Music for Circuit Training
One individual jump rope for each child

Instructional Activities	Teaching Hints

Introductory Activity — Movement Varieties

Move using a basic locomotor movement (i.e., walking, jumping, hopping, skipping, galloping). Then add variety to the movement by asking students to respond to the following factors:
1. Level—low, high, in between.
2. Direction—straight, zigzag, circular, curved, forward, backward, upward, downward.
3. Size—large, tiny, medium movements.
4. Patterns—forming squares, diamonds, triangles, circles, figure-eights.
5. Speed—slow, fast, accelerate.

Use scatter formation.

Emphasize and reinforce creative responses.

Explain concepts of level, direction, size, and speed. Short explanations laced with activity allow students time to recover.

Fitness Development Activity — Circuit Training

Make signs, put them on cones, and place around the perimeter of the teaching area. Students perform the exercise specified at each station while the music is playing.
1. Tortoise and Hare
2. Curl-up variations
3. Hula Hooping on arms
4. Standing Hip Bend
5. Agility run—run back and forth between two designated lines
6. Push-up variations
7. Crab Walk
8. Bend and Twist

Tape alternating segments of silence and music to signal duration of exercise. Music segments (begin at 30 seconds) indicate activity at each station; intervals of silence (10 seconds) announce it is time to stop and move forward to the next station.

Place an equal number of students at each station.

Use activities at the stations that students already know how to perform.

Lesson Focus — Movement Skills and Concepts Using Rope Patterns (6)

A. Rope Patterns
Lay rope lengthwise on floor.
1. Walk as on a balance beam.
   a. Forward
   b. Backward
   c. Sideways
2. Jump/hop down length and back.
   a. Vary time—slow, fast, accelerate, decelerate, even, uneven.
   b. Vary levels and force—light, heavy, high to low.
3. Other locomotor movements.
   a. Crisscross
   b. Jumps with one-half turn
   c. Allow student choice
4. Imitate animals.
5. Crouch jumps.
   a. Various combinations; forward, backward, sideways.
   b. Allow exploration.

Alternate rope pattern activities with rope jumping activities. This offers students time for recovery after rope jumping.

Encourage using both sides of the body. If hopping on the right foot, give equal time to the left foot.

If youngsters have trouble jumping or hopping over the rope, encourage them to step or leap over.

6. Put rope in shapes, letters, numbers.
    a. Move in and out of figures.
    b. Add movements, keeping the body inside figure.
7. Partner work.
    a. Make figure with two ropes. Move in and out of figure.
    b. Using one rope, do follow activity. Take turns.

B. Rope Jumping
1. Hold rope. Jump in time.
2. Perform the slow-time and fast-time rhythm with the rope held in one hand and turned (propellers).
3. Jump the rope and practice slow to fast time.
4. Introduce a few basic steps.
    a. Two-step basic
    b. Alternating basic
    c. Backwards
    d. One foot

Select some children to demonstrate a movement shape or letter. When asking students to demonstrate, be sure they are capable to avoid embarrassment.

This lesson should introduce youngsters to rope jumping. It should not be too instructional, but should be used for the purpose of giving them a positive introduction to rope jumping. Instruction will come in a later lesson.

Game Activity

Change Sides
Supplies: None
Skill: Body management
Identify two parallel lines 30 ft apart with half of the class on each line. On signal, all players cross to the other line, face the center, and stand at attention. The first group to do all three things correctly wins a point. Children must be cautioned to use care when passing through the opposite group. They should be spaced well along each line; this allows room for them to move through each group. Vary the locomotor movements used by specifying skipping, hopping, long steps, sliding, and other varieties of movement. The position to be assumed at the finish can be varied also.

Where's My Partner?
Supplies: None
Skills: Fundamental locomotor movements
Children are in a double circle facing a partner. The inside circle has two or three more players than the outside. When the signal is given, the circles skip (or walk, run, hop, or gallop) to the right. This means that they are skipping in opposite directions. On the command "Halt," the circles face each other to find partners. The players left without a partner go to the friendship pot (the center area of the circle) for one turn. The circles should be reversed after a time.
Variation: The game can also be played with music or a drumbeat. When the music stops, the players seek partners.

Colors
Supplies: Colored paper (construction paper) cut in circles, squares, or triangles for markers
Skills: Color or other perceptual concepts, running
Use five or six different-colored markers with a number of children having the same color. Children start the game standing or seated in a circle each with a marker in front of them. The teacher (or another player) calls out a color. Everyone having that color runs counterclockwise around the circle and back to place. The first player seated upright and motionless is declared the winner. Different kinds of locomotor movement can be specified, such as skipping, galloping, walking, and so on. After a period of play, leave the markers on the floor and have the class move one place to the left so players have a different color.
Variation: Shapes (e.g., circles, triangles, squares, rectangles, stars, and diamonds) can be used instead of colors, as can numbers or other articles or categories, such as animals, birds, or fish.

Instructional Objectives:
To catch a passed ball from a partner
To pass a ball to a partner (both chest and bounce pass)
To dribble a ball

NASPE National Standards:
Introductory Activity: 1, 5
Fitness Activity: 1, 4, 6
Lesson Focus: 1, 2, 3, 5
Game: 1, 5

Equipment Required:
Music for Astronaut Exercises
One 8½" playground ball for each pair of students
Bowling pins for targets (optional)

Instructional Activities	Teaching Hints

Introductory Activity — Airplanes

Children pretend to be airplanes. They take off, zoom with arms out, swoop, turn, and glide. On signal, they drop to the floor in prone position. To take off again, they must "restart" their engines by doing a couple of push-up challenges while making a "vroom, vroom" engine sound.

Encourage creativity by naming different types of airplanes and helicopters.

Use different locomotor movements.

Fitness Development Activity — Astronaut Exercises

Walk, do arm circles	30 seconds	Tape alternating segments of silence
Flexibility and trunk development challenges	30 seconds	and music to signal duration of exercise.
Skip forward, backwards, and sideways	30 seconds	Music segments (30 seconds) indicate
Upper-body strength challenges	30 seconds	aerobic activity; intervals of silence
Slide; change lead leg	30 seconds	(30 seconds) signal flexibility and
Abdominal development challenges	30 seconds	strength development activities.
Jump like a pogo stick	30 seconds	
Upper-body strength challenges	30 seconds	See Chapter 13 for a description of how
Trot lightly in different directions	30 seconds	to perform fitness challenge activities.
Flexibility and trunk development challenges	30 seconds	
Gallop backwards	30 seconds	Allow students to adjust the workload to

Cool down with stretching and walking.

an intensity that is consistent with their ability level.

Lesson Focus — Partner Manipulative Activities Using Balls

1. Rolling a ball back and forth to a partner.
   a. Practice different deliveries, i.e., two-handed, right and left.
   b. Roll at targets such as bowling pins or through the legs of a partner.
2. Dribbling and Passing Skills.
   a. One player guards and the other dribbles. Change on signal. Practice with both hands.
   b. Practice passing back and forth to a partner. Use the chest pass.
   c. Pass back and forth using bounce passes.
   d. Combine passing and dribbling. Dribble the ball 3 times and pass to partner.
3. Rolling and Passing from different positions.
   a. Try rolling and passing skills from different positions, i.e., kneeling, sitting.
4. Passing and Moving
   a. One child remains in place and passes to the other child, who is moving. The moving child can trace different patterns, such as back and forth between two spots or in a circle around the stationary child.
   b. Practice different kinds of throws and passes as both children move in different patterns.
   c. Practice foot skills of dribbling and passing.
   d. Partners hold the ball between their bodies without using the hands or arms. Experiment with different ways to move together.
   e. Carrying a ball, run in different directions while the partner follows. On signal, toss the ball upward so that the child following can catch it. Now change places and repeat the activity.
5. Try following activity; one partner leads a ball activity and the other follows.
6. Allow time for students to explore and create.

Encourage proper skill performance by using instructional cues such as:
"Keep your eyes on the ball."
"Catch the ball with the fingertips."
"Use opposition when passing the ball."

When catching, soft receipt of the ball is achieved by "giving" with the hands and arms. The hands should reach out somewhat to receive the ball and then cushion the impact by bringing the ball toward the body.

To catch a throw above the waist, the hands should be positioned so that the thumbs are together. To receive a throw below the waist, the little fingers should be kept toward each other and the thumbs kept out.

When throwing to a partner, unless otherwise specified, the throw should reach the partner at about chest height. At times, different target points should be specified—high, low, right, left, etc.

Animal Tag

Supplies: None

Skills: Imagery, running, dodging

Two parallel lines are drawn about 40 ft apart. Children are divided into two groups, each of which takes a position on one of the lines. Children in one group get together with their leader and decide what animal they wish to imitate. Having selected the animal, they move over to within 5 ft or so of the other line. There they imitate the animal, and the other group tries to guess the animal correctly. If the guess is correct, they chase the first group back to its line, trying to tag as many as possible. Those caught must go over to the other team. The second group then selects an animal, and the roles are reversed. If the guessing team cannot guess the animal, however, the performing team gets another try. To avoid confusion, children must raise their hands to take turns at naming the animal. Otherwise many false chases will occur. If children have trouble guessing, the leader of the performing team can give the initial of the animal.

Aviator

Supplies: None

Skills: Running, locomotor movements, stopping

Players are parked (in push-up position) at one end of the playing area. The air traffic controller (ATC) is in front of the players and calls out, "Aviators aviators, take off!" Youngsters take off and move like airplanes to the opposite side of the area. The first person to move to the other side and land the plane (get into push-up position facing the ATC) is declared the new ATC. If the ATC yells out some type of stormy weather, all planes must return to the starting line and resume the parked position. Examples of stormy weather commands are lightning, thunder, hurricane, and tornado. Each ATC is allowed to give stormy weather warnings once.

Toe to Toe

Supplies: None

Skills: Fundamental locomotor movements

Youngsters perform a locomotor movement around the area. On signal, each child must find a partner and stand toe to toe (one foot only) with that person. An important skill is to take the nearest person for a partner without searching for a friend. Youngsters who can't find a partner within their immediate area must run quickly to the center of the area (use a marking spot or cone) to find a partner. The goal is to find a nearby partner as quickly as possible and avoid being the last pair formed. If the number of youngsters playing is uneven, the teacher can join in and play. Change locomotor movements often.

Instructional Objectives:
To perform a variety of locomotor
movements by choice
To perform balance skills while
manipulating an object
To manage body weight in space
To absorb force when making contact
with the floor

NASPE National Standards:
Introductory Activity: 1, 3, 5
Fitness Activity: 1, 4, 5
Lesson Focus: 1, 2, 3, 5, 6
Game: 1, 3, 5

Equipment Required:
Secret Movement cards
Six 16" jumping boxes
Six 8" jumping boxes
Ball for game

Instructional Activities	Teaching Hints
Introductory Activity — Secret Movement	
Many different movements and/or combinations of movements are written on large flash cards. Without looking, the teacher or a student selects a card and directs the class to "show me" the secret movement. Youngsters select a movement and perform it until signaled to stop. The card is then revealed to the class to see which youngsters, by chance, guessed the secret movement.	Use the basic locomotor movements when first teaching Secret Movements. Use a variety of movements such as animal walks, stunts, exercises, and sport imitation activities for variety.

Fitness Development Activity — Fitness Games and Challenges

1. Stoop Tag.
2. Freeze; perform stretching activities.
3. Back-to-Back Tag.
4. Freeze; perform abdominal challenges using curl-up variations.
5. Balance Tag.
6. Freeze; perform arm–upper-body strength challenges using push-up variations.
7. Elbow Swing Tag.
8. Freeze; perform trunk development challenges.
9. Color Tag.

Alternate simple tag games with fitness challenge activities. Exercise all parts of the body including upper-body and abdominal strength and flexibility.

Assign many students to be it. Allow a student to quit being "it" if they so choose.

Lesson Focus — Fundamental Skills Using Jumping Boxes

Approaches to the Boxes
1. Basic movements such as skip, hop, jump, etc.
2. Various animal walks.
3. Stunts like heel clicks, half turns, and scooter movements can be used to approach the box.

Activities fall into three basic categories: approaching the box, mounting the box, and dismounting the box. Combining these variables can create a wide range of activities.

Mounting the Box
1. Step, jump, leap, or hop onto the box.
2. Rabbit jump or leap frog onto the box.

Attention should be given to landing in proper form. Lightness, bent-knee action, balance, and body control should be stressed.

Dismounting
1. Jump off with a quarter, half, and full turn.
2. Jump off forward, backward, and sideways.
3. Jump off with different body shapes, i.e., stretch, curl, and jack-knife.
4. Jump off followed by a forward or backward roll.
5. Change the above dismounts by substituting a hop or leap in place of the jump.
6. Hold a hoop in front of the box. Have students jump through the hoop.

Mats should be used to cushion the landing.

No more than four or five children should be assigned to each series of boxes.

Challenge Activities
1. Crouch jump over the boxes.
2. Use a beanbag, toss in air, dismount, and catch.
3. Dribble a playground ball while mounting and dismounting boxes.
4. Hula-hoop to the box, mount and dismount without losing control of hoop.
5. Jump over a wand on the dismount.
6. Jump rope to the box. Mount and dismount maintaining jumping rope.

The use of hoops, wands, and balls can create additional challenges.

Return activities work well with boxes. Children should strive for height and learn to relax as they go through space.

Squirrel in the Trees

Supplies: None

Skills: Fundamental locomotor movements

A number of trees are formed by two players facing each other and holding hands or putting hands on each other's shoulders. A squirrel is in the center of each tree, and one or two extra squirrels are outside. On signal, the trees open up and let the squirrels move around the area. The trees also stay together and move throughout the area. On signal, the trees freeze in place and the squirrels find any available tree. Only one squirrel is allowed in a tree. Rotation is necessary so all students get to be a squirrel. Once the squirrels are in a tree, ask them to face one of the tree players. The person they are facing becomes their partner for a tree and the other person becomes a new squirrel.

Stop Ball

Supplies: A ball

Skills: Tossing, catching

The class is divided into small circles with 5 to 7 players. One player, with their hands over their eyes, stands in the center of the circle. A ball is tossed clockwise or counterclockwise from player to player around the circle. Failing to catch the ball or making a bad toss incurs a penalty. That player takes one long step backward and stays out of the game for one turn. At a time of her own selection, the center player calls, "Stop." The player caught with the ball (or the ball coming to her) steps back and stays out for one turn. The center player should be allowed two or three turns and then changed.

DPE Curriculum Guide – Lesson Plans
Movement Skills and Concepts (7)
Twisting, Turning, Stretching, and Relaxing Movements
Level I – Week 26

Instructional Objectives:	NASPE National Standards:	Equipment Required:

Instructional Objectives:

To apply movement concepts such as body and space awareness, relationships, and qualities of movement to a variety of locomotor and body management skills

To combine locomotor and nonlocomotor skills into movement themes, e.g., supporting body weight, bridges, receiving and transferring weight

NASPE National Standards:

Introductory Activity: 1, 2, 3, 5
Fitness Activity: 1, 3, 4, 5
Lesson Focus: 1, 2, 3, 5
Game: 1, 5

Equipment Required:

Music for Animal Movements
Teacher's choice of equipment for introductory activity and manipulative skills in the lesson focus

---

Instructional Activities	Teaching Hints

Introductory Activity — Creative and Exploratory Opportunities

Put out enough equipment for all children to have a piece. Allow them to explore and create activities while moving. Another alternative is to have students work with a piece of equipment with a partner or small group.

Ask students to move and be active without being told what to do. Encourage independent thinking.

Fitness Development Activity — Animal Movements and Fitness Challenges

1. Puppy Dog Walk—30 seconds.
2. Freeze; perform stretching activities.
3. Measuring Worm Walk—30 seconds
4. Freeze; perform abdominal development challenges.
5. Frog Jump—30 seconds.
6. Freeze; perform push-up position challenges.
7. Elephant Walk—30 seconds.
8. Freeze; do stretching activities
9. Bear Walk—30 seconds.
10. Freeze; perform abdominal challenges.
11. Crab Walk—30 seconds.
12. Freeze; do stretching and relaxing activities.

Tape alternating segments (30 seconds in length) of silence and music to signal duration of exercise. Students do animal movements when the music plays; they do fitness challenges when the music stops.

A variation is to place animal movement signs throughout the area and instruct students to move from sign to sign doing the appropriate animal movement each time they reach a new sign.

Lesson Focus — Movement Skills and Concepts (7)

Fundamental Skill: Twisting

1. Glue your feet to the floor. Can you twist your body to the right and to the left? Can you twist slowly, quickly? Can you bend and twist at the same time? How far can you twist your hands back and forth?
2. Twist two parts of the body at the same time. Try three. More?
3. Can you twist one part of the body in one direction and another in a different direction?
4. Is it possible to twist the upper half of your body without twisting the lower part? How about the reverse?
5. Sit on the floor and see what parts of the body you can twist.
6. Can you twist one part of the body around another? Why or why not?
7. Balance on one foot and twist your body. Can you bend and twist in this position?
8. What different shapes can you make using twisted body parts?

Fundamental Skill: Turning

1. Turn your body left and right with quarter and half turns. Turn clockwise and counterclockwise.

Select a few activities from each category so students can practice a variety of skills. When possible, integrate the manipulative skill activities with fundamental skill activities. A common error is to teach all the activities from one category. Teaching multiple groups of activities enhances motivation.

Teach students the difference between a twist and turn. Twisting is rotating a selected body part around its own long axis. Twisting involves movement around the body part itself. Turning focuses on the space in which the body turns and involves moving the entire body.

2. Post compass directions on the walls—north, south, east, and west. Have children face the correct direction on call. Introduce some other directions—northwest, southeast, etc.
3. Stand on one foot and turn around slowly; quickly; with a series of small hops.
4. Cross your legs with a turn and then sit down. Can you get up without moving your feet?
5. When you hear the signal, turn completely around once. Next time turn the other way. Now try with two full turns; three.
6. Lie on your tummy and turn yourself around in an arc. Try seated position.

Stress maintaining balance while doing turning activities.

Perform twisting and turning movements in both directions. Also, try the movements in sitting or on tummy.

Fundamental Skill: Rocking
1. How many different ways can you rock? Which part of your body can rock the highest?
2. Select a part of the body and show me how you can rock smoothly and slowly. How about smoothly and quickly?
3. Rock like a rocking chair.
4. Lie on your back and rock. Point both hands and feet toward the ceiling and rock on the back.
5. Lie on your tummy and rock. Rock as high as you can. Can you hold your ankles and make giant rocks?
6. Rock in a standing position. Try forward, sideways, and diagonal rocking directions.
7. Select a position where you can rock and twist at the same time.
8. Lie on your back, with knees up, and rock side to side.

Make rocking a smooth and steady rhythm. It should be a controlled movement.

Rocking is usually best done when the body surface is rounded. Discuss how the body can be rounded to make rocking easier.

Manipulative Skill: Student's Choice
Select one or more manipulative activities that need additional development regarding the children's needs and progress. During the week's work, a different activity might be scheduled each individual day.

Since equipment was placed out for the introductory activity, use it for the manipulative skill.

Movement Concept: Stretching and Curling
1. While on your feet, show me a stretched position. A curled position.
2. Go very slowly from your stretched position to the curled one you select. Go rapidly.
3. Keeping one foot in place (on a spot), show how far you can stretch in different directions.
4. Show me a straight (regular) curled position. A twisted curled position. A tight curled position.
5. Select three different curled positions. On signal, go from one to the other rapidly. Repeat with stretch positions.
6. Explore and show the different ways your body can support itself in curled positions.

Stretching and curling are somewhat opposite movements.

Encourage stretching through the full range of movement. The stretch is done slowly and smoothly.

Encourage holding the stretch for 6-10 seconds.

Movement Concept: Tension and Relaxation
1. Make yourself as tense as possible. Now relax.
2. Take a deep breath, hold it tight. Expel the air and relax.
3. Tense and reach as high as you can; slowly relax and droop to the floor.
4. Show how you can tense different parts of the body.
5. Tense one part of the body and relax another. Shift the tenseness to the relaxed part and vice versa.
6. Press your fingers hard against your tensed abdominal muscles. Take your fists and beat lightly against the tensed position. Relax. Repeat.
7. Move forward and stop suddenly in a tensed position. Relax. Repeat.

Relaxation activities are an excellent way to finish the lesson. Help students learn to recognize when a limb and muscles are relaxed.

A quiet atmosphere facilitates relaxing. Soft voices encourage students to "wind down."

Game Activity

Midnight
Supplies: None
Skills: Running, dodging
Establish a safety line about 40 ft from a den in which two or three players, the foxes, are standing. The other players stand behind the safety line and ask "What time is it, Mr. Fox?" Choose one of the foxes to answer with various times, such as "one o' clock," "four o' clock," etc. When the fox says a certain time, the class walks forward that number of steps. For

example, if the fox says "six o'clock," the class moves forward six steps. The fox continues to draw the players toward him. At some point, the fox answers the question by saying "Midnight," and chases the others back to the safety line. Any player who is caught becomes a fox in the den and helps to catch others.

Twins (Triplets)
Supplies: None
Skills: Body management

Have students scatter throughout the area with a partner (twin). Give commands such as "Take three hops and two leaps" or "Walk backward four steps and three skips." When the pairs are adequately separated, the leader calls out "Find your twin!" Players find their twin and stand frozen toe to toe. The goal is to avoid being the last pair to find each other and freeze. Students must move away from each other when following the commands. Alternatives are to find a new twin each time or to have twins start at opposite ends of the playing area.

Variation: The game is more challenging when played in groups of three (triplets). When using this variation, students select new partners each time.

Up Periscope
Supplies: None
Skills: Fundamental locomotor movements

In scattered formation, children move around the area pretending to be ships. Remind the ships to not contact another ship and to keep as much space as possible. When the teacher says "Submarines," players quickly lower their bodies and move at a low level. When the teacher says "Up periscope," students move to their backs and put one leg in the air to imitate a periscope. On "Double periscope," both legs are raised to imitate two periscopes. While the students are in double periscope position, the teacher can quickly give the previous commands to keep students moving. When the teacher says "Surface," the students resume moving through the area as ships.

DPE Curriculum Guide – Lesson Plans
Rhythmic Movement Skills (3)
Level I – Week 27

Instructional Objectives:
To be able to lead other students in
simple locomotor movements
To perform a variety of exercises using
jump ropes
To move rhythmically and learn
simple folk dances

NASPE National Standards:
Introductory Activity: 1, 3, 5
Fitness Activity: 1, 2, 4, 5, 6
Lesson Focus: 1, 3, 5
Game: 1, 3, 5

Equipment Required:
Music for Jump Rope Exercises
Tom-tom
Music for rhythms
Equipment for mini-challenge course

Instructional Activities	Teaching Hints

Introductory Activity — New Leader Warm-Up

Place students in small groups (3–4). Groups move single file around the area, following a leader in the group. On signal, the last person moves to the head of the squad and becomes the leader. Leaders can use various types of locomotor movements and/or exercises to offer variety and challenge.

If students have trouble working small groups, teach the concept of leading and following by working with a partner.

Encourage a variety of responses.

Fitness Development Activity — Jump-Rope Exercises

1. Jump rope—45 seconds. If not able to jump, practice swinging the rope to the side while jumping.
2. Place the rope on the floor and perform locomotor movements around and over the rope. Make different shapes and letters with the rope.
3. Jump rope—45 seconds.
4. Hold the folded rope overhead. Sway from side to side. Twist right and left.
5. Jump rope—45 seconds.
6. Lie on back with rope held with outstretched arms toward ceiling. Bring up one leg at a time and touch the rope with toes. Lift both legs together. Sit up and try to hook the rope over the feet. Release and repeat.
7. Jump rope—45 seconds.
8. Touch toes with the folded rope.
9. Jump rope—45 seconds.
10. Do push-up variations with the rope folded and held between the hands.
11. Jump rope—45 seconds.

Tape alternating segments (45 seconds in length) of silence and music (30 seconds) to signal duration of exercise. Music segments indicate aerobic activity with the jump ropes; intervals of silence announce using the jump ropes to enhance flexibility and strength development.

Space youngsters so they don't hit others with their rope.

Don't worry about nonjumpers. They will learn sooner or later. Give encouragement and keep them motivated.

Lesson Focus — Rhythmic Movement Skills (3)

Make dances easy for students to learn by implementing some of the following techniques:
1. Teach the dances without using partners.
2. Allow youngsters to move in any direction without left-right orientation.
3. Use scattered formation instead of circles.
4. Emphasize strong movements such as clapping and stamping to increase involvement.
5. Play the music at a slower speed when first learning the dance.

Teach a variety of dances rather than one or two in depth in case some students find it difficult to master a specific dance.

Shortnin' Bread (American)

Music Source: WWCD-7050; WWC-7050
Skills: Sliding, turning with a partner
Formation: Scattered with partner
Directions:

Measures	Action
1–2	Clap own hands
3–4	Pat partner's hands
5–6	Clap own hands
7–8	Slap own thighs
9–16	Repeat measures 1–8
17–20	Couples slide to the right holding hands
21–24	Circle holding hands.
25–32	Repeat measures 17–24 moving to the left

Children's Polka (German)

Music Source: WWCD-07042; WWC-07042
Formation: Single circle of couples, partners facing
Skill: Step-draw
Directions:

Measures	Action
1–2	Take two step-draw steps toward the center of the circle, ending with three steps in place. (Draw, draw, step, 2, 3)
3–4	Take two step-draw steps away from the center, ending with three steps in place. (Draw, draw, step, 2, 3)
5–8	Repeat the pattern of measures 1–4.
9	Slap own knees once with both hands; clap own hands once. (Slap, clap)
10	Clap both hands with partner three times. (Clap, 2, 3)
11–12	Repeat the pattern of measures 9 and 10.
13	Hop, placing one heel forward, and shake the forefinger at partner three times. (Scold, 2, 3)
14	Repeat the "scolding" pattern with the other foot and hand. (Scold, 2, 3)
15–16	Turn once around in place with four running steps and stamp three times in place. (Turn, 2, 3, 4; Stamp, 2, 3)

Jump Jim Jo (American)

Music Source: WWCD-1041
Skills: Jumping, running, draw step
Formation: Double circle, partners facing, both hands joined
Directions:

Measures	Action
1–2	Do two jumps sideward, progressing counterclockwise, followed by three quick jumps in place. (Slow, slow, fast, fast, fast)
3–4	Release hands and turn once around in place with four jumps (two jumps per measure). Finish facing partner and rejoin hands. (Jump, turn, 3, 4)
5	Take two sliding steps sideward, progressing counterclockwise. (Slide, slide)
6	Partners face counterclockwise with inside hands joined and tap three times with the toe of the outside foot. (Tap, tap, tap)
7–8	Take four running steps forward, then face partner, join both hands, and end with three jumps in place. (Run, 2, 3, 4; Jump, 2, 3)

Jingle Bells, Var. 1 (Dutch)

Music Source: Any version of Jingle Bells
Skills: Elbow swing, skipping, sliding
Formation: Double circle, partners facing, with both hands joined.
Directions:

Measures	Action
1–2	Partners take eight slides counterclockwise. (Slide, 2, 3, … 8)
3–4	Partners turn so they are standing back to back, and take eight more slides in the line of direction. This move is best made by dropping the front hands and swinging the back hands forward until the dancers are standing back to back. They rejoin the hands that are now in back. Make this move with no loss of rhythm. (Slide, 2, 3, … 8)
5–6	Repeat the action of measures 1 and 2. To get back to the face-to-face position, let go of the back hands and swing the front hands backward, allowing the bodies to pivot and face again. (Slide, 2, 3, … 8)
7–8	Repeat measures 3 and 4. (Slide, 2, 3, … 8)

Chorus	Action
1	Clap own hands three times. (Clap own, 2, 3)
2	Clap both hands with partner three times. (Clap both, 2, 3)
3	Clap own hands four times. (Clap own, 2, 3, 4)
4	Clap both hands with partner once. (Clap both)
5–8	Right elbow swing with partner. Partners hook right elbows and swing clockwise with eight skips. (Swing, 2, 3, 4, 5, 6, 7, 8)
9–12	Repeat the clapping sequence of measures 1–4.
13–16	Left elbow swing with partner for eight skips, finishing in the original starting position, ready to repeat the entire dance with the same partner; or do a left elbow swing with partner for four skips, which is once around, then all children in the inner circle skip forward to the outer dancer ahead and repeat the entire dance from the beginning with a new partner. (Swing, 2, 3, 4, 5, 6, 7, 8)

Seven Steps (Austrian)

Music Source: WWCD-FDN
Skills: Running, hopping
Formation: Double circle with couples facing counterclockwise with inside hands joined
Directions:

Measures	Action
2	Introduction
1–2	Start with outside foot and run 7 steps forward counterclockwise, and then pause with weight on outside foot on 8th count. (Run, 2, 3, 4, 5, 6, 7, pause)
3–4	Start with inside foot and run 7 steps backward (clockwise), and then pause with weight on inside foot on 8th count. (Run, back, 3, 4, 5, 6, 7, pause)
5	Release hands, turn away from partner and starting with the outside foot, run 3 steps away from partner and hop on the outside foot on the 4th count. (Away, 2, 3, hop)
6	Turn and face partner and starting with the inside foot, run 3 steps toward partner and then hop on the inside foot on the 4th count (Back, 2, 3, hop)
7–8	Partner with right hands joined run once around each other with 8 running steps clockwise to the right. (Swing, 2, 3, 4, 5, 6, 7, 8)
9	Release hands, turn away from partner and starting with the outside foot, run 3 steps away from partner; on the 4th count hop and turn on the outside foot to face diagonally toward new partner. (Apart, 2, 3, hop)
10	Take 3 running steps to a new partner (inside partner moves counterclockwise forward diagonally toward new partner and outside partner moves clockwise backward diagonally to next partner. Then hop on the 4th count.
11–12	New partners run once around each other with 8 running steps counterclockwise with left hands joined. Finish in starting position with inside hands joined.

Perform the dance a total of 5 times.

Skip to My Lou (American)

Music Source: WWCD-7054; WWC 7054
Skills: Skipping, changing partners
Formation: Scattered with a partner
Directions: During the chorus, partners skip around the area. At the verse, everyone finds a new partner and continues skipping.

Game Activity

Jack Frost and Jane Thaw

Supplies: Any type of marker to distinguish Jack Frost and Jane Thaw

Skills: Running, dodging, holding position

The class is scattered and moves to avoid being frozen (tagged) by 2 or 3 Jack Frosts, who carry a blue pinnie or streamer in one hand. Frozen children remain immobile until touched (thawed) by the Jane Thaws who are identified by a red streamer or pinnie.

Marching Ponies

Supplies: None

Skills: Marching, running

Two or three children are ringmasters and crouch in the center of a circle of ponies formed by the rest of the class. Two goal lines on opposite sides of the circle are established as safe areas. The ponies march around the circle counting out loud with each step. At a predetermined number of steps (whispered to the ringmasters by the teacher), the ringmasters jump up and attempt to tag the others before they can reach the safety lines. Anyone tagged joins the ringmaster in the center and helps catch others. Reorganize the game after 6 to 8 children have been caught. Try other characterizations, such as lumbering elephants, jumping kangaroos, and the like.

Tag Games

Supplies: None

Skills: Fundamental locomotor movements, dodging

Tag is played in many ways. Children are scattered about the area. One child is it and chases the others, trying to tag one of them. When a tag is made, she says "You're it." The new it chases other children. The following are suggested:

1. Object Tag. Touching a specified type of object (e.g., wood, iron), the floor, or an object of a specified color makes the runner safe.
2. Mimic Tag. Children can be safe by mimicking a particular action or pose.
3. Locomotor Tag. The child who is it specifies how the others should move—skipping, hopping, jumping. The tagger must use the same kind of movement.

Instructional Objectives:
To identify and place body parts on an object
To work cooperatively with others in the parachute activity
To understand safety considerations related to tumbling and inverted balances
To balance the body in a variety of situations
To perform individual self-testing stunts

NASPE National Standards:
Introductory Activity: 1
Fitness Activity: 1, 4, 5, 6
Lesson Focus: 1, 2, 3, 5
Game: 1, 2, 5

Equipment Required:
One beanbag for each student
Music and parachute for fitness
Tumbling mats
Foam balls (8") for games

Instructional Activities	Teaching Hints

Introductory Activity — Body Part Identification

Each student stands near a beanbag placed on the floor. Students are instructed to move over and around the beanbags on the floor. When a body part is called, students place the body part on the nearest beanbag.
Variations:
1. Use different movements.
2. Use different body parts.
3. Call combinations of movements and body parts.

Students should be encouraged to move over and around as many beanbags as possible.

Challenge students by calling out a color. They then must avoid moving over and around all beanbags of that color.

Fitness Development Activity — Parachute Fitness

1. Jog while holding the chute in the left hand. (music)
2. Shake the chute. (no music)
3. Slide while holding the chute with both hands. (music)
4. Sit and perform curl-ups. (no music)
5. Skip. (music)
6. Freeze, face the center, and stretch the chute tightly. Hold for 8–12 seconds. Repeat. (no music)
7. Run in place while holding the chute taut at different levels. (music)
8. Sit with legs under the chute. Do seat walks toward the center. Return to the perimeter. Repeat four to six times. (no music)
9. Place the chute on the ground. Jog away from the chute and return on signal. Repeat. (music)
10. Move into push-up position holding the chute with one hand. Shake the chute. (no music)
11. Shake the chute and jump in place. (music)
12. Lie on back with feet under the chute. Shake the chute with the feet. (no music)
13. Hop to the center of the chute and return. Repeat. (music)
14. Sit with feet under the chute. Stretch by touching the toes with the chute. Relax with other stretches while sitting. (no music)

Tape alternating segments of silence and music to signal duration of exercise. Music segments indicate aerobic activity with the parachute; intervals of silence announce using the chute to enhance flexibility and strength development.

Space youngsters evenly around the chute.

Use different grips (palms up, down, mixed).

All movements should be done under control. Some of the faster and stronger students will have to moderate their performance.

Lesson Focus — Gymnastics Skills (3)

Animal Movements
Siamese Twin Walk
   Stand back to back with a partner. Lock elbows. Walk forward, backward, and sideward in unison.

Tightrope Walk
   Select a line, board, or chalked line on the floor as the high wire. Pretend to be on the high wire and do various tasks with exaggerated loss and control of balance. Add tasks such as jumping rope, juggling balls, and riding a bicycle. Pretend to hold a parasol or a balancing pole while performing.

Five groups of activities in this lesson ensure that youngsters receive a variety of experiences. Pick a few activities from each group and teach them alternately. For example, teach one or two animal movements, then a tumbling and inverted balance, followed by a balance stunt, etc. Give equal time to each group of activities.

Lame Dog Walk

Walk on both hands and one foot. Hold the other foot in the air as if injured. Walk a distance and change feet. The eyes should look forward. Move backward also and in other combinations. Try to move with an injured front leg.

Crab Walk

Squat down and reach back, putting both hands on the floor without sitting down. With head, neck, and body level, walk forward, backward, and sideward.

Tumbling and Inverted Balances

Forward and Backward Roll review

See previous Lesson Plans 7 and 15.

Mountain Climber

This activity is similar to the exercise known as the Treadmill. The weight is taken on the hands with one foot forward and one foot extended back, similar to a sprinter's start. When ready, the performer switches foot position with both feet moving simultaneously.

Switcheroo

This Handstand lead-up activity begins in the front lunge position with the arms overhead. In one continuous movement, bend forward at the hips, place the hands on the mat, and invert the legs over the head. Scissor the legs in the air, and then reverse the position of the feet on the mat. Repeat in a smooth and continuous motion.

Balance Stunts

Forward Balance

Extend one leg backward until it is parallel to the floor. Keeping the eyes forward and the arms out to the sides, bend forward, balancing on the other leg. Hold for 5 seconds without moving. Reverse legs. (This is also called a Forward Scale.)

Hand-and-Knee Balance

Get down on all fours, taking the weight on the hands, knees, and feet, with toes pointed backward. Lift one hand and the opposite knee. Keep the free foot and hand from touching during the hold. Reverse hand and knee positions.

Single-Knee Balance

Perform the same action as in the previous stunt, but balance on one knee (and leg), with both arms outstretched to the sides. Use the other knee.

Individual Stunts

Turn-Over

From a front-leaning rest position, turn over so that the back is to the floor. The body should not touch the floor. Continue the turn until the original position is reassumed. Reverse the direction. Turn back and forth several times.

Thread the Needle

Touch the fingertips together in front of the body. Step through with one foot at a time while keeping the tips in contact. Step back to the original position. Next, lock the fingers in front of the body, and repeat the stunt. Finally, step through the clasped hands without touching the hands.

Heel Slap

From an erect position with hands at the sides, jump upward and slap both heels with the hands.

Pogo Stick

Pretend to be on a pogo stick by keeping a stiff body and jumping on the toes. Hold the hands in front as if grasping the stick. Progress in various directions.

Tumbling and inverted balances require that each student overcome personal fear. Some students may not want to try some of the activities. Offer encouragement but do not require or force these students to perform.

Use many tumbling mats to avoid standing in line (3 or 4 students per mat).

Tumbling and inverted balances demand adequate upper body strength. Students lacking strength (often overweight students) will not be able to safely complete the activities. Allow students to determine their capabilities.

This activity is a lead-up to the handstand and teaches children to support the body weight briefly with the arms.

Balance activities are excellent activities to teach because all students are capable of performing them.

Encourage students to see how long they can hold the balances.

The body should be kept as rigid as possible throughout the turn.

Stress upward propelling action by the ankles and toes, with the body kept stiff, particularly at the knee joints.

Partner and Group Stunts

Double Top

Face partner and join hands. Experiment to see which type of grip works best. With straight arms, lean away from each other and at the same time move the toes close to partner's toes. Spin around slowly in either direction, taking tiny steps.

Try a variation of the Double Top by doing it standing right side to right side.

Game Activity

Charlie Over the Water

Supplies: A volleyball or playground ball

Skills: Skipping, running, stopping, bowling (rolling)

Place the class in circle formation. Two or more children are placed in the center of the circle, holding a ball. One of the center players is designated as Charlie (or Sally). The class skips around the circle to the following chant:

> Charlie over the water,
> Charlie over the sea,
> Charlie caught a bluebird,
> But can't catch me!

On the word *me*, the center players toss their balls in the air while the rest of the class runs and scatters throughout the area. When Charlie catches his ball, he shouts, "Stop!" All of the children stop immediately and must not move their feet. All of the center players roll their ball in an attempt to hit one of their scattered classmates. If a ball is rolled into a scattered player, that child becomes a new Charlie. If a center player misses, they remain in the center, and the game is repeated. If a center player misses twice, however, he picks another person to replace him.

Circle Straddle Ball

Supplies: Two or more 8" foam balls

Skills: Ball rolling, catching

Children are in circle formation, facing toward the center. Each player stands in a wide straddle stance with the side of their foot against their neighbor's. Their hands are placed on the knees. Two or more balls are used. The object of the game is to roll a ball between the legs of other players before they get their hands down to stop the ball. Keep the circles small so students have more opportunities to handle the ball. Players must catch and roll the ball rather than batting it. Hands must be kept on the knees until a ball is rolled at them. After some practice, the following variation can be played.

Variation: Two or more children are in the center, each with a ball. The other children are in the same formation as before. The center players try to roll the ball through the legs of any child, masking intent by using feints and changes of direction. Any child allowing the ball to go through becomes it.

Flowers and Wind

Supplies: None

Skill: Running

Two parallel lines long enough to accommodate the class are drawn about 30 ft apart. Children are divided into two groups. One group is the flowers and the other the wind. Each of the teams takes a position on one of the lines and faces the other team. The flowers secretly select the name of a common flower. When ready, they walk over to the other line and stand about 3 ft away from the wind. The players on the wind team begin to call out flower names—trying to guess the flower chosen. When the flower has been guessed, the flowers run to their goal line, chased by the players of the other team. Any player caught must join the other side. Reverse the roles and repeat the game. If one side has trouble guessing, give a clue about the color or size of the flower or the first letter of its name.

DPE Curriculum Guide – Lesson Plans
Individual Rope-Jumping Skills
Level I – Week 29

Instructional Objectives:
To perform locomotor movements
over a rope
To perform fitness development
activities
To jump a self-turning rope
To identify body changes during jump
roping activities

NASPE National Standards:
Introductory Activity: 1, 5
Fitness Activity: 1, 4, 6
Lesson Focus: 1, 2, 3, 4, 5, 6
Game: 1, 3, 5

Equipment Required:
Music for Four Corners Fitness
One jump rope for each student
Four cones and signs for Four Corners
Fitness
10 beanbags

Instructional Activities	Teaching Hints
Introductory Activity — Locomotor Movements with Equipment	
Each student is given a jump rope and moves around the area using various basic locomotor movements. On signal, they drop the rope, and jump, hop, or leap over as many ropes as possible.	Any piece of equipment can be used. If desired, students can turn and jump the rope.
Fitness Development Activity — Four Corners Fitness	
Outline a large rectangle with a cone at each corner. Place signs with movement tasks on both sides of the cones. Youngsters move around the outside of the rectangle and change movements as they pass each sign. The following movement activities are suggested: Corner 1. Skipping/Jumping/Hopping Corner 2. Sliding/Galloping Corner 3. Various animal movements Corner 4. Sport imitation movements Stop the class after 30 seconds of movement and perform fitness challenges (see Week 5).	Tape alternating segments of silence and music to signal duration of exercise. Music segments (30 seconds) indicate four corner aerobic activity; intervals of silence (45 seconds) announce performance of flexibility and strength development activities. Allow students to select a fitness challenge they feel capable of performing. This implies that not all youngsters are required to do the same workload. Children differ and their ability to perform fitness workloads differs. Make fitness a personal challenge.
Lesson Focus — Individual Rope-Jumping Skills	
The following are lead-up activities for beginning jumpers: 1. Clap hands to a tom-tom beat. 2. Jump in place to a beat without rope. Jump back and forth over rope on floor. 3. Hold both ends of the jump rope in one hand and turn it so a steady rhythm can be made through a consistent turn. Just before the rope hits the ground, the student should practice jumping. 4. Count the rhythm out loud to cue students when to jump. 5. Start jumping the rope one turn at a time—gradually increase the number of turns. 6. Try jogging and jumping rope. The even rhythm of running often makes it easier for some youngsters to jump the rope.	Since rope is a physically taxing activity, it is suggested that time be allowed for recovery. One way to do this is to play less active games between bouts of rope jumping. Background music with a strong beat can be motivating for youngsters. Rope jumping is difficult to master. Be patient and understand that it may take some students a year or two to learn the activity.
Introduce the two basic jumps: 1. Slow time. Jump twice each time the rope turns. One of the jumps is performed when the rope is overhead and serves as a preparatory jump. 2. Fast time. One jump each time the rope makes a complete turn. No preparatory jump is allowed.	Another way to rest students is to have them make shapes, letter, and names with their rope. Tail tag (fold the rope and place it in the waistband) requires trying to pull out the tail of others.

Game Activity

Tommy Tucker's Land

Supplies: About ten beanbags for each game

Skills: Dodging, running

Two or three youngsters, Tommy Tuckers (or Tammi Tuckers, if a girl), stand in the center of a 15-ft square where the beanbags are scattered. The Tuckers are guarding their land and treasure (beanbags). The other children chant:

I'm on Tommy Tucker's land,

Picking up gold and silver.

Children attempt to pick up as much of the treasure as they can while avoiding being tagged by the Tuckers. Any child who is tagged must return the treasure and retire from the game. The game is over when only one child is left or when all of the beanbags have been successfully filched. The teacher may wish to call a halt to the game earlier if a stalemate is reached. New Tuckers are selected.

Change Sides

Supplies: None

Skill: Body management

Identify two parallel lines 30 ft apart with half of the class on each line. On signal, all players cross to the other line, face the center, and stand at attention. The first group to do all three things correctly wins a point. Children must be cautioned to use care when passing through the opposite group. They should be spaced well along each line; this allows room for them to move through each group. Vary the locomotor movements used by specifying skipping, hopping, long steps, sliding, and other varieties of movement. The position to be assumed at the finish can be varied also.

DPE Curriculum Guide – Lesson Plans
Movement Skills and Concepts (8)
Bending, Stretching, and Weight Transfer
Level I – Week 30

Instructional Objectives:
To understand the difference between
  bending and stretching
To bend and stretch in many different
  ways
To be able to transfer weight from one
  body part to another

NASPE National Standards:
Introductory Activity: 1, 2, 5
Fitness Activity: 1, 4, 6
Lesson Focus: 1, 2, 3, 5
Game: 1, 3, 5

Equipment Required:
One hoop for each student
Music for Walk, Trot, and Jog
Tom-tom or tambourine
Parachute

Instructional Activities	Teaching Hints

Introductory Activity — Activity Using Hoops

Issue a hoop for each child and encourage creative activity. If necessary, suggest some of the following challenges:
1. Run or hop with hoop, stop and jump the hoop.
2. Run and roll the hoop like a tire.
3. Spin the hoop and see how many times you can run around it.
4. Roll the hoop and go through it.
5. Combine two hoop activities with two locomotor movements.
6. Try some of the activities learned in the previous hoop lesson focus.

Have the class start moving upon entry into teaching area.
Place the hoops around the perimeter of the area.

While the class is moving, ask students to acquire a hoop and practice jumping in and out of it. Reverse the procedure to put the hoops away.

Fitness Development Activity — Walk, Trot, and Jog

Move to the following signals:
1. One drumbeat—walk.
2. Two drumbeats—trot.
3. Three drumbeats—jog.
4. Whistle—freeze and perform exercises.

Perform various strength and flexibility exercises between bouts of walk, trot, and jog. Examples are:
1. Bend and Twist
2. Sitting Stretch
3. Push-up Challenges
4. Abdominal Challenges
5. Body Twist
6. Standing Hip Bend

Tape alternating segments (20 seconds in length) of silence and music to signal duration of exercise. Music segments indicate walk, trot, and jog activity. Intervals of silence signal performance of the strength and flexibility exercises.

See Chapter 13 for a description of how to perform the exercises. Any exercises can be substituted. Try to maintain the balance of exercising all body parts.

Lesson Focus — Movement Skills and Concepts (8)

Fundamental Skill: Bending
1. Can you bend forward and up?
2. Show how far you can bend backward. Can you see behind you on your backward bend?
3. Combine a forward bend with a backward bend.
4. Bend right and left. Try with your hands out to the sides. Overhead.
5. Explore different ways the body can bend in a standing position.
6. Sit down. How does this affect the bending possibilities of the body? Can you bend forward so your chin touches the floor?
7. How many body parts (joints) can you bend below the waist? Above the waist?
8. Who can lie down and bend two, three, four, five, six parts?
9. Pick two similar parts. Bend one part while unbending the other.
10. Pick two body parts (joints). Beginning at the same time, bend one quickly and one slowly. Bend one smoothly and one with jerks.
11. Make a familiar shape by bending two body parts.
12. Show how you can bend to look funny, happy, sad, slow, and quick.

Select a few activities from each of the categories so students receive a variety of skills to practice. When possible, integrate the manipulative skill activities with fundamental skill activities. A common error is to teach all the activities from one category. The reason for multiple groups of activities is to provide variety and enhance motivation.

Teach the various joints that are bent with different movements.

Explain the difference between bending and stretching.

Fundamental Skill: Stretching

1. Stretch as many body parts as you can.
2. Stretch your arms, legs, and feet in as many ways as possible.
3. At the same time stretch your feet in one direction and your arms in another.
4. Stretch one body part quickly, slowly, smoothly. Try another. Repeat.
5. Bend a body part and tell me which muscles or muscle groups are being stretched.
6. How many ways can you stretch while sitting on the floor?
7. Lie on the floor (prone or supine) and stretch two parts at once. Add others up to five.
8. From any position you like, see if you can at the same time stretch one part quickly (but smoothly) and one part slowly. Try one part quickly and two parts slowly.
9. From a kneeling position, set a mark on the floor where you can reach (stretch) without losing balance. Increase the distance.
10. Stretch your one arm while your other arm curls (bends). Reverse.
11. Can you stretch as tall as a giraffe? As wide as an elephant? As long as a snake?
12. Can you stretch the muscles in your chest, back, ankles, wrist, and fingers? Is this easy?

Encourage smooth controlled stretching. Use cues such as smoothly, gently, without jerking, etc.

Help youngsters understand what muscles are being stretched. They can tell by feeling which muscles are tight and hard.

Discuss why people stretch—to maintain flexibility and be able to have a full range of motion in all joints.

Discuss how adults stretch their muscles prior to vigorous activity.

Manipulative Skill: Parachute Activities

Use locomotor activities with the parachute as the prior activities (bending and stretching) are nonmoving activities. See Week 10 for parachute activities.

Movement Concept: Receiving and Transferring Weight

1. Project yourself high into the air and land. Try to land now with as little noise as possible.
2. Practice projecting yourself into the air and landing in different fashions.
3. Experiment with different landings where one or both hands touch the floor at the completion of the landing.
4. Experiment with turns as you land.
5. Begin your movement through the air with a short run and practice landings.
6. Take a position with the body balanced on two different parts. Transfer the weight to another two parts. Go from three to three.
7. Transfer the weight from a rounded part of the body to the hands and/or the feet. Go back to the rounded part.
8. Jump and land under control. Transfer the weight to another two body parts.
9. Explore different combinations of transferring the weight from various parts to others.

The parachute activity should place emphasis on locomotor movements since the other parts of the lesson are somewhat inactive.

Weight transfer is used in movement to create force. Use throwing as an example of transferring the weight from the rear foot to the forward foot.

Bend the knees when absorbing force from weight transfer. Bent joints are like springs and reduce the chance of injury to joints.

Game Activity

Marching Ponies

Supplies: None
Skills: Marching, running

Two or three children are ringmasters and crouch in the center of a circle of ponies formed by the rest of the class. Two goal lines on opposite sides of the circle are established as safe areas. The ponies march around the circle counting out loud with each step. At a predetermined number of steps (whispered to the ringmasters by the teacher), the ringmasters jump up and attempt to tag the others before they can reach the safety lines. Anyone tagged joins the ringmaster in the center and helps catch others. Reorganize the game after 6 to 8 children have been caught. Try other characterizations, such as lumbering elephants, jumping kangaroos, and the like.

Cat and Mice

Supplies: None
Skills: Running, dodging

Form a large circle. One child is the cat and four others are the mice. The cat and mice cannot leave the circle. On signal, the cat chases the mice inside the circle. As they are caught, the mice join the circle. The last mouse caught becomes the cat for the next round. Start at one point in the circle and progress around the circle to select mice so each child gets a chance to be in the center. Sometimes, one child has difficulty catching the last mouse or any of the mice. The point of the game is for all youngsters to be active. Change mice on a regular time interval rather than waiting until all mice are caught.

DPE Curriculum Guide – Lesson Plans
Movement Skills and Concepts (9)
Leaping, Jump-Rope Targets, and Levels/Speed
Level I – Week 31

Instructional Objectives:
To perform combinations of running
   and leaping steps
To move at different levels and speeds
To understand the concepts of
   acceleration and deceleration

NASPE National Standards:
Introductory Activity: 1, 3
Fitness Activity: 1, 4, 5, 6
Lesson Focus: 1, 2, 3, 5
Game: 1, 5

Equipment Required:
Music and signs for Animal Movements
One jump rope for each child
Tom-tom
Colored paper shapes for game

Instructional Activities	Teaching Hints

Introductory Activity — Locomotor Movement Variations

Using the basic locomotor movements and try the following variations:
1. Changes in speed
2. Weight bearing on different parts of foot (toes, heels, sides of feet)
3. Change directions
4. Making different patterns (triangles, squares, etc.)

The locomotor movements are walking,
running, galloping, skipping, hopping,
jumping, leaping, and sliding.

Encourage students to put together
sequences of various locomotor
movements.

Fitness Development Activity — Animal Movements and Fitness Challenges

1. Puppy Dog Walk—30 seconds.
2. Freeze; perform stretching activities.
3. Measuring Worm Walk—30 seconds
4. Freeze; perform abdominal development challenges.
5. Frog Jump—30 seconds.
6. Freeze; perform push-up position challenges.
7. Elephant Walk—30 seconds.
8. Freeze; perform stretching activities
9. Bear Walk—30 seconds.
10. Freeze; perform abdominal challenges.
11. Crab Walk—30 seconds.
12. Freeze; perform stretching and relaxing activities.

Tape alternating segments (30 seconds
in length) of silence and music to signal
duration of exercise. Music segments
indicate performing animal movements;
intervals of silence announce doing the
fitness challenges.

A variation is to place animal movement
signs throughout the area and instruct
students to move from sign to sign
performing the appropriate animal
movement each time they reach a new
sign.

Lesson Focus — Movement Skills and Concepts (9)

Fundamental Skill: Leaping (taking off on one foot and landing on the other)
1. Run in different directions and practice your leaping. Alternate the leading foot.
2. As you run, try a leap for good height; for distance; for both.
3. Explore the different arm positions you can use in leaping. Which is best?
4. Leap with a quarter or half turn.
5. If there are benches or other obstacles present, leap over these. Put several in
   succession for consecutive leaps.
6. Put one-half the children down scattered in curled position, face to the floor.
   The others leap over as many as possible.
7. Practice making two or three leaps in succession.
8. Practice Leap the Brook.

Movement Concept: Levels and Speed
Find an area to move and explore the following:
1. Show me a slow, low-level movement down and back.
2. What other ways can you go down and back at a slow, low level?
3. Change to a high-level, fast movement.
4. What other ways can you do a high-level, fast movement?
5. Combine a low, fast movement down with a high, slow movement back.
6. Explore other ways to move at different levels and speeds.

Select a few activities from each of the
categories so students receive a variety
of skills to practice. When possible,
integrate the manipulative skill
activities with fundamental skill
activities. A common error is to teach
all the activities from one category. The
reason for multiple groups of activities
is to provide variety and enhance
motivation.

Use instructional cues to stimulate
correct movement:
"Leap as far as possible."
"Lift with your arms."

Explain the terms of speed and levels so
children learn the concepts of altering
movements.

Movement Concept: Partner Activity and Jump Rope Floor Targets

1. Jumping, hopping, cross-steps, scissors steps, heel clicks, etc.
2. Add quarter and half-turns, levels.
3. Take the weight partially on the hands; crouch jumps, bunny jump, cartwheel, etc.
4. Form a selected shape with the rope. Repeat 1, 2, 3. Form the same shape with your body.
5. Matching activity. One partner performs and the other matches the movement.
6. Partner activity. Join hands in some way; hop, jump, or use other movements down the rope or figure. Wheelbarrow or use partner-support activities and move down the rope.

Begin with the rope laid in a straight line along the floor and perform movements down the rope.

Emphasize not touching the rope while moving.

Movement Concept: Acceleration and Deceleration

Teach students what accelerate and decelerate mean.

1. Begin a movement and accelerate.
2. Begin with a fast movement and decelerate.
3. Accelerate to a fast speed and decelerate the same movement.
4. Accelerate with one movement to fast speed, shift to another movement, and decelerate.
5. Can you accelerate one movement of the body while decelerating another at the same time?

Suggested movements for practicing acceleration and deceleration: Stepping in place, running in place, circling body parts, arm thrust movements, jumping, hopping, changing stride.

Game Activity

Mix and Match

Supplies: None

Skills: Fundamental locomotor movements

A dividing line is established through the middle of the area. Half of the children are on one side and half are on the other. Two or three extra persons are placed on one side of the area. A signal is given for youngsters to move as directed on their side of the line. They can be told to run, hop, skip, or make some other movement. On signal, players run to the dividing line and reach across to join hands with a player on the opposite side. The goal is to find a partner and not be left out. Children may reach over but not cross the line. The players left out move to the opposite side so that players without a partner are from alternating sides.

Colors

Use five or six different-colored markers with a number of children having the same color. Children start the game standing or seated in a circle each with a marker in front of them. The teacher (or another player) calls out a color. Everyone having that color runs counterclockwise around the circle and back to place. The first player seated upright and motionless is declared the winner. Different kinds of locomotor movement can be specified, such as skipping, galloping, walking, and so on. After a period of play, leave the markers on the floor and have the class move one place to the left so players have a different color.

Variation: Shapes (e.g., circles, triangles, squares, rectangles, stars, and diamonds) can be used instead of colors, as can numbers or other articles or categories, such as animals, birds, or fish.

DPE Curriculum Guide – Lesson Plans
Rhythmic Movement Skills (4)
Level I – Week 32

Instructional Objectives:
To move rhythmically in simple folk dances
To accept the outcomes of game activities
To show consideration for others in a variety of situations

NASPE National Standards:
Introductory Activity: 1, 3, 5
Fitness Activity: 1, 3, 4, 5, 6
Lesson Focus: 1, 2, 3, 5
Game: 1, 5

Equipment Required:
Hoop or beanbag for each student
Parachute
Music for Parachute Fitness & rhythms
Wand and blindfold for game

Instructional Activities	Teaching Hints

Introductory Activity — Ponies in the Stable

A beanbag or hoop is used to mark each child's stable. On signal, youngsters gallop around the area and in and out of "stables." On a second signal, students return to the nearest stable.
Variations.
1. Use different locomotor movements.
2. Take different positions in the stable such as seated, balanced, collapsed.

To introduce excitement into the activity, remove a few stables and encourage students not to be left out.

Teach directions by asking students to move in a certain direction, i.e., north, south, etc.

Fitness Development Activity — Parachute Fitness

1. Jog while holding the chute in the left hand. (music)
2. Shake the chute. (no music)
3. Slide while holding the chute with both hands. (music)
4. Sit and perform curl-ups. (no music)
5. Skip. (music)
6. Freeze, face the center, and stretch the chute tightly. Repeat five to six times. (no music)
7. Run in place while holding the chute taut at different levels. (music)
8. Sit with legs under the chute. Do a seat walk toward the center. Return to the perimeter. Repeat four to six times. (no music)
9. Place the chute on the ground. Jog away from the chute and return on signal. Repeat. (music)
10. Move into push-up position holding the chute with one hand. Shake the chute. (no music)
11. Shake the chute and jump in place. (music)
12. Lie on back with feet under the chute. Shake the chute with the feet. (no music)
13. Hop to the center of the chute and return. Repeat. (music)
14. Sit with feet under the chute. Stretch by touching the toes with the chute. Relax with other stretches while sitting. (no music)

Tape alternating segments (30 seconds in length) of silence and music to signal duration of exercise. Music segments indicate aerobic activity with the parachute; intervals of silence announce using the chute to enhance flexibility and strength development.

Space youngsters evenly around the chute.

Use different hand grips (palms up, down, mixed).

All movements should be done under control. Some of the faster and stronger students will have to moderate their performance.

Lesson Focus — Rhythmic Movement Skills (4)

Make dances easy for students to learn by implementing some of the following techniques:
1. Teach the dances without using partners.
2. Allow youngsters to move in any direction without left-right orientation.
3. Use scattered formation instead of circles.
4. Emphasize strong movements such as clapping and stamping to increase involvement.
5. Play the music at a slower speed when first learning the dance.

Rhythms should be taught like other sport skills. Avoid striving for perfection so students know it is acceptable to make mistakes. Teach a variety of dances rather than one or two in depth in case some students find it difficult to master a specific dance.

The Muffin Man (American)

Music Source: WWCD-YR002; WWC-YR002

Formation: Single circle, facing center, hands at sides. One child, the Muffin Man, stands in front of another child.

Verses:

1. Oh, have you seen the Muffin Man,
The Muffin Man, the Muffin Man?
Oh, have you seen the Muffin Man,
Who lives on _____ Street?

2. Oh, yes, we've seen the Muffin Man,
The Muffin Man, the Muffin Man.
Oh yes, we've seen the Muffin Man,
Who lives on _____ Street.

Directions:

Verse 1: The children stand still and clap their hands lightly, with the exception of the Muffin Man and his partner. These two join hands and jump lightly in place while keeping time to the music. On the first beat of each measure, a normal jump is taken, followed by a bounce in place (rebound) on the second beat.

Verse 2: The Muffin Man and his partner then skip around the inside of the circle individually and, near the end of the verse, each stands in front of a child, their new partner.

Verse 1 is then repeated, with two sets of partners doing the jumping. During the repetition of verse 2, four children skip around the inside of the circle and choose partners. This procedure continues until all children have been chosen.

Seven Jumps (Danish)

Music Source: WWCD-1043; WWC-3528

Formation: Single circle, hands joined

Directions:

There are seven jumps to the dance. Each jump is preceded by the following action.

Measures	Action
1–8	The circle moves to the right with seven step-hops, one to each measure. On the eighth measure, all jump high in the air and reverse direction. (Step-hop, 2-hop, 3-hop, … 7-hop, change direction)
9–16	Circle to the left with seven step-hops. Stop on measure 16 and face the center. (Step-hop, 2-hop, 3-hop, … 7-hop, face center)
17	All drop hands, place their hands on hips, and lift the right knee upward with the toes pointed downward. (Knee up)
18	All stamp the right foot to the ground on the signal note, then join hands on the next note. (Stamp)
1–18	Repeat measures 1–18, but do not join hands.
19	Lift the left knee, stamp, and join hands.
1–19	Repeat measures 1–19, but do not join hands.
20	Put the right toe backward and kneel on the right knee. Stand and join hands.
1–20	Repeat measures 1–20; do not join hands.
21	Kneel on the left knee. Stand and join hands.
1–21	Repeat measures 1–21; do not join hands.
22	Put the right elbow to the floor with the cheek on the fist. Stand and join hands.
1–22	Repeat measures 1–22; do not join hands.
23	Put the left elbow to the floor with the cheek on the fist. Stand and join hands.
1–23	Repeat measures 1–23; do not join hands.
24	Put the forehead on the floor. Stand and join hands.
1–16	Repeat measures 1–16.

To increase motivation, the dance can be done with a parachute. The dancers hold the parachute taut with one hand during the step-hops. The chute is kept taut with both hands for all jumps except the last, during which the forehead touches the chute on the floor.

Yankee Doodle (American)

Music Source: WWCD-FCN

Formation: Scattered or open circle facing counterclockwise

Directions:

Measures	Action
1–4	All gallop 8 steps (Gallop, 2, … 8)
5–8	All stop, face center, point to cap and bow on word "macaroni." (Stop, point, bow)
9–12	All join hands and take six slides to the right and stamp feet two times on word "dandy." (Slide, 2, 3, … 6; Stamp, stamp)
13–16	All slide six times to the left and clap hands two times on the word "candy." (Slide, 2, 3, … 6; Clap clap)

Change the locomotor movements to fit the age and interest of the group. Have the class create new movement patterns.

Eins Zwei Drei (German)

Music Source: HLP-4026

Formation: Single circle of couples (partner B to partner A's right) facing the center and numbered alternately couple 1, 2, 1, 2

Directions:

Explain that "Eins, Zwei, Drei" means "one, two, three" in German.

Measures	Part I Action
1–2	Couples 1 take three steps toward the center of the circle as they clap their hands by brushing them vertically like cymbals. (Forward, 2, 3, pause)
3–4	Couples 1 repeat measures 1–2, walking backward to place. (Back, 2, 3, pause)
5–8	Couples 1 face, join both hands, and take four slides toward the center of the circle and four slides back to place. Partner A starts with the left foot, partner B with the right. (Slide, 2, 3, 4)
9–16	Couples 2 repeat measures 1–8.
	Part II Action
17	Partner A turns and touches the right heel sideward while shaking the right index finger at partner. Partner B does the same with the left heel and left index finger. (Scold, 2, 3)
18	Repeat measure 17 with the corner, reversing footwork and hands. (Scold, 2, 3)
19–20	Repeat measures 17 and 18.
21–24	All join hands and circle left with eight slides. (Slide, 2, 3, … 8)
25–32	Repeat measures 17–24, reversing the direction of the slides. (Slide, 2, 3, … 8)

Rhythm Sticks—It's a Small, Small World (American)

Music Source: WWC-2015

Skills: Rhythmic tapping and manipulation of sticks

Formation: Children sitting cross-legged individually scattered around the area

Rhythm sticks or Lummi sticks are 12–15 inches in length. Activities may be done individually or in partners. This routine is done individually. The sticks are held in the thumb and the forefinger at about the bottom third of the stick.

Measures	Call	Action
1–2	Down, cross, down, cross	Tap ends of both sticks on the floor, and then cross the arms over tapping the sticks on the floor again.
3–4	Down, cross, down, cross	Repeat
5–6	Down, cross, down, cross	Repeat
7–8	Chorus: It's a small, small world.	Lean forward touching head to knees (curl forward).
9–10	Tap, tap, knees, knees	Tap sticks two times in front of the chest, and then lightly tap the knees twice.
11–12	Tap, tap, knees, knees	Repeat
13–14	Tap, tap, knees, knees	Repeat
15–16	Chorus: It's a small, small world.	Lean forward touching head to knees (curl forward).

The sequence above repeats a number of times with touches to the toes, shoulders, head, and nose. As a variation, youngsters can face a partner and tap both of their sticks to their partner's sticks.

Shoemaker's Dance (Danish)

Music Source: WWCD-1042; WWC-07042

Skills: Skipping, heel and toe

Formation: Double circle, partners facing, with partner A's back to the center of the circle

Directions:

Measures	Part I Action
1	With arms bent and at shoulder height, and with hands clenched to form fists, circle one fist over the other in front of the chest. (Wind the thread)
2	Reverse the circular motion and wind the thread in the opposite direction. (Reverse direction)
3	Pull the elbows back vigorously twice. (Pull and tighten the thread)
4	Clap own hands three times. (Clap, 2, 3)
5–7	Repeat the pattern of measures 1–3.
8	Tap own fists together three times to drive the nails. (Tap, 2, 3)
	Part II Action
9–16	Partners face counterclockwise, inside hands joined. Skip counterclockwise, ending with a bow. (Skip, 2, 3, … 15, bow)

Variation of Part II Action

9	Place the heel of the outside foot forward (counts 1 and), and point the toe of the outside foot in back (2 and).
10	Take three running steps forward, starting with the outside foot and pausing on the last count.
11–12	Repeat the pattern of measures 9–10, starting with the inside foot.
13–16	Repeat the pattern of measures 9–12, entire "heel and toe and run, run, run" pattern dance, four times singing Part II verse.

Bleking (Swedish)

Music Source: WWCD-1044; WWC-07042

Skills: Bleking step, step-hop

Formation: Single circle, partners facing, both hands joined. Partners A face counterclockwise and partners B clockwise.

Directions:

Part I—The Bleking Step: Cue by calling "Slow-slow, fast-fast-fast."

Measures Action

1	Hop on the left foot and extend the right heel forward with the right leg straight. At the same time, thrust the right hand forward. Hop on the right foot, reversing the arm action and extending the left foot to rest on the heel. (Slow, slow)
2	Repeat the action with three quick changes—left, right, left. (Fast, fast, fast)
3–4	Beginning on the right foot, repeat the movements of measures 1 and 2. (Slow, slow, fast, fast, fast)
5–8	Repeat measures 1–4.

Part II—The Windmills: Partners extend their joined hands sideways at shoulder height.

Measures Action

9–16	Partners turn in place with a repeated step-hop. At the same time, the arms move up and down like a windmill. The turning is done clockwise, with A starting on the right foot and B on the left. At the completion of the step-hops (16), the partners should be in their original places ready for Part I again. (Step-hop, 2-hop, 3-hop, … 16-hop)

Variations:

Change from original positions to a double circle, partners facing, As with back to the center. Part I is as described. For Part II, all face counterclockwise, and partners join inside hands. Partners do the basic schottische of "step, step, step, hop" throughout Part II.

Another excellent variation is to do the dance with partners scattered in general space. Part I is as described. For Part II, the children leave their partners and step-hop in various directions around the dancing area. When the music is about to change back to Part I, performers find a partner wherever they can, and the dance is repeated.

Game Activity

Circle Stoop

Supplies: Music or tom-tom

Skills: Moving to rhythm

Children are in a single circle, facing counterclockwise. A march or similar music, or a tom-tom beat, can be used to signal movement. The class marches until the music stops. When the music stops, players stoop and touch both hands to the ground without losing balance. The last person to touch both hands to the ground and those children who lost their balance pay a penalty by going into the mush pot (the center of the circle) for one turn. The music intervals should be varied so youngsters don't anticipate the signal.

Blindfolded Duck

Supplies: A wand and blindfold

Skills: Fundamental locomotor movements

One child, designated the duck (Daisy if a girl, Donald if a boy), stands blindfolded in the center of a circle and holds a wand or similar article. She taps on the floor and tells the class to hop (or perform some other locomotor movement). Children in the circle act accordingly, all moving in the same direction. Daisy then taps the wand twice on the floor, which signals all children to stop. Daisy moves forward with her wand, still blindfolded, to find a child in the circle. She asks, "Who are you?" The child responds, "Quack, quack." Daisy tries to identify this person. If the guess is correct, the identified child becomes the new duck. If the guess is wrong, Daisy must take another turn. After two unsuccessful turns, another child is chosen to be the duck.

DPE Curriculum Guide – Lesson Plans
Fundamental Skills Using Individual Mats
Level I – Week 33

Instructional Objectives:
To be able to identify the eight
    locomotor movements
To perform fitness challenges
    independently
To manage the body in space and on
    the floor

NASPE National Standards:
Introductory Activity: 1, 3, 5
Fitness Activity: 1, 4, 6
Lesson Focus: 1, 2, 3, 5
Game: 1, 3, 5

Equipment Required:
Music for Fitness Challenges
One individual mat for each student

Instructional Activities	Teaching Hints
Introductory Activity — Locomotor Movements and Freeze	
Perform the locomotor movements below; freeze quickly on signal with a wide base of support. A suggestion is to tape alternating segments of silence and music to signal duration of the locomotor movements. Segments of silence to indicate the "freeze" position can be decreased in duration until the desired response latency is reached.	Ask class to start moving upon entry into teaching area.
	If necessary, demonstrate how to perform the movements.
1. Walk 2. Run 3. Jump 4. Hop 5. Skip 6. Gallop 7. Leap 8. Slide	Reinforce stopping without falling.

Fitness Development Activity — Fitness Challenges	
1. Locomotor Movement: Walk for 30 seconds.	Alternate the locomotor movements with the strength and flexibility challenges. Repeat the challenges as necessary.

2. Flexibility and Trunk Development Challenges
    a. Bend in different directions.
    b. Stretch slowly and return quickly.
    c. Combine bending and stretching movements.
    d. Sway back and forth.
    e. Twist one body part; add more body parts.	

	Tape alternating segments (30 seconds in length) of silence and music to signal duration of exercise. Music segments indicate locomotor movements; intervals of silence announce doing the movement challenges.
3. Locomotor Movement: Skip for 30 seconds.	

4. Upper Body Strength Challenges
In a push-up position, do the following challenges:
    a. Lift one foot; the other foot.
    b. Wave at a friend; wave with the other arm.
    c. Scratch your back with one hand; use the other hand.
    d. Walk your feet to your hands.
    e. Turn over and face the ceiling; shake a leg; crab walk.
	Teach youngsters the different challenges and then allow them to select a challenge they can successfully perform.

	The challenges should be enjoyable to perform.
5. Locomotor Movement: Jog for 30 seconds.	

6. Abdominal Development Challenges
From a supine position:
    a. Lift your head and look at your toes.
    b. Lift your knees to your chest.
    c. Wave your legs at a friend.
From a sitting position;
    a. Slowly lay down with hands on tummy.
    b. Lift legs and touch toes.
	Encourage students to focus on trying and feeling successful.
	
	Workloads should be moderate with emphasis on success for all youngsters.

7. Locomotor Movement: Run and leap for 30 seconds.	

Lesson Focus — Fundamental Skills Using Individual Mats

Nonlocomotor Movements

1. Stretch
   a. Different directions.
   b. Different parts of body.
2. Curl
3. Balance
   a. Balance on different body parts.
   b. Balance on different number of parts.
   c. Go from one balance to another.
4. Bridge
   a. Bridge across the short width, long width.
   b. Different parts or number of parts.
   c. Bridge to a full arch.
5. Reach
   a. Keep toes on mat, reach as far as possible.
   b. Keep hand on mat, reach as far as possible.
   c. Keep hand on mat; reach as far as possible with a foot.
6. Rock
   a. On different parts
7. Roll
   a. Different types of rolls.
   b. Roll up in the mat.
8. Twist
   a. Full twist, held.
   b. Moving twists
   c. Twist and untwist.
9. Use other Terms
   a. Straight, curved, narrow, wide, prone melt, shake, fall, collapse.
10. Combination Movements

Give students two or three activities to practice so you have time to move and help. Alternate activities from each of the categories so students receive a variety of skills to practice.

Each student needs a mat. Carpet squares can be used. Indoor-outdoor carpet with rubber backing is best because it doesn't slide.

Encourage students to create as many different varieties of each nonlocomotor movement.

To develop a clear understanding of the movements, challenge the students by changing to different movements quickly.

On and Off the Mats

1. Different locomotor movements- hop, jump, leap.
2. Weight on the hands. Crouch jumps, forward and backward.
3. Animal imitations, i.e., Rabbit, Frog, etc.

Combine sequences of the different non locomotor movements, i.e., rock, bridge, and curl.

Over the Mat

1. Locomotor movements: Add turns, secure height.
2. Weight on the hands.
3. Combinations: Over one way and back another way.
4. How many mats can you jump over in 10 seconds? Change the movements over the mat.
5. Hop over five blue mats. Change the movement, number, and color of the mats.

Encourage youngsters to manage their body when performing the activities. This is an excellent opportunity to encourage moving with falling.

Movements around the Mats

1. Different locomotor movements.
2. Animal Walks, i.e., Dog, Bear, Cat, Rabbit.
3. Keep hands on the mat.
4. Keep feet on the mat.

Mats as a Base

1. Use different magic numbers.
   a. A number of movements out and back.
   b. Different number combinations.
   c. Animal imitations.

Challenge Activities

1. Try some individual and partner stunts with the mats as a base.
   a. Coffee Grinder
   b. Chinese Get-up
   c. Wring the Dishrag

2. Jump from mat to mat without touching the floor. Can you move across the area? Skip from mat to mat.
3. Play "Ring around the Mat." Skip around the mat and all fall down.
4. Move between five mats and cartwheel over two mats. Use different movements and tumbling activities.
5. Put your mat together with a partner and make different shapes, numbers, and letters. Do the same thing in small groups.
6. Magic Carpet Ride—one person pulls a partner sitting on the mat.

Game Activity

Sneak Attack

Supplies: None

Skills: Marching, running

Two parallel lines are drawn about 60 ft apart. The class is divided into two teams. One team takes a position on one of the lines, with their backs to the area. These are the chasers. The other team is on the other line, facing the area. This is the sneak team. The sneak team moves forward on signal, moving toward the chasers. When they get reasonably close, a signal is given, and the sneak team turns and runs back to their line, chased by the other team. Anyone tagged before reaching the line changes to the chase team. The game is then repeated, with the roles exchanged.

Mat Games

Supplies: Individual Mats

Skills: Running, jumping

Each child is seated on a mat. On signal, each rises and jumps over as many different mats as possible. On the next signal, each child takes a seat on the nearest mat. The last child to be seated can pay a penalty. The game can also be played by eliminating one or two mats so that one or two children are left without a home base. The teacher can stand on a mat or turn over mats to put them out of the game. To control roughness, the rule should be that the first child to touch a mat gets to sit on it.

A variation of this game is to have each child touch at least ten mats and then sit cross-legged on his own mat, or a child can be required to alternate touching a mat and jumping over the next mat until a total of ten is reached. "See how many mats you can cartwheel or jump over in 10 seconds." Change the challenge and try again.

Instructional Objectives:
To know the names of fitness activities in Astronaut Exercises
To learn to balance the body while walking a beam
To manipulate an object while walking a beam

NASPE National Standards:
Introductory Activity: 1, 3
Fitness Activity: 1, 4, 6
Lesson Focus: 1, 2, 3, 5
Game: 1, 5

Equipment Required:
Music for Astronaut Exercises
Six balance beam benches or 2" × 4" boards (8 ft long)
Hoops, wands, and beanbags for beam activities

Instructional Activities	Teaching Hints

Introductory Activity — Airplanes

Children pretend to be airplanes. They take off, zoom with arms out, swoop, turn, and glide. On signal, they drop to the floor in prone position. To take off again, they must "restart" their engines by doing a couple of push-up challenges while making a "vroom, vroom" engine sound.

Encourage creativity by naming different types of airplanes and helicopters.

Use different locomotor movements.

Fitness Development Activity — Astronaut Exercises

Walk, do arm circles	30 seconds
Flexibility and trunk development challenges	30 seconds
Skip forward, backwards, and sideways	30 seconds
Upper-body strength challenges	30 seconds
Slide; change lead leg	30 seconds
Abdominal development challenges	30 seconds
Jump like a pogo stick	30 seconds
Upper-body strength challenges	30 seconds
Trot lightly in different directions	30 seconds
Flexibility and trunk development challenges	30 seconds
Gallop backwards	30 seconds

Cool down with stretching and walking.

Tape alternating segments of silence and music to signal duration of exercise. Music segments (30 seconds) indicate aerobic activity; intervals of silence (30 seconds) signal flexibility and strength development activities.

See Chapter 13 for a description of how to perform challenge activities.

Allow students to adjust the workload to an intensity that is consistent with their ability level.

Lesson Focus — Fundamental Skills Using Balance Beams

Balance-beam activities should be done using controlled walking movements. Speed of movement should always be avoided.

Dismounts
All moves across the balance beam should end with a dismount. The following dismounts are examples.
1. Single jump (forward or backward).
2. Jump with turns (half turn, three-quarter turn, or full turn).
3. Jackknife. Jump, kick the legs up, and touch the toes with the fingertips. Keep the feet together.
4. Jackknife Split. Same as the Jackknife, but spread the legs as far as possible.
5. Jump, land, and do a Forward Roll.
6. Backward jump, land, and do a Backward Roll.
7. Side jump to a Side Roll.

Balance Beam Activities
1. Practice walking on floor lines to establish qualities of controlled movement and not looking at feet.
2. Walk length of beam.
   a. Walk forward.
   b. Walk backward.
   c. Walk sideways—lead with both left and right sides of body.
   d. Try other steps—follow steps, heel and toe, on toes, etc.

If balance beams are not available, use 2" × 4" boards placed on the floor. This will give students some elevation off the floor and offer balance challenges.

Place the beams parallel to each other and have a similar number of students lined up behind each one. Students progress down the beam.

After moving the length of the beam, have students do a locomotor movement to the end of the teaching area and return. This will offer students both balance activities and the chance to practice locomotor movements. It also keeps students engaged in activity for a longer period of time and reduces standing and waiting time. Specified movements can be placed on return activity signs.

If a student steps off the beam, have them get back on and progress.

3. Walk different directions and vary arm and body positions.
   a. Hands on hips.
   b. Hand on head.
   c. Arms folded across chest.
   d. Lean to one side or the other.
   e. Body bent forward or backward.
   f. Hands on knees or feet.
4. Perform animal movements across the balance beam.
   a. Puppy dog walk
   b. Bear Walk
   c. Crab Walk
5. Use manipulative equipment while walking the beam.
   a. Balance objects such as beanbags or wands while walking across beam.
   b. Step over a wand or through a hoop while walking the beam.
   c. Toss and catch a beanbag while walking the beam.
   d. Twirl a hoop while walking the beam.
   e. Bounce a ball while walking a beam.
   f. Play catch with a partner while walking the beam.
6. Try to do a stork stand in the middle of the beam (on one foot)

Sometimes, students stop walking the beam and receive little practice. Move with controlled, deliberate movements across the beam. Speed is not a goal.

Game Activity

Toe to Toe
   Supplies: None
   Skills: Fundamental locomotor movements
Youngsters perform a locomotor movement around the area. On signal, each child must find a partner and stand toe to toe (one foot only) with that person. An important skill is to take the nearest person for a partner without searching for a friend. Youngsters who can't find a partner within their immediate area must run quickly to the center of the area (use a marking spot or cone) to find a partner. The goal is to find a nearby partner as quickly as possible and avoid being the last pair formed. If the number of youngsters playing is uneven, the teacher can join in and play. Change locomotor movements often.

Mousetrap
   Supplies: None
   Skills: Skipping, running, dodging
   Half of the class forms a circle with hands joined, facing the center. This is the trap. The other half of the class is on the outside of the circle. These are the mice. Three signals are given for the game. These can be word cues or other signals. On the first signal, the mice skip around, outside the circle, playing happily. On the second signal, the trap is opened. (The circle players raise their joined hands to form arches.) The mice run in and out of the trap. The third signal signals the trap to snap shut. (The arms come down.) All mice caught in the trap join the circle. The game is repeated until most of the mice are caught. The players exchange places and the game begins anew.

Aviator
   Supplies: None
   Skills: Running, locomotor movements, stopping
   Players are parked (in push-up position) at one end of the playing area. The air traffic controller (ATC) is in front of the players and calls out, "Aviators aviators, take off!" Youngsters take off and move like airplanes to the opposite side of the area. The first person to move to the other side and land the plane (get into push-up position facing the ATC) is declared the new ATC. If the ATC yells out some type of stormy weather, all planes must return to the starting line and resume the parked position. Examples of stormy weather commands are lightning, thunder, hurricane, and tornado. Each ATC is allowed to give stormy weather warnings once.

LP 35

Instructional Objectives:	NASPE National Standards:	Equipment Required:

Instructional Objectives:
To recognize variety within locomotor movements
To work independently at circuit training stations
To understand movement concepts of over and under/different ways of moving
To handle a racquet and ball

NASPE National Standards:
Introductory Activity: 1, 3, 5
Fitness Activity: 1, 3, 4, 6
Lesson Focus: 1, 2, 3, 5
Game: 1, 5

Equipment Required:
Music and signs for Circuit Training
One racquet and ball for each child
Hoops (4–6)
8" foam balls (5–7)

Instructional Activities	Teaching Hints

Introductory Activity — Movement Varieties

Move using a basic locomotor movement (i.e., walking, jumping, hopping, skipping, and galloping). Then add variety to the movement by asking students to respond to the following factors:

1. Level—low, high, in between.
2. Direction—straight, zigzag, circular, curved, forward, backward, upward, downward.
3. Size—large, tiny, medium movements.
4. Patterns—forming squares, diamonds, triangles, circles, figure-eights.
5. Speed—slow, fast, accelerate.

Use scatter formation.

Emphasize and reinforce creative responses.

Explain concepts of level, direction, size, and speed. Short explanations laced with activity allow students time to recover.

Fitness Development Activity — Circuit Training

Make signs, put them on cones and place around the perimeter of the teaching area. Students perform the exercise specified at each station while the music is playing.

1. Tortoise and Hare
2. Curl-up variations
3. Hula Hooping on arms
4. Standing Hip Bend
5. Agility run—run back and forth between two designated lines
6. Push-up variations
7. Crab Walk
8. Bend and Twist

Tape alternating segments of silence and music to signal duration of exercise. Music segments (begin at 30 seconds) indicate activity at each station; intervals of silence (10 seconds) announce it is time to stop and move forward to the next station.

Place an equal number of students at each station.

Use activities at the stations that students already know how to perform.

Lesson Focus — Movement Skills and Concepts (10)

Fundamental Skill: Running

1. Run lightly around the area; stop on signal.
2. Run lightly and change directions on signal.
3. Run, turn around with running steps on signal, and continue in a new direction.
4. Pick a spot away from you. Run to it and return without bumping anyone.
5. Run low, gradually increase the height. Reverse.
6. Run patterns. Run inside and around objects.
7. Run with high knee action. Add a knee slap with the hand as you run.
8. Run with different steps—tiny, long, light, heavy, crisscross, wide, and others.
9. Run with arms in different positions—circling, overhead, stiff at sides and others (choice).
10. Free running. Concentrate on good knee lift.
11. Run at different speeds.
12. Touch the ground at times with either hand as you run.

Select a few activities from each of the categories so students receive a variety of skills to practice. When possible, integrate the manipulative skill activities with fundamental skill activities. A common error is to teach all the activities from one category. The reason for multiple groups of activities is to provide variety and enhance motivation.

Encourage running under control. Falling down or collisions should be discouraged. Reinforce students who do run under control.

13. Run backwards, sideways.
14. Run with exaggerated arm movements and/or high bounce.
15. Practice running, crossing from one line to another.
    a. Cross your feet as you run.
    b. Touch the ground with one and both hands as you run.
    c. Run forward, looking backward over your right shoulder.
    d. Same, but look over the left shoulder.
    e. Change direction every few steps.
    f. Run to the center, stop completely, then continue.
    g. Make two stops going across—first with the right side forward and then with the left side forward as you stop.
    h. Run forward and stop. Come back three steps and stop. Continue in forward direction.
    i. Do a two-count stop on the way.
    j. Run sideways across, leading with one side. Next time lead with the other.
    k. Run forward halfway and then backward the rest.
    l. Run backward halfway and then forward the rest.
    m. Make a full turn in the center and continue. Do this right and left.
    n. Provide for student choice.

Use instructional cues:

"Look ahead when running."

"Bend the arms at the elbows and gently move them back and forth."

When teaching running skills, couple them with stopping skills. Encourage effective stopping by bending the knees and lowering the center of gravity.

Manipulative Activity—Racquets and Balls
Individual Activity
1. Place the ball on the racquet face. Roll it around the face.
2. Hit the ball into the air with the racquet. Retrieve and repeat.
3. Bounce the ball into the air, using the racquet. Specify number.
4. Bounce the ball into the air, decreasing the height of the bounce until it rests on the face of the racquet.
5. Bounce the ball on the floor.
6. Alternate bouncing upward and to the floor.
7. Dribble the ball and move while dribbling.
8. Choice activity.

Other pieces of manipulative equipment can be used if racquets and balls are not available.

Place the racquets and balls around the perimeter of the area. On signal, students move and pick up a racquet and ball and begin rolling it around the face of the racquet.

Partner Activity
1. One partner tosses the other hits it back.
2. Try batting it back and forth. If using a tennis ball, let it bounce between hits.
3. Place ball on floor and roll it back and forth.

Partners should be close to each other so control of the ball is maintained.

Movement Concept: Over and Under
1. One partner is an obstacle and the other goes over, under, and around the "obstacle." Reverse positions.
2. Copying action. One partner takes a position and the other goes over and under the first. Reverse positions, but try to copy the same sequence.
3. Progressive sequencing. The first child does a movement (over, under, or around). The second child repeats the movement and adds another. The first child repeats the first two movements and adds a third. The second child repeats and adds a forth.

The goal is to **not** touch the partner who is the obstacle.

Encourage creativity and reinforce new ideas.

Movement Concept: Moving in Different Ways
1. Show me different ways to move when your body is in the air part of the time; when your body is always in contact with the floor.
2. Show me different ways you can progress along the floor without using your hands or feet. Can you "walk" using your seat?
3. What are the different ways you can roll and move?
4. What ways can you move sideways? How can you move on all fours?
5. Move across the floor halfway with one movement and the other half with a decidedly different movement.
6. Explore the different ways you can move when leading with selected parts of the body.

Use student demonstration to encourage variety and creativity. Discuss the many ways of solving a movement problem.

Rollee Pollee

Supplies: Many 8" foam balls

Skills: Ball rolling, dodging

Half of the class forms a circle; the other half is in the center. Balls are given to circle players. The circle players roll the balls at the feet and shoes of the center players, trying to touch them with a ball. The center players move around to avoid the balls. A center player who is touched leaves the center and joins the circle. After a period of time or when all of the children have been touched with a ball, teams trade places. Balls that stop in the center are dead and must be taken back to the circle before being put into play again. The preferable procedure is to have players who recover balls roll them to a teammate rather than return to place with the ball.

Mix and Match

Supplies: None

Skills: Fundamental locomotor movements

A dividing line is established through the middle of the area. Half of the children are on one side and half are on the other. Two or three extra persons are placed on one side of the area. A signal is given for youngsters to move as directed on their side of the line. They can be told to run, hop, skip, or make some other movement. On signal, players run to the dividing line and reach across to join hands with a player on the opposite side. The goal is to find a partner and not be left out. Children may reach over but not cross the line. The players left out move to the opposite side so that players without a partner are from alternating sides.

DPE Curriculum Guide – Lesson Plans
Movement Skills and Concepts (11)
Pushing, Pulling, Rope Jumping, and Balancing the Body
Level I – Week 36

Instructional Objectives:
To make a variety of shapes with the body
To know the difference between pushing and pulling
To know the mechanics of effective pushing and pulling
To understand the difference between making circles with body parts and twisting

NASPE National Standards:
Introductory Activity: 1, 3
Fitness Activity: 1, 4, 6
Lesson Focus: 1, 2, 3, 5
Game: 1, 2, 5

Equipment Required:
Tom-tom & music for Walk, Trot, and Jog
One jump rope for each student
Plastic bottle bat and ball
Batting tee

Instructional Activities	Teaching Hints
Introductory Activity — Run and Assume Shape	
Place emphasis on making a variety of shapes and balances. Vary the locomotor movements. 1. Run and move to a prone (one drumbeat) or supine (two drumbeats) position on signal. 2. Run and move into a balance position. 3. Run and freeze in various shapes.	Place emphasis on running under control and assuming specified shape quickly. Have students move into the activity area in scatter formation.
Fitness Development Activity — Walk, Trot, and Jog	

Move to the following signals:
   1. One drumbeat—walk.
   2. Two drumbeats—trot.
   3. Three drumbeats—jog.
   4. Whistle—freeze and perform exercises.
 	
 Use various strength and flexibility exercises between bouts of walk, trot, and jog to allow students to recover aerobically. Examples are:
   1. Bend and Twist
   2. Sitting Stretch
   3. Push-up challenges
   4. Abdominal Challenges
   5. Body Twist
   6. Standing Hip Bend
	Tape alternating segments (20 seconds in length) of silence and music to signal duration of exercise. Music segments indicate walk, trot, and jog activity. Intervals of silence signal performance of the strength and flexibility exercises.
	
	 Encourage students to move around the area in the same direction.
	
	 See Chapter 13 for a description of how to perform the exercises. Any exercises can be substituted. Exercise all body parts.

Lesson Focus — Movement Skills and Concepts (11)

Fundamental Skill: Pushing
1. Push against a wall first in an erect position and then with knees bent and one foot braced behind the other. Which is better?
2. Push an imaginary object that is very light. Now try pushing a very heavy object.
3. Try to push a partner who is sitting on the floor.
4. Can you push an object with your feet without using your arms and hands? Try with the hands braced behind you.
5. Put your back against an object and push with your feet.
6. Explore different ways to push your object.
7. Find a friend to explore different ways to push him or her over a line.
8. Sit down back to back with your partner and see whether you can move him or her.
9. Lie on the floor and push yourself backward, forward, sideways. Which is easiest?

Select a few activities from each of the categories so students receive a variety of skills to practice. When possible, integrate the manipulative skill activities with fundamental skill activities. A common error is to teach all the activities from one category. The reason for multiple groups of activities is to provide variety and enhance motivation.

Use instructional cues such as:
   "Use a wide stance."
   "Bend your knees and lower your center of gravity."

10. Lie on the floor and push yourself forward with one hand and one foot. Which hand-foot combination is best?
11. Show how you can push a ball to a friend. Push slowly and steadily.

"Place all of your body behind your hands while pushing."

Fundamental Skill: Pulling
1. Reach for an imaginary object near the ceiling and pull the object toward you quickly. Now slowly and smoothly.
2. Clasp your hands together and pull against each hand as hard as you can. Vary the positions of the arms.
3. Hold hands with your partner and try to pull against each other balancing on one foot.
4. Hold hands with partner, drop low, and pull hard against each other.
5. Have partner sit down. Pull partner slowly by the feet.
6. Pretend to pull a heavy object while you are lying on the floor.
7. With partner seated on the floor, pull him or her to his or her feet.

Use instructional cues to enhance pulling skills:
"Lower your body and widen your base of support."
"Lean away from the source of pull."

Use slow controlled pulling. Remind youngsters to ask their partner to stop if the hand grip is slipping.

Manipulative Skills: Rope Jumping
Encourage children to work on needed skill areas. Suggest working first without music and then with music.

Allow students time to practice new jumping skills. Find students who can demonstrate different skills if necessary.

Movement Concepts: Circles in the Body
1. How many joints of the body can do circular motion (circles)?
2. How many different ways can you make the arms circle, using both arms at once?
3. Lie on back, lift your legs. Can you make the arms and legs go in circles? Can you make them go in different circles?
4. In a standing position, show arm circles in horizontal, vertical, and diagonal direction using one arm at a time.
5. Repeat item 4, using both arms.
6. Lie on back and lift the legs. Make circles with the feet first singly and then together.
7. Explore different ways to make two different body parts make circles in different directions.
8. Make a large circle with one part of the body and a small one with another.
9. What joints can twist as well as circle?

Explain that a joint is where different body parts are connected.

Explain the terms horizontal, vertical, and diagonal.

Encourage students to make different size circles in many different directions.

Explain the difference between twisting and circling.

Movement Concept: Balancing the Body
1. On different parts of the body.
2. On different number of body parts, varying from one through five. Different combinations.
3. Balancing on different levels.
4. Work out a sequence of three or four balance poses. Flow from one to the next.
5. Try to balance on both hands.
6. With a partner, form different balances.

Balance skills should emphasize smooth movements that are held 3 to 5 seconds. Students will always try to speed up the balance activity if they are having trouble maintaining balance.

Share balance innovations with peers.

Movement Concept: Sports Imitation Activities
1. Pretend you are a football player—kicking the ball, passing the ball, making a tackle, centering the ball.
2. Pretend you are a basketball player—shooting a basket, dribbling, guarding, jump ball, a free throw shot.
3. Pretend you are a track and field star performing at: the shot-put, the javelin throw, or the discus. Move like a hurdler.
4. Pretend you are a baseball player—pitching, catching a fly ball, fielding a grounder and throwing to first, batting, bunting, sliding into a base.

If desired, pictures of athletes can be used to motivate movement.

Place emphasis on performing the activities with speed and authenticity. Some students may need to see demonstrations of how the skills should be performed.

Change Sides

Supplies: None

Skill: Body management

Identify two parallel lines 30 ft apart with half of the class on each line. On signal, all players cross to the other line, face the center, and stand at attention. The first group to do all three things correctly wins a point. Children must be cautioned to use care when passing through the opposite group. They should be spaced well along each line; this allows room for them to move through each group. Vary the locomotor movements used by specifying skipping, hopping, long steps, sliding, and other varieties of movement. The position to be assumed at the finish can be varied also.

Bottle Bat Ball

Supplies: A plastic bottle bat, whiffle ball, batting tee (optional), home plate, base marker

Skills: Batting, retrieving balls

Batters get three pitches (or swings if a batting tee is used) to hit a fair ball or they are out. The pitches are easy (as in slow-pitch softball) so the batter has a chance to hit the ball. The batter hits the ball and runs around the base marker and back to home plate. If the ball is returned to the pitcher's mound before the batter reaches home, the batter is out. (A marker should designate the pitcher's mound.) Otherwise, the batter has a home run and earns a run for her team. One fielder other than the pitcher is needed, but another can be used. The running distance to first base is critical. It can remain fixed or can be made progressively (one step) longer, until it reaches such a point that the fielders are heavily favored.

DPE Curriculum Guide – Lesson Plans
Fundamental Skills Using Climbing Ropes
Level I – Alternate Lesson Plan

Instructional Objectives:
To be able to recite safety rules for
   rope climbing
To be able to hang on a climbing rope
   for 5 seconds
To be able to swing on a climbing rope

NASPE National Standards:
Introductory Activity:
Fitness Activity:
Lesson Focus: 2, 3, 5
Game:

Equipment Required:
Equipment for Challenge course
Climbing Ropes
Tumbling mats placed under ropes
Benches or Jumping Boxes

Instructional Activities	Teaching Hints

Introductory Activity
Use the introductory activity from the lesson that was replaced.

Fitness Development Activity
Use the fitness activity from the lesson that was replaced.

Lesson Focus — Fundamental Skills Using Climbing Ropes

Supported Pull-Ups

In supported pull-up activities, a part of the body remains in contact with the floor. The pull-up is hand-over-hand and the return is hand-under-hand.

1. Kneel directly under the rope. Pull up to the tiptoes and return to kneeling position.
2. Start in a sitting position under the rope. Pull up; the legs are supported on the heels. Return to sitting position.
3. Start in a standing position. Grasp the rope, rock back on the heels, and lower the body to the floor. Keep a straight body. Return to standing position.

Hangs

In a hang, the body is pulled up in one motion and held up for a length of time (5, 10, or 20 seconds). Progression is important.

1. From a seated position, reach up as high as possible and pull the body from the floor, except for the heels. Hold.
2. Same as the previous stunt, but pull the body completely free of the floor. Hold.
3. From a standing position, jump up, grasp the rope, and hang. This should be a Bent-Arm Hang with the hands about even with the mouth. Hold.
4. Repeat the previous stunt, but add leg movements—one or both knees up, bicycling movement, Half Lever (one or both legs up, parallel to the floor), Full Lever (feet up to the face).

Pull-Ups

In the pull-up, the body is raised and lowered repeatedly. The initial challenge should be to accomplish one pull-up in the defined position. The number of repetitions should be increased with care. All of the activities described for hangs are adaptable to pull-ups. The chin should touch the hands on each pull-up.

Swinging and Jumping

For swinging and jumping, a bench, box, or stool can serve as a takeoff point. To take off, the child reaches high and jumps to a bent-arm position. Landing should be with bent knees.

1. Swing and jump. Add half turns and full turns.
2. Swing and return to the perch. Add single- and double-knee bends.
3. Jump for distance, over a high-jump bar or through a hoop.
4. Swing and pick up a bowling pin and return to the perch.
5. Carry objects (e.g., beanbags, balls, deck tennis rings). A partner, standing to the side away from the takeoff bench, can put articles to be carried back on the takeoff perch by placing each article between the knees or feet.
6. Not using a takeoff device, run toward a swinging rope, grasp it, and gain momentum for swinging.

Teaching Hints

1. Mats should be placed under all ropes.

2. The hand-over-hand method should be used for climbing and the hand-under-hand method for descending.

3. Caution the children not to slide; sliding can cause rope burns on the hands and legs.

4. A climber who becomes tired should stop and rest. Proper rest stops should be taught as part of the swinging and climbing procedure.

5. Children swinging on the ropes should be instructed to make sure that other children are out of the way. Spotters should be used initially for activities in which the body is inverted.

Climbing the Rope

1. *Scissors Grip.* For the Scissors Grip, approach the rope and reach as high as possible, standing with the right leg forward of the left. Raise the back leg, bend at the knee, and place the rope inside the knee and outside the foot. Cross the forward leg over the back leg, and straighten the legs with the toes pointed down. This should give a secure hold. To climb using the Scissors Grip, raise the knees up close to the chest, the rope sliding between them, while supporting the body with the hand grip. Lock the rope between the legs and climb up, using the hand-over-hand method and stretching as high as the hands can reach. Bring the knees up to the chest and repeat the process.

2. *Leg-Around Rest.* Wrap the left leg completely around the rope, keeping the rope between the thighs. The bottom of the rope then crosses over the instep of the left foot from the outside. The right foot stands on the rope as it crosses over the instep, providing pressure to prevent slippage. To provide additional pressure, release the hands and wrap the arms around the rope, leaning away from the rope at the same time. To climb using the Leg-Around Rest, proceed as in climbing with the Scissors Grip, but loosen the grip each time and re-grip higher.

Descending the Rope

There are four methods to descend the rope. The only differences are in the use of the leg locks, as the hand-under-hand is used for all descents.

1. *Scissors Grip.* From an extended scissors grip position, lock the legs and lower the body with the hands until the knees are against the chest. Hold with the hands, and lower the legs to a new position.

2. *Leg-Around Rest.* From the leg-around rest position, lower the body until the knees are against the chest. Lift the top foot, and let the feet slide to a lower position. Secure with the top foot and repeat.

3. *Instep Squeeze.* Squeeze the rope between the insteps by keeping the heels together. Lower the body while the rope slides against the instep.

4. *Stirrup Descent.* Place the rope on the outside of the right foot and carry it over the instep of the left. Pressure from the left foot holds the position. To get into position, let the rope trail along the right leg, reach under, and hook it with the left instep. When the pressure from the left leg is reduced, the rope slides smoothly while the descent is made with the hands.

6. Children should be taught to leave enough margin for a safe descent. No children should go higher than their strength allows.

7. Marks to limit the climb can be put on the rope with adhesive tape. A height of 8 to 10 ft above the floor is reasonable until a child demonstrates proficiency.

8. If the ceiling is higher than 15 or 16 ft, a bright piece of tape should be wrapped around the rope to limit climbing height.

9. Rosin in powdered form and magnesium chalk aid in gripping. It is particularly important that they be used when the rope becomes slippery.

Game Activity

Skunk Tag

Supplies: None

Skills: Fundamental locomotor movements, dodging

Children are scattered about the area. One child is it and chases the others, trying to tag one of them. When a tag is made, she says "You're it." The new it chases other children. Children are safe when they move into the skunk position which is assumed by kneeling and reaching one arm under a knee and holding their nose. The skunk position can only be held for five seconds; students are then eligible to be tagged.

Aviator

Supplies: None

Skills: Running, locomotor movements, stopping

Players are parked (in push-up position) at one end of the playing area. The air traffic controller (ATC) is in front of the players and calls out, "Aviators aviators, take off!" Youngsters take off and move like airplanes to the opposite side of the area. The first person to move to the other side and land the plane (get into push-up position facing the ATC) is declared the new ATC. If the ATC yells out some type of stormy weather, all planes must return to the starting line and resume the parked position. Examples of stormy weather commands are lightning, thunder, hurricane, and tornado. Each ATC is allowed to give stormy weather warnings once.

Objectives:
To develop upper body strength
To be able to explain safety
  precautions when climbing
To be able to climb using the basic
  holds

NASPE National Standards:
Introductory Activity:
Fitness Activity:
Lesson Focus: 2, 3, 5
Game: 1, 5, 6

Equipment Required:
Beanbags
Tumbling mats placed at the base of the
  climbing wall
Climbing wall

Instructional Activities	Teaching Hints

Introductory Activity
Use the introductory activity from the lesson that was replaced.

Fitness Development Activity
Use the fitness activity from the lesson that was replaced.

Lesson Focus — Climbing Wall Activities

Climbing walls are an excellent way to develop strength and coordination while solving climbing challenges. Students can learn to cooperate with others and accomplishment of a climbing task contributes to student self-esteem. Most transverse walls in elementary schools are 8 ft high. Taller walls should have a red-relief line that keeps climbers close to the floor. For additional safety, place mats along the base of the wall. A typical wall may be 40 ft or more wide and have two to three hundred hand holds. The hand holds are often color coded for level of difficulty.

Basic Holds

Teach students the basic ways to climb on the wall. Explain and practice hand and foot holds on the wall at a low level before proceeding to climb. The following are basic holds:

- The Pinch—This basic hold is performed by simply squeezing the hold between the thumb and fingers.

- Finger Grip—Just the fingers are used to hold a rock while adjusting the legs to a stable rock position.

- The Crimp—Grasp the hold with the fingers at the middle joint and wrap the thumb over the first joint of the index finger.

- The Edge—This foothold uses the ball to toe part of the foot. Either side of the shoe can be used, i.e., the front with the toe pointing or the outside edge of the shoe.

Individual Challenge Activities

A positive aspect of climbing walls is that students can use footholds to help them climb. This helps youngsters who are overweight find success. For students who are challenged, do not rush them. Give them activities to do that are near the floor and let them determine when they are ready to challenge themselves. Climbing challenges are individual in nature—each student strives to improve their performance without concern for how others are climbing. The following are examples of climbing activities that can be used to motivate students to stay on the wall and practice their skills.

- Four-Point Hold—Climbers take a four-point rock position (each hand and foot on a separate rock) and move to four new rocks.
- Foothold Climb—Climb high enough to get footholds on rocks.
- Foothold Climbs with Challenges—Similar to the climb above except students are challenged to climb using only certain color rocks.
- Up and Down—Climb and then return to the floor using the same pathway (same rocks).

Climbing walls can be safely used in a physical education setting if students are made aware of and follow appropriate safety rules. Consider the following guidelines:

Climbing walls are only used when a teacher is directly supervising the activity.

Only soft-soled shoes are used during climbing activities.

On walls taller than 8 ft, climbing above the red line is not allowed. The climber's feet must stay below the red line at all times.

Climbers are not to touch or interfere with another climber on the wall.

Only climbers are allowed on the safety mats.

Climb down from the wall—no jumping down is allowed.

- Three-point Hold—Climb off the floor and below the red line. Balance yourself and lift a limb from a hold. Try lifting a different limb.
- Beanbag Climb—Climb with a beanbag on your shoulder. Place the beanbag on a hold and descend. The next person climbs and brings the beanbag down on their shoulder.

Game Activity

Who's leading? (Cooperative Game)

Formation: Entire class in a circle

Supplies: None

The entire class stands shoulder to shoulder in a circle. One student volunteers to go in the middle and cover her eyes. The teacher then selects a volunteer to lead the class in movements while remaining in the circle. This must be done quietly so the person in the middle does not know who the leader is. The teacher will need to provide the leader with examples of movements such as jogging or skipping in place, bicep curls, jumping jacks, etc. The leader will also be instructed to change activities every few seconds. The person in the middle then opens her eyes and watches the movements. She must stay in the middle but may scan the entire class in an effort to find the leader as he changes movements.

Teaching Tip: To add difficulty, encourage the leader to make small changes in movements. For example, start with normal jumping jacks and then move to skier jacks, and then to skiers with no arm movements and finally walking in place. Also, provide the guesser with the idea of watching one-half of the circle. If the activity changes and they don't see anyone do it first, the leader is probably in the other half of the circle. Remind followers to not give the leader away by staring at her.

Is It Raining? (Cooperative Game)

Formation: Entire class in a circle

Supplies: None

This activity works well at the end of a vigorous lesson. Standing in a circle, the teacher initiates a movement that makes a sound and then the child immediately to her right starts the movement and so on in the fashion of a wave at a stadium. When the "wave" gets back to the teacher, another movement is started. The students keep the previous sound until the next one gets around to them. The movements can be any sounds that mimic those heard in nature during a storm. The following are examples:

- Clapping
- Snapping
- Patting quadriceps
- Stamping
- Patting the chest
- Rubbing the hands on the legs
- Rubbing the hands together
- Clucking the tongue
- Making hollow whistles
- Making "Shhhhh" sounds

DPE CURRICULUM GUIDE – LESSON PLANS
Developmental Level II
With Instructional and Academic Integration Activities

WEEK	INTRODUCTORY ACTIVITY	FITNESS DEVELOPMENT ACTIVITY	LESSON FOCUS ACTIVITY	CLOSING ACTIVITY	PAGE
1	Move & Freeze on Signal	Teacher Leader Movement Challenges	Orientation and Class Management Activities	Toe to Toe Whistle Mixer	109
	Spatial awareness	*Skip counting* *Spatial awareness* *Area of a shape* *Components of fitness*	*Grouping* *Shapes* *Parallel lines*	*Grouping* *Listening skills* *Body part identification*	LP 39
2	Fundamental Movements & Stopping	Teacher Leader Exercises	Manipulative Skills Using Wands & Hoops	How Are We Alike? Crows and Cranes (Odds & Evens)	111
	Spatial awareness *Shape recognition*	*Skip counting* *Spatial awareness* *Area of a shape* *Components of fitness*	*Midpoint* *Vertical and horizontal* *90°, 180°, 270°, 360°* *¼, ½, ¾, full turns* *Prediction*	*Spatial awareness* *Scoring* *Parallel lines* *Odd & even* *Math facts with dice*	LP 40
3	Move & Assume Shape	Teacher Leader Exercises	Throwing Skills (1)	Whistle Mixer Couple Tag Partner Stoop	114
	CW & CCW *Perpendicular* *Parallel* *Vertical & horizontal*	*Skip counting* *Spatial awareness* *Working within an area of a shape* *Components of fitness*	*Sequencing of steps* *Velocity* *Adding scores* *Following a checklist*	*Grouping* *Area* *Perimeter* *Estimation* *Circumference*	LP 41
4	New Leader	Hexagon Hustle	Football Skills and Lead-up Activities	Football End Ball	116
	Grouping *Categorizing* *Components of fitness*	*Geometric shape recognition* *CW & CCW* *Skip counting* *Reading signs* *Components of fitness*	*Reading signs* *Measurement of yards* *Opposition*	*Parallel lines* *Skip counting*	LP 42
5	Following Activity	Hexagon Hustle	Introduction to Pedometers	Bounce Ball One Step	118
	Cooperation *Replication of movement patterns* *Sequencing of movements*	*Shape recognition CW & CCW* *Skip counting* *Reading signs* *Components of fitness*	*Pendulums* *Activity monitoring* *Validation of instruments*	*Parallel lines* *Cause & effect* *Scoring*	LP 43

WEEK	INTRODUCTORY ACTIVITY	FITNESS DEVELOPMENT ACTIVITY	LESSON FOCUS ACTIVITY	CLOSING ACTIVITY	PAGE
6	Magic Number Challenges	Circuit Training	Pedometers: Understanding Step Differences & Estimation	Galloping Lizzie Lifeboats	121
	Grouping *Partner pattering* *Component of fitness*	*CW and CCW* *Reading signs* *Counting* *Grouping* *Components of fitness*	*Estimation of time and distance* *Individual differences*	*Grouping* *Parallel lines*	LP 44
7	European Rhythmic Running	Circuit Training	Gymnastics Skills (1)	Whistle Mixer Circle Contests Alaska Baseball	124
	Shape and letter recognition	*CW and CCW* *Reading signs* *Counting* *Grouping* *Components of fitness*	*Sequencing of steps* *Parallel and perpendicular lines* *90°,180°,270°,360°* *¼, ½, ¾, and full turns* *Prediction*	*Grouping* *Circumference* *Skip counting* *Greater than, less than*	LP 45
8	Four Corners Movement	Astronaut Exercises	Soccer Skills and Lead-up Activities (1)	Circle Kickball Diagonal Soccer Soccer Take-Away	128
	Patterns *Math facts* *Even and Odd* *Prime numbers*	*Area and perimeter* *Shape recognition* *CW and CCW* *Components of fitness*	*Rectangle* *Angle of kicking (45°)* *Grouping* *Opposition* *Prediction and estimation* *Reading signs*	*Circumference* *Square and diagonal* *Right triangles* *Scoring*	LP 46
9	Home Base	Astronaut Exercises	Soccer Skills and Lead-up Activities (2)	Diagonal Soccer Dribblerama Bull's-Eye	130
	Grouping *Scoring* *Spatial awareness*	*Area and perimeter* *Shape recognition* *CW & CCW* *Aerobic intensity*	*Rectangle* *Angle of kicking (45°)* *Grouping* *Opposition* *Prediction and estimation* *Reading signs*	*Circumference* *Square and diagonal* *Right triangles* *Area* *Scoring*	LP 47
10	Group Over and Around	Aerobic Fitness	Fundamental Skills Using a Parachute	Indianapolis 500 Attached at the …	133
	Half (½ = 50%) *Number patterns*	*Reading signs* *Choral response* *Target heartrate* *CW & CCW* *Patterning*	*CW & CCW* *Cause & effect* *Circumference, radius, diameter*	*Circumference* *CW & CCW* *Grouping* *Sequencing* *Scoring points*	LP 48

WEEK	INTRODUCTORY ACTIVITY	FITNESS DEVELOPMENT ACTIVITY	LESSON FOCUS ACTIVITY	CLOSING ACTIVITY	PAGE
11	Bend, Stretch & Shake	Aerobic Fitness	Playground Games & Recreational Activities		136
📖	*Body part identification* *Number patterns*	*Reading signs* *Choral response* *Target heartrate* *CW & CCW* *Patterning*	*Grouping* *Reading signs* *Quadrants* *Scoring* *Sequencing*		LP 49
12	Fastest Tag in West	Fitness Orienteering	Walking	New Engineer Just Walk Quiet Cooperation	137
📖	*Spatial Awareness*	*Area and perimeter* *Shape recognition* *CW & CCW* *Aerobic intensity*	*Heart rate calculation* *Determining training zone range* *Geography (Jog across the USA)* *Counting steps (Pedometers)* *Measurements (How many laps in a mile)*	*Grouping* *Reading Signs* *Quadrants* *Scoring* *Sequencing*	LP 50
13	Jumping & Hopping Patterns	Challenge Course	Rhythmic Movement Skills (1)	Whistle March Arches Home Base	139
📖	*Opposites* *Shapes* *Patterns*	*CW & CCW* *Over & Under* *Perimeter* *Reading Signs* *Skip counting*	*Grouping* *Rhythmic counting* *Cultural awareness* *Building sequences*	*Grouping* *Scoring* *CW & CCW*	LP 51
14	Group Tag	Walk, Trot, & Jog	Long-Rope-Jumping Skills	Fly Trap Trades Fox Hunt	143
📖	*Grouping* *Body part identification*	*CW & CCW* *Acceleration & deceleration* *Shape recognition* *Factors of 3, 4, 5*	*Grouping* *Midpoint* *CW & CCW* *Parallel & perpendicular (double Dutch & egg beater)*	*Area of a shape* *Parallel lines* *Choral response* *Grouping*	LP 52
15	Addition Tag	Challenge Course	Gymnastics Skills (2)	Partner Stoop Moving the World	145
📖	*Adding* *Multiplication* *Division*	*CW & CCW* *Over & under* *Perimeter* *Reading signs* *Skip counting*	*Patterning* *Tripod* *Counter balance* *Sequencing*	*Grouping* *Shape recognition* *CW & CCW* *Odds & evens* *Parallel lines* *Addition (with dice)*	LP 53

WEEK	INTRODUCTORY ACTIVITY	FITNESS DEVELOPMENT ACTIVITY	LESSON FOCUS ACTIVITY	CLOSING ACTIVITY	PAGE
16	High Fives	Challenge Course	Rhythmic Movement Skills (2)	Fox Hunt Steal the Treasure Addition Tag	148

	CW & CCW
	Multiples of 5 or any other
	  factor
		CW & CCW
		Over & under
		Perimeter
		Reading signs
		Skip counting
			Grouping
			Rhythmic counting
			Cultural awareness
			Sequencing
			Geometric shapes &
			  cues (semi-circle,
			  star, square)
				Divide by 2
				Parallel lines
				Grouping
					LP 54

17	Squad Leader Movements	Aerobic Fitness & Partner Resistance Exercises	Basketball Skills and Lead-up Activities(1)	Birdie in the Cage Dribblerama	152

	Grouping
	Replication of movement
	  patterns
		Muscle identification
		Health concepts
		Opposition
		Cause & effect
			Sequencing
			Grouping
			Geometric shapes &
			  cues (semi-circle,
			  star, square)
				Parallel lines
				Perimeter & area
				Scoring
					LP 55

18	Bridges by Three	Aerobic Fitness and Partner Resistance Exercises	Basketball Skills and Lead-up Activities(2)	Around the Key	155

	Skip counting
	Grouping
	Spatial awareness
		Muscle identification
		Health concepts
		Opposition
		Cause & effect
			Sequencing
			Grouping
			Geometric shapes &
			  cues (semi-circle,
			  star, square)
				Parallel lines
				Perimeter & area
				Scoring
				Moving within an area
					LP 56

19	Locomotor & Manipulative Activity	Exercises to Music	Throwing Skills (2)	In the Prison Snowball Center Target Throw Target Ball Throw	157
	Sequencing *Skip counting*	*Skip counting* *Listening skills* *Choral response*	*Sequencing of steps* *Velocity* *Adding scores* *Following a chart*	*Grouping* *Parallel lines* *Math facts (scoring)* *Quadrants* *Greater & less than*	LP 57
20	Yarn Ball Fun	Exercises to Music	Cooperative Game Skills	Cageball Kickover Centipede	159
	Skip counting	*Skip counting* *Listening skills* *Choral response*	*Problem solving* *strategies* *Debriefing* *Spelling skills* *Alphabetical order*	*Parallel lines* *Grouping*	LP 58

WEEK	INTRODUCTORY ACTIVITY	FITNESS DEVELOPMENT ACTIVITY	LESSON FOCUS ACTIVITY	CLOSING ACTIVITY	PAGE
21	Movement Varieties	Aerobic, Strength, & Flexibility Jackpot Fitness	Hockey Skills and Lead-up Activities (1)	Circle Keepaway Star Wars Hockey Lane Hockey Circle Straddleball	162
	Shape recognition Directions (N, S, E, W) Size (small, medium, large)	*Reading "jackpots" Components of fitness*	*Vocabulary (offense, defense, forwards, guards, center, tackling, dodging)*	*Circumference Perimeter Segments (thirds, quarters)*	LP 59
22	Run, Stop, and Pivot	Aerobic, Strength, & Flexibility Jackpot Fitness	Hockey Skills and Lead-up Activities (2)	Modified Hockey Lane Hockey	165
	¼, ½, ¾, and full turns CW & CCW	*Reading "jackpots" Components of fitness*	*Vocabulary (offense, defense, forwards, guards, center, tackling, dodging)*	*Circumference Perimeter Segments (thirds, quarters)*	LP 60
23	Moving to Music	Aerobic Fitness	Gymnastics Skills (3)	Steal the Treasure Flippers	167
	Movement patterns	*Reading signs Choral response Target heartrate CW & CCW Patterning*	*Sequencing Directions (diagonal, sideways) Skip counting Estimation*	*Numbers Circumference Parallel lines*	LP 61
24	Stretching and Jogging		Track & Field Skills and Lead-up Activities (1)	Potato Shuttle Relay Shuttle Relays One-on-one Contests	170
		Skip counting Body part identification Speed variations	*Scoring Measurements Reading signs Angle recognition Speed & velocity Place value of time (stopwatch)*	*Shape recognition Perpendicular Parallel*	LP 62
25	Stretching and Jogging		Track & Field Skills and Lead-up Activities (2)	Circular Relays Shuttle Relays One-on-one Contests	173
		Skip counting Body part identification Speed variations	*Scoring Measurements Reading signs Angle recognition Speed & velocity Place value of time (stopwatch)*	*Shape recognition Perpendicular Parallel*	LP 63
26	Move & Perform Task	Racetrack Fitness	Individual Rope-Jumping Skills	Crows & Cranes Is it Raining?	175
	Number patterns	*Reading signs Components of fitness CW & CCW*	*Skip counting Fast & slow time Choral rhyming Jump patterns*	*Scoring Parallel lines*	LP 64

WEEK	INTRODUCTORY ACTIVITY	FITNESS DEVELOPMENT ACTIVITY	LESSON FOCUS ACTIVITY	CLOSING ACTIVITY	PAGE
27	Long Jump Rope Routine	Parachute Fitness	Rhythmic Movement Skills (3)	Jump the Shot Beach Ball Bat Ball Club Guard	177
	Grouping	*CW & CCW* *Circumference* *Skip counting* *Level identification (high, medium, low)*	*Patterning* *Cultural awareness* *Circumference* *Grouping* *Rhythmic counting*	*Circumference* *Parallel lines*	LP 65
28	Squad Leader Movements	Sport Related (Tennis) Fitness Stations	Tennis Skills & Lead-up Activities (1)	Red Light, Green Light Tennis Circle Bump Pass Playground Tennis	181
	Grouping *Replication of movement patterns*	*CW & CCW* *Reading signs* *Health concepts* *Perimeter* *Choral response*	*Sequencing* *Grouping* *Vocabulary*	*Grouping* *Listening* *Scoring* *Quadrants*	LP 66
29	Individual Crows & Cranes	Sport-Related (Tennis) Fitness Stations	Tennis Skills and Lead-up Activities (2)	Caterpillar Alley Rally Playground Tennis	184
	Spatial awareness *Listening skills*	*CW & CCW* *Reading signs* *Health concepts* *Perimeter* *Choral response*	*Sequencing* *Grouping* *Vocabulary*	*Grouping* *Scoring* *Quadrants*	LP 67
30	Marking	Circuit Training	Volleyball Skills and Lead-up Activities (1)	Beach Ball Volleyball Informal Volleyball	187
	Body part identification	*CW & CCW* *Reading signs* *Skip counting* *Grouping*	*Grouping* *Number patterns* *Angles* *Cause & effect* *Shape recognition ("set" with hands in triangle)*	*Grouping* *Parallel lines*	LP 68
31	Home Base	Continuity Drills	Volleyball Skills and Lead-up Activities (2)	Beach Ball Volleyball Informal Volleyball Shower Service Ball	189
	Grouping *Scoring* *Spatial awareness*	*Shape recognition* *CW & CCW* *Skip counting* *Reading signs*	*Grouping* *Number patterns* *Angles* *Shape recognition*	*Grouping* *Parallel lines*	LP 69

WEEK	INTRODUCTORY ACTIVITY	FITNESS DEVELOPMENT ACTIVITY	LESSON FOCUS ACTIVITY	CLOSING ACTIVITY	PAGE
32	Combination Movement Patterns	Racetrack Fitness	Rhythmic Movement Skills (4)	Alaska Baseball Keep It Floating	191
	Patterns *Action verbs*	*Number patterns* *Choral responses* *Math facts*	*Patterning* *Cultural awareness* *Circumference* *Grouping* *Rhythmic counting*	*Grouping* *Perimeter* *Skip counting*	LP 70
33	European Running w/ Variations	Aerobic Fitness	Manipulative Skills Using Frisbees	Frisbee Keep Away Frisbee Golf	195
	Shape recognition *Rhythmic counting* *Letter or number recognition* *CW & CCW*	*Reading signs* *Choral response* *Target heartrate* *CW & CCW* *Patterning*	*Angle recognition* *Parallel* *Sequencing* *Shape cues*	*Parallel* *Reading maps* *Scoring* *Sequencing*	LP 71
34	Tortoise & Hare	Aerobic Fitness	Fundamental Skills Using Balance Beams	Hand Hockey Nonda's Car Lot	197
	Acceleration & deceleration	*Reading signs* *Choral response* *Target heartrate* *CW & CCW* *Patterning*	*Grouping* *Sequencing of steps* *Fractions (¼, ½, ¾, & full turns)* *Degrees (90°, 180°, 270°, 360°)*	*Grouping* *Parallel lines*	LP 72
35	High Fives	Parachute Fitness	Softball Skills and Lead-up Activities (1)	Throw It & Run Two-Pitch Softball Hit & Run	199
	CW & CCW *Multiples of 5 or any other factor*	*CW & CCW* *Circumference* *Skip counting* *Level identification (high, medium, low)*	*Grouping* *Parallel lines* *Arch (pitching)*	*Scoring* *Grouping*	LP 73
36	Tag Games	Partner Fitness Challenges	Softball Skills and Lead-up Activities (2)	Kick Softball Beat Ball	202
	Grouping	*Patterning* *Momentum* *Estimation of time*	*Grouping* *Parallel lines* *Trajectory*	*Scoring* *Grouping*	LP 74

WEEK	INTRODUCTORY ACTIVITY	FITNESS DEVELOPMENT ACTIVITY	LESSON FOCUS ACTIVITY	CLOSING ACTIVITY	PAGE
Alternate Lesson 1	Use the introductory activity from the lesson that was replaced.	Use the fitness activity from the lesson that was replaced.	Fundamental Skills Using Climbing Ropes	Lifeboats Mat Folding	204
			Dismounts *Pendulums (swinging)* *Friction (descending the rope)*	*Cooperative skills* *Problem solving*	LP 75
Alternate Lesson 2	Use the introductory activity from the lesson that was replaced.	Use the fitness activity from the lesson that was replaced.	Fundamental Skills Using Climbing Walls	Zap Keep It Floating	207
			Trusting a partner *Balance* *Vertical and horizontal planes*	*Cooperative problem solving* *Counting in different language* *Body part identification*	LP 76
Alternate Lesson 3	Use the introductory activity from the lesson that was replaced.	Use the fitness activity from the lesson that was replaced.	Manipulative Skills using Playground Balls	Bounce Ball One Step	209
			Sequencing *Grouping* *Vocabulary*	*Grouping* *Listening skills* *Scoring* *Quadrants*	LP 77
Alternate Lesson 4	Use the introductory activity from the lesson that was replaced.	Use the fitness activity from the lesson that was replaced.	Manipulative Skills Using Beanbags	Indianapolis 500 Lily Pads	211
			Sequencing *Grouping* *Vocabulary*	*Grouping* *Scoring* *Quadrants* *Cooperative skills*	LP 78
Alternate Lesson 5	Use the introductory activity from the lesson that was replaced.	Use the fitness activity from the lesson that was replaced.	Fundamental Skills Using Benches	Cageball Kickover Centipede	213
			Dismounts *Fractions (¼, ½, ¾, & full turns)* *Degrees (90°, 180°, 270°, 360°)* *Reading signs*	*Parallel lines* *Grouping*	LP 79

Objectives:
To learn and follow basic management
    activities necessary for
    participation in physical
    education classes

NASPE National Standards:
Introductory Activity: 1
Fitness Activity: 1, 4, 6
Lesson Focus: 2, 5
Game: 2, 5

Equipment Required:
Tom-tom
Music for Fitness Challenges

Instructional Activities	Teaching Hints

Orientation Instructional Procedures

The first week of school should be used to teach students the system you are going to use throughout the year. The following are reminders you might find useful in establishing your expectations and routines.

1. Establish rules and expectations. Discuss your expectations with the class to assure students understand reasons for your guidelines. Explain what the consequences are when rules are not followed. Show where time-out boxes are located and how they will be used.

2. Explain to the class the method you will use to learn names. It might be helpful to ask classroom teachers to have students put their name on a piece of masking tape (nametag). Tell students that you will ask their name on a regular basis until it is learned.

3. Practice entry and exit behaviors for students coming and leaving physical education classes. Have students enter the activity area on the move and continue moving until signaled to stop. Teach students not to touch any equipment that is placed in the teaching area.

4. Decide how excuses for nonparticipation will be handled. If possible, set up a routine where the school nurse determines which students are excused for health reasons.

5. Safety is important. Children should receive instruction on safety rules for apparatus and playground equipment. Safety procedures to be followed in physical education classes should be discussed.

6. Illustrate how you like to stop and start the class. In general, a whistle (or similar loud signal) and a raised hand is effective for stopping the class. A voice command should be used to start the class. Telling the class when before what (Chapter 6) will assure they do not begin before instructions are finished.

7. Discuss the issue, distribution, and care of equipment. Make students responsible for acquiring a piece of equipment and returning it at the end of the lesson. Place your teaching equipment around the perimeter of the area to avoid the rush of students vying to get a ball or beanbag located in one central area.

8. Explain to the class that the format of the daily lesson will include an introductory activity, fitness development, lesson focus, and finish with a game activity. Briefly explain why each part of the lesson is included.

9. Manage students on the move. Have them move throughout the area, freeze, and quickly find a partner. Practice various teaching formations such as open-squad formation and closed-squad formation. Practice moving into a circle while moving (fall-in). Transitions between formations should be done while moving, i.e., jogging from scatter formation into a circular formation.

10. Refer to Chapters 3, 5, and 6 in the text for detailed information about planning, enhancing instructional effectiveness, and class management and discipline strategies.

Introductory Activity — Move and Freeze on Signal

Have students move throughout the area using a variety of locomotor movements. On signal (whistle), they quickly freeze. Try to reduce the response latency by reinforcing students who stop quickly on signal.

The primary objective is to teach students the importance of moving under control (without bumping others or falling down) and quickly freezing.

Fitness Development Activity — Teacher Leader Movement Challenges

1. Locomotor Movement: Walk for 30 seconds.

2. Flexibility and Trunk Development Challenges
   a. Bend in different directions.
   b. Stretch slowly and return quickly.
   c. Combine bending and stretching movements.
   d. Sway back and forth.
   e. Twist one body part; add body parts.

3. Locomotor Movement: Skip for 30 seconds.

4. Shoulder Girdle Challenges
   In a push-up position, do the following challenges:
   a. Lift one foot; the other foot.
   b. Wave at a friend; wave with the other arm.
   c. Scratch your back with one hand; use the other hand.
   d. Walk your feet to your hands.

5. Locomotor Movement: Jog for 30 seconds.

6. Abdominal Development Challenges
   From a supine position:
   a. Lift your head and look at your toes.
   b. Lift your knees to your chest.
   c. Wave your legs at a friend.
   From a sitting position;
   a. Slowly lie down with hands on tummy.
   b. Lift legs and touch toes.

7. Locomotor Movement: Run and leap for 30 seconds.

The goal should be to move students through a number of movement challenges. Emphasis should be placed on starting the fitness activities at a level where all students can feel successful.

Alternate the locomotor movements with the strength and flexibility challenges. Repeat the challenges as necessary.

Tape alternating segments (30 seconds in length) of silence and music to signal duration of exercise. Music segments indicate locomotor movements; intervals of silence announce doing the movement challenges.

Teach youngsters the different challenges and then allow them to select a challenge they can successfully perform.

The challenges should be enjoyable to perform.

Encourage students to focus on effort and feeling successful.

Workloads should be moderate with emphasis on success for all youngsters.

Lesson Focus — Orientation

Since much time during the first week is used for orientation procedures and management, no lesson focus activity is scheduled.

Game Activity — Management Games

Play one or two management games to teach students how to move into partner and small-group formation

Toe to Toe
Supplies: None
Skills: Fundamental locomotor movements
Youngsters perform a locomotor movement around the area. On signal, each child must find a partner and stand toe to toe (one foot only) with that person. An important skill is to take the nearest person for a partner without searching for a friend. Youngsters who can't find a partner within their immediate area must run quickly to the center of the area (use a marking spot or cone) to find a partner. The goal is to find a nearby partner as quickly as possible and avoid being the last pair formed. If the number of youngsters playing is uneven, the teacher can join in and play. Change locomotor movements often.

Whistle Mixer
Supplies: None
Skills: All basic locomotor movements
Children are scattered throughout the area. To begin, they walk around in any direction they wish. A whistle is blown a number of times in succession with short, sharp blasts. Children then form small groups with the number in each group equal to the number of whistle blasts. If there are four blasts, children form groups of four—no more, no less. When players have the correct number, they sit down immediately to signal that no one may leave the group and no one may enter the group. The goal is not to be left out or caught in a circle with the incorrect number of students. Encourage players to move toward the center of the area and raise their hands to facilitate finding others without a group. After the circles are formed, the teacher calls "Walk," and the game continues. In walking, children should move in different directions.

Objectives:
To stop quickly and under control
To maintain the fitness development
  activity
To toss and catch an object in a variety
  of situations

NASPE National Standards:
Introductory Activity: 1
Fitness Activity: 1, 4, 6
Lesson Focus: 2, 3, 5
Game: 1, 3, 5

Equipment Required:
Music tape for exercises
One wand & hoop for each child
Beanbags or fleece balls

Instructional Activities	Teaching Hints

Introductory Activity — Fundamental Movements and Stopping

Use the locomotor movements (run, walk, hop, jump, leap, slide, gallop, and skip) to move throughout the instructional area. On signal, students stop and freeze without falling. Teach proper stopping form, lowering the center of gravity, spreading the feet for a wide base of support, and keeping the body weight over the feet (minimize leaning). This is an excellent activity for teaching students to move in their own space (as far away from others as possible).

Tape alternating segments of silence and music to signal duration of the locomotor movements. Segments of silence that indicate the "freeze" position can be decreased in duration until the desired response latency is reached.

Fitness Development Activity — Teacher Leader Exercises

Arm Circles	25 seconds
Bend and Twist	25 seconds
Treadmill	25 seconds
Abdominal Challenges	25 seconds
Single-Leg Crab Kick	25 seconds
Knee to Chest Curl	25 seconds
Run in Place	25 seconds
Trunk Twister	25 seconds

Follow each exercise with 25 seconds of aerobic activity.

Tape alternating segments (25 seconds) of silence and music. The music signals aerobic activity. During the silent segments the exercises are performed

Allow students to adjust the workload to their personal ability and fitness level. This means that some students may perform more repetitions than others.

Move and help students with the exercises.

Lesson Focus — Manipulative Skills Using Wands and Hoops

Select activities from each of the exercises and challenges groups.

Strength Exercises with Wands
1. Pull the Wand Apart. Place the hands 6 in. apart near the center of the wand. With a tight grip to prevent slippage and with arms extended, pull the hands apart. Change grip and position.
2. Push the Wand Together. Hold the wand as above and push the hands together.
3. Wand Twist. Hold the wand with both hands about 6 in. apart. Twist the hands in opposite directions.
4. Bicycle. Holding the wand horizontally throughout and using an overhand grip, extend the wand outward and downward. Bring it upward near the body, completing a circular movement. On the downward movement, push the wand together, and on the upward movement, pull the wand apart.
5. Arm Spreader. Hold the wand overhead with hands spread wide. Attempt to compress the stick. Reverse force, and attempt to pull the stick apart.
6. Dead Lift. Partially squat and place the wand under the thighs. Place the hands between the legs and try to lift. Try also with hands on the outside of the legs.
7. Abdominal Tightener. From a standing position, place the wand behind the buttocks. With hands on the ends of the wand, pull forward and resist with the abdominal muscles.

Wands can be made from ¾ in. maple dowels or from a variety of broom and mop handles. They should be cut to a length of 36 in. Wands are noisy when they hit the floor. Putting rubber crutch tips on the ends of a wand alleviates most of the noise and makes them easier to pick up.

The isometric exercises with wands presented can be performed with a variety of grips. With the wand horizontal, use either the overhand or underhand grip. With the wand in vertical position, grip with the thumbs pointed up, down, or toward each other.

Repeat each exercise with a different grip. Exercises can also be repeated with the wand in different positions: in front of the body (either horizontal or

Stretching Exercises with Wands

1. Side Bender. Grip the wand and extend the arms overhead with feet apart. Bend sideways as far as possible, maintaining straight arms and legs. Recover, and bend to the other side.
2. Body Twist. Place the wand behind the neck, with arms draped over the wand from behind. Rotate the upper body first to the right as far as possible and then to the left. The feet and hips should remain in position. The twist is at the waist.
3. Body Twist to Knee. Assume body twist position. Bend the trunk forward and twist so that the right end of the wand touches the left knee. Recover, and touch the left end to the right knee.
4. Shoulder Stretcher. Grip the wand at the ends in a regular grip. Extend the arms overhead and rotate the wand, arms, and shoulders backward until the stick touches the back of the legs. The arms should be kept straight. Those who find the stretch too easy should move their hands closer to the center of the wand.
5. Toe Touch. Grip the wand with the hands about shoulder width apart. Bend forward, reaching down as far as possible without bending the knees. The movement should be slow and controlled. Try the same activity from a sitting position.
6. Over the Toes. Sit down, flex the knees, place the wand over the toes, and rest it against the middle of the arch. Grip the stick with the fingers at the outside edge of the feet. Slowly extend the legs forward, pushing against the stick and trying for a full extension of the legs.

Wand Challenges

1. Can you reach down and pick up your wand without bending your knees?
2. Try to balance your wand on different body parts. Watch the top of the wand to get cues on how to retain the balance.
3. Can you hold your stick against the wall and move over it? Gradually raise the height of the wand.
4. Let's see whether you can hold the stick at both ends and move through the gap.
5. Can you twirl the wand and keep it going like a windmill?
6. Let's see how many different ways you can move over and around your wand when it is on the floor.
7. Put one end of the wand on the floor and hold the other end. How many times can you run around your wand without getting dizzy?
8. Place one end of the wand against a wall. Holding the other end and keeping the wand against the wall, duck underneath. Place the wand lower and lower on the wall and go under.
9. Place the wand between your feet and hop around as though you are on a pogo stick.
10. Toss the wand from one hand to the other.
11. Hold the wand vertically near the middle. Can you release your grip and catch the wand before it falls to the floor?
12. Have a partner hold a wand horizontally above the floor. Jump, leap, and hop over the wand. Gradually raise the height of the wand.
13. Put your wand on the floor and try making different kinds of bridges over it.
14. Place the wand on the floor. Curl alongside it, just touching it. Curl at one end of the wand.
15. Balance the wand vertically on the floor. Release the wand and try to complete different stunts--clapping the hands, doing a heel click, touching different body parts—before the wand falls to the floor.
16. Put the wand on the floor and see how many ways you can push it, using different body parts.

Hoop Activities

1. Hula-hoop using various body parts such as waist, neck, knees, arms, and fingers.
    a. While hula-hooping on the arms, try to change the hoop from one arm to the other.

vertical), overhead, or behind the back. Hold each exercise for 8 to 12 seconds.

Be gentle when stretching. Reach and stretch the muscles, hold the stretch for a few seconds and relax. Repeat a number of times.

Because wands are noisy when dropped, youngsters should hold their wands with both hands or put them on the floor during instruction.

An adequate amount of space is needed for each individual because wand stunts demand room.

Children may easily be injured using wands improperly. Teach children proper use of wands. Emphasize the need to use care when handling wands to avoid injury to self and others. Do not allow any improper use of wands.

Hoops produce noisy activity. It is helpful to have the children place their hoops on the floor when listening.

In activities that require children to

b. Change hoop from one partner to another while hula-hooping.
   c. Try leg-skippers—hula-hoop with one leg and jump the hoop with the other leg.
2. Jump rope with the hoop—forward, sideways, and backward. Begin with a back-and-forth swing.
3. Roll hoop and run alongside it. Run in front of it.
4. Roll hoop with a reverse spin to make it return to the thrower.
5. Roll with a reverse spin and see how many times a partner can go through it.
6. Balance the hoop on your head, try to walk through it ("thread the needle") forward, backward, and sideways.
7. Try partner activities:
   a. Play catch with hoop.
   b. Hula-hoop on one arm, toss to partner who catches it on one arm.
   c. Use two hoops for catching.
   d. Hoop with one hoop and play catch with other.
   e. Move through a hoop held by a partner.

jump through hoops, instruct the holder to grasp the hoop lightly, so as not to cause an awkward fall if a performer hits it.

Hoops can serve as a "home" for various activities. For instance, children might leave their hoops to gallop in all directions and then return quickly to the hoop on command.

When teaching the reverse spin with hoops, have the students throw the hoop up, in place, rather than forward along the floor. After they learn the upward throw, they can progress to the forward throw for distance.

Game Activity

How Are We Alike? (Cooperative Activity)
   Formation: Partners
   Supplies: None
   This activity is excellent for the beginning of the school year physical education orientation when students are getting to know each other and the teacher. Students join with a partner and discuss, "How are we alike?" The teacher should give a few categories such as appearance, family, activities they like, birthdays, and then let the students talk. Before grouping students with a different partner or a group of 4 to repeat the activity, allow volunteers to share their findings.
   Teaching Tips: After "How are we alike?" have students find out "How are we different?" This sets the tone for physical education that we all have similarities and we all have differences and that is okay. It is important for students to understand early on that respecting similarities and differences is an important component of working with others.

Crows and Cranes
   Supplies: None
   Skills: Running, dodging
   Establish two goal lines on opposite sides of the area. The class is divided into two groups—the crows and the cranes. The groups face each other at the center of the area, about 5 ft apart. The leader calls out either "Crows" or "Cranes," using a cr-r-r-r-r sound at the start of either word to mask the result. If "Crows" is the call, the crows chase the cranes to the goal line. If "Cranes" is the call, the cranes chase. Any player caught goes over to the other side and becomes a member of that group. The team that has the most players when the game ends is the winner.

DPE Curriculum Guide – Lesson Plans
Throwing Skills (1)
Level II – Week 3

Objectives:
To recognize a variety of shapes and
   move the body into the correct
   shape
To perform continuous fitness activity
To know the elements of proper
   throwing
To throw with maximum velocity

NASPE National Standards:
Introductory Activity: 1
Fitness Activity: 1, 4, 6
Lesson Focus: 2, 3, 5
Game: 1, 3, 5

Equipment Required:
Music for Teacher Leader Exercises
Many types of balls for throwing
Throwing targets; hoops, mats, bowling
   pins, and/or cageball
Whistle

Instructional Activities	Teaching Hints

Introductory Activity — Move and Assume Shape

Have students move using a variation of a basic movement. Freeze on signal and assume a designated shape. Some suggestions are:
   a. Balance
   b. Stretch
   c. Curl
   d. Bridge

Encourage creativity in movements and poses.

Reinforce moving under control.

Use scatter formation.

Fitness Development Activity — Teacher Leader Exercises

Arm Circles	25 seconds
Bend and Twist	25 seconds
Treadmill	25 seconds
Abdominal Challenges	25 seconds
Single-Leg Crab Kick	25 seconds
Knee to Chest Curl	25 seconds
Run in Place	25 seconds
Trunk Twister	25 seconds

Follow each exercise with 25 seconds of aerobic activity.

Tape alternating segments (25 seconds) of silence and music. The music signals aerobic activity. During the silent segments the exercises are performed.

Allow students to adjust the workload to their personal ability and fitness level. This means that some students may perform more repetitions than others.

Move and help students with the exercises.

Lesson Focus — Throwing Skills (1)

Individual activities
1. Throw balls against the wall. Emphasize the following points:
   a. Start with the feet together.
   b. Start with nonthrowing side to the wall.
   c. Lift both the throwing and nonthrowing arm (to form a "T") in order to assure the throwing arm elbow is lifted and the nonthrowing arm points at the target.
   d. Begin the throw with a step forward with the foot opposite the throwing arm.
   e. Throw as hard as possible.
2. Throw from one side of the gym and try to hit the other wall.
3. If outside, throw as hard and far as possible.

Throwing takes a great deal of practice to master. Two major issues to consider when teaching throwing are:
1. How can I arrange my class so students receive the most opportunity to throw?
2. How can I arrange my class so students get to throw with maximum velocity? A mature pattern of throwing cannot be learned if students are not allowed to throw with maximum force.

Throwing for form
1. Arrange activities to emphasize proper throwing form. Some suggestions are:
   a. Throwing off a tumbling mat. The slight step down off the mat helps some students develop the forward step with the nonthrowing side foot. The student stands on the edge of the mat and steps to the floor with the nonthrowing side foot as the throw begins. (The other foot remains on the mat.) Use the cues, "step, elbow leads, and throw."
   b. Starting a throw with both feet in a hoop. The thrower must lift the front foot to step out of the hoop. Begin with the nonthrowing side of the body

Proper form and velocity of throws are closely related. A reason for practicing form is to encourage students to think about technique.

Give each student 4 or 5 balls to throw. They can be placed in a Frisbee to keep them from rolling around. When all students are done throwing, they

facing the target and both feet inside the hoop. As the throw begins, a forward step is taken with the nonthrowing foot out of the hoop.

c. Touching a cone behind the thrower. The thrower lines up with a cone about an arm's-length away and near the throwing side (away from the target). As the throwing arm is extended on the backswing, a slight backward reach is made to encourage reaching back in preparation to throw.

Throwing for velocity

1. Throw at mats on the wall
   a. Throw fleece balls hard from 15 to 20 ft.
   b. Retrieve only if the balls roll behind the throwing line.
2. Throw at hoops leaning against the wall and try to knock them down.
3. Throw at bowling pins
4. Throw outside for distance.

retrieve the same number of balls they have thrown.

Throwing for velocity is exciting for youngsters. It can also increase the activity level of the lesson as youngsters retrieve the thrown objects.

A cageball is an excellent target for encouraging throwing velocity. When it is hit, it will move slightly. A goal can be made to move the cageball across a goal line.

Game Activity

Whistle Mixer
Supplies: A whistle
Skills: All basic locomotor movements

Children are scattered throughout the area. To begin, they walk around in any direction they wish. A whistle is blown a number of times in succession with short, sharp blasts. Children then form small groups with the number in each group equal to the number of whistle blasts. If there are four blasts, children form groups of four—no more, no less. When players have the correct number, they sit down immediately to signal that no one may leave the group and no one may enter the group. The goal is not to be left out or caught in a circle with the incorrect number of students. Encourage players to move toward the center of the area and raise their hands to facilitate finding others without a group. After the circles are formed, the teacher calls "Walk," and the game continues. In walking, children should move in different directions.

Variation: A fine version of this game is done with the aid of a tom-tom. Different beats indicate different locomotor movements—skipping, galloping, slow walking, normal walking, running. The whistle is still used to set the number for each circle.

Couple Tag
Supplies: None
Skills: Running, dodging

Establish two goal lines on opposite sides of the area. Players run in pairs, with inside hands joined. All pairs, except two, line up on one of the goal lines. The pairs in the center are it. They call "Come," and the children, keeping hands joined, run to the other goal line. The pairs in the center, also retaining joined hands, try to tag any other pair. As soon as a couple is caught, they help the center couple. The game continues until all are caught. The last couple caught is it for the next game.

Variation: *Triplet Tag.* The game can be played with sets of threes. Tagging is done with any pair of joined hands. If a triplet breaks joined hands, that group is considered caught.

Partner Stoop
Supplies: Music
Skills: Marching rhythmically

The game follows the same basic principle of stooping as in Circle Stoop, but is played with partners. The group forms a double circle in one direction with one partner on the inside and one on the outside. When the music begins, all march in the line of direction. After a short period of marching, a signal (whistle) is sounded, and the inside circle reverses direction and marches the other way. The partners are thus separated. When the music stops, the outer circle stands still, and the partners making up the inner circle walk (or run) in any direction to rejoin their respective outer circle partners. As soon as players reach their partner, they get toe to toe and stoop without losing balance. The last couple to stoop and those who lose their balance go to the center of the circle and wait out the next round. Start the game walking and gradually pick up the speed of the movements when the class moves under control.

DPE Curriculum Guide – Lesson Plans
Football Skills and Lead-up Activities
Level II – Week 4

Objectives:
To lead other students in New Leader
    activities
To independently perform hustle
    activities
To be able to throw and catch a
    football
To be able to center a football

NASPE National Standards:
Introductory Activity: 1, 3, 5
Fitness Activity: 1, 4, 6
Lesson Focus: 2, 3, 5
Game: 2, 3, 5

Equipment Required:
Signs and music for Hexagon Hustle
One foam rubber junior football for
    each two students
Pinnies to identify teams

Instructional Activities		Teaching Hints

Introductory Activity — New Leader

Make groups of 3–4 students, assigning one of the students to be a leader. The groups move around the area, following the leader. On signal, the last person moves to the head of the squad and become the leader. Various types of locomotor movements and/or exercises should be used.

Movement should be continuous unless an exercise is being performed.

Encourage students to design their personal movement patterns

Fitness Development Activity — Hexagon Hustle

Hustle	20 seconds	Outline a large hexagon with 6 cones.
Push-Up from Knees	30 seconds	Place signs with directions on both sides
Hustle	20 seconds	of the cones. The signs identify the
Bend and Twist (8 counts)	30 seconds	hustle activity students are to perform as
Hustle	20 seconds	they approach a cone. Tape alternating
Jumping Jacks (4 counts)	30 seconds	segments of silence and music to signal
Hustle	20 seconds	duration of exercise. Music segments
Abdominal Challenges (2 counts)	30 seconds	indicate aerobic activity; intervals of
Hustle	20 seconds	silence announce flexibility and strength
Double Leg Crab Kick	30 seconds	development activities.
Hustle	20 seconds	
Sit and Stretch (8 counts)	30 seconds	See Chapter 13 for a description of
Hustle	20 seconds	exercises and activities.
Power Jumper	30 seconds	
Hustle	20 seconds	
Squat Thrust (4 counts)	30 seconds	

Lesson Focus — Football Skills

Skills
Practice the following skills:
1. Forward Passing
    The ball should be gripped lightly behind the middle with the fingers on the lace. The thumbs and fingers should be relaxed. In throwing, the opposing foot should point in the direction of the pass, with the body turned sideways. In preparation for the pass, the ball is raised up and held over the shoulders. The ball is delivered directly forward with an overhand movement of the arm and with the index finger pointing toward the line of flight.
2. Catching
    When making a catch, the receiver should keep both eyes on the ball and catch it in the hands with a slight give. As soon as the ball is caught, it should be tucked into the carrying position. The little fingers are together for most catches.
3. Centering
    Centering involves transferring the ball, on a signal, to the quarterback. In elementary school, the shotgun formation is most often used. This requires snapping the ball a few yards backward to the quarterback. A direct snap involves placing the hands under the buttocks of the center. The ball is then lifted, rotated a quarter turn, and snapped into the hands of the quarterback.

Use instructional cues to improve throwing techniques:
1. Turn the nonpassing side toward the direction of the target.
2. Pass the ball with an overhand motion.
3. Step toward the pass receiver.

The following instructional cues will focus on catching technique:
1. Thumbs together for a high pass (above shoulder level).
2. Thumbs apart for a low pass (below shoulder level).
3. Reach for the ball, give, and bring the ball to the body.

The centering player takes a position with the feet well spread and toes pointed straight ahead. Knees are bent and close enough to the ball to reach it with a slight stretch. The right hand takes about the same grip as is used in passing. The other hand is on the side near the back of the ball and merely acts as a guide. On signal from the quarterback, the center extends the arms backward through the legs and centers the ball to the quarterback.

Instructional cues for centering include the following:
1. Reach forward for the ball.
2. Snap the ball with the dominant hand.
3. Guide the ball with the nondominant hand.

Drills
Set up stations for skill practice. Rotate students to each station.

Station 1—Stance Practice

Students work with a partner and practice getting into the proper stance position. When stance form is mastered, partners can practice getting into position and racing to cones five yards away.

Station 2—Centering to a Partner

Students work in pairs and practice centering to each other.

Station 3—Passing and Receiving with a Partner

Students work in pairs and practice passing and receiving the ball. Place emphasis on proper throwing and catching technique.

Station 4—Pass Defense Drill

Work in groups of three. One player is the passer, one the receiver, and one the defensive player. The passer takes the ball, calls the signal for the receiver to run a pattern, and passes to the receiver who is covered by the defensive player

Signs that describe key points for each skill should be placed on cones at each station. Instructional cues should also be placed on the signs so students can analyze their form and performance.

Use foam rubber footballs with third and fourth graders. This helps students learn the skills without fear of being hurt by the ball.

Football Lead-up Activities

Football End Ball

Supplies: Foam rubber junior footballs

Skills: Passing, catching

The court is divided in half by a centerline. End zones are marked 3 ft wide, completely across the court at each end. Players on each team are divided into three groups: forwards, guards, and ends. The object is for a forward to throw successfully to one of the end-zone players. End-zone players take positions in one of the end zones. Their forwards and guards then occupy the opposite half of the court farthest from this end zone. The forwards are near the centerline, and the guards are back near the end zone in their half of the court. When a team gets the ball, the forwards try to throw over the heads of the opposing team to an end-zone player. To score, an end-zone player must have both feet inside the zone and catch the ball. No moving with the ball is permitted by any player. After each score, the ball is immediately turned over to the other team.

A penalty results in loss of the ball to the other team. Penalties are assessed for the following.

1. Holding a ball for more than 5 seconds
2. Stepping over the end line or stepping over the centerline into the opponent's territory
3. Pushing or holding another player

In case of an out-of-bounds ball, the ball belongs to the team that did not cause it to go out. The nearest player retrieves the ball at the sideline and returns it to a player of the proper team. Fast, accurate passing is encouraged. Players in the end zones must practice jumping high to catch the ball while still landing with both feet inside the end-zone area. A system of rotation is desirable. Each time a score is made, players on that team can rotate one person. To outline the end zones, tumbling mats (4 by 7 ft or 4 by 8 ft) can be used. Three or four mats forming each end zone delineate a definite area and eliminate the problem of defensive players (guards) stepping into the end zone.

DPE Curriculum Guide – Lesson Plans
Introduction to Pedometers
Level II – Week 5

Objectives:
To learn how pedometers work
To learn how to find an accurate
    placement point for the pedometer
To learn how to monitor physical
    activity in physical education class

NASPE National Standards:
Introductory Activity: 1
Fitness Activity: 1, 4, 2
Lesson Focus: 2, 5
Game: 2, 5

Equipment Required:
Six cones & signs for Hexagon Hustle
Pencils & containers for pedometers
One pedometer for each student
Belts for pedometers (if needed)
Record sheets for recording data
Balls or beanbags for games

Instructional Activities	Teaching Hints

Introductory Activity — Following Activity

One partner leads and performs combinations of locomotor and nonlocomotor movements. The other partner follows and performs the same movements. This can also be used with groups of 3–4 students following a leader.

Change the leaders often so all students get a chance to create some movements.

Fitness Development Activity — Hexagon Hustle

Hustle	25 seconds	Outline a large hexagon with 6 cones.
Push-Up from Knees	30 seconds	Place signs with directions on both sides
Hustle	25 seconds	of the cones. The signs identify the
Bend and Twist (8 counts)	30 seconds	hustle activity students are to perform
Hustle	25 seconds	as they approach a cone. Tape
Jumping Jacks (4 counts)	30 seconds	alternating segments of silence and
Hustle	25 seconds	music to signal duration of exercise.
Abdominal Challenges (2 counts)	30 seconds	Music segments indicate aerobic
Hustle	25 seconds	activity; intervals of silence announce
Double Leg Crab Kick	30 seconds	flexibility and strength development
Hustle	25 seconds	activities.
Sit and Stretch (8 counts)	30 seconds	
Hustle	25 seconds	Encourage students to do their best.
Power Jumper	30 seconds	Workloads should be personalized by
Hustle	25 seconds	each student by performing activities
Squat Thrust (4 counts)	30 seconds	they feel able to do.

Lesson Focus — Introductory Pedometer Procedures

Activity 1: How Pedometers Work

1. Organize the class into small groups of 5–6 students. Place the pedometers (6) in containers around the area. On entering the activity area, students move to their assigned container and pick up their assigned pedometer. When all students have a pedometer, freeze the class.

2. If the pedometers have a cover, show them how to open the pedometer. Practice opening and closing it a few times until it becomes easy for them. With a multifunction pedometer, practice using the mode button to move to different functions.

3. Show the class how the pedometer must be oriented to count accurately. Have them hold the pedometer (where they can see the display). Show the class how little up and down movement is required to record a step. Challenge them to make the smallest movement possible. Tilt the pedometer in all planes to see when it stops counting. Have students try a number of positions so they learn how the pedometer must be placed on the body to receive an accurate measurement.

4. Continue your planned activities. Leave a few minutes at the end of the lesson to check the steps and activity time students have accumulated and answer any questions they might have about the workings of a pedometer.

Pedometers should be numbered and assigned to a student.

Many students will want to force the pedometers open. Teach them to push on the latch with their thumb to open the pedometer.

Shaking the pedometer too hard will prevent the pedometer from counting accurately. The pedometer measures very small up and down movement.

Many reset buttons have a 2–3 second delay so youngsters won't accidentally reset the pedometer when they open it. To reset, hold the button down.

Replace the pedometers in the proper containers after they have been reset.

Activity 2: Finding an Accurate Pedometer Placement

1. Explain that the best location for the pedometer is usually on the waist over the midpoint of the kneecap. However, for some people, other placements may be more accurate. The objective of this activity is to identify the most accurate placement for each student.

2. Ask students to place the pedometer on the waistband in line with the kneecap. Ask them to reset the pedometer so the step display shows zero steps. Have them walk and count (quietly) 30 steps. Stop on the 30th step and check the pedometer display. Ask the class to write down or remember the number of steps their pedometer counted. Then go to Step 3.

3. Show the class how to move the pedometer a few inches toward their hip. Have them reset the pedometer and repeat Step 2 above. Record or remember the number of steps the pedometer counted. When finished, go to Step 4.

4. Ask the class to move the pedometer a few inches past their hip so the pedometer rests on their back. They may need a friend to help them put the pedometer on their waist band. Have them reset the pedometer and repeat Step 2 above. Record or remember the number of steps the pedometer counted.

5. If some students' pedometers are still not recording accurately, have them try a belt of some type such as a flag football or team belt. Another possibility is to fasten it on a pocket that is level (parallel to the floor).

6. Ask students which spot was the most accurate for them. The pedometers leave the factory tested to be accurate within one step. An accurate placement spot will give a reading of ±3 steps when taking 30 steps.

Use a belt, team belt, or flag football belt for students who do not have an adequate place to clip on the pedometer.

Pedometer accuracy is quite sensitive to placement. Since the pedometer measures ground force, it must be fixed and snug to the body to sense the motion. Loose clothing will make accuracy problematic.

Being overweight or having an uneven gait makes finding an accurate spot much more difficult. It can be done, but such students may require more help.

If the pedometer still records inaccurately, try changing pedometers to assure that the pedometer's battery is not low or the pedometer not recording accurately.

Activity 3: Procedures for Monitoring Class Activity

1. On entering the activity area, students move to their assigned container, pick up their assigned pedometer and put it on the waistband while walking or jogging. When all students have the pedometers in place, freeze the class and have them reset their pedometers.

2. Continue your planned regular lesson. Leave five minutes at the end of the lesson for carrying out the following activities:

   a. Ask the class to move and secure a step and activity time record sheet. Each student should pick up a sheet and pencil and place their name, pedometer container number, and pedometer number on the sheet. Explain to the class that they will pick up the same numbered pedometer each time they come to class.

   b. Have them record the number of steps (and activity time, if applicable) they accumulated.

   c. Ask them to reset their pedometers and place them in the same box where they originally picked them up. At the same time, they will place their record sheets next to their assigned container.

When using pedometers with multiple modes, have students push the mode button until activity time is on the display.

Decide whether you will ultimately use step or activity time goals as the most useful unit of measure.

Caution students to leave the pedometer fastened to the waistband. If the pedometer is removed, they may lose the privilege of using it.

After students have their names on their record sheets and learn the recording protocol, a student from the current class can place record sheets for the next class near the pedometer containers.

Game Activity

Bounce Ball

Supplies: Volleyballs or rubber playground balls of about the same size

Skills: Throwing, ball rolling

The court is divided into halves. The class is divided into two teams and each team occupies one half of the court and is given a number of balls. Two players from each team should be assigned to retrieve balls that go behind their end lines. The object of the game is to bounce or roll the ball over the opponents' end line. A ball thrown across the line on a fly does not count. Two scorers are needed, one at each end line. Players can move wherever they wish in their own area but cannot cross the centerline. After the starting signal, the balls are thrown back and forth at will.

One Step

Supplies: A ball or beanbag for each pair of children

Skills: Throwing, catching

Two players stand facing each other about 3 ft apart. One has a ball or beanbag. The object of the game is to throw or toss the item so that the partner can catch it without moving her feet. When the throw is completed successfully, the thrower takes one step backward and waits for a throw from her partner. Players try to increase the distance one step at a time until they reach an established line. When either player misses or moves their feet, the partners move forward and start over.

Variables that provide interest and challenge are types of throws, types of catches, and different steps. Throwing can be underhand, overhand, two-handed, under one leg, around the back, and so on. Catching can be two-handed, left-handed, right-handed, to the side, and so on. The step can be a giant step, a tiny step, a hop, a jump, or a similar movement.

Objectives:
To understand why people may walk the same distance but have different step counts
To develop skills of estimation related to steps, time, and distance

NASPE National Standards:
Introductory Activity: 1
Fitness Activity: 1, 4, 2
Lesson Focus: 2, 5
Game: 2, 5

Equipment Required:
Signs & music for circuit training
Magic number cards
Pencils & containers for pedometers
One pedometer for each student
Belts for pedometers (if needed)
Record sheets for recording data
Beanbag for game activity

Instructional Activities	Teaching Hints

Introductory Activity — Magic Number Challenges

Students are challenged to put together a combination of locomotor movements corresponding to the magic numbers designated (e.g., 10, 8, and 7). Students would have to do three different movements 10, 8, and 7 times, respectively. Use cards with specified numbers. Think of new activities for each series of numbers.

The number of movements, the repetitions and the types of movements can be changed to offer a wide variety of challenges.

Fitness Development Activity — Circuit Training

Students do the best they can at each station within the time limit. This implies that not all youngsters are required to do the same workload.
Rope Jumping
Triceps Push-Ups
Agility Run
Body Circles
Hula Hoop
Knee Touch Curl-Ups
Crab Walk
Tortoise and Hare
Bend and Twist

Tape alternating segments of silence and music to signal duration of exercise. Music segments (begin at 30 seconds) indicate activity at each station; intervals of silence (10 seconds) announce it is time to stop and move forward to the next station.

Use signals such as start, stop, and move up to ensure rapid movement to the next station.

Conclude circuit training with 2–4 minutes of walking, jogging, rope jumping, or other aerobic activity.

Ask students to do the best they can. Expect workloads to differ.

Lesson Focus — Understanding Step Differences and Estimation

Activity 1: Understanding Step Count Differences

1. Ask students to find a partner who is different in height or build.

2. Have the class press the mode button until the step counter is showing. Reset the pedometers and tell the class to begin walking with their partner in a "Follow the Leader" manner until the "freeze" signal is given.

3. Partners stop on signal and record their step counts.

4. Have partners compare their step counts and discuss why there is a difference. As the discussion evolves, offer some of the following possibilities:
   a. Their partner was taller or shorter.
   b. Their pedometer or the placement of the pedometer wasn't accurate.
   c. They didn't follow their partner exactly around the course.
   d. Their partner had longer or shorter stride lengths.
   e. Their clothes were loose fitting and made the pedometer inaccurate.

A different size partner is not crucial, more than likely there will be individual differences. However, students who differ in stature will usually show the greatest differences in step counts.

Help students understand that people differ in the number of steps required to cover the same distance. That makes it difficult to compare the number of steps they took to cover a distance with the number of steps it took a friend. In other words, step counts are most meaningful to the person who accumulated the steps.

These differences illustrate why a single standard, i.e., 10,000 steps for all students does not make sense. It would be easier or harder for some students to reach a uniform standard.

Activity 2: Jogging versus Walking—How Many Steps?

1. Set up or use an existing walking or jogging track. Mark the track off with cones so it is easy for students to see the entire course.

2. Explain that they will move around the course twice. The first time they will walk the track and the second time they will jog. The objective for this activity will be to guess which takes more steps—walking or jogging. The second goal is to guess which takes longer (activity time)—walking or jogging.

3. Have the students get a record sheet to record each of their four guesses, i.e., walking steps, jogging steps, walking time, and jogging time.

4. Ask students to find a starting point (they can start and finish at a selected cone along the track). Have the class reset their pedometers and walk the course at a comfortable speed. Tell them to stop at the end of the course and record their actual walking steps and activity time.

5. Repeat Step 4, except have the class jog (or fast walk for those students who find jogging too demanding).

6. Discuss the factors that can impact the number of steps they accumulate when walking or jogging such as:
    a. the type of activity such as playing a game or walking.
    b. the length of strides.
    c. the speed of the activities.

Activity 3: Estimating Steps required to Travel a Distance

1. The purpose of the activity is to estimate how many steps it takes to cover a specified distance. Set up a walking course for students. The course should be large enough so students will not be crowded as they walk. Students can start at one of the three corners of the course to reduce the number of students starting at the same spot.

2. Give students a record sheet to record their step guesses and actual step counts. Have them guess and record how many steps they think it will take to walk each side of the triangle.

3. Get the class to the starting point and ask them to press the mode button until the step counter is showing. Ask them to reset their pedometers.

4. Walk side one of the triangle, stop and record the actual number of steps it took to cover the distance.

5. Ask students to reset their pedometers after walking each leg of the triangle and repeat Step 4 for the other two sides of the triangle.

6. Ask students to compare the actual number of steps they took with the number of steps they guessed.

Activity 4: Estimating Walking Time (requires a pedometer that monitors activity time)

1. The purpose of this activity is to guess the amount of time it will take to cover a specified distance. Have students repeat the steps used in Activity 3 above.

Prepare a record sheet that offers room for four guesses and four actual scores.

The guesses will be walking steps, jogging steps, walking time, and jogging time. The actual scores will be walking steps, jogging steps, walking time, and jogging time.

Discuss with students why there are differences. Is the pedometer able to measure the intensity of your physical activity?

Since all students are doing the same thing in this activity, why are there differences in the number of steps accumulated at each of the speeds?

Are there people who are "efficient" movers who are able to accomplish movement goals in fewer steps? Could this make weight management more difficult?

A suggestion is to use 3 cones to mark off a large triangular course. If the area is small, set up three different small courses.

This activity can be repeated with different courses so students start to realize how many steps it takes to move a certain distance.

Lessons can be started by asking the class to guess how many steps it will take to cover a specified distance. They then walk that course to warm up and compare actual steps with their guesses.

Ask students to get an important adult to play this guessing game with them at home or in an afterschool activity.

Game Activity

Galloping Lizzie

    Supplies: A beanbag or fleece ball
    Skills: Throwing, dodging, running
    Two or more players are it and have a beanbag or fleece ball. The other players are scattered around the playground. The players with the bag or ball run after the others and attempt to hit other players below the waist with the object. The person hit becomes it, and the game continues. The tagger must throw the bag or ball, not merely touch another person with it.

Lifeboats (Cooperative Activity)

Formation: Groups of 8–12

Supplies: 2–3 individual mats or hoops, 2 scooters, and 1 long jump rope per group

The group is positioned on one side of the gym (a slow sinking ship) and given a scooter (lifeboat) and a long jump rope. The objective is to get the entire group from the sinking ship to the mainland (the other side of the gym) using only their lifeboats. Spaced randomly between the starting and stopping points are 3 individual mats (or hoops), which are islands in the ocean. Any students that touch the gym floor (water) must return to the starting point or island they were on (if hoops are used as islands, inside the hoop does not count as water). Thus, all students must remain on a mat at all times unless they are traveling across the ocean in a lifeboat (scooter). Students may be pulled with the jump rope but they may not be pushed. Students who are transported across the ocean must remain on the mainland and cannot return to the island or lifeboats; however, if they step into the "water" trying to rescue a teammate, they must return to the final island.

DPE Curriculum Guide – Lesson Plans
Gymnastics Skills (1)
Level II – Week 7

Objectives:
To move rhythmically to a drumbeat
To support the body weight in a variety of tumbling and stunt activities
To control the body weight in a variety of tumbling and stunt activities
To enjoy participation in group games

NASPE National Standards:
Introductory Activity: 1,5
Fitness Activity: 1, 2, 4, 5
Lesson Focus: 1, 3, 4, 6
Game: 1, 2, 3, 5

Equipment Required:
Tom-tom or tambourine
Circuit training music and signs
5–6 hoops and individual jump ropes
Tumbling mats
Balls & bowling pins for game activities

Instructional Activities	Teaching Hints

Introductory Activity — European Rhythmic Running

To introduce a group of children to Rhythmic Running, have them clap to the beat of the drum. Next, as they clap, have them walk in place, keeping time. Following this, have them run in place, omitting the clapping. Finally, the class can run in single-file formation, develop the ability to follow a leader, maintain proper spacing and move to the rhythm of the tom-tom.

A variation is to have a leader move in different shapes and designs. Have class freeze and see if they can identify the shape or formation.

Fitness Development Activity — Circuit Training

Rope Jumping
Triceps Push-Ups
Agility Run
Body Circles
Hula Hoop
Knee Touch Curl-Ups
Crab Walk
Tortoise and Hare
Bend and Twist

Conclude circuit training with 2–4 minutes of walking, jogging, rope jumping, or other aerobic activity.

Tape alternating segments of silence and music to signal duration of exercise. Music segments (begin at 30 seconds) indicate activity at each station; intervals of silence (10 seconds) announce it is time to stop and move forward to the next station.

Use signals such as start, stop, and move up to ensure rapid movement to the next station.

Ask students to do the best they can. Expect workloads to differ.

Lesson Focus — Gymnastics Skills (1)

Animal Movements
Cricket Walk
   Squat. Spread the knees. Put the arms between the knees and grasp the outside of the ankles with the hands. Walk forward or backward. Chirp like a cricket. Turn around right and left. See what happens when both feet are moved at once!

Frog Jump
   From a squatting position, with hands on the floor slightly in front of the feet, jump forward a short distance, landing on the hands and feet simultaneously. Note the difference between this stunt and the Rabbit Jump. Emphasis eventually should be on both height and distance. The hands and arms absorb part of the landing impact to prevent excessive strain on the knees.

Seal Crawl
   Start in the front-leaning rest position, the weight supported on straightened arms and toes. Keeping the body straight, walk forward, using the hands for propelling force and dragging the feet. Keep the body straight and the head up.

Reverse Seal Crawl
   Do the Seal Crawl with the tummy facing up and dragging the heels.

Six groups of activities in this lesson ensure that youngsters receive a variety of experiences. Pick a few activities from each group and teach them alternately. For example, teach one or two animal movements, then a tumbling and inverted balance, followed by a balance stunt, etc. Give equal time to each group of activities.

Scatter tumbling mats throughout the area so that there is little standing in line waiting for a turn. No more than 3–4 students per mat.

Youngsters can do the animal walks around their mats. Many of the activities in this unit do not have to be performed on the mat.

Tumbling and Inverted Balances

Forward Roll

Stand facing forward, with the feet apart. Squat and place the hands on the mat, shoulder width apart, with elbows against the insides of the thighs. Tuck the chin to the chest and make a rounded back. A push-off with the hands and feet provides the force for the roll. Carry the weight on the hands, with the elbows bearing the weight of the thighs. If the elbows are kept against the thighs and the weight is assumed there, the force of the roll is transferred easily to the rounded back. Try to roll forward to the feet. Later, try with the knees together and no weight on the elbows.

A major concern for safety is the neck and back region. Overweight children are at greater risk and can be allowed to avoid tumbling and inverted balances. Substitute a logroll.

Forward Roll to a Walkout

Perform the Forward Roll as described previously, except walk out to a standing position. The key to the Walkout is to develop enough momentum to allow a return to the feet. The leg that first absorbs the weight is bent while the other leg is kept straight.

Do not perform many repetitions of tumbling and inverted balances. For most children, limiting the number of forward or backward roll repetitions to four or five will prevent fatigue and injury.

Review the Backward Curl (taught in grades K–2)

Approach this activity in three stages. For the first stage, begin in a sitting position, with the knees drawn up to the chest and the chin tucked. The hands are clasped and placed behind the head with the elbows held out as far as possible. Gently roll backward until the weight is on the elbows. Roll back to starting position.

In stage two, perform the same action as before, but place the hands alongside the head on the mat while rolling back. The fingers are pointed in the direction of the roll, with palms down on the mat. (A good cue is "Point your thumbs toward your ears and keep your elbows close to your body.")

For stage three, perform the same action as in stage two, but start in a crouched position on the feet with the back facing the direction of the roll. Momentum is secured by sitting down quickly and bringing the knees to the chest.

The Backward Curl should be used to learn to roll back and forth. No youngster should be expected to roll over if it is difficult. In stunts and tumbling, it is important that the student decide if they are capable and confident enough to try the activity.

The Backward Curl is a lead-up to the Backward Roll. Teach children to push against the floor to take pressure off the back of the neck.

Backward Roll (Handclasp Position)

Clasp the fingers behind the neck, with elbows held out to the sides. From a crouched position, sit down rapidly, bringing the knees to the chest for a tuck to secure momentum. Roll completely over backward, taking much of the weight on the forearms. With this method, the neck is protected.

The handclasp position backward roll should be learned before the traditional backward roll. The handclasp method, in contrast to the traditional backward roll, does not require adequate arm strength to lift the body off the floor and release the head.

Climb-Up (taught in grades K–2)

Begin on a mat in a kneeling position, with hands placed about shoulder width apart and the fingers spread and pointed forward. Place the head forward of the hands, so that the head and hands form a triangle on the mat. Walk the body weight forward so that most of it rests on the hands and head. Climb the knees to the top of the elbows. (This stunt is a lead-up to the Headstand.)

The Climb-Up should only be performed by youngsters who have sufficient strength to support the body weight. Overweight children will find this to be a difficult activity.

Balance Stunts

One-Leg Balance Reverse

Assume a forward balance position by balancing on one leg, bending over at the waist until the chest is parallel with the floor, and extending the arms. In a quick movement, to give momentum, swing the free leg down and change to the same forward balance position facing in the opposite direction (a 180-degree turn). No unnecessary movement of the supporting foot should be made after the turn is completed. The swinging foot should not touch the floor.

With the exception of the tumbling and inverted balances group, all the activities in this unit can be performed by all youngsters. If in doubt about an activity in the tumbling and inverted balances group, avoid teaching it.

Tummy Balance

Lie prone on the floor with arms outstretched forward or to the sides, with palms down. Raise the arms, head, chest, and legs from the floor and balance on the tummy. The knees should be kept straight.

This activity is excellent for back strength. It also reinforces students who are flexible in the back area.

Leg Dip

Extend both hands and one leg forward, balancing on the other leg. Lower the body to sit on the heel and return without losing the balance or touching the floor with any part of the body. Try with the other foot.

When doing the Leg Dip, another student can assist from the back by applying upward pressure to the elbows.

Individual Stunts

Reach-Under

Take a position with the feet pointed ahead (spaced about 2 ft apart) and toes against a line or a floor board. Place a beanbag two boards in front of, and midway between, the feet. Without changing the position of the feet, reach one hand behind and between the legs to pick up the beanbag. Now pick up with the other hand. Repeat, moving the beanbag a board farther away each time.

If a beanbag is unavailable, youngsters can see how far they can gradually reach and note the distance in relationship to a tile, piece of grass, or board in the floor.

Stiff Person Bend

Place the feet about shoulder width apart and pointed forward. Place a beanbag a few inches behind the right heel. Grasp the left toes with the left hand, thumb on top. Without bending the knees, reach the right hand outside the right leg and pick up the beanbag without releasing the hold on the left toes

These are enjoyable challenges for youngsters. Increase the challenge by gradually increasing the distance of the reach. Reverse sides of the body.

Coffee Grinder

Put one hand on the floor and extend the body to the floor on that side in a side-leaning rest position. Walk around the hand, making a complete circle and keeping the body straight.

The Coffee Grinder should be done slowly, with controlled movements. The body should remain as straight as possible throughout the circle movement.

Scooter

Sit on the floor with legs extended, arms folded in front of the chest, and chin held high. To scoot, pull the seat toward the heels, using heel pressure and lifting the seat slightly. Extend the legs forward again and repeat the process.

Partner and Group Stunts

Partner Hopping

Partners coordinate hopping movements for short distances and in different directions and turns. Three combinations are suggested.
1. Stand facing each other. Extend the right leg forward to be grasped at the ankle by partner's left hand. Hold right hands and hop on the left leg.
2. Stand back to back. Lift the leg backward, bending the knee, and have partner grasp the ankle. Hop as before.
3. Stand side by side with inside arms around each other's waist. Lift the inside foot from the floor and make progress by hopping on the outside foot.

Find a partner who is similar in ability.

If either partner begins to fall, the other should release the leg immediately. Reverse foot positions.

Partner Twister

Partners face and grasp right hands as if shaking hands. One partner swings the left leg over the head of the other and turns around, taking a straddle position over partner's arm. The other swings the right leg over the first partner, who has bent over, and the partners are now back to back. First partner continues with the right leg and faces in the original direction. Second partner swings the left leg over the partner's back to return to the original face-to-face position.

Partners need to duck to avoid being kicked by each other's feet as the legs are swung over.

Partner Pull-Up

Partners sit facing each other in a bent-knee position, with heels on the floor and toes touching. Pulling cooperatively, they come to a standing position.

The goal is to *simultaneously* come to the standing position, instead of one standing and pulling the other to their feet.

Game Activity

Whistle Mixer

Supplies: A whistle
Skills: All basic locomotor movements
Children are scattered throughout the area. To begin, they walk around in any direction they wish. A whistle is blown a number of times in succession with short, sharp blasts. Children then form small groups with the number in each group equal to the number of whistle blasts. If there are four blasts, children form groups of four—no more, no less. When players have

the correct number, they sit down immediately to signal that no one may leave the group and no one may enter the group. The goal is not to be left out or caught in a circle with the incorrect number of students. Encourage players to move toward the center of the area and raise their hands to facilitate finding others without a group. After the circles are formed, the teacher calls "Walk," and the game continues. In walking, children should move in different directions.

Circle Contests

Supplies: Volleyballs or 8" foam rubber balls, two bowling pins

Skills: Throwing, catching

Two teams arranged in independent circles compete against each other. The circles should be the same diameter; lines can be drawn on the floor to ensure this. The players of each team are numbered consecutively so each player in one circle corresponds to a player in the other circle. Two numbered players, in sequence, go to the center of the opponents' circle to compete for their team in either of the following activities.

1. *Circle Club Guard.* The two center players guard a bowling pin. The ball is rolled at the club. The circle that knocks down the club first wins a point.

2. *Touch Ball.* The circle players pass the ball from one to another while the two center players try to touch it. The center player who touches the ball first wins a point for the respective team. In case neither player is able to touch the ball in a reasonable period of time, the action should be cut off without awarding a point.

After all players have competed, the team with the most points wins. For *Circle Club Guard*, there must be three passes to different people before the ball can be rolled at the club. Establishing circle lines may be necessary to regulate throwing distance.

Alaska Baseball

Supplies: A volleyball or soccer ball

Skills: Kicking, batting, running, ball handling

Players are divided into two teams; one is at bat while the other is in the field. A straight line provides the only out-of-bounds line, and the team at bat is behind this line midway between the ends of the line. The other team is scattered around the fair territory. One player propels the ball, either batting a volleyball or kicking a stationary soccer ball. Her teammates are in a close file behind her. As soon as the batter sends the ball into the playing area, she starts to run around her own team. Each time the runner passes the head of the file, the team gives a loud count.

There are no outs. The first fielder to get the ball stands still and starts to pass the ball back overhead to the nearest teammate, who moves directly behind to receive it. The remainder of the team in the field must run to the ball and form a file behind the fielder. The ball is passed back overhead, with each player handling the ball. When the last field player in line has a firm grip on it, she shouts "Stop." At this signal, a count is made of the number of times the batter ran around her team. To score more accurately, half rounds can be counted. Five batters or half of the team should bat; then the teams should change places. This is better than allowing an entire team to bat before changing to the field, because players in the field fatigue from many consecutive runs.

DPE Curriculum Guide – Lesson Plans
Soccer Skills and Lead-up Activities (1)
Level II – Week 8

Objectives:
To strike a foam rubber soccer ball
  with a variety of body parts
To dribble a foam rubber soccer ball
  with the feet
To trap a foam rubber ball with a
  variety of body parts
To play a soccer lead-up activity and
  understand the joy of participation

NASPE National Standards:
Introductory Activity: 1, 2
Fitness Activity: 1, 4, 2
Lesson Focus: 2, 3, 5
Game: 2, 3, 5

Equipment Required:
Music tape for Astronaut Exercises
8" foam rubber or 8½" playground ball
  for each student
Pinnies (optional)
Cones for marking the drill areas and
  goals

Instructional Activities	Teaching Hints

Introductory Activity — Four Corners Movement

Lay out a rectangle with a cone at each corner. As the child passes each corner, he changes to a different locomotor movement.

Challenge students to perform various qualities of movement (i.e., soft, heavy, slow, fast).

Fitness Development Activity — Astronaut Exercises

Walk, do arm circles	35 seconds	
Crab full-leg extension	30 seconds	
Skip sideways	35 seconds	
Body twist	30 seconds	
Slide; change lead leg	35 seconds	
Jumping Jack variations	30 seconds	
Crab Walk	35 seconds	
Curl-Ups with twist	30 seconds	
Hop to center and back	35 seconds	
Four count push-ups	30 seconds	
Gallop backwards	35 seconds	
Bear hugs	30 seconds	
Grapevine Step (Carioca)	35 seconds	
Trunk Twisters	30 seconds	
Power Jumper	35 seconds	

Cool down with stretching and walking.

Tape alternating segments of silence (30 seconds) and music (35 seconds) to signal the duration of exercise. Music segments indicate aerobic activity while intervals of silence announce flexibility and strength development activities.

See Chapter 13 for a description of how to perform the exercises.

Allow students to adjust the workload to an intensity that is consistent with their ability level.

Use scatter formation; ask students to change directions from time to time in order to keep spacing.

Lesson Focus — Soccer Skills (1)

Skills
Practice the following skills:
1. Dribbling
   Dribbling is moving the ball with a series of taps or pushes to cover ground and still retain control. It allows a player to change direction quickly and to avoid opponents. The best contact point is the inside of the foot, but the outside of the foot will be used at faster running speeds. The ball should be kept close to the player to maintain control.
2. Inside-of-the-Foot Pass (Push Pass)
   The inside-of-the-foot pass is used for accurate passing over distances of up to 15 yards. Because of the technique used, this pass is sometimes referred to as the push pass. The nonkicking foot is placed well up, alongside the ball. As the kicking foot is drawn back, the toe is turned out. During the kick, the toe remains turned out so that the inside of the foot is perpendicular to the line of flight. The sole is kept parallel to the ground. At contact, the knee of the kicking leg should be well forward, over the ball, and both knees should be slightly bent.

When teaching students beginning skills, have them place their hands behind their back to avoid the temptation of touching the ball with the hands.

Keep the ball near the body so it can be controlled. (Don't kick it too far in front of the body.) Dribble the ball with a controlled tap.

Place the nonkicking foot alongside the ball. Keep the head down and eyes focused on the ball during contact.

Make contact with the outside or inside of the foot rather than with the toe.

3. Inside-of-the-Foot Trap

This is the most common method of control, and is used when the ball is either rolling along the ground or bouncing up to knee height. The full surface of the foot, from heel to toe, should be presented perpendicular to the ball.

Move in line with the path of the ball and reach with the foot to meet the ball. Give when ball contact is made to absorb force.

Drills

Use the following partner drills to practice the skills above:

1. Dribbling, marking, and ball recovery. Pairs are scattered, with one player in each pair having a soccer ball. That player dribbles in various directions, and the second player attempts to stay close to the first (marking). As skill development occurs, the defensive player can attempt to recover the ball from the dribbler. If successful, roles are reversed.

Each student should practice dribbling and handling the ball individually. Use drills after students have had time to practice the skills individually. Working with a partner increases the motivational level.

2. Dribbling, Passing, and Trapping. One player of the pair has a ball and dribbles in different directions. On signal, she passes to her partner, who traps the ball and begins dribbling, continuing until another signal is given.

Emphasize controlled activity. The goal is not to see how far or hard the ball can be kicked.

Soccer Lead-up Activities

Circle Kickball

Supplies: Two soccer balls or 8" foam rubber balls
Skills: Kicking, controlling

Players are in circle formation. Using the side of the foot, players kick the balls back and forth inside the circle. The object is to kick a ball out of the circle beneath the shoulder level of the circle players. A point is scored against each of the players where a ball leaves the circle between them. If, however, a lost ball is clearly the fault of a single player, then the point is scored against that player only. Any player who kicks a ball higher than the shoulders of the circle players has a point scored against him. Players with the fewest points scored against them win. A player is not penalized if he leaves the circle to recover a ball and the second ball goes through the vacated spot.

Diagonal Soccer

Supplies: A soccer ball, pinnies (optional)
Skills: Kicking, passing, dribbling, some controlling, defending, blocking shots

Two corners are marked off with cones 5 ft from the corners on both the sides, outlining triangular dead areas. Each team lines up and tries to protect two adjacent sides of the square. To begin competition, three players from each team move into the playing area in their own half of the space. These are the active players who may roam anywhere in the square. The other players act as goalkeepers.

The object of the game is for active players to kick the ball through the opposing team's line (beneath shoulder height) to score. After 30 to 45 seconds, active players rotate to the sidelines and new players take their place. Players on the sidelines may block the ball with their bodies and use their hands. The team against whom the point was scored starts the ball for the next point. Only active players may score. Scoring is much the same as in Circle Kickball in that a point is awarded for the opponents when any of the following occur:

1. A team allows the ball to go through its line below the shoulders.
2. A team touches the ball illegally.
3. A team kicks the ball over the other team above shoulder height.

Soccer Take-Away

Supplies: A soccer ball for each student
Skills: Dribbling and defensive skills

Four or five players are designated as defensive players. Each of the rest of the students have a soccer ball and dribble it around the area. The defensive players try to take away a ball from the offensive players. When a successful steal is made, the player losing control of the ball becomes a defensive player.

DPE Curriculum Guide – Lesson Plans
Soccer Skills and Lead-up Activities (2)
Level II – Week 9

Objectives:
To strike a foam rubber soccer ball
   with a variety of body parts
To dribble a foam rubber soccer ball
   with the feet
To trap a foam rubber ball with a
   variety of body parts
To play a soccer lead-up activity and
   understand the joy of participation

NASPE National Standards:
Introductory Activity: 1, 3, 5
Fitness Activity: 1, 4, 6
Lesson Focus: 2, 3, 5
Game: 2, 3, 5

Equipment Required:
6 marking spots
Music tape for Astronaut Exercises
One 8" foam rubber or 8½" playground
   ball for each student
Pinnies for games (optional)
Cones for marking the drill areas and
   goals

Instructional Activities	Teaching Hints

Introductory Activity — Home Base

The class is divided into teams of 5–6 players. One player in each group is designated the captain. Rubber spots are placed throughout the teaching area equal to the number of teams. Each spot serves as a home base for one of the squads. The teams begin in a straight line with the captain standing on a spot and the rest of the team lined up behind her. The teacher calls out a locomotor movement that the players use to move throughout the area. When the teacher calls "home base!" each team lines up in starting formation with the captain first in line. The first team to return to proper position wins that round.

This is an excellent game to teach youngsters how to get in small-group formations quickly.

If desired, use the call "find your home" to assemble the class in pre-assigned squads. Some teachers use squads for station teaching and dividing the class into teams.

Fitness Development Activity — Astronaut Exercises

Walk, do arm circles	35 seconds
Crab full-leg extension	30 seconds
Skip sideways	35 seconds
Body twist	30 seconds
Slide; change lead leg	35 seconds
Jumping Jack variations	30 seconds
Crab Walk	35 seconds
Curl-Ups with twist	30 seconds
Hop to center and back	35 seconds
Four count push-ups	30 seconds
Gallop backwards	35 seconds
Bear Hugs	30 seconds
Grapevine Step (Carioca)	35 seconds
Trunk Twisters	30 seconds
Power Jumper	35 seconds

Cool down with stretching and walking.

Tape alternating segments of silence (30 seconds) and music (35 seconds) to signal the duration of exercise. Music segments indicate aerobic activity; intervals of silence announce flexibility and strength development activities.

See Chapter 13 for a description of how to perform the exercises.

Allow students to adjust the workload to an intensity that is consistent with their ability level.

Use scatter formation; ask students to change directions from time to time in order to keep spacing.

Lesson Focus — Soccer Skills (2)

Skills

Divide the skills into four stations and place necessary equipment at each station. Students can practice skills they learned in last week's lesson.
1. Review and practice the long pass. Set up a station with plenty of room and students with a partner. They long pass back and forth to each other.
2. Review the inside-of-the foot pass and trapping: Work with a partner and practice passing and trapping.
3. Practice dribbling skills: Give each student a ball and have them practice dribbling. Move the ball with a series of taps. Start slowly and keep the ball in front of the body.
4. Dribbling and Passing: Students work with a partner. One dribbles the ball a short distance and then passes it to their partner.

Make signs that tell students the skills they are to practice at each station. Set the signs on cones in the areas where students are to practice.

The foam training balls are best for teaching introductory soccer skills. They don't hurt students when kicked or when they are struck by a ball.

Drills Using Three Players

With one ball for three players, many of the possibilities suggested for pair practice are still possible. An advantage of drills for three players is that fewer balls are needed.

1. Passing and controlling. The trio of players set up a triangle with players about 10 yards apart. Controlled passing and practice in ball control should occur.
2. Dribbling and passing. A shuttle-type drill can be structured where players keep going back and forth continuously. Player 1 has the ball and dribbles to player 2, who dribbles the ball back to player 3, who in turn dribbles to player 1. Players can dribble the entire distance or dribble a portion of the distance and then pass the ball to the end player. Obstacles can be set up to challenge players to dribble through or around each obstacle.
3. Dribbling and stopping the ball. Three dribblers are in line, each with a ball. The leader moves in various directions, followed by the other two players. On signal, each player controls her ball. The leader circles around to the back ball, and the other two move one ball forward. The dribbling continues for another stop. A third stop puts the players back in their original positions.
4. Passing. Players stand in three corners of a 10-yard square. After a player passes, he must move to the empty corner of the square, which is sometimes a diagonal movement.
5. Passing and defense. One player is the feeder and rolls the ball to either player. As soon as she rolls the ball, she attempts to block or tackle the player receiving the ball to prevent a pass to the third player, who, if the pass is completed, attempts to pass back.

Grids with areas that are approximately 10 yards square can be marked off with marking spots or cones. The drills are then conducted with a threesome in each area.

The drills can also be set up as individual stations where students rotate after a specified time.

Many of the drills are simple game activities. Students enjoy the opportunity to play with friends.

Emphasis should be on form and practicing the skills. If students are unable to control the ball, drills may not work and students should be given time to practice individually.

Soccer Lead-up Activities

Diagonal Soccer

Supplies: A soccer ball, pinnies (optional)

Skills: Kicking, passing, dribbling, some controlling, defending, blocking shots

Two corners are marked off with cones 5 ft from the corners on both the sides, outlining triangular dead areas. Each team lines up and tries to protect two adjacent sides of the square. To begin competition, three players from each team move into the playing area in their own half of the space. These are the active players who may roam anywhere in the square. The other players act as goalkeepers.

The object of the game is for active players to kick the ball through the opposing team's line (beneath shoulder height) to score. After 30 to 45 seconds, active players rotate to the sidelines and new players take their place. Players on the sidelines may block the ball with their bodies and use their hands. The team against whom the point was scored starts the ball for the next point. Only active players may score. Scoring is much the same as in Circle Kickball in that a point is awarded for the opponents when any of the following occur:

1. A team allows the ball to go through its line below the shoulders.
2. A team touches the ball illegally.
3. A team kicks the ball over the other team above shoulder height.

Dribblerama

Supplies: One soccer ball for each player

Skills: Dribbling, protecting the ball

The playing area is a large circle or square, clearly outlined. All players dribble within the area. The game is played on two levels.

Level 1: Each player dribbles throughout the area, controlling the ball so it does not touch another ball. If a touch occurs, both players go outside the area and dribble around the area. Once youngsters have completed dribbling one lap, they may re-enter the game.

Level 2: Two equal playing areas are delineated. All players start in one of the areas. While dribbling and controlling the ball, each player attempts to kick any other ball out of the area. When a ball is kicked out, the player owning that ball takes it to the other area and dribbles. As more players move to the second area, a second game ensues. Players in this area move back to the opposite side. This keeps all players actively involved in the games.

Bull's-Eye

Supplies: One soccer ball per player

Skills: Dribbling, protecting the ball

The playing area is a large outlined area—circle, square, or rectangle. One player holds a ball in her hands, which serves as the bull's-eye. The other players dribble within the area. The player with the bull's-eye attempts to throw her ball (basketball push shot) at any other ball. The ball that is hit now becomes the new bull's-eye. The old bull's-eye becomes one of the dribblers. A new bull's-eye cannot hit back immediately at the old bull's-eye. If the group is large, have two bull's-eyes. No score is kept and no one is eliminated.

LP 48

Objectives:	NASPE National Standards:	Equipment Required:
To perform a variety of fitness activities rhythmically	Introductory Activity: 1, 5	Music and signs for Aerobic Fitness
To work together with peers to accomplish parachute activities	Fitness Activity: 1, 4, 5, 6	Parachute, beanbags, jump ropes, and cageball
To develop strength through parachute activities	Lesson Focus: 2, 3, 5	Box and 4 balls
	Game: 1, 3, 5	

Instructional Activities	Teaching Hints

Introductory Activity — Group Over and Around

One half of the class is scattered. Each is in a curled position. The other half of the class leaps or jumps over the down children. On signal, reverse the group quickly. In place of a curl, the down children can bridge while the other youngsters move around them.	The down children can also alternate between curl and bridge, as well as move around the area while in a bridged position.

Fitness Development Activity — Aerobic Fitness

1. Rhythmic run with clap	Use music to stimulate effort. Any combination of movements can be used.
2. Bounce turn and clap	
3. Rhythmic 4-count curl-ups (knees, toes, knees, back)	
4. Rhythmic Crab Kicks (slow time)	Keep the steps simple and easy to perform. Some students will become frustrated if the learning curve is steep.
5. Jumping Jack combination	
6. Double knee lifts	
7. Lunges (right, left, forward) with single-arm circles (on the side lunges) and double-arms circles (on the forward lunge)	Signs that explain the aerobic activities will help students remember performance cues.
8. Rhythmic trunk twists	
9. Directional run (forward, backward, side, turning)	
10. Rock side to side with clap	
11. Side-leg raises (alternate legs)	Don't stress or expect perfection. Allow students to perform the activities as best they can.
12. Rhythmic 4-count push-ups (If these are too difficult for students, substitute single-arm circles in the push-up position.)	
	Alternate bouncing and running movements with flexibility and strength development movements.

Lesson Focus — Fundamental Skills Using a Parachute

Parachute Warm-Up Activities. These activities are useful for starting children on the parachute. They are demanding activities that allow students to use excess energy.	One parachute is generally sufficient for a class of 30 children. Parachutes come in different sizes, but those with diameters ranging from 24 to 32 ft are suitable for a regular class. The size with most utility is the 28-ft parachute. Each parachute has an opening near the top to allow trapped air to escape and to keep the parachute shaped properly. Most parachutes are constructed of nylon. A parachute should stretch tight and not sag in the middle when it is pulled snug by children spaced around it.
Shaking the Rug and Making Waves	
Shaking the Rug involves rapid movements of the parachute, either light or heavy. Making Waves involves large movements to send billows of cloth up and down.	
Chute Crawl	
Half of the class, either standing or kneeling, stretches the chute at waist level parallel to the ground. The remaining children crawl under the chute to the opposite side from their starting position.	
Kite Run	
The class holds the chute on one side with one hand. The leader points in the direction they are to run while holding the chute aloft like a kite.	
Running Number Game	
The children around the chute count off by fours; then they run lightly, holding the chute in one hand. The teacher calls out one of the numbers. Children with that number immediately release their grip on the chute and run forward to the next place vacated. They must put on a burst of speed to move ahead.	

Parachute Exercise Activities. Exercises should be done vigorously and with enough repetitions to challenge the children. In addition to the exercises presented, others can be adapted to parachute play.

Toe Toucher

Sit with feet extended under the parachute and hold the chute taut with a two-hand grip, drawing it up to the chin. Bend forward and touch the grip to the toes. Return parachute to stretched position.

Curl-Up

Extend the body under the parachute in curl-up position, so that the chute comes up to the chin when held taut. Do Curl-Ups, returning each time to the stretched chute position.

Dorsal Lift

Lie prone, with head toward the parachute and feet pointed back, away from it. Grip the chute and slide toward the feet until there is some tension on it. Raise the chute off the ground with a vigorous lift of the arms, until head and chest rise off the ground. Return.

V-Sit

Lie supine, with head toward the chute. Do V-Sit by raising the upper and lower parts of the body simultaneously into a V-shaped position. The knees should be kept straight.

Backward Pull

Face the parachute and pull back, away from its center. Pulls can be made from a sitting, kneeling, or standing position.

Parachute Activities with Equipment

Ball Circle

Place a basketball or a cageball on the raised chute. Make the ball roll around the chute in a large circle, controlling it by raising or lowering the chute. Try the same with two balls. A beach ball is also excellent.

Popcorn

Place a number of beanbags (from 6 to 10) on the chute. Shake the chute to make them rise like corn popping.

Team Ball

Divide the class in half, each team defending half of the chute. Using from 2 to 6 balls of any variety, try to bounce the balls off the opponents' side, scoring 1 point for each ball.

Poison Snake

Divide into teams. Place from 6 to 10 jump ropes on the chute. Shake the chute and try to make the ropes hit players on the other side. For each rope that touches one team member, that team has a point scored against it. The team with the lower score is the winner.

Parachute Dome Activities To make a dome, children begin with the parachute on the floor, holding with two hands and kneeling on one knee. To trap air under the chute, children stand up quickly, thrusting their arms above the head, and then return to starting position.

Students under the Chute

Tasks for under the chute can be specified, such as turning a certain number of turns with a jump rope, throwing and catching a beanbag, or bouncing a ball a number of times. The needed objects should be under the chute before the dome is made.

Number Exchange

Children are numbered from 1 to 4. The teacher calls a number as the dome is made, and those with the number called must change position to be under the dome before the chute comes down. Locomotor movements can be varied.

Punching Bag

Children make a dome and stand on the edges. They then punch at the chute while slowly and gently walking the edges of the chute toward the center.

The grips used in handling the parachute are comparable to those employed in hanging activities on an apparatus. Grips can be with one or two hands, overhand (palms facing away), underhand (palms facing toward), or mixed (one hand underhand and the other overhand).

For preliminary explanations, the parachute can be stretched out on the ground in its circular pattern, with the children seated so that they cannot touch the parachute during instructions. When the children hold the parachute during later explanations, they should retain their hold lightly, letting the center of the parachute drop to the ground. Children must be taught to exercise control and not to manipulate the parachute while explanations are in progress.

Walking on the parachute should be discouraged, since it is a slippery surface and may increase the chance of falls.

Teach the proper technique of lifting the parachute. Youngsters should start with one knee on the floor; as the hands lift upward, stand and make the legs do the work. As the stand occurs, take a step toward the center of the chute and lift upward. Lifting should be done with the legs and arms.

Blooming Flower

Children make a dome and kneel with both knees on the edge of the chute. They hold hands around the chute and lean in and out to represent a flower opening.

Lights Out

While making a dome, the children take two steps toward the center and sit inside the chute. The chute can be held with the hands at the side or by sitting on it.

Mushroom Activities

To form a mushroom, students begin with the chute on the ground, kneeling on one knee and holding with two hands. They stand up quickly, thrusting the arms overhead. Keeping the arms overhead, each walks forward three or four steps toward the center. The arms are held overhead until the chute is deflated.

Mushroom Release

All children release at the peak of inflation and either run out from under the chute or move to the center and sit down, with the chute descending on top of them.

Mushroom Run

Children make a mushroom. As soon as they move into the center, they release holds and run once around the inside of the chute, counterclockwise, back to place.

Game Activity

Indianapolis 500

Supplies: None

Skills: Running, tagging

Players start in a large circle and are numbered off in threes or fours. A race starter says "Start your engines," and then calls out a number. Those players with the corresponding number run in the same direction around the circle and try to tag players in front of them. If the leader yells "Pit stop," all runners have to stop and return to their original position. If "Car crash" is called by the leader, all runners change direction and continue running. Change starters often.

Attached at the … (Cooperative Activity)

Formation: Partners

Supplies: One beanbag or ball for each set of partners

Partners stand on one side of the activity area. The challenge is to get to the other sideline or end line while attached at the hip, head, back, ankle, elbow, hamstring, etc. Locomotor movements can be specified for moving across the area. For a more difficult activity, provide a beanbag or ball for the students to put between the "attached" body parts.

Teaching Tip: To add difficulty, after completing tasks with a partner, challenge students to work in groups of 3, 4, or more.

DPE Curriculum Guide – Lesson Plans
Playground and Recreational Activities
Level II – Week 11

Objectives:
To learn the rules of games that are common on local playgrounds
To learn the etiquette of games that are common on local playgrounds
To understand the recreational and self-directed nature of playground games

NASPE National Standards:
Introductory Activity: 1, 5
Fitness Activity: 1, 4, 5, 6
Lesson Focus: 2, 3, 5, 6
Game: 2, 3, 5, 6

Equipment Required:
Tambourine
Signs and music for Aerobic Fitness
Equipment needed for playground games

Instructional Activities	Teaching Hints

Introductory Activity — Bend, Stretch and Shake

Students should alternate between various bending and stretching activities. On signal, students shake and relax various body parts. Teach a variety of bending and stretching activities.

Use a tambourine to signal changes in bending and stretching. Shake it to signal shaking activities.

Fitness Development Activity — Aerobic Fitness

The following aerobic movements are suggestions only. Also, stop the aerobic fitness movements and do flexibility and strength development activity to allow students time to recover aerobically.

1. Rhythmic run with clap
2. Bounce, turn, and clap
3. Rhythmic 4-count curl-ups (knees, toes, knees, back)
4. Rhythmic Crab Kicks (slow time)
5. Jumping Jack combination
6. Double knee lifts
7. Lunges (right, left, forward) with single-arm circles (on the side lunges) and double-arms circles (on the forward lunge)
8. Rhythmic trunk twists
9. Directional run (forward, backward, side, turning)
10. Rock side to side with clap
11. Side-leg raises (alternate legs)
12. Rhythmic 4-count push-ups (If these are too difficult for students, substitute single-arm circles in the push-up position.)

Use music to stimulate effort. Any combination of movements can be used.

Keep the steps simple and easy to perform. Some students will become frustrated if the learning curve is steep.

Signs that explain the aerobic activities will help students remember performance cues.

Don't stress or expect perfection. Allow students to perform the activities as best they can.

Alternate bouncing and running movements with flexibility and strength development movements.

Lesson Focus and Game Activity — Playground Games and Recreational Activities

Playground and Recreational Activities

The objective of this lesson should be to teach youngsters the rules and methods for playing games during their free time. Emphasis should be on self-direction so students do not need supervision.

1. Tetherball
2. Four Square
3. Two Square
4. Volley Tennis
5. Basketball
   a. Around the Key
   b. Twenty-One
   c. Freeze Out
6. Hopscotch
7. Jump Rope
8. Soccer (2 on 2)
9. Frisbee Golf
10. Wall Handball
11. Any playground and recreational activities played at your school.

The focus of this lesson is to teach students the rules and etiquette required to play recreational activities. Take time to discuss questions students might have about the activities.

Playground games listed here are examples. Most schools have a number of games that are popular. Ask youngsters what games are popular and allow some upper-grade students to teach them.

If desired, set up stations and divide students into four groups. All students to rotate to each group during the lesson focus time. Use signs on cones that explain the activities to be done at each station.

DPE Curriculum Guide – Lesson Plans
Walking Activities
Level II – Week 12

Objectives:

To travel throughout the area and be able to avoid or catch another individual

To understand the differences in aerobic capacities among classmates

To find a walking pace that is comfortable for an extended time

NASPE National Standards:

Introductory Activity: 1, 5
Fitness Activity: 1, 4, 6
Lesson Focus: 4, 5, 6
Game: 2, 3, 5, 6

Equipment Required:

Music for fitness orienteering routine
Stations and signs for fitness orienteering
Laminated map card of checkpoint stations
Letters for the checkpoints
Beanbag or baton and cones for walking activities

Instructional Activities	Teaching Hints

Introductory Activity — Fastest Tag in the West

All students are it. On signal, they try to tag each other. If they are tagged, they must freeze, but they are eligible to tag other students who pass near them. If two or more players tag each other simultaneously, they are both/all "frozen."

The focus of this game is activity. Don't overemphasize rules. When about half of the class is frozen, start the game over.

Fitness Development Activity — Fitness Orienteering

Students work together as members of a team. Eight to ten stations are placed around the area in random fashion. Each squad is given a laminated "map" card of exercise stations. Each of the maps has the stations in different order so that there is only one squad at a "landmark." The team members exercise together (each member performing at their own pace) and "hunt" for the next exercise station listed on their map card when signaled. When they complete the station activity, one member of the squad picks up a letter from the "checkpoint" and the team moves to the next station. The goal is to complete the fitness orienteering stations, pick up a letter at each station, and return to the original starting point to unscramble "the secret word."

Examples of checkpoint stations on the exercise map card are:

1. Run to the Northwest corner of the gym and pick up your letter now. When the music starts, continue to run to a different corner until the music stops.
2. Move to the individual mats and perform push-up challenges until the music stops.
3. Run to the benches and perform step-ups until the music stops. The count should be "up, up, down, down," with your steps.
4. Move to the red marking spots and perform two different stretches until the music stops.
5. Run and find the jump ropes. When the music starts, pick up the ropes and do some jump-rope tricks you learned earlier.
6. Skip to the tumbling mats. When the music starts, perform abdominal challenges.
7. As a group, jog to the 3 green marking spots and pick up your letter. Jog and try to touch at least 5 walls, 2 different red lines, and 3 different black lines. Stay together with your group.
8. Jog to the "jumping jacks" sign and perform jumping jacks with at least 4 different variations in arm or foot patterns.

Intervals of music (30 seconds) and silence (15 seconds) signal when to exercise and when to change to a new station.

See Chapter 13 for a description of how to perform the exercises.

Allow students to adjust the workload to an intensity that is consistent with their ability level.

Set up the stations prior to the lesson. Each day the course is run, the order of the checkpoint stations can be changed.

Lesson Focus — Walking

This should be a relaxed lesson with emphasis on developing activity patterns that can be used outside of the school environment. An educational approach to this lesson teaches students that walking is done without equipment and offers excellent health benefits. Walking can be done throughout the lifespan. The following are suggestions for implementing this unit of instruction:

1. Youngsters should be allowed to find a friend with whom they want to walk. The result is usually a friend of similar ability level. A way to judge correct pace is to be able to talk with a friend without undue stress. If students are too winded to talk, they are probably moving too fast. A selected friend will encourage talking and help assure that the experience is positive and within the student's aerobic capacity.

2. Walking should be done in individual directions rather than doing laps on a track. Doing laps on a track is one of the surest ways to discourage less-mobile youngsters. They always finish last and are open to chiding by the rest of the class.

3. Walking should be done for a specified time rather than a specified distance. All youngsters should not have to move the same distance. This goes against the philosophy of accompanying individual differences and varying aerobic capacities. Walking for a set amount of time will allow the less-able child to move without fear of ridicule. For health benefits, it is best to move for a longer time at a slower speed than to run at top speed for a shorter distance.

Walking Activities

New Engineer

Playing Area: Gymnasium or defined activity area

Players: Groups of 6–8

Supplies: A small piece of equipment (beanbag or baton) for a group of 4–6 students

Skills: Walking, pacing,

Groups of 4–6 students stand in a single file line and begin walking with the leader (engineer) holding the piece of equipment and leading the group throughout the teaching area. On signal, the leader hands the piece of equipment to the second person who hands it to the third and so on. This is all done while the line is still walking. When the equipment gets back to the last person (the caboose), the caboose begins speed walking to the front of the line to become the "new engineer."

Teaching Tip: Challenge students to move with a brisk walk. At different intervals, stop and change the makeup of the teams to provide renewed interest.

Just Walk

Playing Area: Outside walking area

Players: Groups of 1–4

Supplies: Cones

Skills: Walking, pacing

A walking course is set up using cones. If desired, a map can be drawn to provide path directions to students. If a map is used, this activity serves as a precursor to an orienteering lesson presented below. Students can walk along, with a partner, or in groups. The only rule is that they have to be moving and remain on the course for a predetermined time. This activity is not intended to take an entire period. In fact, 10–15 minutes is sufficient. This offers an excellent opportunity for teachers to walk with students and get to know them as individuals.

Quiet Cooperation (Cooperative Activity)

Formation: Groups of 10–12

Supplies: 1 marking spot for each student

Students stand in a line shoulder to shoulder with a marking spot under their feet. Without talking, making any noise, or touching the gym floor, students get in order using these criteria:

1. Number of pets (fewest to most).
2. Alphabetical by first name (father's, mother's, or pet name can also be used).
3. Alphabetical by last name.
4. Month of birthday (January to December or vice versa).
5. Shortest to tallest.

Objectives:

To perform a locomotor movement and manipulate an object simultaneously

To perform rhythmic movements in folk dances

To appreciate the origin of folk dances

To understand the cultural differences among students from different backgrounds

NASPE National Standards:

Introductory Activity: 1, 3, 5
Fitness Activity: 1, 4, 5, 6
Lesson Focus: 1, 2, 3, 4
Game: 1, 3, 5

Equipment Required:

Equipment for the Challenge Course
Music for games
Music for rhythmic activities

Instructional Activities	Teaching Hints
Introductory Activity — Jumping and Hopping Patterns	
Students jump or hop to a target area and return with a different pattern. Many combinations can be devised with the basic idea being to develop a pattern to get to the target and another to return to home spot. An example is: Jump in all directions and hop back to place; or three jumps forward and a half twist, three jumps back to place, and a half twist.	Encourage students to develop personal combinations of movement. Increase the distance of movement as the patterns are developed.
Fitness Development Activity — Challenge Course	
Design a course around the perimeter of the area using the following ideas: 1. Step on jumping box, dismount to tumbling mat and do a forward roll. 2. Run and weave through four wands held upright by cones. 3. Handwalk across a horizontal ladder or do a flexed-arm hang from a climbing rope for 5 seconds. 4. Step on and off three jumping boxes (small-large-small). 5. Agility run through hoops. 6. Perform jump turns. 7. Leap over a magic rope held taut with two chairs or jumping boxes. 8. Hop on one foot. 9. Do a logroll across a tumbling mat. 10. Alternate going over and under six obstacles (cones and wands or hoops). 11. Crouch jump or scooter movements the length of a balance-beam bench. 12. Slide through a parallel tumbling mat maze (mats stood on their sides).	Move through the challenge course with quality movements rather than speed. Distribute youngsters throughout the course instead of starting them at one common point. Stop the class at regular intervals to perform flexibility and strength development activities. Change directions periodically. This helps prevent a build-up of students at slower moving stations.

Lesson Focus — Rhythmic Movement Skills (1)

Make dances easy for students to learn by implementing some of the following techniques:

Rhythms should be taught like other sport skills. Avoid striving for perfection so students know it is acceptable to make mistakes. Teach a variety of dances rather than one or two in depth in case some students find it difficult to master a specific dance.

1. Teach the dances without using partners.
2. Allow youngsters to move in any direction without left-right orientation.
3. Use scattered formation instead of circles.
4. Emphasize strong movements such as clapping and stamping to increase involvement.
5. Play the music at a slower speed when first learning the dance.

The Bird Dance (Chicken Dance)

Music Source: WWCD-4903; WWC-9126

Formation: Circle or scatter formation, partners facing

Directions:

Measures	Part I Action
1	Four snaps—thumb and fingers, hands up
2	Four flaps—arms up and down, elbows bent
3	Four wiggles—hips, knees bent low
4	Four claps
5–16	Repeat action of measures 1–4 three times

Measures Part II Action

1–8 With a partner either do a right-hand star with 16 skips or 16 walking steps, or do an elbow swing. (Skip, 2, 3, … 15, change hands)

9–16 Repeat with the left hand. On the last four counts of the last swing, everyone changes partners. If dancing in a circle formation, partners B advance forward counterclockwise to the next partner A. If dancing in a scattered formation, everyone scrambles to find a new partner. (Skip, 2, 3, … 12, change partners)

Csebogar (Hungarian)

Music Source: WWCD 1042;

Formation: Single circle, partners facing center, hands joined with partners B on the right

Directions:

Measures Part I Action

1–4 Take seven slides to the left. (Slide, 2, 3, 4, 5, 6, 7, change)

5–8 Take seven slides to the right. (Back, 2, 3, 4, 5, 6, 7, stop)

9–12 Take three skips to the center and stamp on the fourth beat. Take three skips backward to place and stamp on the eighth beat. (Forward, 2, 3, stamp; Backward, 2, 3, stamp)

13–16 Hook right elbows with partner and turn around twice in place, skipping. (Swing, 2, 3, 4, 5, 6, 7, 8)

Part II Action (Partners face each other in a single circle with hands joined.)

17–20 Holding both of partner's hands, take four draw steps (step, close) toward the center of the circle. (Step-close, 2-close, 3-close, 4-close)

21–24 Take four draw steps back to place. (Step-close, 2-close, 3-close, 4-close)

25–26 Go toward the center of the circle with two draw steps. (In-close, 2-close)

27–28 Take two draw steps back to place. (Out-close, 2-close)

29–32 Hook elbows and repeat the elbow swing, finishing with a shout and facing the center of the circle in the original formation. (Swing, 2, 3, 4, 5, "Csebogar")

Crested Hen (Danish)

Music Source: WWCD-1042

Formation: Sets of three. One child is designated the center child.

Directions:

Measures Part I Action

1–4 Dancers in each set form a circle. Starting with a stamp with the left foot, each set circles to the left, using step-hops. (Stamp and, 2 and, 3 and, 4 and, 5 and, 6 and, 7 and, stop)

5–8 The figure is repeated. Dancers reverse direction, beginning again with a stamp with the left foot and following with step-hops. The change of direction should be vigorous and definite, with the left foot crossing over the right. At the end of the sequence, two dancers release each other's hands to break the circle and stand on either side of the center person, forming a line of three while retaining joined hands with the center dancer. (Stamp and, 2 and, 3 and, 4 and, 5 and, 6 and, 7 and, line)

Part II Action (During this part, the dancers use the step-hop continuously while making the pattern figures)

9–10 The dancer on the right moves forward in an arc to the left and dances under the arch formed by the other two. (Under and, 2 and, 3 and, 4 and)

11–12 After the right dancer has gone through, the two forming the arch turn under (dishrag), to form once again a line of three. (Turn and, 2 and, 3 and, 4 and)

13–16 The dancer on the left then repeats the pattern, moving forward in an arc under the arch formed by the other two, who turn under to unravel the line. (Under and, 2 and, 3 and, 4 and; Turn and, 2 and, 3 and, circle)

As soon as Part II is completed, dancers again join hands in a small circle. The entire dance is repeated. Another of the three can be designated the center dancer.

Bingo (American)

Music Source: WWCD-FDN

Skills: Walking, right-and-left grand

Formation: Double circle, partners side by side and facing counterclockwise, partners A on the inside and inside hands joined.

Note: Bingo is a favorite of young people. The singing must be brisk and loud. The dance is in three parts.

Directions:

Part I: Partners walk counterclockwise around the circle, singing the following refrain. (Walk, 2, 3, … 15, face center)

Part II: All join hands to form a single circle, partner B on partner A's right. They sing (spelling out) with these actions.

Action

All take four steps into the center.

All take four steps backward.

All take four steps forward again.

Take four steps backward, drop hands, and face partner.

Part III: Shake right hands with the partner, calling out B on the first heavy note. All walk forward, passing their partner, to meet the oncoming person with a left handshake, calling out I on the next chord. Continue to the third person with a right handshake, sounding out the N. Pass on to the fourth person, giving a left handshake and a G. Instead of a handshake with the fifth person, face each other, raise the arms high above the head, shake all over, and sound out a long, drawn-out O. The fifth person becomes the new partner, and the dance is repeated.

Variation: The dance can be adapted to the use of a parachute. At the end of Part II (the end of the line "And Bingo was his name") partners A face the chute and hold it with both hands, lifting it to shoulder level. Partners B drop their hands from the parachute and get ready to move clockwise. On each of the letters B-I-N-G-O, they move inside the first A, outside the next, and so on, for five changes. They then take a new place as indicated and get ready to repeat the dance. The next sequence can have partners B remaining in place, holding the chute, while partners A move counterclockwise.

Grand March (American)

Music Source: WWCD-WOF2 or any good march or square dance record

Skills: Controlled walking, marching, grand march figures

Formation: Partners B are on the left side of the room, facing the end, and partners A are on the right side, facing the same end. This is the foot of the hall. The teacher or caller stands at the other end of the room, the head of the hall. An alternative formation is to put half of the class on each side of the room and to designate each half with different colored pinnies.

Directions:

Call	Action
Down the center by twos.	The lines march forward to the foot of the hall, turn the corner, meet at the center of the foot of the hall, and march in couples toward the caller, with inside hands joined. The B's line should be on the proper side so that, when the couples come down the center, A is on B's left. Odd couples are numbered 1, 3, 5, and so on. Even couples are numbered 2, 4, 6, and so on.
Twos left and right.	The odd couples go left and the even couples go right around the room and meet at the foot of the hall.
Down the center by fours.	The couples walk down the center, four abreast.
Separate by twos.	When they approach the caller, odd couples go left and even couples right. They meet again at the foot of the hall.
Form arches.	Instead of coming down the center, odd couples form arches and even couples tunnel under. Each continues around the sides of the hall to meet at the head.
Other couples arch.	Even couples arch, and odd couples tunnel under. Each continues around the sides of the room to the foot.
Over and under.	The first odd couple arches over the first even couple, then ducks under the second even couple's arch. Each couple goes over the first couple and under the next. Continue around to the head of the hall.
Pass right through.	As the lines come toward each other, they mesh and pass through each other in the following fashion: All drop handholds. Each B walks between the A and B of the opposite couple and continues walking to the foot of the hall.
Down the center by fours.	Go down the center four abreast.
Fours left and right.	The first four go left around the room, and the second four go right. The fours meet at the foot of the hall.
Down the center by eights.	Go eight abreast down the center.
Grapevine.	All persons in each line join hands and keep them joined. The leader takes either end of the first line and starts around the room with the line trailing. The other lines hook on to form one long line.
Wind it up.	The leader winds up the group in a spiral formation, like a clock spring. The leader makes the circles smaller and smaller until he or she is in the center.
Reverse (unwind).	The leader turns and faces in the opposite direction and walks between the lines of winding dancers. The leader unwinds the line and leads it around the room.
Everybody swing.	After the line is unwound, everybody does a square dance swing.

Apat Apat (Philippines)

Music Source: WWCD-RM4; WWC-572
Skills: Walking; star hold
Formation: Double circle of partners facing counterclockwise with inside hands joined

Directions:

Measures	Action
	Introduction
1	All face counterclockwise with inside hands joined and walk forward 4 steps. On count 4, release hands and execute a half turn right to face clockwise. (Walk, 2, 3, turn)
2	Take 4 walking steps forward clockwise. Release hands on the fourth step and face partner. (Walk, 2, 3, face)
3	Walk 4 steps backward away from partner. (Away, 2, 3, 4)
4	Walk 4 steps forward toward partner with each partner taking a quarter turn to the right on the fourth count. Partners will be facing in opposite directions. (Forward, 2, 3, right turn)
5	Walk forward 4 steps with partners moving in opposite directions. (Forward, 2, 3, 4)
6	Walk backward 4 steps to meet partner. (Backward, 2, 3, 4)
7	Face partner. With right hand star (join right hands with elbows bent) walk clockwise around partner 4 steps in place. (Star, 2, 3, 4)
8	Release hands, inside circle youngsters walk forward 4 steps counterclockwise to meet next partner. Outside circle youngsters turn a half turn in place to wait for new partner.

Repeat the dance.

Game Activity

Whistle March

Supplies: Music
Skill: Moving rhythmically

Brisk marching music is useful for this game. Children are scattered around the room, walking in various directions and keeping time to the music. A whistle is blown a number of times. On this signal, lines are formed of that precise number of children, no more and no fewer. To form the lines, children stand side by side with elbows touching. As soon as a line of the proper number is formed, they begin to march to the music around the room. Any children left over go to the center of the room and remain there until the next signal. On the next whistle signal (a single blast), the lines break up, and all walk individually around the room in various directions. When forming new lines, it may be helpful to stipulate that players must group with different players each time.

Arches

Supplies: Music
Skills: Moving rhythmically

The game is similar to London Bridge. An arch is placed in the playing area. (To form an arch, two players stand facing one another with hands joined and arms raised.) When the music starts, the other players move in a circle, passing under the arch. Suddenly, the music stops, and the arch is brought down by dropping the hands. All players caught in an arch immediately pair off to form other arches, keeping in a general circle formation. If a caught player does not have a partner, he waits in the center of the circle until one is available. The last players caught (or left) form arches for the next game.
Variation: Different types of music can be used, and children can move according to the pattern of the music.

Home Base

Supplies: Cones to delineate the area, four pinnies
Skills: Reaction time, locomotor movements, body management

Place a number of marking spots on the floor throughout the area. Divide the class into groups of 5 or 6. Ask each group to quickly line up with one person on a marking spot and the rest of the players behind in single file. The person on the spot is designated as the team captain. A locomotor movement is called and all players do this movement throughout the area. When "Home base" is called, the captains quickly find the closest spot and their respective squad members line up behind them. The first team to return to proper position (standing in a straight line) is declared the winner. Avoid calling "Home base" until the students are thoroughly mixed. A number of different formations can be specified that students must assume upon return to their home base.

Objectives:
To travel throughout the area and be able to avoid or catch another individual

To jump a rope turned by others

To know the difference in long-rope jumping between entering front and back doors

NASPE National Standards:
Introductory Activity: 1, 2, 5
Fitness Activity: 1, 4, 6
Lesson Focus: 2, 3, 4, 5
Game: 1, 3, 5

Equipment Required:
Music for Walk, Trot, and Jog
Long jump ropes (two for each group of four children)

Instructional Activities	Teaching Hints

Introductory Activity — Group Tag

A number of players are designated to be it. On signal, they try to tag other players. If a player is tagged, that player becomes it and must try to tag another. In other words, each person who is it tags only one player. If players want to be "safe," they must stand toe-to-toe in a group of three or more students.

Encourage students to say "you're it" when they tag someone.

If students can't catch someone, they can give up being it.

Fitness Development Activity — Walk, Trot, and Jog

Move to the following signals:
1. One drumbeat—walk.
2. Two drumbeats—trot.
3. Three drumbeats—jog.
4. Whistle—freeze and perform exercises.

Perform various strength and flexibility exercises between bouts of walk, trot, and jog. Examples are:
1. Bend and Twist
2. Sitting Stretch
3. Push-Up Challenges
4. Abdominal Challenges
5. Trunk Twister
6. Body Circles
7. Crab Walk

Tape alternating segments of silence and music to signal duration of exercise. Music segments indicate aerobic activity (30–45 seconds); intervals of silence announce flexibility and strength development activities (30 seconds).

Assure that students run under control (not as fast as they can) and in the same direction.

Allow students to perform at a level they feel comfortable. Youngsters are genetically different and should not be expected to do the same amount of exercise repetitions.

Lesson Focus — Long-Rope-Jumping Skills

1. Run through turning rope from front-door approach.
2. Run through turning rope from back-door approach.
3. Try different approaches, a few jumps and varied exits
   a. Run in front door, out back door.
   b. Run in front door and out front door.
   c. Run in back door and out back door.
   d. Run in back door and out front door.
   e. Run in front or back door, jump and do a quarter, half, and full turn.
   f. Add individual rope.
4. Hot Pepper: *Gradually* increase the speed of the rope
5. High Water: *Gradually* raise the height of the rope while it is turned.
6. Have more than one child jump at a time. Students can enter in pairs or any other combination. Have jumpers change positions while jumping.
7. Have jumper attempt to jump while holding a beanbag or playground ball between the knees.
8. Have one of the turners jump the long rope.
9. Play catch with a partner while jumping the rope.
10. Egg Beater: Two long ropes are turned simultaneously with four turners.

Turning the rope is a difficult skill for young children. It must be practiced regularly until children can maintain an even, steady rhythm. Effective turning is requisite to successful jumping. If turning is not rhythmic, skilled jumpers will have problems. Youngsters must be taught: Learn to turn first, then learn to jump.

Front door means entering from the side where the rope is turning forward and toward the jumper after it reaches its peak. Back door means entering from the side where the rope is turning backward and away from the jumper. To enter front door, the jumper follows the rope in and jumps when it completes the turn.

11. Double Dutch: Requires two long ropes turned alternately. Rope near jumper is turned back door and far rope front door. To start turning, begin with the ropes held tight. Start turning in small circles and gradually move together. To enter back door, the jumper waits until the rope reaches its peak and moves in as the rope moves downward.

Game Activity

Fly Trap

Supplies: None

Skills: Fundamental locomotor movements

Half of the class is scattered around the playing area, sitting on the floor in cross-legged fashion. These children form the trap. The rest of the players are flies and they buzz around the seated children. When a whistle is blown, the flies must freeze where they are. If any of the trappers can touch a fly, that youngster sits down at that spot and becomes a trapper. The trappers must keep their seats glued to the floor. The game continues until all of the flies are caught. Some realism is given to the game if the flies make buzzing sounds and move their arms as wings. Some experience with the game enables the teacher to determine how far apart to place the seated children. After most of the flies have been caught, the groups trade places. Change the method of locomotion.

Trades

Supplies: None

Skills: Imagery, running, dodging

Designate two lines at opposite ends of the area. The class is divided into two teams of equal number. One team, the chasers, stands on one of the lines. The other team, the runners, starts on the other line. The runners move toward the chasers while reciting the following dialogue:

Runners: *Here we come.*
Chasers: *Where from?*
Runners: *New Orleans.*
Chasers: *What's your trade?*
Runners: *Lemonade.*
Chasers: *Show us some.*

The runners move close to the other team's goal line and proceed to act out an occupation or a specific task that they have chosen previously. The opponents try to guess what the pantomime represents. When a correct guess is made, the chasers try to tag the running team before they reach the goal line. Any runner tagged must join the chasers. The game is repeated with roles reversed. The team ending with the greater number of players is the winner. If a team has trouble guessing the pantomime, the other team should provide hints. Teams also should be encouraged to have a number of activities selected so that little time is consumed in choosing the next activity to be pantomimed.

Fox Hunt

Supplies: None

Skills: Running, dodging

Two players form trees by facing each other and holding hands. The third member of the group is a fox and stands between the hands of the trees. Three players are identified as foxes without trees and three players are designated as hounds. The hounds try to tag the foxes that are not in trees. The extra foxes may move to a tree and displace the fox that is standing in the tree. In addition, the foxes in trees may leave the safety of their trees at any time. If the hound tags a fox, their roles are reversed immediately, the fox becoming the hound. The game should be stopped at regular intervals to allow the players who are trees to change places with the foxes and hounds. Different locomotor movements can be specified to add variety to the game.

LP 53

Objectives:
To hear and move to different rhythms
To support and control body weight in
a variety of stunts and tumbling
activities
To participate in game activities in a
cooperative manner

NASPE National Standards:
Introductory Activity: 1, 2, 5
Fitness Activity: 1, 3, 4, 6
Lesson Focus: 1, 2, 3, 5
Game: 1, 3

Equipment Required:
Equipment for Challenge Course
Tumbling mats
Music for game

Instructional Activities	Teaching Hints

Introductory Activity — Addition Tag

Two couples are it, and each stands with inside hands joined. These are the taggers. The other children run individually. The couples move around the playground, trying to tag with the free hands. The first person tagged joins the couple, making a trio. The three then chase until they catch a fourth. Once a fourth person is caught, the four divide and form two couples, adding another set of taggers to the game. This continues until all children are tagged.

The game moves faster if started with two couples.

A tag is legal only when the couple or group of three keeps their hands joined.

Fitness Development Activity — Challenge Course

Design a course around the perimeter of the area using the following ideas:
1. Step on jumping box, dismount to tumbling mat and do a forward roll.
2. Run and weave through four wands held upright by cones.
3. Handwalk across a horizontal ladder or do a flexed-arm hang from a climbing rope for 5 seconds.
4. Step on and off three jumping boxes (small-large-small).
5. Agility run through hoops.
6. Perform jump turns.
7. Leap over a magic rope held taut with two chairs or jumping boxes.
8. Hop on one foot.
9. Do a logroll across a tumbling mat.
10. Alternate going over and under six obstacles (cones and wands or hoops).
11. Crouch jump or scooter movements the length of a balance-beam bench.
12. Slide through a parallel tumbling mat maze (mats stood on their sides).

Move through the challenge course with quality movements rather than speed.

Distribute youngsters throughout the course instead of starting them at one common point.

Stop the class at regular intervals to perform flexibility and strength development activities.

Change directions periodically. This helps prevent a build-up of students at slower moving stations.

Lesson Focus — Gymnastics Skills (2)

Animal Movements

Measuring Worm

From a front-leaning rest position, keeping the knees stiff, inch the feet up as close as possible to the hands. Regain position by inching forward with the hands. Keep the knees straight, with the necessary bending occurring at the hips.

Mule Kick

Stoop down and place the hands on the floor in front of the feet. The arms are the front legs of the mule. Kick out with the legs while the weight is supported momentarily on the arms. Taking the weight on the hands is important. The stunt can be learned in two stages. First, practice taking the weight momentarily on the hands. Next, add the kick.

Walrus Walk

Begin in a front-leaning rest position, with fingers pointed outward. Make progress by moving both hands forward at the same time. Try to clap the hands with each step.

Six groups of activities in this lesson ensure that youngsters receive a variety of experiences. Pick a few activities from each group and teach them alternately. For example, teach one or two animal movements, then a tumbling and inverted balance, followed by a balance stunt, etc. Give equal time to each group of activities.

Scatter tumbling mats throughout the area so that there is little standing in line waiting for a turn.

Youngsters can do the animal walks around their mats. Many of the activities in this unit do not have to be performed on the mat.

Tumbling and Inverted Balances
Frog Handstand (Tip-Up)

Squat down on the mat, placing the hands flat, with fingers pointing forward and elbows inside and pressed against the inner part of the knees. Lean forward, using the leverage of the elbows against the knees, and balance on the hands. Hold for 5 seconds. Return to position. The head does not touch the mat at any time. The hands may be turned in slightly if this makes better contact between the elbows and the insides of the thighs.

Half Teeter-Totter

This is continued lead-up activity for the Handstand. Begin in the lunge position and shift the weight to the hands. Kick the legs up in the air to a 135-degree angle, then return to the feet. This activity is similar to the Switcheroo, except that the feet are kicked higher without switching foot position.

Cartwheel

Start with the body in an erect position, arms outspread and legs shoulder width apart. Bend the body to the right and place the right hand on the floor. Follow this, in sequence, by the left hand, the left foot, and the right foot. Perform with a steady rhythm. Each body part should touch the floor at evenly spaced intervals. The body should be straight and extended when in the inverted position. The entire body must be in the same plane throughout the stunt, and the feet must pass directly overhead.

Balance Stunts
Leg Dip

Extend both hands and one leg forward, balancing on the other leg. Lower the body to sit on the heel and return without losing the balance or touching the floor with any part of the body. Try with the other foot.

Balance Jump

With hands and arms out to the sides and body parallel to the ground, extend one leg back and balance the weight on the other leg. Quickly change balance to the other foot, maintaining the initial position but with the feet exchanged. Keep the body parallel to the ground during the change of legs. Try with arms outstretched forward.

Seat Balance

Sit on the floor, holding the ankles in front, with elbows inside the knees. The feet are flat on the floor, and the knees are bent at approximately a right angle. Raise the legs (toes pointed) so that the knees are straight, and balance on the seat for 5 seconds.

Individual Stunts
Heelstand

Begin in a full-squat position with the arms dangling at the sides. Jump upward to full leg extension with the weight on both heels and fling the arms out diagonally. Hold momentarily, then return to position. Several movements can be done rhythmically in succession.

Wicket Walk

Bend over and touch the floor with the weight evenly distributed on the hands and feet, thus forming a wicket. Walk the wicket forward, backward, and sideward.

Knee Jump to Standing

Kneel, with seat touching the heels and toes pointing backward (shoelaces against the floor). Jump to a standing position with a vigorous upward swing of the arms. It is easier to jump from a smooth floor than from a mat, because the toes slide more readily on the floor.

A major concern for safety is the neck and back region. Overweight children are at greater risk and might be allowed to avoid tumbling and inverted balances.

All tumbling and inverted balances should be done on tumbling mat.

Children who have difficulty with the cartwheel should be instructed to concentrate on taking the weight of the body on the hands in succession (like the spokes of a wheel). They need to get the feel of the weight support and later can concentrate on getting the body into proper position. After the class has had some practice in doing cartwheels, a running approach with a skip can be added before takeoff.

Working in pairs can be helpful. One student critiques the other's performance to make sure that the key performance and safety areas are addressed.

After the activities are learned, place emphasis on correct performance emphasizing three phases:
1. Starting position
2. Execution
3. Finishing position

Keep the arms and legs as nearly vertical as possible when doing the Wicket Walk. A common error in the execution of this stunt is to keep the hands positioned too far forward of the feet.

Partner and Group Stunts

Rowboat

   Partners sit on the floor or on a mat, facing each other with legs apart and feet touching. Both grasp a wand with both hands. Pretend to row a boat. Seek a wide range of movement in the forward-backward rowing motion.

The stunt can be done without a wand by having children grasp hands.

Leapfrog

   One student forms a back. A leaper takes a running start, lays hands flat on the back at the shoulders, and vaults over the low student. Backs are formed at various heights. To form a low back, crouch down on the knees, curling into a tight ball with the head tucked well down. To form a medium back, reach down the outside of the legs from a standing position and grasp the ankles. The feet should be reasonably spread and the knees straight.

The bottom position must be stable in order to absorb the shock of the leaper. To form a high back, stand stiff-legged, bend over, and brace arms against the knees. The feet should be spread, the head down, and the body braced to absorb the vault.

Wheelbarrow

   One partner gets down on the hands with feet extended to the rear and legs apart. The other partner (the pusher) grasps partner's legs about halfway between the ankles and the knees. The wheelbarrow walks forward on the hands, supported by the pusher. Movements should be under good control.

Children have a tendency to grasp the legs too near the feet. The pusher must not push too fast. The wheelbarrow should have the head up and look forward. The pusher should carry the legs low and keep the arms extended.

Game Activity

Partner Stoop

   Supplies: Music

   Skills: Marching rhythmically

   The game follows the same basic principle of stooping as in Circle Stoop, but is played with partners. The group forms a double circle in one direction with one partner on the inside and one on the outside. When the music begins, all march in the line of direction. After a short period of marching, a signal (whistle) is sounded, and the inside circle reverses direction and marches the other way. The partners are thus separated. When the music stops, the outer circle stands still, and the partners making up the inner circle walk (or run) in any direction to rejoin their respective outer circle partners. As soon as players reach their partner, they get toe-to-toe and stoop without losing balance. The last couple to stoop and those who lose their balance go to the center of the circle and wait out the next round. Start the game walking and gradually pick up the speed of the movements when the class moves under control.

Moving the World (Cooperative Activity)

   Formation: Entire class scattered throughout area

   Supplies: One large cageball

   Using a cageball or other large ball as the world, the world is transported to different locations in the gym. The ball may not be kicked, thrown, or struck and all class members must be involved:

1. No hands can touch the world.
2. Only feet can touch the ball.
3. Half of the team must be lying on their back.
4. Only backs can touch the ball.
5. Only elbows can touch the ball and no talking is allowed.
6. Students must crab-walk.

   Teaching Tip: Directions such as "move the ball 30 ft northwest" or "move the world 25 ft in the same direction you would travel from Arcanum to Pittsburg" can be used.

Objectives:

To control body movements while moving through the Challenge Course

To perform a variety of locomotor movements in a rhythmic setting

To understand the difference between compliance and noncompliance of rules

NASPE National Standards:

Introductory Activity: 1, 5
Fitness Activity: 1, 4, 5, 6
Lesson Focus: 1, 2, 3, 5
Game: 1, 5

Equipment Required:

Equipment for Challenge Course
Music for Rhythmic Activities
Bowling pins and balls for game

Instructional Activities	Teaching Hints
Introductory Activity — High Fives	
Students move in different directions throughout the area. On signal, they are challenged to run toward a partner, jump, and give a "high five" (slap hands) while moving. Emphasis should be placed on timing so that the "high five" is given at the top of the jump.	Change the type of high fives, i.e., low, under leg, roundhouse. High fives should be given gently. No hard slapping.
Fitness Development Activity — Challenge Course	
Design a course around the perimeter of the area using the following ideas: 1. Step on jumping box, dismount to tumbling mat and do a forward roll. 2. Run and weave through four wands held upright by cones. 3. Handwalk across a horizontal ladder or do a flexed-arm hang from a climbing rope for 5 seconds. 4. Step on and off three jumping boxes (small-large-small). 5. Agility run through hoops. 6. Perform jump turns. 7. Leap over a magic rope held taut with two chairs or jumping boxes. 8. Hop on one foot. 9. Do a logroll across a tumbling mat. 10. Alternate going over and under six obstacles (cones and wands or hoops). 11. Crouch jump or scooter movements the length of a balance-beam bench. 12. Slide through a parallel tumbling mat maze (mats stood on their sides).	Move through the challenge course with quality movements rather than speed. Distribute youngsters throughout the course instead of starting them at one common point. Stop the class at regular intervals to perform flexibility and strength development activities. Change directions periodically. This helps prevent a build-up of students at slower moving stations.

Lesson Focus — Rhythmic Movement Skills (2)

Begin each lesson with a review of one or two dances youngsters know and enjoy. Review dances from lesson plan Week 13 as desired before teaching new ones.

Rhythms should be taught like other sport skills. Avoid striving for perfection so students know it is acceptable to make mistakes. Teach a variety of dances rather than one or two in depth in case some students find it difficult to master a specific dance. Make dances easy for students to learn by implementing some of the following techniques:
  1. Teach the dances without using partners.
  2. Allow youngsters to move in any direction without left-right orientation.
  3. Use scattered formation instead of circles.
  4. Emphasize strong movements such as clapping and stamping to increase involvement.
  5. Play the music at a slower speed when first learning the dance.

Wild Turkey Mixer (American)

Music Source: WWC-FFD or any music with a definite rhythm
Formation: Trios abreast facing counterclockwise around the circle
Directions:

Measures	Action
1–8	In lines of three, with the right and left person holding the near hand of the center person, all walk 16 steps forward. (Walk, 2, 3, … 16)
9–12	The center person (Wild Turkey) turns the right-hand person once around with the right elbow. (Turn, 2, 3, 4, 5, 6, 7, 8)
13–16	The Wild Turkey turns the left-hand person with the left elbow, and then moves forward to repeat the dance with the two new people ahead. (Turn, 2, 3, 4; Forward, 2, 3, 4)

This dance can be adapted to other pieces of music. With a faster tempo, the elbow swings are done with a skip instead of a walk.

Patty Cake (Heel and Toe) Polka (International)

Music Source: WWCD-FDN

Formation: Double circle, partners facing, A partners in the inner circle with back to the center. Both hands are joined with partner. A's left and B's right foot are free.

Directions:

Measures	Part I Action
1–2	Heel-toe twice with A's left and B's right foot. (Heel, toe, heel, toe)
3–4	Take four slides sideward to A's left, progressing counterclockwise. Do not transfer the weight on the last count. Finish with A's right and B's left foot free. (Slide, 2, 3, 4)
5–8	Repeat the pattern of measures 1–4, starting with A's right and B's left foot, progressing clockwise. Finish with the partners separated and facing. (Heel, toe, heel, toe; slide, 2, 3, 4)

Measures	Part II Action
9	Clap right hands with partner three times. (Right, 2, 3)
10	Clap left hands with partner three times. (Left, 2, 3)
11	Clap both hands with partner three times. (Both, 2, 3)
12	Slap own knees three times. (Knees, 2, 3)
13–14	Right elbow swing with partner. Partners hook right elbows and swing once around with four walking steps, finishing with A's back to center. (Swing, 2, 3, 4)
15–16	Progress left to a new partner with four walking steps. (Left, 2, 3, 4)

Repeat the entire dance with the new partner.

Oh, Susanna (American)

Music Source: WWCD-1043

Formation: Single circle, all facing center, partner B on the right

Directions:

Measures	Part I Action
1–4	Partners B walk forward four steps and back four, as partners A clap hands. (Forward, 2, 3, 4; Back, 2, 3, 4)
5–8	Reverse, with A's walking forward and back, and B's clapping time. (Forward, 2, 3, 4; Back, 2, 3, 4)

Measures	Part II Action
1–8	Partners face each other, and all do a grand right and left by grasping the partner's right hand, then passing to the next person with a left-hand hold. Continue until reaching the seventh person, who becomes the new partner. (Face, 2, 3, 4, 5, 6, 7, 8)

Measures	Chorus
1–16	All join hands in promenade position with the new partner and walk counterclockwise around the circle for two full choruses singing: "Oh Susanna, oh don't you cry for me, For I come from Alabama with my banjo on my knee." (Promenade, 2, 3, … 16)

Repeat the dance from the beginning, each time with a new partner. For variety in the chorus, skip instead of walk, or walk during the first chorus and swing one's partner in place during the second chorus.

Troika (Russian)

Music Source: WWCD-3528; WWC-3528

Formation: Trios face counterclockwise. Start with hands joined in a line of three. The body weight is on the left foot; the right foot is free.

Directions:

Measures	Part I Action
1	Take four running steps diagonally forward right, starting with the right foot. (Diagonal, 2, 3, 4)
2	Take four running steps diagonally forward left, starting with the right foot. (Diagonal, 2, 3, 4)
3–4	Take eight running steps in a forward direction, starting with the right foot. (Forward, 2, 3, 4, 5, 6, 7, 8)

| 5–6 | The center dancer and the left-hand partner raise joined hands to form an arch and run in place. Meanwhile, the right-hand partner moves counterclockwise around the center dancer with eight running steps, goes under the arch, and back to place. The center dancer unwinds by turning under the arch. (Under, 2, 3, 4; Turn, 2, 3, 4) |
| 7–8 | Repeat the pattern of measures 5 and 6, with the left-hand partner running under the arch formed by the center dancer and the right-hand partner. (Under, 2, 3, 4; Turn, 2, 3, circle) |

Measures	**Part II Action**
9–11	The trio joins hands and circles left with 12 running steps. (Run, 2, 3, 4, 5, 6, 7, 8, 9, 10, 11, 12)
12	Three stamps in place (counts 1–3), pause (count 4). (Stamp, 2, 3, pause)
13–15	The trio circles right with 12 running steps, opening out at the end to re-form in lines of three facing counterclockwise. (Run, 2, 3, 4, 5, 6, 7, 8, open, 10, 11, 12)
16	The center dancer releases each partner's hand and runs under the opposite arch of joined hands to advance to a new pair ahead.

Right- and left-hand partners run in place while waiting for a new center dancer to join them in a new trio. (Stamp, 2, line, pause)

Green Sleeves (English)

Music Source: WWCD-1042

Skills: Walking, star formation, over and under

Formation: Double circle with couples in sets of four, facing counterclockwise. Two couples form a set and are numbered 1 and 2. Inside hands of each couple are joined.

Directions:

Measures	Call	Action
1–8	Walk	Walk forward 16 steps.
9–12	Right-hand star	Each member of couple 1 turns individually to face the couple behind. All join right hands and circle clockwise (star) for eight steps
13–16	Left-hand star	Reverse direction and form a left-hand star. This should bring couple 1 back to place facing in the original direction.
17–20	Over and under	Couple 2 arches and couple 1 backs under four steps while couple 2 moves forward four steps. Couple 1 then arches and couple 2 backs under (four steps for each).
21–24	Over and under	Repeat the action of measures 17–20.

La Raspa (Mexican)

Music Source: WWCD-05117

Skills: Bleking step, running, elbow swing

Formation: Partners are facing, couples scattered around the room.

Directions: La raspa means "the rasp" or "the file," and the dance movements are supposed to represent a rasp or file in action. Directions are the same for both partners.

Part I: To begin, the partners face each other, partner B with hands at sides and partner A with hands behind the back.

Measures	**Action**
1–4	Beginning right, take one Bleking step. (Slow, slow, fast, fast, fast)
5–8	Turn slightly counterclockwise away from partner (right shoulder to right shoulder) and, beginning with a jump on the left foot, repeat measures 1–4. (Slow, slow, fast, fast, fast)
9–12	Repeat action of measures 1–4, facing opposite direction (left shoulder to left shoulder). (Slow, slow, fast, fast, fast)
13–16	Repeat action of measures 1–4, facing partner. (Slow, slow, fast, fast, fast)

Part II: Partners hook right elbows; left elbows are bent and left hands are pointed toward the ceiling.

Measures	**Action**
1–4	Do a right elbow swing, using eight running or skipping steps. Release and clap the hands on the eighth count. (Swing, 2, 3, 4, 5, 6, 7, clap)
5–8	Do a left elbow swing, using eight running or skipping steps. Release and clap the hands on the eighth count. (Swing, 2, 3, 4, 5, 6, 7, clap)
9–16	Repeat the actions of measures 1–8.

Variations:

Face partner (all should be in a single-circle formation for this version) and do a grand right and left around the circle. Repeat Part I with a new partner.

All face center or face a partner and do the Bleking step. On each pause, clap own hands twice.

Pata Pata (African)

Music Source: WWCD-3528; WWC-3528
Skills: Toe touches, knee lift, quarter turns
Formation: Single lines facing in one direction
Directions:

Measures	Action
1–2	Start with feet together; touch right foot sideward right and return next to left foot. (Right touch, together)
3–4	Same as above with left foot. (Left touch, together)
5	With feet together, move toes out keeping heels on the ground. (Toes out)
6	Turn heels out keeping toes on the ground. (Heels out)
7	Turn heels in keeping toes on the ground. (Heels in)
8	Turn toes in keeping heels on the ground. The feet should now be together. (Toes in)
9–12	Raise right knee diagonally in front of the body and then touch right foot next to left foot. Repeat for counts 11–12. (Lift, touch, lift, touch)
13–16	Kick left foot forward while turning a ¼ turn to the right with weight on the right foot. Step backward left, right, left. Feet should be together at the end of count 16. (Kick, left, right, left)

Repeat the dance.

Variation: When youngsters learn the footwork, it is enjoyable to add some arm movements to the dance. At count 5, with elbows close to the body, raise hands up and straight out palms up. Count 6 turn palms down with elbows out. Count 7, turn palms up. Count 8, turn palms down.

Game Activity

Fox Hunt

Supplies: None

Skills: Running, dodging

Two players form trees by facing each other and holding hands. The third member of the group is a fox and stands between the hands of the trees. Three players are identified as foxes without trees and three players are designated as hounds. The hounds try to tag the foxes that are not in trees. The extra foxes may move to a tree and displace the fox that is standing in the tree. In addition, the foxes in trees may leave the safety of their trees at any time. If the hound tags a fox, their roles are reversed immediately, the fox becoming the hound. The game should be stopped at regular intervals to allow the players who are trees to change places with the foxes and hounds. Different locomotor movements can be specified to add variety to the game.

Steal the Treasure

Supplies: A bowling pin

Skill: Dodging

A playing area about 20 ft square is outlined, with a small circle in the center. A bowling pin placed in the small circle (hula hoop) as the treasure. Two guards are selected to protect the treasure. The guards can move as far from the treasure as they like to tag a player. Anyone tagged must retire and wait for the next game. To successfully steal the treasure, a player must pick it up cleanly without getting tagged. The guards tag them when they come too near. If the treasure is knocked over by a player trying to steal it, that player must also wait out a turn. There is a delicate balance for the guards between being too far from the treasure and staying too near the treasure and never tagging anyone. If the guards tag all players, they are declared billionaires.

Addition Tag

Supplies: None

Skills: Running, dodging

Two or more couples are it and each stands with inside hands joined. These are the taggers. The rest of the class runs individually. The couples move around the area, trying to tag with the free hands. The first person tagged joins the couple, making a trio. The three then chase until they catch a fourth. Once a fourth person is caught, the four divide and form two couples, adding another set of taggers to the game. This continues until the majority of the players are tagged. The game moves faster if started with two couples. A tag is legal only when the couple or group of three keeps their hands joined. The game can be used as an introductory activity, since all children are active.

DPE Curriculum Guide – Lesson Plans
Basketball Skills and Lead-up Activities (1)
Level II – Week 17

Objectives:
To understand the basic rules of
   basketball
To dribble, pass and shoot a basketball
   with proper form
To participate in basketball lead-up
   games

NASPE National Standards:
Introductory Activity: 1, 5
Fitness Activity: 1, 4, 5, 6
Lesson Focus: 2, 3, 5
Game: 2, 3, 5

Equipment Required:
Music for Aerobic Fitness
One junior basketball or playground ball
   per student
8 hoops or individual mats
Pinnies

Instructional Activities	Teaching Hints

Introductory Activity — Squad Leader Movements

Organize class into small groups of 3–4 students. Each group moves around the area, following a leader. When a change is signaled, the last person goes to the head of the line and becomes the squad leader.

Encourage leaders to keep the group moving. The minimum activity is jogging in place.

Fitness Development Activity — Aerobic Fitness and Partner Resistance Exercises

Students find a partner and lead each other in aerobic activities. Partners switch leader and follower roles after each partner resistance exercise. This routine assumes that students have previous aerobic fitness experience. If not, the aerobic activities will have to be led by the teacher.

Bounce and clap	25 seconds
Arm curl-up	45 seconds
Jumping Jack variations	25 seconds
Camelback	45 seconds
Lunge variations	25 seconds
Fist pull apart	45 seconds
Directional runs	25 seconds
Scissors	45 seconds
Rhythmic running	25 seconds
Butterfly	45 seconds
Bounce with body twist	25 seconds
Resistance push-up	45 seconds

Walk, stretch, and relax for a minute or two.

Tape alternating segments of silence and music to signal duration of exercise. Music segments indicate aerobic activity (25 seconds); intervals of silence announce partner resistance exercises (45 seconds).

Teach the exercises first. See Chapter 13 in the text for complete descriptions. A sign with aerobic activities on one side and partner resistance exercises on the other helps students remember the activities. The signs can be held upright by cones and shared by 2–4 students.

Take 6–10 seconds to complete a resistance exercise.

Lesson Focus — Basketball Skills (1)

Skills
Practice the following skills:
1. Chest (or Two-Hand) Pass

   For the chest, or two-hand, pass, one foot is ahead of the other, with the knees flexed slightly. The ball is released at chest level, with the fingers spread on each side of the ball. The elbows remain close to the body, and the ball is released by extending the arms and snapping the wrists as one foot moves toward the receiver.
2. Catching

   Receiving the ball is a most important fundamental skill. Many turnovers involve failure to handle a pass properly. The receiver should move toward the pass with the fingers spread and relaxed, reaching for the ball with elbows bent and wrists relaxed. The hands should give as the ball comes in.
3. Dribbling

   Dribbling is used to advance the ball, break for a basket, or maneuver out of a difficult situation. The dribbler's knees and trunk should be slightly flexed, with hands and eyes forward. The fingertips propel the ball with the hand cupped and relaxed. There is little arm motion. Younger children tend to slap at the ball rather than push it. The dribbling hand should be alternated, and practice in changing hands is essential.

Instructional cues help students focus on proper performance of passing.
1. Fingers spread with thumbs behind the ball.
2. Elbows in; extend through the ball.
3. Step forward, extend arms, and rotate hands slightly inward.
4. Throw at chest level to the receiver.
5. For bounce passes, bounce the ball past the halfway point nearer the receiver.

Instructional cues for catching include the following:
1. Move into the path of the ball.
2. Reach and give with the ball (absorb the force of the ball by reaching and bringing the ball to the chest).

4. Shooting—One-Hand (set) Push Shot

The one-hand push shot is used as a set shot for young children. The ball is held at shoulder-eye level in the supporting hand with the shooting hand slightly below center and behind the ball. As the shot begins, the supporting (nonshooting) hand remains in contact as long as possible. The shooting hand then takes over with fingertip control, and the ball rolls off the center three fingers. The hand and wrist follow through, finishing in a flexed position. Vision is focused on the hoop during the shot. Proper technique should be emphasized rather than accuracy.

Drills

Passing and Catching Drills

1. Slide Circle Drill

In the slide circle drill, a circle of 4–6 players slides around a person in the center. The center person passes to and receives from the sliding players. After the ball has gone around the circle twice, another player takes the center position.

2. Circle-Star Drill

With only 5 players, a circle-star drill is particularly effective. Players pass to every other player, and the path of the ball forms a star. The star drill works well as a relay. Any odd number of players will cause the ball to go to all participants, assuring that all receive equal practice.

Dribbling Drills

3. Random Dribbling

Each child has a ball. Dribbling is done in place, varied by using left and right hands. Develop a sequence of body positions (i.e., standing, kneeling, lying on the side, on two feet and one hand). Encourage players to develop a sequence by dribbling a certain number of times in each selected position. Dribble with each hand.

4. One-Hand Control Drill

Begin with the right hand holding the ball. Make a half circle around the right leg to the back. Bounce the ball between the legs (back to front) and catch it with the right hand and move it around the body again. After continuing for a short time, switch to the left hand.

Shooting Drills

5. Basic Shooting Drill

In one simple shooting drill, players form files of no more than 4 people, and take turns shooting a long and a short shot or some other prescribed series of shots.

6. Set-Shot Drill

In the set-shot drill, players are scattered around a basket in a semicircle, with a leader in charge. Players should be close enough to the basket so that they can shoot accurately. The leader passes to each in turn to take a shot. The leader chases the ball after the shot. A bit of competition can be injected by allowing a successful shooter to take one step back for the next shot, or a player can shoot until he misses.

Instructional cues for dribbling include the following:
1. Push the ball to the floor. Don't slap it.
2. Push the ball forward when moving.
3. Eyes forward and head up.

Shooting instructional cues focus on proper form:
1. Keep the shooting elbow near the body.
2. Bend the knees and use the legs.
3. Release the ball off the fingertips.

Baskets should be lowered to 8 or 9 ft, depending on the size of the youngsters.

Lowered baskets help students shoot with proper form. Shooting is not a throw. If students have to throw the ball at the basket, it is too high.

Practice the skills in an individual manner as much as possible. The best alternative is a ball for every student to shoot and dribble. Reduce taking turns as much as possible when practicing skills.

Use junior basketballs or smaller for third and fourth grade students. It is difficult for students to learn skills with regulation size balls. They are too heavy and too large in diameter for youngsters.

Basketball Lead-up Activities

Birdie in the Cage

Supplies: A soccer ball, basketball, or volleyball

Skills: Passing, catching, intercepting

Players are placed in circle formation with two or more children in the center of the circle. The object of the game is for the center players to try to touch the ball while circle players are passing it. After a brief time (15–20 seconds) choose new players to enter the circle. If scoring is desired, center players can count the number of touches they made. The ball should move rapidly. Passing to a neighboring player is not allowed. Play can be limited to a specific type of pass (bounce, two-hand, push).

Dribblerama

Supplies: One basketball for each player

Skills: Dribbling and protecting the ball

Dribblerama can be played at two levels of difficulty.

Level 1: All players dribble throughout the area, controlling their ball so that it does not touch another ball. If a touch occurs, both players go outside the area and dribble around the area. Once youngsters have completed dribbling around the area, they reenter the game.

Level 2: The area is divided in half and all players move to one of the halves. While dribbling and controlling a ball, each player attempts to cause another player to lose control of his ball. When control is lost, that player takes his/her ball and moves to the opposite half of the area. When 5 or 6 players remain, bring all players back into the game and start over.

Objectives:

To cooperatively resist a partner performing exercises

To perform defensive skills

To shoot the layup shot

To participate as a team member in basketball lead-up games

NASPE National Standards:

Introductory Activity: 1, 5

Fitness Activity: 1, 4, 5, 6

Lesson Focus: 2, 3, 5

Game: 2, 3, 5

Equipment Required:

Music for Aerobic Fitness

One junior basketball or playground ball per student

8 hoops or individual mats

Pinnies

Instructional Activities	Teaching Hints

Introductory Activity — Bridges by Three

Form groups of three. Two of the children make bridges, and the third child goes around both bridges and sets up a bridge. Each child in turn goes around the bridges of the other two. Different kinds of bridges can be specified. To assure adequate activity, specify how many steps the youngster must run after going around both bridges. For example, "do 10 skips before making your bridge."

Encourage students to develop personal combinations of movement.

Increase the distance of movement that students move after going through both bridges.

Fitness Development Activity — Aerobic Fitness and Partner Resistance Exercises

Students find a partner and lead each other in aerobic activities. Partners switch leader and follower roles after each partner resistance exercise. This routine assumes that students have previous aerobic fitness experience. If not, the aerobic activities will have to be led by the teacher.

Bounce and clap	25 seconds
Arm curl-up	45 seconds
Jumping Jack variations	25 seconds
Camelback	45 seconds
Lunge variations	25 seconds
Fist pull apart	45 seconds
Directional runs	25 seconds
Scissors	45 seconds
Rhythmic running	25 seconds
Butterfly	45 seconds
Bounce with body twist	25 seconds
Resistance push-up	45 seconds

Walk, stretch, and relax for a minute or two.

Tape alternating segments of silence and music to signal duration of exercise. Music segments indicate aerobic activity (25 seconds); intervals of silence announce partner resistance exercises (45 seconds).

Teach the exercises first. See Chapter 13 in the text for complete descriptions. A sign with aerobic activities on one side and partner resistance exercises on the other help students remember the activities. The signs can be held upright by cones and shared by 2–4 students.

Take 6–10 seconds to complete a resistance exercise.

Lesson Focus — Basketball Skills (2)

Skills:

Review skills from the previous lesson plan which include passing, catching, dribbling, and set shot. Introduce new skills:

1. Defending

Defending involves bending the knees slightly, spreading the feet, and facing the opponent at a distance of about 3 ft. The weight should be distributed evenly on both feet to allow for movement in any direction. Sideward movement is done with a sliding motion. The defender should wave one hand to distract the opponent and to block passes and shots.

2. Layup Shot

The layup is a short shot taken when going in toward the basket either after receiving a pass or at the end of a dribble. In a shot from the right side, the takeoff is with the left foot, and vice versa. The ball is carried with both hands early in the shot and then shifted to one hand for the final push. The ball, guided by the fingertips, should be laid against the backboard with a minimum of spin.

Instructional cues for proper defending are as follows:

1. Keep the knees bent.
2. Keep the hands up.
3. Don't cross the feet when moving.

Instructional cues for the layup shot are:

1. Take off on the foot opposite the shooting hand
2. Lay the ball on the backboard above the basketball.
3. Jump upward and slightly forward on the takeoff.

Drills:

Review previous drills learned in the previous lesson and introduce the following:

1. Group Defensive Drill

   For the group defensive drill, the entire class is scattered on a basketball floor, facing one of the sides. The instructor or the student leader stands on the side, near the center. The leader points in one direction (forward, backward, or to one side) and gives the command "Move." When the students have moved a short distance, the leader commands, "Stop." Players keep good defensive position throughout.

2. Layup Drill

   Two short lines of players are placed; one to the left of the basket and the other on the right side of the basket. One line passes to the other line for layup shots. Shooters come in from the right side first (this is easier), then from the left, and finally from the center. Each player goes to the end of the other line.

Commands can be changed so that movement is continuous. Commands are "Right," "Left," "Forward," "Backward," and "Stop." The leader must watch that movement is not so far in any one direction that it causes players to run into obstructions. Commands can be given in order, and pointing can accompany commands.

Basketball Lead-up Activities

Around the Key

Supplies: A basketball

Skill: Shooting

Spots are arranged for shooting around the key. A player begins at the first spot and continues until a miss. When a miss occurs, the player can stop and wait for her next opportunity and begin from the point where the miss occurred, or she can "risk it" and try another shot immediately from the point where the first try was missed. If the shot is made, the player continues. If the shot is missed, the player must start over on the next turn. The winner is the player who completes the key first or who makes the most progress.

Objectives:

To cooperatively participate in a
    simple tag game
To perform continuous fitness activity
To know the elements of proper
    throwing
To throw with maximum velocity

NASPE National Standards:

Introductory Activity: 1, 2, 3, 5
Fitness Activity: 1, 2, 5, 6
Lesson Focus: 2, 3, 5
Game: 1, 2, 3, 5

Equipment Required:

Beanbags for Introductory Activity
Music for exercises
Many types of balls for throwing
Throwing targets; hoops, mats, bowling
    pins, and/or cageball

Instructional Activities	Teaching Hints

Introductory Activity — Locomotor and Manipulative Activity

Each child is given a beanbag and moves around the area using various basic locomotor movements. Students toss and catch their beanbags while moving. On signal, they drop the beanbags and jump and/or hop over as many bags as possible.

Vary the challenge by specifying the number or color of beanbags to move over or around.

Fitness Development Activity — Exercises to Music

Crab Kicks	25 seconds
Rope jumping	30 seconds
Windmills	25 seconds
Walk and do arm circles	30 seconds
Abdominal Crunchers	25 seconds
Jumping Jack variations	30 seconds
Side Flex	25 seconds
Two-Step or gallop	30 seconds
Triceps push-ups	25 seconds
Aerobic jumping	30 seconds
Push-up challenges	25 seconds
Leg extensions	30 seconds
Walking to cool down	30 seconds

Select music that has a strong rhythm and easy-to-hear beat. When the music is on, students perform aerobic activities (for 25 seconds). When the music is not playing, students perform the strength development and flexibility exercises (30 seconds).

See Chapter 13 of the textbook for descriptions of the exercises.

Use scatter formation.

Lesson Focus — Throwing Skills (2)

Review and practice throwing for form

1. Review proper throwing form outlined in Week 3.
    a. Throw yarn balls from a standing position 20 feet from the wall. Throw 5 balls, retrieve and repeat.
    b. Throw yarn balls or tennis balls using the proper grip. Throw at bowling pins or hoops leaning against the wall and encourage trying to knock down the hoops. Gradually increase the distance from the wall.

Review and practice throwing for velocity

1. Review throwing for velocity in Week 3. Set up activities using large targets so students will throw forcefully.
    a. Throw at mats on the wall. Throw tennis balls hard from 16–20 ft. Retrieve only if the balls roll beyond the throwing line.
    b. Throw at hoops leaning against mats on the wall.
    c. Large target throw. Use a circle or square 4 ft in diameter placed on the wall. Students should throw from 20–35 ft.

Practice throwing at targets

1. Use targets to increase motivation. The targets should encourage throwing for velocity rather than accuracy. Some examples of targets are:
    a. Throw through hoops suspended from basketball goals.
    b. Use large boxes for targets and try to throw inside the box
    c. Cageball throw. Throwers try to move it into the corner by throwing at it.
    d. Many bowling pins set near the walls.
    e. Graduated-size targets. Use with 4 ft, 3 ft, and 2 ft diameter circles.

Throwing takes a great deal of practice to master. Two major issues to consider when teaching throwing are:
1. How can I arrange my class so students receive the most opportunity to throw?
2. How can I arrange my class so students get to throw with maximum velocity? A mature pattern of throwing cannot be learned if students are not allowed to throw with maximum force.

Proper form and velocity of throws are closely related. A reason for practicing form is to encourage students to think about technique.

Give each student 4 or 5 balls to throw. On signal, when all the balls have been thrown students go retrieve the same number of balls they have thrown.

Make throwing targets large so students throw with velocity rather than accuracy. Throwing for targets is exciting for youngsters.

In the Prison

Supplies: 15–20 throwing balls

Skill: Throwing

Two teams, one assigned to each half of the gym. Balls (15–20) are placed on the center line. On signal, each team throws the balls to the other side of the gym. The object of the game is to get all the balls into the other team's backcourt area (or prison), which extends 10 ft from the wall. The teacher stops play by blowing a whistle, then counting the number of balls in the "prison."

Snowball

Supplies: 36 yarn balls

Skill: Throwing

Two teams, one assigned to each half of the gym. Each student has a yarn ball. Players can be hit three times. Each time they are hit they call out the number (1, 2, 3) of times they have been hit. After the third hit they must go to the side of the area and count to 25 before they can reenter. Teams must stay in their half of the gym.

Center Target Throw

Supplies: Twenty 8" gray foam balls and 20 bowling pins

Skill: Throwing

The area is divided into quadrants. Two teams compete, and each team has its own set of targets (bowling pins) set on a centerline. Half of each team is placed in opposing quadrants with the pins in the middle. Team A, on the left half of the area, has players on both sides of the center line behind restraining lines 15–20 ft away from the center target line. Team B is positioned the same way on the right half of the area. Each team tries to knock down all of its bowling pins as quickly as possible.

Target Ball Throw

Supplies: Ten 18" beach balls and 36 yarn balls

Skill: Throwing

Beach balls are placed on the center line of the gym. There are two teams and each must stay in its half of the gym. Players have yarn balls. The object of the game is to roll the beach balls into the other team's court by hitting them with the yarn balls. The team that has the least number of beach balls on its side when the teacher blows the whistle is the winner.

LP 58

Objectives:
To apply fundamental skills in a
unique situation
To learn and practice personal and
social skills
To work cooperatively in a group
setting

NASPE National Standards:
Introductory Activity: 2, 3, 5
Fitness Activity: 1, 2, 5, 6
Lesson Focus: 1, 2, 3, 5, 6
Game: 1, 2, 3, 5, 6

Equipment Required:
Music for Exercises
Tumbling mats
Yarn balls
Marking spots
Hoops
Tinikling poles & basketballs
Frisbees
Scoops

Instructional Activities	Teaching Hints
Introductory Activity — Yarn Ball Fun	
Each child has a yarn ball. Allow students to kick, throw, or move with the ball for a designated time. On signal, place the balls on the floor and perform movements around, between and over the balls.	Place the yarn balls around the perimeter of the area. When students enter, they can move to a yarn ball and begin handling it.

Fitness Development Activity — Exercises to Music

Crab Kicks	25 seconds	Select music that has a strong rhythm
Rope jumping	30 seconds	and easy-to-hear beat. When the music
Windmills	25 seconds	is on, students perform aerobic activities
Walk and do arm circles	30 seconds	(for 25 seconds). When the music is not
Abdominal Crunchers	25 seconds	playing, students perform the strength
Jumping Jack variations	30 seconds	development and flexibility exercises
Side Flex	25 seconds	(30 seconds).
Two-Step or gallop	30 seconds	
Triceps push-ups	25 seconds	See Chapter 13 of the textbook for
Aerobic jumping	30 seconds	descriptions of the exercises.
Push-up challenges	25 seconds	
Leg extensions	30 seconds	Use scatter formation.
Walking to cool down	30 seconds	

Lesson Focus and Game Activity — Cooperative Game Skills
Presenting Cooperative Skill Activities

1. **Set the Stage**: During this first step it is the teacher's job to sell the activity with the following information:
   What is the challenge?
   What are the rules?
   What are the consequences for breaking the rules?
   Are there any safety issues that need to be addressed?
   During this step, only the essential information to get the group going is provided. This information can be presented in the form of a descriptive and often imaginary story.

2. **Facilitate:** Once the stage has been set, the teacher's role is to step back and let the students work. For many teachers this is a difficult task because they want to tell students how to accomplish the task or at least give them a few hints. During this step, it is best to simply answer questions and monitor the group for safety. Success does not always mean the task is accomplished; learning to cooperate is more important than completing the task. Much can be learned and gained from simply working on the task. It is critical that teachers allow time for the final step.

3. **Debrief**: Debriefing may be the most important component in effectively implementing cooperative activities. The foundation of debriefing is open-ended questions. Question such as "Did that work?" or "Would you do that again?" require a yes or no response and do not foster discussion. The following are examples of open-ended questions:
   What did you have to do in order to accomplish the goal?
   What does "communicate" mean?
   What happened that was positive?
   What happened that could have been better?

How could you have changed things?

What does it mean to be patient?

How can you compromise?

What would you have done differently? The same?

Cooperative Activities

Mat Folding

Formation: Groups of 4–5 students

Supplies: One tumbling mat for each group

The group is given one tumbling mat and instructed to stand on it. While keeping their feet on the mat at all times, teams are given the following challenges:

1. Rotate the mat 360 degrees.
2. Move the mat 15 ft.
3. Without using any hands, fold the mat into fourths.
4. Unfold the mat without using any hands.

Attached at the …

Formation: Partners

Supplies: One beanbag or ball for each set of partners

Partners stand on one side of the activity area. The challenge is to get to the other sideline or end line while attached at the hip, head, back, ankle, elbow, hamstring, etc. Locomotor movements can be specified for moving across the area. For a more difficult activity, provide a beanbag or ball for the students to put between the "attached" body parts.

Teaching tip: To add difficulty, after completing tasks with a partner, challenge students to work in groups of 3, 4, or more.

Quiet Cooperation

Formation: Groups of 10–12 students

Supplies: One marking spot for each student

Students stand in a line shoulder to shoulder with a marking spot under their feet. Without talking, making any noise, or touching the gym floor, students get in order using these criteria:

1. Number of pets (fewest to most).
2. Alphabetical by first name (father's, mother's, or pet name can also be used).
3. Alphabetical by last name.
4. Month of birthday (January to December or vice versa).
5. Shortest to tallest.

All Aboard

Formation: Entire class scattered with hoops spread through area

Supplies: 15 hoops

Students are challenged to get as many students as possible into one hoop placed on the ground. In order for a person to be considered "on board," one foot must be touching the ground inside of the hoop and no body parts touching the floor outside the hoop. One technique to lead up to this activity is to play Musical Hoops. Hoops are scattered throughout the gym and music is playing. When the music stops students move to a hoop, placing at least one foot inside the hoop. More than one student can be in a hoop. Each time the music plays the teacher removes one or two hoops until only enough hoops remain for all students to be aboard.

Human Spelling Bee

Formation: Squads of 5–6 players

Supplies: None

Groups of 5–6 students are challenged with spelling out words, letter by letter, with their bodies while lying on the floor. All team members must be in the letter and the team must identify the bottom of the letter. Physical education terms or spelling words may be used. Also, students can spell out answers to questions asked by the teacher. Mathematical equations could also be written (i.e., $7 \times 7 = 49$), one number and symbol at a time.

Scoop Ball

Formation: Squads of 6–8 students

Supplies: Four basketballs, one hoop, four Tinikling poles, and two scoops for every team

Teams of 6–8 students attempt to move four basketballs approximately 50 ft, without touching the basketballs with any body parts, and place the balls into a hoop. Four Tinikling poles and two scoops are provided. The following rules apply:

1. If a ball touches the floor or a student, the ball must be returned to the starting point.
2. Players may not walk with the balls.
3. The balls may not be thrown, kicked, or passed.

4. Balls that roll or bounce out of the hoop must be returned to the starting point.
5. Students are only permitted to hold one scoop at a time.

Flippers

Formation: Entire class divided into two teams

Supplies: 30–40 flying disks

The flying disks are spread throughout the teaching area and two teams formed. One team is charged with flipping the disks so they are face up, while the other team attempts to flip the disks to a face-down position. After a practice game, the following stipulations can be used.

1. No hands.
2. Feet only.
3. Students must crab-walk or bear crawl.
4. Feet only, and only one foot can touch the disk at a time.
5. Knees only.

DPE Curriculum Guide – Lesson Plans
Hockey Skills and Lead-up Activities (1)
Level II – Week 21

Objectives:
To understand and translate into
    movement the concepts of level,
    direction, and size
To demonstrate how the hockey stick
    should be handled for safety
To practice passing and fielding a
    hockey puck
To design drills for practicing hockey
    skills

NASPE National Standards:
Introductory Activity: 1, 3, 5
Fitness Activity: 1, 4, 5, 6
Lesson Focus: 2, 3, 5
Game: 2, 5, 6

Equipment Required:
Music and jump ropes for Jackpot
    Fitness
One puck (or whiffle ball) and hockey
    stick for each student
Marking spots for Lane Hockey
Tumbling mats for goals

Instructional Activities	Teaching Hints

Introductory Activity — Movement Varieties

Move using a basic locomotor movement. Then add variety to the movement by asking students to respond to the following factors:
1. Level—low, high, in-between.
2. Direction—straight, zigzag, circular, curved, forward, backward, upward, downward.
3. Size—large, tiny, medium movements.

Help students understand the concepts of level, direction, and size by briefly discussing them.

Encourage creativity by reinforcing novel responses.

Fitness Development Activity — Aerobic, Strength, and Flexibility Jackpot Fitness

    Three different "jackpots" (boxes) are filled with fitness exercises and activities are placed around the teaching area. One jackpot is filled with a variety of strength development activities written on small index cards. A second jackpot is filled with flexibility activities. The third jackpot contains aerobic activities. Students can work individually or with a partner. They begin at one of the jackpots of choice and randomly pick out an activity to perform. If with a partner, they take turns selecting the card from the box. The only stipulations are that they must rotate to a different box each time and cannot select an activity they previously performed. If they pick an activity they performed on a previous stop, they return it to the jackpot and select another.

Aerobic Jackpot
1. Carioca around the basketball court.
2. Perform a "mirror drill" with your partner for 30 seconds.
3. Jump rope using both slow and fast time.
4. Tortoise and Hare/Running in place.
5. Marching with high steps around the area.

Strength Jackpot
1. Perform Abdominal Challenges
2. Perform Push-up Challenges
3. Do the Treadmill exercise
4. Do as many Power Jumpers as possible
5. Perform as many Crab Kicks as possible.

Flexibility Jackpot
1. Perform the Bend and Twist exercise.
2. Stretch using the Sitting Stretch.
3. Stretch using the Lower Leg Stretch.
4. Do the Standing Hip Bend.
5. Perform the Body Twist.

Allow students to adjust the workload to their level. This implies resting if the rope jumping is too strenuous.

A music interval of 30 seconds signals the duration of fitness activity followed by 10–15 second interval used for selecting a new activity from a different jackpot.

Students are expected to perform as many repetitions as possible while the music is playing.

Lesson Focus — Hockey Skills (1)

Skills

Practice the following skills:

1. Gripping and carrying the stick.

    The hockey stick should be held with both hands and carried as low to the ground as possible. The basic grip puts the left hand at the top of the stick and the right hand 6–12 in. below the left.

    To ensure accuracy as well as safety, the stick must not be swung above waist height.

2. Controlled Dribble.

    The controlled dribble consists of a series of short taps in the direction in which the player chooses to move. The hands should be spread 10–14 in. apart to gain greater control of the stick. As the player becomes more skilled, the hands can be moved closer together. The stick is turned so that the blade faces the ball. The grip should not be changed, but rather, the hands should be rotated until the back of the left hand and the palm of the right hand face the ball. The ball can then be tapped just far enough in front of the player to keep it away from the feet but not more than one full stride away from the stick.

    Dribbling instructional cues:
    1. Control the puck. It should always be within reach of the stick.
    2. Hold the stick firmly.
    3. Keep the elbows away from the body.

3. Front Field.

    For the front field, the student must keep an eye on the ball, move to a point in line with its path, and extend the flat side of the blade forward to meet the ball. The faster the ball approaches, the more she must learn to give with the stick to absorb the momentum of the ball. The player should field the ball in front of the body and not permit it to get too close.

    Front fielding instructional cues:
    1. Field with a "soft stick." This means holding the stick with relaxed hands.
    2. Allow the puck to hit the stick and then "give" to make a soft reception.
    3. Keep the hands apart on the stick.

4. Forehand Pass.

    The forehand pass is a short pass that usually occurs from the dribble. It should be taught before driving, because the quick hit requires accuracy rather than distance. The player spreads the feet with toes pointed slightly forward when striking. Approach the ball with the stick held low and bring the stick straight back, in line with the intended direction of the hit. The hands should be the same distance apart as in the carrying position, and the stick should be lifted no higher than waist level. The player's right hand guides the stick down and through the ball. The head should be kept down with the eyes on the ball. A short follow-through occurs after contact.

    Forehand passing instructional cues:
    1. Approach the puck with the side facing the direction of the pass.
    2. Keep the head down and eyes on the puck.
    3. Keep the stick below waist level at all times.
    4. Drive the stick through the puck.

Drills

Use the following drills to practice the skills above:

1. Dribbling
    a. Each student has a stick and ball. On signal, change directions while maintaining control of the ball.
    b. Dribble and dodge imaginary tacklers or dodge around a set of cones. Partners may act as tacklers.
    c. Students in pairs—20 ft apart. One partner dribbles toward the other, goes around him or her, and returns to starting point. The first student then drives the ball to the second, who completes the same sequence.
2. Forehand Passing and Front Fielding
    a. From 8–10 ft apart, partners forehand pass and front field the ball back and forth to each other both from moving and stationary positions.
    b. Partners 20 ft apart—players pass the ball back and forth with emphasis on *fielding* and *immediately* hitting the ball back.

Hockey is a rough game when children are not taught the proper methods of stick handling. They need to be reminded often to use caution and good judgment when handling hockey sticks.

Ample equipment increases individual practice time and facilitates skill development. A stick and a ball or puck for each child are desirable.

If hockey is played on a gym floor, a plastic puck or yarn ball should be used. If played on a carpeted area or outdoors, a whiffle ball is used. An 8-ft folding mat set on end makes a satisfactory goal.

Hockey Lead-up Activities

Circle Keep-Away

Supplies: One stick per person, a puck or ball

Skills: Passing, fielding

Players are spaced evenly around the circle, with two or more players in the center. The object of the game is to keep the players in the center from touching the puck. The puck is passed back and forth, with emphasis on accurate passing and fielding. Center players see how many touches they can make during their turn. Change the center players after a time limit so all youngsters have an opportunity to be center players.

Star Wars Hockey

Supplies: One stick per player, four pucks or balls

Skill: Dribbling

Each team forms one side of a square formation. The game is similar to Star Wars, with the following exceptions:

1. Four pucks (or balls) are used. When a number is called, each player with that number goes to a puck and dribbles it out of the square through the opening they previously occupied, around the square counterclockwise, and back to the original spot. Circles 12 in. in diameter are drawn on the floor to provide a definite place where the puck must be returned. If the game is played outdoors, marking spots can be used to mark where the pucks must be returned.

2. No player is permitted to use anything other than the stick in making the circuit and returning the puck to the inside of the hoop. The penalty for infractions is disqualification.

Lane Hockey

Supplies: Hockey stick per player, puck, two goals

Skills: All hockey skills

The field is divided into 8 lanes. A defensive and an offensive player are placed in each of the 8 lanes. A goalkeeper for each team is also positioned in front of the goal area. Players may not leave their lane during play. A shot on goal may not be taken until a minimum of two passes has been completed. This rule encourages passing to someone in a better position before taking a shot on goal. Encourage players to maintain their spacing during play. The purpose of the lanes is to force players to play a zone rather than swarming to the puck. Rules used for regulation hockey enforce situations not described here. A free hit (unguarded) is awarded a team if a foul occurs. Players should be rotated after a goal is scored or at regular time intervals.

Circle Hockey Straddleball

Supplies: Hockey sticks and pucks or yarn balls

Skills: Passing and fielding

Children are in circle formation, facing in. Each player stands in a wide straddle stance 2–3 ft apart. The object of the game is to pass one of the pucks between the legs of another. Each time a puck goes between the legs of an individual, a point is scored. The players having the fewest points scored against them are winners. Keep the circles small so students have more opportunities to handle the puck.

Objectives:
To practice passing and fielding a hockey puck
To design drills for practicing hockey skills
To understand and perform goaltending skills

NASPE National Standards:
Introductory Activity: 1, 5
Fitness Activity: 1, 4, 5, 6
Lesson Focus: 2, 3, 5
Game: 2, 3, 5

Equipment Required:
Music and jump ropes for Jackpot Fitness
Hockey sticks and pucks or yarn balls
Marking spots and cones
Tumbling mats for goals

Instructional Activities	Teaching Hints

Introductory Activity — Run, Stop and Pivot

The class should run, stop on signal, and pivot. Vary the activity by having the class pivot on the left or right foot and increase the circumference of the pivot. Movement should be continuous. Students pivot and then continue running.

Relate the pivot to a sport such as basketball and explain how it involves rotating around one foot.

Fitness Development Activity — Aerobic, Strength, and Flexibility Jackpot Fitness

Three different "jackpots" (boxes) are filled with fitness exercises and activities are placed around the teaching area. One jackpot is filled with a variety of strength development activities written on small index cards. A second jackpot is filled with flexibility activities. The third jackpot contains aerobic activities. Students can work individually or with a partner. They begin at one of the jackpots of choice and randomly pick out an activity to perform. If with a partner, they take turns selecting the card from the box. The only stipulations are that they must rotate to a different box each time and cannot select an activity they previously performed. If they pick an activity they performed on a previous stop, they return it to the jackpot and select another.

Aerobic Jackpot
1. Carioca around the basketball court.
2. Perform a "mirror drill" with your partner for 30 seconds.
3. Jump rope using both slow and fast time.
4. Tortoise and Hare/Running in place.
5. Marching with high steps around the area.

Strength Jackpot
1. Perform Abdominal Challenges
2. Perform Push-up Challenges
3. Do the Treadmill exercise
4. Do as many Power Jumpers as possible
5. Perform as many Crab Kicks as possible.

Flexibility Jackpot
1. Perform the Bend and Twist exercise.
2. Stretch using the Sitting Stretch.
3. Stretch using the Lower Leg Stretch.
4. Do the Standing Hip Bend.
5. Perform the Body Twist.

Allow students to adjust the workload to their level. This implies resting if the rope jumping is too strenuous.

A music interval of 30 seconds signals the duration of fitness activity followed by 10–15 second interval used for selecting a new activity from a different jackpot.

Students are expected to perform as many repetitions as possible while the music is playing.

Lesson Focus — Hockey Skills (2)

Skills:
Review and practice skills introduced last week:
1. Gripping and carrying the stick
2. Controlled dribble
3. Front field
4. Forehand pass

Introduce new skills:
1. Driving.
   Driving is used to hit the ball moderate to long distances and to shoot at the goal. It differs from other passes in that the hands are brought together more toward the end of the stick. This gives the leverage necessary to apply greater force to

the ball and results in more speed and greater distance. The swing and hit are similar to the quick hit. Stick control should be stressed so that wild swinging does not occur.

2. Tackling

The tackle is a means of taking the ball away from an opponent. The tackler moves toward the opponent with the stick held low. The tackle is timed so that the blade of the stick is placed against the ball when the ball is off the opponent's stick. The tackler then quickly dribbles or passes in the direction of the goal. Throwing the stick or striking carelessly at the ball should be discouraged. Players need to remember that a successful tackle is not always possible.

3. Goalkeeping

The goalie may kick the ball, stop it with any part of the body, or allow it to rebound off the body or hand. He may not, however, hold the ball or throw it toward the other end of the playing area. The goalkeeper is positioned in front of the goal line and moves between the goal posts. When a ball is hit toward the goal, the goalie should attempt to move in front of the ball and to keep his feet together. This allows the body to block the ball should the stick miss it. After the block, the ball is passed immediately to a teammate.

Review the drills presented last week:
1. Dribbling
2. Forehand Passing and Front Fielding

Introduce new drills:

Passing and Fielding drills

1. The shuttle turn-back drill, in which two files of 4–5 players face each other, can be used. The first person in the file passes to the first person in the other file, who in turn fields the ball and returns the pass. Each player, when finished, goes to the end of the file.

2. The downfield drill for passing and fielding skills for on the move. Three files of players start at one end of the field. One player from each file proceeds downfield, passing to and fielding from the others until the other end of the field is reached. A goal shot can be made at this point. The players should remain close together for short passes until a high level of skill is reached.

3. Practice driving for distance and accuracy with a partner.

Dodging and Tackling Drills

1. Players spread out on the field, each with a ball. On command, they dribble left, right, forward, and backward. On the command "Dodge," the players dodge an imaginary tackler. Players should concentrate on ball control and dodging in all directions.

2. Players work in pairs. One partner dribbles toward the other, who attempts to make a tackle. If the tackle is successful, roles are reversed. This drill should be practiced at moderate speeds in the early stages of skill development.

Hockey Lead-up Activities

Modified Hockey

Supplies: One stick per person, a puck or ball

Skills: Dribbling, passing, dodging, tackling, face-off

The teams take any position on the field as long as they remain inside the boundaries. The object of the game is to hit the puck through the opponent's goal. No goalies are used. At the start of the game and after each score, play begins with a face-off. Each goal is worth one point. The distance between goal lines is flexible but should be on the long side. If making goals is too easy or too difficult, the width of the goals can be adjusted accordingly.

Lane Hockey

Supplies: Hockey stick per player, puck, two goals

Skills: All hockey skills

The field is divided into eight lanes. A defensive and an offensive player are placed in each of the 8 lanes. A goalkeeper for each team is also positioned in front of the goal area. Players may not leave their lane during play. A shot on goal may not be taken until a minimum of two passes has been completed. This rule encourages looking for teammates and passing to someone in a better position before taking a shot on goal. Encourage players to maintain their spacing during play. The purpose of the lanes is to force players to play a zone rather than swarming to the puck. Rules used for regulation hockey enforce situations not described here. A free hit (unguarded) is awarded a team if a foul occurs. Players should be rotated after a goal is scored or at regular time intervals.

DPE Curriculum Guide – Lesson Plans
Gymnastics Skills (3)
Level II – Week 23

Objectives:

To put together a combination of
movements in a smooth and
flowing manner

To support the body weight in a variety
of settings

To work cooperatively with a partner

NASPE National Standards:

Introductory Activity: 1, 3, 5
Fitness Activity: 1, 4, 6
Lesson Focus: 1, 2, 3, 5
Game: 1, 5

Equipment Required:

Music for introductory activity and
Aerobic Fitness
Tumbling Mats
4–6 bowling pins for game

Instructional Activities	Teaching Hints

Introductory Activity — Moving to Music

Use a different music to stimulate various locomotor and nonlocomotor
movements. Different dance steps such as polka, two-step, and schottische could
be practiced.

The primary purpose of this activity is
to help students sense different rhythms
and move to the rhythm.

Fitness Development Activity — Aerobic Fitness

1. Rhythmic run with clap
2. Bounce turn and clap
3. Rhythmic 4-count curl-ups (knees, toes, knees, back)
4. Rhythmic Crab Kicks (slow time)
5. Jumping Jack combination
6. Double knee lifts
7. Lunges (right, left, forward) with single-arm circles (on the side lunges) and
   double-arms circles (on the forward lunge)
8. Rhythmic trunk twists
9. Directional run (forward, backward, side, turning)
10. Rock side to side with clap
11. Side-leg raises (alternate legs)
12. Rhythmic 4-count push-ups (If these are too difficult for students, substitute
    single-arm circles in the push-up position.)

Use music to stimulate effort. Any
combination of movements can be used.

Keep the steps simple and easy to
perform. Some students will become
frustrated if the learning curve is steep.

Signs that explain the aerobic activities
will help students remember
performance cues.

Don't stress or expect perfection. Allow
students to perform the activities as best
they can.

Alternate bouncing and running
movements with flexibility and strength
development movements.

Lesson Focus — Gymnastics Skills (3)

Animal Movements

Double-Lame Dog

   Support the body on one hand and one leg. Move forward in this position,
maintaining balance. The distance should be short (5–10 ft), as this stunt is
strenuous. Different leg-arm combinations should be employed such as cross-
lateral movements (right arm with left leg and left arm with right leg).

Turtle

   Hold the body in a wide push-up position with the feet apart and the hands
widely spread. From this position, move in various directions, keeping the plane of
the body always about the same distance from the floor.

Walrus Slap

   From the front-leaning rest position, push the body up in the air quickly by
force of the arms, clap the hands together, and recover to position.

Tumbling and Inverted Balances

Forward Roll Combinations

   Review the Forward Roll (see Week 7). Combinations such as the following
can be introduced.

*Five groups of activities in this lesson
ensure that youngsters receive a
variety of experiences. Pick a few
activities from each group and teach
them alternately. For example, teach
one or two animal movements, then a
tumbling and inverted balance,
followed by a balance stunt, etc. Give
equal time to each group of activities.*

Youngsters can do the animal walks
around their mats. Many of the
activities in this unit do not have to be
performed on the mat.

Scatter tumbling mats throughout the
area so that there is little standing in
line waiting for a turn.

a. Do a Forward Roll preceded by a short run.
b. Do two Forward Rolls in succession.
c. Do a Forward Roll to a vertical jump in the air, and repeat.

Balance Stunts
Seat Balance
Sit on the floor, holding the ankles in front, with elbows inside the knees. The feet are flat on the floor, and the knees are bent at approximately a right angle. Raise the legs (toes pointed) so that the knees are straight, and balance on the seat for 5 seconds.

Face-to-Knee Touch
Begin in a standing position with feet together. Placing the hands on the hips, balance on one foot, with the other leg extended backward. Bend the trunk forward and touch the knee of the supporting leg with the forehead. Recover to original position.

Finger Touch
Put the right hand behind the back with the index finger straight and pointed down. Grasp the right wrist with the left hand. From an erect position with the feet about 6 in. apart, squat down and touch the floor with the index finger. Regain the erect position without losing balance.

Individual Stunts
Stoop and Stretch
Hold a beanbag with both hands. Stand with heels against a line and feet about shoulder width apart. Keeping the knees straight, reach between the legs with the beanbag and place it as far back as possible. Reach back and pick it up with both hands.

Tanglefoot
Stand with heels together and toes pointed out. Bend the trunk forward and extend both arms down between the knees and around behind the ankles. Bring the hands around the outside of the ankles from behind and touch the fingers to each other. Hold for a 5-second count. Balance for 5 seconds without releasing the handclasp.

Egg Roll
In a sitting position, assume the same clasped-hands position as for the Tanglefoot. Roll sideways over one shoulder, then to the back, then to the other shoulder, and finally back up to the sitting position. The movements are repeated in turn to make a full circle back to place.

Toe Touch Nose
From a sitting position on the floor, touch the toes of either foot to the nose with the help of both hands. Do first one foot and then the other. More flexible youngsters will be able to place the foot on top of the head or even behind the neck. Although this is a flexibility exercise, caution should be used; the leg can be forced too far.

Toe Tug Walk
Bend over and grasp the toes with thumbs on top. Keep the knees bent slightly and the eyes forward. Walk forward without losing the grip on the toes. Walk backward and sideward to provide more challenge.

Partner and Group Stunts
Camel Lift and Walk
In the wheelbarrow position, the wheelbarrow raises the seat as high as possible, forming a camel. Camels can lower themselves or walk in the raised position.

Children who have difficulty with forward rolls should not have to do them.

A major concern for safety is the neck and back region. Overweight children are at greater risk and might be allowed to avoid tumbling and inverted balances.

All tumbling and inverted balances should be done on a tumbling mat. Limit the number of children per mat to 3 or 4.

Working in pairs can be helpful. One student critiques the other's performance to make sure that the key performance and safety areas are addressed.

After the activities are learned, place emphasis on correct performance emphasizing three phases:
1. Starting position
2. Execution
3. Finishing position

The secret to the egg roll is a vigorous sideward movement to secure initial momentum. If mats are used, two should be placed side by side to cover the extent of the roll. (Some children can do this stunt better from a crossed-ankle position.)

Dump the Wheelbarrow

Get into the wheelbarrow position. Lift the legs and return to normal position.

Dromedary Walk

One child (the support) gets down on the hands and knees. The other child sits on the support, facing the rear, and fixes the legs around the support's chest. The top child leans forward, to grasp the back of the support's ankles. The top child's arms are reasonably extended. The support takes the weight off the knees and walks forward with the top child's help.

Centipede

One child, the stronger and larger individual, gets down on the hands and knees. The other child faces the same direction, places the hands about 2 ft in front of the support's, then places the legs and body on top of the support. The knees should be spread apart and the heels locked together. The centipede walks with the top child using hands only and the supporting child using both hands and feet. The support should gather the legs well under while walking and not be on the knees.

Game Activity

Steal the Treasure

Supplies: A bowling pin
Skill: Dodging

A playing area about 20 ft square is outlined, with a small circle in the center. A bowling pin placed in the small circle (hula hoop) as the treasure. Two guards are selected to protect the treasure. The guards can move as far from the treasure as they like to tag a player. Anyone tagged must retire and wait for the next game. To successfully steal the treasure, a player must pick it up cleanly without getting tagged. The guards tag them when they come too near. If the treasure is knocked over by a player trying to steal it, that player must also wait out a turn. There is a delicate balance for the guards between being too far from the treasure and staying too near the treasure and never tagging anyone. If the guards tag all players, they are declared billionaires.

Flippers (Cooperative Activity)

Formation: Entire class divided into 2 teams
Supplies: 30–40 flying disks

Flying disks (30–40) are spread throughout the teaching area and two teams formed. One team is charged with flipping the disks so they are face up, while the other team attempts to flip the disks to a face down position. After a practice game, the following stipulations can be used.
1. No hands.
2. Feet only.
3. Students must crab walk or bear crawl.
4. Feet only, and only one foot can touch the disk at a time.
5. Knees only.
6. Heel only.

DPE Curriculum Guide – Lesson Plans
Track and Field Skills and Lead-up Activities (1)
Level II – Week 24

Objectives:
To understand how to stretch prior to
  strenuous activity
To recognize the wide range of
  individual differences among peers

NASPE National Standards:
Introductory Activity: 1, 4, 6
Fitness Activity: 2, 4
Lesson Focus: 2, 3, 5
Game: 2, 3, 5

Equipment Required:
Stopwatches
Track and field equipment

Instructional Activities	Teaching Hints

Introductory and Fitness Development Activities — Stretching and Jogging

Combine the introductory and fitness activities during the track and field unit. This will help students understand how to stretch and warm up for a demanding activity such as track and field.

Jog	1–2 minutes	
Standing Hip Bend	30 seconds	
Sitting Stretch	30 seconds	
Partner Rowing	60 seconds	
Bear Hug (stretch each leg)	40 seconds	
Side Flex (stretch each leg)	40 seconds	
Trunk Twister	30 seconds	
Jog	3–4 minutes	

Emphasis should be on jogging and stretching to prepare for strenuous activity.

Encourage smooth and controlled stretching. Hold each stretch for 6–10 seconds.

Lesson Focus — Track and Field Skills and Lead-up Activities (1)

Skills

Standing Start

The standing start has a variety of uses in physical education activities. Many children find it more comfortable than the sprinter's start. When practical, however, children should use the sprinter's start for track work. In the standing start, the feet should be in a comfortable half-stride position. An extremely long stride is to be avoided. The body leans forward so that the center of gravity is forward. The weight is on the toes, and the knees are flexed slightly. The arms can be down or hanging slightly back.

The goal of track and field is self-improvement and developing proper techniques. Each student must accept responsibility for self-directed work and should be encouraged to try all activities.

Sprinter's Start

The "On your mark" position places the toe of the front foot from 4–12 in. behind the starting line. The thumb and first finger are just behind the line, with other fingers adding support. The knee of the rear leg is placed just opposite the front foot or ankle.

For the "Get set" position, the seat is raised so that it is nearly parallel to the ground. The knee of the rear leg is raised off the ground, and the shoulders are moved forward over the hands. The weight is evenly distributed over the hands and feet. The head is not raised, as the runner should be looking at a spot a few feet in front of the starting line.

On the "Go" signal, the runner pushes off sharply with both feet, with the front leg straightening as the back leg comes forward for a step. The body should rise gradually rather than pop up suddenly. The instructor should watch for a stumbling action on the first few steps. This results from too much weight resting on the hands in the "Get set" position.

The program should offer something for all—boys and girls, the highly skilled and the less skilled, and those with physical problems. Children with weight problems need particular attention. They must be stimulated and encouraged, since their participation will be minimal if little attention is paid to them. Special goals can be set for overweight children, and special events and goals can also be established for children with handicaps.

Sprinting

In proper sprinting form, the body leans forward, with the arms swinging in opposition to the legs. The arms are bent at the elbows and swing from the shoulders in a forward and backward plane, not across the body. Forceful arm action aids sprinting. The knees are lifted sharply forward and upward and are brought down with a vigorous motion, followed by a forceful push from the toes.

The goal of the program should be to allow students to develop at their own rate. The instructor needs to be perceptive enough to determine whether students are working too hard or too little. Special attention must be given to those who appear disinterested, dejected, emotionally upset, or

Distance Running

In distance running, as compared with sprinting, the body is more erect and the motion of the arms is less pronounced. Pace is an important consideration. Runners should try to concentrate on the qualities of lightness, ease, relaxation, and looseness. Relaxed striding action, a slight body lean, and good head position are also important. Encourage runners to strike the ground with the heel first and then push off with the toes.

Standing Long Jump

In the standing long jump, the jumper toes the line with feet flat on the ground and fairly close together. The arms are brought forward in a preliminary swing and are then swung down and back. The jump is made with both feet as the arms are swung forcibly forward to assist in lifting the body upward and forward. In the air, the knees should be brought upward and forward, with the arms held forward to sustain balance.

Long Jump

For the running long jump, a short run is needed. The run should be timed so that the toes of the jumping foot contact the board in a natural stride. The jumper takes off from one foot and strives for height. The landing is made on both feet after the knees have been brought forward. The landing should be in a forward direction, not sideward.

A fair jump takes off behind the scratch line. A foul (scratch) jump is called if the jumper steps beyond the scratch line or runs into or through the pit. Each contestant is given a certain number of trials (jumps). A scratch jump counts as a trial. Measurement is from the scratch line to the nearest point of touch.

High Jumping

The Scissors Jump is recommended for group instruction because of safety factors. The high-jump bar is approached from a slight angle. The takeoff is by the leg that is farther from the bar. The near leg is lifted and goes over, followed quickly in a looping movement by the rear leg. A good upward kick with the front leg, together with an upward thrust of the arms, is needed. The knees should be straightened at the highest point of the jump. The landing is made on the lead foot followed by the rear foot.

Hurdles

The hurdler should step so that the takeoff foot is planted 3–5 ft from the hurdle. The lead foot is extended straight forward over the hurdle; the rear (trailing) leg is bent, with the knee to the side. The lead foot reaches for the ground, quickly followed by the trailing leg. The hurdler should avoid floating over the hurdle. Body lean is necessary. A hurdler may lead with the same foot over consecutive hurdles or may alternate the leading foot. Some hurdlers like to thrust both arms forward instead of a single arm. A consistent step pattern should be developed.

Drills—Station (Small-Group) Instruction

Divide the group into four groups and send an equal number of students to each station. Practice the skills at each station. Finish the lesson by running the relay activities listed in the game section below.

Station 1—Starting, Sprinting, and Hurdling

Practice starting form. Work with a partner who gives the commands for starting. Sprint 40–60 yards and walk back to the starting line. Reverse roles.

Station 2—Standing Long Jump and High Jump

The standing long jump can be done on a tumbling mat or the ground. A tape measure can be taped to the mat or placed on the ground so students can see how far they are jumping. Swing the arms forward on the takeoff.

Station 3—Running Long Jump

Practice the running long jump by taking a short run, making contact with the takeoff board and jumping into the pit.

withdrawn.

The long jump pit must be maintained properly. It should be filled with fresh sand of a coarse variety.

If stopwatches and tape measures are used, it is important to make them highly visible. Tie bright colored cord to them or anchor to cones to assure that they are not misplaced.

Make signs for each of the stations. The signs should include appropriate performance techniques, what is to be done at each station, and appropriate safety precautions.

The high-jump bar should be at a height that offers challenge but allows concentration on technique rather than on height. Too much emphasis on competition for height quickly eliminates the poorer jumpers, who need the experience most. Safety is of utmost importance. Using a flexible elastic rope as a crossbar and avoiding any type of flop will prevent injury. The practice of keeping the entire class together on a single high-jump facility is poor methodology. This arrangement determines who are the best jumpers in class but does little else.

Station 4—Distance Running for Pace

Outline a track with cones and have children run at a pace they can continue. If they need to stop frequently, they are running too fast. The running should be loose and relaxed. Work at this station is for learning a proper pace rather than racing.

Track and Field Lead-up Activities

Potato Shuttle Relay

A small box about a foot square is placed 5 ft in front of each lane. Four 12-in. circles are drawn at 5-ft intervals beyond the box. This makes the last circle 25 ft from the starting point. Four blocks or beanbags are needed for each team. To start, the blocks are placed in the box in front of each team. The first runner goes to the box, takes a single block, and puts it into one of the circles. She repeats this performance until there is a block in each circle, then she tags off the second runner. This runner brings the blocks back to the box, one at a time, and tags off the third runner, who returns the blocks to the circles, and so on. Paper plates or Frisbees can be used instead of circles drawn on the floor.

Variation: The race can also be done with bowling pins. Instead of being placed in a box, they are in a large circle at the start.

Shuttle Relays

Since the runner is moving toward a stationary person, a difficulty in running shuttle relays is control of the exchange. In the excitement, the next runner may leave too early, and the tag or exchange is then made ahead of the restraining line. A high-jump standard or cone can be used to prevent early exchanges. The next runner awaits the tag with an arm around the standard or a hand on a cone.

One-on-One Contests

Allow students to find a friend and have a number of personal contests in track and field events such as sprints, hurdling, high jump, and standing long jump.

LP 63

Objectives:
To understand how to stretch prior to strenuous activity
To recognize the wide range of individual differences among peers

NASPE National Standards:
Introductory Activity: 1, 3, 5
Fitness Activity: 1, 4, 6
Lesson Focus: 1, 2, 4, 5
Game: 1, 5

Equipment Required:
Stopwatches
Track and Field Equipment

Instructional Activities	Teaching Hints
Introductory and Fitness Development Activities — Stretching and Jogging	

Combine the introductory and fitness activities during the track and field unit. This will help students understand how to stretch and warm up for a demanding activity such as track and field.

Jog	1–2 minutes
Standing Hip Bend	30 seconds
Sitting Stretch	30 seconds
Partner Rowing	60 seconds
Bear Hug (stretch each leg)	40 seconds
Side Flex (stretch each leg)	40 seconds
Trunk Twister	30 seconds
Jog	3–4 minutes

Emphasis should be on jogging and stretching to prepare for strenuous activity.

Encourage smooth and controlled stretching. Hold each stretch for 6–10 seconds

Lesson Focus — Track and Field Skills (2)

Skills
Review the skills taught in the previous lesson. Introduce the following skills:
Baton Passing

The right hand to left hand method is used in longer distance relays and is the best choice for elementary school children as it is easy and offers a consistent method for passes. This pass allows the receiver to face the inside of the track while waiting to receive the baton in the left hand. The oncoming runner holds the baton in the right hand like a candle when passing it to a teammate. The receiver reaches back with the left hand, fingers pointing down, thumb to the inside, and begins to run as the runner advances to within 3–5 yards. The receiver grasps the baton and shifts it from the left to the right hand while moving. If the baton is dropped, it must be picked up, or the team is disqualified. An alternative way to receive the baton is to reach back with the hand facing up; however, the fingers-down method is considered more suitable for sprint relays.

Hop-Step-and-Jump

The hop-step-and-jump event requires a takeoff board and a jumping pit. The distance from the takeoff board to the pit should be one that even less skilled jumpers can make. The event begins with a run similar to that for the running long jump. The takeoff is with one foot, and the jumper must land on the same foot to complete the hop. He then takes a step followed by a jump. The event finishes like the long jump, with a landing on both feet.

The jumper must not step over the takeoff board in the first hop, under penalty of fouling. Distance is measured from the front of the takeoff board to the closest place where the body touches. This is usually a mark made by one of the heels, but it could be a mark made by an arm or another part of the body if the jumper landed poorly and fell backward.

Drills—Station (Small-Group) Instruction
Divide the group into four groups and send an equal number of students to each station. See Lesson Week 24 for a description of activities not listed here. Practice the skills at each station. Finish the lesson by running the relay activities listed in the game section below.

The goal of track and field is self-improvement and developing proper techniques. Each student must accept responsibility for self-directed work and should be encouraged to try all activities.

The program should offer something for all—boys and girls, the highly skilled and the less skilled, and those with physical problems. Children with weight problems need particular attention. They must be stimulated and encouraged, since their participation will be minimal if little attention is paid to them. Special goals can be set for overweight children, and special events and goals can also be established for children with handicaps.

Pits for the long jump and the hop-step-and-jump must be maintained properly. They should be filled with fresh sand of a coarse variety.

The goal of the program should be to allow students to develop at their own rate. The instructor needs to be perceptive enough to determine whether students are working too hard or too little. Special attention must be given to those who appear disinterested, dejected, emotionally upset, or withdrawn.

Station 1—Starting, Sprinting, and Hurdling

Practice starting form. Work with a partner who gives the commands for starting. Sprint 40–60 yards and walk back to the starting line. Reverse roles.

Station 2—Hop-Step-and-Jump and High Jump

Set up the hop-step-and-jump with instructions on proper form set on a cone.

Station 3—Baton Passing

Practice the running long jump by taking a short run, making contact with the takeoff board and jumping into the pit.

Station 4—Distance Running for Pace

Outline a track with cones and have children run at a pace they can continue. If they need to stop frequently, they are running too fast. The running should be loose and relaxed. Work at this station is for learning a proper pace rather than racing.

If stopwatches and tape measures are used, it is important to make them highly visible. Tie bright colored cord to them or anchor to cones to assure that they are not misplaced.

Make signs for each of the stations. The signs should include appropriate performance techniques, what is to be done at each station, and appropriate safety precautions.

Track and Field Lead-up Activities

Circular (Pursuit) Relays

Circular relays make use of the regular circular track. The baton exchange technique is important, and practice is needed. On a 220-yard or 200-meter track, relays can be organized in a number of ways, depending on how many runners are spaced for one lap. Four runners can do a lap, each running one-quarter of the way; two can do a lap, each running one half of the distance; or each runner can complete a whole lap. In these races, each member of the relay team runs the same distance. Relays can also be organized so team members run different distances.

Shuttle Relays

Since children are running toward each other, one great difficulty in running shuttle relays is control of the exchange. In the excitement, the next runner may leave too early, and the tag or exchange is then made ahead of the restraining line. A high-jump standard or cone can be used to prevent early exchanges. The next runner awaits the tag with an arm around the standard or a hand on a cone.

One-on-One Contests

Allow students to find a friend and have a number of personal contests in track and field events such as sprints, hurdling, high jump, and standing long jump.

Objectives:
To create novel movement tasks
To understand the differences in
aerobic capacities among
classmates
To be able to jump slow and fast time
with a self-turned rope

NASPE National Standards:
Introductory Activity: 1, 3, 5
Fitness Activity: 1, 4, 5, 6
Lesson Focus: 1, 2, 4, 5
Game: 1, 5

Equipment Required:
Music and signs for Racetrack Fitness
Jump rope for each student
Beanbags for games

Instructional Activities	Teaching Hints

Introductory Activity — Move and Perform Task

Move around the area using any desired locomotor movement; on signal, stop and perform a task such as an exercise or stunt. Some suggested activities are: Heel Click, Push-up, Stork Stand, Sit-up, or any desired stretch.

Allow students to demonstrate novel responses in order to increase the range of student response.

Fitness Development Activity — Racetrack Fitness

Five or six fitness activities are arranged in the center (the Pit) of a large circle outlined with marking spots (the race track). If desired, tumbling mats can be placed in the center of the race track to delineate the pit stop area. Students work with a partner and alternate running (or doing other locomotor movements) around the race track and going to the pit to perform a strength or flexibility exercise. A different exercise should be performed each time so students assure variety in their workout.

The following are some examples of exercises that can be used for Pit exercises.
1. Arm circles
2. Bend and twist
3. Abdominal challenges
4. Knee to chest curl
5. Push-up challenges
6. Trunk twister

Intervals of 30 seconds of music with 10 seconds of silence can be used to signal role changes. The student who was running the track now goes to the pit to exercise and vice versa.

Assure that students run under control (not as fast as they can) and in the same direction.

Allow students to perform at a level they feel comfortable. Youngsters are genetically different and should not be expected to do the same amount of exercise repetitions.

Lesson Focus — Individual Rope-Jumping Skills

1. For students who are having trouble jumping the rope, try some of the following activities:
   a. Jump in place to a tom-tom beat without rope.
   b. Hold both ends of the jump rope in one hand (practice with right and left hands) and turn it to the side so a steady rhythm can be made through a consistent turn. Just before the rope hits the ground, the student should practice jumping.
   c. Start jumping the rope one turn at a time—gradually increase the number of turns.
2. Introduce the two basic jump rhythms:
   a. Slow-time rhythm. In slow-time rhythm, the performer jumps the rope and then takes a second jump while the rope is overhead. The jump while the rope is overhead is usually a small, light rebound jump. In slow time, the rope makes one full turn for each two jumps.
   b. Fast-time rhythm. In fast-time rhythm, the student jumps the rope with every jump. The rope makes one full turn for every jump.
3. Introduce some of the basic step variations. The basic steps can be done in slow or fast time.
   a. Side Swing. Swing the rope, held with both hands to one side of the body. Switch and swing the rope on the other side of the body.
   b. Double Side Swing and Jump. Swing the rope once on each side of the body. Follow the second swing with a jump over the rope. The sequence should be swing, swing, jump.

The length of the rope is dependent on the height of the jumper. It should be long enough so that the ends reach to the armpits or slightly higher when the child stands on its center. Grades 3–4 students need mostly 8-ft ropes, with a few 7- and 9-ft lengths. Ropes or handles can be color-coded for length.

Two types of ropes are available; the beaded (plastic segment) and the plastic (licorice) rope. The beaded ropes are heavier and seem easier to turn for beginning jumpers. The drawback to the beaded ropes is that they hurt when they hit another student. Also, if the segments are made round, the rope will roll easily on the floor children may fall when they step on it. The plastic licorice ropes are lighter and give less wind resistance.

c. Alternate-Foot Basic Step. In the Alternate-Foot Basic Step, as the rope passes under the feet, the weight is shifted alternately from one foot to the other, raising the unweighted foot in a running position.

d. Bird Jumps. Jump with the toes pointed in (pigeon walk) and with the toes pointed out (duck walk). Alternate toes in and toes out.

e. Swing-Step Forward. The Swing-Step Forward is the same as the Alternate-Foot Basic Step, except that the free leg swings forward. The knee is kept loose and the foot swings naturally.

f. Rocker Step. In executing the Rocker Step, one leg is always forward in a walking-stride position. As the rope passes under the feet, the weight is shifted from the back foot to the forward foot. The rebound is taken on the forward foot while the rope is above the head. On the next turn of the rope, the weight is shifted from the forward foot to the back foot, repeating the rebound on the back foot.

4. Individual Rope Jumping with a Partner. One student turns and jumps the rope while her partner enters and jumps simultaneously. Entering is sometimes difficult for beginners, so it may be necessary to begin in position and then start turning the rope. The following are some challenges partners can try:

a. Run in and face partner, and both jump.

b. Run in and turn back to partner, and both jump.

c. Decide which steps are to be done; then run in and match steps.

d. Repeat with the rope turning backward.

Instructional cues to use for improving jumping technique are as follows:

a. Keep the arms at the side of the body while turning. (Many children lift the arms to shoulder level trying to move the rope overhead. This makes it impossible for the youngster to jump over the elevated rope.)

b. Turn the rope by making small circles with the wrists.

c. Jump on the balls of the feet.

d. Bend the knees slightly to absorb the force of the jump.

e. Don't jump too high. Make a small jump over the rope.

Game Activity

Is it Raining? (Cooperative Activity)

Formation: Entire class in a circle

Supplies: None

This activity works well at the end of a vigorous lesson. Standing in a circle, the teacher initiates a movement and then the child immediately to her right starts the movement and so on in the fashion of a wave at a stadium. When the "wave" gets back to the teacher another movement is started. The students keep the previous sound until the next one gets around to them. The movements can be any sounds that mimic those heard in nature during a storm. The following are examples of potential moves for the teacher:

Clapping

Snapping

Patting quadriceps

Stamping

Patting the chest

Hands rubbing on legs

Hands rubbing together

Clucking the tongue

Hollow whistles

Making "Shhhhh" sounds

Teaching Tips: Allow students to create movements and lead the changes. Instruct students to close their eyes and rely on their hearing to not only listen for the sound to come around, but to also see if they can figure out what the new movement is.

Crows and Cranes

Supplies: None

Skills: Running, dodging

Establish two goal lines on opposite sides of the area. The class is divided into two groups—the crows and the cranes. The groups face each other at the center of the area, about 5 ft apart. The leader calls out either "Crows" or "Cranes," using a cr-r-r-r-r sound at the start of either word to mask the result. If "Crows" is the call, the crows chase the cranes to the goal line. If "Cranes" is the call, the cranes chase. Any player caught goes over to the other side and becomes a member of that group. The team that has the most players when the game ends is the winner.

LP 65

Objectives:
To be able to turn and jump a long
    rope
To cooperatively perform parachute
    fitness activities
To perform locomotor movements to
    rhythm
To understand strategies in simple
    game activities

NASPE National Standards:
Introductory Activity: 1, 2, 4, 5
Fitness Activity: 1, 4, 5, 6
Lesson Focus: 1, 2, 3, 5
Game: 1, 2, 3, 5

Equipment Required:
8–10 long jump ropes
Parachute for fitness
Music for rhythmic activities
Tinikling equipment
Clubs, balls, jump the shot rope, and
    beach balls for games

Instructional Activities	Teaching Hints

Introductory Activity — Long Jump Rope Routine

Have the squad form a loose column and hold a long jump rope in the right hand.

Group youngsters into fours

1. On the first signal: Run in a column with one child leading the way.
2. Second signal: Shift the rope overhead from right hand to left hand without stopping.
3. Third signal: Two inside children let go of rope, outside children begin turning the rope for the two who have released the rope. They continue jumping the rope until the next signal.
4. Fourth signal: The outside youngsters move to the inside positions and vice versa. The sequence is then repeated.

Encourage students to think of other
activities to perform with the rope on
the second signal.

If desired, the groups can carry two
ropes and practice double Dutch on the
third and fourth signals.

Fitness Development Activity — Parachute Fitness

1. Jog in circle with chute held in left hand. Reverse directions and hold with right hand. (music)
2. Standing, raise the chute overhead, lower to waist, lower to toes, raise to waist, etc. (no music)
3. Slide to the right; return slide to the left. (music)
4. Sit and perform abdominal challenges. (no music)
5. Skip. (music)
6. Freeze; face the center, and stretch the chute tightly with bent arms. Hold for 8–12 seconds. Repeat five to six times. (no music)
7. Run in place, hold the chute at waist level and hit the chute with lifted knees. (music)
8. Sit with legs under the chute. Do a seat walk toward the center. Return to the perimeter. Repeat four to six times. (no music)
9. Place the chute on the ground. Jog away from the chute and return on signal. Repeat. (music)
10. On sides with legs under the chute, perform Side Flex and lift chute with legs. (no music)
11. Hop to the center of the chute and return. Repeat. (music)
12. Assume the push-up position with the legs aligned away from the center of the chute. Shake the chute with one arm while the other arm supports the body. (no music)
13. Lie on back with legs under the chute. Shake the chute with the feet. (music)
14. Sit with feet under the chute. Stretch by touching the toes with the chute. Relax with other stretches while sitting. (no music)

Tape alternating segments (25–30
seconds in length) of silence and music
to signal duration of exercise. Music
segments indicate aerobic activity with
the parachute; intervals of silence
announce using the chute to enhance
flexibility and strength development.

Space youngsters evenly around the
chute.

Use different hand grips (palms up,
down, mixed).

All movements should be done under
control. Some of the faster and stronger
students will have to moderate their
performance.

Lesson Focus — Rhythmic Movement Skills (3)

Begin each lesson with a review of one or two dances youngsters know and enjoy. Review dances from Weeks 13 and 16 as
desired before teaching new ones.

Rhythms should be taught like other sport skills. Avoid striving for perfection so students know it is acceptable to make mistakes. Teach a variety of dances rather than one or two in depth in case some students find it difficult to master a specific dance. Make dances easy for students to learn by implementing some of the following techniques:

1. Teach the dances without using partners.
2. Allow youngsters to move in any direction without left-right orientation.
3. Use scattered formation instead of circles.
4. Emphasize strong movements such as clapping and stamping to increase involvement.
5. Play the music at a slower speed when first learning the dance.

E-Z Mixer

Music Source: WWC-FFD or any music with a definite rhythm
Formation: Circle formation with couples in promenade position, inside hands joined, facing counterclockwise.
Directions:

Measures	Action
1–2	With partner B on the right, walk forward four steps. (Forward, 2, 3, 4) Back out to face center in a single circle. (Circle, 2, 3, 4)
3–4	Partners B walk to the center. (In, 2, 3, 4) Back out of the center. (Out, 2, 3, 4)
5–6	Partners A take four steps to the center, turning one half left face on the fourth step. (In, 2, 3, turn left face) They take four steps toward the corner. (Out, 2, 3, 4)
7–8	As swing the corner B twice around, opening up to face counterclockwise, back in starting position, to begin the dance again. (Swing, 2, 3, open)

Irish Washerwoman (Irish)

Music Source: WWCD-1043
Formation: Single circle, couples facing center, partner B to the right, hands joined
Directions: Dancers follow the call.

Call	Action
All join hands and go to the middle.	Beginning left, take four steps to the center. (Center, 2, 3, 4)
And with your big foot keep time to the fiddle.	Stamp four times in place (Stamp, 2, 3, 4)
And when you get back, remember my call.	Take four steps backward to place (Back, 2, 3, 4)
Swing your corner and promenade all.	Swing the corner and promenade in the line of direction. (Swing, 2, 3, promenade)

Dancers keep promenading until they hear the call again to repeat the pattern.

Gustaf's Skoal (Swedish)

Music Source: WWCD-1044; WWCD-FDN
Formation: The formation is similar to a square dance set of four couples, each facing center. Partner A is to the left of partner B. Couples join inside hands; the outside hand is on the hip. Two of the couples facing each other are designated the head couples. The other two couples, also facing each other, are the side couples.
Directions: The dance is in two parts. During Part I, the music is slow and stately. The dancers perform with great dignity. The music for Part II is light and represents fun.

Measures	Part I Action
1–2	The head couples, inside hands joined, walk forward three steps and bow to the opposite couple. (Forward, 2, 3, bow)
3–4	The head couples take three steps backward to place and bow to each other. (The side couples hold their places during this action.) (Back, 2, 3, bow)
5–8	The side couples repeat action of measures 1–4 while the head couples hold their places. (Forward, 2, 3, bow; Back, 2, 3, bow)
9–16	The dancers repeat measures 1--8.

Measures	Part II Action
17–22	The side couples raise joined hands to form an arch. Head couples skip forward four steps, release partners' hands, join inside hands with opposite person, and skip under the nearest arch with new partner. After going under the arch, they drop hands and head back home to their original partner. (Head couples: Skip, 2, 3, 4; Under, 2, 3, 4; Around, 2, 3, 4)
23–24	All couples join both hands with partners and swing once around with four skipping steps. (Swing, 2, 3, 4)
25–30	Head couples form arches while side couples repeat the action of measures 17–22. (Side couples: Skip, 2, 3, 4; Under, 2, 3, 4; Around, 2, 3, 4)
31–32	All couples then repeat the movements in measures 23–24. (Swing, 2, 3, 4)

Tinikling (Philippine Islands)

Music Source: WWCD-8095; WWC-9015

Formation: Sets of four scattered around the room. Each set has two strikers and two dancers.

Directions: Two 8-ft bamboo poles and two crossbars on which the poles rest are needed for the dance. A striker kneels at each end of the poles; both strikers hold the end of a pole in each hand. The music is in waltz meter, 3/4 time, with an accent on the first beat. The strikers slide and strike the poles together on count 1. On the other two beats of the waltz measure, the poles are opened about 15 in. apart, lifted an inch or so, and tapped twice on the crossbars in time to counts 2 and 3. The rhythm "close, tap, tap" is continued throughout the dance, each sequence constituting a measure.

Basically, the dance requires that a step be done outside the poles on the close (count 1) and that two steps be done inside the poles (counts 2 and 3) when the poles are tapped on the crossbars. Many step combinations have been devised. The basic tinikling step should be practiced until it is mastered. The step is done singly, although two dancers are performing. Each dancer takes a position at an opposite end and on the opposite side so that the dancer's right side is to the bamboo poles.

Count 1: Step slightly forward with the left foot.
Count 2: Step with the right foot between the poles.
Count 3: Step with the left foot between the poles.
Count 4: Step with the right outside to dancer's own right.
Count 5: Step with the left between the poles.
Count 6: Step with the right between the poles.
Count 7: Step with the left outside to the original position.

The initial step (count 1) is used only to get the dance under way. The last step (count 7) to original position is actually the beginning of a new series (7, 8, 9–10, 11, 12).

Tinikling steps also can be adjusted to 4/4 rhythm ("close, close, tap, tap"), which requires the poles to be closed on two counts and open on the other two. The basic foot pattern is two steps outside the poles and two inside. For the sake of conformity, we present all routines in the original 3/4 time ("close, tap, tap"). If other rhythms are used, adjust accordingly.

Dancers can go from side to side, or can return to the side from which they entered. The dance can be done singly, with the two dancers moving in opposite directions from side to side, or the dancers can enter from and leave toward the same side. Dancers can do the same step patterns or do different movements. They can dance as partners, moving side by side with inside hands joined, or facing each other with both hands joined.

Teaching suggestions:

Steps should be practiced first with stationary poles or with lines drawn on the floor. Jump ropes can be used as stationary objects over which to practice. Students handling the poles should concentrate on watching each other rather than the dancer to avoid becoming confused by the dancer's feet.

To gain a sense of the movement pattern for 3/4 time, slap both thighs with the hands on the "close," and clap the hands twice for movements inside the poles. For 4/4 time, slap the right thigh with the right hand, then the left thigh with the left hand, followed by two claps. This routine should be done to music, with the poles closing and opening as indicated. Getting the feel of the rhythm is important.

Polly Wolly Doodle (American)

Music Sources: WWCD-1041

Skills: Sliding, turning, walking

Formation: Double circle of dancers, partners facing with both hands joined, partner A with back to the center of the circle.

Directions:

Measures	Part I Action
1–4	All slide four steps—A to left, B to right, counterclockwise. (Slide, 2, 3, 4)
5–8	Drop hands and all turn solo circle, A to left, B to right, with five stamps in this rhythm: 1-2-1, 2, 3. (Stamp on the word "polly," stamp on the other foot on the word "doodle," and take three quick stamps on the word "day.") (Turn, 2, stamp, 2, 3)
9–16	Repeat measures 1–8, but in the opposite direction, A moving to right and B to left. (Slide, 2, 3, 4; Turn, 2, stamp 2, 3)

Measures	Part II Action
1–4	Both bow to each other, A with hands on hips, B with hands at sides. (A bow; B bow)
5–8	With four walking steps (or skipping steps), both move backward, away from each other. (Back, 2, 3, 4)
9–12	Both move diagonally forward to own left to meet a new partner. (Diagonal, 2, 3, 4)
13–16	With the new partner, elbow swing in place using a skipping step. (Swing, 2, 3, 4) Repeat the dance from the beginning with the new partner.

Pop Goes the Weasel (American)

Music Source: WWCD-1043; WWCD-FDN

Skills: Walking, skipping, turning under

Formation: Double circle of sets of four; couples facing with partner B on partner A's right. Couples facing clockwise are number 1 couples; couples facing counterclockwise are number 2 couples.

Directions:

Measures	Action
1–4	Join hands in a circle of four and circle left, once around, with eight skipping or sliding steps. (Circle, 2, 3, 4, 5, 6, 7, 8)
5–6	Take two steps forward, raising the joined hands, and two steps backward, lowering the hands. (Forward, 2; Back, 2)
7–8	"Ones" pop the "Twos" under (i.e., couples number 1 raise their joined hands to form an arch and pass the number 2 couples under). All walk ahead to meet a new couple. (Forward, and pop through)

Repeat as desired.

Variations:

1. Dancers are in sets of three, all facing counterclockwise. Each forms a triangle with one child in front and the other two with joined hands forming the base. The front dancer reaches back and holds the outside hands of the other two dancers. The groups of three are in a large circle formation.

Measures	Action
1–2	Sets of three dancers skip forward four times. (Forward, 2, 3, 4)
3–4	Sets of three skip backward four times. (Backward, 2, 3, 4)
5–6	Sets of three skip forward four times. (Forward, 2, 3, 4)
7–8	On "Pop goes the weasel," the two back dancers raise their joined hands, and the front dancer backs up underneath to the next set. This set, in the meantime, has "popped" its front dancer back to the set behind it. (Raise and pop under)

2. "Pop Goes the Weasel" is excellent for stimulating creative movement. The music actually consists of a verse and a chorus part. During the verse part, the children can slide, gallop, or skip until the "Pop" line, at which time they make a half or full turn in the air. During the chorus, they can do jerky nonlocomotor movements. Other options include ball routines, in which the children dribble in time to the music during the verse and pass the ball around various parts of the body during the chorus. Another variation involves ropes. The children carry a jump rope while skipping, sliding, or galloping. During the chorus, they jump in time to the music, and on the word "Pop," they try to do a double jump.

Game Activity

Jump the Shot

Supplies: A jump-the-shot rope

Skill: Rope jumping

The players stand in circle formation. One player with a long rope stands in the center. A soft object is tied to the free end of the rope to give it some weight. An old, deflated ball or beanbag makes a good weight (tie the rope to it and use duct tape to keep it from becoming untied). The center player turns the rope under the feet of the circle players, who must jump over it. A player who touches the rope with the feet must move up to the next group. Change the center player after one or two misses. The center player should be cautioned to keep the rope near the ground. The rope speed can be varied. An effective way to turn the rope is to sit cross-legged and turn it over the head. Different tasks can be performed such as hopping, jumping and turning, or jumping and clapping.

Beach Ball Bat Ball

Supplies: 4–6 beach balls

Skills: Batting, tactile handling

Two games are played across the gymnasium area. The teams are scattered throughout the area without restriction as to where they may move. To begin the game, the balls are placed on the centerline dividing the court area. Four to eight beach balls are in play at the same time. A score occurs when the beach ball is batted over the end line. Once the ball moves across the end line it is dead. Players concentrate on the remaining balls in play. If a ball is on the floor, it is picked up and batted into play. At no time may a ball be carried. After all the balls are scored, the game ends. A new game is started after teams switch goals.

Club Guard

Supplies: A juggling club or bowling pin and foam rubber ball

Skill: Throwing

A circle about 15 ft in diameter is drawn. Inside the circle at the center, an 18-in. circle is drawn. The club is placed in the center of the small circle. Two or three youngsters guard the club. The other players stand outside the large circle, which is the restraining line for them. The circle players throw the ball at the club and try to knock it down. The guards try to block the throws with the legs and body but must stay out of the small inner circle. The outer circle players pass the ball around rapidly so that one of the players can get an opening to throw as the guards maneuver to protect the club. Rotate in new guards after a short period of time (15–20 seconds).

Objectives:
To know the proper method of holding
  a racquet
To learn to handle a racquet while
  moving
To hit a ball in a predetermined
  direction with a racquet

NASPE National Standards:
Introductory Activity: 1, 3, 5
Fitness Activity: 1, 4, 5, 6
Lesson Focus: 2, 3, 5
Game: 1, 2, 3, 5

Equipment Required:
Signs for sport-related fitness stations
One racquet and cut foam training ball
  for each student
Tumbling mats or net (volleyball etc.)
Rubber marking spots

Instructional Activities	Teaching Hints

Introductory Activity — Squad Leader Movements

Organize class into small groups of 3–4 students. Each group moves around the area, following a leader. When a change is signaled, the last person goes to the head of the line and becomes the squad leader.

Encourage leaders to keep the group moving. The minimum activity is jogging in place.

Fitness Development Activity — Sport-Related (Tennis) Fitness Stations

Design your circuit so youngsters alternate strength and flexibility activities with sport-related fitness activities. Students do the best they can at each station within the time limit. Children differ and their ability to perform fitness workloads differs.
1. Rope jumping
2. Tennis shuffle—similar to the agility run, Mark two lines about 30 ft apart. While holding the racquet in the ready position, slide back and forth between the lines. Change appropriately to the backhand and forehand position when moving.
3. Shoulder girdle development challenges
4. Run and set—Students move with a racquet in hand. They run a short distance, place their feet in proper position and swing at an imaginary ball. Repeat as many times as possible using the forehand and backhand.
5. Flexibility and trunk development challenges
6. Racquets and beanbag toss—Students work with a partner or small group and toss a beanbag back and forth and catch it with racquet. Avoid using hands.
7. Abdominal development challenges
8. Quarter turn sets—Start in a front-facing position with racquet held in the ready position. Follow a leader and do a quarter jump turn (to forehand or backhand setup position). Go back to front facing position each time. Each leader gets to lead 5 jump turns.

Tape alternating segments of silence and music to signal duration of exercise. Music segments (begin at 30 seconds) indicate activity at each station while intervals of silence (10 seconds) announce it is time to stop and move forward to the next station.

See the Week 1 lesson plan for strength and flexibility challenges.

Use signals such as start, stop, and move up to ensure rapid movement to the next station.

Ask students to do the best they can. Expect workloads to differ.

Lesson Focus — Tennis Skills

Racquet Handling Skills
1. Show the forehand grip. Have the student hold the racquet perpendicular to the floor and shake hands with it.
   a. The thumb and forefinger make a "V" down the handle.
   b. Keep the wrist firm

2. Place ball on racquet and attempt to roll it around the edge of the racquet without allowing it to fall off the racquet. Flip the racquet over (backhand grip) and roll ball.

3. Balance the ball on the racquet using the forehand grip while trying the following challenges:
   a. Touch the floor with hand.
   b. Move to knees and back to feet.
   c. Sit down and get back on feet.
   d. Lie down and get back on feet.
   e. Skip, gallop, or any other locomotor movement.

Explain the difference between forehand and backhand in these activities, i.e., with the forehand, the palm of the hand is up. With the backhand, the palm of the hand is down.

When students are receiving instruction, teach them to cross their arms and hug the racquet. If instructions are longer than 15 seconds, have students place their racquet and ball on the floor and take one step backwards. Limit instructional episodes to 30 seconds.

Don't chase a ball that is out of your area. When performing drills, teach students to stay at least an arm plus a racquet length from other players.

4. Flip the racquet over (backhand grip) and balance the ball while trying the following challenges:
   a. Pat your knees with the off hand.
   b. While moving, do a full turn and keep walking.
   c. Walk 5 steps forward and 5 steps backward. Repeat.
   d. Lie down and get back on feet.
   e. See how high you can balance the ball. How low can you carry the ball?

5. Beanbag Toss and Catch Activities.
   a. Toss the beanbag in the air and catch it on the racquet.
   b. Toss the beanbag in the air from the racquet and catch it with the off-hand.
   c. Toss the beanbag in the air from the racquet and catch it with the racquet.
   d. Toss the beanbag a few feet in front with the off-hand, move, and catch it with the racquet.

The purpose of these activities is to learn to keep the racquet in a level plane. Also, students can begin to see the difference between the forehand and backhand stroke.

Have students hold their racquet overhead. The top of the racquet is the highest level they should toss the beanbag. Limiting the height of the tosses will maximize safety and reduce management problems.

Moving and Tracking Skills

1. Beanbag Balance. Students balance a beanbag on the face of the racquet while moving around the area. Ask them to sit down, do a full turn, and heel click while maintaining control of the beanbag. Ask students to think of challenges to perform with their racquet and ball.

2. Edgy Beanbag Balance. Increase the challenge by asking the students to balance the beanbag on the edge of the racquet. Play "Stop & Go" with the beanbag on the edge of the racquet (students run and freeze quickly without losing control of the beanbag). Try some of the challenges created in the previous activity.

3. Racquet Balance. Change the pace of the lesson by practicing getting the racquet to stand by itself. Balance the racquet, let go of it, swing your leg over the racquet, and catch it with the same hand. Try doing it with the nondominant legs as well.

4. Racquet Balance with a Partner. Partners are about 3 ft apart while balancing their racquets. On signal, they release their racquet and try to catch their partner's racquet before it falls to the ground. If both partners catch their racquet, they each step back one step and repeat the challenge. An additional challenge is to make a full turn after the release and before catching the racquet.

5. Beanbag Pass and Catch. Partners pass a beanbag back and forth to each other and catch the beanbag on their racquet. Begin with partners in a stationary position and then increase the challenge by passing the beanbag to one side of the catching partner (move and catch). Another challenge is to have the catching partner circle around the tossing partner. The catching partner returns the beanbag with a toss.

6. Ready Position and Catch. One player is the tosser and the other player is in ready position with the racquet. The tosser will toss the beanbag to one side or the other of the player in ready position. Their goal is to catch it on the racquet (forehand or backhand) and learn to move into position rather than reaching for the ball. Switch positions after 4 tosses.

Beanbags are used in this lesson to help students find success quickly. Place emphasis on learning to watch the moving object.

When youngsters are having trouble mastering an activity, they can go back to the previously learned activities. All students do not have to be on the same activity at the same time. Since these are individual activities, youngsters can feel comfortable moving at a pace that works for them. Students will go off-task when an activity is too difficult for them.

Change partners regularly so that the class learns to work together. Practicing with different partners will create friendships. Part of tennis is the social experience and learning to enjoy an activity with a friend. Remind students that "Everybody Counts! Make New Friends!"

If a class or some students master the beanbag activities, the transition ball can be used to increase the challenge.

Tennis Lead-up Activities

Red Light, Green Light Tennis

Supplies: One racquet and one cut foam ball per student
Skills: Racquet and ball control; reaction time

This game is played somewhat like the original *Red Light, Green Light* game except that each player has a cut foam ball balanced on their racquet. If a player loses control of their ball (it falls off the racquet or they touch it with the other hand), when "Red Light" is called, they have a point scored against them. "Green Light" starts them moving again. The goal is to avoid accumulating points. To add variety to the game, use other commands like left turn, right turn, "U-turn," and "hit the brakes."

Circle Bump Pass

Supplies: One racquet for each player and a cut foam ball for each group
Skills: Bumping the ball to another player

Divide the class into three or four groups in circle formation. Circles are competing against each other. Each circle is given 5 points. All players have a racquet and there is one ball per circle. The goal is to bump pass the ball to other group members. The ball may bounce as many times as desired. However, once it stops bouncing, it is out of play and a point is taken from that team. The goal is for each circle to keep their points as long as possible. Rather than wait for all teams to lose their points with one remaining, start the game over frequently. The purpose of the game is for all students to have a chance to practice their skills.

Playground Tennis

Supplies: One racquet per student and one cut foam ball per game.

Skills: Racquet and ball control, bumping the ball, team play

Playground Tennis is a team game that uses no more than 4 players per team (4 against 4) per court. Players "bump" the cut foam ball over the net rather than taking wild swings. Racquet control is the instructional cue. A stretch magic rope, volleyball net or similar equipment can be used to delineate the net. There is no spiking, all balls must have an upward trajectory. Score by ones, the first team to five is the winner and a new game starts.

There are three ways to win/lose a point.

    1. If the ball rolls, it is dead and the point goes to the other team.

    2. If the first bounce after the ball crosses the net does not land in the court, the point goes to the other team.

    3. If the server double faults, the point goes to the other team.

If players converge on the ball rather than stay in their area, establish quadrants where they must stay. Rotate youngsters to different quadrants so they have a chance to play in all areas.

The serve is drop-hit (i.e., one bounce on the court and then bumped over the net) from anywhere on the court. Two serves per point are allowed. Servers are rotated after every other point (serve two points and change servers).

Once the ball is served, it may bounce as many times as the receiving team wants it to, no matter where it goes. When a team bumps the ball over the net, the first bounce must land inside the doubles court lines. After that, the ball is in play as long as the ball is bouncing, even if it goes outside of the doubles court. The team tries to scoop it up and bump it back over the net. If the ball is hit into the net, but is still bouncing, it is still in play and the team can continue to try to scoop it up and bump it over the net.

Teaching Tip: Play 3 on 3 with less able students and 2 on 2 with more proficient students.

DPE Curriculum Guide – Lesson Plans
Tennis Skills and Lead-up Activities (2)
Level II – Week 29

Objectives:
To know the proper method of holding the racquet for forehand and backhand strokes
To volley with a partner using the forehand and backhand strokes

NASPE National Standards:
Introductory Activity: 1, 3, 5
Fitness Activity: 1, 4, 5, 6
Lesson Focus: 2, 3, 5
Game: 1, 2, 3, 5

Equipment Required:
Signs for sport-related fitness stations
One racquet and cut foam training ball for each student
Tumbling mats or net (volleyball, etc.)
Rubber marking spots

Instructional Activities	Teaching Hints

Introductory Activity — Individual Crows and Cranes

All students have a partner and line up along two lines facing each other. The lines are about 3 ft apart. This is an individual game. The partners alternate calling out "Crows!" When one of the partners decides to call out "Cranes," the other partner must take off and run back to a safety line without being tagged. If the chaser tags them, the chaser gets a point. Players start over immediately.

Assure students are spread out so they don't run into each other.

Tagging is done with the back of the hand on the shoulder.

Fitness Development Activity — Sport-Related (Tennis) Fitness Stations

Design your circuit so youngsters alternate strength and flexibility activities with sport-related fitness activities. Students do the best they can at each station within the time limit. Children differ and their ability to perform fitness workloads differs.
1. Rope jumping
2. Tennis shuffle—similar to the agility run, Mark two lines about 30 ft apart. While holding the racquet in the ready position, slide back and forth between the lines. Change appropriately to the backhand and forehand position when moving.
3. Shoulder girdle development challenges
4. Run and set—Students move with a racquet in hand. They run a short distance, place their feet in proper position and swing at an imaginary ball. Repeat as many times as possible using the forehand and backhand.
5. Flexibility and trunk development challenges
6. Racquets and beanbag toss—Students work with a partner or small group and toss a beanbag back and forth and catch it with racquet. Avoid using hands.
7. Abdominal development challenges
8. Quarter turn sets—Start in a front facing position with racquet held in the ready position. Follow a leader and do a quarter jump turn (to forehand or backhand setup position). Go back to front facing position each time. Each leader gets to lead 5 jump turns.

Tape alternating segments of silence and music to signal duration of exercise. Music segments (begin at 30 seconds) indicate activity at each station; intervals of silence (10 seconds) announce it is time to stop and move forward to the next station.

See the Week 1 lesson plan for strength and flexibility challenges.

Use signals such as start, stop, and move up to ensure rapid movement to the next station.

Ask students to do the best they can. Expect workloads to differ.

Lesson Focus — Tennis Skills

The Forehand—Individual Activities
1. Begin the lesson by reviewing some racquet handling activities from the previous lessons.
2. Without excessive talking, show students the forehand bump against the wall and let them find a wall space to practice. Give students a minute or two to practice the forehand stroke. Focus on keeping the non-racquet side of the body toward the wall. Teach students to have their feet in proper alignment for hitting the ball to the wall in front of them.
3. Select the corrective feedback you will offer students. Teach to one point at a time and offer time for practice. Some points that often need practice are:
   a. Set up with your nonracquet side toward the wall.
   b. Make your swing move low to high (start low & follow through high).
   c. Move your body into position so you can make contact with the ball when it is in line with the front foot.

Allow students to try a skill first before offering corrective feedback. This helps them see the need for help in improving their performance and allows you to see where they need help.

There are a number of ways to simulate nets for students in the physical education setting. Tumbling mats can be laid folded and on-edge as a net. Cafeteria tables can also be used. Some teachers use two cones with a jump rope stretched between them for a net. Other alternatives are to use a lowered

The Backhand—Individual Activities

1. Demonstrate the two-hand backhand stroke for the class. Have students practice performing backhand shots without a ball.
2. Backhand bump-ups with bounce. Practice bumping the ball in the air with a backhand and letting it bounce to the floor.
3. Backhand bump-ups without a bounce. Practice bumping the ball in the air continuously with the backhand.
4. Drop hit bump-ups into the air. Drop hit the ball into the air. This requires a firm wrist to elevate the ball. Remind students to drop the ball from shoulder height.
5. Backhands against the wall. Practice hitting backhand shots against the wall with a gentle bump stroke. Keep the distance from student to wall short so the ball doesn't travel too far off course.
6. Forehand and backhand bump-ups. Offer the opportunity for students to practice using the forehand and backhand strokes to perform bump-ups. To make sure they know the difference between forehand and backhand, have them call out the stroke they are using.

Note: Don't over emphasize "how many in a row" can you perform? This has a tendency to have students focus on accumulating a number of hits without concern for how they perform their strokes.

The Forehand and Backhand Strokes—Station Activities: Move to stations and allow students to practice independently at each station.

Station 1. Forehand and backhand bump-ups with bounce. Practice bumping the ball in the air with a forehand and letting it bounce to the floor. Follow with a backhand and bounce.

Station 2. Forehand and backhand bump-ups without a bounce. Practice bumping the ball in the air continuously with the forehand. Repeat with backhand.

Station 3. Drop hit bump-ups into the air. Drop hit the ball into the air. This requires a firm wrist to elevate the ball. Remind students to drop the ball from shoulder height.

Station 4. Forehands and backhands against the wall. Practice hitting forehand and backhand shots against the wall with a gentle bump stroke. Keep the distance from student to wall short so the ball doesn't travel too far off course.

volleyball net or caution tape tied between floor standards. The purpose is to give students a target to hit the ball over.

Remind the class that bump-ups should not go higher than eye level.

Tell students the "top of the hand" leads the way on the backhand.
Remind students to look before they chase a ball they have missed.

Use a change of pace activity if students start to go off-task. Play one of the games below if necessary. Students will begin to go off-task if they have to concentrate on learning new skills for a long period of time.

Divide the class into groups of 4 using the Whistle Mixer technique. Then assign one person from each group to the first station, a second person from each group to the second station, etc.

2–3 minutes per station will allow ample opportunity for practice.

Ask students to put the equipment back where they acquired it at their station when they rotate to a new station.

Tennis Lead-up Activities

Caterpillar

Supplies: One racquet for each player and cut foam balls

Skills: Handling the ball on the racquet while moving

Divide the class into groups of three. Have the players line up, side by side (shoulder to shoulder) behind the baseline. Each player has a racquet and holds it out in front to him/her with the racquet face pointing upward. Only the last person in the line has a ball and it is balanced on the strings. On "go," players with the ball roll it to the teammate next to them without touching it with the off hand. When the ball is on the teammate's racquet, he/she runs to the front of the line and touches shoulders with the teammate there. Players should run behind the line after they pass the ball. This is continued over and over until the team makes its way to the designated finish line. A beanbag may be used if the players are having difficulty with the ball.

Alley Rally

Supplies: One racquet per student; three cut foam balls per pair of students

Skills: Bumping balls over the net

Have players pair up with a partner. The partners stand 3–5 ft away from one another, anywhere in the court area. Each player puts a ball down in front of his/her feet on the court. Each player takes one step away form the ball in front of them and another step to the left or right (depending on whether the player is left or right handed), so that the partners' forehand contact points (racquet face) are in a direct line across from each other. The players then bump a ball back and forth trying to hit their partner's ball that is lying on the court. Play a game to five and start over. Change partners often. Some variations are to increase the distance between the players or change the targets on the court. For example, hoops or marking spots could be used as larger targets.

Playground Tennis

Supplies: One racquet per student and one cut foam ball per game.

Skills: Racquet and ball control, bumping the ball, team play

Playground Tennis is a team game that uses no more than 4 players per team (4 against 4) per court. Players "bump" the cut foam ball over the net rather than taking wild swings. Racquet control is the instructional cue. A stretch magic rope, volleyball net, or similar equipment can be used to delineate the net. There is no spiking, all balls must have an upward trajectory. Score by ones, the first team to five is the winner and a new game starts.

There are three ways to win/lose a point.

1. If the ball rolls, it is dead and the point goes to the other team.
2. If the first bounce after the ball crosses the net does not land in the court, the point goes to the other team.
3. If the server double faults, the point goes to the other team.

If players converge on the ball rather than stay in their area, establish quadrants where they must stay. Rotate youngsters to different quadrants so they have a chance to play in all areas.

The serve is drop-hit (i.e., one bounce on the court and then bumped over the net) from anywhere on the court. Two serves per point are allowed. Servers are rotated after every other point (serve two points and change servers).

Once the ball is served, it may bounce as many times as the receiving team wants it to, no matter where it goes. When a team bumps the ball over the net, the first bounce must land inside the doubles court lines. After that, the ball is in play as long as the ball is bouncing, even if it goes outside of the doubles court. The team tries to scoop it up and bump it back over the net. If the ball is hit into the net, but is still bouncing, it is still in play and the team can continue to try to scoop it up and bump it over the net.

Teaching Tip: Play 3 on 3 with less able students and 2 on 2 with more proficient students

Objectives:

To perform overhand and underhand
volleyball passing skills

To volley the ball a number of times
against a wall

To practice skills successfully with a
partner

To learn the basic rules of volleyball

NASPE National Standards:

Introductory Activity: 1, 3, 5

Fitness Activity: 1, 2, 4, 5

Lesson Focus: 1, 3, 4, 6

Game: 2, 3, 5

Equipment Required:

Tambourine

Music and signs for Circuit Training

One beach ball, 8" foam rubber, or
volleyball trainer for each student

Volleyball net (6 ft height)

Instructional Activities	Teaching Hints

Introductory Activity — Marking

Each child has a partner who is somewhat equal in ability. Under control, one partner runs, dodges, and tries to lose the other, who tries to stay within 3 ft of the runner. On signal, both freeze. The chaser must be close enough to touch her partner to say that they have marked (scored a point) them. Partners then reverse roles.

1. Use different locomotor movements.
2. Allow a point to be scored only when they touch a specified body part (i.e., knee, elbow, left hand).

Fitness Development Activity — Circuit Training

Students do the best they can at each station within the time limit. This implies that not all youngsters are required to do the same workload. Children differ and their ability to perform fitness workloads differs. Make fitness a personal challenge.

Rope Jumping
Triceps Push-Ups
Agility Run
Body Circles
Hula Hoop
Knee Touch Curl-Ups
Crab Walk
Tortoise and Hare
Bend and Twist

Conclude circuit training with 2–4 minutes of walking, jogging, rope jumping, or other aerobic activity.

Tape alternating segments of silence and music to signal duration of exercise. Music segments (begin at 30 seconds) indicate activity at each station while intervals of silence (10 seconds) announce it is time to stop and move forward to the next station.

Use signals such as start, stop, and move up to ensure rapid movement to the next station.

Ask students to do the best they can. Expect workloads to differ.

Lesson Focus — Volleyball Skills

Skills

Practice the following skills:

Overhand Pass

To execute an overhand pass, the player moves underneath the ball and controls it with the fingertips. The cup of the fingers is made so that the thumbs and forefingers are close together and the other fingers are spread. The hands are held forehead high, with elbows out and level with the floor. The player, when in receiving position, looks ready to shout upward through the hands. The player contacts the ball above eye level and propels it with the force of spread fingers, not with the palms. At the moment of contact, the legs are straightened and the hands and arms follow through.

Forearm Pass (Underhand Pass)

The hands are clasped together so that the forearms are parallel. The clasp should be relaxed, with the type of handclasp a matter of choice. The thumbs are kept parallel and together, and the fingers of one hand make a partially cupped fist, with the fingers of the other hand overlapping the fist. The wrists are turned downward and the elbow joints are reasonably locked. The forearms are held at the proper angle to rebound the ball, with contact made with the fists or forearms between the knees as the receiver crouches.

Using beach balls and trainer volleyballs will allow youngsters time to move into the path of the volleyball instead of reaching for the ball. Proper footwork is critical to the success of volleyball; using proper balls will help assure that youngsters learn correctly.

Instructional cues of passing include the following:
1. Move into the path of the ball; don't reach for it.
2. Bend the knees prior to making contact.
3. Contact the ball with the fingertips (overhand pass).
4. Extend the knees upon contact with the ball.
5. Follow through after striking the ball.

Individual Passing Drills

1. Practice wall rebounding: Stand 6 ft away from a wall. Pass the ball against the wall and catch it.
2. From a spot 6 ft from the wall, throw the ball against the wall and alternate an overhand pass with a forearm pass.
3. Throw the ball to one side (right or left) and move to the side to pass the ball to the wall. Catch the rebound.
4. Pass the ball directly overhead and catch it. Try making two passes before catching the ball. Later, alternate an overhand pass with a forearm pass and catch the ball. This is a basic drill and should be mastered before proceeding to others.

Partner Passing Drills

1. Players are about 10 ft apart. Player A tosses the ball (controlled toss) to player B, who passes the ball back to A, who catches the ball. Continue for several exchanges and then change throwers.
2. Two players are about 15 ft apart. Player A passes to himself or herself first and then makes a second pass to player B, who catches the ball and repeats. Follow with a return by B.
3. Players A and B try to keep the ball in the air continuously.
4. Players are about 15 ft apart. Player A remains stationary and passes in such a fashion that player B must move from side to side. An option is to have player B move forward and backward.
5. Players are about 10 ft apart. Both have hoops and attempt to keep one foot in the hoop while passing. Try keeping both feet in the hoop.
6. Player A passes to player B and does a complete turnaround. B passes back to A and also does a full turn. Other stunts can be used.

The usual basketball court should be divided into two volleyball courts on which players play crosswise. Nets should be lowered to 6 ft and raised 6 to 12 in. as children mature.

In the primary grades, children should have had ball-handling experiences related to volleyball skills. Rebounding and controlling balloons is an excellent related experience, particularly for younger children. Included in ball-handling experiences with beach balls or foam rubber training balls should be exploratory work in batting with the hands and other body parts.

Regulation volleyballs should not be used with third and fourth grade students. An 8-in. foam rubber training ball has much the same feel as a volleyball but does not cause pain. The foam balls should be used for skill practice. Another excellent ball is the volleyball trainer, which closely resembles a volleyball but is larger in diameter and lighter in weight. Either ball helps keep children from developing a fear of the fast-moving object.

Game Activity — Volleyball Lead-up Activities

Beach Ball Volleyball

Supplies: A beach ball 16–20 in. in diameter

Skills: Most passing skills, modified serving

The players of each team are in two lines on their respective sides of the net. The player on the right side of the back line serves, as in regulation volleyball. The distance is shortened, however, because serving a beach ball successfully from the normal volleyball serving distance is difficult. The player serves from the normal playing position on the court in the right back position. Scoring is similar to regulation volleyball. Play continues until the ball touches the floor. A team loses a point to the other team when it fails to return the ball over the net by the third volley or when it returns the ball over the net but the ball hits the floor out of bounds without being touched by the opposing team. The server continues serving as long as his team scores. Rotation is as in regulation volleyball. Position the server as close to the net as possible while still remaining in the right back position on the court.

Informal Volleyball

Supplies: A trainer volleyball

Skills: Passing

This game is similar to regulation volleyball, but there is no serving. Each play begins with a student on one side tossing the ball overhead and passing it over the net. Points are scored for every play, as there is no "side out." As soon as a point is scored, the nearest player takes the ball and immediately puts it into play. Otherwise, basic volleyball rules govern the game. Rotation occurs as soon as a team has scored 5 points, with the front and back lines changing place. Action is fast, and the game moves rapidly, as every play scores a point for one team or the other.

Objectives:

To perform overhand and underhand
    volleyball passing skills
To volley the ball a number of times
    against a wall
To hit an underhand serve over a 6' net
To learn the basic rules of volleyball

NASPE National Standards:

Introductory Activity: 1, 3, 5
Fitness Activity: 1, 4, 6
Lesson Focus: 2, 3, 5
Game: 2, 3, 5

Equipment Required:

Marking spots for Home Base
Music for Continuity Drills
One beach ball, 8" foam rubber, or
    volleyball trainer for each student
Volleyball net (6 ft height)

Instructional Activities	Teaching Hints

Introductory Activity — Home Base

The class is divided into teams of 5–6 players. One player in each group is
designated the captain. Rubber spots are placed throughout the teaching area equal
to the number of teams. Each spot serves as a home base for one of the squads.
The teams begin in a straight line with the captain standing on a spot and the rest
of the team lined up behind her. The teacher calls out a locomotor movement that
the players use to move throughout the area. When the teacher calls "home base!"
each team lines up in starting formation with the captain first in line. The first
team to return to proper position wins that round.

This is an excellent game to teach
youngsters how to get in small-group
formations quickly.

If desired, use the call "find your home"
to assemble the class in pre-assigned
squads. Some teachers use squads for
station teaching and dividing the class
into teams.

Fitness Development Activity — Continuity Drills

Rope jumping—forward	25 seconds	Make a tape with music segments
Double Crab Kick	30 seconds	(25 seconds) alternated with silence
Rope jumping—backward	25 seconds	(30 seconds). When the music is
Knee Touch Curl-Up	30 seconds	playing, students jump rope; when
Jump and turn body	25 seconds	silence occurs, students do a flexibility
Push-ups	30 seconds	and strength development exercise.
Rocker Step	25 seconds	
Bend and Twist	30 seconds	Exercises can be done in two-count
Swing-Step forward	25 seconds	fashion. Exercises are done when the
Side Flex	30 seconds	leader says "Ready." The class answers
Free jumping	25 seconds	"One-two" and performs a repetition.

Relax and stretch for a short time.

Allow students to adjust the workload to
their level. This implies resting if the
rope jumping is too strenuous.

Lesson Focus — Volleyball Skills

Skills

Review skills taught in the previous week:
Overhand Pass
Forearm Pass (Underhand pass)

Introduce a new skill:
Underhand Serve
    Directions are for a right-handed serve. The player stands facing the net with
the left foot slightly forward and the weight on the right (rear) foot. The ball is
held in the left hand with the left arm across and a little in front of the body. On
the serving motion, step forward with the left foot, transfer the weight to the front
foot, and at the same time bring the right arm back in a preparatory motion. The
right hand swings forward and contacts the ball just below center. The ball can be
hit with an open hand or with the fist (facing forward or sideward).

The serve is used to start play. The
underhand serve is easiest for elementary
school children to learn even though the
overhand (floater) serve is the most
effective. Few youngsters will be capable
of mastering the overhand serve.

The following instructional cues focus
on correct performance of the serve:

1. Use opposition. Place the opposite
foot of the serving hand forward.
2. Transfer the weight to the forward
foot.
3. Keep the eyes on the ball.
4. Decide prior to the serve where it
should be placed.

Drills
Individual Passing Drills
1. Pass the ball 3 ft or so to one side, move under the ball, and pass it back to the original spot. The next pass should be to the other side.
2. Pass the ball directly overhead. On the return, jump as high as possible and make a second pass. Continue.
3. Stand with one foot in a hoop. Pass the ball overhead and attempt to continue passing while keeping one foot in the hoop. Try with both feet in the hoop.

Partner Passing Drills:
1. Players are about 15 ft apart. Player A remains stationary and passes in such a fashion that player B must move from side to side. An option is to have player B move forward and backward.
2. Players are about 10 ft apart. Both have hoops and attempt to keep one foot in the hoop while passing. Try keeping both feet in the hoop.
3. Player A passes to player B and does a complete turnaround. B passes back to A and also does a full turn. Other stunts can be used.

Partner Serving and Passing Drills
1. Partners are about 20 ft apart. Partner A serves to partner B, who catches the ball and returns the serve to partner A.
2. Partner A serves to partner B, who makes a pass back to partner A. Change responsibilities.
3. Service One-Step. Partners begin about 10 ft apart. Partner A serves to partner B, who returns the serve with partner A catching. If there is no error and if neither receiver moved the feet to catch, both players take one step back. This is repeated each time that no error or foot movement by the receivers occurs. If an error occurs or if appreciable foot movement is evident, the players revert to the original distance of 10 ft and start over.

5. Follow through; don't punch at the ball.

Regulation volleyballs should not be used with third and fourth grade students. An 8-in. foam rubber training ball has much the same feel as a volleyball but does not cause pain. The foam balls should be used for skill practice. Another excellent ball is the volleyball trainer, which closely resembles a volleyball but is larger in diameter and lighter in weight. Either ball helps keep children from developing a fear of the fast-moving object.

The use of the fist to hit balls on normal returns causes poor control and interrupts play. Except for dig passes, both hands should be used to return the ball. Teachers should rule hitting with the fist a loss of a point if the practice persists.

Volleyball Lead-up Games

Continue playing the games listed in the Week 30. The lead-up games for this age are:
   Beach Ball Volleyball
   Informal Volleyball

Introduce the following game:
Shower Service Ball
   Supplies: 4–6 trainer volleyballs
   Skills: Serving, catching
   A line parallel to the net is drawn through the middle of each court to define the serving area. Players are scattered in no particular formation. The game involves the skills of serving and catching. To start the game, 2–3 volleyballs are given to each team and are handled by players in the serving area. Balls may be served at any time and in any order by a server, who must be in the back half of the court. Any ball served across the net is to be caught by any player near the ball. The person catching or retrieving a ball moves quickly to the serving area and serves. A point is scored for a team whenever a served ball hits the floor in the other court or is dropped by a receiver. Two scorers are needed, one for each side. As youngsters improve, all serves should be made from behind the baseline.

Objectives:

To put together a combination of
  movements in a smooth and
  flowing manner
To evade or stay near a partner while
  traveling
To perform rhythmic activities while
  handling manipulative equipment

NASPE National Standards:

Introductory Activity: 1, 5
Fitness Activity: 1, 2, 4, 5, 6
Lesson Focus: 1, 3, 4, 5
Game: 1, 2, 5

Equipment Required:

1 jump rope for each student
Music for Racetrack Fitness
2 Lummi sticks for each student
1 playground ball for each student

Instructional Activities	Teaching Hints

Introductory Activity — Combination Movement Patterns

Explore some of the following movement combinations:
1. Run, leap, and roll.
2. Run, collapse, and roll.
3. Hop, turn around, and shake.
4. Run, change direction, and collapse.
5. Hop, make a shape in the air, and balance.

Encourage a variety of responses

Try having students work in pairs and
generate different combinations. They
can mimic each other's ideas.

Fitness Development Activity — Racetrack Fitness

Five or six fitness activities are arranged in the center (the Pit) of a large circle
outlined with marking spots (the race track). If desired, tumbling mats can be
placed in the center of the race track to delineate the pit stop area. Students work
with a partner and alternate running (or doing other locomotor movements) around
the race track and going to the pit to perform a strength or flexibility exercise. A
different exercise should be performed each time so students assure variety in
their workout.

The following are some examples of exercises that can be used for Pit exercises.
1. Arm Circles
2. Bend and Twist
3. Abdominal Challenges
4. Knee to Chest Curl
5. Push-up Challenges
6. Trunk Twister

Intervals of 30 seconds of music with 10
seconds of silence are used to signal role
changes. The student who was running
the track now goes to the pit to exercise
and vice versa.

Assure that students run under control
(not as fast as they can) and in the same
direction.

Allow students to perform at a level
they feel comfortable. Youngsters are
genetically different and should not be
expected to do the same amount of
exercise repetitions.

Lesson Focus — Rhythmic Movement Skills (4)

Rope-Jumping Skills to Music
1. Perform the slow-time and fast-time rhythm with the rope held in one hand
   and turned.
2. Jump the rope and practice changing back and forth from slow to fast time.
3. Review basic steps students have learned in the earlier lesson plan on rope
   jumping (Week 29).
4. Allow student time to put together a simple routine to music using some of the
   steps they have learned.

Ball Skills to Music
Perform a number of ball skills to the rhythm of the music. See Week 5 for a
refresher of skills learned previously.
  a. Bounce and catch.
  b. Bounce, clap, catch; bounce, turn, catch—also use toss.
  c. Dribble continuously in place and while moving.
  d. Work with a partner or in groups, passing one or more balls to one another
     in rhythm.
  e. Create different movements such as swings, spins, and around the body.
  f. Develop a routine utilizing some of the skills above.

Music selected should have a steady and
unchanging beat. It should be played
loud so that it can easily be heard above
the noise of jump ropes and/or balls.

Jumping rope is a demanding activity.
Even though music will motivate
youngsters to practice, it can't be done
for long. Take a break and practice ball
skills. If desired, come back to rope
jumping after practicing ball skills.

Encourage students to bounce the ball
on the beat of the rhythm. It may help to
hit a tom-tom or tambourine to make the
beat easy to feel.

Lummi Sticks

Music Source: WWCD-2015 or 2014; WWC-2000

Formation: Couples scattered throughout the area

Directions: Lummi sticks are smaller versions of wands; they are 12–15 in. long. Most Lummi stick activities are done by partners, although some can be done individually. Each child sits cross-legged, facing a partner at a distance of 18–20 in. Children adjust this distance as the activities demand. The sticks are held in the thumb and fingers (not the fist) at about the bottom third of the stick. Routines are based on sets of six movements; each movement is completed in one count. Many different routines are possible. Only the basic ones are presented here. The following one-count movements are used to make up routines.

- a. Vertical tap: Tap both sticks upright on the floor.
- b. Partner tap: Tap partner's stick (right stick to right stick, or left to left).
- c. End tap: Tilt the sticks forward or sideward and tap the ends on the floor.
- d. Cross-tap: Cross hands and tap the upper ends to the floor.
- e. Side tap: Tap the upper ends to the side.
- f. Flip: Toss the stick in air, giving it a half turn, and catch other end.
- g. Tap together: Hold the sticks parallel and tap them together.
- h. Toss right (or left): Toss the right-hand stick to partner's right hand, at the same time receiving partner's right-hand stick.
- i. Pass: Lay the stick on the floor and pick up partner's stick.
- j. Toss right and left: Toss quickly right to right and left to left, all in the time of one count.

A number of routines, incorporating the movements described, are presented here in sequence of difficulty. Each routine is to be done four times to complete the 24 beats of the chant.

- a. Vertical tap, tap together, partner tap right, vertical tap, tap together, partner tap left.
- b. Vertical tap, tap together, pass right stick, vertical tap, tap together, pass left stick.
- c. Vertical tap, tap together, toss right stick, vertical tap, tap together, toss left stick.
- d. Repeat numbers 1, 2, and 3, but substitute an end tap and flip for the vertical tap and tap together. Perform the stated third movement (e.g., end tap, flip, partner tap right, end tap, flip, partner tap left).
- e. Vertical tap, tap together, toss right and left quickly, end tap, flip, toss right and left quickly.
- f. Cross-tap, cross-flip, vertical tap (uncross arms), cross-tap, cross-flip, vertical tap (uncross arms).

Popcorn (American)

Music Source: WWCD-RM7; WWC-RM7

Skills: Toe touches, knee lifts, jumps, ¼ turns

Formation: Single lines of students; no partners

Directions:

Counts	Measures
24	Wait 24 counts; gently bounce up and down by bending the knees during the introduction
1–4	Touch right toe in front and return; repeat. (Right, together, Right, together)
5–8	Touch left toe in front and return; repeat. (Left, together, left, together)
9–12	Touch right toe in back and return; repeat. (Back, together, back, together)
13–16	Touch left toe in front and return; repeat. (Back, together, back, together)
17–20	Lift right knee up in front of left knee and return; repeat. (Knee up, return, knee up, return)
21–24	Lift left knee up in front of right knee and return; repeat. (Knee up, return, knee up, return)
25–26	Lift right knee up in front of left knee and return. (Knee up, return)
27–28	Lift left knee up in front of right knee and return. (Knee up, return)
29–30	Clap both hands together once. (clap)
31–32	Jump and turn ¼ turn to the right. (jump and turn)

Repeat entire dance to the end of the music.

Red River Valley (American)

Music Source: WWCD-FDN

Skills: Walk, buzz swing

Formation: Triple circle with 3 dances side by side in sets of 6 dancers—2 trios facing each other. Half the trios face counterclockwise and half face clockwise

Directions:

Measures	Part I Action
4	Introduction
1–4	Middle person of each trio leads partners forward to right to meet oncoming trio using 8 walking steps. (Walk, 2, 3, … 8)
5–8	Join hands with oncoming trio and circle to the left (clockwise) 4 walking steps; then reverse direction and circle right using 4 walking steps. (Circle, left, 3, 4; circle, right, 3, 4)

9–12	Middle person swings around with person on left using 8 buzz (shuffling) steps. (Swing, 2, 3, … 8)
13–16	Middle person swings around with person on right using 8 buzz (shuffling) steps. (Swing, 2, 3, … 8)
	Part II Action
1–8	Repeat action of measures 1–8 in Part I. (Walk, 2, 3, … 8)
9–12	The 4 outside youngsters form a right-hand star in the center of the set and walk around once to starting point using 8 walking steps. (Star, 2, 3, … 8)
13–16	The two middle youngsters "do-si-do" around each other, returning to own place using 8 walking steps. (Do-si-do, 2, 3, … 8)
	Part III Action
1–8	Repeat action of measures 1–8 in Part I. (Walk, 2, 3, … 8)
9–12	The two left-hand outside youngsters change places diagonally across using 8 walking steps. (Left, diagonal, 3, … 8)
13–16	The two right-hand outside youngsters change places diagonally across using 8 walking steps. The middle person now has different partners. (Right, diagonal, 3, … 8)

The entire dance is repeated 2 times.

Sicilian Circle (American)

Music Source: WWCD-FDN
Skills: Walking, two-hand swing (either walking or buzz turn), wheel turn
Formation: Double circle composed of groups of two couples facing each other with partners side by side. Couples are numbered 1 and 2 with #1 couples moving counterclockwise and #2 couples clockwise.
Directions:

Measures	Action
4	Introduction
1–4	The sets of two couples join hands and walk 8 steps to the left ending where they started and drop hands. (Circle, left, 2, 3, 4, … 8)
5–8	Partners join both hands and swing once around to the left using 8 walking or buzz steps. (Swing, left, 2, 3, 4, … 8)
9–12	Couples advance toward each other and pass right shoulders through to opposite's place using 4 walking steps. As soon as across, couples do a wheel-turn around with partner on the left walking backward 4 steps and moving into place on partner's left who turns in place using 4 steps. If desired, left partner can hold left hand with partner's left hand and right hand around back of partner's waist. Hands are dropped. (Pass, through, 3, 4; wheel, turn, 3,4)
13–16	Couples pass through again as described in measures 9–12. (Back, through, 3, 4; wheel, turn, 3,4)
17–20	Right-hand partners advance toward each other, join right hands briefly, pass each other by right shoulders, drop hands, and join left hand with opposite left partner using 4 steps. The opposite left partner does a wheel turn as described in measures 9–12 using 4 steps. (Right partner, chain, 3, 4; wheel, turn, 3,4)
21–24	Right-hand partner chain back again and turn as in measure 17–20 using 8 steps and end with left hands joined with partner. (Chain, back, 3, 4; wheel, turn, 3,4)
25–28	Partners join hands in promenade position and advance 4 steps toward opposite and 4 steps backward to place. (Forward, 2, 3, 4; Back, 2, 3, 4)
29–32	Each couple with hands in promenade position advance to the left of the opposite couple to the next couple using 8 steps. (New couple, 2, 3, … 8)

Dance is repeated 3 times.

Savila Se Bela Loza (Serbian)

Music Source: WWCD-TCZ; WWC-572
Skills: Running step, crossover step, hop
Formation: Broken circle or line; joined hands held down
Directions: Explain Savila Se Bela Loza (pronounced SAH-vee-lah say BAY-lah LOH-zah) means a "grapevine entwined in itself."

Measures	Part I Action
	Introduction
1–20	Face slightly to right, move right starting with the right foot taking 18 small running steps forward. Do a step-hop on the 19th and 20th steps. (Run, 2, 3, … 18, step, hop)
21–40	Face slightly left and repeat above action starting with the left foot. Finish with a step hop on the left foot. (Run, 2, 3, … 18, step, hop)
	Part II Action
41–44	Beginning with right, take one schottische step moving right. Translated this is a step to the right sideward on right foot, a step with the left foot behind the right followed by a step-hop on the right foot. (Right, left, right, hop)

45–48   Beginning with left, take one schottische step moving left. This is done with a step to the left sideward on left foot, a step with the right foot behind the left followed by a step-hop on the left foot. (Left, right left, hop)

49–64   Repeat the action of counts 41–48 two more times.

Repeat the dance. During the music for Part I, the leaders on the ends of the lines may lead the line anywhere, winding or coiling the line like a grapevine.

Ve David (Israeli)

Music Source: WWCD-RM3; WWC-RM3

Skills: Walking, pivoting, buzz-step turn

Formation: Double circle, couples facing counterclockwise, partner B on partner A's right. Inside hands joined, right foot free.

Directions:

Measures	Part I Action
1–2	All walk forward and form a ring. Take four walking steps forward, starting with the right foot and progressing counterclockwise, then back out, taking four walking steps to form a single circle, facing center, with all hands joined. (Walk, 2, 3, 4; Single, circle, 3, 4)
3–4	All forward and back. Four steps forward to center and four steps backward, starting with the right foot. (Forward, 2, 3, 4; Back, 2, 3, 4)

Part II Action

1–2	B's forward and back; A's clap. Partner B, starting with the right foot, walk four steps forward to the center and four steps backward to place while Partner A clap. (B's in, 2, 3, 4; Out 2, 3, 4)

Part III Action

1–2	Partner A forward, circle to the right, and progress to a new partner; all clap. A's, clapping hands, walk four steps forward to the center, starting with the right foot. They turn right about on the last "and" count and walk forward four steps, passing their original partner and progressing ahead to the next. (As in, 2, 3, 4; Turn to new partner)
3–4	Swing the new partner. The A and the new partner B swing clockwise with right shoulders adjacent, right arms around each other across in front, and left arms raised—pivoting with right foot for an eight count "buzz-step" swing. (Swing, 2, 3, 4, 5, 6, 7, 8)

Repeat the entire dance.

Game Activity

Alaska Baseball

Supplies: A volleyball or soccer ball

Skills: Kicking, batting, running, ball handling

Players are divided into two teams; one is at bat while the other is in the field. A straight line provides the only out-of-bounds line, and the team at bat is behind this line midway between the ends of the line. The other team is scattered around the fair territory. One player propels the ball, either batting a volleyball or kicking a stationary soccer ball. Her teammates are in a close file behind her. As soon as the batter sends the ball into the playing area, she starts to run around her own team. Each time the runner passes the head of the file, the team gives a loud count.

There are no outs. The first fielder to get the ball stands still and starts to pass the ball back overhead to the nearest teammate, who moves directly behind to receive it. The remainder of the team in the field must run to the ball and form a file behind the fielder. The ball is passed back overhead, with each player handling the ball. When the last field player in line has a firm grip on it, she shouts "Stop." At this signal, a count is made of the number of times the batter ran around her team. To score more accurately, half rounds can be counted. Five batters or half of the team should bat; then the teams should change places. This is better than allowing an entire team to bat before changing to the field, because players in the field fatigue from many consecutive runs.

Keep It Floating (Cooperative Activity)

Formation: Groups of 4–8

Supplies: For each group, two balloons, one beach ball, and one hoop for every two youngsters

Students form a circle and join hands. Their challenge is to keep a balloon up for as many hits as possible without letting go of hands. After a few rounds, another balloon is added to increase the difficulty. Finally, a beach ball and one balloon are used.

Teaching Tips: For advanced classes, place one hoop between each set of students. Student must keep one foot in each hoop on either side of them. This advanced challenge is best with only one balloon. To integrate other academic content, have the students do the following while participating in the initial version of the challenge:

1. State a different fruit or vegetable with each hit.
2. Count in a foreign language.
3. Count by 2's, 3's, 4's, etc.
4. Attempt to strike the balloon with a different bone or muscle each time and call out the name of that body part.
5. Call out a different lifetime activity with each hit.

Objectives:
To learn the unique throwing style
   required with Frisbees
To learn the rules of Frisbee golf
To perform continuous fitness activity

NASPE National Standards:
Introductory Activity: 1, 5
Fitness Activity: 1, 4, 6
Lesson Focus: 2, 3, 5
Game: 2, 3, 5

Equipment Required:
Tom-tom or tambourine
Signs and music for Aerobic Fitness
One Frisbee per student
Cones and hoops for Frisbee Golf

Instructional Activities	**Teaching Hints**

Introductory Activity — European Rhythmic Running with Variations

Students clap to the beat of the tambourine and run in single-file formation. Practice some of the following variations:
1. Clap hands the first beat of a four beat rhythm.
2. Stamp foot and clap hands on the first beat.
3. On signal, make a complete turn, using four running steps.

Encourage students to originate different variations of rhythmic running.

After the rhythm is learned, stop striking the tambourine and let the class maintain the rhythm.

Fitness Development Activity — Aerobic Fitness

1. Rhythmic run with clap
2. Bounce turn and clap
3. Rhythmic 4-count curl-ups (knees, toes, knees, back)
4. Rhythmic Crab Kicks (slow time)
5. Jumping Jack combination
6. Double knee lifts
7. Lunges (right, left, forward) with single-arm circles (on the side lunges) and double-arms circles (on the forward lunge)
8. Rhythmic trunk twists
9. Directional run (forward, backward, side, turning)
10. Rock side to side with clap
11. Side-leg raises (alternate legs)
12. Rhythmic 4-count push-ups (If these are too difficult for students, substitute single-arm circles in the push-up position.)

Use music to stimulate effort. Any combination of movements can be used.

Keep the steps simple and easy to perform. Some students will become frustrated if the learning curve is steep.

Signs that explain the aerobic activities will help students remember performance cues.

Don't stress or expect perfection. Allow students to perform the activities as best they can.

Alternate bouncing and running movements with flexibility and strength development movements.

Lesson Focus — Manipulative Skills Using Frisbees

Throwing the Disk
Backhand Throw
   The backhand grip is used most often. The thumb is on top of the disk, the index finger along the rim, and the other fingers underneath. To throw the Frisbee with the right hand, stand in a sideways position with the right foot toward the target. Step toward the target and throw the Frisbee in a sideways motion across the body, snapping the wrist and trying to keep the disk flat on release.
Underhand Throw
   The underhand throw uses the same grip as in the backhand throw, but the thrower faces the target and holds the disk at the side of the body. Step forward with the leg opposite the throwing arm while bringing the Frisbee forward. When the throwing arm is out in the front of the body, release the Frisbee. The trick to this throw is learning to release the disk so that it is parallel to the ground.

Catching the Disk
Thumb-Down Catch
   The thumb-down catch is used for catching when the disk is received at waist level or above. The thumb is pointing toward the ground.

Use the following instructional cues to improve skill performance:

a. Release the disk parallel to the ground. If it is tilted, a curved throw results.

b. Step toward the target and follow through on release of the disk.

c. Snap open the wrist and make the Frisbee spin.

If space is limited, all Frisbees should be thrown in the same direction.

Thumb-Up Catch

The thumb-up catch is used when the Frisbee is received below waist level. The thumb points up, and the fingers are spread.

Throwing and Catching Activities:
  a. Throw the Frisbee at different levels to partner.
  b. Throw a curve—to the left, right, and upward. Vary the speed of the curve.
  c. Throw a bounce pass—try a low and a high pass.
  d. Throw the disc like a boomerang. Must throw at a steep angle into the wind.
  e. Throw the Frisbee into the air, run and catch. Increase the distance of the throw.
  f. Throw the Frisbee through a hoop held by a partner.
  g. Catch the Frisbee under your leg. Catch it behind your back.
  h. Throw the Frisbees into hoops that are placed on the ground as targets. Different-colored hoops can be given different values. Throw through your partner's legs.
  i. Frisbee bowling—One partner has a bowling pin, which the other partner attempts to knock down by throwing the Frisbee.
  j. Play catch while moving. Lead your partner so he doesn't have to break stride.
  k. See how many successful throws and catches you can make in 30 seconds.
  l. Frisbee Baseball Pitching—Attempt to throw the Frisbee into your partner's "Strike Zone."

Youngsters can develop both sides of the body by learning to throw and catch the disk with either hand. The teacher should design the activities so that youngsters get both right-hand and left-hand practice.

Since a Frisbee is somewhat different from the other implements that children usually throw, devote some time to teaching form and style in throwing and catching. Avoid drills that reward speed in throwing and catching.

Frisbee Game Activities

Frisbee Keep Away

Supplies: Frisbees

Skills: Throwing and catching Frisbees

Students break into groups of three. Two of the players in the group try to keep the other player from touching the Frisbee while they are passing it back and forth. If the Frisbee is touched by a defensive player, the person who threw the Frisbee becomes the defensive player. Begin the game by asking students to remain stationary while throwing and catching. Later, challenge can be added by allowing all players in the group to move.

Frisbee Golf

Supplies: One Frisbee per person, hoops for hole markers, cones

Skills: Frisbee throwing for accuracy

Frisbee Golf or disk golf is a favorite game of many students. Boundary cones with numbers can be used for tees, and holes can be boxes, hula hoops, trees, tires, garbage cans, or any other available equipment on the school grounds. Draw a course on a map for students and start them at different holes to decrease the time spent waiting to tee off. Regulation golf rules apply. The students can jog between throws for increased activity.

Disk golf is played like regular golf. One stroke is counted for each time the disk is thrown and when a penalty is incurred. The object is to acquire the lowest score. The following rules dictate play:

Tee-throws: Tee-throws must be completed within or behind the designated tee area.

Lie: The lie is the spot on or directly underneath the spot where the previous throw landed.

Throwing order: The player whose disk is the farthest from the hole throws first. The player with the least number of throws on the previous hole tees off first.

Fairway throws: Fairway throws must be made with the foot closest to the hole on the lie. A run-up is allowed.

Dog leg: A dog leg is one or more designated trees or poles in the fairway that must be passed on the outside when approaching the hole. There is a two-stroke penalty for missing a dog leg.

Putt throw: A putt throw is any throw within 10 ft of the hole. A player may not move past the point of the lie in making the putt throw. Falling or jumping putts are not allowed.

Unplayable lies: Any disk that comes to rest 6 ft or more above the ground is unplayable. The next throw must be played from a new lie directly underneath the unplayable lie (one-stroke penalty).

Out-of-bounds: A throw that lands out-of-bounds must be played from the point where the disk went out (one-stroke penalty).

Course courtesy: Do not throw until the players ahead are out of range.

Completion of hole: A disk that comes to rest in the hole (box or hoop) or strikes the designated hole (tree or pole) constitutes successful completion of that hole.

DPE Curriculum Guide – Lesson Plans
Fundamental Skills Using Balance Beams
Level II – Week 34

Objectives:
To design rhythmic activities for aerobic fitness
To maintain balance while doing a variety of beam challenges
To demonstrate controlled balance while manipulating equipment

NASPE National Standards:
Introductory Activity: 1
Fitness Activity: 1, 4, 6
Lesson Focus: 1, 2, 3, 5
Game: 1, 2, 5

Equipment Required:
Music and signs for Aerobic Fitness
6 balance beams and 6 tumbling mats
Desired equipment for balance beam challenges
8" foam balls for Hand Hockey

Instructional Activities	Teaching Hints

Introductory Activity — Tortoise and Hare

When the leader calls out the word "tortoise," students run in place slowly. On the word "hare," they change to a rapid run. Students can work in small groups to allow for more leaders.

Try some different variations such as:
1. Moving throughout the area.
2. Performing various stretching activities.
3. Moving in different directions.

Fitness Development Activity — Aerobic Fitness

1. Rhythmic run with clap
2. Bounce turn and clap
3. Rhythmic 4-count curl-ups (knees, toes, knees, back)
4. Rhythmic Crab Kicks (slow time)
5. Jumping Jack combination
6. Double knee lifts
7. Lunges (right, left, forward) with single-arm circles (on the side lunges) and double-arms circles (on the forward lunge)
8. Rhythmic trunk twists
9. Directional run (forward, backward, side, turning)
10. Rock side to side with clap
11. Side-leg raises (alternate legs)
12. Rhythmic 4-count push-ups (If these are too difficult for students, substitute single-arm circles in the push-up position.)

Use music to stimulate effort. Any combination of movements can be used.

Keep the steps simple and easy to perform. Some students will become frustrated if the learning curve is steep.

Signs that explain the aerobic activities will help students remember performance cues.

Don't stress or expect perfection. Allow students to perform the activities as best they can.

Alternate bouncing and running movements with flexibility and strength development movements.

Lesson Focus — Fundamental Skills Using Balance Beams

Perform balance beam activities using controlled walking movements. Speed of movement should always be avoided.

Dismounts
Complete all moves across the balance beam with a dismount. The following are examples of effective dismounts. Place a tumbling mat at the end of each beam so youngsters can dismount safely.
1. Single jump (forward or backward)
2. Jump with turns (half turn, three-quarter turn, or full turn).
3. Jackknife. Jump, kick the legs up, and touch the toes with the fingertips. Keep the feet together.
4. Jackknife Split. Same as the Jackknife, but spread the legs as far as possible.
5. Jump, land, and do a Forward Roll.
6. Backward jump, land, and do a Backward Roll.
7. Side jump to a Side Roll.

If balance beams are not available, use 2" × 4" boards placed on the floor. This will give students some elevation off the floor and offer balance challenges.

Place the beams parallel to each other and have a similar number of students lined up behind each one. Students progress down the beam.

After moving the length of the beam, have students do a locomotor movement (return activity) to the end of the teaching area and return. This offers students balance activities and the chance to practice locomotor movements.

Balance Beam Activities

1. Walk length of beam.
   a. Walk forward.
   b. Walk backward.
   c. Walk sideways—lead with both left and right sides of body.
2. Walk different directions and vary arm and body positions.
   a. Hands on hips.
   b. Hands on head.
   c. Hands folded across chest.
   d. Lean to one side or the other.
   e. Body bent forward or backward.
   f. Hands on knees or feet.
   g. Exploratory activity.
3. Balance objects such as beanbags, erasers, or wands while walking across beam.
4. Move across the beam in various directions using the following movements:
   a. Slide
   b. Heel and toe
   c. Tiptoes
   d. Grapevine
   e. Dip step
5. Perform animal movements across the balance beam.
   a. Puppy dog walk
   b. Bear Walk
   c. Crab Walk
6. Use manipulative equipment while walking the beam.
   a. Play catch with beanbags. Try different throws and movements.
   b. Bounce a playground ball and catch it, dribble it, play catch with a partner.
   c. Step over a wand, go under a wand, change directions.
   d. Go through a hoop.

Return activities keep students engaged in activity for a longer period of time and reduce standing and waiting time. Specified movements can be placed on return activity signs.

If a student steps off the beam, have them get back on and progress. Sometimes, students stop walking the beam and receive little practice.

Move with controlled, deliberate movements across the beam. Speed is not a goal.

Game Activity

Hand Hockey

Supplies: 8" gray foam balls

Skills: Striking, volleying

Players are divided into two teams. Half of the players on each team are guards and are stationed on the goal line as defenders. The other half are active players and are scattered throughout the playing area in front of their goal line. The object of the game is to bat or push the ball with either hand so that it crosses the goal line the other team is defending. Players may move the ball as in hockey but may not throw, hoist, or kick it. The defensive goal line players are limited to one step into the playing field when playing the ball.

The ball is put into play by being rolled into the center of the field. After a goal has been scored or after a specified period, guards become active players, and vice versa. An out-of-bounds ball goes to the opposite team and is put into play by being rolled from the sidelines into the playing area. If the ball becomes entrapped among players, play is stopped, and a roll of the ball from the referee resumes play. Players must play the ball and not resort to rough tactics. A player who is called for unnecessary roughness or for illegally handling the ball must go to the sidelines (as in hockey) and remain in the penalty area until the players change positions. Players should scatter and attempt to pass to each other rather than bunch around the ball. Once youngsters learn the game, introduce more than one ball to increase the amount of activity.

Nonda's Car Lot

Supplies: None

Skills: Running, dodging

Two or three players are it and stand in the center of the area between two lines established at opposite ends of the playing area. The class selects four brands of cars (e.g., Honda, Corvette, Toyota, Cadillac). Each student then selects a car from the four but does not tell anyone what it is. One of the taggers calls out a car name. All students who selected that name attempt to run to the other line without getting tagged. The tagger calls out the cars until all students have run. When a child (car) gets tagged, he sits down at the spot of the tag. He cannot move but may tag other students who run nearby. When the one who is it calls out "Car lot," the entire class runs. Change taggers often.

Objectives:
To throw and catch a softball
To hit a softball
To be able to field softball grounders
  and fly balls

NASPE National Standards:
Introductory Activity: 1, 5
Fitness Activity: 1, 4, 5, 6
Lesson Focus: 2, 3, 5
Game: 2, 3, 5

Equipment Required:
Parachute and exercise music
Whiffle balls
Plastic bats for whiffle balls
Batting tee and bases
Playground ball

Instructional Activities	Teaching Hints

Introductory Activity — High Fives

Students move in different directions throughout the area. On signal, they are challenged to run toward a partner, jump, and give a "high five" (slap hands) while moving. Emphasis should be placed on timing so that the "high five" is given at the top of the jump.

Change the type of high fives, i.e., low, under leg, roundhouse.

High fives should be given gently. No hard slapping.

Fitness Development Activity — Parachute Fitness

1. Jog in circle with chute held in left hand. Reverse directions and hold with right hand. (music)
2. Standing, raise the chute overhead, lower to waist, lower to toes, raise to waist, etc. (no music)
3. Slide to the right; return slide to the left. (music)
4. Sit and perform abdominal challenges. (no music)
5. Skip. (music)
6. Freeze; face the center, and stretch the chute tightly with bent arms. Hold for 8–12 seconds. Repeat five to six times. (no music)
7. Run in place, hold the chute at waist level and hit the chute with lifted knees. (music)
8. Sit with legs under the chute. Do a seat walk toward the center. Return to the perimeter. Repeat four to six times. (no music)
9. Place the chute on the ground. Jog away from the chute and return on signal. Repeat. (music)
10. On sides with legs under the chute, perform Side Flex and lift chute with legs. (no music)
11. Hop to the center of the chute and return. Repeat. (music)
12. Assume the push-up position with the legs aligned away from the center of the chute. Shake the chute with one arm while the other arm supports the body. (no music)
13. Lie on back with legs under the chute. Shake the chute with the feet. (music)
14. Sit with feet under the chute. Stretch by touching the toes with the chute. Relax with other stretches while sitting. (no music)

Tape alternating segments (25–30 seconds in length) of silence and music to signal duration of exercise. Music segments indicate aerobic activity with the parachute while intervals of silence announce using the chute to enhance flexibility and strength development.

Space youngsters evenly around the chute.

Use different hand grips (palms up, down, mixed).

All movements should be done under control. Some of the faster and stronger students will have to moderate their performance.

Lesson Focus — Softball Skills

Skills
Practice the following skills:
1. Overhand Throw
   For the overhand throw, the hand with the ball is then brought back over the head so that it is well behind the shoulder at about shoulder height. The left side of the body is turned in the direction of the throw, and the left arm is raised in front of the body. The weight is on the back (right) foot, with the left foot advanced and the toe touching the ground. The arm comes forward with the elbow leading, and the ball is thrown with a downward snap of the wrist. The body weight is brought forward into the throw, shifting to the front foot. There should be good follow-through so that the palm of the throwing hand faces the ground at completion of the throw. The eyes should be on the target throughout, and the arm should be kept free and loose during the throw.

Whiffle balls and plastic bats are a much safer alternative for children this age. It is easier for them to swing plastic bats and the fear of getting hit by a softball will not be an issue.

Instructional cues for **throwing** are:
1. Place the throwing arm side of the body away from the target.
2. Step toward the target with the foot opposite the throwing hand.
3. Bend and raise the arm at the elbow. Lead with the elbow.

2. Pitching

Official rules call for the pitcher to have both feet in contact with the pitcher's rubber, but few elementary schools possess a rubber. Instead, the pitcher can stand with both feet about even, facing the batter, and holding the ball momentarily in front with both hands. The pitcher takes one hand from the ball, extends the right arm forward, and brings it back in a pendulum swing, positioning the ball well behind the body. A normal stride taken toward the batter with the left foot begins the throwing sequence for a right-handed pitcher. The arm is brought forward with an underhanded slingshot motion, and the weight is transferred to the leading foot. Only one step is permitted.

Instructional cues for **pitching** are:
1. Face the plate.
2. Keep your eyes on the target.
3. Swing the pitching arm backward and step forward.

3. Fielding Grounders

To field a grounder, the fielder should move as quickly as possible into the path of the ball and then move forward and play the ball on a good hop. The eyes must be kept on the ball, following it into the hands or glove. The feet are spread, the seat is kept down, and the hands are carried low and in front. The weight is on the balls of the feet or on the toes, and the knees are bent to lower the body. As the ball is caught, the fielder straightens up, takes a step in the direction of the throw, and makes the throw.

Instructional cues for **fielding** are:
1. Move into line with the path of the ball.
2. Give when catching the ball.
3. Use the glove to absorb the force of the ball.
4. For grounders, keep the head down and watch the ball move into the glove.

4. Batting (Right-Handed)

The batter stands with the left side of the body toward the pitcher. The feet are spread and the weight is on both feet. The body should be facing the plate. The bat is held with the trademark up, and the left hand grasps the bat lower than the right. The bat is held over the right shoulder, pointing both back and up. The elbows are away from the body. The swing begins with a hip roll and a short step forward in the direction of the pitcher. The bat is then swung level with the ground at the height of the pitch. The eyes are kept on the ball until it is hit. After the hit, there must be good follow-through.

Instructional cues for **batting** are:
1. Keep the hands together.
2. Swing the bat horizontally.
3. Swing through the ball.
4. Hold the bat off the shoulder.
5. Watch the ball hit the bat.

Station (Small Group) Instruction
Station 1—Batting
Use a batting tee. For each station, two tees are needed, with a bat and at least two balls for each tee. Three to five children are assigned to each tee. There should be a batter, a catcher to handle incoming balls, and fielders. When only three children are in a unit, the catcher should be eliminated. Each batter is allowed a certain number of swings before rotating to the field. The catcher becomes the next batter, and a fielder moves up to catcher.

Hitters should avoid the following: lifting the front foot high off the ground, stepping back with the rear foot, or bending forward.

Station 2—Throwing and Catching
Work with a partner and practice some of the following throwing drills:
    a. Throw back and forth, practicing various throws.
    b. Gradually increase the distance of the throws.
    c. Focus on accuracy; if the throws are not caught, reduce the distance between players.

Stand about 7–10 yards apart when practicing throwing.

For youngsters who are afraid of the ball, use a whiffle ball.

Station 3—Pitching
Students find a partner and pitch and catch with each other. Set out a number of bases at each station so pitchers can pitch and catch using a base as a target (home plate).
    a. Pitch to another player over a plate.
    b. Call balls and strikes. One player is the pitcher, the second is the catcher, and the third is the umpire. A fourth player can be a stationary batter to provide a more realistic pitching target.

Face the batter, both feet on the rubber and the ball held in front with both hands. One step is allowed, and the ball must be delivered on that step.
Ball must be pitched underhanded.
No motion or fake toward the plate can be made without delivering the ball.

Station 4—Fielding
Players find a partner and practice throwing grounders and fly balls to each other.
    a. One partner throws a grounder, the other partner fields the ball and throws it back to the other. Reverse roles.
    b. Do the same thing above except throw fly balls.

Show form for high and low catch.

Move into the path of the ball.

Softball Lead-up Activities

Throw It and Run
    Supplies: A softball or similar ball
    Skills: Throwing, catching, fielding, base running

Throw It and Run softball is played like regular softball with the following exception. With one team in the field at regular positions, the pitcher throws the ball to the batter, who, instead of batting the ball, catches it and immediately throws it into the field. The ball is then treated as a batted ball, and regular softball rules prevail. No stealing is permitted, however, and runners must hold bases until the batter throws the ball. A foul ball is an out.

Variations:

1. Under-Leg Throw. Instead of throwing directly, the batter can turn to the right, lift the left leg, and throw the ball under the leg into the playing field.

2. Beat-Ball Throw. The fielders, instead of playing regular softball rules, throw the ball directly home to the catcher. The batter, in the meantime, runs around the bases. A point is scored for each base that she touches before the catcher receives the ball. A ball caught on the fly would mean no score. Similarly, a foul ball would not score points but would count as a turn at bat.

Two-Pitch Softball

Supplies: A softball, a bat

Skills: Most softball skills, except regular pitching

Two-Pitch Softball is played like regular softball with the following changes:

1. A member of the team at bat pitches. A system of rotation should be set up so that every child takes a turn as pitcher.

2. The batter gets only two pitches to make a hit and must hit a fair ball on one of these pitches or is out. The batter can foul the first ball, but if the second is fouled, the batter is out. There is no need to call balls or strikes.

3. The pitcher does not field the ball. A member of the team in the field acts as the fielding pitcher.

4. If the batter hits the ball, regular softball rules are followed. No stealing is permitted, however.

Since the pitcher is responsible for pitching a ball that can be hit, the pitching distance can be shortened to give the batter ample opportunity to hit the ball. The instructor can act as the pitcher.

Hit and Run

Supplies: A volleyball, soccer ball, or playground ball, home plate, base markers

Skills: Catching, throwing, running, dodging

One team is at bat, and the other is scattered in the field. Boundaries must be established, but the area does not have to be shaped like a baseball diamond. The batter stands at home plate with the ball. In front of the batter, 12 ft away, is a short line over which the ball must be hit to be in play. In the center of the field, about 40 ft away, is the base marker. The distance the batter runs around the base marker may have to be shortened or lengthened, depending on the ability of the players.

The batter bats the ball with the hands or fists so that it crosses the short line and lands inside the area. She then attempts to run down the field, around the base marker, and back to home plate without being hit by the ball. The members of the other team field the ball and throw it at the runner. The fielder may not run or walk with the ball but may throw to a teammate who is closer to the runner. A run is scored each time a batter runs around the marker and back to home plate without getting hit by the ball. A run also is scored if a foul is called on the fielding team for walking or running with the ball.

The batter is out in any of the following circumstances.

1. A fly ball is caught.

2. He is hit below the shoulders with the ball.

3. The ball is not hit beyond the short line.

4. The team touches home plate with the ball before the runner returns. (This out is used only when the runner stops in the field and does not continue.)

The game can be played in innings of three outs each, or a change of team positions can be made after all members of one team have batted.

DPE Curriculum Guide – Lesson Plans
Softball Skills and Lead-up Activities (2)
Level II – Week 36

Objectives:
To throw and catch a softball size ball
To hit a softball
To be able to field softball grounders
    and fly balls

NASPE National Standards:
Introductory Activity: 1, 2, 5
Fitness Activity: 1, 2, 4, 5, 6
Lesson Focus: 2, 3, 5
Game: 2, 3, 5

Equipment Required:
Music for Partner Fitness Challenges
Whiffle balls
Plastic bats for whiffle balls
Batting tee and bases
Soccer ball

Instructional Activities	Teaching Hints

Introductory Activity — Tag Games

Teach a tag game or two selected by students. Examples of previous tag games learned are Addition Tag, Fastest Tag in the West, and Group Tag.

Select tag games that keep all students involved in activity.

Fitness Development Activity — Partner Fitness Challenges

Try to pair students with someone of similar ability and size. Emphasis should be placed on continuous movement and activity. The following are examples of partner activities that are both challenging and enjoyable.

Circle Five
Partner 1 stands stationary in the center of the circle with one palm up. Partner 2 runs in a circle around partner 1 and "gives a high five" when passing the upturned palm. The size of the circle is gradually increased. Reverse roles on signal.

Foot Tag
Partners stand facing each other. On signal, they try to touch each other's toes with their feet. Emphasize the importance of a touch, as contrasted to a stamp or kick.

Knee Tag
Partners stand facing each other. On signal, they try to tag the other person's knees. Each time a tag is made, a point is scored. Play for a designated amount of time.

Mini Merry-Go-Round
Partners face each other with the feet nearly touching and the hands grasped in a double wrist grip. Partners slowly lean backward while keeping the feet in place until the arms are straight. Spin around as quickly as possible. It is important that partners be of similar size.

Around and Under
One partner stands with the feet spread shoulder width apart and hands held overhead. The other partner goes between the standing partner's legs, stands up, and slaps the partner's hands. Continue the pattern for a designated time.

Partner challenges are fitness activities that can be used with intermediate-grade youngsters. They can be used to develop aerobic endurance, strength, and flexibility. Another advantage of partner challenges is that they can be performed indoors as a rainy-day activity.

Use 30 second intervals of music and silence to signal starting and stopping the partner fitness challenges. During the music interval, students perform the fitness challenges. During the silent intervals, they perform flexibility and strength development activities.

Lesson Focus — Softball Skills

Skills
Review skills learned last week:
1. Overhand Throw
2. Pitching
3. Fielding Grounders
4. Batting

Whiffle balls and plastic bats are a much safer alternative for children this age. It is easier for them to swing plastic bats and the fear of getting hit by a softball will not be an issue.

Station (Small-Group) Instruction
Station 1—Play Pepper (Hitting and Fielding)
A line of 3–4 players is about 10 yards in front of and facing a batter. The players toss the ball to the batter, who attempts to hit controlled grounders back to them. The batter stays at bat for a period of time and then rotates to the field.

If youngsters are not able to hit the ball, they can catch and throw it to the fielders.

Station 2—Pitching and Umpiring

Students find a partner and pitch and catch with each other. Set out a number of bases at each station so pitchers can pitch and catch using a base as a target (home plate).

    a. Pitch to another player over a plate.

    b. Call balls and strikes. One player is the pitcher, the second is the catcher, and the third is the umpire. A fourth player can be a stationary batter to provide a more realistic pitching target.

When umpiring, strikes are called by raising the right hand and balls require raising the left hand.

Station 3—Infield Practice

1. Throw around the bases clockwise and counterclockwise.
2. Roll ball to infielders and make the play at first. After each play, throw around the infield.
3. If enough skill, bat the ball to the infielders in turn.

While having infield practice, one person at the station can run the bases and try to complete a circuit around the bases before the ball does.

Station 4—Batting Practice

Each batter takes six swings and then rotates to the field. Catcher becomes batter and pitcher moves up to catcher.

Have more than one ball at the stations so the pitching can continue when a ball is hit or not caught.

Softball Lead-up Activities

Kick Softball

    Supplies: A soccer ball or another ball to be kicked

    Skills: Kicking a rolling ball, throwing, catching, running bases

    The batter stands in the kicking area, a 3-ft-square home plate. The batter kicks the ball rolled on the ground by the pitcher. The ball should be rolled at moderate speed. An umpire calls balls and strikes. A strike is a ball that rolls over the 3-ft square. A ball rolls outside this area. Strikeouts and walks are called the same as in regular softball. The number of foul balls allowed should be limited. No base stealing is permitted. Otherwise, the game is played like softball.

Variations:

1. The batter kicks a stationary ball. This saves time, since there is no pitching.
2. **Punch Ball**. The batter can hit the ball as in a volleyball serve or punch a ball pitched by the pitcher.

Beat Ball

    Supplies: Soft softball, bat, batting tee (optional)

    Skills: All softball skills

    One team is at bat and the other team in the field. The object of the game is to hit the ball and run around the bases before the fielding team can catch the ball, throw it to first base, and then throw it to the catcher at home plate. If the ball beats the hitter home or a fly ball is caught, it is an out. If the hitter beats the ball to home plate, a run is scored. All players on a team bat once before switching positions with the fielding team. The ball must be hit into fair territory before the hitter can run. Only three pitches are allowed each hitter.

Variations:

1. Depending on the maturity of the players, a batting tee may be used. The hitter can be allowed the option of using the batting tee or hitting a pitched ball.
2. The pitcher can be selected from the batting team. This assures that an attempt will be made to make pitches that can be hit.
3. The distance can be varied so that hitters have a fair opportunity to score. If hitters score too easily, another base can be added.

DPE Curriculum Guide – Lesson Plans
Fundamental Skills Using Climbing Ropes
Level II – Alternate Lesson Plan #1

Objectives:
To be able to recite safety rules for
 rope climbing
To be able to hang on a climbing rope
 for 5 seconds
To be able to hang and swing on a
 climbing rope

NASPE National Standards:
Introductory Activity:
Fitness Activity:
Lesson Focus: 2, 3, 5
Game: 5, 6

Equipment Required:
Climbing Ropes
Tumbling mats placed under ropes
Benches or Jumping Boxes

Instructional Activities	Teaching Hints

Introductory Activity
Use the introductory activity from the lesson that was replaced.

Fitness Development Activity
Use the fitness activity from the lesson that was replaced.

Lesson Focus – Fundamental Skills using Climbing Ropes

Supported Pull-Ups
In supported pull-up activities, a part of the body remains in contact with the floor.
 The pull-up is hand-over-hand and the return is hand-under-hand.
1. Kneel directly under the rope. Pull up to the tiptoes and return to kneeling
position.
2. Start in a sitting position under the rope. Pull up; the legs are supported on the
heels. Return to sitting position.
3. Start in a standing position. Grasp the rope, rock back on the heels, and lower
the body to the floor. Keep a straight body. Return to standing position.

Hangs
In a hang, the body is pulled up in one motion and held up for a length of time (5,
10, or 20 seconds). Progression is important.
1. From a seated position, reach up as high as possible and pull the body from the
floor, except for the heels. Hold.
2. Same as the previous stunt but pull the body completely free of the floor. Hold.
3. From a standing position, jump up, grasp the rope, and hang. This should be a
Bent-Arm Hang with the hands about even with the mouth. Hold.
4. Repeat the previous stunt, but add leg movements—one or both knees up,
bicycling movement, Half Lever (one or both legs up, parallel to the floor), Full
Lever (feet up to the face).

Pull-Ups
In the pull-up, the body is raised and lowered repeatedly. The initial challenge
should be to accomplish one pull-up in the defined position. The number of
repetitions should be increased with care. All of the activities described for hangs
are adaptable to pull-ups. The chin should touch the hands on each pull-up.

Swinging and Jumping
For swinging and jumping, a bench, box, or stool can serve as a takeoff point. To
take off, the child reaches high and jumps to a bent-arm position. Landing should
be with bent knees.
1. Swing and jump. Add half turns and full turns.
2. Swing and return to the perch. Add single- and double-knee bends.
3. Jump for distance, over a high-jump bar or through a hoop.
4. Swing and pick up a bowling pin and return to the perch.
5. Carry objects (e.g., beanbags, balls, deck tennis rings). A partner, standing to
the side away from the takeoff bench, can put articles to be carried back on the
takeoff perch by placing each article between the knees or feet.

1. Mats should be placed under all
ropes.

2. The hand-over-hand method should
be used for climbing and the hand-
under-hand method for descending.

3. Caution the children not to slide;
sliding can cause rope burns on the
hands and legs.

4. A climber who becomes tired should
stop and rest. Proper rest stops should be
taught as part of the climbing procedure.

5. Children also should be taught to
leave enough margin for a safe descent.
No children should go higher than their
strength allows.

6. Spotters should be used initially for
activities in which the body is inverted.

7. Rosin in powdered form and
magnesium chalk aid in gripping. It is
particularly important that they be used
when the rope becomes slippery.

8. Children swinging on the ropes
should be instructed to make sure that
other children are out of the way.

9. Marks to limit the climb can be put
on the rope with adhesive tape. A height
of 8–10 ft above the floor is reasonable
until a child demonstrates proficiency.

10. If the ceiling is higher than 15–16 ft,

6. Not using a takeoff device, run toward a swinging rope, grasp it, and gain momentum for swinging.

a bright piece of tape should be wrapped around the rope to limit climbing height.

Climbing the Rope

1. *Scissors Grip*. For the Scissors Grip, approach the rope and reach as high as possible, standing with the right leg forward of the left. Raise the back leg, bend at the knee, and place the rope inside the knee and outside the foot. Cross the forward leg over the back leg, and straighten the legs with the toes pointed down. This should give a secure hold. To climb using the Scissors Grip, raise the knees up close to the chest, the rope sliding between them, while supporting the body with the hand grip. Lock the rope between the legs and climb up, using the hand-over-hand method and stretching as high as the hands can reach. Bring the knees up to the chest and repeat the process.

2. *Leg-Around Rest*. Wrap the left leg completely around the rope, keeping the rope between the thighs. The bottom of the rope then crosses over the instep of the left foot from the outside. The right foot stands on the rope as it crosses over the instep, providing pressure to prevent slippage. To provide additional pressure, release the hands and wrap the arms around the rope, leaning away from the rope at the same time. To climb using the Leg-Around Rest, proceed as in climbing with the Scissors Grip, but loosen the grip each time and re-grip higher.

Descending the Rope

There are four methods to descend the rope. The only differences are in the use of the leg locks, as the hand-under-hand is used for all descents.

1. *Scissors Grip*. From an extended scissors grip position, lock the legs and lower the body with the hands until the knees are against the chest. Hold with the hands, and lower the legs to a new position.

2. *Leg-Around Rest*. From the leg-around rest position, lower the body until the knees are against the chest. Lift the top foot, and let the feet slide to a lower position. Secure with the top foot and repeat.

3. *Instep Squeeze*. Squeeze the rope between the insteps by keeping the heels together. Lower the body while the rope slides against the instep.

4. *Stirrup Descent*. Place the rope on the outside of the right foot and carry it over the instep of the left. Pressure from the left foot holds the position. To get into position, let the rope trail along the right leg, reach under, and hook it with the left instep. When the pressure from the left leg is reduced, the rope slides smoothly while the descent is made with the hands.

Stunts Using Two Ropes

Two ropes hanging close together are needed for the following activities.

Straight-Arm Hang. To do the Straight-Arm Hang, jump up, grasp one rope with each hand, and hang with the arms straight.

Bent-Arm Hang. Perform as for the Straight-Arm Hang, but bend the arms at the elbows.

Arm Hangs with Different Leg Positions
  a. Do single- and double-knee lifts.
  b. Do a Half Lever. Bring the legs up parallel to the floor and point the toes.
  c. Do a Full Lever. Bring the feet up to the face and keep the knees straight.
  d. Do a Bicycle. Pedal as on a bicycle.

Pull-Ups. The Pull-Up is the same as on a single rope, except that each hand grasps a rope.

Inverted Hangs.
  a. Hang with the feet wrapped around the ropes.
  b. Hang with the feet against the inside of the ropes.
  c. Hang with the toes pointed and the feet not touching the ropes

Skin the Cat. From a bent-arm position, kick the feet overhead and continue the roll until the feet touch the mat. Return to the starting position.

Lifeboats (Cooperative Activity)

Formation: Groups of 8–12

Supplies: 2–3 individual mats or hoops, 2 scooters, and 1 long jump rope per group.

The group is positioned on one side of the gym (a slow sinking ship) and given a scooter (lifeboat) and a long jump rope. The objective is to get the entire group from the sinking ship to the mainland (the other side of the gym) using only their lifeboats. Spaced randomly between the starting and stopping points are 3 individual mats (or hoops), which are islands in the ocean. Any students that touch the gym floor (water) must return to the starting point or island they were on (if hoops are used as islands, inside the hoop does not count as water). Thus, all students must remain on a mat at all times unless they are traveling across the ocean in a lifeboat (scooter). Students may be pulled with the jump rope but they may not be pushed. Students who are transported across the ocean must remain on the mainland and cannot return to the island or lifeboats; however, if they step into the "water" trying to rescue a teammate, they must return to the final island.

Mat Folding (Cooperative Activity)

Formation: Groups of 4–5 students

Supplies: One tumbling mat for each group

The group is given one tumbling mat and instructed to stand on it. While keeping their feet on the mat at all times, teams are given the following challenges:

1. Rotate the mat 360 degrees.
2. Move the mat 15 ft.
3. Without using any hands, fold the mat into fourths.
4. Unfold the mat without using any hands.

Teaching Tip: This is an enjoyable activity to use at the end of a gymnastics lesson.

DPE Curriculum Guide – Lesson Plans
Fundamental Skills using Climbing Walls
Level II – Alternate Lesson Plan #2

Objectives:
To develop upper body strength
To be able to explain safety
precautions when climbing
To be able to climb using the basic
holds

NASPE National Standards:
Introductory Activity:
Fitness Activity:
Lesson Focus: 2, 3, 5
Game: 1, 5, 6

Equipment Required:
Balloons, beanbags, & hoops
Tumbling mats placed at the base of the
climbing wall
Climbing wall
Jump or stretch ropes

Instructional Activities	Teaching Hints

Introductory Activity
Use the introductory activity from the lesson that was replaced.

Fitness Development Activity
Use the fitness activity from the lesson that was replaced.

Lesson Focus – Climbing Wall Activities
Climbing walls are an excellent way to develop strength and coordination while solving climbing challenges. Students can learn to cooperate with others and the accomplishment of a climbing task contributes to student self-esteem. Most transverse walls in elementary schools are 8 ft high. Taller walls should have a red-relief line that keeps climbers close to the floor. For additional safety, place mats along the base of the wall. A typical wall may be 40 ft or more wide and have 200–300 hand holds. The hand holds are often color coded for level of difficulty.

Basic Holds
Teach students the basic ways to climb on the wall. Explain and practice hand and foot holds on the wall at a low level before proceeding to climb. The following are basic holds:

- The Pinch—This basic hold is performed by simply squeezing the hold between the thumb and fingers.

- Finger Grip—Just the fingers are used to hold a rock while adjusting the legs to a stable rock position.

- The Crimp—Grasp the hold with the fingers at the middle joint and wrap the thumb over the first joint of the index finger.

- The Edge—This foothold uses the ball to toe part of the foot. Either side of the shoe can be used, i.e., the front with the toe pointing or the outside edge of the shoe.

- The Lock-Off—The crimp grip is used on the hold and the arm is bent at the elbow and held close to the climber's body. This hold is used to stabilize the body close to the wall so the other arm can be used to reach for a new hold.

Climbing walls can be safely used in a physical education setting if students are made aware of and follow appropriate safety rules. Consider the following:
1. Climbing walls are only used when a teacher is directly supervising the activity.
2. Only soft-soled shoes are used during climbing activities.
3. On walls taller than 8 ft, climbing above the red line is not allowed. The climber's feet must stay below the red line at all times.
4. Climbers are not to touch or interfere with another climber on the wall.
5. Only climbers are allowed on the safety mats.
6. Climb down from the wall—no jumping down is allowed.

Individual Challenge Activities
- Four-Point Hold—Climbers take a four-point rock position (each hand and foot on a separate rock) and move to four new rocks.

- Foothold Climb—Climb high enough to get footholds on rocks.

- Foothold Climbs with Challenges—Similar to the climb above except students are challenged to climb using only certain color rocks.

- Up and Down—Climb and then return to the floor using the same pathway (same rocks).

A positive aspect of climbing walls is that students can use footholds to help them climb. This helps youngsters who are overweight find success. For students who are challenged, do not rush them.

Give them activities to do that are near the floor and let them determine when they are ready to challenge themselves.

- Three-point Hold—Climb off the floor and below the red line. Balance yourself and lift a limb from a hold. Try lifting a different limb.

- Beanbag Climb—Climb with a beanbag on your shoulder. Place the beanbag on a hold and descend. The next person climbs and brings the beanbag down on their shoulder.

Partner Activities
- Point and Move—One partner is on the floor while the other partner assumes a four-point hold on the wall. The floor partner points to a hand or foot hold that is the next move the climber must take. The purpose is to challenge partners with reasonable moves, not impossible tasks. Change roles after 5 moves.

- Sightless Climbing—The climbing partner puts on a blindfold and is guided by their partner on the floor. Partners describe the direction and distance of the move to the climber.

Climbing challenges are individual in nature—each student strives to improve their performance without concern for how others are climbing. The following are examples of climbing activities that can be used to motivate students to stay on the wall and practice their skills.

Partner activities are motivating because they bring a social and cooperative aspect to climbing. Allow students to change partners regularly so they learn to understand individual differences. Encourage students to be helpful, but not touch their partner while they are climbing.

Game Activity

Zap (Cooperative Game)
Formation: Groups of 4–10 students
Supplies: One tumbling mat, one stretch rope or jump rope, two volleyball standards or device to attach the ropes
The rope is attached on either side of the mat and approximately 3–4 ft off the ground, depending on the age of the children. For this activity the challenge is to get the entire group over the rope and to the other side without touching, or getting "zapped," by the rope. However, to enhance the challenge and keep it safe, jumping over the rope is not allowed. In addition, to start, the group forms a circle and joins hands to form a "closed chain." This chain must remain closed throughout the challenge. If anyone is zapped by the rope or the chain is broken (two people let go hands), the entire group must go back to the other side and start over.

Keep It Floating
Formation: Groups of 4–8 students
Supplies: For each group, two balloons, one beach ball, and one hoop for every two youngsters
Students form a circle and join hands. Their challenge is to keep a balloon up for as many hits as possible without letting go of hands. After a few rounds, another balloon is added to increase the difficulty. Finally, a beach ball and one balloon are used. Teaching Tip: For advanced classes, place one hoop between each set of students. Students must keep one foot in each hoop on either side of them. This advanced challenge is best with only one balloon. To integrate other academic content, have the students do the following while participating in the initial version of the challenge:
1. State a different fruit or vegetable with each hit.
2. Count in a foreign language.
3. Count by twos, threes, fours, etc.
4. Attempt to strike the balloon with a different bone or muscle each time and call out the name of that body part.
5. Call out a different lifetime activity with each hit.

DPE Curriculum Guide – Lesson Plans
Manipulative Skills Using Playground Balls
Level II – Alternate Lesson Plan #3

Objectives:
To sequence a series of locomotor
   movements
To participate in physical activity that
   exercises all body parts
To throw and catch a playground ball
To control a playground ball with the
   feet

NASPE National Standards:
Introductory Activity:
Fitness Activity:
Lesson Focus: 1, 2, 3, 5
Game: 1, 2, 3

Equipment Required:
One 8½" playground ball or foam
   rubber ball for each student

Instructional Activities	Teaching Hints

Introductory Activity
Use the introductory activity from the lesson that was replaced.

Fitness Development Activity
Use the fitness activity from the lesson that was replaced.

Lesson Focus — Manipulative Skills Using Playground Balls

Individual Activities

Controlled rolling and handling
1. Sit, stand, or lie on back--roll ball around and handle it between legs, behind
   back to develop a proper "feel" of the ball.

Bounce and catch
1. Two hands, one hand.
2. Bounce at different levels.
3. Bounce between legs.
4. Close eyes and bounce.
5. Dribble ball in a stationary and/or moving position.
6. Dribble and follow the commands, such as: move forward, backward, in a
   circle, sideways, while walking, galloping, trotting, etc.

Toss and catch
1. Toss and catch, vary height.
2. Add various challenges while tossing (i.e., touch floor, clap hands, turn, make
   body turns, sit down, lie down).
3. Toss and let bounce. Also add some challenges as above.
4. Toss up and catch behind back—toss from behind back and catch in front.
5. Create moving challenges (i.e., toss, run five steps, catch, toss, back up five
   hops, and catch).

Bat the ball (as in volleyball) to self (teach a low-controlled bat).
1. Bat the ball—use palm, back, and side of hand.
2. Bat the ball using different body parts.

Foot skills
1. Pick the ball up with both feet and catch. Both front and rear of body catch.
2. From a sitting position, ball between feet, toss ball up and catch with hands.
3. While sitting, toss ball up with hands and catch with feet.
4. Put ball between feet or knees and play tag games.
5. Keep ball in air by using feet, knees, head. How many times can you bounce it
   in succession?

Teaching Hints:

Give students two or three activities to
practice so you have time to move and
help youngsters. Alternate activities
from each of the categories so students
receive a variety of skills to practice.

When catching, soft receipt of the ball is
achieved by "giving" with the hands
and arms. The hands should reach out
somewhat to receive the ball and then
cushion the impact by bringing the ball
in toward the body in a relaxed way.

Toss high as you can and still maintain
control.

To catch a throw above the waist, the
hands should be positioned so that the
thumbs are together. To receive a throw
below the waist, the little fingers should
be kept toward each other and the
thumbs kept out.

Laterality is an important consideration.
Right and left members of the body
should be given practice in turn.

When throwing to a partner, unless
otherwise specified, the throw should
reach the partner at about chest height.
At times, different target points should
be specified—high, low, right, left, at
the knee, and so on.

Partner Activities
Passing skills
1. Two-handed, right and left.
2. Throw to various targets—high, low, right, and left.
3. Odd throws—under leg, around body, football center, shot-put, windmill, discus.
4. Push-shot types. Straight push, arch.
5. Roll the ball to partner. Flick it in the air with foot and catch.
6. Have one partner dribble and the other attempt to take it away without fouling.

Distance between partners should be short at first and should be lengthened gradually.

Control the passes. Move closer together if necessary.

Game Activity

Bounce Ball

Supplies: Volleyballs or rubber playground balls of about the same size

Skills: Throwing, ball rolling

The court is divided into halves. The class is divided into two teams and each team occupies one half of the court and is given a number of balls. Two players from each team should be assigned to retrieve balls that go behind their end lines. The object of the game is to bounce or roll the ball over the opponents' end line. A ball thrown across the line on a fly does not count. Two scorers are needed, one at each end line. Players can move wherever they wish in their own area but cannot cross the centerline. After the starting signal, the balls are thrown back and forth at will.

One Step

Supplies: A ball or beanbag for each pair of children

Skills: Throwing, catching

Two players stand facing each other about 3 ft apart. One has a ball or beanbag. The object of the game is to throw or toss the item so that the partner can catch it without moving her feet. When the throw is completed successfully, the thrower takes one step backward and waits for a throw from her partner. Players try to increase the distance one step at a time until they reach an established line. When either player misses or moves their feet, the partners move forward and start over.

Variables that provide interest and challenge are types of throws, types of catches, and different steps. Throwing can be underhand, overhand, two-handed, under one leg, around the back, and so on. Catching can be two-handed, left-handed, right-handed, to the side, and so on. The step can be a giant step, a tiny step, a hop, a jump, or a similar movement.

Objectives:
To be able to lead and follow peers performing activity
To perform fitness activities independently
To develop visual-tactile skills

NASPE National Standards:
Introductory Activity:
Fitness Activity:
Lesson Focus: 1, 2, 3, 5
Game: 6

Equipment Required:
One beanbag per student
12 bowling pins and 12 foam balls

Instructional Activities	Teaching Hints

Introductory Activity
Use the introductory activity from the lesson that was replaced.

Fitness Development Activity
Use the fitness activity from the lesson that was replaced.

Lesson Focus — Beanbag Activities

In place, Tossing to self
1. Toss and catch with both hands—right hand, left hand
2. Toss and catch with the back of hands. This will encourage children to catch with "soft hands."
3. Toss the beanbag to increasingly high level, *emphasizing* a straight overhead toss. To encourage straight tossing, have the child sit down.

Give students two or three activities to practice so you have time to move and help youngsters. Alternate activities from each of the categories so students receive a variety of skills to practice.

In Place, Adding Stunts
1. Toss overhead and perform the following stunts and catch the bag.
   a. 1/4 and 1/2 turns, right and left
   b. Full turn
   c. Touch floor
   d. Clap hands
   e. Clap hands around different parts of body, behind back, under legs
   f. Heel click
   g. Student choice

Stress a soft receipt of the beanbag by giving with the hands, arms, and legs. "Giving" involves the hands going out toward the incoming beanbag and bringing it in for a soft landing.

Remind students to keep their eyes on the beanbag when catching.

In place, kicking to self
1. Place beanbag on foot, kick up and catch—right foot, left foot.
2. Try above activity from sitting and lying positions.
3. Kick up and catch behind back.
4. Kick up overhead, make ½ turn and catch.
5. Put beanbag between feet, jump up and catch beanbag.
6. Toss beanbag with one foot and catch with the other foot.

When tossing and catching, toss slightly above eye level. Overly high tosses should be discouraged until catching is mastered.

Locomotor movements (Toss, Move and Catch)
1. Toss overhead, move to another spot and catch.
2. Toss, do a locomotor movement and catch.
3. Move from side to side.
4. Toss overhead behind self, move, and catch.
5. Exploratory movements.

Beanbags should be at least 6 in. square. This size balances well and can be controlled on various parts of the body, thus offering greater challenge.

Balance the beanbag
1. Balance on the following body parts:
   a. Head
   b. Back of hand
   c. Shoulder
   d. Knee
   e. Foot
   f. Elbow

Stress laterality and directionality when teaching manipulative skills. Children should be taught to throw, catch, and balance beanbags with both the left and right sides of their body. They should learn to catch and throw at different levels.

2. Balance and move as follows:
   a. Walk
   b. Run
   c. Skip
   d. Gallop
   e. Sit down
   f. Lie down
   g. Turn around
   h. Balance beanbag on body part and move on all fours.

See who can balance the beanbag longest on various body parts while moving.

Emphasize quality not quantity. Motivation is often enhanced by practicing an activity for a short time and returning to it later.

Partner activities
1. Toss back and forth using the following throws:
   a. Two-handed throws—overhead, underhand, side, and over shoulder.
   b. One-handed throws and catches.
   c. Throw at different levels and targets such as high, low, left, right.
   d. Throw under leg, around body, from behind back, center, as in football, etc.
   e. Sit down and play catch—try different throws and catches.
   f. Toss in various directions to make partner move and catch. Have one partner move around other in a circle while catching and throwing.
   g. Propel more than one beanbag back and forth. Toss both beanbags together, as well as at opposite times.

Children should toss at chest height to a partner, unless a different type of throw is specified. Teach all types of return: low, medium, high, left, and right.

In partner work, keep distances between partners reasonable, especially in introductory phases. Fifteen feet or so seems to be a reasonable starting distance. Throwing too hard or out of range, to cause the partner to miss, should be discussed.

Game Activity

Indianapolis 500
   Supplies: None
   Skills: Running, tagging
   Players start in a large circle and are numbered off in threes or fours. A race starter says "Start your engines," and then calls out a number. Those players with the corresponding number run in the same direction around the circle and try to tag players in front of them. If the leader yells "Pit stop," all runners have to stop and return to their original position. If "Car crash" is called by the leader, all runners change direction and continue running. Change starters often.

Lily Pads (Cooperative Activity)
   Formation: Teams of 6–15 students
   Supplies: One poly spot per child
   Students will begin standing on their poly spots, or lily pads, in a straight line. Each lily pad should be about 12" apart. The team's challenge is to reverse their order so that the two youngsters on the end switch places, the second to last switch places, etc. See below for a visual explanation. The catch is that each member of the team must have at least one foot on a lily pad at all times. If either of these rules is broken, the teams must start over in the original order.

      Start   Finish
  1 2 3 4 5 6 7 8   8 7 6 5 4 3 2 1

   Teaching Tip: If poly spots are not available, this activity can also be done using a line or a long piece of tape. Simply make the rule that one foot must be on the tape at all times.

Objectives:
To be able to move continuously in moderately active activities
To learn the rules of recreational activities
To play in recreational activities independently without adult supervision

NASPE National Standards:
Introductory Activity:
Fitness Activity:
Lesson Focus: 1, 2, 3, 5
Game: 1, 5

Equipment Required:
6 benches and tumbling mats
Cageball, pinnies, and stopwatch for games

Instructional Activities	Teaching Hints

Introductory Activity
Use the introductory activity from the lesson that was replaced.

Fitness Development Activity
Use the fitness activity from the lesson that was replaced.

Lesson Focus — Fundamental Skills Using Benches

Present activities from each of the categories so students receive a variety of skills to practice.

1. Animal movements on bench.
   a. Seal Crawl
   b. Cat Walk
   c. Lame Dog Walk
   d. Rabbit Jump
   e. Crab Walk
2. Locomotor movements.
   a. Skip on the bench
   b. Gallop on the bench
   c. Step on and off the bench
   d. Jump on and off the bench
   e. Hop on and off the bench
   f. Jump or hop over the bench
3. Pulls—pull body along the bench in various positions.
   a. Prone position—head first, feet first
   b. Supine position—head first, feet first
   c. Side position—head first, feet first
4. Pushes—same as above activity except push with the arms in all positions.
5. Movements alongside the benches—proceed alongside the bench in the following positions.
   a. Prone position—hands on bench
   b. Supine position—hands on bench
   c. Turn over—proceed along bench changing from prone to supine positions with hands on bench
   d. All of the above positions performed with the feet on the bench.
6. Scooter movements—sit on bench and proceed along bench without using hands.
   a. Regular scooter—feet leading
   b. Reverse scooter—legs trailing
   c. Seat walk—walk on the buttocks
7. Crouch jumps.
   a. Straddle jump
   b. Regular jump
   c. One hand, two feet
   d. One hand, one foot

1. Mats should be placed at the ends of the benches to facilitate the dismount and various rolls and stunts executed after the dismount.

2. Four to five children is the maximum number that should be assigned to one bench.

3. The child next in turn should begin when the performer ahead is about three-quarters of the way across the bench.

4. All activities on the benches should be broken down into three distinct parts: the approach to and mounting of the bench, the actual activity on the bench, and the dismount from the bench.

5. When students have completed their movement across the bench, perform a jump dismount to complete the activity.

6. All bench activities should end with a dismount. Some examples of dismounts are:
   a. Single jump—forward or backward
   b. Jump with turns—1/2 or 3/4 or full
   c. Jackknife (Pike)
   d. Jackknife split (straddle)
   e. Jump, forward roll
   f. Back jump, back roll
   g. Side jump, side roll
   h. Jump, Shoulder roll
   i. Jump sideways, Cartwheel

Cageball Kickover

Supplies: A cageball, 24- or 30-in. size

Skill: Kicking

Players are divided into two teams and sit facing each other, with legs outstretched and soles of the feet about 6–12 ft apart. While maintaining the sitting position, each player leans back and supports his weight on the hands, which are placed slightly to the rear. The cageball is rolled between the two teams. The object of the game is to kick the ball over the other team, thereby scoring a point. After a point is scored, restart the game by rolling the ball into play again. Rotate players by having a player on the left side of the line take a place on the right side after a point is scored, thus moving all the players one position to the left. When the ball is kicked out at either end, no score results and the ball is rolled into play again.

Centipede (Cooperative Activity)

Formation: Entire class shoulder to shoulder

Supplies: None

All students stand shoulder to shoulder on a sideline, facing the same direction, and feet touching the person next to them. The entire class must move to the other sideline without breaking the chain of touching feet. If the chain breaks, the group must take three steps back. Students may put their arms around each other if desired.

Teaching Tip: Some classes may require a progression starting with partners, then small groups, and finally the entire class.

DPE CURRICULUM GUIDE – LESSON PLANS
Developmental Level III
With Instructional and Academic Integration Activities

WEEK	INTRODUCTORY ACTIVITY	FITNESS DEVELOPMENT ACTIVITY	LESSON FOCUS ACTIVITY	CLOSING ACTIVITY	PAGE
1	Move and Freeze on Signal	Teacher Leader Exercises	Orientation and Class Management Activities	Toe to Toe Whistle Mixer	223
	Geometric shape recognition *Letter recognition* *CW & CCW*	*Spatial Awareness* *Heart rate calculation* *Skip counting*	*Grouping*	*Grouping* *Listening skills* *Body part identifications*	LP 80
2	European Running	Teacher–Leader Exercises	Manipulative Skills Using Wands & Hoops	Balance Beam Mixer Jolly Ball Circle Touch	225
	Geometric shape recognition *Letter recognition 4/4 time* *CW & CCW*	*Spatial awareness* *Heart rate calculation* *Skip counting*	*Midpoint* *Vertical & horizontal* *¼, ½, ¾ & full turns* *Degrees (90°, 180°, 270°, 360°)* *Prediction*	*Geometric shape recognition* *Mental math problems (to call numbers)*	LP 81
3	Move and Freeze	Teacher–Leader Exercises	Long-Rope Jumping Skills	Cageball Target Throw Sunday Wolfe's Beanbag Exchange	228
	Geometric shape recognition *Letter recognition* *CW & CCW*	*Spatial awareness* *Heart rate calculation* *Skip counting*	*Grouping* *Midpoint* *Parallel lines (Double Dutch)* *Perpendicular lines (Egg Beater)*	*Cause and Effect* *Parallel lines* *Grouping*	LP 82
4	Move and Manipulate	Hexagon Hustle	Football Skills and Lead-up Activities (1)	Football End Ball Speed Football Kick-Over	230
	Levels (Low, medium, and high) *Fractions* *Percentages*	*Shape recognition* *CW & CCW* *Skip counting* *Reading signs*	*Reading signs* *Measurement of yards* *Opposition*	*Parallel lines* *Skip counting* *Measurement of yards* *Scoring*	LP 83
5	Fastest Tag in the West	Hexagon Hustle	Football Skills and Lead-up Activities (2)	Speed Football Fourth Down Flag Football	233
	Area of a shape *Perimeter*	*Shape recognition* *CW & CCW* *Skip counting* *Reading signs*	*Reading signs* *Measurement of yards* *Opposition*	*Measurement of yards* *Scoring*	LP 84

WEEK	INTRODUCTORY ACTIVITY	FITNESS DEVELOPMENT ACTIVITY	LESSON FOCUS ACTIVITY	CLOSING ACTIVITY	PAGE
6	Following Activities	Circuit Training	Advanced Pedometer Skills	Moving Together Who's Leading	236
	Grouping *Patterning* *Categorization (components of fitness)*	*CW & CCW* *Reading signs* *Fitness components* *Skip counting* *Grouping* *Choral responses* *Time recognition (What station is at _ o'clock?)*	*Personal goal setting* *Comparing time and step counts* *Determining stride length* *Converting steps to distance*	*Cause and effect* *Body part identification*	LP 85
7	Medic Tag	Circuit Training	Gymnastics Skills (1)	Mat Folding Octopus Pin Knockout	240
	Body part identification	*CW & CCW* *Reading signs* *Sequence of fitness components* *Skip counting* *Grouping* *Choral responses* *Time recognition (What station is at _ o'clock?)*	*Angles (acute, obtuse, and right angles)* *Parallel lines* *Patterning*	*Trajectory* *Velocity* *Grouping* *Skip Counting*	LP 86
8	Hospital Tag	Astronaut Exercises	Soccer Skills and Lead-up Activities (1)	Dribblerama Sideline Soccer Line Soccer Mini-Soccer	244
	Body part identification	*Area and perimeter* *Shape recognition* *CW & CCW* *Aerobic intensity*	*Reading signs* *Opposition* *Rectangles* *Angle for kicking (45°)* *Grouping* *Prediction*	*Shape recognition* *Perimeter* *Parallel lines* *Grouping* *Rotation (of players)* *Scoring*	LP 87
9	PACER Run	Astronaut Exercises	Soccer Skills and Lead-up Activities (2)	Bull's-Eye Line Soccer Mini-Soccer Regulation Soccer	247
	Estimation and prediction (How many times?)	*Area and perimeter* *Shape recognition* *CW & CCW* *Aerobic intensity*	*Reading signs* *Opposition* *Rectangles* *Angle for kicking (45°)* *Grouping* *Prediction*	*Shape recognition* *Perimeter* *Parallel lines* *Grouping* *Rotation (of players)* *Scoring*	LP 88

WEEK	INTRODUCTORY ACTIVITY	FITNESS DEVELOPMENT ACTIVITY	LESSON FOCUS ACTIVITY	CLOSING ACTIVITY	PAGE
10	Beanbag Touch & Go	Aerobic Fitness	Juggling Skills and Pyramids	Fast Pass One-Base Tagball	250
📖	*Ratio* *Anatomical Terms* *Muscle Identification*	*Reading signs* *Target heart rate* *Fitness components*	*Reading signs* *Opposition* *Rectangles* *Angle for kicking (45°)* *Grouping* *Prediction*	*Shape recognition* *Perimeter* *Parallel lines* *Grouping* *Rotation (of players)* *Scoring*	LP 89
11	Jog & Stretch	Aerobic Fitness	Recreational Activities		253
📖	*CW & CCW* *Skip Counting* *Body part identification*	*Reading signs* *Target heart rate* *Patterning of fitness components*	*Reading Signs* *Grouping* *Sequencing* *Quadrants* *Addition and multiplication (scoring)*		LP 90
12	Vanishing Beanbags	Fitness Orienteering	Walking Activities	Walking Interviews Giant Map Construction New Engineer	254
📖	*Greater than/Less than* *Space/Area*	*Area and perimeter* *Shape recognition* *CW & CCW* *Aerobic and intensity*	*Target heart rate* *Training zone* *Geography (jog across the USA)* *Counting steps (pedometers)* *Calculating stride length* *Steps per mile (pedometers)* *Measurement (laps per mile)*	*Reading Signs* *Grouping* *Sequencing* *Quadrants* *Addition and multiplication (scoring)*	LP 91
13	Hospital Tag	Challenge Course	Rhythmic Movement Skills (1)	Triplet Stoop Pacman	256
📖	*Body part identification*	*CW & CCW* *Perimeter* *Skip counting* *Reading signs* *Following a course*	*Grouping* *Rhythmic Counting* *Cultural Awareness* *Triplets (3's)* *Building sequences*	*Grouping* *Triplets (3's)* *Circumference* *Shape recognition*	LP 92
14	Stretching		Orienteering Skills and Activities	Scavenger Hunt School Ground Orienteering	259
📖	*Skip counting* *Body part identification*		*Problem solving* *Counting steps* *Addition of scores (team score)*	*Reading Signs* *Grouping* *Sequencing* *Quadrants* *Addition and multiplication (scoring)*	LP 93

WEEK	INTRODUCTORY ACTIVITY	FITNESS DEVELOPMENT ACTIVITY	LESSON FOCUS ACTIVITY	CLOSING ACTIVITY	PAGE	
15	Marking	Challenge Course	Gymnastics Skills (2)	All Aboard Over the Wall	261	
	Body part identification	*CW & CCW* *Perimeter* *Skip counting* *Reading signs* *Following a course*	*Patterning* *Perpendicular* *Balance* *Base of Support* *Body part identification*	*Patterning* *Shape Recognition* *Scoring*		LP 94
16	European Running with Variations	Challenge Course	Rhythmic Movement Skills (2)	Cageball Target Throw Stranded	265	
	Shape recognition *Rhythmic counting* *CW & CCW*	*CW & CCW* *Perimeter* *Skip counting* *Reading signs* *Following a course*	*Grouping* *Rhythmic counting* *Cultural awareness* *Triplets (3's)* *Building of sequences*	*Cause and effect* *Parallel lines* *Grouping* *Division (Chain Tag)*		LP 95
17	Dribble and Pivot	Partner Aerobic Fitness & Resistance Exercises	Basketball Skills and Lead-up Activities (1)	Sideline Basketball	269	
	¼, ½, ¾, and Full Turns *Degrees of pivot (90°, 180°, 270°, and 360°)*	*Health Concepts* *Opposition and resistance* *Cause and effect* *Muscle Recognition*	*Sequencing* *Grouping* *Geometric shapes (semi-circle, star, square)*	*Parallel lines* *Scoring* *Moving within an area* *Perimeter*		LP 96
18	Barker's Hoopla	Partner Aerobic Fitness & Resistance Exercises	Basketball Skills and Lead-up Activities (2)	Twenty-One Lane Basketball One Goal Basketball	272	
	Grouping *Scoring*	*Health Concepts* *Opposition and resistance* *Cause and effect* *Muscle Recognition*	*Sequencing* *Grouping* *Geometric shape (semi circle, star, square)*	*Parallel lines* *Scoring* *Moving within an area* *Perimeter*		LP 97
19	Run, Stop, & Pivot	Exercises to Music	Throwing Skills	In the Prison Snowball Cageball Target Throw Target Ball Throw	275	
	¼, ½, ¾, and Full Turns *Degrees of pivot (90°, 180°, 270°, and 360°)*	*Skip counting* *Listening skills*	*Sequencing* *Grouping* *Geometric shapes (semi-circle, star, square)*	*Parallel lines* *Scoring* *Moving within an area* *Perimeter*		LP 98
20	Agility Run	Exercises to Music	Cooperative Game Skills		277	
	Estimation and prediction (How many times?)	*Skip counting* *Listening skills*	*Area and perimeter* *Shape recognition* *Problem Solving* *Cooperative skills*			LP 99

WEEK	INTRODUCTORY ACTIVITY	FITNESS DEVELOPMENT ACTIVITY	LESSON FOCUS ACTIVITY	CLOSING ACTIVITY	PAGE
21	Rubber Band	Aerobic, Strength, & Flexibility Jackpot Fitness	Hockey Skills and Lead-up Activities (1)	Lane Hockey Goalkeeper Hockey Sideline Hockey	280
	Grouping *Patterning*	*Reading "jackpots"* *Components of Fitness*	*Grouping* *Parallel* *Vocabulary (Offense, defense, guards, forwards, centers, dodging, tackling)*	*Grouping* *Parallel lines*	**LP 100**
22	Move & Exercise on Signal	Aerobic, Strength, & Flexibility Jackpot Fitness	Hockey Skills and Lead-up Activities (2)	Sideline Hockey Regulation Hockey	284
	CW & CCW *Grouping* *Components of fitness*	*Number pattern responses* *Rhyming responses (choral)* *States and capitols* *Math facts*	*Grouping* *Parallel* *Vocabulary (Offense, defense, guards, forwards, centers, dodging, tackling)*	*Grouping* *Parallel lines*	**LP 101**
23	Pyramid Power	Aerobic Fitness	Gymnastics Skills (3)	Lilly Pads Flag Chase Jolly Ball	287
	Grouping	*Reading signs* *Target heart rate* *Patterning of fitness components*	*Sequencing steps* *Right angels* *Parallel* *Perpendicular* *Prediction* *Center of gravity* *Pattern of movements*	*Grouping* *Math facts* *CW & CCW* *Predicting* *Greater and less than* *Geometric shapes*	**LP 102**
24	Stretching Activities		Track & Field Skills and Lead-up Activities (1)	Circular Relays Shuttle Relays One-on-One Contests	291
		Body part identification *Skip Counting*	*Timing (stop watch)* *Measurements* *Reading signs* *Angle recognition* *Speed and velocity*	*Shape recognition* *Perpendicular* *Parallel*	**LP 103**
25	Stretching Activities		Track & Field Skills and Lead-up Activities (2)	Circular Relays Shuttle Relays Flippers	294
		Body part identification *Skip Counting*	*Timing (stop watch)* *Measurements* *Reading signs* *Angle recognition* *Speed and velocity*	*Shape recognition* *Perpendicular* *Parallel*	**LP 104**

WEEK	INTRODUCTORY ACTIVITY	FITNESS DEVELOPMENT ACTIVITY	LESSON FOCUS ACTIVITY	CLOSING ACTIVITY	PAGE
26	Racetrack Fitness		Track & Field Skills and Lead-up Activities (3)	Circular Relays Shuttle Relays One-on-One Contests	296
📖		*Reading signs* *Components of Fitness* *CW & CCW*	*Timing (stop watch)* *Measurements* *Reading signs* *Angle recognition* *Speed and velocity*	*Shape recognition* *Perpendicular* *Parallel*	**LP 105**
27	Following Activity	Parachute Fitness	Rhythmic Movement Skills (3)	Whistle Ball Zap	297
📖	*Grouping* *Partner patterning* *Categorization (components of fitness)*	*CW & CCW* *Circumference* *Skip counting* *Segments* *Level identification (high, medium, & low)*	*Patterning* *Grouping* *Rhythmic counting* *Cultural awareness* *Spacing*	*Grouping* *Circumference*	**LP 106**
28	High Fives	Sport-Related Fitness Stations	Tennis Skills and Lead-up Activities	Tennis Volleyball Playground Tennis	301
📖	*Skip counting* *CW & CCW* *Multiples of 5 (or another number)*	*CW & CCW* *Circumference* *Skip counting* *Segments* *Level identification (high, medium, & low)*	*Parallel* *Perpendicular* *Number patterns*	*Grouping* *Scoring*	**LP 107**
29	Individual Crows and Cranes	Sport-Related Fitness Stations	Tennis Skills and Lead-up Activities	Tennis Volleyball Volley-Shuttle Run Playground Tennis	304
📖	*Grouping* *Sequencing of patterns*	*Skip counting* *Listening skills*	*Slow time and Fast time* *90°(elbow)* *Revolutions (turning)* *Target heart rate* *Sequencing of steps*	*Directions (N/S/E/W)* *Right/Left* *Parallel lines* *Perpendicular lines* *Skip counting*	**LP 108**
30	New Leader	Circuit Training	Volleyball Skills and Lead-up Activities (1)	Pass and Dig Mini-Volleyball Regulation Volleyball	307
📖	*Grouping* *Quadrants*	*CW & CCW* *Reading signs* *Sequence of fitness components* *Skip counting* *Grouping* *Choral responses* *Time recognition (What station is at _ o'clock?)*	*Grouping* *Number patterns* *Angles* *Cause and effect* *Shape recognition (Hands like a triangle)*	*Grouping* *Skip counting* *Patterning* *Parallel lines*	**LP 109**

WEEK	INTRODUCTORY ACTIVITY	FITNESS DEVELOPMENT ACTIVITY	LESSON FOCUS ACTIVITY	CLOSING ACTIVITY	PAGE
31	Ball Activities	Continuity Drills	Volleyball Skills and Lead-up Activities (2)	Three and Over Volleyball Rotation Volleyball	310
	Shape recognition *Patterning of movements*	*Shape recognition* *CW & CCW* *Skip counting* *Reading signs*	*Grouping* *Number patterns* *Angles* *Cause and effect* *Shape recognition (Hands like a triangle)*	*Grouping* *Skip counting* *Patterning* *Parallel lines*	LP 110
32	Group Over & Around	Racetrack Fitness	Rhythmic Movement Skills (4)	Pig Ball Touchdown Chain Tag	312
	Grouping *Sequencing*	*Reading Signs* *Components of Fitness* *CW & CCW*	*Grouping* *Rhythmic counting* *Cultural awareness* *Sequencing*	*Parallel lines* *Addition* *Angles*	LP 111
33	Moving to Music	Squad Leader Exercises with Task Cards	Frisbee Skills	Frisbee Keep-Away Frisbee Golf	316
	Movement patterns *Recall of information*	*Skip counting* *Reading signs* *Grouping*	*Angel recognition* *Parallel lines* *Sequencing of steps* *Geometric shape recognition*	*Parallel lines* *Following a map* *Scoring* *Sequencing*	LP 112
34	Personal Choice	Parachute Fitness	Gymnastics Skills (4)	Pin Knockout Dot Bridge	318
	Recall of information *Sequencing of fitness components*	*CW & CCW* *Circumference* *Skip counting* *Segments* *Level identification (high, medium, & low)*	*Low center of gravity* *Wide base of support* *Grouping* *Sequencing of steps* *¼, ½, ¾, and full turns* *Degrees ((90°, 180°, 270°, and 360°)*	*Parallel lines* *Estimation (How many pins will be knocked down?)*	LP 113
35	Personal Choice	Squad Leader Exercises with Task Cards	Softball Skills and Lead-up Activities (1)	Scrub (Work-up)	320
	Recall of information *Sequencing fitness components*	*Skip counting* *Reading signs* *Grouping*	*Grouping* *Parallel lines* *Sequencing of steps* *CW & CCW* *Geometric shapes* *Arch*	*Scoring* *Grouping*	LP 114

WEEK	INTRODUCTORY ACTIVITY	FITNESS DEVELOPMENT ACTIVITY	LESSON FOCUS ACTIVITY	CLOSING ACTIVITY	PAGE
36	Personal Choice	Partner Fitness Challenges	Softball Skills and Lead-up Activities (2)	Slow-Pitch Softball Three-Team Softball	322
	Recall of information Sequencing fitness components	*Patterning Momentum Estimation of time*	*Grouping Parallel lines Sequencing of steps CW & CCW Geometric shapes Arch*	*Scoring Grouping*	LP 115
Alternate Lesson 1	Stretching Activities		Cross-Country Running and Walking Skills	Individual or Recreational Activities	324
	Skip Counting Body Part Identification		*Problem solving Counting steps Addition of scores (team scores)*	*Map reading Directions (N/S/E/W) Distance*	LP 116
Alternate Lesson 2	Use the introductory activity from the lesson that was replaced.	Use the fitness activity from the lesson that was replaced.	Racquet Sports Skills	Volley Tennis One-Wall Handball and Racquetball	325
			Parallel Perpendicular Number Patterns	*Grouping Scoring Quadrants*	LP 117
Alternate Lesson 3	Use the introductory activity from the lesson that was replaced.	Use the fitness activity from the lesson that was replaced.	Individual Rope-Jumping Skills	Right Face, Left Face One Base Tagball	327
			Slow time/Fast time Revolutions (turning) Target heart rate Sequencing of Steps	*Directions (N/S/E/W) Parallel lines Perpendicular lines Skip counting*	LP 118
Alternate Lesson 4	Use the introductory activity from the lesson that was replaced.	Use the fitness activity from the lesson that was replaced.	Fundamental Skills Using Climbing Ropes	Moving Together Who's Leading	330
			Dismounts Pendulums (swinging) Friction (descending the rope)	*Cooperative Skills Problem solving*	LP 119

LP 80

Objectives:
To learn and follow basic management activities necessary for participation in physical education classes

NASPE National Standards:
Introductory Activity: 1
Fitness Activity: 1,4, 2
Lesson Focus: 2, 5
Game: 2, 5

Equipment Required:
Tom-tom
Tape player and music for fitness challenges

Instructional Activities	**Teaching Hints**

Orientation Instructional Procedures

The first week of school should be used to teach students the system you are going to use throughout the year. The following are reminders you might find useful in establishing your expectations and routines.

1. Establish rules and expectations. Discuss your expectations with the class to assure students understand reasons for your guidelines. Explain what the consequences are when rules are not followed. Show where time-out boxes are located and how they will be used.

2. Explain to the class the method you will use to learn names. It might be helpful to ask classroom teachers to have students put their name on a piece of masking tape (nametag). Tell students that you will ask them their name on a regular basis until it is learned.

3. Develop entry and exit behaviors for students coming and leaving physical education classes. Students should know how to enter the instructional area and to leave equipment alone until told to use it. If squads are used for instruction, place students into squads and practice moving into formation on signal.

4. Decide how excuses for nonparticipation will be handled. If possible, set up a routine where the school nurse determines which students are excused for health reasons.

5. Safety is important. Children should receive safety rules to be followed on apparatus and playground equipment. Safety procedures to be followed in physical education classes should be discussed.

6. Illustrate how you will stop and start the class. In general, a whistle (or similar loud signal) and a raised hand is effective for stopping the class. A voice command should be used to start the class. Telling the class when before what (Chapter 6 will assure they do not begin before instructions are finished.

7. Discuss the issue, distribution, and care of equipment. Make students responsible for acquiring a piece of equipment and returning it at the end of the lesson. Place equipment around the perimeter of the teaching area to reduce the chance of students fighting over a piece of equipment.

8. Explain to the class that the format of the daily lesson will include an introductory activity, fitness development, lesson focus, and finish with a game activity.

9. Practice various teaching formations such as open-squad formation and closed-squad formation. Practice moving into a circle while moving (fall-in). Transitions between formations should be done while moving, i.e., jogging from scatter formation into a circular formation.

10. Refer to Chapter 3, 5, and 6 in the text for detailed information about planning, developing an effective learning environment, and class management strategies.

Introductory Activity — Move and Freeze on Signal

Have students move throughout the area using a variety of locomotor movements. On signal (whistle), they quickly freeze. Try to reduce the response latency by reinforcing students who stop quickly on signal.

The primary objective is to teach students the importance of moving under control (without bumping others or falling down) and quickly freezing.

Fitness Development Activity — Teacher–Leader Exercises

Arm Circles	30 seconds
Bend and Twist	30 seconds
Treadmill	30 seconds
Abdominal Challenges	30 seconds
Single-Leg Crab Kick	30 seconds
Knee to Chest Curl	30 seconds
Run in Place	30 seconds
Trunk Twister	30 seconds

Follow each exercise with 30 seconds of aerobic activity.

Tape alternating segments (30 seconds) of silence and music. The music signals aerobic activity. During the silent segments, the exercises are performed.

Allow students to adjust the workload to their personal ability and fitness level. This means that some students may perform more repetitions than others.

Move and help students with the exercises.

Lesson Focus — Orientation

Since much time during the first week is used for orientation procedures and management, no lesson focus activity is scheduled.

Game Activity — Management Games

Play one or two management games to teach students how to move into partner and small-group formation.

Toe to Toe

Supplies: None

Skills: Fundamental locomotor movements

Youngsters perform a locomotor movement around the area. On signal, each child must find a partner and stand toe to toe (one foot only) with that person. An important skill is to take the nearest person for a partner without searching for a friend. Youngsters who can't find a partner within their immediate area must run quickly to the center of the area (use a marking spot or cone) to find a partner. The goal is to find a nearby partner as quickly as possible and avoid being the last pair formed. If the number of youngsters playing is uneven, the teacher can join in and play. Change locomotor movements often.

Whistle Mixer

Supplies: None

Skills: All basic locomotor movements

Children are scattered throughout the area. To begin, they walk around in any direction they wish. A whistle is blown a number of times in succession with short, sharp blasts. Children then form small groups with the number in each group equal to the number of whistle blasts. If there are four blasts, children form groups of four—no more, no less. When players have the correct number, they sit down immediately to signal that no one may leave the group and no one may enter the group. The goal is not to be left out or caught in a circle with the incorrect number of students. Encourage players to move toward the center of the area and raise their hands to facilitate finding others without a group. After the circles are formed, the teacher calls "Walk," and the game continues. In walking, children should move in different directions.

Objectives:

To run rhythmically to the beat of a
tambourine

To demonstrate activities designed to
improve cardiovascular fitness

To develop manipulative skills using
hoops and wands in a variety of
challenges

NASPE National Standards:

Introductory Activity: 1, 5
Fitness Activity: 1, 4, 6
Lesson Focus: 2, 3, 5
Game: 1, 3, 5

Equipment Required:

Tambourine
One wand and one hoop for each student
Cageball
12 yarn balls

Instructional Activities	Teaching Hints

Introductory Activity — European Running

Students move around the area to the beat of a tambourine. The step is a trot with the knees lifted. Emphasize proper spacing and moving rhythmically. Stop on a double beat of the tambourine.

Have the leader move in different shapes and designs. Have class freeze and see if they can identify the shape or formation.

Fitness Development Activity — Teacher Leader Exercises

Arm Circles	30 seconds
Bend and Twist	30 seconds
Treadmill	30 seconds
Abdominal Challenges	30 seconds
Single-Leg Crab Kick	30 seconds
Knee to Chest Curl	30 seconds
Run in Place	30 seconds
Trunk Twister	30 seconds

Follow each exercise with 30 seconds of aerobic activity.

Tape alternating segments (30 seconds) of silence and music. The music signals aerobic activity. During the silent segments, the exercises are performed

Allow students to adjust the workload to their personal ability and fitness level. This means that some students may perform more repetitions than others.

Move and help students with the exercises.

Lesson Focus — Manipulative Skills Using Wands and Hoops

Select activities from each of the exercises and challenges groups.

Strength Exercises with Wands

1. Pull the Wand Apart. Place the hands 6 in. apart near the center of the wand. With a tight grip to prevent slippage and with arms extended, pull the hands apart. Change grip and position.
2. Push the Wand Together. Hold the wand as previously, except push the hands together.
3. Wand Twist. Hold the wand with both hands about 6 in. apart. Twist the hands in opposite directions.
4. Bicycle. Holding the wand horizontally throughout and using an overhand grip, extend the wand outward and downward. Bring it upward near the body, completing a circular movement. On the downward movement, push the wand together, and on the upward movement, pull the wand apart.
5. Arm Spreader. Hold the wand overhead with hands spread wide. Attempt to compress the stick. Reverse force, and attempt to pull the stick apart.
6. Dead Lift. Partially squat and place the wand under the thighs. Place the hands between the legs and try to lift. Try also with hands on the outside of the legs.
7. Abdominal Tightener. From a standing position, place the wand behind the buttocks. With hands on the ends of the wand, pull forward and resist with the abdominal muscles.

Stretching Exercises with Wands

1. Side Bender. Grip the wand and extend the arms overhead with feet apart. Bend sideways as far as possible, maintaining straight arms and legs. Recover, and bend to the other side.

Wands can be made from ¾ in. maple dowels or from a variety of broom and mop handles. They should be cut to a length of 36 in. Wands are noisy when they hit the floor. Putting rubber crutch tips on the ends of a wand alleviates most of the noise and makes them easier to pick up.

The isometric exercises with wands presented can be performed with a variety of grips. With the wand horizontal, use either the overhand or underhand grip. With the wand in vertical position, grip with the thumbs pointed up, down, or toward each other.

Repeat each exercise with a different grip. Exercises can also be repeated with the wand in different positions: in front of the body (either horizontal or vertical), overhead, or behind the back. Hold each exercise for 8 to 12 seconds.

2. Body Twist. Place the wand behind the neck, with arms draped over the wand from behind. Rotate the upper body first to the right as far as possible and then to the left. The feet and hips should remain in position. The twist is at the waist.

3. Body Twist to Knee. Assume body twist position. Bend the trunk forward and twist so that the right end of the wand touches the left knee. Recover, and touch the left end to the right knee.

4. Shoulder Stretcher. Grip the wand at the ends in a regular grip. Extend the arms overhead and rotate the wand, arms, and shoulders backward until the stick touches the back of the legs. The arms should be kept straight. Those who find the stretch too easy should move their hands closer to the center of the wand.

5. Toe Touch. Grip the wand with the hands about shoulder width apart. Bend forward, reaching down as far as possible without bending the knees. The movement should be slow and controlled. Try the same activity from a sitting position.

6. Over the Toes. Sit down, flex the knees, place the wand over the toes, and rest it against the middle of the arch. Grip the stick with the fingers at the outside edge of the feet. Slowly extend the legs forward, pushing against the stick and trying for a full extension of the legs.

Be gentle when stretching. Reach and stretch the muscles, hold the stretch for a few seconds and relax. Repeat a number of times.

Because wands are noisy when dropped, youngsters should hold their wands with both hands or put them on the floor during instruction.

Wand Challenges

1. Can you reach down and pick up your wand without bending your knees?
2. Try to balance your wand on different body parts. Watch the top of the wand to get cues on how to retain the balance.
3. Can you hold your stick against the wall and move over it? Gradually raise the height of the wand.
4. Let's see whether you can hold the stick at both ends and move through the gap.
5. Put one end of the wand on the floor and hold the other end. How many times can you run around your wand without getting dizzy?
6. Place one end of the wand against a wall. Holding the other end and keeping the wand against the wall, duck underneath. Place the wand lower and lower on the wall and go under.
7. Toss the wand from one hand to the other.
8. Hold the wand vertically near the middle. Can you release your grip and catch the wand before it falls to the floor?
9. Have a partner hold a wand horizontally above the floor. Jump, leap, and hop over the wand. Gradually raise the height of the wand.
10. Balance the wand vertically on the floor. Release the wand and try to complete different stunts—clapping the hands, doing a heel click, touching different body parts—before the wand falls to the floor.

An adequate amount of space is needed for each individual, because wand stunts demand room.

Children may easily be injured using wands improperly. Teach children proper use of wands. Emphasize the need to use care when handling wands to avoid injury to self and others. Do not allow any improper use of wands.

Hoop Activities

1. Hula-hoop using various body parts such as waist, neck, knees, arms and fingers.
   a. While hula-hooping on the arms, try to change the hoop from one arm to the other.
   b. Change hoop from one partner to another while hula-hooping.
   c. Try leg-skippers—hula-hoop with one leg and jump the hoop with the other leg.
2. Jump rope with the hoop—forward, sideways, and backward. Begin with a back-and-forth swing.
3. Roll hoop and run alongside it. Run in front of it.
4. Roll hoop with a reverse spin to make it return to the thrower.
5. Roll with a reverse spin and see how many times a partner can go through it.
6. Roll the hoop with a reverse spin, jump over it, and catch it as it returns. Roll the hoop with a reverse spin, and as it returns, hoist it with the foot and catch it. Roll the hoop with a reverse spin, kick it up with the toe, and go through the hoop. Roll the hoop with a reverse spin, run around it, and catch it. Roll the hoop with a reverse spin, pick it up, and begin hooping on the arm—all in one motion.
7. Balance the hoop on your head; try to walk through it ("thread the needle") forward, backward, and sideways.

Hoops produce noisy activity. You may find it helpful to have the children lay their hoops on the floor when they are to listen.

The key to the reverse spin is to pull down (toward the floor) on the hoop as it is released. When teaching the reverse spin with hoops, have the students throw the hoop up, in place, rather than forward along the floor. After they learn the upward throw, they can progress to the forward throw for distance.

8. Try partner activities:
   a. Play catch with hoop.
   b. Hula-hoop on one arm, toss to partner who catches it on one arm.
   c. Use two hoops for catching.
   d. Hoop with one hoop and play catch with other.
   e. Move through a hoop held by a partner.

Game Activity

Balance Beam Mixer (Cooperative Activity)

Formation: Groups of 8–10

Supplies: One low balance beam or bench per group

Students stand shoulder to shoulder on a low balance beam or bench (for younger students) with mats alongside the beam for safety. While remaining on the balance beam or bench, students are challenged to get in order based on the following criteria:

1. Alphabetical order by first name from left to right.
2. Alphabetical order by first name from right to left.
3. Tallest to shortest.
4. Month of birth date (January to December or vice versa).

Jolly Ball

Supplies: A cageball 24 in. or larger (or a 36- to 48–in. pushball)

Skill: Kicking

Four teams are organized, each of which forms one side of a square. Children sit down, facing in, with hands braced behind them. The members of each team are numbered consecutively. Players wait until their number is called. Four active players (one from each team) move in crab position and try to kick the cageball over any one of the three opposing teams. The sideline players can also kick the ball. Ordinarily, the hands are not used, but can be allowed in the learning stages of the game.

A point is scored against a team that allows the ball to go over its line. A ball that goes out at the corner between teams is dead and replayed. After a short bout of time (10 to 20 seconds), the active children retire to their teams and another number is called. The team with the fewest points wins the game. This game is strenuous for the active players, so rotate them often. Two children from each team can be active at once.

Circle Touch

Supplies: Yarn balls

Skills: Dodging, body management

One child plays against three others, who form a small circle with joined hands. The object of the game is for the lone child to touch a designated child (on the shoulders) in the circle with a yarn ball. The other two children in the circle, by dodging and maneuvering, attempt to keep the tagger away from the third member of the circle. The circle players may maneuver and circle in any direction but may not release their hand grips. The tagger, in attempting to touch the protected circle player, must go around the outside of the circle. He is not permitted to go underneath or through the joined hands of the circle players. To avoid roughness, the game should be played in short, 20-second bouts with a new tagger for each bout.

DPE Curriculum Guide – Lesson Plans
Long-Rope Jumping Skills
Level III – Week 3

Objectives:
To jump a rope turned by others
To know the difference in long-rope
jumping between entering front
and back doors
To understand how to enter and exit in
double Dutch rope jumping

NASPE National Standards:
Introductory Activity: 1, 4
Fitness Activity: 1, 4, 6
Lesson Focus: 2, 3, 4, 5
Game: 1, 2, 5

Equipment Required:
Music for exercises and rope jumping
6–12 long jump ropes (16 ft long)
Cageball and 12–15 throwing balls for
game

Instructional Activities	Teaching Hints

Introductory Activity — Move and Freeze

1. Review the run, walk, hop, jump, leap, slide, gallop, and skip with proper stopping.
2. Practice moving and stopping correctly—emphasize basics of proper movement.

Add variety by asking students to respond to the some of the following movement factors such as high, low, zigzag, large, small, square, triangles, circles.

Fitness Development Activity — Teacher Leader Exercises

Arm Circles	35 seconds
Bend and Twist	35 seconds
Treadmill	35 seconds
Abdominal Challenges	35 seconds
Single-Leg Crab Kick	35 seconds
Knee to Chest Curl	35 seconds
Run in Place	35 seconds
Trunk Twister	35 seconds

Follow each exercise with 35 seconds of aerobic activity.

Tape alternating segments (35 seconds) of silence and music. The music signals aerobic activity. During the silent segments, the exercises are performed

Allow students to adjust the workload to their personal ability and fitness level. This means that some students may perform more repetitions than others.

Move and help students with the exercises.

Lesson Focus — Long-Rope Jumping Skills

Single Long-Rope Activities

1. Review previously learned jumping skills. Teach the difference between entering front and back doors. Front door means entering from the side where the rope is turning forward and toward the jumper after it reaches its peak. Back door means entering from the side where the rope is turning backward and away from the jumper. To enter front door, the jumper follows the rope in and jumps when it completes the turn. To enter back door, the jumper waits until the rope reaches its peak and moves in as the rope moves downward. Learning to enter at an angle is usually easier, but any path that is comfortable is acceptable.
2. Have more than one youngster jump at a time. Students can enter in pairs or triplets.
3. Jump while holding a beanbag or playground ball between the knees.
4. While turning rope, rotate under the rope and jump. Continue jumping and rotate back to the turning position.
5. Play catch with a playground ball while jumping.
6. Do the Egg Beater: Two or more long ropes are turned simultaneously. The ropes are aligned perpendicular to each other; the jumper jumps the rope where they cross.
7. Try combinations of three or four ropes turning. The ropes are aligned parallel to each other and students jump and move through to the next rope.

Four children is an appropriate group size for practicing long-rope skills. Two members of the group turn the rope while the others practice jumping. A plan for rotating turners is important so that all children receive similar amounts of practice jumping.

Long ropes should be 16 feet in length.

Instructional cues to teach long-rope jumping skills are:
a. Turn the rope with the forearm.
b. Lock the wrist and keep the thumb up while turning.
c. Stand perpendicular to the rope.
d. Barely touch the floor with the turning rope.
e. Don't cross the midline of the body with the forearm while turning the rope.
f. Jump on the balls of the feet.

Double Dutch (two ropes) Activities

1. Teach entering and exiting. Basic jump on both feet. Land on the balls of the feet, keeping ankles and knees together with hands across the stomach.
   Entering: When entering, stand beside a turner and run into the ropes when the back rope (farther from the jumper) touches the floor. Turners should be taught to say "Go" each time the back rope touches the floor.
   Exiting: Exit the ropes by facing and jumping toward one turner and exiting immediately after jumping. The exit should be made as close to the turner's shoulder as possible.
2. Jogging Step. Run in place with a jogging step. Increase the challenge by circling while jogging.
3. Scissors Jump. Jump to a stride position with the left foot forward and the right foot back about 8 in. apart. Each jump requires reversing the position of the feet.
4. Straddle Jump. Jump to the straddle position and return to closed position. Try a Straddle Cross Jump by crossing the legs on return to the closed position. The straddle jumps should be performed facing away from the turners.
5. Turnaround. Circle left or right using the basic jump. Begin circling slowly at first and then increase speed. To increase the challenge, try the turnaround on one foot.
6. Hot Peppers. Use the Jogging Step and gradually increase the speed of the ropes.
7. Half Turn. Perform a half turn with each jump. Remember to lead the turn with the head and shoulders.
8. Ball Tossing. Toss and catch a playground ball while jumping.
9. Individual Rope Jumping. Enter double Dutch with an individual rope and jump. Face the turner and decrease the length of the individual jump rope.

Arm positions and turning motions are similar to turning a single long rope. In short, keep the upper arm stationary, rotate at the elbow with locked wrist, and keep the thumb up. Avoid crossing the midline of the body, and establish an even cadence. Rotate the hands inward toward the midline of the body (right forearm counterclockwise and left forearm clockwise).

Double Dutch turning takes considerable practice. Take time to teach it as a skill that is necessary for successful jumping experiences.

Students should concentrate on the sound of the ropes hitting the floor so that they make an even and rhythmic beat.

Concentrate on jumping in the center of the ropes facing a turner. Use white shoe polish to mark a jumping target.

Game Activity

Cageball Target Throw

Supplies: A cageball (18- to 30-in.), 12 to 15 smaller balls of various sizes
Skill: Throwing

An area about 20 ft wide is marked across the center of the playing area, with a cageball in the center. The object of the game is to throw the smaller balls against the cageball, thus forcing it across the goal line in front of the other team. Players may come up to the line to throw, but they may not throw while inside the cageball area. A player may enter the area, however, to recover a ball. No one is to touch the cageball at any time, nor may a ball in the hands of a player push the cageball. If the cageball seems to roll too easily, it should be deflated slightly. The throwing balls can be of almost any size—soccer balls, volleyballs, playground balls, for example.

Sunday

Supplies: None
Skills: Running, dodging

Two parallel lines are delineated at each end of the playing area. Three or more players are it and stand in the center of the area between the two lines. The rest of the class is placed on one of the designated lines. The object is to cross to the other line without being tagged or making a false start. All line players stand with their front foot on the line. The line players must run across the line immediately when one of the taggers calls "Sunday." Anyone who does not run immediately is considered caught. The tagger can call other days of the week to confuse the runners. No player can move if another day of the week is called. "Making a start" must be defined clearly. To begin, it can be defined as a player moving either foot. Later, when children get better at the game, any movement of the body constitutes a start.

Wolfe's Beanbag Exchange

Supplies: One beanbag per child
Skills: Running, dodging, tossing, catching

Five or six children are identified as taggers. The remaining players start scattered throughout the area, each with a beanbag in hand. The taggers chase the players with beanbags. When a tag is made, the tagged player must freeze, keeping her feet still and beanbag in hand. To unfreeze a player, a nonfrozen player can exchange his beanbag for a beanbag held by a frozen player. If two frozen players are within tossing distance, they can thaw each other by exchanging their beanbags through the air using a toss and catch. Both tosses have to be caught or the beanbags are retrieved and tried again from their previous location. After students have learned the game, taggers can interfere with the tossing of beanbags between two frozen players by batting them to the floor. The toss is tried again and the players remain frozen until both players make successful catches.

DPE Curriculum Guide – Lesson Plans
Football Skills and Lead-up Activities (1)
Level III – Week 4

Objectives:
To participate in a balanced fitness
routine
To learn the basic rules of football
To perform the basic skills of football
To enjoy participating in football lead-
up activities

NASPE National Standards:
Introductory Activity: 1, 3, 5
Fitness Activity: 1, 4, 6
Lesson Focus: 2, 3, 5
Game: 2, 3, 5

Equipment Required:
Signs, cones, and music for Hexagon
Hustle
10–15 foam rubber junior size footballs
4 soccer balls or 8" foam rubber
balls
12 cones for boundaries
Pinnies and flags for lead-up games

Instructional Activities	Teaching Hints
Introductory Activity — Move and Manipulate	
Each student is given a piece of equipment and moves around the area using locomotor movements. Students toss and catch the equipment while moving. On signal, the equipment is dropped, and students move over and around equipment.	Use any type of equipment available. The goal is to move and be able to manipulate an object.

Fitness Development Activity — Hexagon Hustle

Tape alternating segments of silence and music to signal duration of exercise.
Music segments (25 seconds) indicate moving around the hexagon, while intervals
of silence (30 seconds) announce flexibility and strength development activities.

Hustle	25 seconds	
Push-Up from Knees	30 seconds	
Hustle	25 seconds	
Bend and Twist (8 counts)	30 seconds	
Hustle	25 seconds	
Jumping Jacks (4 counts)	30 seconds	
Hustle	25 seconds	
Curl-Ups (2 counts)	30 seconds	
Hustle	25 seconds	
Crab Kick (2 counts)	30 seconds	
Hustle	25 seconds	
Sit and Stretch (8 counts)	30 seconds	
Hustle	25 seconds	
Power Jumper	30 seconds	
Hustle	25 seconds	
Squat Thrust (4 counts)	30 seconds	

Conclude the Hexagon Hustle with a slow jog or walk.

Teaching Hints for Hexagon Hustle:

Outline a large hexagon with six cones.
Place signs with locomotor movements
on both sides of the cones. Locomotor
movements to use are: jogging,
skipping, galloping, hopping, jumping,
sliding, leaping, and animal movements.
Sport movements such as defensive
sliding, running backwards, and running
and shooting jump shots can also be
used. The signs identify the hustle
activity students are to perform as they
approach a cone.

During the hustle, faster moving
students should pass on the outside of
the hexagon.

Change directions at times to keep
students spaced out properly.

Lesson Focus — Football Skills (1)

Skills
Practice the following skills:
1. Forward Passing
   The ball should be gripped lightly behind the middle with the fingers on the
lace. The thumbs and fingers should be relaxed. In throwing, the opposing foot
should point in the direction of the pass, with the body turned sideways. In
preparation for the pass, the ball is raised up and held over the shoulders. The ball
is delivered directly forward with an overhand movement of the arm and with the
index finger pointing toward the line of flight.
2. Catching
   When making a catch, the receiver should keep both eyes on the ball and
catch it in the hands with a slight give. As soon as the ball is caught, it should be
tucked into the carrying position. The little fingers are together for most catches.
3. Centering
   Centering involves transferring the ball, on a signal, to the quarterback. In
elementary school, the shotgun formation is most often used. This requires

Use instructional cues for throwing:
1. Turn the nonthrowing side toward the
direction of the throw.
2. Throw the ball with an overhand
motion.
3. Step toward the pass receiver.

Instructional cues help improve catching
technique:
1. Thumbs together for a high pass
(above shoulder level).
2. Thumbs apart for a low pass (below
shoulder level).
3. Reach for the ball, give, and bring the
ball to the body.

snapping the ball a few yards backward to the quarterback. A direct snap involves placing the hands under the buttocks of the center. The ball is then lifted, rotated a quarter turn, and snapped into the hands of the quarterback.

The centering player takes a position with the feet well spread and toes pointed straight ahead. Knees are bent and close enough to the ball to reach it with a slight stretch. The right hand takes about the same grip as is used in passing. The other hand is on the side near the back of the ball and merely acts as a guide. On signal from the quarterback, the center extends the arms backward through the legs and centers the ball to the quarterback.

4. Punting

The kicker stands with the kicking foot slightly forward. The fingers are extended in the direction of the center. The eyes should be on the ball from the time it is centered until it is kicked, and the kicker should actually see the foot kick the ball. After receiving the ball, the kicker takes a short step with the kicking foot and then a second step with the other foot. The kicking leg is swung forward and, at impact, the leg is straightened to provide maximum force. The toes are pointed, and the long axis of the ball makes contact on the top of the instep. The leg should follow through well after the kick. Emphasis should be placed on dropping the ball properly. Beginners have a tendency to throw it in the air, making the punt more difficult.

Instructional cues for centering include the following:
1. Reach forward for the ball.
2. Snap the ball with the dominant hand.
3. Guide the ball with the nondominant hand.

Instructional cues for punting are:
1. Drop the football; don't toss it upward.
2. Keep the eyes focused on the ball.
3. Kick upward and through the ball.
4. Contact the ball on the outer side of the instep.

Signs that describe key points for each skill should be placed on cones at each station. Instructional cues should also be placed on the signs so students can analyze their form and performance.

Drills

Set up stations for skill practice. Rotate students to each station.

Station 1—Stance Practice

Students work with a partner and practice getting into the proper stance position. When stance form is mastered, partners can practice getting into position and racing to cones 5 yd away. Offensive players should use a 3-point stance with toes pointed forward and head up. Defensive players usually use a 4-point stance with more weight on hands. Blockers should avoid falling and should stay on their toes and in front of defensive player.

Station 2—Centering and Carrying the Ball

Students work in pairs and practice centering to each other. The player receiving the ball tucks the ball in and runs 5 to 10 yd.

Station 3—Passing and Receiving with a Partner

Students work in pairs and practice passing and receiving the ball. Place emphasis on proper throwing and catching technique. Begin practice with short passes to a stationary receiver. After success, practice throwing to moving receivers, placing emphasis on leading the receiver with the pass.

Station 4—Punting

Concentrate on technique rather than distance when teaching punting. Emphasize keeping the head down with the eyes on the ball. Drop the football rather than tossing it upward prior to the kick. Work in groups of three. One player is the punter, one the receiver, and one receives the pass from the punt receiver.

Junior size footballs are best for this age group. Regulation size footballs are unacceptable because youngster's hands are too small and the balls are too heavy.

The ball should be carried with the arm on the outside and the end of the ball tucked into the notch formed by the elbow and arm. The fingers add support for the carry.

For beginning punters, using a round foam rubber ball will be easier than kicking a football. Foam rubber footballs are the next step before using junior size footballs.

Football Lead-up Games

Football End Ball

Supplies: Foam rubber junior footballs

Skills: Passing, catching

The court is divided in half by a centerline. End zones are marked 3 ft wide, completely across the court at each end. Players on each team are divided into three groups: forwards, guards, and ends. The object is for a forward to throw successfully to one of the end-zone players. End-zone players take positions in one of the end zones. Forwards and guards then occupy the half of the court farthest from this end zone. The forwards are near the centerline, and the guards are back near the end zone of their half of the court. The ball is put into play with a center jump between the two tallest opposing forwards. When a team gets the ball, the forwards try to throw over the heads of the opposing team to an end-zone player. To score, the ball must be caught by an end-zone player with both feet inside the zone. No moving with the ball is permitted by any player. After each score, play is resumed by a jump ball at the centerline.

A penalty results in loss of the ball to the other team. Penalties are assessed for the following.

1. Holding a ball for more than 5 seconds
2. Stepping over the end line or stepping over the centerline into the opponent's territory
3. Pushing or holding another player

In case of an out-of-bounds ball, the ball belongs to the team that did not cause it to go out. The nearest player retrieves the ball at the sideline and returns it to a player of the proper team. Encourage fast, accurate passing. Players in the end zones need to jump high to catch the ball, while still landing with both feet inside the end-zone area. A system of rotation is desirable. Each time a score is made, players on that team can rotate one person.

To outline the end zones, some instructors use folding mats (4 by 7 ft or 4 by 8 ft). Three or four mats forming each end zone make a definite area and eliminate the problem of defensive players (guards) stepping into the end zone.

Speed Football

Supplies: Foam rubber junior footballs, flag for each player

Skills: Passing, catching, running with ball

The ball can be kicked off or started at the 20-yd line. The object is to move the ball across the opponent's goal by running or passing. If the ball drops to the ground or a player's flag is pulled when carrying the ball, it is a turnover and the ball is set into play at that spot. Interceptions are turnovers and the intercepting team moves on offense. Teams must make at least four complete passes before they are eligible to move across the opponent's goal line. No blocking is allowed.

Playing more than one game at a time on smaller fields will allow more students to be actively involved in the game. This is also an enjoyable game when played with Frisbees.

Kick-Over

Playing area: Football field with a 10-yd end zone

Players: Six to ten on each team

Supplies: Foam rubber junior footballs

Skills: Kicking, catching

Teams are scattered on opposite ends of the field. The object is to punt the ball over the other team's goal line. If the ball is caught in the end zone, no score results. A ball kicked into the end zone and not caught scores a goal. If the ball is kicked beyond the end zone on the fly, a score is made regardless of whether the ball is caught. One team starts play with a punt from a point 20 to 30 ft in front of its own goal line. On a punt, if the ball is not caught, the team must kick from the spot of recovery. If the ball is caught, three long strides are allowed to advance the ball for a kick.

The player kicking next should move quickly to the area from which the ball is to be kicked. Players should be numbered and should kick in rotation. If the players do not kick in rotation, one or two aggressive players will dominate the game.

DPE Curriculum Guide – Lesson Plans
Football Skills and Lead-up Activities (2)
Level III – Week 5

LP 84

Objectives:
To critique football throwing
   techniques of peers
To learn the basic rules of football
To perform the basic skills of football
To enjoy participating in football lead-
   up activities

NASPE National Standards:
Introductory Activity: 1, 5
Fitness Activity: 1, 4, 6
Lesson Focus: 2, 3, 5
Game: 2, 3, 5

Equipment Required:
Signs, cones, and music for Hexagon
   Hustle
8 foam rubber junior footballs, 12
   cones for boundaries
One flag belt and one pinnie for each
   student

Instructional Activities	Teaching Hints

Introductory Activity — Fastest Tag in the West

All students are it. On signal, they try to tag each other. If they are tagged, they must freeze, but they are eligible to tag other students who pass near them. If two or more players tag each other simultaneously, they are both/all "frozen."

The idea of the game is to get all students involved in activity. Restart the game often rather than waiting for all students to be tagged.

Fitness Development Activity — Hexagon Hustle

Tape alternating segments of silence and music to signal duration of exercise. Music segments indicate moving around the hexagon while intervals of silence announce flexibility and strength development activities.

Hustle	25 seconds	
Push-Up from Knees	30 seconds	
Hustle	25 seconds	
Bend and Twist (8 counts)	30 seconds	
Hustle	25 seconds	
Jumping Jacks (4 counts)	30 seconds	
Hustle	25 seconds	
Curl-Ups (2 counts)	30 seconds	
Hustle	25 seconds	
Crab Kick (2 counts)	30 seconds	
Hustle	25 seconds	
Sit and Stretch (8 counts)	30 seconds	
Hustle	25 seconds	
Power Jumper	30 seconds	
Hustle	25 seconds	
Squat Thrust (4 counts)	30 seconds	

Outline a large hexagon with six cones. Place signs with locomotor movements on both sides of the cones. Locomotor movements to use are: jogging, skipping, galloping, hopping, jumping, sliding, leaping, and animal movements. Sport movements such as defensive sliding, running backwards, and running and shooting jump shots can also be used. The signs identify the hustle activity students are to perform as they approach a cone.

During the hustle, faster moving students should pass on the outside of the hexagon.

Change directions at times to keep students spaced out properly.

Lesson Focus — Football Skills (2)

Since this is the second week of football, emphasis should be placed on playing some of the lead-up football games. Review last week's skills and introduce the new skills. Devote the rest of the time to playing the games.

Skills
Review the skills taught last week:
1. Forward Passing
2. Catching
3. Centering
4. Punting

Introduce new skills:
1. Lateral Passing
   Lateral passing is a simple underhand toss of the ball to a teammate. The ball must be tossed sideward or backward to qualify as a lateral. It should be tossed with an easy motion, and no attempt should be made to make it spiral like a forward pass.

Students can work with a partner and practice the skills they learned last week. A ball for each two players will assure the most practice time.

The lateral pass is used when a ball carrier wants to get rid of the ball before being stopped.

2. Blocking

In blocking for Flag Football, the blocker must maintain balance and not fall to the knees. The elbows are out and the hands are held near the chest. The block should be more of an obstruction than a takeout and should be set with the shoulder against the opponent's shoulder or upper body. Making contact from the rear in any direction not only is a penalty but also could cause serious injury.

Instructional cues for blocking technique are the following:
1. Keep feet spread and knees bent.
2. Keep head up.
3. Stay in front of the defensive player.
4. Move your feet; stay on the balls of the feet.

Football Lead-up Activities

Speed Football

See the Week 4 Lesson Plan, Football Skills for a complete game description.

Fourth Down

Supplies: Foam rubber junior football

Skills: Most football skills, except kicking and blocking

Every play is a fourth down, which means that the play must score or the team loses the ball. No kicking is permitted, but players may pass at any time from any spot and in any direction. There can be a series of passes on any play, either from behind or beyond the line of scrimmage.

The teams line up in an offensive football formation. To start the game, the ball is placed into the center of the field, and the team that wins the coin toss has the chance to put the ball into play. The ball is put into play by centering. The back receiving the ball runs or passes to any of his teammates. The one receiving the ball has the same privilege. No blocking is permitted. After each touchdown, the ball is brought to the center of the field, and the team against which the score was made puts the ball into play.

To down a runner or pass receiver, a two-handed touch above the waist is made. The back first receiving the ball from the center has immunity from tagging, provided that he does not try to run. All defensive players must stay 10 ft away unless he runs. The referee should wait for a reasonable length of time for the back to pass or run. If the ball is still held beyond that time, the referee should call out, "Ten seconds." The back must then throw or run within 10 seconds or be rushed by the defense.

The defensive players scatter to cover the receivers. They can use a one-on-one defense, with each player covering an offensive player, or a zone defense. Since the team with the ball loses possession after each play, the following rules are used to determine where the ball should be placed when the other team takes possession.

1. If a ball carrier is tagged with two hands above the waist, the ball goes to the other team at that spot.

2. If an incomplete pass is made from behind the line of scrimmage, the ball is given to the other team at the spot where the ball was put into play.

3. When an incomplete pass is made by a player beyond the line of scrimmage, the ball is brought to the spot from which it was thrown.

The team in possession should be encouraged to pass as soon as is practical, because children tire from running around to become free for a pass. The defensive team can score by intercepting a pass. Since passes can be made at any time, on interception the player should look down the field for a pass to a teammate.

Variation: The game can be called Third Down, with the offensive team having two chances to score.

Flag Football

Supplies: Foam rubber junior football, two flags per player (about 3 in. wide and 24 in. long)

Skills: All football skills

The field is divided into three zones by lines marked off at 20-yd intervals. There also should be two end zones, from 5 to 10 yd in width, defining the area behind the goal in which passes may be caught. Flag Football is played with two flags on each player. The flag is a length of cloth that is hung from the side at the waist of each player. To down (stop) a player with the ball, one of the flags must be pulled.

Flag Football should rarely, if ever, be played with 11 players on a side. This results in a crowded field and leaves little room to maneuver. If six or seven are on a team, four players are required to be on the line of scrimmage. For eight or nine players, five offensive players must be on the line.

The game consists of two halves. A total of 25 plays make up each half. All plays count in the 25, except the try for the point after a touchdown and a kickoff out-of-bounds.

The game is started with a kickoff. The team winning the coin toss has the option of selecting the goal it wishes to defend or choosing to kick or receive. The loser of the toss takes the option not exercised by the first team. The kickoff is from the goal line, and all players on the kicking team must be onside. The kick must cross the first zone line or it does not count as a play. A kick that is kicked out-of-bounds (and is not touched by the receiving team) must be kicked again. A second consecutive kick out-of-bounds gives the ball to the receiving team in the center of the field. The kicking team may not recover the kickoff unless it is caught and then fumbled by the receivers.

A team has four downs to move the ball into the next zone or they lose the ball. If the ball is legally advanced into the last zone, then the team has four downs to score. A ball on the line between zones is considered in the more forward zone.

Time-outs are permitted only for injuries or when called by the officials. Unlimited substitutions are permitted. Each must report to the official.

The team in possession of the ball usually huddles to make up the play. After any play, the team has 30 seconds to put the ball into play after the referee gives the signal.

Blocking is done with the arms close to the body. Blocking must be done from the front or side, and blockers must stay on their feet.

A player is down if one of her flags has been pulled. The ball carrier must make an attempt to avoid the defensive player and is not permitted to run over or through the defensive player. The tackler must play the flags and not the ball carrier. Good officiating is needed, because defensive players may attempt to hold or grasp the ball carrier until they are able to remove one of her flags.

All forward passes must be thrown from behind the line of scrimmage. All players on the field are eligible to receive and intercept passes.

All fumbles are dead at the spot of the fumble. The first player who touches the ball on the ground is ruled to have recovered the fumble. When the ball is centered to a back, she must gain definite possession of it before a fumble can be called. She is allowed to pick up a bad pass from the center when she does not have possession of the ball.

All punts must be announced. Neither team can cross the line of scrimmage until the ball is kicked. Kick receivers may run or use a lateral pass. They cannot make a forward pass after receiving a kick.

A pass caught in an end zone scores a touchdown. The player must have control of the ball in the end zone. A ball caught beyond the end zone is out-of-bounds and is considered an incomplete pass.

A touchdown scores 6 points, a completed pass or run after touchdown scores 1 point, and a safety scores 2 points. A point after touchdown is made from a distance of 3 ft from the goal line. One play (pass or run) is allowed for the extra point. Any ball kicked over the goal line is ruled a touchback and is brought out to the 20-yd line to be put into play by the receiving team. A pass intercepted behind the goal line can be a touchback if the player does not run it out, even if she is tagged behind her own goal line.

A penalty of 5 yd is assessed for the following:
1. Being offside
2. Delay of game (too long in huddle)
3. Failure of substitute to report
4. Passing from a spot not behind line of scrimmage (This also results in loss of down.)
5. Stiff-arming by the ball carrier, or not avoiding a defensive player
6. Failure to announce intention to punt
7. Shortening the flag in the belt, or playing without flags in proper position
8. Faking the ball by the center, who must center the pass on the first motion

The following infractions are assessed a 15-yd loss:
1. Holding, illegal tackling
2. Illegal blocking
3. Unsportsmanlike conduct (This also can result in disqualification.)

Teaching suggestions: Specifying 25 plays per half eliminates the need for timing and lessens arguments about a team's taking too much time in the huddle. Using the zone system makes the first-down yardage point definite and eliminates the need for a chain to mark off the 10 yd needed for a first down.

DPE Curriculum Guide – Lesson Plans
Advanced Pedometer Skills
Level III – Week 6

Objectives:
To understand why people may walk
    the same distance but have
    different step counts
To be able to calculate baseline activity
    and set personal activity goals

NASPE National Standards:
Introductory Activity: 3, 4
Fitness Activity: 1, 4, 6
Lesson Focus: 2, 3, 5
Game: 2, 5

Equipment Required:
Music Tape for Circuit Training
Pedometers
Pencils and worksheets
30' distance identified with cones

Instructional Activities	Teaching Hints

Introductory Activity — Following Activities

One partner leads and performs various kinds of movements. The other partner follows and performs the same movements. This can also be done with small groups, with the group following a leader.

Encourage students to challenge their partner. Change partners once or twice to maintain interest in the activity.

Fitness Development Activity — Circuit Training

Students do the best they can at each station within the time limit. This implies that not all youngsters are required to do the same workload. Children differ and their ability to perform fitness workloads differs. Make fitness a personal challenge.
Rope Jumping
Triceps Push-Ups
Agility Run
Body Circles
Hula Hoops
Reverse Curls
Crab Walk
Tortoise and Hare
Bend and Twist

Conclude circuit training with 2–4 minutes of walking, jogging, rope jumping, or other self-paced aerobic activity

Tape alternating segments of silence and music to signal duration of exercise. Music segments (begin at 30 seconds) indicate activity at each station while intervals of silence (10 seconds) announce it is time to stop and move forward to the next station.

Use signals such as start, stop, and move up to ensure rapid movement to the next station.

Ask students to do their personal best. Expect workloads to differ.

Lesson Focus — Advanced Pedometer Skills

Comparing Steps and Activity Time

1. Teach students to switch their display between step counts and activity time using the mode button. Have them reset the pedometer, gently shake it, and check both displays so they are familiar with the mode button.

2. The purpose of this activity is to see which measure is most meaningful for teachers and students. Ask students to find a partner who is taller or shorter. The purpose is to try to match students with different stride length.

3. Have students reset their pedometers and prepare to walk alongside their partner until the stop signal is given.

4. Start the students and have them walk for a couple of minutes. Give a "freeze" signal and ask students to open their pedometers and compare both steps and activity time.

5. Ask students to discuss with their partner why step counts are different but activity times are quite similar.

6. Which measurement is the most accurate way to gauge how active students have been during P.E. (or at any other time)?

Before starting this activity, make sure students understand how to view steps counts and activity time (by pressing the mode button).

Step counts are impacted by stride length. Students may cover the same distance but have unequal step counts. This can be discouraging to the student with fewer steps. Using activity time will minimize this discrepancy.

Discuss the following:
1. Why might step counts be different?
2. Did you walk the same distance?
3. Were you active the same amount of time?
4. Can we set the same step goal for all people?
5. Can we set the same time goal for all people?
6. Which measurement has the least possibility for individual differences?

Calculating Baseline Step Counts & Activity Time

1. Students will secure a pedometer and a Baseline Step Count & Physical Activity worksheet. For four days (eight days for secondary school students) during physical education class, students will monitor their step counts and minutes of physical activity. At the end of each physical education class, students will record their step counts and activity time on the worksheet. To calculate an accurate baseline, the periods of measure must be equal, for example, 30-minute periods.

2. At the end of the four-day period, have students calculate their average physical education step counts and activity time by totaling the four days and dividing by 4.

3. Baseline Step Count & Physical Activity is defined as the average amount of steps and activity each student accumulates each physical education period.

4. The ultimate goal is for students to learn about their average daily step counts and physical activity time. As an intermediate step to 24-hour surveillance, begin by having students identify their school day baseline. Establish a set time for students to start recording steps and activity and a time to record the data at the end of the day. After students are able to record their data independently, a sample of students can begin to collect daily baseline data on themselves for a 24-hour period.

The purpose of this activity is to determine the average amount of activity students accumulate in a set amount of time.

This activity is also an effective check for the physical education teacher to see how many minutes of physical activity each student is receiving in physical education.

Baselines will be used for a future activity: goal setting. Eight days of activity are needed to establish a baseline for secondary students because they have more control over their choice of activity.

Students who show interest and an adequate level of responsibility can be allowed to use them outside of the school environment.

Calculating Personal Activity Goals

1. Baseline step count and physical activity baseline data must have been gathered in the previous lesson prior to completing this activity.

2. Teach students to calculate their personal activity time goals by increasing their baseline activity level by 10 percent. For example, if a student's baseline activity is 12 minutes, they will increase their activity goal to 13 minutes. Note that partial minutes (.2) have been ignored. This makes it much easier for students to calculate.

3. Have students calculate their personal step count goals by increasing their step counts by 10 percent. For example, if a student's baseline step count is 1200 in their physical education class, they will increase their step count goal by 120 steps to 1320 steps.

4. Students then pursue their goal for the next 14 days. If they achieve their goal a majority of the days (8 or more), they increase their goal by another 10 percent of their baseline. If they do not achieve the goal a majority of the days, the existing goal is maintained.

5. Teach students that goal setting is appropriate until a reasonable terminal goal is reached. The question to discuss with students is "How much is enough?"

The purpose of this activity is to learn to calculate personal step count and physical activity goals based on baseline data.

Round off activity time to the nearest minute. Ignore the seconds when doing this activity.

Discuss with students how to design effective goals, e.g., setting a goal that is within reach, but not too difficult or easy to accomplish.

Goals can be set for different time periods such as recess, lunch hour, physical education classes, afterschool programs, and 24-hour surveillance.

Determining Stride Length

1. Set up a stride length measurement station by placing two lines 30 ft apart. Mark the starting and end points with cones so it is easy for students to see the station points.

2. Students will count the number of steps it takes to travel between the lines. Have students start 10–15 ft behind the starting line and walk toward the line at a normal pace. Students count their first step as the one that touches the ground inside the start line. Continue walking and counting steps until a foot touches outside the finish line. That is the number of steps they will use to calculate their stride length.

3. Have students record the number of steps it took to cover the distance.

4. Use the table below to find stride length.

Set up multiple measurement stations around the area to speed up the process.

Stride length is not as accurate a measure as steps and exercise time because of the variation in stride length during a typical day of activity. For example, uphill means shorter strides, while fast walking will result in longer strides.

Calculating how far one has traveled is an excellent math integration activity. Spreadsheets are useful for these types of math activities.

5. Wet Foot Walk. Another way to measure stride length is to walk through a water puddle or wet grass onto dry pavement and measure the distance from heel to heel that the wet footprints leave. The key here is to measure heel to heel or from toe to toe not from one heel to the other toe.

Teaching students to multiply feet and inches times steps is a difficult task. You may want to teach students to change the inches to 10ths of an foot so it can be multiplied easier.

Number of Steps over a 30 ft distance	Stride Length in Feet and inches
7	4' 3"
8	3' 9"
9	3' 4"
10	3' 0"
11	2' 9"
12	2' 6"
13	2' 4"
14	2' 2"
15	2' 0"
16	1' 11"
17	1' 9"
18	1' 8"
19	1' 7"
20	1' 6"
21	1' 5"
22	1' 4"

Converting Steps to Distance

1. Have students place the pedometer in the step count mode and reset them.

2. Tell students they will walk for 10 minutes. Ask them to guess how far (in miles) they will be able to walk in that amount of time.

3. Have students walk for approximately 10 minutes. The purpose of the activity will be for each student to see how far they actually travel in relation to their guess.

4. Stop the class at the end of the 10 minute walking period and have students open their pedometers and check the number of steps they accumulated on their calculation sheet.

5. Ask students to multiply the number of steps they accumulated by their stride length (determined in the previous activity). Convert the distance to mileage by dividing their distance in feet by 5,280. To calculate their miles per hour, have students multiply their distance in miles by 6. That will be their speed if they have walked 10 minutes as described in Step 2.

This activity is for middle/high school students.

Any amount of time is satisfactory. The purpose of the activity is to teach students an understanding of how far they walk in a certain amount of time.

Moderate to vigorous activity is often defined by walking 3 to 3.5 miles per hour.

If possible, have students walk on different terrain, uphill and downhill. This will help them understand how hills and valleys can impact their walking speed. For example, hikers and mountain climbers would not cover that much distance because of the rough terrain.

Game Activity

Moving Together (Cooperative Activity)
Formation: Groups of 4 students
Supplies: none
Groups of 4 students form teams on the sidelines of the teaching area. The objective is for the team to move to the other sideline with the following stipulations:
1. Six feet touching the floor and all team members touching an ankle.
2. Eight body parts (no heads) touching the ground at all times.
3. Half of the team at a high level and half the team at a low level.
4. Every foot touching one other foot.
5. Only four feet can touch the ground.
6. Four feet and one hand must be on the ground.
7. Move with the fewest number of feet as possible touching the floor.
8. Move with the most hands and fewest feet touching the floor.
   Teaching Tips: Additional challenges can be made by providing the teams with different pieces of equipment to carry

while attempting the challenges. To minimize competition, provide each group with a list of challenges. Once they have completed one challenge, they choose their next challenge from the list. This provides continuous activity for all groups.

Who's Leading? (Cooperative Activity)

Formation: Entire class in a circle

Supplies: None

The entire class stands shoulder to shoulder in a circle. One student volunteers to go in the middle and cover her eyes. The teacher then selects a volunteer to lead the class in movements while remaining in the circle. This must be done quietly so the person in the middle does not know who the leader is. The teacher will need to provide the leader with examples of movements such as jogging or skipping in place, bicep curls, jumping jacks, etc. The leader will also be instructed to change activities every few seconds. The person in the middle then opens her eyes and watches the movements. She must stay in the middle but may scan the entire class in an effort to find the leader as he changes movements.

Teaching Tips: To add difficulty, encourage the leader to make small changes in movements. For example, start with normal jumping jacks and then move to skier jacks, and then to skiers with no arm movements and finally walking in place. Also, provide the guesser with the idea of watching one half of the circle. If the activity changes and they don't see anyone do it first, the leader is probably on the other half of the circle. Remind followers to not give the leader away by staring at her.

DPE Curriculum Guide – Lesson Plans
Gymnastics Skills (1)
Level III – Week 7

Objectives:
To exercise independently in the
  circuit training activity
To understand the principles of
  stability and balance
To control the body weight in a variety
  of tumbling and stunt activities
To participate in "one-on-one"
  competition and accept the outcome

NASPE National Standards:
Introductory Activity: 1, 5
Fitness Activity: 1, 3, 4, 6
Lesson Focus: 1, 2, 3, 5
Game: 2, 3, 5

Equipment Required:
Circuit training music, signs, and cones
10–12 tumbling mats
Flags for "Grab the Flag"
8 to 12 bowling pins
10 to 15 8" foam rubber balls
Pinnies for Team Handball

Instructional Activities	Teaching Hints

Introductory Activity — Medic Tag

Three or four students are designated as "taggers." They try to tag the others; when tagged, a student kneels down as if injured. Another student (not one of the taggers) can "rehabilitate" the injured player, enabling her to reenter play.

Different types of rehabilitation can be used. The easiest is to touch a body part or run a full circle around the person.

Fitness Development Activity — Circuit Training

Students do the best they can at each station within the time limit. This implies that not all youngsters are required to do the same workload. Children differ and their ability to perform fitness workloads differs. Make fitness a personal challenge.
Rope Jumping
Triceps Push-Ups
Agility Run
Body Circles
Hula Hoops
Reverse Curls
Crab Walk
Tortoise and Hare
Bend and Twist

Conclude circuit training with 2–4 minutes of walking, jogging, rope jumping, or other self-paced aerobic activity

Tape alternating segments of silence and music to signal duration of exercise. Music segments (begin at 30 seconds) indicate activity at each station, while intervals of silence (10 seconds) announce it is time to stop and move forward to the next station.

Use signals such as start, stop, and move up to ensure rapid movement to the next station.

Ask students to do their personal best. Expect workloads to differ.

Lesson Focus — Gymnastics Skills (1)

Tumbling and Inverted Balances
Review the Forward Roll
    Stand facing forward, with the feet apart. Squat and place the hands on the mat, shoulder width apart, with elbows against the insides of the thighs. Tuck the chin to the chest and make a rounded back. A push-off with the hands and feet provides the force for the roll. Carry the weight on the hands, with the elbows bearing the weight of the thighs. If the elbows are kept against the thighs and the weight is assumed there, the force of the roll is transferred easily to the rounded back. Try to roll forward to the feet. Later, try with the knees together and no weight on the elbows.

Review the Backward Roll (Handclasp Position)
    Clasp the fingers behind the neck, with elbows held out to the sides. From a crouched position, sit down rapidly, bringing the knees to the chest for a tuck to secure momentum. Roll completely over backward, taking much of the weight on the forearms. With this method, the neck is protected.

Forward and Backward Roll Combinations
    Begin with a Forward Roll, coming to a standing position with feet crossed. Pivot the body to uncross the feet and to bring the back in the line of direction for a

Five groups of activities in this lesson ensure that youngsters receive a variety of experiences. Pick a few activities from each group and teach them alternately. For example, teach one or two balance stunts, then a tumbling and inverted balance, followed by a combative, etc. Give equal time to each group of activities.

Scatter tumbling mats throughout the area so that there is little standing in line waiting for a turn.

Do not perform many repetitions of tumbling and inverted balances. For most children, limiting the number of forward or backward roll repetitions to four or five will prevent fatigue and injury.

Backward Roll.

Hold the toes, heels, ankles, or a wand while rolling. Use different arm positions, such as out to the sides or folded across the chest. Use a wide straddle position for both the Forward Roll and the Backward Roll.

Balance Stunts
V-Up

Lie on the back, with arms overhead and extended. Keeping the knees straight and the feet pointed, bring the legs and the upper body up at the same time to form a V shape. The entire weight is balanced on the seat. Hold the position for 5 seconds.

Push-Up Variations

Begin the development of push-up variations by reviewing proper push-up techniques. The only movement is in the arms. The body should come close to, but not touch, the floor. Explore the following variations.

a. Monkey Push-Up. Point the fingers toward each other. Next, bring the hands close enough for the fingertips to touch.

b. Circle-O Push-Up. Form a circle with each thumb and forefinger.

c. Fingertip Push-Up. Get up high on the fingertips.

d. One-Legged Push-Up. Lift one leg from the floor.

Flip-Flop

From a push-up position, propel the body upward with the hands and feet, doing a Turn-Over. Flip back. The stunt should be done on a mat.

Individual Stunts
Wall Walk-Up

From a push-up position with feet against a wall, walk up the wall backward to a handstand position. Walk down again.

Skier's Sit

Assume a sitting position against a wall with the thighs parallel to the floor and the knee joints at right angles. (The position is the same as if sitting in a chair, but, of course, there is no chair.) The hands are placed on the thighs with the feet flat on the floor and the lower legs straight up and down. Try to sit for 30 seconds, 45 seconds, and 1 minute.

Rocking Horse

Lie facedown on a mat with arms extended overhead, palms down. With back arched, rock back and forth.

Heel Click (Side)

Balance on one foot, with the other out to the side. Hop on the supporting foot, click the heels, and return to balance. Try with the other foot.

Partner and Group Stunts
Double Scooter

Two children about the same size face each other, sitting on each other"'s feet. With arms joined, scoot forward or backward with cooperative movements. When one child moves the seat, the other child should help by lifting with the feet. Progress is made by alternately flexing and extending the knees and hips.

Tandem Bicycle

One child forms a bicycle position, with back against a wall and knees bent, as if sitting. The feet should be placed under the body. The second child backs up and sits down lightly on the first child's knees. Other children may be added in the same fashion, their hands around the waist of the player immediately in front for support. Moving the feet on the same side together makes forward progress.

No youngster should be expected to roll if they are fearful or think it is too difficult. In stunts and tumbling, it is important that the student decide if they are capable and confident enough to try the activity.

Youngsters can do many of the activities around their mats. Many of the activities in this unit do not have to be performed on the mat.

A major concern for safety is the neck and back region. Overweight children are at greater risk and might be allowed to avoid tumbling and inverted balances.

When doing partner stunts and combatives, consider the following instructional procedures:

1. Safety factors must be emphasized. Youngsters should be matched for size; a common method is to ask students to pair up with someone who is similar in height. The length of bouts should be short—usually 5–10 seconds of contesting is adequate. Children should freeze immediately when the whistle is blown. In tug-of-war contests, no one should let go suddenly to avoid sending other children sprawling backward.

2. Instructions for combatives should be as explicit as necessary. Starting positions should be defined so that both contestants begin in an equal and neutral position. What constitutes a win and the number of trials permitted should be defined.

3. Fair play should be stressed. Children should be encouraged to find strategies and maneuvers to gain success, but always within the framework of the rules.

Circle High Jump

Stand in circles of three, each circle having children of somewhat equal height. Join hands. One child tries to jump over the opposite pair of joined hands. To be completely successful, each circle must have each child jump forward in turn over the opposite pair of joined hands. (Jumping backward is not recommended.) To reach good height, an upward lift is necessary. Try two small preliminary jumps before exploding into the jump over the joined hands.

Combatives

Hand Wrestle

Starting Position: Contestants place right foot against right foot and grasp right hands in a handshake grip. The left foot is planted firmly to the rear for support.

Action: Try to force the other, by hand and arm pressure, to move either foot. Any movement by either foot means a loss.

Finger Fencing

Starting Position: Contestants stand on the right foot and hold the left foot with the left hand.

Action: Hook index fingers of the right hands and try to push the opponent off balance. Change feet and hands. Any movement of the supporting foot means a loss.

Touch Knees

Starting Position: Contestants stand on both feet and face each other.

Action: Touch one of the opponent's knees without letting the opponent touch yours. Five touches determine the victor.

Grab the Flag

Starting Position: Opponents are on their knees, facing each other on a tumbling mat. Each has a flag tucked in the belt near the middle of the back.

Action: Remain on the knees at all times. Try to grab the flag from the other.

Rooster Fight

Starting Position: Players stoop down and clasp hands behind the knees.

Action: Try to upset the other player or cause the handhold to be released.

4. The teacher can start contests on signal, or children can be allowed to start contests on their own. If children are not self-disciplined, it is best for the instructor to start and stop all contests.

5. To add variety, contests should be done with the right side (arm or leg), the left side, and both sides. Body position can be varied. Children can stand, crouch, sit, or lie for the same contest.

6. Develop a system of rotation, so youngsters have more than one opponent. Rotating assures that one child will not continually dominate another.

Game Activity

Mat Folding (Cooperative Activity)

Formation: Groups of 4 to 5 students

Supplies: One tumbling mat for each group

The group is given one tumbling mat and instructed to stand on it. While keeping their feet on the mat at all times, teams are given the following challenges:

1. Rotate the mat 360 degrees.
2. Move the mat 15 feet.
3. Without using any hands, fold the mat into fourths.
4. Unfold the mat without using any hands.

Teaching Tip: This is an enjoyable activity to use at the end of a gymnastics lesson.

Octopus

Supplies: None

Skills: Maneuvering, problem solving

Octopus is a game that gets its name from the many hands joined together in the activity. Children stand shoulder to shoulder in a tight circle. Everyone thrusts their hands forward and reaches through the group of hands to grasp other hands across the circle. Players may not hold both hands of the same player. Players also may not hold the hand of an adjacent player. The object is to untangle the mess created by the joined hands by going under, over, or through fellow players. No one is permitted to release a handgrip during the unraveling. What is the end result? Perhaps one large circle or two smaller connected circles. If, after a period of time, the knotted hands do not seem to unravel, call a pause. The teacher and group can decide where the difficulty is and allow a change in position of those hands until the knot is dissolved. This is a good example of a cooperative game that requires close teamwork.

Pin Knockout

Supplies: 8 to 12 bowling pins per team, 10 to 12 foam rubber balls

Skill: Throwing

Two teams of equal number play the game. Each team is given many playground balls and six bowling pins. A court with a centerline is needed. The size of the court depends on the number of children in the game. The object of the game is to knock down all of the opponents' bowling pins. The balls are used for rolling at the opposing team's pins. Each team stays in its half of the court.

A player is eliminated if any of the following occurs:

1. He is touched by any ball at any time, regardless of the situation (other than picking up a ball).

2. She steps over the centerline to roll or retrieve a ball. (Any opposing team member hit as a result of such a roll is not eliminated.)

3. He attempts to block a rolling ball with a ball in his hands and the rolling ball touches him in any manner.

A foul is called when a player holds a ball longer than 10 seconds without rolling at the opposing team. The ball must be immediately given to the opposing team. The bowling pins are placed anywhere in the team's area. Players may guard the pins, but must not touch them. When a pin is down, even if a member of the defending team knocked it over unintentionally, it is removed immediately from the game. The game is over when all pins on one side have been knocked down.

DPE Curriculum Guide – Lesson Plans
Soccer Skills and Lead-up Activities (1)
Level III – Week 8

Objectives:
To participate in tag games in a
    cooperative fashion
To strike a ball with a variety of body
    parts
To dribble a ball with the feet
To trap a with a variety of body parts
To play a soccer lead-up activity and
    understand the joy of participation

NASPE National Standards:
Introductory Activity: 1, 5
Fitness Activity: 1, 4, 6
Lesson Focus: 2, 3, 5
Game: 2, 3, 5

Equipment Required:
Cones and music for Astronaut
    Exercises
8" foam rubber or junior soccerball for
    each student
Pinnies (optional)
Cones for marking the drill areas and
    goals

Instructional Activities	Teaching Hints

Introductory Activity — Hospital Tag

All students are it. When tagged, they must cover that area of their body with one hand. Students may be tagged twice, but they must be able to hold both tagged spots and keep moving. When a student is tagged three times, he must freeze.

Restart the game when the majority of students have been frozen. It is counterproductive to wait until the last student is frozen.

Fitness Development Activity — Astronaut Exercises

Walk, do arm circles	35 seconds	Tape alternating segments of silence (30 seconds) and music (35 seconds) to signal the duration of exercise. Music segments indicate aerobic activity, while intervals of silence announce flexibility and strength development activities.
Crab Full-Leg Extension	30 seconds	
Skip sideways	35 seconds	
Body Twist	30 seconds	
Slide; change lead leg	35 seconds	
Jumping Jack variations	30 seconds	
Crab Walk	35 seconds	
Curl-ups with twist	30 seconds	See Chapter 13 for a description of how to perform the exercises.
Hop to center and back	35 seconds	
Four count push-ups	30 seconds	
Gallop backwards	35 seconds	Allow students to adjust the workload to an intensity that is consistent with their ability level.
Bear Hugs	30 seconds	
Grapevine Step (Carioca)	35 seconds	
Trunk Twisters	30 seconds	
Power Jumper	35 seconds	Use scatter formation; ask students to change directions from time to time in order to keep spacing.

Cool down with stretching and walking.

Lesson Focus — Soccer Skills (1)

Skills
Practice the following skills:
1. Dribbling
    Dribbling is moving the ball with a series of taps or pushes to cover ground and still retain control. It allows a player to change direction quickly and to avoid opponents. The best contact point is the inside of the foot, but the outside of the foot will be used at faster running speeds. The ball should be kept close to the player to maintain control.

Contact the ball with the inside, outside, or instep of the foot.

Keep the ball near the body so it can be controlled. (Don't kick it too far in front of the body.) Dribble the ball with a controlled tap.

2. Inside-of-the-Foot Pass (Push Pass)
    The inside-of-the-foot pass is used for accurate passing over distances of up to 15 yd. Because of the technique used, this pass is sometimes referred to as the push pass. The nonkicking foot is placed well up, alongside the ball. As the kicking foot is drawn back, the toe is turned out. During the kick, the toe remains turned out so that the inside of the foot is perpendicular to the line of flight. The sole is kept parallel to the ground. At contact, the knee of the kicking leg should be well forward, over the ball, and both knees should be slightly bent.

Place the nonkicking foot alongside the ball. Keep the head down and eyes focused on the ball during contact.

3. Inside-of-the-Foot Trap

This is the most common method of control, and is used when the ball is either rolling along the ground or bouncing up to knee height. The full surface of the foot, from heel to toe, should be presented perpendicular to the ball.

4. Goalkeeping

Goalkeeping involves stopping shots by catching, stopping, or otherwise deflecting the ball. Goalkeepers should become adept at catching low rolling balls, diving on rolling balls, catching airborne balls at waist level and below, and catching airborne balls at waist height and above.

When trapping, move in line with the path of the ball and reach with the foot to meet the ball. Give when ball contact is made to absorb force.

Goalkeepers should practice catching low rolling balls by getting down on one knee, with their body behind the ball to act as a backstop, and catching the ball with both hands, fingers pointing toward the ground.

Drills Using Four or More Players

Use the following partner drills to practice the skills above. Drills for four or more players should be organized so that a rotation gives all players an equal opportunity to practice skills.

1. Dribbling. Two teams of four players are lined up and facing each other about 10 yd apart. Each player at the front of the team has a ball. Both front players dribble to the center, where they exchange balls and continue dribbling to the other side. The next players perform similarly.

A variation is to have the two players meet at the center, exchange balls, and dribble back to their starting point. Action should be continuous.

2. Shooting, goalkeeping, and defense. A shooting drill against defense can be run with four players and a 15-ft goal set off with cones or other markers. One player has the ball. He advances and attempts to maneuver around a second player so that he can shoot past the goalkeeper guarding a goal. A fourth player acts as the retriever. Rotate positions.

Use foam rubber balls for goalkeeping drills to avoid hurting someone with the ball.

3. Dribbling. Four or five players, each with a ball, form a line. A "coach" stands about 15 yd in front of the line. Each player, in turn, dribbles up to the coach, who indicates with a thumb in which direction the player should dribble past. The coach should give the direction at the last possible moment.

Make sure all students get a chance to be the "coach."

4. Passing, controlling, and defense. Four players stand in the four corners of a square, 10 yd on a side. Two defensive players are inside the square. The corner players stay in place within the square and attempt to pass the ball among themselves, while the two defenders attempt to recover the ball. After a period of time, another two players take over as defenders.

This is a traditional game of keep-away using soccer balls. Encourage students to avoid body contact.

Play the soccer lead-up games after sufficient time has been allotted for skills and drills.

Soccer Lead-up Activities

Dribblerama

Supplies: One soccer ball for each player

Skills: Dribbling, protecting the ball

The playing area is a large circle or square, clearly outlined. All players dribble within the area. The game is played on two levels.

Level 1: Each player dribbles throughout the area, controlling the ball so it does not touch another ball. If a touch occurs, both players go outside the area and dribble around the area. Once youngsters have completed dribbling one lap, they may reenter the game.

Level 2: Two equal playing areas are delineated. All players start in one of the areas. While dribbling and controlling the ball, each player attempts to kick any other ball out of the area. When a ball is kicked out, the player owning that ball takes it to the other area and dribbles. As more players move to the second area, a second game ensues. Players in this area move back to the opposite side. This keeps all players actively involved in the games.

Sideline Soccer

Supplies: A soccer ball, four cones, pinnies (optional)

Skills: Most soccer skills, competitive play

Teams line up on the sidelines of the rectangle. Three or four active players from each team are called from the end of the team line. These players remain active until a point is scored; then they rotate to the other end of the line. The object is to kick the ball between cones (goals) that define the scoring area. The active players on each team compete against each other, aided by their teammates on the sidelines.

To start play, the ball can be given to one team or dropped between two opposing players at the center of the field. To score, the ball must be kicked last by an active player and must go through the goal at or below shoulder height. A goal counts one point. Sideline players can pass to other sideline players or an active teammate, but a sideline kick cannot score a goal.

Regular soccer rules generally prevail, with special attention to the restrictions of no pushing, holding, tripping, or other rough play. Rough play is a foul and causes a point to be awarded to the other team.

For an out-of-bounds ball, the team on the side of the field where the ball went out-of-bounds is awarded a free kick near that spot. No score can result from a free kick. Violation of the touch rule also results in a free kick.

Rotate in a new set of players after 30 to 45 seconds. More active players can be added when the class is large. A number of passes to sideline players can be mandated before a shot on goal can be taken. After some expertise is acquired, the cones should be moved in to narrow the goal area. If the ball goes over the end line but not through the goal area, the ball is put into play by a defender with a kick.

Line Soccer

Supplies: A soccer ball, four cones, pinnies

Skills: Most soccer skills, competitive play

Two goal lines are drawn 80 to 120 ft apart. A restraining line is drawn 15 ft in front of and parallel to each goal line. Field width can vary from 50 to 80 ft. Each team stands on one goal line, which it defends. The referee stands in the center of the field and holds a ball. At the whistle, three players (more if the teams are large) run from the right side of each line to the center of the field and become active players. The referee drops the ball to the ground, and the players try to kick it through the other team defending the goal line. The players in the field may advance by kicking only.

A score is made when an active player kicks the ball through the opposing team and over the end line (provided that the kick was made from outside the restraining line). Cones should be put on field corners to define the goal line. One point is scored when the ball is kicked over the opponent's goal line below shoulder level. One point is also scored in case of a personal foul involving pushing, kicking, tripping, and the like.

Line players act as goalies and are permitted to catch the ball. Once caught, however, the ball must be laid down immediately and either rolled or kicked. It cannot be punted or drop-kicked.

For illegal touching by the active players, a direct free kick from a point 12 yd in front of the penalized team's goal line is given. All active players on the defending team must stand to one side until the ball is kicked. Only goalies defend. An out-of-bounds ball is awarded to the opponents of the team last touching it. The regular soccer throw-in from out of bounds should be used. If the ball goes over the shoulders of the defenders at the end line, any endline player may retrieve the ball and put it into play with a throw or kick.

A time limit of 1 minute is set for any group of active players. After time is up, play is halted and the players are changed. Use a system of player rotation so all participants get to play.

Mini-Soccer

Supplies: A soccer ball, pinnies or colors to mark teams, four cones for the corners

Skills: All soccer skills

Each end of the field has a 21-ft-wide goal marked by jumping standards. A 12-yd semicircle on each end outlines the penalty area. The center of the semicircle is at the center of the goal.

The game follows the general rules of soccer, with one goalie for each side. One new feature, the corner kick is incorporated in this game. This kick is used when the ball, last touched by the defense, goes over the end line but not through the goal. The ball is taken to the nearest corner for a direct free kick, and a goal can be scored from the kick. In a similar situation, if the attacking team last touched the ball, the goalkeeper kick is awarded. The goalie puts the ball down and placekicks it forward.

The players are designated as center forward, outside right, outside left, right halfback, left halfback, fullback, and goalie. Players should rotate positions. The forwards play in the front half of the field, and the guards in the back half. Neither position, however, is restricted to these areas entirely, and all may cross the centerline without penalty.

A foul by the defense within its penalty area (semicircle) results in a penalty kick, taken from a point 12 yd distant, directly in front of the goal. Only the goalie is allowed to defend. The ball is in play, with others waiting outside the penalty area.

Position play should be emphasized. The lines of three should be encouraged to spread out and stay in their area. The number of players can vary, with some games using as few as three on a side in a more restricted area.

DPE Curriculum Guide – Lesson Plans
Soccer Skills and Lead-up Activities (2)
Level III – Week 9

LP 88

Objectives:
To strike a soccer ball with a variety of body parts
To dribble a ball with the feet
To trap a ball with a variety of body parts
To play a soccer lead-up activity and understand the joy of participation

NASPE National Standards:
Introductory Activity: 1, 5
Fitness Activity: 1, 4, 6
Lesson Focus: 2, 3, 5
Game: 2, 3, 5

Equipment Required:
Cones and tape for Astronaut Exercises
One 8" foam rubber ball or junior soccer ball per student
Pinnies for lead-up games
Cones for marking the drill areas and goals

Instructional Activities	**Teaching Hints**

Introductory Activity — PACER Run

Pick two lines or markers 20 m apart. Students run (or use other locomotor movements) back and forth between the lines in a specified time (i.e., 10 seconds). Students can add a personal challenge by seeing how many times they can move back and forth within the given time limit.

Students can try this with a partner they pick. They can race each other to the lines and back.

Students can walk when necessary.

Fitness Development Activity — Astronaut Exercises

Walk, do arm circles	35 seconds
Crab Full-Leg Extension	35 seconds
Skip sideways	35 seconds
Body Twist	35 seconds
Slide; change lead leg	35 seconds
Jumping Jack variations	35 seconds
Crab Walk	35 seconds
Curl-ups with twist	35 seconds
Hop to center and back	35 seconds
Four count push-ups	35 seconds
Gallop backwards	35 seconds
Bear Hugs	35 seconds
Grapevine Step (Carioca)	35 seconds
Trunk Twisters	35 seconds
Power Jumper	35 seconds

Cool down with stretching and walking.

Tape alternating segments of silence (35 seconds) and music (35 seconds) to signal the duration of exercise. Music segments indicate aerobic activity, while intervals of silence announce flexibility and strength development activities.

See Chapter 13 for a description of how to perform the exercises.

Allow students to adjust the workload to an intensity that is consistent with their ability level.

Use scatter formation; ask students to change directions from time to time in order to keep spacing.

Lesson Focus — Soccer Skills (2)

Skills
Divide the skills into four stations and place necessary equipment at each station. Students should practice skills they learned in last week's lesson.
1. Review and practice the long pass. Set up a station with plenty of room and students with a partner. They long pass back and forth to each other.
2. Review the inside-of-the foot pass and trapping: Work with a partner and practice passing and trapping.
3. Practice dribbling skills: Give each student a ball and have them practice dribbling. Move the ball with a series of taps. Start slowly and keep the ball in front of the body.
4. Goalkeeping and shooting: Students work with a partner. One dribbles the ball a short distance and then takes shot at goal. The other partner tries to prevent the score.

Make signs that tell students the skills they are to practice at each station. Set the signs on cones in the areas where students are to practice. Ask students to read the signs before they begin.

The foam training balls are best for teaching introductory soccer skills. They don't hurt students when kicked or when they are struck by a ball.

Drills Using Four or More Players
Use the following partner drills to practice the skills above. Drills for four or more players should be organized so that a rotation gives all players an equal opportunity to practice skills.

1. Shooting. For two-way goal practice, 2 to 6 players are divided, half on each side of the goal. The width of the goal can vary, depending on the skill of the players. Two types of shooting should be practiced: (a) kicking a stationary ball from 10 to 20 yd out and (b) preceding a kick with a dribble. In the second type, a restraining line 12 to 15 yd out is needed. Use spots or cones to mark this line. Use at least 4 balls for this two-way drill. After a period of kicking, the groups should change sides. Ball chasers are the players at the end of each line.

2. Shooting and goalkeeping. Scoring can also be practiced with a goalkeeper. Practice should be done with a stationary ball from 12 yd out (penalty distance) and with kicks preceded by a dribble. The goalie and the chaser should remain for one complete round and then rotate. Having a second ball to play with saves time because play can continue while the chaser is recovering the previous ball.

3. Kicking and trapping. This is an excellent squad drill. Approximately 8 players form a circle 15 yd in diameter. Two balls are passed back and forth independently. Passes should be kept low, using primarily the side-of-the-foot kick. Using 3 balls can be tried also.

4. Passing and shooting. The drill can be done with 4 to 6 players. Two balls are needed. A passer is stationed about 15 yd from the goal, and a retriever is behind the goal. The shooters are in line, 20 yd from the goal and to the right. The first shooter passes to the passer, and then runs forward. The passer returns the ball to the shooter. The shooter tries to time her run forward so that she successfully shoots the pass through the goal. Both the passer and the retriever should stay in position for several rounds of shooting and then rotate to become shooters. The first pass can be from a stationary ball. Later, however, the kicker can be allowed to dribble forward a short distance before making the first pass. Reverse the field and practice from the left, shooting with the nondominant leg.

Using cones or chalk, a grid system of 10-yd squares can be marked on a playing field. The grid can be useful when organizing drills, activities, and small-sized games. The number of squares needed depends on the size of the class, but at least one square for every three students is recommended. The drills can also be set up as individual stations where students rotate after a specified time.

In soccer drills, two approaches should be recognized. The first is the practice of technique with no opposition from any defense. The second is the skill approach, which involves both offensive and defensive players and perhaps a target. In drills using the skill approach, the goal is to outmaneuver the opponent. Some drills begin with the technique approach and then move to the skill approach.

Soccer Lead-up Activities

Bull's-Eye

Supplies: One soccer ball per player
Skills: Dribbling, protecting the ball

The playing area is a large outlined area—circle, square, or rectangle. One player holds a ball in her hands, which serves as the bull's-eye. The other players dribble within the area. The player with the bull's-eye attempts to throw her ball (basketball push shot) at any other ball. The ball that is hit now becomes the new bull's-eye. The old bull's-eye becomes one of the dribblers. A new bull's-eye cannot hit back immediately at the old bull's-eye. If the group is large, have two bull's-eyes. No score is kept and no one is eliminated.

Line Soccer

See the Lesson Plan, Week 8 for a complete game description.

Mini-Soccer

See the Lesson Plan, Week 8 for a complete game description.

Regulation Soccer

Supplies: A soccer ball, pinnies
Skills: All soccer skills

A team usually consists of 3 forwards, 3 midfield players, 4 backline defenders, and 1 goalkeeper. Forwards are the main line of attack. They need to develop good control, dribbling, and shooting skills, and they must have a strong desire to score. They should be encouraged to shoot frequently. Midfield players tend to be the powerhouse of the team. They need good passing and tackling skills as well as a high level of cardiovascular fitness. Defenders should work well together and know when to tackle. They should play safely by clearing the ball away from their own penalty area, and not risk dribbling or passing toward their own goal unless it is absolutely safe to do so. Goalkeepers must be quick and agile, be good decision makers, and have ball-handling skills.

On the toss of the coin, the winning team gets its choice of kicking off or selecting which goal to defend. The loser exercises the option not selected by the winner.

On the kickoff, the ball must travel forward about 1 yd, and the kicker cannot touch it again until another player has kicked it. The defensive team must be 10 yd away from the kicker. After each score, the team not winning the point gets to kick off. Both teams must be onside at the kickoff. The defensive team must stay onside and out of the center circle until the ball is kicked. Regular soccer rules call for scoring by counting the number of goals made.

Elementary school children usually play 6-minute quarters. There should be a rest period of 1 minute between quarters and 10 minutes between halves.

When the ball goes out-of-bounds on the sideline, it is put into play with a throw-in from the spot where it crossed the line. No goal may be scored, nor may the thrower play the ball a second time until it has been touched by another player. All opponents are to be 10 yd back at the time of the throw.

If the ball is caused to go out-of-bounds on the end line by the attacking team, a goal kick is awarded. The ball is placed in the goal area and kicked beyond the penalty area by a defending player, who may not touch the ball twice in succession. If the ball is touched by a player before it goes out of the penalty area, it is not yet in play and should be kicked again.

If the defensive team causes the ball to go out-of-bounds over the end line, a corner kick is awarded. The ball is placed 1 yd from the corner of the field and kicked into the field of play by an attacking player. The 10-yd restriction also applies to defensive players.

If the ball is touched by two opponents at the same time and caused to go out-of-bounds, a drop ball is called. The referee drops the ball between two opposing players, who cannot kick it until it touches the ground. A drop ball also is called when the ball is trapped among downed players.

If a player is closer to the opponent's goal line than to the ball at a time when the ball is played in a forward direction, it is an offside infraction. Exceptions exist, and a player is not offside when she is in her half of the playing field, when two opponents are nearer their goal line than the attacking player at the moment when the ball is played, or when the ball is received directly from a corner kick, a throw-in, or a goal kick.

Personal fouls involving unnecessary roughness are penalized. Tripping, striking, charging, holding, pushing, and jumping an opponent intentionally are forbidden.

It is a foul for any player, except the goalkeeper, to handle the ball with the hands or arms. The goalkeeper is allowed only four steps and must then get rid of the ball. After the ball has left her possession, the goalkeeper may not pick it up again until another player has touched it. Players are not allowed to screen or obstruct opponents, unless they are in control of the ball.

Penalties are as follows:

1. A direct kick is awarded for all personal fouls and handballs. A goal can be scored from a direct free kick. Examples of infringements are pushing, tripping, kicking a player, and holding.

2. A penalty kick is awarded if direct free-kick infringements are committed by a defender in his own penalty area.

3. An indirect free kick is awarded for off-sides, obstruction, dangerous play such as high kicking, a goalkeeper's taking more than four steps or repossessing the ball before another player has touched it, and playing the ball twice after a dead-ball situation. The ball must be touched by a second player before a goal can be scored. The referee should signal if the kick is indirect by pointing one arm upward vertically.

Teaching suggestions: Players should be encouraged to use the space on the field to the best advantage. When a team is in possession of the ball, players should attempt to find a position from which they can pass either behind the player with the ball to give support, or toward the goal to be in a better position to shoot. When a team is forced into defense, the defenders should get "goal-side" of attackers (between the attackers and their own goal) to prevent them from gaining an advantage.

From an early stage, players should be taught to give information to each other during the game, especially when they have possession of the ball. Valuable help can be given by shouting instructions such as "Man on," "You have time," or "Player behind," and also by calling for the ball when in a good position to receive a pass.

DPE Curriculum Guide – Lesson Plans
Juggling Skills and Pyramids
Level III – Week 10

Objectives:
To be able to juggle three scarves
To be able to juggle two balls
To participate in low-organized games
    and contribute to the team outcome

NASPE National Standards:
Introductory Activity: 1, 5, 7
Fitness Activity: 1, 2, 4, 5, 7
Lesson Focus: 3, 5, 6, 7
Game: 1, 3, 6

Equipment Required:
Music and signs for fitness
Juggling scarves (3 for each student)
Different types of balls for juggling
Base and balls for game activities

Instructional Activities	Teaching Hints

Introductory Activity — Beanbag Touch and Go

Spread beanbags throughout the area. On signal, students move and touch as many beanbags as possible. Different body parts can be specified for touching (i.e., "Touch five yellow beanbags with your right knee.")

Stipulate students touch different colors of beanbags
Challenge to move over and around beanbags

Fitness Development Activity — Aerobic Fitness

The following aerobic movements are suggestions only. When youngsters begin to fatigue, stop the aerobic fitness movements and do some of the flexibility and strength development activities learned in previous lessons. This will allow students time to recover aerobically.
1. Rhythmic run with clap
2. Bounce turn and clap
3. Rhythmic 4-count curl-ups (knees, toes, knees, back)
4. Rhythmic Crab Kicks (slow time)
5. Jumping Jack combination
6. Double knee lifts
7. Lunges (right, left, forward) with single-arm circles (on the side lunges) and double-arms circles (on the forward lunge)
8. Rhythmic trunk twists
9. Directional run (forward, backward, side, turning)
10. Rock side to side with clap
11. Side leg raises (alternate legs)
12. Rhythmic 4-count push-ups (If these are too difficult for students, substitute single-arm circles in the push-up position.)

Use music to stimulate effort. Any combination of movements can be used.

Keep the steps simple and easy to perform. Some students will become frustrated if the learning curve is steep.

Signs that explain the aerobic activities will help students remember performance cues.

Don't stress or expect perfection. Allow students to perform the activities as best they can.

Alternate bouncing and running movements with flexibility and strength development movements.

Lesson Focus — Juggling Skills and Pyramids

Juggling with Scarves

Scarves are held near the center by the fingertips. To throw the scarf, it should be lifted and pulled into the air above eye level. Scarves are caught by clawing, a downward motion of the hand, and grabbing the scarf from above as it is falling.

Cascading—Cascading is the easiest pattern for juggling three objects. The following sequence can be used to learn this basic technique.
a. One scarf. Hold the scarf in the center. Quickly move the arm across the chest and toss the scarf with the palm out. Reach out with the other hand and catch the scarf in a straight-down motion (clawing). Toss the scarf with this hand using the motion and claw it with the opposite hand. Continue the tossing and clawing sequence over and over.
b. Two scarves and one hand. Hold the scarves with the fingertips in one hand. Toss the first scarf upward. As the first scarf reaches its zenith, toss the second scarf and catch the first one. Continue.
c. Two scarves and two hands. Hold a scarf with the fingertips of each hand. Toss the first one across the body as described above. Toss the second scarf across the body in the opposite direction.
d. Three-scarf cascading. A scarf is held in each hand by the fingertips as described above. The third scarf is held with the ring and little fingers against the palm of the hand. The first scarf to be thrown will be from the hand that is holding two scarves.

Reverse Cascading—Reverse cascading involves tossing the scarves from the waist level to the outside of the body and allowing the scarves to drop down the midline of the body.
a. One scarf.
b. Two scarves.
c. Three scarves.

Column Juggling—Column juggling is so named because the scarves move straight up and down as though they were inside a large pipe or column and do not cross the body.

Showering—Start with two scarves in the right hand and one in the other. Begin by throwing the first two scarves from the right hand. Toss the scarves in a large circle away from the midline of the body and overhead as high as possible. As soon as the second scarf is released, toss the scarf from the left to the right hand and throw it in the same path with the right hand. All scarves are caught with the left hand and passed to the right hand.

Juggling Challenges
a. While cascading, toss a scarf under one leg.
b. While cascading, toss a scarf from behind the back.
c. Instead of catching one of the scarves, blow it upward with a strong breath of air.
d. Begin cascading by tossing the first scarf into the air with a foot. Lay the scarf across the foot and kick it into the air.
e. Try juggling three scarves with one hand. Do not worry about establishing a pattern, just catch the lowest scarf each time. Try both regular and reverse cascading, as well as column juggling.
f. While doing column juggling, toss up one scarf, hold the other two and make a full turn. Resume juggling.
g. Try juggling more than three scarves (up to six) while facing a partner.
h. Juggle three scarves while standing beside a partner with inside arms around each other. This is easy to do since it is regular three-scarf cascading.

Juggling with Balls
Instructional Procedures
1. Juggling requires accurate, consistent tossing, and this should be the first emphasis. The tosses should be thrown to the same height on both sides of the body, about 2 ft upward and across the body, since the ball is tossed from one hand to the other. Practice tossing the ball parallel to the body; the most common problem in juggling is that the balls are tossed forward and the juggler has to move forward to catch them.
2. The fingers, not the palms, should be used in tossing and catching. Stress relaxed wrist action.
3. The student should look upward to watch the balls at the peak of their flight, rather than watching the hands. Focus on where the ball peaks, not the hands.
4. The balls should be caught about waist height and released a little above this level.
5. Two balls must be carried in the starting hand, and the art of releasing only one must be mastered.
6. Progression should be working successively with first one ball, then two balls, and finally three balls.

Recommended Progression for Cascading
1. Using one ball and one hand only, toss the ball upward (2 to 2 ft), and catch it with the same hand. Begin with the dominant hand, and later practice with the other. Toss quickly, with wrist action. Then handle the ball alternately with right and left hands, tossing from one hand to the other.
2. Now, with one ball in each hand, alternate tossing a ball upward and catching it in the same hand so that one ball is always in the air. Begin again with a ball in each hand. Toss across the body to the other hand. To keep the balls from colliding, toss under the incoming ball. After some expertise has been acquired, alternate the two kinds of tosses by doing a set number (4 to 6) of each before shifting to the other.
3. Hold two balls in the starting hand and one in the other. Toss one of the balls in the starting hand, toss the ball from the other hand, and then toss the third ball.

Pyramids
Emphasis is on making small pyramid groups. Stunts using two performers should be practiced as preliminary to pyramid building with three students. Groups larger than three are not recommended since it is difficult to supervise safely. Place a number of signs or pictures around the area to encourage different types of pyramids.

Closing Activities
Group Juggling (Cooperative Activity)
Formation: Squads of 5 to 6 students
Supplies: 1 ball or beanbag for each student
Teams of 5–6 students are formed and each student has a ball or beanbag. A variety of types of balls will add to the excitement of this activity. On signal (e.g. "1, 2, ready, toss"), each team member tosses his ball to another teammate and then catches a ball tossed to him. The objective is to see how many successful tosses can be made in unison. Typically students will toss to the same person each time. A successful toss occurs when all team members catch the ball tossed to them. After several tosses, the teacher gives each group the responsibility of selecting one team to give the signal for their group.

Fast Pass

Supplies: One 8" foam rubber ball, pinnies

Skills: Passing, catching, moving to an open area

One team begins with the ball. The object is to complete five consecutive passes without the ball touching the floor. The team without the ball attempts to intercept the ball or recover an incomplete pass. Each time a pass is completed, the team shouts the number of consecutive passes completed it represents. Each time a ball touches the floor or is intercepted, the count starts over. Players may not contact each other. Emphasis should be placed on spreading out and using the entire court area. If players do not spread out, the area can be broken into quadrants and players restricted to one quadrant.

One-Base Tagball

Supplies: A base (or standard), a volleyball (8" foam ball for younger children)

Skills: Running, dodging, throwing

A home line is drawn at one end of the playing space. A base or standard is placed about 50 ft in front of the home line. Two teams are formed. One team is scattered around the fielding area, the boundaries of which are determined by the number of children. The other team is lined up in single file behind the home line.

The object of the game is for the fielding team to tag the runners with the ball. Two runners at a time try to round the base and head back for the home line without being tagged. The game is continuous, meaning that as soon as a running team player is tagged or crosses the home line, another player starts immediately. The fielding team may run with the ball and pass it from player to player, trying to tag one of the runners. The running team scores a point for each player who runs successfully around the base and back to the home line.

At the start of the game, the running team has two players ready at the right side of the home line. The others on the team are in line, waiting for a turn. The teacher throws the ball anywhere in the field, and the first two runners start toward the base. They must run around the base from the right side. After all of the players have run, the teams exchange places. The team scoring the most points wins.

To facilitate tagging a runner, players on the fielding team should make passes to a person close to the runner. They must be alert, because two children at a time are running. The next player on the running team must watch carefully in order to start the instant one of the two preceding runners is back safely behind the line or has been hit.

Objectives:

To be able to move continuously in moderately active activities

To learn the rules of recreational activities

To play in recreational activities independently without adult supervision

NASPE National Standards:

Introductory Activity: 1, 2, 4, 7
Fitness Activity: 1, 2, 4, 7
Lesson Focus: 1, 4, 5, 6
Game: 2, 3, 5, 6

Equipment Required:

Music and signs for Aerobic Fitness
Equipment for recreational activities

Instructional Activities	Teaching Hints

Introductory Activity — Jog and Stretch

The class jogs around the area. On signal, they stop and stretch a body part. Students work independently and are responsible for stretching as many body parts as possible.

Use students to demonstrate a variety of stretches.

Fitness Development Activity — Aerobic Fitness

The following aerobic movements are suggestions only. When youngsters begin to fatigue, stop the aerobic fitness movements and do some of the flexibility and strength development activities learned in previous lessons. This will allow students time to recover aerobically.

1. Rhythmic run with clap
2. Bounce turn and clap
3. Rhythmic 4-count curl-ups (knees, toes, knees, back)
4. Rhythmic Crab Kicks (slow time)
5. Jumping Jack combination
6. Double knee lifts
7. Lunges (right, left, forward) with single-arm circles (on the side lunges) and double-arms circles (on the forward lunge)
8. Rhythmic trunk twists
9. Directional run (forward, backward, side, turning)
10. Rock side to side with clap
11. Side leg raises (alternate legs)
12. Rhythmic 4-count push-ups (If these are too difficult for students, substitute single-arm circles in the push-up position.)

Use music to stimulate effort. Any combination of movements can be used.

Keep the steps simple and easy to perform. Some students will become frustrated if the learning curve is steep.

Signs that explain the aerobic activities will help students remember performance cues.

Don't stress or expect perfection. Allow students to perform the activities as best they can.

Alternate bouncing and running movements with flexibility and strength development movements.

Lesson Focus and Game Activity — Recreational Activities

The purpose of this unit is to teach children activities that they can play during the time when school is not in session.

1. Shuffleboard
2. Four Square
3. Double Dutch rope jumping
4. Team Handball
5. Around the Key Basketball
6. Beach Ball Volleyball (2 on 2)
7. Jacks
8. Marbles
9. Sidewalk Tennis
10. Horseshoes
11. Rope Quoits
12. Tetherball
13. Tennis Volleyball

Teach students the rules of recreational activities so they are able to participate effectively during free time.

Teach games that are traditional in your area. Older youngsters may be a good source of advice for often-played games.

If desired, set up a number of stations and have youngsters rotate to different stations during the lesson.

DPE Curriculum Guide – Lesson Plans
Walking Activities
Level III – Week 12

Objectives:

To appreciate the fitness outcomes of orienteering

To participate in vigorous activity for an extended period of time

To understand the opportunities that walking offers for socializing with friends

NASPE National Standards:

Introductory Activity: 1, 5
Fitness Activity: 1, 4, 6
Lesson Focus: 4, 5, 6
Game: 2, 3, 5, 6

Equipment Required:

One beanbag per student
Music for fitness orienteering routine
Stations and signs for fitness orienteering
Laminated map card of checkpoint stations
Letters for the checkpoints

Instructional Activities	Teaching Hints

Introductory Activity — Vanishing Beanbags

Beanbags (one per student) are spread throughout the area. Students move throughout the area. On signal, they find a beanbag and sit on it. On the next signal or command, the students move again, with a few beanbags being removed during the interval. On signal, they once again sit on a beanbag. The object is to try not to be left without a beanbag move than five times.

There are no ties when finding a beanbag to sit on. If students feel it is a tie, both must leave that bag and find another.

Specify placing different body parts on the beanbag.

Fitness Development Activity — Fitness Orienteering

Students work together as members of a team. Eight to ten stations are placed around the area in random fashion. Each squad is given a laminated "map" card of exercise stations. Each of the maps has the stations in different order so that there is only one squad at a "landmark." The team members exercise together (each member performing at their own pace) and "hunt" for the next exercise station listed on their map card when signaled. When they complete the station activity, one member of the squad picks up a letter from the "checkpoint" and the team moves to the next station. The goal is to complete the fitness orienteering stations, pick up a letter at each station, and return to the original starting point to unscramble "the secret word."

Examples of checkpoint stations on the exercise map card are:

1. Run to the Northwest corner of the gym and pick up your letter now. When the music starts, continue to run to a different corner until the music stops.
2. Move to the individual mats and perform push-up challenges until the music stops.
3. Run to the benches and perform step-ups until the music stops. The count should be "up, up, down, down," with your steps.
4. Move to the red marking spots and perform two different stretches until the music stops.
5. Run and find the jump ropes. When the music starts, pick up the ropes and do some jump rope tricks you learned earlier.
6. Skip to the tumbling mats. When the music starts perform abdominal challenges.
7. As a group, jog to the three green marking spots and pick up your letter. Jog and try to touch at least 5 walls, 2 different red lines, and 3 different black lines. Stay together with your group.
8. Jog to the "jumping jacks" sign and perform jumping jacks with at least 4 different variations in arm or foot patterns.

Intervals of music (30 seconds) and silence (15 seconds) signal when to exercise and when to change to a new station.

See Chapter 13 for a description of how to perform the exercises.

Allow students to adjust the workload to an intensity that is consistent with their ability level.

Set up the stations prior to the lesson. Each day the course is run, the order of the checkpoint stations can be changed.

Lesson Focus — Walking Instruction

This should be a relaxed lesson with emphasis on developing activity patterns that can be used outside of the school environment. An educational approach to this lesson teaches students that walking is done without equipment and offers excellent health benefits. Walking is an activity that can be done throughout the lifespan. The following are suggestions for implementing this unit of instruction:

1. Youngsters should be allowed to find a friend with whom they want to walk. The result is usually a friend of similar ability level. A way to judge correct pace is to be able to talk with a friend without undue stress. If students are too winded to talk, they are probably moving too fast. A selected friend will encourage talking and help assure that the experience is positive and within the student's aerobic capacity.

2. Walking should be done in individual directions rather than doing laps on a track. Doing laps on a track is one of the surest ways to discourage less mobile youngsters. They always finish last and are open to chiding by the rest of the class.

3. Walking should be done for a specified time rather than a specified distance. All youngsters should not have to move the same distance. This goes against the philosophy of accompanying individual differences and varying aerobic capacities. Walking for a set amount of time will allow the less able child to move without fear of ridicule. For health benefits, it is best to move for a longer time at a slower speed than to run at top speed for a shorter distance.

Walking Activities

Walking Interviews

Playing Area: Gymnasium or outside walking course
Players: Partners
Supplies: 4 × 6 index cards with interview questions
Skills: Walking, communication, pacing

Children choose a partner. Each set of partners is given an index card with a series of questions. For this activity, students simply walk with their partner and interview them using the questions provided. Once all of the questions are asked, the partners switch roles using the questions on the back side of the card. Examples of interview questions include:

What is your favorite physical activity? Why?
What is your favorite movie and why?
How many people are in your family?
What do you usually do after school?
What is your favorite subject in school?
Who was your teacher last year?
What is your favorite fruit or vegetable?

Teaching Tip: Minimize the number of questions so students have to change partners often. This increases the number of peers students will get to know. Another idea is to allow students to create their own questions.

Giant Map Construction

Playing Area: Gymnasium or defined teaching area
Players: Groups of 2–3
Supplies: One sheet of paper and a pencil for each set of partners
Skills: Walking, map reading, cooperation

In an activity setting defined by cones, each set of partners maps a route they will walk together. Shapes, words, or letters can be used as routes. They then walk the route with their partner. For example, a spelling word for the week may be "Intensity." Using the entire activity area as their "mapping area," the partners walk and spell out the word "Intensity" from left to right.

Teaching Tip: The key to this activity is to get students to use the entire designated area for the trail they will map and walk. If pedometers are used, have students guess the number of steps it will take one or both partners to finish the route. Sets of partners can test the number of steps or amount of activity time it takes to walk the route and then swap maps with another group.

New Engineer

Playing Area: Gymnasium or defined activity area
Players: Groups of 6–8
Supplies: A small piece of equipment (beanbag or baton) for a group of 4–6 students
Skills: Walking, pacing,

Groups of 4 to 6 students stand in a single file line and begin walking with the leader (engineer) holding the piece of equipment and leading the group throughout the teaching area. On signal, the leader hands the piece of equipment to the second person who hands it to the third and so on. This is all done while the line is still walking. When the equipment gets back to the last person (the caboose), the caboose begins speed walking to the front of the line to become the "new engineer."

Teaching Tip: Challenge students to move with a brisk walk. At different intervals, stop and change the makeup of the teams to provide renewed interest.

When youngsters are finished walking and jogging, allow them the opportunity to participate in a choice of individual or recreational activities.

DPE Curriculum Guide – Lesson Plans
Rhythmic Movement Skills (1)
Level III – Week 13

Objectives:
To perform a number of physical
   challenges with body control
To move rhythmically in a variety of
   situations
To participate cooperatively in a game
   setting

NASPE National Standards:
Introductory Activity: 1, 5
Fitness Activity: 1, 4, 5, 6
Lesson Focus: 1, 2, 3, 5
Game: 1, 3, 5

Equipment Required:
Equipment for Challenge Course
Music for Challenge Course
Music for rhythmic activities
Markers for Pacman game

Instructional Activities	Teaching Hints

Introductory Activity — Hospital Tag

All students are it. When tagged, they must cover that area of their body with one hand. Students may be tagged twice, but they must be able to hold both tagged spots and keep moving. When a student is tagged three times, he must freeze.

Restart the game when the majority of students have been frozen. It is counterproductive to wait until the last student is frozen.

Fitness Development Activity — Challenge Course

Design a course around the perimeter of the area using some of the following ideas:
1. Step on jumping box, dismount to tumbling mat, and do a forward roll.
2. Run and weave through four wands held upright by cones.
3. Handwalk across a horizontal ladder or do a flexed-arm hang from a climbing rope for 5 seconds.
4. Step on and off three jumping boxes (small-large-small).
5. Agility run through hoops.
6. Perform jump turns.
7. Leap over a magic rope held taut with two chairs or jumping boxes.
8. Hop on one foot.
9. Do a log roll across a tumbling mat.
10. Alternate going over and under six obstacles (cones and wands or hoops).
11. Crouch jump or scooter movements the length of a balance-beam bench.
12. Slide through a parallel tumbling mat maze (mats stood on their sides).

Use taped intervals of music and silence. When the music is playing, students travel through the challenge course. When the music stops, youngsters do some stretching and strength development exercises. This gives them a chance to recover aerobically.

Distribute students thoughout the course rather than lining them up at a starting point. Faster moving students can pass on the outside.

Change directions periodically to prevent a build-up of students at one station.

Lesson Focus — Rhythmic Movement Skills (1)

Make dances easy for students to learn by implementing some of the following techniques:
Rhythms should be taught like other sport skills. Avoid striving for perfection so students know it is acceptable to make mistakes. Teach a variety of dances rather than one or two in depth in case some students find it difficult to master a specific dance.
1. Teach the dances without using partners.
2. Allow youngsters to move in any direction without left-right orientation.
3. Use scattered formation instead of circles.
4. Emphasize strong movements such as clapping and stamping to increase involvement.
5. Play the music at a slower speed when first learning the dance.

Jessie Polka (American)

Music Source: WWCD-RM8
Formation: Circle, couples facing counterclockwise with inside arms around each other's waist
Directions:

Measures	Part I Action
1	Beginning left, touch the heel in front, then step left in place. (Left heel, together)
2	Touch the right toe behind. Then touch the right toe in place, or swing it forward, keeping the weight on the left foot. (Right toe, touch)
3	Touch the right heel in front, then step right in place. (Right heel, together)
4	Touch the left heel to the left side, sweep the left foot across in front of the right. Keep the weight on the right. (Left heel, crossover)

Measures Part II Action

5–8   Take four two-steps or polka steps forward in the line of direction. (Step, close, step; step, close, step; step, close, step; step, close, step)

Inside-Out Mixer

Music Source: Any music with a pronounced beat suitable for walking at a moderate speed

Formation: Triple circle (three children standing side by side), facing counterclockwise, with inside hands joined. A pinnie can be worn by the center person for identification.

Directions:

Measures Action

1–4   Take eight walking steps forward. (Forward, 2, 3, 4, 5, 6, 7, 8)

5–8   Form a small circle and circle left in eight steps back to place. (Circle, 2, 3, 4, 5, 6, 7, 8)

9–12   The center person walks forward under the raised arms opposite, pulling the other two under to turn the circle inside out. (Inside-out, 2, 3, 4, 5, 6, 7, 8)

13–16   The trio circles left in eight steps, returning to place. When almost back to place, drop hands. The center person walks forward counterclockwise, and the other two walk clockwise (the way they are facing) to the nearest trio for a change of partners. (Circle, 2, 3, 4, mix, 6, 7, 8)

Cotton-Eyed Joe (American)

Music Source: WWCD-FDN

Formation: Double circle of couples with partner B on the right, holding inside hands and facing counterclockwise. Varsouvienne position can also be used.

Directions:

Measures Action

1–2   Starting with the left foot, cross the left foot in front of the right foot, kick the left foot forward. (Cross, kick)

3–4   Take one two-step backward. (Left, close, left)

5–6   Cross the right foot in front of the left foot; kick the right foot forward. (Cross, kick)

7–8   Do one two-step backward. (Right, close, right)

9–16   Repeat measures 1--8.

17–32   Perform eight two-steps counterclockwise beginning with the left foot. (Step, close, step; repeat eight times)

Alley Cat (American)

Music Source: WWCD-4903

Skills: Grapevine step, touch step, knee lifts

Formation: None, although all should face the same direction during instruction.

Directions:

Measures Action

1–2   Do a grapevine left and kick: Step sideward left, step right behind left, step left again, and kick. Repeat to the right. (Left, behind, left, kick; right, behind, right, kick)

3–4   Touch the left toe backward, bring the left foot to the right, touch the left toe backward again, bring the left foot to the right, taking the weight. Repeat, beginning with the right toe. (Left and, left and; right and, right and)

5–6   Raise the left knee up in front of the right knee and repeat. Raise the right knee up twice, similarly. (Left and, left and; right and, right and)

7–8   Raise the left knee and then the right knee. Clap the hands once and make a jump quarter turn to the left. (Left and, right and, clap and, jump)

After the routine is repeated three times, the dancer should be facing in the original direction.

Big Sombrero Circle Mixer (American)

Music Source: WWC-FFD

Skills: Circling, do-si-do, star, swing

Formation: Sicilian Circle. Couples facing couples clockwise and counterclockwise around the circle.

Directions:

Measures	Action
2	Introduction (8 counts total)
1–2	Join hands with the facing couple and circle left using 8 walking steps. (Circle, 2, 3, ... 8)
3–4	Keep hands joined circle right using 8 walking steps. (Circle right, 2, 3, ... 8)
5–6	Face partner and do-si-do using 8 walking steps. (Do-si-do, 2, 3, ... 8)
7–8	Face opposite and do-si-do using 8 walking steps. (Opposite, 2, 3, ... 8)
9–10	All four circle while doing a right hand star using 8 walking steps. (Star, 2, 3, ... 8)

11–12	All four circle while doing a left hand star using 8 walking steps. (Star, 2, 3, … 8)
13–14	Swing partner by linking right elbows and swinging once or twice. (Swing, 2, 3, … 8)
15–16	Pass through the opposite couple passing right shoulders and walk to the next couple using 8 steps. (Pass, through, 3, 4, … 8)

Repeat the dance to the end of the music. Youngsters should always return back to their starting position after every 8 count movement.

Circle Virginia Reel (American)

Music Source: WWCD-57; WWC-57
Skills: Star, swing, do-si-do, swing, promenade
Formation: Couples facing in a double circle with dancers about 4 ft apart
Directions:

Measures	Action
1–4	Partners walk forward 4 and backward 4 steps; repeat. (Forward, 2, 3, 4; back, 2, 3, 4; forward, 2, 3, 4; back, 2, 3, 4)
5–8	Partners make a star by joining right hands (with bent elbows) and circling around once clockwise in 8 steps. Reverse direction and star with left hands back to place in 8 steps. (Right star, 2, 3, … 8; left star, 2, 3, … 8)
9–10	Partners join hands with bent elbows held chest high and circle clockwise back to place in 8 steps. (Circle, 2, 3, … 8)
11–12	Partners walk forward and do-si-do passing right shoulders and stepping to the right when passing back to back. After passing, each partner moves diagonally (veers) to the right to end in front of a new partner. (Do-si-do, 2, 3, 4, veer, 2, 3, 4)
13–16	Facing a new partner and joining hands, inside circle partner begins with left foot and outside circle begins with right foot doing a 2 heel-toe steps and 4 slide steps counterclockwise. Repeat to the other side sliding clockwise. (Heel, toe, heel toe, slide, slide, slide, slide; heel, toe, heel, toe, slide, slide, slide, slide)
17–20	Partners do a right elbow swing in place for 12 counts using a walking step and use 4 counts to end in promenade position. (Swing, 2, 3, …12, promenade position 15, 16)
21–24	In promenade position, partners walk forward counterclockwise 16 steps and end facing each other. (Promenade, 2, 3, … 16)

Game Activity

Triplet Stoop

Supplies: Music
Skill: Moving rhythmically

Break the class into groups of three. The groups march abreast around the area. On signal, the outside person of the three continues marching in the same direction. The middle person stops and marches in place. The inside player reverses direction and marches in the opposite direction. When the music stops, the groups of three reunite at the spot where the middle player stopped. The last three to join hands and stoop move to the center to wait out one turn. The game can also be played with two or three students designated as extras. They can march wherever they desire. When the music stops, they can join any middle player. Any excluded person becomes an extra.

Pacman

Supplies: Markers in the shape of Pacman
Skills: Fleeing, reaction time

Three students are it and carry the Pacman marker. The remainder of the class is scattered throughout the area, standing on a floor line. Movement can only be made on a line. Begin the game by placing the three taggers at the corners of the perimeter lines. Play is continuous; a player who is tagged takes the marker and becomes a new tagger. If a player leaves a line to escape being tagged, that player must secure a marker and become an additional tagger.

Objectives:

To develop a personalized warm-up
routine that enhances flexibility

To learn the basic concepts of
orienteering

To work with peers to solve
orienteering problems

To show respect for peers regardless of
individual differences in ability

NASPE National Standards:

Introductory Activity: 4, 5, 6
Fitness Activity: 4, 5, 6
Lesson Focus: 4, 5, 6
Game: 2, 3, 5, 6

Equipment Required:

Map direction signs

An orienteering map, instructions,
envelope for each control, and a
clue for each control

Map of school grounds with controls
and landmarks

Instructional Activities	Teaching Hints
Introductory Activity and Fitness Development Activity — Stretching	

Combine the introductory and fitness activities during the track and field unit. This workout helps students learn to stretch and warm up for cross-country running.

Standing Hip Bend	30 seconds
Sitting Stretch	30 seconds
Partner Rowing	60 seconds
Bear Hug (do each leg)	40 seconds
Side Flex (do each leg)	40 seconds
Trunk Twister	30 seconds

Keep stretching activities smooth and sustained. Stretches can be held for 6 to 10 seconds.

Allow students to lead each other in their warm-up routine. A goal should be for students to develop a personal warm-up routine they can use when they are away from school.

Youngsters should work independently during their warm-up. If they desire, they can work with a friend.

Lesson Focus — Orienteering Skills

Orienteering is a navigation and sport activity that incorporates walking or jogging, determining directions, and map reading. The object of the activity is to use a map and compass to locate specific points in a given area. Competitive orienteering can involve skills such as skiing, mountain biking, compass readings and point tracking while navigating a wilderness course designed to test the skills of participants. At the elementary level, the focus of orienteering is to teach students fundamental concepts such as recognizing directions (north, south, east, and west) and map reading.

Determining directions

For many students, learning directions is difficult. One strategy is to mark the walls in the gymnasium with an N, S, E, or W to identify compass directions. This allows students to learn the relationship of each direction. For example, when facing east, north is to the left. Another strategy is to mark landmarks on the school grounds. The slide on the south side of the playground could have an "S" painted on it. Similarly, the fence on the east side of the school grounds could have an "E" painted, or hung, on it. These strategies allow teachers to teach directions inside and outside.

Older children can be taught to determine directions by looking at the sun. The sun always rises in the east. Thus, if students are looking at the sun in the morning, west is always behind them. Another way to teach this concept is to know that in the morning one's shadow points west. Next, students can transfer what was learned in the gym and know that if they are facing east, to the left is north and to the right is south. Conversely, in the afternoon, when students look at the sun, their shadow points east; to the right is north and to the left is south. This will take time for students to process and understand. Since most physical education classes occur at the same time each day, students will be able to learn one method before another is presented.

Introduce map directions by placing a large N, S, E, and W on the appropriate walls.

Refer to the walls as the East wall or the North wall when giving directions. For example, "When I say go, hustle to the red line closest to the East wall."

Use small instructional bouts such as "If we run from this wall (pointing to the East wall) to that wall (pointing to the west wall) what direction are we moving" to introduce directional travel. Presenting this information in a variety of lessons leading up to orienteering will help set the stage for those lessons. For example, if working on basketball passing with a partner direction might be "When I say go, work on your overhead pass with one partner facing north and one facing south."

Introduce students to basic symbols used to designate landmarks and controls. Controls refer to the specific locations students are challenged to find

Reading a map

Most classrooms have maps and globes that help students understand the idea of a map reading. Reading a map involves determining landmarks and directions. For elementary students in a gymnasium, this could be recognizing doors, the clock, or posters on a wall when shown a map of the gymnasium. This will involve students recognizing symbols.

In order to read a map, students must orient the map. This involves turning the map until what is in front of the student in the gymnasium is in front of the student on the map. For example, students may be standing in the four square court in the southeast corner of the gym facing the side door on the west wall. They would then turn the map until the southeast corner of the gym on the map is closest to them and the west wall is farthest away. Teachers can give instruction such as "Standing where you are, orient your map to the clock." Students can also be taught to keep their thumb where they are on the map and move their thumb as they move. This is called "thumbing."

on an orienteering course. See Chapter 23 of *DPE* test for examples of maps with symbols.

If pencils are needed, for safety reasons, provide students with a pencil box or folder to carry all of their materials (maps, pencils, etc.).

Orienteering Activities

Scavenger Hunt

Playing Area: Entire gymnasium or designated teaching area
Players: Individuals, partners, or small groups of 3–4
Supplies: An orienteering map, instructions, an envelope for each control, a clue for each control
Skills: Map reading, problem solving

An orienteering course is set up similar to those presented above. The activity is taught and participated in just as an orienteering course. The only exception is that at each control, youngsters collect a clue that is part of a series of clues to be collected at each control. At the conclusion of the course, each team must then use the clues to solve the puzzle. The following is a list of possible puzzles to be solved.

- At each control students collect an index card with a single letter. All of the letters together spell out O-R-I-E-N-T-E-E-R-I-N-G.
- A picture is cut into the same number of pieces as there are controls and pasted onto an index card. At each control, groups collect a piece of the puzzle that they will assemble into a picture after completing the course.
- Each word of a question such as "What is an important part of a healthy lifestyle?" Each group will probably come up with a different answer such as, physical activity, a balanced diet, or not smoking.
- The letters to two or three of a class's spelling words could be used as well. This will require students to unscramble the letters to spell the words. This is also an excellent method of reinforcing classroom content without sacrificing physical education objectives.

School Ground Orienteering

Playing Area: School grounds
Players: Groups of 1, 2, 3, or 4
Supplies: Map of school grounds with landmarks and controls
Skills: Map reading, cooperation

This activity is a follow-up, or progression, from **Gymnasium Orienteering** (see Chapter 23 in *DPE*). Thus, the process of planning is identical. Depending on the classes' familiarity with finding N, S, E, and W outside, the instructions may have to change. For example, rather than an instruction of "Move northwest from control #7 to find control #8," the control may read "From control #7, move towards the slide to find control #8." Make all controls visible so you can keep all students in sight. Prior to this activity students should be given instructions regarding what area they will use. For example, students could be told that there will be no controls on the K–2 playground, or in front of the school.

Teaching tips: For additional challenge, remove the numbers from each control. Just as with *Gymnasium Orienteering*, students will have to use the instructions and their map-reading skills to find the controls.

Objectives:
To understand the principles of
  stability and balance
To control the body weight in a variety
  of tumbling and stunt activities
To participate in "one-on-one"
  competition and accept the outcome

NASPE National Standards:
Introductory Activity: 1
Fitness Activity: 1, 4, 5, 6
Lesson Focus: 2, 3, 5
Game: 1, 3

Equipment Required:
Music and equipment for Challenge
  Course
Tumbling mats
Hoops for game activity

Instructional Activities	Teaching Hints

Introductory Activity — Marking

Each child has a partner who is somewhat equal in ability. Under control, one partner runs, dodges, and tries to lose the other, who must stay within 3 ft of the runner. On signal, both stop. Chasers must be able to touch their partners to say that they have marked them. Partners then change roles.

Allow a point to be scored only when they touch a specified body part (i.e., knee, elbow, left hand).

Fitness Development Activity — Challenge Course

Design a course around the perimeter of the area using some of the following ideas:
1. Step on jumping box, dismount to tumbling mat, and do a forward roll.
2. Run and weave through four wands held upright by cones.
3. Handwalk across a horizontal ladder or do a flexed-arm hang from a climbing rope for 5 seconds.
4. Step on and off three jumping boxes (small-large-small)
5. Agility run through hoops.
6. Perform jump turns.
7. Leap over a magic rope held taut with two chairs or jumping boxes.
8. Hop on one foot.
9. Do a log roll across a tumbling mat.
10. Alternate going over and under six obstacles (cones and wands or hoops).
11. Crouch jump or scooter movements the length of a balance-beam bench.
12. Slide through a parallel tumbling mat maze (mats stood on their sides).

Use taped intervals of music and silence. When the music is playing, students travel through the challenge course. When the music stops, youngsters do some stretching and strength development exercises. This gives them a chance to recover aerobically.

Distribute students throughout the course rather than lining them up at a starting point. Faster moving students can pass on the outside.

Change directions periodically to prevent a build-up of students at one station.

Lesson Focus — Gymnastics Skills (2)

Tumbling and Inverted Balances
Judo Roll

For a left Judo Roll, stand facing the mat with the feet well apart and the left arm extended at shoulder height. Bring the arm down and throw the left shoulder toward the mat in a rolling motion, with the roll made on the shoulder and the upper part of the back. Reverse for a right Judo Roll. Both right and left Judo Rolls should be practiced. Later, a short run and a double-foot takeoff should precede the roll. The Judo Roll is essentially a Forward Roll with the head turned to one side. The point of impact is the back of one shoulder and the finish is a return to the standing position.

Cartwheel

Start with the body in an erect position, arms outspread and legs shoulder width apart. Bend the body to the right and place the right hand on the floor. Follow this, in sequence, by the left hand, the left foot, and the right foot. Perform with a steady rhythm. Each body part should touch the floor at evenly spaced intervals. The body should be straight and extended when in the inverted position. The entire body must be in the same plane throughout the stunt, and the feet must pass directly overhead.

Cartwheel and Round-Off

Practice the Cartwheel, adding a light run with a skip for a takeoff. To change to a Round-Off, place the hands somewhat closer together during the early Cartwheel action. Bring the feet together and make a quarter turn to land on both feet, with the body facing the starting point. A Backward Roll can follow the Round-Off.

Five groups of activities in this lesson ensure that youngsters receive a variety of experiences. Pick a few activities from each group and teach them alternately. For example, teach an individual stunt or two, then a tumbling skill or inverted balance, followed by a balance stunt, etc. Give equal time to each group of activities.

Children who have difficulty with the Cartwheel should be instructed to concentrate on taking the weight of the body on the hands in succession. They need to get the feel of the weight support and later can concentrate on getting the body into proper position. After the class has had some practice in doing Cartwheels, a running approach with a skip can be added before takeoff.

Advanced Forward and Backward Roll Combinations

Put together different combinations of Forward Rolls and Backward Rolls. The emphasis should be on choice, exploration, and self-discovery. Variations can involve different approaches, execution acts, and finishes.

Try the following variations of the Forward Roll.

1. Roll while holding the toes, heels, ankles, or a wand.
2. As above, but cross the hands.
3. Roll with hands on the knees or with a ball between the knees.

Try the following suggestions with the Backward Roll.

1. Begin with a Stiff-Legged Sit-down and go into the roll.
2. Roll to a finish on one foot only.
3. Roll with a ball between the knees.

Balance Stunts

Long Reach

Place a beanbag about 3 ft in front of a line. Keeping the toes behind the line, lean forward on one hand and reach out with the other hand to touch the beanbag. Recover in one clean, quick movement to the original position, lifting the supporting hand off the floor. Increase the distance of the bag from the line.

Toe Jump

Hold the left toes with the right hand. Jump the right foot through without losing the grip on the toes. Try with the other foot. (Teachers should not be discouraged if only a few can do this stunt; it is quite difficult.)

Front Seat Support

Sit on the floor, with the legs together and forward. Place the hands flat on the floor, somewhat between the hips and the knees, with fingers pointed forward. Push down so the hips come off the floor, with the weight supported on the hands and heels. Next, lift the heels and support the entire weight of the body on the hands for 3 to 5 seconds. (Someone can help the performer get into position by giving slight support under the heels.)

Individual Stunts

Walk-Through

From a front-leaning rest position, walk the feet through the hands, using tiny steps, until the body is fully extended with the back to the floor. Reverse the body to original position. The hands stay in contact with the floor throughout.

Jump-Through

Starting in a front-leaning rest position, jump the feet through the arms in one motion. Reverse with another jump and return to original position. The hands must push off sharply from the floor, so the body is high enough off the floor to allow the legs to jump under. (Some children may find it easier to swing a little to the side with one leg, going under the lifted hand.)

Circular Rope Jump

Crouch down in a three-quarter knee bend, holding a folded jump rope in one hand. Swing the rope under the feet in a circular fashion, jumping it each time. Reverse the direction of the rope. Work from both right and left sides with either a counterclockwise or clockwise turn of the rope.

Bouncer

Start in a push-up position. Bounce up and down with the hands and feet leaving the ground at the same time. Try clapping while doing this. Move in various directions. Turn around.

Partner and Group Stunts

Two-Way Wheelbarrow

One child holds two wheelbarrows, but with one in front and one behind. The child secures the front wheelbarrow first in a normal wheelbarrow position. The back wheelbarrow assumes position by placing the ankles over the already established hand position of the holder.

Scatter tumbling mats throughout the area so that there is little standing in line waiting for a turn.

Do not perform many repetitions of tumbling and inverted balances. For most children, limiting the number of forward or backward roll repetitions to four or five will prevent fatigue and injury.

No youngster should be expected to roll over if they fear getting hurt. In stunts and tumbling, it is important that the student decide if they are capable and confident enough to try the activity.

Youngsters can do many of the activities around their mats. Many of the activities in this unit do not have to be performed on the mat.

A major concern for safety is the neck and back region. Overweight children are at greater risk and might be allowed to avoid tumbling and inverted balances.

Circular Rope Jump Variations:
1. Perform the rope jump with a partner.
2. Jump using different foot patterns (e.g., one foot or alternate feet) and using slow and fast time.
3. Establish standards for declaring a class champion in different areas. Some categories could be maximum number of turns in 30 seconds, most unique routine, and most jumps without a miss.

Partner Rising Sun

Partners lie facedown on the floor, with heads together and feet in opposite directions. They hold a volleyball or a basketball (or a ball of similar size) between their heads. Working together, they stand up and return to position while retaining control of the ball. Do not touch the ball with the hands.

Triple Roll

Three children get down on their hands and knees on a mat, with heads all in the same direction to one of the sides. The performers are about 4 ft apart. Each is numbered—1, 2, or 3—with the number 1 child in the center. Number 2 is on the right and number 3 is on the left. Number 1 starts rolling toward and under number 2, who projects upward and over number 2. Number 2 is then in the center and rolls toward number 3, who projects upward and over number 2. Number 3, in the center, rolls toward and under number 1, who, after clearing number 3, is back in the center. Each performer in the center thus rolls toward and under the outside performer.

Partner Rising Sun: A slightly deflated ball works best. Some caution is necessary to prevent bumping heads if the ball is suddenly squeezed out.

Triple Roll: Children should be taught that as soon as they roll to the outside, they must get ready to go over the oncoming child from the center. There is no time for delay. The upward projection of the body to allow the rolling child to go under is important.

Combatives

Palm Push

Starting Position: Contestants face each other, standing 12 in. apart. They place the palms of their hands together and must keep them together throughout the contest.

Action: Try to push the opponent off balance.

Bulldozer

Starting Position: Opponents are on their hands and feet (not knees), facing each other, with right shoulders touching.

Action: Try to push (not bump) each other backward. Pushing across the mat or across a restraining line determines the winner. Change shoulders and repeat.

Breakdown

Starting Position: Opponents are in a front-leaning rest (push-up) position, facing each other.

Action: Using one hand, try to break down the other's position by pushing or dislodging his support while maintaining your own position.

Elbow Wrestle

Starting Position: Contestants lie on the floor or sit at a table and face each other. Their right hands are clasped, with right elbows bent and resting on the surface, and right forearms pressed against each other.

Action: Force the other's arm down while keeping the elbows together. Raising the elbow from the original position is a loss.

When doing combatives consider the following instructional procedures:

Safety factors must be emphasized. Youngsters should be matched for size; a common method is to ask students to pair up with someone who is similar in height. The length of bouts should be short—usually 5–7 seconds of contesting is adequate. Children should freeze immediately when the whistle is blown.

Instructions for the contest should be as explicit as necessary. Starting positions should be defined so that both contestants begin in an equal and neutral position. What constitutes a win and the number of trials permitted should be defined.

Develop a system of rotation, so that youngsters have more than one opponent. Rotating assures that one child will not continually dominate another.

Game Activity

All Aboard (Cooperative Activity)

Formation: Entire class scattered with hoops spread through area

Supplies: 15 hoops

Students are challenged to get as many students as possible into one hoop placed on the ground. In order for a person to be considered "on board," one foot must be touching the ground inside of the hoop and no body parts touching the floor outside the hoop. One technique to lead up to this activity is to play Musical Hoops. Hoops are scattered throughout the gym and music is playing. When the music stops, students move to a hoop placing at least 1 ft inside the hoop. More than 1 student can be in a hoop. Each time the music plays the teacher removes 1 or 2 hoops until only enough hoops remain for all students to be aboard.

Over the Wall

Supplies: None

Skills: Running, dodging

Two parallel goal lines are drawn about 60 ft apart. Two additional parallel lines about 3 ft apart are laid out parallel to the goal lines in the middle of the game area. This is the wall. Two or three players are it and stand on the wall. All of the other players are behind one of the goal lines. The tagger calls "Over the wall." All of the players must then run across the wall to the other goal line. The taggers try to tag any crossing player. Anyone caught helps catch the others. Players also are considered caught when they step on the wall. They must clear it with a leap or a jump and cannot step on it anywhere, including on the lines. After crossing over to the other side safely, players wait for the next call. The game can be made more difficult by increasing the width of the wall. Taggers can step on or run through the wall at will.

Objectives:

To run rhythmically to the beat of a
tambourine

To perform sustained fitness activity

To be able to perform a variety of folk
dances

To understand the social significance
of folk dances

NASPE National Standards:

Introductory Activity: 1, 5

Fitness Activity: 1, 3, 4, 5, 6

Lesson Focus: 1, 3, 5, 6

Game: 1, 2, 3, 5

Equipment Required:

Equipment and music for Challenge
Course

Music for rhythmic activities

Cageball and 15 foam balls (8")

Pinnies

Instructional Activities	Teaching Hints

Introductory Activity — European Running with Variations

Students move around the area to the beat of a tambourine. The step is a trot with
the knees lifted. Emphasize proper spacing and moving rhythmically. Stop on a
double beat of the tambourine. Try some of the following variations:

1. Clap hands on every fourth beat.
2. Stamp foot on every second beat.
3. On signal, make a complete turn using four running steps.
4. On signal, stop, pivot and move in the opposite direction.
5. Let a student lead the class through various formations.

Have the leader move in different shapes
and designs. Have class freeze and see if
they can identify the shape or formation.

At times, stop the drumbeat and have the
class continue running. Challenge them to
maintain the rhythm with their feet.
Avoid the tendency to speed the rhythm.

Fitness Development Activity — Challenge Course

Design a course around the perimeter of the area using some of the following ideas:

1. Step on jumping box, dismount to tumbling mat, and do a forward roll.
2. Run and weave through four wands held upright by cones.
3. Handwalk across a horizontal ladder or do a flexed-arm hang from a climbing
   rope for 5 seconds.
4. Step on and off three jumping boxes (small-large-small).
5. Agility run through hoops.
6. Perform jump turns.
7. Leap over a magic rope held taut with two chairs or jumping boxes.
8. Hop on one foot.
9. Do a log roll across a tumbling mat.
10. Alternate going over and under six obstacles (cones and wands or hoops).
11. Crouch jump or scooter movements the length of a balance-beam bench.
12. Slide through a parallel tumbling mat maze (mats stood on their sides).

Use taped intervals of music and silence.
When the music is playing, students
travel through the challenge course.
When the music stops, youngsters do
some stretching and strength
development exercises. This gives them a
chance to recover aerobically.

Distribute students throughout the
course rather than lining them up at a
starting point. Faster moving students
can pass on the outside.

Change directions periodically to prevent
a build-up of students at one station.

Lesson Focus — Rhythmic Movement Skills (2)

Make dances easy for students to learn by implementing some of the following techniques:

Rhythms should be taught like other sport skills. Avoid striving for perfection so students know it is acceptable to make
mistakes. Teach a variety of dances rather than one or two in depth in case some students find it difficult to master a specific
dance.

1. Teach the dances without using partners.
2. Allow youngsters to move in any direction without left-right orientation.
3. Use scattered formation instead of circles.
4. Emphasize strong movements such as clapping and stamping to increase involvement.
5. Play the music at a slower speed when first learning the dance.

Hora (Hava Nagila) (Israeli)

Music Source: WWCD-3528; WWC-3528

Formation: Single circle, facing center, hands joined. The circle can be partial.

Note: The hora is regarded as the national dance of Israel. It is a simple dance that expresses joy. The traditional hora is done
in circle formation, with the arms extended sideward and the hands on the neighbors' shoulders. It is easiest to introduce the
dance step individually. Once the step is learned, youngsters can join hands and practice the circle formation
counterclockwise or clockwise. The clockwise version is presented here.

Directions:

Measures	Action
1–3	Step left on the left foot. Cross the right foot in back of the left, with the weight on the right. Step left on the left foot and hop on it, swinging the right foot forward. Step-hop on the right foot and swing the left foot forward. The same step is repeated over and over. (Side, behind, side, swing; side, swing)

The circle may move to the right also, in which case the same step is used, but the dancers begin with the right foot.

Limbo Rock

Music Source: WWCD-4903

Formation: Single circle or scattered

Directions:

Measures	Part I Action
1–2	Touch left foot in. Touch left foot out. Three steps in place. (In, out, left, right, left)
3–4	Repeat measures 1 and 2 beginning with opposite foot. (In, out, right, left, right)
5–8	Repeat measures 1–4.

Measures	Part II Action
9–10	Swivel toes right, swivel heels right. Repeat and straighten feet. (Swivel, 2, 3, straighten)
11–12	Repeat beats 1 and 2 beginning with swivel toes left.
13–14	Jump in, clap; jump out, clap. (Jump, clap, jump, clap)
15–16	Repeat measures 13 and 14. Variation:

Teton Mountain Stomp (American)

Music Source: WWCD-FDN

Formation: Single circle of partners in closed dance position, partners A facing counterclockwise, partners B facing clockwise.

Directions:

Measures	Action
1–4	Step to the left toward the center of the circle on the left foot, close right foot to the left, step again to the left on the left foot, stomp right foot beside the left but leave the weight on the left foot. Repeat this action, but start on the right foot and move away from the center. (Side, close; side, stomp; side, close; side, stomp)
5–8	Step to the left toward the center on the left foot; stomp the right foot beside the left. Step to the right away from the center on the right foot, and stomp the left foot beside the right. In "banjo" position (modified closed position with right hips adjacent), partner A takes four walking steps forward, while partner B takes four steps backward, starting on the right foot. (Side, stomp, side, stomp; walk, 2, 3, 4)
9–12	Partners change to sidecar position (modified closed position with left hips adjacent) by each making a one half turn to the right in place, A remaining on the inside and B on the outside. A walks backward while B walks four steps forward. Partners change back to banjo position with right hips adjacent by each making a left-face one half turn; then they immediately release from each other. A walks forward four steps to meet the second B approaching, while B walks forward four steps to meet the second A approaching. (Change, 2, 3, 4; new partner, 2, 3, 4)
13–16	New partners join inside hands and do four two-steps forward, beginning with A's right foot and B's left. (Step, close, step; repeat four times)

D'Hammerschmiedsgselln (Bavarian)

Music Source: WWCD-TC1; WWC-TC1

Skills: Clapping routine, step-hops

Formation: Circle of four

Directions: Translated, the title of the dance means "The Journey Blacksmith."

Measures	Action
1–16	First opposites do a clapping pattern beginning on the first count of measure 1, while the other pair does a clapping pattern beginning on the first count of measure 2. The six-count pattern is performed as follows: With both hands, slap own thighs (count 1), slap own chest (count 2), clap own hands (count 3), clap right hands (count 4), clap left hands (count 5), and clap opposite's hands (count 6). (Thighs, chest, together, right, left, both) Repeat the six-count pattern seven additional times.
	Part I
17–24	Join hands and circle left with eight step-hops. (Step-hop, 2-hop, … 8-hop)
25–32	Circle right in the same manner. (Step-hop, 2-hop, … 8-hop)
33–48	Repeat the chorus action.
	Part II—Star
49–56	Right-hand star with eight step-hops. (Step-hop, 2-hop, … 8-hop)
57–64	Left-hand star in the same manner. (Step-hop, 2-hop, … 8-hop)
65–80	Repeat the chorus action.

Part III—Big Circle

81–88   Circles of four open to form one large circle, and circle left with eight step-hops. (Step-hop, 2-hop, ... 8-hop)

89–96   Reverse direction, continuing with eight step-hops. (Step-hop, 2-hop, ... 8-hop)

Variation: As a mixer, try the following sequence.

Measures Action

1–16   Use the chorus clapping pattern described.

17–24   As in Part I or II, circle left, or do a right-hand star with step-hops (or simple walking steps).

25–32   Do eight step-hops with the corner in general space or in any comfortable position, progressing anywhere.

Repeat the entire sequence with a new foursome.

Doudlebska Polka (Czechoslovakian)

Music Source: WWCD-572; WWC-572

Skills: Polka step, walking, clapping pattern

Formation: Make either one large circle or several smaller circles scattered around the floor. The following description is for one large circle.

Directions:

Measures Part I Action

1–16   Partners assume the Varsouvienne position and do 16 polka steps around the circle, one couple following another. (Polka, 2, 3, ... 16)

Part II Action

17–32   Partner A puts the right arm around partner B's waist as they stand side by side, while B puts the left hand on A's right shoulder. A puts the left hand on the shoulder of the A in front. This closes the circle. Partner A moves sideward to the center to catch up with the A ahead. In this position, all march forward counterclockwise and sing loudly "La, la, la," and so forth. This takes 32 walking steps. (Walk, 2, 3, ... 32)

Part III Action

33–48   Partner A face the center, and partner B drop behind their partner. B turns to face the other way, clockwise, and polka around the circle (around A) with their hands on hips. At the same time, A, face center, clap a rhythm as follows: Clap hands twice, then extend both hands, palms outward, toward the neighbor on each side, and clap hands once with the neighbor. Repeat this pattern over and over. For variation, A may slap a thigh occasionally, or duck down, or cross her arms when clapping the neighbor's hand. (A: Clap, clap, out; Repeat 16 times) (B: Polka, 2, 3, ... 16)

At the end of Part III, partner A turns around, takes whichever partner B is behind them, and resume the dance from the beginning. If some children are without a partner, they move to the center and find a partner.

Extra children can enter the dance during the clapping part for partner A, and some can join the ring to polka around the outside. Those left without a partner wait for the next turn. When the group is large, several circles can be made, and it is perfectly proper for unpartnered children to steal into another circle. The polka in this case is done anywhere around the room. During the march, make circles of any number of people.

Kalvelis (Little Blacksmith) (Lithuanian)

Music Source: WWCD-WOF3

Skills: Polka step, swing, clapping pattern, grand right and left

Formation: Single circle of couples facing center, partner B on partner A's right, all hands joined in a single circle with the right foot free.

Directions:

Measures Part I Action

1–8   Circle right with seven polka steps, ending with three stamps. (Circle and, 2 and, 3 and, 4 and, 5 and, 6 and, 7 and, stamp, stamp, stamp)

9–16   Circle left with seven polka steps, ending with three stamps. (Circle and, 2 and, 3 and, 4 and, 5 and, 6 and, 7 and, stamp, stamp, stamp)

Chorus

1–2   Clap own hands four times, alternating, left hand onto own right, then right hand onto own left. (Clap, 2, 3, 4)

3–4   Right elbow swing with four skips. (Swing, 2, 3, 4)

5–6   Repeat the clapping pattern of measures 1 and 2. (Clap, 2, 3, 4)

7–8   Left elbow swing with four skips. (Swing, 2, 3, 4)

9–16   Repeat the pattern of measures 1–8.

Part II Action

1–8   Partner B dance three polka steps forward toward the center, ending with three stamps. Then turn to face their partner and return to place with three polka steps forward, ending with three stamps, facing center again. (Step-close-step-hop; step-close-step-hop; step-close-step-hop; stamp, stamp, stamp)

| 9–16 | Partner A repeat the pattern of measures 1–8, but dance more vigorously, stamping on the first beat of each measure. (Step-close-step-hop; step-close-step-hop; step-close-step-hop; stamp, stamp, stamp) |

Chorus

| 1–16 | As described above. |

Part III Action

| 1–16 | Grand right and left around the circle with 16 polka steps, meeting a new partner on the last measure. (Step-close-step-hop; repeat 16 times) |

Chorus

| 1–16 | As described, but with a new partner. |

Game Activity

Cageball Target Throw

Supplies: A cageball or large beach ball (18" to 30".), 15 foam balls (8")

Skill: Throwing

An area about 20 ft wide is marked across the center of the playing area, with a cageball in the center. The object of the game is to throw the foam balls against the cageball, thus forcing it across the line in front of the other team. Players may come up to the line to throw, but they may not throw while inside the cageball area. A player may enter the area, however, to recover a ball. No one is to touch the cageball at any time, nor may the cageball be pushed with a ball in the hands of a player. If the cageball seems to roll too easily, it should be deflated slightly.

Stranded (Cooperative Activity)

Formation: Squads of 5 to 6 students

Supplies: 1 tumbling mat, 3 hoops (or volleyball standards), 2 scooters, and 1 long jump rope per team

The objective of this challenge is to get all team members from a capsized, but floating, boat (represented by a tumbling mat), across the river via 3 islands in the river, to the shore. Each island (represented by a hoop) is approximately 15 ft apart from the others and has two team members on it. The remainder of the team is positioned on a boat, or mat. The students on the boat have 2 scooters and a 16 to 20 ft. long jump rope. While on the scooters, students may not be pushed by other students or pulled using the rope; they must find a way to move without touching the "water." Any student touching the water must return to the boat.

Objectives:
To learn the basic rules of basketball
To participate in a self-directed
manner in basketball drills
To work with teammates in basketball
lead-up games

NASPE National Standards:
Introductory Activity: 1, 2, 5
Fitness Activity: 1, 4, 5, 6
Lesson Focus: 2, 3, 5
Game: 2, 3, 5

Equipment Required:
One junior basketball or 8" foam ball
for each student
Cones, signs, and tape for Partner
Aerobic and Resistance Exercises
Flags and pinnies for lead-up games
Hoops or individual mats for lead-up
games

Instructional Activities	Teaching Hints

Introductory Activity — Dribble and Pivot

Students acquire a basketball or playground ball and begin dribbling around the area. On signal, they stop and pivot. On the command "go," they begin dribbling again.

Alternate right and left hands while dribbling.

Change the pivot foot every other time.

Fitness Development Activity — Partner Aerobic Fitness and Resistance Exercises

Students find a partner and lead each other in aerobic activities. Partners switch leader and follower roles after each partner resistance exercise. This routine assumes that students have previous aerobic fitness experience. If not, the aerobic activities will have to be led by the teacher.

Bounce and Clap	25 seconds
Arm Curl-Up	45 seconds
Jumping Jack variations	25 seconds
Camelback	45 seconds
Lunge variations	25 seconds
Fist pull apart	45 seconds
Directional Runs	25 seconds
Scissors	45 seconds
Rhythmic Running	25 seconds
Butterfly	45 seconds
Bounce with Body Twist	25 seconds
Resistance Push-Up	45 seconds

Walk, stretch, and relax for a minute or two.

Tape alternating segments of silence and music to signal duration of exercise. Music segments indicate aerobic activity (25 seconds), while intervals of silence announce partner resistance exercises (45 seconds).

Teach the exercises first; see Chapter 13 for complete descriptions. A sign with aerobic activities on one side and partner resistance exercises on the other help students remember the activities. The signs can be held upright by cones and shared by 2–4 students.

Take 6–10 seconds to complete a resistance exercise.

Lesson Focus — Basketball Skills (1)

Skills
Practice the following skills:
1. Chest (or Two-Hand) Pass
    For the chest, or two-hand pass, one foot is ahead of the other, with the knees flexed slightly. The ball is released at chest level, with the fingers spread on each side of the ball. The elbows remain close to the body, and the ball is released by extending the arms and snapping the wrists as one foot moves toward the receiver.
2. Catching
    Receiving the ball is a most important fundamental skill. Many turnovers involve failure to handle a pass properly. The receiver should move toward the pass with the fingers spread and relaxed, reaching for the ball with elbows bent and wrists relaxed. The hands should give as the ball comes in.
3. Dribbling
    Dribbling is used to advance the ball, break for a basket, or maneuver out of a difficult situation. The dribbler's knees and trunk should be slightly flexed, with hands and eyes forward. The fingertips propel the ball with the hand cupped and relaxed. There is little arm motion. Students tend to slap at the ball rather than push it. The dribbling hand should be alternated.

Instructional cues help students focus on proper performance of passing.
1. Fingers spread with thumbs behind the ball.
2. Step forward, extend arms, and rotate hands slightly inward.
3. Throw at chest level to the receiver.
4. For bounce passes, bounce the ball past the halfway point nearer the receiver.

Instructional cues for catching include the following:
1. Move into the path of the ball.
2. Spread the fingers and catch with the fingertips.
3. Reach and give with the ball (absorb the force of the ball by reaching and bringing the ball to the chest).

4. Shooting—One-Hand (set) Push Shot

The one-hand push shot is used as a set shot for young children. The ball is held at shoulder–eye level in the supporting hand with the shooting hand slightly below center and behind the ball. As the shot begins, the supporting (nonshooting) hand remains in contact as long as possible. The shooting hand then takes over with fingertip control, and the ball rolls off the center three fingers. The hand and wrist follow through, finishing in a flexed position. Vision is focused on the hoop during the shot. Proper technique should be emphasized rather than accuracy.

Drills

Passing and Catching Drills

1. Slide Circle Drill

In the slide circle drill, a circle of 4 to 6 players slides around a person in the center. The center person passes to and receives from the sliding players. After the ball has gone around the circle twice, another player takes the center position.

2. Circle-Star Drill

With only 5 players, a circle-star drill is particularly effective. Players pass to every other player, and the path of the ball forms a star. The star drill works well as a relay. Any odd number of players will cause the ball to go to all participants, assuring that all receive equal practice.

Dribbling Drills

3. Random Dribbling

Each child has a ball. Dribbling is done in place, varied by using left and right hands. Develop a sequence of body positions (i.e., standing, kneeling, lying on the side, on two feet and one hand). Dribble with each hand.

4. One-Hand Control Drill

Begin with the right hand holding the ball. Make a half circle around the right leg to the back. Bounce the ball between the legs (back to front) and catch it with the right hand and move it around the body again. Change hands.

5. Obstacle, or Figure-Eight, Dribbling

For obstacle, or figure-eight, dribbling, three or more obstacles are positioned about 5 ft apart. The first player at the head of each file dribbles in and around each obstacle, changing hands so that the hand opposite the obstacle is the one always used.

Dribbling and Pivoting Drills

6. File Drill

For the file drill, each player in turn dribbles forward to a designated line, stops, pivots, faces the file, passes back to the next player, and runs to a place at the end of the line. The next player repeats the pattern.

7. Dribble-and-Pivot Drill

For the dribble-and-pivot drill, players are scattered by pairs around the floor. One ball is required for each pair. On the first whistle, the front player of the pair dribbles in any direction and fashion on the court. On the second whistle, she stops and pivots back and forth. On the third whistle, she dribbles back and passes to the partner, who immediately dribbles forward, repeating the routine.

Shooting Drills

8. Basic Shooting Drill

In one simple shooting drill, players form files of no more than 4 people, and take turns shooting a long and a short shot or some other prescribed series of shots.

9. Set-Shot Drill

In the set-shot drill, players are scattered around a basket in a semicircle, with a leader in charge. Players should be close enough to the basket so that they can shoot accurately. The leader passes to each in turn to take a shot. The leader chases the ball after the shot.

Instructional cues for dribbling include the following:
1. Push the ball to the floor. Don't slap it.
2. Push the ball forward when moving.
3. Eyes forward and head up.

Shooting instructional cues focus on proper form:
1. Keep the shooting elbow near the body.
2. Bend the knees and use the legs.
3. Release the ball off the fingertips.

Baskets should be lowered to 8 or 9 ft, depending on the size of the youngsters.

Lowered baskets help students shoot with proper form. Shooting is not a throw. If students have to throw the ball at the basket, it is too high.

Practice the skills in an individual manner as much as possible. The best alternative is a ball for every student to shoot and dribble. Reduce taking turns as much as possible when practicing skills.

Use junior basketballs or smaller for third and fourth grade students. It is difficult for students to learn skills with regulation size balls. They are too heavy and large in diameter for youngsters.

Basketball Lead-up Activities

Sideline Basketball

Supplies: A junior basketball, pinnies

Skills: All basketball skills

Divide the class into two teams, each lined up along one side of the court, facing the other. Three or four active players from each team enter the floor to play regulation basketball. The remainder of the players, who stand on the sideline, can catch and pass the ball to the active players. Sideline players may not shoot, nor may they enter the playing floor. They must keep one foot completely out of bounds at all times.

The active players play regulation basketball, with the addition that they must pass and receive the ball three times from sideline players before they can attempt a goal. Sideline players may pass to each other but must pass back to an active player after three sideline passes. The game starts with active players occupying their half of the court. The ball is taken out of bounds under its own basket by the team that was scored on. Play continues until a period of time (1 minute) elapses. The active players then go to the end of their line and three new active players come out from the right. All other players move down and adjust to fill the space left by the new players.

No official out of bounds on the sides is called. The players on that side of the floor simply recover the ball and put it into play with a pass to an active player without delay. Out of bounds on the ends is the same as in regular basketball. If one of the sideline players enters the court and touches the ball, it is a violation, and the ball is awarded out of bounds on the other side to a sideline player of the other team. Free throws are awarded when a player is fouled.

LP 97

DPE Curriculum Guide – Lesson Plans
Basketball Skills and Lead-up Activities (2)
Level III – Week 18

Objectives:
To learn the basic rules of basketball
To participate in a self-directed
    manner in basketball drills
To work with teammates in basketball
    lead-up games

NASPE National Standards:
Introductory Activity: 1, 3, 5
Fitness Activity: 1, 4, 5, 6
Lesson Focus: 2, 3, 5
Game: 2, 3, 5

Equipment Required:
Five hoops and 30 beanbags for
    Barker's Hoopla
Cones, signs, and tape for Partner
    Aerobics and Resistance Exercises
One junior basketball or 8" foam ball
    for each student
Pinnies for lead-up games

Instructional Activities	Teaching Hints

Introductory Activity — Barker's Hoopla

Place one hoop in each of four corners and in the middle of a square playing area. A distance between hoops of 25–30 feet is challenging. Five or six beanbags are placed in each hoop. There are five teams, one beside each hoop (home base). The object is to take beanbags from other hoops and return them to the home base hoop.

Beanbags must be taken *out* of home base hoop and placed in other hoops. It is not acceptable to pass or throw beanbags. No more than one beanbag may moved at one time.

Fitness Development Activity — Partner Aerobic Fitness and Resistance Exercises

Students find a partner and lead each other in aerobic activities. Partners switch leader and follower roles after each partner resistance exercise. This routine assumes that students have previous aerobic fitness experience. If not, the aerobic activities will have to be led by the teacher.

Bounce and Clap	25 seconds
Arm Curl-Up	45 seconds
Jumping Jack variations	25 seconds
Camelback	45 seconds
Lunge variations	25 seconds
Fist pull apart	45 seconds
Directional runs	25 seconds
Scissors	45 seconds
Rhythmic running	25 seconds
Butterfly	45 seconds
Bounce with Body Twist	25 seconds
Resistance Push-Up	45 seconds

Walk, stretch, and relax for a minute or two.

Tape alternating segments of silence and music to signal duration of exercise. Music segments indicate aerobic activity (25 seconds), while intervals of silence announce partner resistance exercises (45 seconds).

Teach the exercises first; see Chapter 13 for complete descriptions. A sign with aerobic activities on one side and partner resistance exercises on the other help students remember the activities. The signs can be held upright by cones and shared by 2–4 students.

Take 6–10 seconds to complete a resistance exercise.

Lesson Focus — Basketball Skills (2)

Skills

Review previously learned skills (lesson #17) including: Chest and bounce passes, catching, dribbling and pivoting, and the one-hand set shot.

Introduce new skills:
1. Defending
    Defending involves bending the knees slightly, spreading the feet, and facing the opponent at a distance of about 3 ft. The weight should be distributed evenly on both feet to allow for movement in any direction. Sideward movement is done with a sliding motion. The defender should wave one hand to distract the opponent and to block passes and shots.
2. Layup Shot
    The layup is a short shot taken when going in toward the basket either after receiving a pass or at the end of a dribble. In a shot from the right side, the takeoff is with the left foot, and vice versa. The ball is carried with both hands early in the shot and then shifted to one hand for the final push. The ball, guided by the fingertips, should be laid against the backboard with a minimum of spin.

Instructional cues for proper defending are:
1. Keep the knees bent.
2. Keep the hands up.
3. Don't cross the feet when moving.

Instructional cues for the layup shot are:
1. Take off on the foot opposite the shooting hand.
2. Lay the ball on the backboard above the basketball.

272

3. Jump Shot

The jump should be straight up, rather than at a forward or backward angle. The ball should be released at the height of the jump. Since the legs cannot be used to increase the force applied to the ball, the jump shot is difficult for the majority of elementary school youngsters. It may be best to avoid teaching the shot to youngsters who lack enough strength to shoot the ball correctly and resort to throwing it. If the jump shot is presented, the basket should be at the lowest level available and a junior-sized basketball used to develop proper shooting habits.

3. Jump upward and slightly forward on the takeoff.

4. Two-Hand Overhead Pass

The two-hand overhead pass is effective against a shorter opponent. The passer is in a short stride position, with the ball held overhead. The momentum of the pass comes from a forceful wrist and finger snap. The pass should take a slightly downward path.

Another way to practice proper form with the jump shot is to use gray foam balls. They are light and can be shot easily by children. Concentrate on proper form rather than making baskets. Reinforce students who use good technique.

Drills

Review and introduce drills from last week's lesson (#17). Introduce the following new drills:

Jump-Shot Drill

The jump-shot drill is similar to the layup drill, except that the incoming shooter receives the ball, stops, and takes a jump shot. The line of shooters should move back so that there is room for forward movement to the shooting spot. As soon as the passer releases the ball to the shooter, he moves to the end of the shooter's line. The shooter goes to the passer's line after shooting

The jump shot drill may be inappropriate for less strong players. They can choose to shoot the layup shot in lieu of the jump shot.

Three Lane Rush Drill

This is a lead-up to the three-player weave, which is difficult for elementary school youngsters to learn. Youngsters are in three lines across one end of the area. The first three players move parallel down the court while passing the ball back and forth to each other. A layup shot can be taken as players near the basket.

1. Use chest and/or bounce passes.
2. "Lead" the receiver with the pass.
3. Follow your pass, going behind the receiver; then cut for basket, awaiting receipt of a pass.

Basketball Lead-up Activities

Sideline Basketball

See the Lesson Plan, Basketball Skills (Week 17) for a complete game description.

Twenty-One

Supplies: A junior basketball

Skills: Shooting

Players are in file formation by teams. Each player is permitted a long shot (from a specified distance) and a follow-up shot. The long shot, if made, counts 2 points and the short shot counts 1 point. The follow-up shot must be made from the spot where the ball was recovered from the first shot. The normal one-two-step rhythm is permitted on the short shot from the place where the ball was recovered. The first player scoring a total of 21 points is the winner. If the ball misses the backboard and basket altogether on the first shot, the second shot must be taken from the corner.

Variations:

1. Start with a simpler game that allows dribbling before the second shot.
2. Allow players to shoot as long as every shot is made. This means that if both the long and the short shot are made, the player goes back to the original position for a third shot. All shots made count and the shooter can continue until a miss.
3. Play with team competition, with each player contributing to the team score.
4. Use various combinations and types of shots.

Lane Basketball

Supplies: Junior basketball, pinnies, cones to mark zones

Skills: All basketball skills

The court is divided into six lanes. Players must stay in their lane and cannot cross the midcourt line. Regular basketball rules prevail, with the exception that players cannot dribble more than three times. Play is started with a jump ball. At regular intervals, youngsters rotate to the next lane to assure they get to play offense and defense. A number of rule changes can be implemented to change the focus of the game. For example, three passes may be required before shooting may occur. Also, to increase the amount of activity, youngsters can move the entire length of the floor within their lane.

One-Goal Basketball

Supplies: A junior basketball, pinnies (optional)

Skills: All basketball skills

This is an excellent class activity if four or more baskets are available. The game is played by two teams according to the rules of basketball but with the following exceptions.

1. When a defensive player recovers the ball, either from the backboard or on an interception, the ball must be taken out beyond the foul-line circle before offensive play is started and an attempt at a goal is made.

2. After a basket is made, the ball is taken in the same fashion away from the basket to the center of the floor, where the other team starts offensive play.

3. Regular free throw shooting can be observed after a foul, or some use can be made of the rule whereby the offended team takes the ball out-of-bounds.

4. An offensive player who is tied up in a jump ball loses the ball to the other team.

5. Individuals are responsible for calling fouls on themselves.

LP 98

Objectives:

To run, stop, and pivot under control
 without falling
To know the elements of proper
 throwing
To throw with maximum velocity

NASPE National Standards:

Introductory Activity: 1, 5
Fitness Activity: 1, 4, 5, 6
Lesson Focus: 2, 3, 5
Game: 1, 2, 3, 5

Equipment Required:

Exercise to music CD
Many types of balls for throwing
Throwing targets; hoops, mats, bowling
 pins, and/or cageball

Instructional Activities	Teaching Hints

Introductory Activity — Run, Stop, and Pivot

The class runs, stops on signal, and pivots. Vary the activity by pivoting on the left foot or the right foot, increasing the circumference, and performing pivots in quick succession. Teach both the stride stop (one foot in front of the other) and the jump stop (with both feet parallel to each other) prior to the pivot.

Emphasize bending the knees and lowering the center of gravity.

Students should continue running after the pivot.

Fitness Development Activity — Exercises to Music

Crab Kicks	25 seconds	Select music that has a strong rhythm
Rope jumping	30 seconds	and easy-to-hear beat. When the music
Windmills	25 seconds	is on, students perform aerobic activities
Walk and do arm circles	30 seconds	(for 30 seconds). When the music is not
Abdominal Crunchers	25 seconds	playing, students perform the strength
Jumping Jack variations	30 seconds	development and flexibility exercises
Side Flex	25 seconds	(25 seconds).
Two-Step or gallop	30 seconds	
Triceps push-ups	25 seconds	See Chapter 13 of the textbook for
Aerobic jumping	30 seconds	descriptions of the exercises.
Push-up challenges	25 seconds	
Leg extensions	30 seconds	Use scatter formation.
Walking to cool down	30 seconds	

Lesson Focus — Throwing Skills

Individual activities

1. Throw balls against the wall. Emphasize the following points:
    a. Start with the feet together.
    b. Start with nonthrowing side to the wall.
    c. Lift both the throwing and nonthrowing arm (to form a "T") in order to assure the throwing arm elbow is lifted and the nonthrowing arm points at the target.
    d. Begin the throw with a step forward with the foot opposite the throwing arm.
    e. Throw as hard as possible.
2. Throw from one side of the gym and try to hit the other wall.
3. If outside, throw as hard and far as possible.

Throwing for form

1. Arrange activities to emphasize proper throwing form. Some suggestions are:
    a. Throwing off a tumbling mat. The slight step down off the mat helps some students develop the forward step with the nonthrowing side foot. The student stands on the edge of the mat and steps to the floor with the nonthrowing side foot as the throw begins. (The other foot remains on the mat.) Use the cues, "step, elbow leads, and throw."
    b. Starting a throw with both feet in a hoop. The thrower must lift the front foot to step out of the hoop. Begin with the nonthrowing side of the body facing the target and both feet inside the hoop. As the throw begins, a forward step is taken with the nonthrowing foot out of the hoop.

Throwing takes a great deal of practice to master. Two major issues to consider when teaching throwing are:
1. How can I arrange my class so students receive the most opportunity to throw?
2. How can I arrange my class so students get to throw with maximum velocity? A mature pattern of throwing cannot be learned if students are not allowed to throw with maximum force.

Proper form and velocity of throws are closely related. A reason for practicing form is to encourage students to think about technique.

Give each student 4 or 5 balls to throw. They can be placed in a Frisbee to keep them from rolling around. When all students are done throwing, they retrieve the same number of balls they have thrown. Another alternative is to

c. Touching a cone behind the thrower. The thrower lines up with a cone about an arm's-length away and near the throwing side (away from the target). As the throwing arm is extended on the backswing, a slight backward reach is made to encourage reaching back in preparation to throw.

d. Throw yarn balls from a standing position 20 ft from the wall. Throw 5 balls, retrieve, and repeat.

e. Throw yarn balls or tennis balls using the proper grip. Throw at bowling pins or hoops leaning against the wall and encourage trying to knock down the hoops. Gradually increase the distance from the wall.

Throwing for velocity

Throwing is a complex skill that cannot be learned by slowing it down. To learn the proper throwing form, students must throw as hard as possible.

1. Throw at mats on the wall
   a. Throw fleece balls hard from 15 to 20 ft.
   b. Retrieve only if the balls roll behind the throwing line.
2. Throw at hoops leaning against the wall and try to knock them down.
3. Throw at bowling pins.
4. Throw outside for distance.
5. Throw at a cageball.

put out a number of buckets filled with balls and place students with a partner. One partner feeds the other a certain number of balls and then they change roles.

Ask a tennis pro or high school for used and worn balls. They work well for throwing.

Throwing for velocity is exciting for youngsters. It can also increase the activity level of the lesson as youngsters retrieve the thrown objects.

A cageball is an excellent target for encouraging throwing velocity. When it is hit, it will move slightly. A goal can be made to move the cageball across a goal line.

Game Activity

In the Prison

Supplies: 15–20 throwing balls

Skill: Throwing

Two teams, one assigned to each half of the gym. Balls (15–20) are placed on the center line. On signal, each team throws the balls to the other side of the gym. The object of the game is to get all the balls into the other team's backcourt area (or prison), which extends 10 ft from the wall. The teacher stops play by blowing a whistle, then counting the number of balls in the "prison."

Snowball

Supplies: 36 yarn balls

Skill: Throwing

Two teams, one assigned to each half of the gym. Each student has a yarn ball. Players can be hit three times. Each time they are hit they call out the number (1, 2, 3) of times they have been hit. After the third hit they must go to the side of the area and count to 25 before they can reenter. Teams must stay in their half of the gym.

Center Target Throw

Supplies: Twenty 8" gray foam balls and 20 bowling pins

Skill: Throwing

The area is divided into quadrants. Two teams compete, and each team has its own set of targets (bowling pins) set on a centerline. Half of each team is placed in opposing quadrants with the pins in the middle. Team A, on the left half of the area, has players on both sides of the center line behind restraining lines 15 to 20 ft away from the center target line. Team B is positioned the same way on the right half of the area. Each team tries to knock down all of its bowling pins as quickly as possible.

Target Ball Throw

Supplies: Ten 18" beach balls and 36 yarn balls

Skill: Throwing

Beach balls are placed on the center line of the gym. There are two teams and each must stay in its half of the gym. Players have yarn balls. The object of the game is to roll the beach balls into the other team's court by hitting them with the yarn balls. The team that has the least number of beach balls on its side when the teacher blows the whistle is the winner.

DPE Curriculum Guide – Lesson Plans
Cooperative Game Skills
Level III – Week 20

To apply fundamental skills in a
   unique situation
To learn and practice personal and
   social skills
To work cooperatively in a group setting

NASPE National Standards:
Introductory Activity: 1
Fitness Activity: 1, 4, 5, 6
Lesson Focus: 1, 2, 3, 5, 6
Game: 1, 2, 3, 5, 6

Equipment Required:
Exercise to music CD
Individual mats or hoops
Scooters
Long jump ropes
Balance beams or benches
Balls or beanbags
Tumbling mats
Blindfolds
Marking spots

Instructional Activities	Teaching Hints
Introductory Activity — Agility Run	
Pick two lines or markers 5–10 yd apart. Students run (or use other locomotor movements) back and forth between the lines for a specified time (10, 15, or 20 seconds). Students can add a personal challenge by seeing how many times they can move back and forth within the given time limit.	Students can try this with a partner they pick. They can race each other to the lines and back. Students can walk when necessary.

Fitness Development Activity — Exercises to Music		
Crab Kicks	25 seconds	Select music that has a strong rhythm
Rope jumping	30 seconds	and easy-to-hear beat. When the music
Windmills	25 seconds	is on, students perform aerobic activities
Walk and do arm circles	30 seconds	(for 30 seconds). When the music is not
Abdominal Crunchers	25 seconds	playing, students perform the strength
Jumping Jack variations	30 seconds	development and flexibility exercises
Side Flex	25 seconds	(25 seconds).
Two-Step or gallop	30 seconds	
Triceps push-ups	25 seconds	See Chapter 13 of the textbook for
Aerobic jumping	30 seconds	descriptions of the exercises.
Push-up challenges	25 seconds	
Leg extensions	30 seconds	Use scatter formation.
Walking to cool down	30 seconds	

Lesson Focus and Game Activity — Cooperative Game Skills

Teaching Cooperative Game Skills

1. Set the Stage: During this first step it is the teacher's job to sell the activity with the following information:
   What is the challenge?
   What are the rules?
   What are the consequences for breaking the rules?
   Are there any safety issues that need to be addressed?
   During this step, only the essential information to get the group going is provided. This information can be presented in the form of a descriptive and often imaginary story.

2. Facilitate: Once the stage has been set, the teacher's role is to step back and let the students work. For many teachers this is a difficult task because they want to tell students how to accomplish the task or at least give them a few hints. During this step, it is best to simply answer questions and monitor the group for safety. Success does not always mean the task is accomplished; learning to cooperate is more important than completing the task. Much can be learned and gained from simply working on the task. It is critical that teachers allow time for the final step.

3. Debrief: Debriefing may be the most important component in effectively implementing cooperative activities. The foundation of debriefing is open-ended questions. Question such as "Did that work?" or "Would you do that again?" require a yes or no response and do not foster discussion. The following are examples of open-ended questions:

What did you have to do in order to accomplish the goal?
What does "communicate" mean?
What happened that was positive?
What happened that could have been better?
How could you have changed things?
What does it mean to be patient?
How can you compromise?
What would you have done differently? The same?

Cooperative Activities
Lifeboats
Formation: Groups of 8 to 12 students

Supplies: Two to three individual mats or hoops, two scooters, and one long jump rope per group

The group is positioned on one side of the gym (a slow sinking ship) and given a scooter (lifeboat) and a long jump rope. The objective is to get the entire group from the sinking ship to the mainland (the other side of the gym) using only their lifeboats. Spaced randomly between the starting and stopping points are three individual mats (or hoops), which are islands in the ocean. Any students that touch the gym floor (water) must return to the starting point or island they were on (if hoops are used as islands, inside the hoop does not count as water). Thus, all students must remain on a mat at all times unless they are traveling across the ocean in a lifeboat (scooter). Students may be pulled with the jump rope but they may not be pushed. Students who are transported across the ocean must remain on the mainland and cannot return to the island or lifeboats; however, if they step into the "water" trying to rescue a teammate, they must return to the final island.

Moving Together
Formation: Groups of 4 students

Supplies: None

Groups of 4 students form teams on the sidelines of the teaching area. The objective is for the team to move to the other sideline with the following stipulations:
1. Six feet touching the floor and all team members touching an ankle.
2. Eight body parts (no heads) touching the ground at all times.
3. Half of the team at a high level and half the team at a low level.
4. Every foot touching one other foot.
5. Only four feet can touch the ground.
6. Four feet and one hand must be on the ground.
7. Move with the fewest number of feet possible touching the floor.
8. Move with the most hands and fewest feet touching the floor.

Teaching Tip: Additional challenges can be made by providing the teams with different pieces of equipment to carry while attempting the challenges. To minimize competition provide each group with a list of challenges. Once they have completed one challenge, they choose their next challenge from the list. This provides continuous activity for all groups.

Balance Beam Mixer
Formation: Groups of 8–10 students

Supplies: One low balance beam or bench per group

Students stand shoulder to shoulder on a low balance beam or bench (for younger students) with mats alongside the beam for safety. While remaining on the balance beam or bench, students are challenged to get in order based on the following criteria:
1. Alphabetical order by first name from left to right.
2. Alphabetical order by first name from right to left.
3. Tallest to shortest.
4. Month of birth date (January to December or vice versa).

Group Juggling
Formation: Squads of 5–6 students

Supplies: One ball or beanbag for each student

Teams of 5–6 students are formed and each student has a ball or beanbag. A variety of types of balls will add to the excitement of this activity. On signal (e.g., "one, two, ready, toss"), each team member tosses his ball to another teammate and then catches a ball tossed to him. The objective is to see how many successful tosses can be made in unison. Typically students will toss to the same person each time. A successful toss occurs when all team members catch the ball tossed to them. After several tosses, the teacher gives each group the responsibility of selecting one team to give the signal for their group.

Stranded
Formation: Squads of 5–6 students

Supplies: One tumbling mat, three hoops (or volleyball standards), two scooters, and one long jump rope per team

The objective of this challenge is to get all team members from a capsized, but floating, boat (represented by a tumbling mat), across the river via three islands in the river, to the shore. Each island (represented by a hoop) is approximately 15 ft apart from the others and has two team members on it. The remainder of the team is positioned on a boat, or mat. The students on the boat have two scooters and a 16- to 20-foot-long jump rope. While on the scooters, students may not be pushed by other students or pulled using the rope; they must find a way to move without touching the "water." Any student touching the water must return to the boat.

Centipede

Formation: Entire class shoulder to shoulder

Supplies: None

All students stand shoulder to shoulder on a sideline, facing the same direction, with feet touching the person next to them. The entire class must move to the other sideline without breaking the chain of touching feet. If the chain breaks, the group must take three steps back. Students may put their arms around each other if desired.

Teaching Tip: Some classes may require a progression starting with partners, then small groups, and finally the entire class.

DPE Curriculum Guide – Lesson Plans
Hockey Skills and Lead-up Activities (1)
Level III – Week 21

Objectives:
To lead other students through warm-up activities
To learn hockey skills and apply them in lead-up games
Accept decisions made by game officials in hockey lead-up activities
To play group games and cooperate with teammates

NASPE National Standards:
Introductory Activity: 1
Fitness Activity: 1, 4, 5, 6
Lesson Focus: 2, 3, 5
Game: 2, 3, 5

Equipment Required:
Music and jump ropes for Jackpot Fitness
One jump rope for each student
Hockey stick and puck (fleece ball) for each student
Cones or tumbling mats for goals

Instructional Activities	Teaching Hints

Introductory Activity — Rubber Band

Students begin from a central point with the teacher. On signal, students move away from the teacher with a designated movement such as run, hop sideways, skip backward, double-lame dog, or Carioca. On signal, they sprint back to the central point.

An alternative way of doing rubber band is to give students 5 seconds to see how far they can move. On signal, they return and see if they reach the original point in 5 seconds.

Fitness Development Activity — Aerobic, Strength, and Flexibility Jackpot Fitness

Three different "jackpots" (boxes) are filled with fitness exercises and activities are placed around the teaching area. One jackpot is filled with a variety of strength development activities written on small index cards. A second jackpot is filled with flexibility activities. The third jackpot contains aerobic activities. Students can work individually or with a partner. They begin at one of the jackpots of choice and randomly pick out an activity to perform. If with a partner, they take turns selecting the card from the box. The only stipulations are that they must rotate to a different box each time and cannot select an activity they previously performed. If they pick an activity they performed on a previous stop, they return it to the jackpot and select another.

Allow students to adjust the workload to their level. This implies resting if the rope jumping is too strenuous.

A music interval of 30 seconds signals the duration of fitness activity followed by 10 to 15 second interval used for selecting a new activity from a different jackpot.

Students are expected to perform as many repetitions as possible while the music is playing.

Aerobic Jackpot
1. Carioca around the basketball court.
2. Perform a "mirror drill" with your partner for 30 seconds.
3. Jump rope using both slow and fast time.
4. Tortoise and Hare/Running in place.
5. Marching with high steps around the area.

Strength Jackpot
1. Perform Abdominal Challenges
2. Perform Push-up Challenges
3. Do the Treadmill exercise
4. Do as many Power Jumpers as possible
5. Perform as many Crab Kicks as possible.

Flexibility Jackpot
1. Perform the Bend and Twist exercise.
2. Stretch using the Sitting Stretch.
3. Stretch using the Lower Leg Stretch.
4. Do the Standing Hip Bend.
5. Perform the Body Twist.

Lesson Focus — Hockey Skills (1)

Skills
Practice the following skills:
1. Gripping and carrying the stick.
   The hockey stick should be held with both hands and carried as low to the ground as possible. The basic grip puts the left hand at the top of the stick and the right hand 6 to 12 inches below the left.

To ensure accuracy as well as safety, the stick must not be swung above waist height.

2. Controlled Dribble.

The controlled dribble consists of a series of short taps in the direction in which the player chooses to move. The hands should be spread 10 to 14 inches apart to gain greater control of the stick. As the player becomes more skilled, the hands can be moved closer together. The stick is turned so that the blade faces the ball. The grip should not be changed, but rather, the hands should be rotated until the back of the left hand and the palm of the right hand face the ball. The ball can then be tapped just far enough in front of the player to keep it away from the feet but not more than one full stride away from the stick.

3. Front Field.

For the front field, the student must keep an eye on the ball, move to a point in line with its path, and extend the flat side of the blade forward to meet the ball.

The faster the ball approaches, the more she must learn to give with the stick to absorb the momentum of the ball. The player should field the ball in front of the body and not permit it to get too close.

4. Forehand Pass.

The forehand pass is a short pass that usually occurs from the dribble. It should be taught before driving, because the quick hit requires accuracy rather than distance. The player spreads the feet with toes pointed slightly forward when striking. Approach the ball with the stick held low and bring the stick straight back, in line with the intended direction of the hit. The hands should be the same distance apart as in the carrying position, and the stick should be lifted no higher than waist level. The player's right hand guides the stick down and through the ball. The head should be kept down with the eyes on the ball. A short follow-through occurs after contact.

5. Face-Off

The face-off is used at the start of the game, after a goal, or when the ball is stopped from further play by opposing players. Two players take the face-off, each facing a sideline, with their right sides facing the goal that their team is defending. Each player hits the ground on her side of the ball and the opponent's stick over the ball, alternately, three times. After the third hit the ball is played, and each player attempts to control the ball or to pass it to a teammate. The right hand can be moved down the stick to facilitate a quick, powerful movement. An alternate means of starting action is for a referee to drop the ball between the players' sticks.

6. Goalkeeping

The goalie may kick the ball, stop it with any part of the body, or allow it to rebound off the body or hand. He may not, however, hold the ball or throw it toward the other end of the playing area. The goalkeeper is positioned in front of the goal line and moves between the goal posts. When a ball is hit toward the goal, the goalie should attempt to move in front of the ball and to keep his feet together. This allows the body to block the ball should the stick miss it. After the block, the ball is passed immediately to a teammate.

Drills
The following drills can be used to practice the skills above:
1. Dribbling
   a. Each student has a stick and ball. On signal, change directions while maintaining control of the ball.
   b. Dribble and dodge imaginary tacklers or dodge around a set of cones. Partners may act as tacklers.
   c. Students in pairs—20 ft apart. One partner dribbles toward the other, goes around him or her, and returns to starting point. The first student then drives the ball to the second, who completes the same sequence.
2. Forehand Passing and Front Fielding
   a. From 8–10 ft apart, partners forehand pass and front field the ball back and forth to each other both from moving and stationary positions.
   b. Partners 20 ft apart—players pass the ball back and forth with emphasis on fielding and immediately hitting the ball back.

Dribbling instructional cues:
1. Control the puck. It should always be within reach of the stick.
2. Hold the stick firmly.
3. Keep the elbows away from the body.

Front fielding instructional cues:
1. Field with a "soft stick." This means holding the stick with relaxed hands.
2. Allow the puck to hit the stick and then "give" to make a soft reception.
3. Keep the hands apart on the stick.

Forehand passing instructional cues:
1. Approach the puck with the side facing the direction of the pass.
2. Keep the head down and eyes on the puck.
3. Keep the stick below waist level at all times.
4. Drive the stick through the puck.

Hockey is a rough game when children are not taught the proper methods of stick handling. They need to be reminded often to use caution and good judgment when handling hockey sticks.

Ample equipment increases individual practice time and facilitates skill development. A stick and a ball (puck) for each child are desirable.

If hockey is played on a gym floor, a plastic puck or yarn ball should be used. If played on a carpeted area or outdoors, a whiffle ball is used. An 8-ft folding mat set on its end makes a satisfactory goal.

c. The shuttle turn-back formation, in which two files of 4 or 5 players face each other, can be used. The first person in the file passes to the first person in the other file, who in turn fields the ball and returns the pass. Each player, when finished, goes to the end of the file.

d. The downfield drill is useful for polishing passing and fielding skills while moving. Three files of players start at one end of the field. One player from each file proceeds downfield, passing to and fielding from the others until the other end of the field is reached. A goal shot can be made at this point. The players should remain close together for short passes until a high level of skill is reached.

3. Dodging and Tackling Drills

a. Players are spread out on the field, each with a ball. On command, they dribble left, right, forward, and backward.

On the command "Dodge," the players dodge an imaginary tackler. Players should concentrate on ball control and dodging in all directions.

b. Players work in pairs. One partner dribbles toward the other, who attempts to make a tackle. If the tackle is successful, roles are reversed. This drill should be practiced at moderate speeds in the early stages of skill development.

c. A three-on-three drill affords practice in many skill areas. Three players are on offense and three are on defense. The offense can concentrate on passing, dribbling, and dodging, while the defense concentrates on tackling. A point is given to the offense when they reach the opposite side of the field. The defensive team becomes the offensive team after a score.

Hockey is a team game that is more enjoyable for all when the players pass to open teammates. Excessive control of the ball by one person should be discouraged.

An individual who is restricted to limited activity can be designated as a goalie. This is an opportunity for children with disabilities to participate and receive reinforcement from peers. An asthmatic child, for example, might serve as a goalkeeper.

If fatigue becomes a problem, use rotation and rest periods.

Hockey Lead-up Activities

Lane Hockey

Supplies: Hockey stick per player, puck, two goals
Skills: All hockey skills

The field is divided into 8 lanes (see Chapter 26 for a diagram). A defensive and an offensive player are placed in each of the 8 sections. A goalkeeper for each team is also positioned in front of the goal area. Players may not leave their lane during play. A shot on goal may not be taken until a minimum of two passes has been completed. This rule encourages looking for teammates and passing to someone in a better position before taking a shot on goal.

Encourage players to maintain their spacing during play. The purpose of the lanes is to force players to play a zone rather than swarming to the puck. Rules used for regulation hockey enforce situations not described here. A free hit (unguarded) is awarded a team if a foul occurs. Players should be rotated after a goal is scored or at regular time intervals.

Variation: Increase the number of lanes to 10 or 12. This involves a larger number of players. On a large playing area, the lanes may be broken into thirds rather than halves. Increase the number of passes that should be made prior to a shot on goal.

Goalkeeper Hockey

Supplies: One stick per player, a puck or ball
Skills: Passing, fielding, goalkeeping

Each team occupies two adjacent sides of the square (see Chapter 26 for a diagram). The puck or ball is placed in the center of the square. Team members are numbered consecutively from left to right. The instructor calls two or three numbers. These players enter the playing area and attempt to capture the ball and pass it through the opposing team. A point is scored when the ball goes through the opponent's side. Sideline players are goalies and have the opportunity to practice goalkeeping skills. When a score is made, the active players return to their positions, and new players are called.

Keep track of the numbers called so all players have an equal opportunity to play. Different combinations of numbers can be called.

Sideline Hockey

Supplies: One hockey stick per player, a puck or ball, two 4-by-8-ft folding tumbling mats
Skills: Most hockey skills, except goaltending

Each team is divided into two groups. Three to six players from each team move onto the court; these are the active players. The others will actively participate on the sidelines. No goalkeeper is used. A face-off at the center starts the game and puts the ball into play after each score. Each team on the field, aided by the sideline players, attempts to score a goal. The sideline players help keep the ball in bounds and can pass it onto the court to the active players. Sideline players may pass to an active player or to each other.

Any out-of-bounds play on a sideline belongs to the team guarding that sideline and is immediately put into play with a pass. An out-of-bounds shot over the end line that does not score a goal is put into play by the team defending the goal. The group of players on the field changes places with the sideline players on their team as soon as a goal is scored or after a specified time period.

Illegal touching, sideline violations, and other minor fouls result in loss of the ball to the opposition. Roughing fouls and illegal striking should result in banishment to the sideline for the remainder of the competitive period. Try to encourage team play and passing strategies rather than having all players charge and swarm the puck. An effective rule is to require active players to make three passes to their teammates before taking a shot on goal. This makes all players an important part of the game.

DPE Curriculum Guide – Lesson Plans
Hockey Skills and Lead-up Activities (2)
Level III – Week 22

Objectives:

To keep away an object (puck) from opponents in three-on-three game

To strike a hockey puck so it travels in the desired direction

To understand the basic rules of hockey

NASPE National Standards:

Introductory Activity: 1, 3, 5

Fitness Activity: 1, 4, 5, 6

Lesson Focus: 2, 3, 5

Game: 2, 3, 5

Equipment Required:

Music and jump ropes for Jackpot Fitness

Hockey stick and puck for each student

Cones or tumbling mats for goals

Instructional Activities	Teaching Hints

Introductory Activity — Move and Exercise on Signal

Students do a locomotor movement, stop on signal and perform an exercise such as the following suggested activities: Push-Ups, Curl-Ups, Crab Kick, V-Ups, and Treadmills.

Use any locomotor movement. Students should get up and move as soon as they have completed the exercise.

Fitness Development Activity — Aerobic, Strength, and Flexibility Jackpot Fitness

Three different "jackpots" (boxes) are filled with fitness exercises and activities are placed around the teaching area. One jackpot is filled with a variety of strength development activities written on small index cards. A second jackpot is filled with flexibility activities. The third jackpot contains aerobic activities. Students can work individually or with a partner. They begin at one of the jackpots of choice and randomly pick out an activity to perform. If with a partner, they take turns selecting the card from the box. The only stipulations are that they must rotate to a different box each time and cannot select an activity they previously performed. If they pick an activity they performed on a previous stop, they return it to the jackpot and select another.

Aerobic Jackpot
1. Carioca around the basketball court.
2. Perform a "mirror drill" with your partner for 30 seconds.
3. Jump rope using both slow and fast time.
4. Tortoise and Hare/Running in place.
5. Marching with high steps around the area.

Strength Jackpot
1. Perform Abdominal Challenges.
2. Perform Push-up Challenges.
3. Do the Treadmill exercise.
4. Do as many Power Jumpers as possible.
5. Perform as many Crab Kicks as possible.

Flexibility Jackpot
1. Perform the Bend and Twist exercise.
2. Stretch using the Sitting Stretch.
3. Stretch using the Lower Leg Stretch.
4. Do the Standing Hip Bend.
5. Perform the Body Twist.

Allow students to adjust the workload to their level. This implies resting if the rope jumping is too strenuous.

A music interval of 30 seconds signals the duration of fitness activity, followed by 10 to 15 second interval used for selecting a new activity from a different jackpot.

Students are expected to perform as many repetitions as possible while the music is playing.

Lesson Focus — Hockey Skills (2)

Since this is the final lesson of hockey, devote more time to playing hockey lead-up activities. For specific teaching hints, see the previous Lesson Plan, Week 21.

Skills

Review skills taught in previous lesson:
1. Gripping and carrying the stick
2. Controlled dribble
3. Front Field
4. Forehand Pass
5. Face-off
6. Goalkeeping

Introduce new skills:

1. Tackling

The tackle is a means of taking the ball away from an opponent. The tackler moves toward the opponent with the stick held low. The tackle is timed so that the blade of the stick is placed against the ball when the ball is off the opponent's stick. The tackler then quickly dribbles or passes in the direction of the goal. Throwing the stick or striking carelessly at the ball should be discouraged. Players need to remember that a successful tackle is not always possible.

2. Dodging

Dodging is a means of evading a tackler and maintaining control of the ball. The player dribbles the ball directly at the opponent. At the last instant, the ball is pushed to one side of the tackler, depending on the direction the player is planning to dodge. If the ball is pushed to the left, the player should move around the right side of the opponent to regain control of the ball, and vice versa. Selecting the proper instant to push the ball is the key to successful dodging. Dodging should not be attempted if a pass would be more effective.

Introduce the following drills:

1. Three-on-Three Drill. Set up many goals and allow 6 students to work in small groups of 3 offensive and 3 defensive players.
2. Shooting Drill. Mats are set up as goals (3 or 4 on each end of the floor). Half of class on each half of the floor. Each team attempts to hit pucks into opponents' goals without crossing centerline of gym. Use a large number of pucks.
3. Dodging and Tackling Drill. Players work in pairs. One partner dribbles toward the other, who attempts to make a tackle. If the tackle is successful, roles are reversed. This drill should be practiced at moderate speeds in the early stages of skill development.

Hockey Lead-up Activities

Sideline Hockey

See the Lesson Plan, Hockey Skills (Week 21) for a complete game description.

Regulation Elementary Hockey

Supplies: One stick per player, a puck or ball

Skills: All hockey skills

In a small gymnasium, the walls can serve as the boundaries. In a large gymnasium or on an outdoor field, the playing area should be delineated with traffic cones. The area should be divided in half, with a 12-ft restraining circle centered on the midline. This is where play begins at the start of the periods, after goals, or after foul shots. The official goal is 2 ft high by 6 ft wide, with a restraining area 4 ft by 8 ft around the goal to protect the goalie. Each team has a goalkeeper, who stops shots with her hands, feet, or stick; a center, who is the only player allowed to move full court and who leads offensive play (the center has her stick striped with black tape); two guards, who cannot go beyond the centerline into the offensive area and who are responsible for keeping the puck out of their defensive half of the field; and two forwards, who work with the center on offensive play and who cannot go back over the centerline into the defensive area.

A game consists of three periods of 8 minutes each, with a 3-minute rest between periods. Play is started with a face-off by the centers at midcourt. Other players cannot enter the restraining circle until the ball has been hit by the centers. The clock starts when the puck is put into play and runs continuously until a goal is scored or a foul is called. Substitutions can be made only when the clock is stopped. If the ball goes out-of-bounds, it is put back into play by the team that did not hit it last.

Whenever the ball passes through the goal on the ground, 1 point is scored. If, however, the ball crosses the goal line while in the air, it must strike against the mat or back wall to count for a score. Under no circumstances can a goal be scored on a foul. The puck can deflect off a player or equipment to score, but it cannot be kicked into the goal.

The goalkeeper may use her hands to clear the puck away from the goal, but she may not hold or throw it toward the other end of the playing area. She is charged with a foul for holding the puck. The goalkeeper may be pulled from the goal area but cannot go beyond the centerline. No other player may enter the restraining area without being charged with a foul.

The following are fouls and are penalized by loss of the puck at the spot of the foul.

1. Illegally touching the puck with the hands
2. Swinging the stick above waist height (called sticking)
3. Guards or forwards moving across the centerline
4. Player other than the goalie entering the restraining area
5. Goalie throwing the puck
6. Holding, stepping on, or lying on the puck

Defenders must be 5 yd back when the puck is put into play after a foul. If the spot where the foul occurred is closer than 5 yd to the goal, only the goalkeeper may defend. The puck is then put into play 5 yd directly out from the goal.

Personal fouls include any action or rough play that endangers other players. A player committing a personal foul must retire to the sidelines for 2 minutes. The following are personal fouls:
1. Hacking or striking with a stick
2. Tripping with either the foot or the stick
3. Pushing, blocking

Objectives:
To understand the principles of
  stability and balance
To control the body weight in a variety
  of tumbling and stunt activities
To participate in "one-on-one"
  competition and accept the outcome
To play group games and cooperate
  with teammates

NASPE National Standards:
Introductory Activity: 5, 6, 7
Fitness Activity: 1, 2, 4
Lesson Focus: 3, 5, 6, 7
Game: 1, 3, 6, 7

Equipment Required:
Aerobic fitness tape
Beanbags and wands
Tumbling mats
Cageball, four bowling pins, and flags
  for game activities

Instructional Activities	Teaching Hints

Introductory Activity — Pyramid Power

Pyramid Power
Students move throughout the area. On signal, they find a partner and build a simple partner support stunt or pyramid (i.e., double bear, table, hip–shoulder stand, statue). On the next signal, pyramids are quickly and safely dismantled and students move again.

Select a partner of similar size.

Remind students to stand on the proper points of body support.

Fitness Development Activity — Aerobic Fitness

The following aerobic movements are suggestions only. When youngsters begin to fatigue, stop the aerobic fitness movements and do some of the flexibility and strength development activities learned in previous lessons. This will allow students time to recover aerobically.
1. Rhythmic run with clap
2. Bounce turn and clap
3. Rhythmic 4-count curl-ups (knees, toes, knees, back)
4. Rhythmic Crab Kicks (slow time)
5. Jumping Jack combination
6. Double knee lifts
7. Lunges (right, left, forward) with single-arm circles (on the side lunges) and double-arms circles (on the forward lunge)
8. Rhythmic trunk twists
9. Directional run (forward, backward, side, turning)
10. Rock side to side with clap
11. Side leg raises (alternate legs)
12. Rhythmic 4-count push-ups (If these are too difficult for students, substitute single-arm circles in the push-up position.)

Use music to stimulate effort. Any combination of movements can be used.

Keep the steps simple and easy to perform. Some students will become frustrated if the learning curve is steep.

Signs that explain the aerobic activities will help students remember performance cues.

Don't stress or expect perfection. Allow students to perform the activities as best they can.

Alternate bouncing and running movements with flexibility and strength development movements.

Lesson Focus — Gymnastics Skills (3)

The following five groups of activities in this lesson ensure that youngsters receive a variety of experiences. Pick a few activities from each group and teach them alternately.

Tumbling and Inverted Balances
Headstand

Begin on a mat in a kneeling position, with hands placed about shoulder width apart and the fingers spread and pointed forward. Place the head forward of the hands, so that the head and hands form a triangle on the mat. Walk the body weight forward so that most of it rests on the hands and head. Go directly into a Headstand, using a kick-up to achieve the inverted position. Maintain the triangle position of the hands and the head. In the final inverted position, the feet should be together, with legs straight and toes pointed. The weight is evenly distributed among the three points—the two hands and the forward part of the head. The body should be aligned as straight as possible.

The safest way to come down from the inverted position is to return to the mat in the direction that was used in going up. Bending at both the waist and the knees helps recovery. The child should be instructed, in the case of overbalancing, to tuck the head under and go into a Forward Roll. Both methods of recovery from the inverted position should be included in the instructional sequences early in the presentation.

Spotting the Headstand: The spotter is stationed directly in front of the performer and steadies as needed. The spotter can first apply support to the hips and then transfer to the ankles as the climb-up position is lengthened into a Headstand. If unable to control the performer, the spotter must be alert to moving out of the way when the performer goes into a Forward Roll to come out of the inverted position.

Backward Roll Combinations

Review the Backward Roll. Continue emphasis on the Push-Off with the hands. Try some of the following combinations:

1. Do a Backward Roll to a standing position. A strong push by the hands is necessary to provide enough momentum to land on the feet.
2. Do two Backward Rolls in succession.
3. Do a Crab Walk into a Backward Roll.
4. Add a jump in the air at the completion of a Backward Roll.

Balance Stunts

Long Reach

Place a beanbag about 3 ft in front of a line. Keeping the toes behind the line, lean forward on one hand and reach out with the other hand to touch the beanbag. Recover in one clean, quick movement to the original position, lifting the supporting hand off the floor. Increase the distance of the bag from the line.

Toe Jump

Hold the left toes with the right hand. Jump the right foot through without losing the grip on the toes. Try with the other foot. (Teachers should not be discouraged if only a few can do this stunt; it is quite difficult.)

Individual Stunts

Pretzel

Touch the back of the head with the toes by raising the head and trunk and bringing the feet to the back of the head. Try first to bring the toes close enough to the head so the head-to-toe distance can be measured by another child with a hand span (the distance between the thumb and little finger when spread). If this distance is met, then try touching one or both feet to the back of the head.

Jackknife

Stand erect with hands out level to the front and a little to the side. Jump up and bring the feet up quickly to touch the hands. Vary by starting with a short run. Be sure the feet come up to the hands, rather than the hands moving down to the feet. Do several Jackknives in succession. The takeoff must be with both feet, and good height must be achieved.

Heel-and-Toe Spring

Place the heels against a line. Jump backward over the line while bent over and grasping the toes. (Lean forward slightly to allow for impetus and then jump backward over the line.) Try jumping forward to original position. To be successful, the child should retain the grasp on the toes. The teacher can introduce the stunt by first having children grasp their ankles when making the jumps. This is less difficult.

Single-Leg Circle (Pinwheel)

Assume a squatting position, with both hands on the floor, left knee between the arms and right leg extended to the side. Swing the right leg forward and under the lifted right arm, under the left leg and arm, and back to starting position. Several circles should be made in succession. Reverse position and try with the left leg.

Partner and Group Stunts

Quintuplet Roll

Five children can make up a roll series. They are numbered 1 through 5. Numbers 3 and 5 begin by going over numbers 2 and 4, respectively, who roll under. Number 1 goes over number 3 as soon as possible. Each then continues to go alternately over and under.

Dead Person Lift

One child lies on her back, with body stiff and arms at the sides. Two helpers stand, one on each side of the "dead" person, with hands at the back of the neck and fingers touching. Working together, they lift the child, who remains rigid, to a standing position. From this position, the child is released and falls forward in a Dead Body Fall.

Injured Person Carry

The "injured" child lies on the back. Six children, three on each side, kneel down to do the carry. The lifters work their hands, palms upward, under the person to form a human stretcher, and then lift up. (The "injured" child must maintain a stiff position.) They walk a short distance and set the person down carefully.

Merry-Go-Round

From 8–12 children are needed. Half of the children form a circle with joined hands, using a wrist grip. The remaining children drape themselves (each over a pair of joined hands) to become riders. The riders stretch out their bodies, faces up, toward the center of the circle, with the weight on the heels. Each rider then leans back on a pair of joined hands and connects hands, behind the circle of standing children, with the riders on either side. There are two sets of joined hands—the first circle, or merry-go-round, and the riders.

Combatives

Catch-and-Pull Tug-of-War

Starting Position: Two teams face each other across a line.

Action: Try to catch hold of and pull any opponent across the line. A player pulled across the line waits in back of the opposing team until time is called. The team capturing the most players wins.

Stick Twist

Starting Position: Contestants face each other with their feet approximately 12 in. apart. They hold a wand above their heads with both hands, the arms completely extended.

Action: On signal, try to bring the wand down slowly without changing the grip. The object is to maintain the original grip and not to let the wand twist in the hands. The wand does not have to be forced down, but rather should be moved down by mutual agreement. It can be moved down completely only if one player allows it to slip.

Toe Touch

Starting Position: Contestants form a large circle.

Action: On signal, try to step lightly on the opponent's toes (those on the left and right side), while not allowing the opponent to step on your toes. Keep score by counting the number of touches made.

Crab Contest

Starting Position: Both contestants are in crab position with seats held high.

Action: On signal, try, by jostling and pushing, to force the other's seat to touch the mat.

Game Activity

Lily Pads (Cooperative Activity)

Formation: Teams of 6–15 students

Supplies: One poly spot per child

Students will begin standing on their poly spots, or lily pads, in a straight line. Each lily pad should be about 12" apart. The team's challenge is to reverse their order so that the two youngsters on the end switch places, the second to last switch places, etc. See below for a visual explanation. The catch is that each member of the team must have at least one foot on a lily pad at all times. If either of these rules is broken, the teams must start over in the original order.

Start	Finish
1 2 3 4 5 6 7 8	8 7 6 5 4 3 2 1

Teaching Tip: If poly spots are not available, this activity can also be done using a line or a long piece of tape. Simply make the rule that one foot must be on the tape at all times.

Flag Chase

Supplies: Flags, stopwatch

Skills: Running, dodging

The class is divided into two teams. One team wears flags positioned in the back of the belt. The flag team scatters throughout the area. On signal, the object is for the chasing team to capture as many flags as possible in a designated amount of time. The flags are placed in a box. Players cannot use their hands to ward off a chaser. Roles are reversed. The team pulling the most flags is declared the winner.

Jolly Ball

Supplies: A cageball 24 in. or larger (or a 36- to 48-in. pushball)

Skill: Kicking

Four teams are organized, each of which forms one side of a square. Children sit down, facing in, with hands braced behind them. The members of each team are numbered consecutively. Players wait until their number is called. Four active players (one from each team) move in crab position and try to kick the cageball over any one of the three opposing teams. The sideline players can also kick the ball. Ordinarily, the hands are not used, but can be allowed in the learning stages of the game.

A point is scored against a team that allows the ball to go over its line. A ball that goes out at the corner between teams is dead and replayed. After a short bout of time (10 to 20 seconds), the active children retire to their teams and another number is called. The team with the fewest points wins the game. This game is strenuous for the active players, so rotate them often. Two children from each team can be active at once.

Objectives:

To demonstrate activities designed to improve flexibility

To demonstrate proper starting techniques

To perform the scissors high jump properly

NASPE National Standards:

Introductory Activity: 1, 4, 5, 6

Fitness Activity: 1456

Lesson Focus: 2, 3, 5

Game: 2, 3, 5

Equipment Required:

High jump equipment

Batons, stopwatches, and tape measures

Hurdles

Instructional Activities	Teaching Hints
Introductory and Fitness Development Activities — Stretching Activities	

Combine the introductory and fitness activities during the track and field unit. This will help students understand how to stretch and warm up for a demanding activity such as track and field.

Jog	1–2 minutes
Standing Hip Bend	30 seconds
Sitting Stretch	30 seconds
Partner Rowing	60 seconds
Bear Hug (20 seconds each leg)	40 seconds
Side Flex (20 seconds each leg)	40 seconds
Trunk Twister	30 seconds

Emphasis should be on jogging and stretching to prepare for a strenuous activity.

See the textbook, Chapter 13, for a description of exercises.

Encourage smooth and controlled stretching. Hold each stretch for 6–10 seconds.

Lesson Focus — Track and Field Skills (1)

Skills

Teach the following skills if students haven't learned them in earlier grades.

Standing Start

The standing start should be practiced, for this type of start has a variety of uses in physical education activities. Many children find it more comfortable than the sprinter's start. When practical, however, children should use the sprinter's start for track work. In the standing start, the feet should be in a comfortable half-stride position. An extremely long stride is to be avoided. The body leans forward so that the center of gravity is forward. The weight is on the toes, and the knees are flexed slightly. The arms can be down or hanging slightly back.

Sprinter's Start

"On your mark" position places the toe of the front foot from 4–12 in. behind the starting line. The thumb and first finger are just behind the line, with other fingers adding support. The knee of the rear leg is placed just opposite the front foot or ankle.

For the "Get set" position, the seat is raised so that it is nearly parallel to the ground. The knee of the rear leg is raised off the ground, and the shoulders are moved forward over the hands. The weight is evenly distributed over the hands and feet. The head is not raised, as the runner should be looking at a spot a few feet in front of the starting line.

On the "Go" signal, the runner pushes off sharply with both feet, with the front leg straightening as the back leg comes forward for a step. The body should rise gradually rather than pop up suddenly. The instructor should watch for a stumbling action on the first few steps. This results from too much weight resting on the hands in the "Get set" position.

Sprinting

In proper sprinting form, the body leans forward, with the arms swinging in opposition to the legs. The arms are bent at the elbows and swing from the shoulders in a forward and backward plane, not across the body. Forceful arm action aids sprinting. The knees are lifted sharply forward and upward and are brought down with a vigorous motion, followed by a forceful push from the toes.

The goal of track and field is self-improvement and developing proper techniques. Each student must accept responsibility for self-directed work and should be encouraged to try all activities.

The program should offer something for all—boys and girls, the highly skilled and the less skilled, and those with physical problems. Children with weight problems need particular attention. They must be stimulated and encouraged, since their participation will be minimal if little attention is paid to them. Special goals can be set for overweight children, and special events and goals can also be established for children with handicaps.

The long jump must be maintained properly. It should be filled with fresh sand of a coarse variety.

Baton Passing

The right hand to left hand method is the best choice for elementary school children as it is easy and offers a consistent method for passes. This pass allows the receiver to face the inside of the track while waiting to receive the baton in the left hand. The oncoming runner holds the baton in the right hand like a candle when passing it to a teammate. The receiver reaches back with the left hand, fingers pointing down and thumb to the inside, and begins to run as the runner advances to within 3–5 yd. The receiver grasps the baton and shifts it from the left to the right hand while moving. If the baton is dropped, it must be picked up, or the team is disqualified. An alternative way to receive the baton is to reach back with the hand facing up; however, the fingers-down method is considered more suitable for sprint relays.

Receivers can look over their shoulders to see the oncoming runner or can look forward in the direction of the run. Looking backward is called a visual pass and is slower than passing while looking forward (called a blind pass). However, there is a greater chance for error when the receiver is not looking backward and at the baton during the pass. The visual pass is recommended for elementary school children.

Distance Running

In distance running, as compared with sprinting, the body is more erect and the motion of the arms is less pronounced. Pace is an important consideration. Runners should try to concentrate on the qualities of lightness, ease, relaxation, and looseness. Good striding action, a slight body lean, and good head position are also important. Runners should be encouraged to strike the ground with the heel first and then push off with the toes.

If stopwatches and tape measures are used, it is important to make them highly visible. Tie bright-colored cord to them or anchor to cones to assure that they are not misplaced.

High Jumping—Scissors Jump

The scissors jump is by far the safest high jump and should be used for elementary school children when direct supervision is not available. For the scissors jump, the high-jump bar is approached from a slight angle. The takeoff is by the leg that is farther from the bar. The near leg is lifted and goes over, followed quickly in a looping movement by the rear leg. A good upward kick with the front leg, together with an upward thrust of the arms, is needed. The knees should be straightened at the highest point of the jump. The landing is made on the lead foot followed by the rear foot.

High-jump techniques are developed by practice. The bar should be at a height that offers challenge but allows concentration on technique rather than on height. Too much emphasis on competition for height quickly eliminates the poorer jumpers, who need the experience most.

Long Jump

For the running long jump, a short run is needed. The run should be timed so that the toes of the jumping foot contact the board in a natural stride. The jumper takes off from one foot and strives for height. The landing is made on both feet after the knees have been brought forward. The landing should be in a forward direction, not sideward.

A fair long jump takes off behind the scratch line. A foul (scratch) jump is called if the jumper steps beyond the scratch line or runs into or through the pit. Each contestant is given a certain number of trials (jumps). A scratch jump counts as a trial. Measurement is from the scratch line to the nearest point of touch.

Hop-Step-and-Jump

The hop-step-and-jump event is increasing in popularity, particularly because it is now included in Olympic competition. A takeoff board and a jumping pit are needed. The distance from the takeoff board to the pit should be one that even less skilled jumpers can make. The event begins with a run similar to that for the running long jump. The takeoff is with one foot, and the jumper must land on the same foot to complete the hop. He then takes a step followed by a jump. The event finishes like the long jump, with a landing on both feet. The pattern can be changed to begin with the left foot. A checkpoint should be used, as for the running long jump.

The jumper must not step over the takeoff board in the first hop, under penalty of fouling. Distance is measured from the front of the takeoff board to the closest place where the body touches. This is usually a mark made by one of the heels, but it could be a mark made by an arm or another part of the body if the jumper landed poorly and fell backward.

Hurdles

The hurdler should step so that the takeoff foot is planted 3–5 ft from the hurdle. The lead foot is extended straight forward over the hurdle; the rear (trailing) leg is bent, with the knee to the side. The lead foot reaches for the ground, quickly followed by the trailing leg. The hurdler should avoid floating over the hurdle. Body lean is necessary. A hurdler may lead with the same foot over consecutive hurdles or may alternate the leading foot. Some hurdlers like to thrust both arms forward instead of a single arm. A consistent step pattern should be developed.

Station (Small-Group) Instruction

The teacher should instruct at a different station each day. Start at the station that demands the most instruction. Set up a system of rotation that assures all stations will be covered during the unit.

Make signs for each of the stations. The signs should include appropriate performance techniques, what is to be done at each station, and appropriate safety precautions.

Station 1

Starting and Sprinting

1. Front foot 4–12" behind line.
2. Thumb and first finger behind line, other fingers support.
3. Knee of other leg placed just opposite front foot.
4. On "get set," seat is raised, the down knee comes up a little, and the shoulders move forward over the hands.
5. On "go," push off sharply and take short, driving steps.

Hop-Step-and-Jump (Triple Jump)

1. Important to get the sequence and rhythm first, then later try for distance.
2. Sprinting.

Station 2

Running High Jump

1. Keep stretch rope low enough so all can practice.
2. Approach at 45 degrees.
3. Good kick-up and arm action.

Baton Passing

1. Decide on method of passing.
2. Incoming runner passes with left hand to right hand of receiver.
3. After receiving, change to the left hand.
4. Estimate how fast to take off with respect to the incoming runner.

Station 3

Running Long Jump

1. Decide on jumping foot.
2. Establish checkpoint.
3. Control last four steps.
4. Seek height.

Standing Long Jump or Shuttle Relays

Station 4

Hurdling

1. At beginning, use one or two hurdles.
2. Leading foot is directly forward.

Practice Striding for Distance Running

1. Work on pace.
2. Easy, relaxed strides.

The goal of the program should be to allow students to develop at their own rate. The instructor needs to be perceptive enough to determine whether students are working too hard or too little. Special attention must be given to those who appear disinterested, dejected, emotionally upset, or withdrawn.

The high jump bar should be at a height that offers challenge but allows concentration on technique rather than on height. Too much emphasis on competition for height quickly eliminates the poorer jumpers, who need the experience most. Safety is of utmost importance. Using a flexible elastic rope as a crossbar and avoiding any type of flop will prevent injury. The practice of keeping the entire class together on a single high-jump facility is poor methodology. This arrangement determines who are the best jumpers in class but does little else.

Track and Field Lead-up Activities

Circular (Pursuit) Relays

Circular relays make use of the regular circular track. The baton exchange technique requires practice. On a 220-yd or 200-m track, relays can be organized in a number of ways, depending on how many runners are spaced for one lap. Four runners can do a lap, each running one-quarter of the way; two can do a lap, each running one half of the distance; or each runner can complete a whole lap. In these races, each member of the relay team runs the same distance. Relays can also be organized so members run different distances.

Shuttle Relays

Because children are running toward each other, one great difficulty in running shuttle relays is control of the exchange. In the excitement, the next runner may leave too early, and the tag or exchange is then made ahead of the restraining line. A high-jump standard or cone can be used to prevent early exchanges. The next runner awaits the tag with an arm around the standard or a hand on a cone.

One-on-One Contests

Allow students to find a friend and have a number of personal contests in track and field events such as sprints, hurdling, high jump, and standing long jump.

Objectives:
To understand how to stretch prior to strenuous activity
To recognize the wide range of individual differences among peers
To enjoy one-on-one competition in track and field activities

NASPE National Standards:
Introductory Activity: 1, 4, 5, 6
Fitness Activity: 1, 4, 5, 6
Lesson Focus: 2, 3, 5
Game: 2, 3, 5

Equipment Required:
High jump equipment
Batons, stopwatches, and tape measures
Hurdles

Instructional Activities	Teaching Hints
Introductory and Fitness Development Activities — Stretching Activities	

Combine the introductory and fitness activities during the track and field unit. This will help students understand how to stretch and warm up for a demanding activity such as track and field.

Jog	1–2 minutes
Standing Hip Bend	30 seconds
Sitting Stretch	30 seconds
Partner Rowing	60 seconds
Bear Hug (20 seconds each leg)	40 seconds
Side Flex (20 seconds each leg)	40 seconds
Trunk Twister	30 seconds

Emphasis should be on jogging and stretching to prepare for a strenuous activity.

See the textbook, Chapter 13, for a description of exercises.

Encourage smooth and controlled stretching. Hold each stretch for 6–10 seconds.

Lesson Focus — Track and Field Skills (2)

Skills
Introduce the following skills before proceeding to small-group instruction.
Striding
    In distance running, as compared with sprinting, the body is more erect and the motion of the arms is less pronounced. Pace is an important consideration. Runners should try to concentrate on the qualities of lightness, ease, relaxation, and looseness. Good striding action, a slight body lean, and good head position are also important. Runners should be encouraged to strike the ground with the heel first and then push off with the toes

Hurdling
    Several key points govern good hurdling technique. The runner should adjust his stepping pattern so that the takeoff foot is planted 3–5 ft from the hurdle. The lead foot is extended straight forward over the hurdle; the rear (trailing) leg is bent, with the knee to the side. The lead foot reaches for the ground, quickly followed by the trailing leg. The hurdler should avoid floating over the hurdle. Body lean is necessary. A hurdler may lead with the same foot over consecutive hurdles or may alternate the leading foot. Some hurdlers like to thrust both arms forward instead of a single arm. A consistent step pattern should be developed.
    Wands supported on blocks or cones can also be used as hurdles. Hurdles should begin at about 12 in. in height and increase to 18 in. They should be placed about 25 ft apart.

Station (Small-Group) Instruction
Review skills that were taught last week, if necessary. The teacher should instruct at a different station each day. Start at the station that demands the most instruction. Set up a system of rotation that assures all stations will be covered during the unit. Allow youngsters to work with a partner of somewhat equal ability. At each station, set out signs that tell students what they are to practice and list key performance points.

Station 1
Sprinting—Partners time each other over different distances.
1. 60-yd distance.
2. 75-yd distance.
3. Record best performance.

Hop-Step-and-Jump—Partners take turns practicing the hop, step, and jump.
1. Three trials.
2. Record best performance.

Station 2

High Jump—Partners practice the scissors jump
1. Each jump begins at a height they desire. If the jump is made, they can dictate how much to raise the height.
2. Three trials.
3. Record best performance.

Baton Passing—Practice passing the baton with partner while waiting for high jump turn.

Station 3

Running Long Jump - Partners take turns performing the running long jump.
1. Three trials.
2. Record best performance.

Shuttle Relays - Partners practice with another set of partners, about 20 yd apart and facing each other. See below for a description of shuttle relays.

Station 4

Hurdling—Partners time each other over a three hurdle course.
1. Set up 60-yd hurdle course.
2. Two trials.
3. Record best performance.

Striding Practice—Striding practice can be done while waiting for turns on the hurdles.

Track and Field Lead-up Activities

Circular (Pursuit) Relays

Circular relays make use of the regular circular track. The baton exchange technique is important, and practice is needed. On a 220-yd or 200-m track, relays can be organized in a number of ways, depending on how many runners are spaced for one lap. Four runners can do a lap, each running one-quarter of the way; two can do a lap, each running one half of the distance; or each runner can complete a whole lap. In these races, each member of the relay team runs the same distance. Relays can also be organized so team members run different distances.

Shuttle Relays

Since children are running toward each other, one great difficulty in running shuttle relays is control of the exchange. In the excitement, the next runner may leave too early, and the tag or exchange is then made ahead of the restraining line. A high-jump standard or cone can be used to prevent early exchanges. The next runner awaits the tag with an arm around the standard or a hand on a cone.

Flippers (Cooperative Activity)

Formation: Entire class divided into two teams

Supplies: 30–40 flying disks

Flying disks (30–40) are spread throughout the teaching area and two teams formed. One team is charged with flipping the disks so they are faceup, while the other team attempts to flip the disks to a facedown position. After a practice game, the following stipulations can be used.
1. No hands.
2. Feet only.
3. Students must crab walk or bear crawl.
4. Feet only, and only one foot can touch the disk at a time.
5. Knees only.
6. Heel only.

Objectives:

To understand how to stretch prior to strenuous activity

To recognize the wide range of individual differences among peers

To enjoy one-on-one competition in track and field activities

NASPE National Standards:

Introductory Activity: 1, 4, 5, 6

Fitness Activity: 1, 4, 5, 6

Lesson Focus: 2, 3, 5

Game: 2, 3, 5

Equipment Required:

Music tape for Racetrack Fitness

High jump equipment

Batons, stopwatches, and tape measures

Hurdles

Instructional Activities	Teaching Hints
Fitness Development Activity — Racetrack Fitness	
Five or six fitness activities are arranged in the center (the Pit) of a large circle outlined with marking spots (the race track). If desired, tumbling mats can be placed in the center of the race track to delineate the pit stop area. Students work with a partner and alternate running (or doing other locomotor movements) around the race track and going to the pit to perform a strength or flexibility exercise. A different exercise should be performed each time so students assure variety in their workout.	Intervals of 30 seconds of music with 10 seconds of silence can be used to signal role changes. The student who was running the track now goes to the pit to exercise and vice versa.
The following are some examples of exercises that can be used for Pit exercises. 1. Arm Circles 2. Bend and Twist 3. Abdominal Challenges 4. Knee to Chest Curl 5. Push-Up Challenges 6. Trunk Twister	Assure that students run under control (not as fast as they can) and in the same direction. Allow students to perform at a level they feel comfortable. Youngsters are genetically different and should not be expected to do the same amount of exercise repetitions.

Lesson Focus — Track and Field Skills (3)

Track and Field Skills

1. Utilize the last week of this unit to conduct a track and field meet. The same rotation plan and groups of students started the previous two weeks can be continued for the meet.
2. Utilize the same stations, events, number of trials, and scoring procedures outlined in last week's track and field lesson.

Track and Field Lead-up Activities

Circular (Pursuit) Relays

Circular relays make use of the regular circular track. The baton exchange technique is important, and practice is needed. On a 220-yd or 200-m track, relays can be organized in a number of ways, depending on how many runners are spaced for one lap. Four runners can do a lap, each running one-quarter of the way; two can do a lap, each running one half of the distance; or each runner can complete a whole lap. In these races, each member of the relay team runs the same distance. Relays can also be organized so team members run different distances.

Shuttle Relays

Since children are running toward each other, one great difficulty in running shuttle relays is control of the exchange. In the excitement, the next runner may leave too early, and the tag or exchange is then made ahead of the restraining line. A high-jump standard or cone can be used to prevent early exchanges. The next runner awaits the tag with an arm around the standard or a hand on a cone.

One-on-One Contests

Allow students to find a friend and have a number of personal contests in track and field events such as sprints, hurdling, high jump, and standing long jump.

Objectives:

To work cooperatively with peers in parachute fitness activities

To perform locomotor movements to rhythm

To understand strategies in simple game activities

To hear changes in musical accompaniment and move accordingly

NASPE National Standards:

Introductory Activity: 1, 3, 5
Fitness Activity: 1, 3, 4, 5, 6
Lesson Focus: 2, 3, 5
Game: 1, 3, 5

Equipment Required:

Parachute and music tape for fitness
Tinikling equipment
Music for rhythmic activities
Pinnies
6 playground balls or coated foam balls
Jump the shot rope

Instructional Activities	Teaching Hints

Introductory Activity — Following Activity

One partner leads and performs various kinds of movements. The other partner follows and performs the same movements. This can also be done with small groups, with the group following a leader.

Encourage students to challenge their partner. Change partners once or twice to maintain interest in the activity.

Fitness Development Activity — Parachute Fitness

1. Jog in circle with chute held in left hand. Reverse direction and hold with right hand.
2. Standing, raise the chute overhead, lower to waist, lower to toes, raise to waist, etc.
3. Slide to the right; return slide to the left.
4. Sit and perform curl-ups with a twist.
5. Skip.
6. Freeze, face the center, and stretch the chute tightly with bent arms. Hold for 8–12 seconds. Repeat.
7. Run in place, hold the chute at waist level, and hit the chute with lifted knees.
8. Sit with legs under the chute. Do a seat walk toward the center. Return to the perimeter. Repeat four to six times.
9. Place the chute on the ground. Jog away from the chute and return on signal. Repeat.
10. On sides with legs under the chute. Perform Side Flex and lift chute with legs.
11. Lie on back with legs under the chute. Shake the chute with the feet.
12. Hop to the center of the chute and return. Repeat.
13. Assume the push-up position with the legs aligned away from the center of the chute. Shake the chute with one arm while the other arm supports the body.
14. Sit with feet under the chute. Stretch by touching the toes with the chute. Relax with other stretches while sitting.

Tape alternating segments (25–30 seconds in length) of silence and music to signal duration of exercise. Music segments indicate aerobic activity with the parachute, while intervals of silence announce using the chute to enhance flexibility and strength development.

Space youngsters evenly around the chute.

Use different hand grips (palms up, down, mixed).

All movements should be done under control. Some of the faster and stronger students will have to moderate their performance.

Lesson Focus — Rhythmic Movement Skills (3)

Make dances easy for students to learn by implementing some of the following techniques:

Rhythms should be taught like other sport skills. Avoid striving for perfection so students know it is acceptable to make mistakes.

Teach a variety of dances rather than one or two in depth in case some students find it difficult to master a specific dance.

1. Teach the dances without using partners.
2. Allow youngsters to move in any direction without left-right orientation.
3. Use scattered formation instead of circles.
4. Emphasize strong movements such as clapping and stamping to increase involvement.
5. Play the music at a slower speed when first learning the dance.

Jugglehead Mixer (American)

Music Source: Any music with a definite and steady beat.
Formation: Double circle facing counterclockwise in promenade position.
Directions: Actions described are for the inside partner; directions are opposite for the partner on the outside of the circle.

Measures   Action

1–4   Do a two-step left and two-step right and take four walking steps forward.

5–8   Repeat measures 1–4.

9–10   Inside partner takes the outside partner's right hand and walks around to face the person behind.

11–12   Inside partner turns the person behind with the left hand.

13–14   Inside partner turns partner with the right hand going all the way around.

15–16   Inside partner steps up one place to the outside person ahead, who becomes the new partner.

Ten Pretty Girls (American)

Music Source: WWCD-1042

Formation: Circle of groups of any number, with arms linked or hands joined, all facing counterclockwise.

Directions:

Measures   Action

1–2   Starting with the weight on the right foot, touch the left foot in front, swing the left foot to the left and touch, swing the left foot behind the right foot and put the weight on the left foot, step to the right, close the left foot to the right. (Front, side, back-side, together)

3–4   Repeat, starting with the weight on the left foot and moving to the right. (Front, side, back-side, together)

5–6   Take four walking or strutting steps forward, starting on the left foot. (Walk, 2, 3, 4)

7–8   Swing the left foot forward with a kicking motion; swing the left foot backward with a kicking motion; stamp left, right, left, in place. (Swing, swing, stamp, stamp, stamp)

Repeat the entire dance 11 times, starting each time with the alternate foot. The dance can be used as a mixer when performed in a circle by groups of three. On measures 7–8, have the middle person move forward to the next group during the three stamps.

Klumpakojis (Swedish)

Music Source: WWCD-1042

Formation: Couples in a circle, side by side, all facing counterclockwise, with partner B to the right.

Directions:

Measures   Part I Action

1–4   With inside hands joined, free hand on hip, all walk briskly around the circle for 8 steps counterclockwise. (Walk, 2, 3, 4, 5, 6, 7, turn)

5–8   Turn individually to the left, reverse direction, change hands, and walk 8 steps clockwise. (Walk, 2, 3, 4, 5, 6, 7, turn)

Measures   Part II Action

9–12   Face partner and make a star by joining right hands (making certain that the right elbow is bent). The left hand is on the hip. With partner, walk around clockwise for 8 walking steps. Change hands and repeat the 8 steps, reversing direction. (Star, 2, 3, 4, 5, 6, 7, 8; reverse, 2, 3, 4, 5, 6, 7, 8)

Measures   Part III Action

13–16   Listen to the musical phrase, then stamp 3 times on the last two counts. Listen to the phrase again, then clap own hands 3 times. (Listen, listen, stamp, 2, 3; listen, listen, clap, 2, 3)

17–20   Shake the right finger in a scolding motion at partner. (Scold, 2, 3) Shake the left finger. (Scold, 2, 3)

21–24   Turn solo to the left, clapping partner's right hand once during the turn. Use 2 walking steps to make the turn, and finish facing partner. (Turn, 2, stamp, 2, 3)

25–32   Repeat the action of measures 13–24.

Measures   Part IV Action

33–40   With inside hands joined, do 16 polka steps (or two-steps) forward, moving counterclockwise. (Later, as the dance is learned, change to the promenade position.) On polka steps 15 and 16, partner A moves forward to take a new partner B while handing the original partner B to the A in back. New couple joins inside hands. (Step, close, step, hop; step, close, step, hop; repeat for a total of 16 polka steps)

Tinikling (Philippine Islands)

Music Source: WWCD-8095; WWC-9015

Formation: Sets of 4 scattered around the room. Each set has 2 strikers and 2 dancers.

Directions: Two 8-foot bamboo poles and two crossbars on which the poles rest are needed for the dance. A striker kneels at each end of the poles; both strikers hold the end of a pole in each hand. The music is in waltz meter, 3/4 time, with an accent on the first beat.

The strikers slide and strike the poles together on count 1. On the other two beats of the waltz measure, the poles are opened about 15 inches apart, lifted an inch or so, and tapped twice on the crossbars in time to counts 2 and 3. The rhythm "close, tap, tap" is continued throughout the dance. Basically, the dance requires that a step be done outside the poles on the close (count 1) and that two steps be done inside the poles (counts 2 and 3) when the poles are tapped on the crossbars. Many step combinations have been devised.   The basic tinikling step should be practiced until it is mastered. The step is done singly, although two dancers are performing. Each dancer takes a position at an opposite end and on the opposite side so that the dancer's right side is to the bamboo poles.

Count 1: Step slightly forward with the left foot.

Count 2: Step with the right foot between the poles.

Count 3: Step with the left foot between the poles.

Count 4: Step with the right outside to dancer's own right.

Count 5: Step with the left between the poles.

Count 6: Step with the right between the poles.

Count 7: Step with the left outside to the original position.

The initial step (count 1) is used only to get the dance under way. The last step (count 7) to original position is actually the beginning of a new series (7, 8, 9–10, 11, 12).

Tinikling steps also can be adjusted to 4/4 rhythm (close, close, tap, tap), which requires the poles to be closed on two counts and open on the other two. The basic foot pattern is two steps outside the poles and two inside. For the sake of conformity, we present all routines in the original 3/4 time (close, tap, tap). If other rhythms are used, adjust accordingly.

Dancers can go from side to side, or can return to the side from which they entered. The dance can be done singly, with the two dancers moving in opposite directions from side to side, or the dancers can enter from and leave toward the same side. Dancers can do the same step patterns or do different movements. They can dance as partners, moving side by side with inside hands joined, or facing each other with both hands joined.

Teaching suggestions:

Steps should be practiced first with stationary poles or with lines drawn on the floor. Jump ropes can be used as stationary objects over which to practice. Students handling the poles should concentrate on watching each other rather than the dancer to avoid becoming confused by the dancer's feet.

To gain a sense of the movement pattern for 3/4 time, slap both thighs with the hands on the "close," and clap the hands twice for movements inside the poles. For 4/4 time, slap the right thigh with the right hand, then the left thigh with the left hand, followed by two claps. This routine should be done to music, with the poles closing and opening as indicated. Getting the feel of the rhythm is important.

Old Dan Tucker (American)

Music Source: WWCD-57; WWC-57

Skills: Slide, grand right and left, swing, promenade

Formation: Couples in a single circle with hands joined facing the center. One person is in the center as "Dan Tucker" and will take someone's partner.

Directions:

Counts	Part I Action
1–8	All take 4 walking steps forward and 4 steps backward. (Forward, 2, 3, 4; back, 2, 3, 4)
9–16	Partners face, join both hands, and take 4 slides in and 4 slides out. (Slide in, 2, 3, 4; slide out, 2, 3, 4)
17–24	Repeat walking steps as described in counts 1–8. (Forward, 2, 3, 4; back, 2, 3, 4)
25–32	Repeat slide steps as described in counts 9–16. (Slide in, 2, 3, 4; slide out, 2, 3, 4)
	Part II Action
1–16	Partners face and do a grand right and left for 16 walking steps and passing 7 partners before taking the 8th and preparing to swing. (Right, 2, left, 4, right, 6 … right, 14, left, new partner)
	Part III Action
17–24	On the call, "swing," each person takes the nearest partner (they should have passed 7 partners and be swinging the 8th) and swings 4 times. The person in the middle of the ring ("Dan Tucker") takes a partner anywhere in the ring. The person without a partner goes to the center of the circle. (Swing 1, swing 2, swing 3, swing 4)
	Part IV Action
1–16	On the call, "promenade," couples promenade 16 steps around the circle counterclockwise and end facing the center. (Promenade, 2, 3, … 15, face center)

Repeat the dance until the end of the music.

Shindig in the Barn (American)

Music Source: WWC-FFD

Skills: Walking, do-si-do, swinging, sliding

Formation: Contra style (two lines with partners facing each other). Seven couples will fit the music.

Directions:

Measures	Action
2	Introduction. (8 counts total)
1–2	Everybody walk forward 4 steps and back 4 steps. (Forward, 2, 3, 4; back, 2, 3, 4)

3–4	All pass through to the other side by walking forward 4 steps toward partner, do a half turn while passing right shoulder of partner, and walk 4 steps backward. (Walk, 2, 3, 4, turn, 6, 7, 8)
5–6	Everybody forward and back—repeat measures 1–2 above. (Forward, 2, 3, 4; back, 2, 3, 4)
7–8	Everybody pass through to the other side with 8 steps—repeat measures 3–4 above. (Walk, 2, 3, 4, turn, 6, 7, 8)
9–10	All couples do-so-do by passing right shoulders and back. (Do-si-do, 2, 3, … 8)
11–12	All couples do a two-hand swing one time around to the left using 8 steps. After the swing, all couples except the head couple go back to their original position. The head couples remain in the middle with their hands joined facing each other. (Swing, 2, 3, … 8)
13–14	The head couple takes 8 sliding (sashay) or skipping steps to the foot of the line. All the other couples clap to the beat and watch. (Slide, 2, 3, … 8)
15–16	Head couple does a right elbow swing at the foot of the line for 8 counts and remains at the foot of the line creating a new head couple. (Swing, 2, 3, … 8)

Repeat dance to the end of the music.

Game Activity

Whistle Ball

Supplies: A ball for each group of 6–8 players.

Skills: Passing, catching

Eight or fewer children move into circle formation. A ball is passed rapidly back and forth among them in any order. The object is to stay in the game as long as possible. A player sits down in place after making any of the following errors:

1. A player has the ball or the ball is on the way when the signal occurs. (Time intervals can be signaled with music on–off taped segments of 5 to 15 seconds.)

2. A poor throw is made or a catch is not made after a catchable throw.

3. A pass is made back to the person from whom it was received.

Another way to control the time periods is to appoint a child as timer and to give her a list of the time periods, a whistle, and a stopwatch. The timer should be cautioned not to give any advance indication of when the stop signal will be blown. Start the game over when there are 4 or 5 players left so players sit out for a short time.

Zap (Cooperative Activity)

Formation: Groups of 4–10

Supplies: One tumbling mat, one magic rope or jump rope, two volleyball standards or device to attach the ropes.

The rope is attached on either side of the mat and approximately 3–4 ft off the ground depending on the age of the children. For this activity the challenge is to get the entire group over the rope and to the other side without touching, or getting "zapped," by the rope. However, to enhance the challenge and keep it safe, jumping over the rope is not allowed. In addition, to start, the group forms a circle and joins hands to form a "closed chain." This chain must remain closed throughout the challenge. If anyone is zapped by the rope or the chain is broken (2 people let go hands), the entire group must go back to the other side and start over.

Objectives:

To practice the forehand stroke and
backhand strokes

To be able to bump and volley a cut
foam training ball with a partner

To play tennis lead-up activities

NASPE National Standards:

Introductory Activity: 1, 3, 5

Fitness Activity: 1, 4, 5, 6

Lesson Focus: 2, 3, 5

Game: 1, 2, 3, 5

Equipment Required:

Signs for sport-related fitness stations

One racquet and cut foam training ball
for each student

Tumbling Mats or net (volleyball, etc.)

Rubber marking spots

Instructional Activities	Teaching Hints

Introductory Activity — High Fives

Students move in different directions throughout the area. On signal, they are
challenged to run toward a partner, jump, and give a "high five" (slap hands)
while moving. Emphasis should be placed on timing so that the "high five" is
given at the top of the jump.

Combinations of changing the level of
the high five and changing the speed of
the locomotor movement can be
developed.

Fitness Development Activity — Sport-Related Fitness Stations

Design your circuit so youngsters alternate strength and flexibility activities with
sport-related fitness activities. Students do the best they can at each station within
the time limit. Children differ and their ability to perform fitness workloads
differs.

1. Rope jumping.
2. Tennis shuffle—similar to the agility run. Mark two lines about 30 ft apart.
    While holding the racquet in the ready position, slide back and forth between
    the lines. Change appropriately to the backhand and forehand position when
    moving.
3. Shoulder girdle development challenges.
4. Run and set—Students move with a racquet in hand. They run a short
    distance, place their feet in proper position and swing at an imaginary ball.
    Repeat as many times as possible using the forehand and backhand.
5. Flexibility and trunk development challenges.
6. Racquets and beanbag toss—Students work with a partner or small group and
    toss a beanbag back and forth and catch it with racquet. Avoid using hands.
7. Abdominal development challenges.
8. Quarter turn sets—Start in a front facing position with racquet held in the
    ready position. Follow a leader and do a quarter jump turn (to forehand or
    backhand setup position). Go back to front facing position each time. Each
    leader gets to lead 5 jump turns.

Tape alternating segments of silence and
music to signal duration of exercise.
Music segments (begin at 30 seconds)
indicate activity at each station, while
intervals of silence (10 seconds)
announce it is time to stop and move
forward to the next station.

See the *DPE* textbook, Chapter 13, for
strength and flexibility challenges and
exercises.

Use signals such as start, stop, and move
up to ensure rapid movement to the next
station.

Ask students to do the best they can.
Expect workloads to differ.

Lesson Focus — Tennis Skills

Footwork and Ball Handling Skills

The focus of this lesson is to develop quality footwork. Encourage players to hold
their racquets in proper position while moving.

1. Roll and Racquet Catch. Working with a partner, one partner rolls the ball to
    the other who moves in front of the ball, lets it roll up the racquet and taps it in
    the air. Reverse the sequence with the other partner rolling etc.

2. Toss and Racquet Catch. Performed as above except the ball is tossed in the
    air to partner. Catch the ball on the racquet and reverse the sequence.

3. Toss, Volley, and Racquet Catch. One partner tosses the ball to the other who
    volleys it back to the tosser, who catches it with a racquet catch. Reverse roles
    after five tosses.

4. Balance ball on racquet and move. Begin in ready position with ball on racquet.
    A student or the instructor moves the group forward, backward, and sideways.
    Goal is to keep the ball under control by shuffling with a smooth step.

If some students find it too challenging
to use a transition ball, allow them to
practice the activities with a beanbag.
Developing a positive attitude toward
tennis is more important than learning
any specific skills.

Just bump the ball. Avoid wild and
uncontrolled swings.

Stay in your own space. Don't chase a
ball that is out of your area without
looking to see if it safe. When
performing drills, teach students to stay
at least an arm plus a racquet length
from other players.

5. Racquet and ball handling skills.
    a. Pick up the ball with foot and racquet.
    b. Toss ball into the air with foot and racquet and catch it on the racquet.
    c. Tap or toss the ball in the air, make a full turn and catch the ball on the racquet. Let it bounce once if too difficult.
    d. Create challenges using heel clicks, touching the floor, or sitting down after tossing or tapping the ball in the air.

Forehand and Backhand Combinations

Students will practice hitting forehand and backhand strokes. Since it is important to immediately move into position for a forehand or backhand, students should move to the ready position after a return so they are ready to return the next shot. Fundamentals of the ready position are:
    a. Weight evenly balanced on the balls of both feet with the knees slightly bent.
    b. The racquet is held in front of the body with the head of the racquet near eye level.
    c. The racquet is held with both hands and the body is squared up parallel with the net.
The following skills can be practiced with the class as a whole or set up for station teaching.

1. Alternate Forehand and Backhand Bumps against the Wall. After each stroke, players return to the ready position. Let the ball bounce more than once so there is time to get in position.

2. Toss and Hit Forehands and Backhands with a Partner. One partner tosses the ball to the forehand or backhand side. After each stroke return to ready position. Change roles after 6 tosses.

3. Toss and Hit One Step. One partner tosses the ball to either the forehand or backhand side. With each successful return, the player takes one step away from the tosser. The goal is to continue to return the ball accurately to the tosser. Change roles after 6 tosses.

4. Partner Rally. Begin the rally with a drop-hit serve. Both forehand and backhand serves can be used during play. A point can only be scored after 4 successful returns. A point is scored when one partner misses a return or hits a return that is out of reach.

5. Partner Target Rally. Begin the rally with a drop-hit serve. After the serve, every shot that goes in the target (a hoop or carpet square) earns a point. Change partners regularly after one minute of play.

6. Partner Rally over a Net. Play is similar to Partner Target Rally above with the exception that a point is scored when the ball is not returned over the net. A point is not scored if the opponent is unable to reach the return.

These activities take considerable space, so emphasis must be placed on controlled bumps rather than wild swinging.

If students become frustrated, put the equipment down and play a simple game such as tag or "Simon Says."

Allow students to try a skill first before offering corrective feedback. This helps them see the need for help in improving their performance and allows you to see where they need help.

Change partners when going to a new activity.

Emphasize having quick feet so the return to the ready position is done quickly.

When tossing feeds to a partner, emphasize the need for doing it in a manner that makes it easy to hit. Talk about "friendly feeds."

Short games allow students to meet many players and not end up losing by a large margin if they stayed with the same partner.

There are a number of ways to simulate nets for students in the physical education setting. Tumbling mats can be laid folded and on-edge as a net. Cafeteria tables can also be used. Some teachers use 2 cones with a jump rope stretched between them for a net. The purpose is to give students a target to hit the ball over.

Students should try to hit to their partner in all of these games. Since there are no out-of-bound lines, points can only be scored if the ball is returnable by the opponent.

Tennis Lead-up Activities

Tennis Volleyball

Supplies: One racquet per student and cut foam training balls.
Skills: Bumping and volleying

Divide the class in half. A player at the baseline hits the ball over the net. Once the ball lands in the appropriate half of the court, anyone on the team may hit the ball to a teammate or directly over the net. The ball can be hit any number of times on one side on any number of bounces. The ball is dead when it rolls. No boundaries make this an interesting and exciting game. Points can be scored on or off serve. Play to 11 points and start over. Change the makeup of the teams often.

Playground Tennis

Supplies: One racquet per student and one cut foam training ball per game.

Skills: Racquet and ball control, bumping the ball, team play

Playground Tennis is a team game that uses no more than 4 players per team (4 against 4) per court. Players "bump" the cut foam ball over the net rather than taking wild swings. Racquet control is the instructional cue. A stretch magic rope, volleyball net or similar equipment can be used to delineate the net. There is no spiking, all balls must have an upward trajectory. Score by ones, the first team to 5 points is the winner and a new game starts.

There are three ways to win/lose a point.

1. If the ball rolls, it is dead and the point goes to the other team.
2. If the first bounce after the ball crosses the net does not land in the court, the point goes to the other team.
3. If the server double faults, the point goes to the other team.

If players converge on the ball rather than stay in their area, establish quadrants where they must stay. Rotate youngsters to different quadrants so they have a chance to play in all areas.

The serve is drop-hit (i.e., one bounce on the court and then bumped over the net) from anywhere on the court. Two serves per point are allowed. Servers are rotated after every other point (serve 2 points and change servers).

Once the ball is served, it may bounce as many times as the receiving team wants it to, no matter where it goes. When a team bumps the ball over the net, the first bounce must land inside the doubles court lines. After that, the ball is in play as long as the ball is bouncing, even if it goes outside of the doubles court. The team tries to scoop it up and bump it back over the net. If the ball is hit into the net, but is still bouncing, it is still in play and the team can continue to try to scoop it up and bump it over the net.

Teaching Tip: Play 3 on 3 with less able students and 2 on 2 with more proficient students

DPE Curriculum Guide – Lesson Plans
Tennis Skills and Lead-up Activities (2)
Level III – Week 29

Objectives:

To be able to bump and volley a cut foam tennis ball with a partner

To practice basic tennis skills

To play tennis lead-up activities

NASPE National Standards:

Introductory Activity: 1, 3, 5

Fitness Activity: 1, 4, 5, 6

Lesson Focus: 2, 3, 5

Game: 1, 2, 3, 5

Equipment Required:

Signs for sport-related fitness stations

One racquet and cut foam training ball for each student

Tumbling Mats or net (volleyball, etc.)

Rubber marking spots

Instructional Activities	**Teaching Hints**

Introductory Activity — Individual Crows and Cranes

All students have a partner and line up along two lines facing each other. The lines are about 3 ft apart. This is an individual game. The partners alternate calling out "Crows!" When one of the partners decides to call out "Cranes," the other partner must take off and run back to a safety line without being tagged. If the chaser tags them, the chaser gets a point. Players start over immediately.

Assure students are spread out so they don't run into each other.

Tagging is done with the back of the hand on the shoulder.

Fitness Development Activity — Sport-Related Fitness Stations

Design your circuit so youngsters alternate strength and flexibility activities with sport-related fitness activities. Students do the best they can at each station within the time limit. Children differ and their ability to perform fitness workloads differs.

1. Rope jumping.
2. Tennis shuffle—similar to the agility run. Mark two lines about 30 ft apart. While holding the racquet in the ready position, slide back and forth between the lines. Change appropriately to the backhand and forehand position when moving.
3. Shoulder girdle development challenges.
4. Run and set—Students move with a racquet in hand. They run a short distance, place their feet in proper position and swing at an imaginary ball. Repeat as many times as possible using the forehand and backhand.
5. Flexibility and trunk development challenges.
6. Racquets and beanbag toss—Students work with a partner or small group and toss a beanbag back and forth and catch it with racquet. Avoid using hands.
7. Abdominal development challenges.
8. Quarter turn sets—Start in a front facing position with racquet held in the ready position. Follow a leader and do a quarter jump turn (to forehand or backhand setup position). Go back to front facing position each time. Each leader gets to lead five jump turns.

Tape alternating segments of silence and music to signal duration of exercise. Music segments (begin at 30 seconds) indicate activity at each station, while intervals of silence (10 seconds) announce it is time to stop and move forward to the next station.

See the *DPE* textbook, Chapter 13, for strength and flexibility challenges and exercises.

Use signals such as start, stop, and move up to ensure rapid movement to the next station.

Ask students to do the best they can. Expect workloads to differ.

Lesson Focus – Tennis Skills

Volleying

A volley is any return that is hit before it bounces. The volley can be explained to students as a blocked shot that is hit with the racquet held firmly in the path of a ball like a "stop sign." There is no swing or follow-through with the volley shot and the ball is hit out in front of the body. The following are key points of emphasis for the volley shot.

1. The shake hands grip is used for the volley shot. The wrist is held firm in either case.
2. The side of the body is turned sideways to the target before contacting the ball.
3. The ball is contacted in front of the body; the ball is blocked, not hit. There is no follow-through.

For the following activities, a beanbag or fleece ball can be used in early stages. The beanbag will drop to the floor and is easy to block. The fleece ball can be volleyed a short distance so students can work with a partner. The final progression would be to the transition ball. Have students "choke up" on the racquet when they are first learning the volley.

When introducing the volley, have students practice setting up in the forehand and backhand volley position and checking the direction of their racquet face. Remind them that the angle of the racquet face determines which way the ball will travel.

Focus on the forehand volley first because it is easier for students to perform. The racquet is easier for them to see so they can set the racquet face at the right angle. If students are having trouble with the backhand volley, stick to the forehand volley. Success is more important than presenting an activity that is too difficult for them to accomplish.

1. Partner Toss, Volley, and Catch. Using a fleece ball, one partner tosses to the forehand or backhand of their partner. The partner volleys it back to their partner who catches it. Begin with partners three steps apart. Change roles after six tosses.

2. Partner Bump Feed, Volley, and Trap. Using a fleece ball, one partner bump feeds the ball to the other. The ball is returned with a volley to the feeder who traps the ball against their racquet. Change roles after 6 tosses. For a variation, start students 3 steps apart and allow the feeder to back up a step each time a successful volley and trap is made.

3. Circle Volley. Begin by using a fleece ball and then progress to a transition ball. Place students in a circle of 3 students. The goal is to have players volley the ball so it goes around the circle twice. The ball can only be volleyed once by a player. Circles score a point if they make it around twice. They must start over after a miss by any player.

Skill Practice Stations
Station 1: Racquet and ball-handling skills.
   a. Pick up the ball with foot and racquet.
   b. Toss ball into the air with foot and racquet and catch it on the racquet.
   c. Tap or toss the ball in the air, make a full turn and catch the ball on the racquet. Let it bounce once if too difficult.
   d. Bounce ball in the air, switch racquet to the other hand.
Station 2: Drop and Hit Forehands.
   Partners use a rope or line as a net. One partner drops and hits the ball over the net using a forehand stroke and a rally ensues. The other partner begins the next rally.
Station 3: Forehand and Backhand Hits.
   Partners are about 10 ft from each other. One partner starts with a drop hit forehand. Partners try to rally the ball and accumulate 4 returns using both forehand and backhand strokes. Roles are reversed for the next drop and hit after a completed rally.
Station 4: Partner Target Rally.
   Begin the rally with a drop-hit serve. After the serve, every shot that goes in the target (a hoop or carpet square) earns a point. Change partners regularly after 1 minute of play.
Station 5: Toss, Turn, and Serve.
   Using fleece balls, players toss the ball, turn and serve the ball at the wall. Focus on tossing the ball until you find an acceptable toss. Follow through with the racquet.
Station 6: Partner Bump Feed, Volley, and Trap.
   Using a fleece ball, one partner bump feeds the ball to the other. The ball is returned with a volley to the feeder who traps the ball against their racquet. Change roles after 6 tosses.

Punch at the ball rather than swing. Hold the racquet firm and block the ball. Volleying requires quick feet. In the early stages of teaching the volley, have students start in the ready position. Call out forehand or backhand and get them in the habit of moving their feet into position for the volley.

If the range of ability varies somewhat in a class, different objects can be used at the students' discretion. They can choose the object they would like to volley based on their ability level. Care must be taken to assure there is room for using different objects such as beanbags and transition balls.

Allow 2–3 minutes at each station for students to practice. Place emphasis on working in a responsible manner.

Using stations to teach tennis skills offers a chance to work individually with students who need additional help.

Set up the tennis station signs around the perimeter of the teaching area. If necessary, explain one station at a time. It is usually counterproductive to sit the class down and explain all the stations. They can't remember all in explanations and fidget because they want to get started. Move between stations and explain the stations while students are engaged.

Put the necessary equipment at each station and ask students to replace the equipment where they found it before they move to the next station.

It usually takes about 15–20 seconds for students to put back the equipment and move up to a new station.

Tennis Lead-up Activities

Tennis Volleyball
   Supplies: One racquet per student and cut foam training balls.
   Skills: Bumping and volleying
   Divide the class in half. A player at the baseline hits the ball over the net. Once the ball lands in the appropriate half of the court, anyone on the team may hit the ball to a teammate or directly over the net. The ball can be hit any number of teams on one side on any number of bounces. The ball is dead when it rolls. No boundaries make this an interesting and exciting game. Points can be scored on or off serve. Play to 11 points and start over. Change the makeup of the teams often.

Volley-Shuttle Run
   Supplies: One racquet per student and one cut foam training ball per group.
   Skills: Volleying
   Divide the class into groups of 6 students. Each player has a racquet. Place half of each team (3 students) on one side of the net and half on the opposite side. Teams line up in single file 6–10 ft from the net. The first player volleys the ball and then runs around the net to get into the line on that side. Players concentrate on hitting controlled volleys. The activity continues in a shuttle relay fashion.

Playground Tennis

Supplies: One racquet per student and one cut foam training ball per game

Skills: Racquet and ball control, bumping the ball, team play

Playground Tennis is a team game that uses no more than 4 players per team (4 against 4) per court. Players "bump" the cut foam ball over the net rather than taking wild swings. Racquet control is the instructional cue. A stretch magic rope, volleyball net, or similar equipment can be used to delineate the net. There is no spiking, all balls must have an upward trajectory. Score by ones, the first team to 5 points is the winner and a new game starts.

There are three ways to win/lose a point.

1. If the ball rolls, it is dead and the point goes to the other team.

2. If the first bounce after the ball crosses the net does not land in the court, the point goes to the other team.

3. If the server double faults, the point goes to the other team.

If players converge on the ball rather than stay in their area, establish quadrants where they must stay. Rotate youngsters to different quadrants so they have a chance to play in all areas.

The serve is drop-hit (i.e., one bounce on the court and then bumped over the net) from anywhere on the court. Two serves per point are allowed. Servers are rotated after every other point (serve 2 points and change servers).

Once the ball is served, it may bounce as many times as the receiving team wants it to, no matter where it goes. When a team bumps the ball over the net, the first bounce must land inside the doubles court lines. After that, the ball is in play as long as the ball is bouncing, even if it goes outside of the doubles court. The team tries to scoop it up and bump it back over the net. If the ball is hit into the net, but is still bouncing, it is still in play and the team can continue to try to scoop it up and bump it over the net.

Teaching Tip: Play 3 on 3 with less able students and 2 on 2 with more proficient students.

Objectives:
To lead other students through warm-up activities
To serve a volleyball in a predetermined direction
To understand basic principles of training

NASPE National Standards:
Introductory Activity: 1, 3, 5
Fitness Activity: 1, 2, 3, 6
Lesson Focus: 2, 3, 5
Game: 2, 3, 5

Equipment Required:
Signs and music for Circuit Training
One beach ball, volleyball trainer, or foam training ball for each student
Volleyball net or magic stretch ropes

Instructional Activities	Teaching Hints

Introductory Activity — New Leader

Divide class into small groups and appoint one member in each group to lead. Groups move around the area following any movement the leader does. On signal, another person in the group becomes the leader. The leader can use various types of locomotor movements and/or exercises.

Assign each group a specific area if desired. Each area could include a piece of equipment to aid in the activity (beanbag, fleece ball, etc.).

Fitness Development Activity — Circuit Training

Students do the best they can at each station within the time limit. This implies that not all youngsters are required to do the same workload. Children differ and their ability to perform fitness workloads differs. Make fitness a personal challenge.
Rope Jumping
Push-Ups
Agility Run
Lower Leg Stretch
Juggling Scarves
Curl-Ups with Twist
Alternate Leg Extension
Tortoise and Hare
Bear Hug

Conclude circuit training with 2–4 minutes of walking, jogging, rope jumping, or other self-paced aerobic activity

Tape alternating segments of silence and music to signal duration of exercise. Music segments (begin at 35 seconds) indicate activity at each station, while intervals of silence (10 seconds) announce it is time to stop and move forward to the next station.

Use signals such as start, stop, and move up to ensure rapid movement to the next station.

Ask students to do their personal best. Expect workloads to differ.

Lesson Focus — Volleyball Skills (1)

Skills
Practice the following skills:
Overhand Pass

To execute an overhand pass, the player moves underneath the ball and controls it with the fingertips. The cup of the fingers is made so that the thumbs and forefingers are close together and the other fingers are spread. The hands are held forehead high, with elbows out and level with the floor. The player, when in receiving position, looks ready to shout upward through the hands. The player contacts the ball above eye level and propels it with the force of spread fingers, not with the palms. At the moment of contact, the legs are straightened and the hands and arms follow through.

Forearm Pass (Underhand Pass)

The hands are clasped together so that the forearms are parallel. The clasp should be relaxed, with the type of handclasp a matter of choice. The thumbs are kept parallel and together, and the fingers of one hand make a partially cupped fist, with the fingers of the other hand overlapping the fist. The wrists are turned downward and the elbow joints are reasonably locked. The forearms are held at the proper angle to rebound the ball, with contact made with the fists or forearms between the knees as the receiver crouches.

Using beach balls or trainer volleyballs will allow youngsters time to move into the path of the volleyball instead of reaching for the ball. Proper footwork is critical to the success of volleyball; using proper balls will help assure that youngsters learn correctly.

Instructional cues for passing include the following:
1. Move into the path of the ball; don't reach for it.
2. Bend the knees prior to making contact.
3. Contact the ball with the fingertips (overhand pass).
4. Extend the knees upon contact with the ball.
5. Follow through after striking the ball.

Underhand Serve

Directions are for a right-handed serve. The player stands facing the net with the left foot slightly forward and the weight on the right (rear) foot. The ball is held in the left hand with the left arm across and a little in front of the body. On the serving motion, the server steps forward with the left foot, transfers the weight to the front foot, and at the same time brings the right arm back in a preparatory motion. The right hand now swings forward and contacts the ball just below center. The ball can be hit with an open hand or with the fist (facing forward or sideward). Children should explore the best way to strike the ball, with the flat of the hand or the fist. Each player can select the method that is personally most effective.

Setup

The term *setup* applies to a pass that sets the ball for a possible spike. The object is to raise the ball with a soft, easy pass to a position 1 or 2 ft above the net and about 1 ft away from it. The setup is generally the second pass in a series of three. An overhand pass is used for the setup. It is important for the back line player, who has to tap to the setter, to make an accurate and easily handled pass.

Individual Passing Drills

1. Practice wall rebounding: Stand 6 ft away from a wall. Pass the ball against the wall and catch it.
2. From a spot 6 ft from the wall, throw the ball against the wall and alternate an overhand pass with a forearm pass.
3. Throw the ball to one side (right or left) and move to the side to pass the ball to the wall. Catch the rebound.
4. Pass the ball directly overhead and catch it. Try making two passes before catching the ball. Later, alternate an overhand pass with a forearm pass and catch the ball. This is a basic drill and should be mastered before proceeding to others.

Partner Passing Drills

1. Players are about 10 ft apart. Player A tosses the ball (controlled toss) to player B, who passes the ball back to A, who catches the ball. Continue for several exchanges and then change throwers.
2. Two players are about 15 ft apart. Player A passes to themselves first and then makes a second pass to player B, who catches the ball and repeats. Follow with a return by B.
3. Players A and B try to keep the ball in the air continuously.
4. Players are about 15 ft apart. Player A remains stationary and passes in such a fashion that player B must move from side to side. An option is to have player B move forward and backward.
5. Players are about 10 ft apart. Both have hoops and attempt to keep one foot in the hoop while passing. Try keeping both feet in the hoop.
6. Player A passes to player B and does a complete turnaround. B passes back to A and also does a full turn. Other stunts can be used.

Partner Work (Serving and Passing)

1. Partners are about 20 ft apart. Partner A serves to partner B, who catches the ball and returns the serve to partner A.
2. Partner A serves to partner B, who makes a pass back to partner A. Change responsibilities.
3. Service One-Step. Partners begin about 10 ft apart. Partner A serves to partner B, who returns the serve with partner A catching. If there is no error and if neither receiver moved the feet to catch, both players take one step back. This is repeated each time no error or foot movement by the receivers occurs. If an error occurs or if appreciable foot movement is evident, the players revert to the original distance of 10 ft and start over.
4. A player stands at the top of the key on a basketball court. The object is to serve the ball into the basket. Scoring can be as in other basket-making drills: 3 points for a basket, 2 points for hitting the rim, and 1 point for hitting the backboard but not the rim. Partner retrieves the ball.

Instructional cues for the serve:
1. Use opposition. Place the opposite foot of the serving hand forward.
2. Transfer the weight to the forward foot.
3. Keep the eyes on the ball.
4. Decide prior to the serve where it should be placed.
5. Follow through; don't punch at the ball.

The usual basketball court should be divided into two volleyball courts on which players play crosswise. Nets should be lowered to 6 ft and raised 6–12 in. as children mature.

Volleyball Lead-up Activities

Pass and Dig

Supplies: A trainer volleyball for each team

Skills: Overhand, forearm, and dig passes

Each team forms a small circle of not more than 8 players. The object of the game is to see which team can make the greater number of volleys in a specified time or which team can keep the ball in the air for the greater number of consecutive volleys without error.

On the signal "Go," the game is started with a volley by one of the players. The following rules are in force.

1. Balls are volleyed back and forth with no specific order of turns, except that the ball cannot be returned to the player from whom it came.

2. A player may not volley a ball twice in succession.

3. Any ball touching the ground does not count and ends the count.

Teaching suggestions: Players should be responsible for calling illegal returns on themselves and thus interrupting the consecutive volley count. The balls used should be of equal quality, so that one team cannot claim a disadvantage. Groups should be taught to count the volleys out loud, so that their progress is known.

Mini-Volleyball

Supplies: A volleyball or trainer volleyball

Skills: Most volleyball skills

Mini-Volleyball is a modified activity designed to offer opportunities for successful volleyball experiences to children between the ages of 9 and 12. The playing area is 15 ft wide and 40 ft long. The spiking line is 10 ft from the centerline. Many gymnasiums are marked for badminton courts that are 20 by 44 ft with a spiking line 6.5 ft from the center. This is an acceptable substitute court.

The modified rules used in Mini-Volleyball are as follows.

1. A team consists of 3 players. Two substitutions may be made per game.

2. Players are positioned for the serve so that there are two front-line players and one back-line player. After the ball is served, the back-line player may not spike the ball from the attack area or hit the ball into the attack area unless the ball is below the height of the net.

3. The height of the net is 6 ft, 10 in.

4. Players rotate positions when they receive the ball for serving. The right front-line player becomes the back-line player, and the left front-line player becomes the right front-line player.

5. A team wins a game when it scores 15 points and has a 2-point advantage over the opponent. A team wins the match when it wins two out of three games.

The back-line player cannot spike and thus serves a useful function by allowing the front players to receive the serves while he moves to the net to set up for the spikers.

Modify the game to suit the needs of participants. Sponge training balls work well in the learning stages of Mini-Volleyball.

Regulation Volleyball

Supplies: A volleyball

Skills: All volleyball skills

Regulation volleyball should be played with one possible rule change: In early experiences, it is suggested that the server be allowed a second chance if she fails to get the first attempt over the net and into play. This should apply only to the initial serve. Some instructors like to shorten the serving distance during the introductory phases of the game. It is important for the serving to be done well enough to keep the game moving.

A referee should supervise the game. There are generally three calls.

1. "Side out." The serving team fails to serve the ball successfully to the other court, fails to make a good return of a volley, or makes a rule violation.

2. "Point." The receiving team fails to make a legal return or is guilty of a rule violation.

3. "Double foul." Fouls are made by both teams on the same play, in which case the point is replayed. No score or side out results.

Backcourt players should be encouraged to pass to frontcourt players rather than merely batting the ball back and forth across the net.

DPE Curriculum Guide – Lesson Plans
Volleyball Skills and Lead-up Activities (2)
Level III – Week 31

Objectives:
To handle a ball in a variety of
    situations
To show respect for peers with
    different skill levels
To accept decisions made by officials
To enjoy a variety of volleyball games

NASPE National Standards:
Introductory Activity: 1, 2, 3
Fitness Activity: 1, 4, 6
Lesson Focus: 2, 3, 5
Game: 2, 3, 5

Equipment Required:
Music tape for Continuity Drills
One beach ball, volleyball trainer, or
    foam training ball for each student
Volleyball net or magic stretch ropes

Instructional Activities	Teaching Hints

Introductory Activity — Ball Activities

Each student has a ball and dribbles around the area. On signal, stop and perform a number of activities with the ball. Examples are passing the ball behind the back, under a leg, and overhead. Try variations such as tossing the ball into the air instead of dribbling while moving or play catch with a friend while moving.

Focus on ball control and quality movement.

Place the balls around the perimeter of the area for quick acquisition and immediate activity.

Fitness Development Activity — Continuity Drills

Rope jumping—forward	25 seconds	
Double Crab Kick	30 seconds	
Rope jumping—backward	25 seconds	
Knee Touch Curl-Up	30 seconds	
Jump and turn body	25 seconds	
Push-Ups	30 seconds	
Rocker Step	25 seconds	
Bend and Twist	30 seconds	
Swing -Step forward	25 seconds	
Side Flex	30 seconds	
Free jumping	25 seconds	

Relax and stretch for a short time.

Make a tape with music segments (25 seconds) alternated with silence (30 seconds). When the music is playing, students jump rope; when silence occurs, students do a flexibility and strength development exercise.

Exercises can be done in two-count fashion. Exercises are done when the leader says "Ready." The class answers "One-two" and performs a repetition.

Allow students to adjust the workload to their level. This implies resting if the rope jumping is too strenuous.

Lesson Focus — Volleyball Skills (2)

Skills
Review the skills learned last week. Use some of the drills introduced in the previous lesson to practice the skills.
    a. Underhand serve
    b. Overhand pass
    c. Serving
    d. Setup
Introduce a new skill.
Blocking
    A member of the defensive team forms a screen by extending hands and arms straight up while jumping straight up. The ball is not struck, but rebounds from the blocker's stiffened hands and arms.

Blocking involves one or more members of the defensive (receiving) team forming a screen of arms and hands near the net to block a spike. At the elementary school level, a single individual usually does blocking, and little attention is given to multiple blocking. To block a ball, a player jumps high with arms outstretched overhead, palms facing the net, and fingers spread. The jump must be timed with that of the spiker, and the blocker must avoid touching the net.

Drills
Leave time for playing volleyball lead-up games.
Station (Small-Group) Instruction
Divide the class into four equal groups. Set up a system of rotation that assures all stations will be covered.

The ball is not struck but rather rebounds from the blocker's stiffened hands and arms. Students should know about blocking even if it is used infrequently in elementary play.

Station 1—Individual Volleying

1. Volley the ball directly overhead and catch. Try two consecutive volleys before the catch. Next, alternate a bump with an overhand pass before the catch. Finally, try to keep the ball going five or six times in a row with one kind of volley; alternate kinds of volleys.

2. Volley the ball 15 ft overhead, make a full turn and pass the ball again. Vary with other stunts (i.e., touching the floor, a heel click, clapping the hands at two different spots).

Station 2—Volleying with a Partner

Players are 10 ft apart. One player tosses the ball to the other, who volleys it back to the first player, who catches it. After several volleys by one player, exchange tossers. Players can try to keep the ball going back and forth with a designated number of volleys before one player catches the ball.

Station 3—Serving to a Partner

One partner serves to the other, who volleys the ball back. Exchange responsibilities after several serves and return volleys.

Station 4—Setting and Blocking

For blocking, three players are positioned alongside the net, each with a ball. The players take turns on the other side of the net, practicing blocking skills. Each spiker tosses the ball to himself for spiking. A defensive player moves along the line to block consecutively a total of three spikes. The next step is to have two players move along the line to practice blocking by pairs.

Station work is facilitated if signs are made directing students what to do at each station. List key points and how to do the drills. Signs allow students to work independently

Many of the drills can be done without a net. This allows better use of space since nets restrict how much of the area is used.

Volleyball Lead-up Activities

Mini-Volleyball

See the Lesson Plan, Volleyball Skills (Week 30) for a complete game description.

Regulation Volleyball

See the Lesson Plan, Volleyball Skills (Week 30) for a complete game description.

Three and Over Volleyball

Supplies: A volleyball
Skills: All volleyball skills

The game Three and Over emphasizes the basic offensive strategy of volleyball. The game follows regular volleyball rules with the exception that the ball must be played three times before going over the net. The team loses the serve or the point if the ball is not played three times.

Rotation Mini-Volleyball

Supplies: A volleyball
Skills: All volleyball skills

If four teams are playing in two contests at the same time, a system of rotation can be set up. Divide the available class time roughly into three parts, less the time allotted for logistics. Each team plays the other three teams on a timed basis. At the end of a predetermined time period, whichever team is ahead wins the game. A team may win, lose, or tie during any time period, with the score determined at the end of the respective time period. The best win-loss record wins the overall contest.

DPE Curriculum Guide – Lesson Plans
Rhythmic Movement (4)
Level III – Week 32

Objectives:
To jump a self-turned rope for an
  extended period of time
To develop an appreciation of folk
  dances and their respective
  cultures
To cooperate in a social setting (folk
  dancing)

NASPE National Standards:
Introductory Activity: 1, 3
Fitness Activity: 1, 4, 5, 6
Lesson Focus: 1, 2, 3, 5
Game: 1, 3, 5

Equipment Required:
Music tape for Racetrack Fitness
One jump rope for each student
15 scooters and cageball
Small object for Touchdown game

Instructional Activities	Teaching Hints

Introductory Activity — Group Over and Around

One half of the class is scattered. Each is in a curled position. The other half of the class leaps, jumps over, or moves around the down children. On signal, reverse group roles quickly. In place of a curl, the down children can bridge and make other shapes.

The down children can move slowly around the area.

Emphasize controlled movement.

Fitness Development Activity — Racetrack Fitness

Five or six fitness activities are arranged in the center (the Pit) of a large circle outlined with marking spots (the race track). If desired, tumbling mats can be placed in the center of the race track to delineate the pit stop area. Students work with a partner and alternate running (or doing other locomotor movements) around the race track and going to the pit to perform a strength or flexibility exercise. A different exercise should be performed each time so students assure variety in their workout.

The following are some examples of exercises that can be used for Pit exercises.
1. Arm Circles
2. Bend and Twist
3. Abdominal Challenges
4. Knee to Chest Curl
5. Push-Up Challenges
6. Trunk Twister

Intervals of 30 seconds of music with 10 seconds of silence can be used to signal role changes. The student who was running the track now goes to the pit to exercise and vice versa.

Assure that students run under control (not as fast as they can) and in the same direction.

Allow students to perform at a level they feel comfortable. Youngsters are genetically different and should not be expected to do the same amount of exercise repetitions.

Lesson Focus — Rhythmic Movement (4)

Make dances easy for students to learn by implementing some of the following techniques:
Rhythms should be taught like other sport skills. Avoid striving for perfection so students know it is acceptable to make mistakes. Teach a variety of dances rather than one or two in depth in case some students find it difficult to master a specific dance.
1. Teach the dances without using partners.
2. Allow youngsters to move in any direction without left-right orientation.
3. Use scattered formation instead of circles.
4. Emphasize strong movements such as clapping and stamping to increase involvement.
5. Play the music at a slower speed when first learning the dance.

Jiffy Mixer

Music Source: WWCD-FDN
Formation: Double circle, partners facing.
Directions: The Windsor record has an introduction. Directions are for partners A; B's actions are opposite.
Measures Introduction—use with Windsor record only
1–4 Wait, wait, balance apart (push away on the left foot and touch the right). Balance together (forward on the right and touch the left).
Measures Action
1–4 Strike the left heel diagonally out and return to touch the toe near the right foot. Repeat. Do a side step left with a touch. (Heel, toe; heel, toe; side, close; side, touch)

5–8   Repeat while moving in the opposite direction, beginning with the right foot. (Heel, toe; heel, toe; side, close; side, touch)

9–12   Take four chug steps backward clapping on the up beat. (Chug, clap, chug, clap, chug, clap, chug, clap)

13–16   Starting with the left foot, take four slow, swaggering steps diagonally to the right, progressing to a new partner. (Walk, 2, 3, 4)

The chug step is done by jumping and dragging both feet backward. The body is bent slightly forward.

Horse and Buggy Schottische (American)

Music Source: WWCD-1046

Formation: Couples in sets of four in a double circle, facing counterclockwise. Couples join inside hands and give outside hands to the other couple.

Directions:

Measures   Action

1–2   Moving forward, perform two schottische steps. (Step, step, step, hop; step, step, step, hop)

3–4   Progress in line of direction performing four step-hops. (Step-hop, 2-hop, 3-hop, 4-hop)

During the four step-hops, either of the following patterns can be done.

   1. The lead couple drops inside hands and step-hops around the outside of the back couple, who move forward during the step-hops. The lead couple then joins hands behind the other couple, and the positions are reversed.

   2. The lead couple continues to hold hands and move backward under the upraised hands of the back couple, who untwist by turning away from each other.

Alunelul (Romanian)

Music Source: WWCD-TC1; WWC-TC1

Formation: Single circle, hands on shoulders to both sides, arms straight ("T" position)

Directions: The Romanians are famous for rugged dances. This dance is called "Little Hazelnut." The stomping action represents the breaking of the hazelnuts. The title is pronounced "ah-loo-NAY-loo."

Measures   Part I Action

1–2   Sidestep right, step left behind right, sidestep right, step left behind right, sidestep right, stomp left foot twice. (Side, back, side, back, side, stomp, stomp)

3–4   Beginning with the left foot, repeat the action but with reverse footwork. (Side, back, side, back, side, stomp, stomp)

5–8   Repeat the action of measures 1–4.

Measures   Part II Action

9–10   Sidestep right, left behind right, sidestep right, stomp. (Side, back, side, stomp)

11–12   Sidestep left, right behind left, sidestep left, stomp. (Side, back, side, stomp)

13–16   Repeat the action of measures 9–12.

Measures   Part III Action

17–18   In place, step right, stomp left; step left, stomp right; step right, stomp left twice. (Side, stomp, side, stomp, side, stomp, stomp)

19–20   In place, step left, stomp right; step right, stomp left; step left, stomp right twice. (Side, stomp, side, stomp, side, stomp, stomp)

21–24   Repeat action of measures 17–20. Teaching suggestions:

The stamps should be made close to the supporting foot. In teaching the dance, scatter the dancers in general space so they can move individually.

Korobushka (Russian)

Music Source: WWCD-572; WWC-572

Formation: Double circle, partner A back to the center, with partners facing and both hands joined. A's left and B's right foot are free.

Directions:

Measures   Part I Action

1–2   Take one schottische step away from the center (partner A moving forward, partner B backward) starting with A's left and B's right foot. (Out, 2, 3, hop)

3–4   Repeat the pattern of measures 1 and 2, reversing direction and footwork. (In, 2, 3, hop)

5–6   Repeat the pattern of measures 1 and 2, ending on the last count with a jump on both feet in place. (Out, 2, 3, jump)

7–8   Hop on the left foot, touching the right toes across in front of the left foot (count 1). Hop on the left foot, touching the right toes diagonally forward to the right (count 2). Jump on both feet in place, clicking the heels together (count 1), pause, and release the hands (count 2). (Across, apart, together)

Measures   Part II Action

9–10   Facing partner and beginning with the right foot, take one schottische step right, moving sideways away from partner. (Side, back, side, hop)

11–12   Facing and beginning with the left foot, take one schottische step left, returning to partner. (Side, back, side, hop)

13–14	Joining right hands with partner, balance forward and back: Step forward on the right foot (count 1), pause (count 2), rock back on the left foot in place (count 3), pause (count 4). (Forward, hop, back, hop)
15–16	Take four walking steps forward, starting with the right foot, and change places with partner. (Walk, 2, 3, 4)
17–24	Repeat the pattern of measures 9–16, returning to place.

Oh Johnny (American)

Music Source: WWCD-05114; WWC-57

Skills: Shuffle step, swing, allemande left, do-si-do, promenade

Formation: Single circle of couples facing inward with partner B on the right.

Directions: A shuffle step is used throughout this dance.

Action

All join hands and circle for eight steps.

All stop and swing with partner.

A's turn to their left and swing the corner B.

Swing with partner again.

A's turn to their left and do an allemande left with their corner.

A's turn to their right and do a do-si-do with their partner.

A's promenade with the corner B, who becomes the new partner for the next repetition.

Teaching hint: To simplify the dance, begin in scattered formation and teach each call with students changing from partner to corner using any nearby person. Since this is a fast-moving dance, the music should be slowed down until students can successfully complete the dance.

Virginia Reel (American)

Music Source: WWCD-05114

Skills: Skipping, arm turn, do-si-do, sliding (sashay), reeling

Formation: Six couples in a longways set of two lines facing. Partners on one end of the set are designated the head couple.

Directions:

Measures	Call	Action
1–4	All go forward and back.	Take three steps forward, curtsy or bow. Take three steps back and close.
5–8	Right hands around.	Move forward to partner, turn once in place using a right forearm grasp and return to position.
9–12	Left hands around.	Repeat measures 5–8 with a left forearm grasp.
13–16	Both hands around.	Partners join both hands, turn once in a clockwise direction, and move backward to place.
17–20	Do-si-do your partner.	Partners pass each other right shoulder to right shoulder and then back to back and move backward to place.
21–24	All go forward and back.	Repeat the action of measures 1–4.
25–32	Head couple sashay.	The head couple, with hands joined, takes eight slides down to the foot of the set and eight slides back to place.
33–64	Head couple reel.	The head couple begins the reel with linked right elbows and turns one and one-half times to face the next couple in line. Each member in the head couple then links left elbows with the person facing and turns once in place. The head couple meets again in the center and turns once with a right elbow swing. The next dancers down the line are turned with a left elbow swing and then the head couple returns to the center for another right elbow turn. The head couple thus progresses down the line, turning each dancer in order. After the head couple has turned the last dancers, they meet with a right elbow swing, turn halfway around, and sashay (slide) back to the head of the set.
65–96	Everybody march.	All couples face toward the head of the set with the head couple in front. The person on the right turns to the right, while the person on the left turns to the left and goes behind the line followed by the other dancers. When the head couple reaches the foot of the set, they join hands and make an arch, under which all other couples pass. The head couple is now at the foot of the set and the dance is repeated with a new head couple.

The dance is repeated until each couple has had a chance to be the head couple.

Trio Fun Mixer (American)

Music Source: WWC-FFD

Skills: Walking, Do-si-do, star

Formation: Lines of three facing lines of three in a large circle.

Directions:

Measures	Action
1–4	Facing threesomes (six dancers) join hands and circle left one time around back to place. (circle, 2, 3, … 16)
5–6	Center student in each threesome does a do-si-do with each other. (Do-si-do, 2, 3, … 8)
7–8	Right youngsters in each threesome move diagonally to do-si-do with each other. (Do-si-do, 2, 3, … 8)
9–10	Left youngsters in each threesome move diagonally to do-si-do with each other. (Do-si-do, 2, 3, … 8)
11–12	Center person in each threesome faces the person on the right and turns that person with a right hand star and then turns the person on the left with a left hand star and goes back to place. (Star, 2, 3, 4; left, 2, 3, 4)
13–14	Lines of three go forward 4 counts and back 4 counts. (Forward, 2, 3, 4; back, 2, 3, 4)
15–16	Lines of three walk forward passing right shoulders and move forward to the next group of three (Forward pass, 2, 3, … 8)

Repeat to the end of the music.

Game Activity

Pig Ball (Cooperative Activity)

Formation: Two equal teams

Supplies: A rubber pig. If not available a deflated playground ball will work.

This activity is a continuous version of Alaskan Baseball. Team A stands in a single file line with the last person in line holding the pig. To start the game, the pig is thrown anywhere in the teaching area. The teacher will have to delineate this area. Team B then hustles to the pig and stands in a single file line behind the first person to reach the pig. They then hand the pig to the back of the line alternating between over the head and between the legs. This is best described as "Over and Under, Over and Under." While Team B is doing this, the person that threw the pig is hustling around her team which is still standing in a single file line. Each time an end of the line is passed, the team receives a point. This allows all children to score at least one run for their team. When the pig gets to the last person on Team B, the team yells "PIG," and the pig is thrown anywhere in the teaching area. At this time the person that threw the pig begins running around his teammates who remain in a single file line. At the same time, Team A is hustling to the pig and beginning the over and under passing. The game continues in this fashion for as long as desired.

Teaching Tips: This game is very rigorous. For this reason, after 3–4 rounds the game should be stopped and some type of instruction given. The instruction could be about cardiovascular health and why the heart is beating faster, why Pig Ball is cooperative, or strategy for the game. However, after a short bout of instruction and rest, students will be ready for more. Also, the teacher can identify a specific locomotor movement or animal movement that all students must use.

Touchdown

Supplies: A small object that can be concealed in the hand.

Skills: Running, dodging

Two parallel lines are placed at each end of the playing area. The class is divided into two teams with one team on each of the two lines. One team (offensive) huddles, placing their hands in the center. Players choose one player to carry the object to the opponents' goal line. The offensive team moves out of the huddle and spreads out along the line. On the signal "Hike," the offensive players move toward the opponents' goal line holding their hands closed so it is impossible to tell who is carrying the object. On the charge signal, the defensive team runs forward and tries to tag all the players. When tagged, players must freeze immediately and open both hands to show whether they have the object. If the player carrying the object reaches the goal line without being tagged, she calls "Touchdown" and scores 6 points. The defensive team now becomes the offensive team and vice versa.

Chain Tag

Supplies: None

Skills: Running, dodging

Two parallel lines are established at opposite ends of the playing area. Two groups of three players form a chain with joined hands and occupy the center. The players with free hands on either end of the chain do the tagging. All other players line up on one of the parallel lines. The players in the center call "Come on over," and children cross from one line to the other. The chains try to tag the runners. Anyone caught joins the chain. When the chain grows to six players, it divides into two groups of three players.

DPE Curriculum Guide – Lesson Plans
Frisbee Skills
Level III – Week 33

Objectives:
To learn the unique throwing style required with Frisbees
To learn the rules of Frisbee golf
To play a round of Frisbee golf in a cooperative manner

NASPE National Standards:
Introductory Activity: 1, 5
Fitness Activity: 1, 2, 3, 5
Lesson Focus: 2, 3, 5
Game: 2, 3, 5

Equipment Required:
Moving to Music tape
Music, cones, and signs for Squad Leader Exercises
Frisbees (one for each pair of students)
Scorecards and clipboards
Hoops, bowling pins, and cones

Instructional Activities	Teaching Hints
Introductory Activity — Moving to Music	
Use different types of music to stimulate various locomotor and nonlocomotor movements. Dance steps such as the polka, two-step, schottische, and grapevine could be practiced.	If youngsters have trouble sensing the rhythm, use a tom-tom or tambourine to accentuate the beat.

Fitness Development Activity — Squad Leader Exercises with Task Cards

Suggested exercises to be placed on task cards:

Sitting Stretch
Push-Up challenges
Body Circles
Jumping Jack variations
Crab Kick combinations
Abdominal challenges
Treadmills
Toe Touchers
Leg Extensions

If there is a delay in starting an exercise, the squad should walk or jog.

The class is divided into groups of four to five students. Each group is given a task card that lists 8 to 10 exercises. One of the group members begins as the leader and leads the group through an exercise. Each time an exercise is completed, the card is passed to a new leader.

Use alternating intervals of music to signal exercising (30 seconds) with silence (5–8 seconds) to indicate passing the card.

Lesson Focus — Frisbee Skills

Throwing the Disk
Backhand Throw
    The backhand grip is used most often. The thumb is on top of the disk, the index finger along the rim, and the other fingers underneath. To throw the Frisbee with the right hand, stand in a sideways position with the right foot toward the target. Step toward the target and throw the Frisbee in a sideways motion across the body, snapping the wrist and trying to keep the disk flat on release.
Underhand Throw
    The underhand throw uses the same grip as in the backhand throw, but the thrower faces the target and holds the disk at the side of the body. Step forward with the leg opposite the throwing arm while bringing the Frisbee forward. When the throwing arm is out in the front of the body, release the Frisbee. The trick to this throw is learning to release the disk so that it is parallel to the ground.

Catching the Disk
Thumb-Down Catch
    The thumb-down catch is used for catching when the disk is received at waist level or above. The thumb is pointing toward the ground. The Frisbee should be tracked from the thrower's hand. This clues the catcher about any tilt on the disk that may cause it to curve.
Thumb-Up Catch
    The thumb-up catch is used when the Frisbee is received below waist level. The thumb points up and the fingers are spread.

Throwing and Catching Activities:
a. Throw the Frisbee at different levels to partner.
b. Throw a curve—to the left, right and upward. Vary the speed of the curve.

Use the following instructional cues to improve skill performance:

a. Release the disk parallel to the ground. If it is tilted, a curved throw results.

b. Step toward the target and follow through on release of the disk.

c. Snap open the wrist and make the Frisbee spin.

If space is limited, all Frisbees should be thrown in the same direction. Students can line up on either side of the area and throw across to each other.

Most activities are best practiced by pairs of students using one disk.

c. Throw a bounce pass—try a low and a high pass.
d. Throw the disc like a boomerang. Must throw at a steep angle into the wind.
e. Throw the Frisbee into the air, run and catch. Increase the distance of the throw.
f. Throw the Frisbee through a hoop held by a partner.
g. Catch the Frisbee under your leg. Catch it behind your back.
h. Throw the Frisbees into hoops that are placed on the ground as targets. Different-colored hoops can be given different values. Throw through your partner's legs.
i. Frisbee bowling—One partner has a bowling pin, which the other partner attempts to knock down by throwing the Frisbee.
j. Play catch while moving. Lead your partner so he doesn't have to break stride.
k. See how many successful throws and catches you can make in 30 seconds.
l. Frisbee Baseball Pitching—Attempt to throw the Frisbee into your partner's "Strike Zone."

Youngsters can develop both sides of the body by learning to throw and catch the disk with either hand. The teacher should design the activities so that youngsters get both right-hand and left-hand practice.

Since a Frisbee is somewhat different from the other implements that children usually throw, devote some time to teaching form and style in throwing and catching. Avoid drills that reward speed in throwing and catching.

Frisbee Game Activities

Frisbee Keepaway
Supplies: Frisbees
Skills: Throwing and catching Frisbees

Students break into groups of three. Two of the players in the group try to keep the other player from touching the Frisbee while they are passing it back and forth. If a defensive player touches the Frisbee, the person who threw the Frisbee becomes the defensive player. Begin the game by asking students to remain stationary while throwing and catching. Later, challenge can be added by allowing all players in the group move.

Frisbee Golf
Supplies: One Frisbee per person, hoops for hole markers, cones
Skills: Frisbee throwing for accuracy

Frisbee Golf or disk golf is a favorite game of many students. Boundary cones with numbers can be used for tees, and holes can be boxes, hula hoops, trees, tires, garbage cans, or any other available equipment on the school grounds. Draw a course on a map for students and start them at different holes to decrease the time spent waiting to tee off. Regulation golf rules apply. The students can jog between throws for increased activity.

Disk golf is played like regular golf. One stroke is counted for each time the disk is thrown and when a penalty is incurred. The object is to acquire the lowest score. The following rules dictate play:

Tee-throws: Tee-throws must be completed within or behind the designated tee area.

Lie: The lie is the spot on or directly underneath the spot where the previous throw landed.

Throwing order: The player whose disk is the farthest from the hole throws first. The player with the least number of throws on the previous hole tees off first.

Fairway throws: Fairway throws must be made with the foot closest to the hole on the lie. A run-up is allowed.

Dog leg: A dog leg is one or more designated trees or poles in the fairway that must be passed on the outside when approaching the hole. There is a two-stroke penalty for missing a dog leg.

Putt throw: A putt throw is any throw within 10 ft of the hole. A player may not move past the point of the lie in making the putt throw. Falling or jumping putts are not allowed.

Unplayable lies: Any disk that comes to rest 6 ft or more above the ground is unplayable. The next throw must be played from a new lie directly underneath the unplayable lie (one-stroke penalty).

Out-of-bounds: A throw that lands out-of-bounds must be played from the point where the disk went out (one-stroke penalty).

Course courtesy: Do not throw until the players ahead are out of range.

Completion of hole: A disk that comes to rest in the hole (box or hoop) or strikes the designated hole (tree or pole) constitutes successful completion of that hole.

Objectives:

To understand the principles of
   stability and balance

To control the body weight in a variety
   of tumbling and stunt activities

To participate in "one-on-one"
   competition and accept the
   outcome

To play group games and cooperate
   with teammates

NASPE National Standards:

Introductory Activity: 1, 5
Fitness Activity: 1, 4, 5, 6
Lesson Focus: 1, 2, 3, 5
Game: 1, 3

Equipment Required:

Music for Parachute Fitness
Parachute
Tumbling mats
15–20 foam balls (8") or playground
   balls
12–16 bowling pins

Instructional Activities	Teaching Hints

Introductory Activity — Personal Choice

Students select any type of activity they wish to use to warm up. They may use one they have previously learned in class, or they may create one of their own. Emphasis should be on a balanced approach that works all major muscle groups.

If desired, students can work with a partner and share ideas with each other for desired activities.

Fitness Development Activity — Parachute Fitness

1. Jog in circle with chute held in left hand. Reverse directions and hold with right hand.
2. Standing, raise the chute overhead, lower to waist, lower to toes, raise to waist, etc.
3. Slide to the right; return slide to the left.
4. Sit and perform curl-ups with a twist.
5. Skip.
6. Freeze, face the center, and stretch the chute tightly with bent arms. Hold for 8–12 seconds. Repeat.
7. Run in place, hold the chute at waist level, and hit the chute with lifted knees.
8. Sit with legs under the chute. Do a seat walk toward the center. Return to the perimeter. Repeat four to six times.
9. Place the chute on the ground. Jog away from the chute and return on signal. Repeat.
10. On sides with legs under the chute. Perform Side Flex and lift chute with legs.
11. Lie on back with legs under the chute. Shake the chute with the feet.
12. Hop to the center of the chute and return. Repeat.
13. Assume the push-up position with the legs aligned away from the center of the chute. Shake the chute with one arm while the other arm supports the body.
14. Sit with feet under the chute. Stretch by touching the toes with the chute. Relax with other stretches while sitting.

Tape alternating segments (25–30 seconds in length) of silence and music to signal duration of exercise. Music segments indicate aerobic activity with the parachute, while intervals of silence announce using the chute to enhance flexibility and strength development.

Space youngsters evenly around the chute.

Use different grips (palms up, down, mixed).

All movements should be done under control. Some of the faster and stronger students will have to moderate their performance.

Lesson Focus — Gymnastics Skills (4)

Five groups of activities in this lesson ensure that youngsters receive a variety of experiences. Pick a few activities from each group and teach them alternately. For example, teach an individual stunt or two, then a tumbling skill or inverted balance, followed by a balance stunt, etc. Give equal time to each group of activities.

Review activities taught in previous gymnastics lesson plans.

   a. Tumbling and Inverted Balances

   b. Balance Stunts

   c. Individual Stunts

   d. Partner and Group Stunts

   e. Combatives

Pin Knockout

Supplies: Many 8" foam balls or playground balls, 12 bowling pins

Skills: Rolling, dodging

Divide the team in half and give each team many playground balls and 6 bowling pins. A court with a centerline is needed. The size of the court depends on the number of children in the game. The object of the game is to knock down all of the opponents' bowling pins. The balls are used for rolling at the opposing team's pins. Each team stays in its half of the court.

A player is eliminated if any of the following occurs:

1. He is touched by any ball at any time, regardless of the situation (other than picking up a ball).

2. She steps over the centerline to roll or retrieve a ball. (Any opposing team member hit as a result of such a roll is not eliminated.)

3. He attempts to block a rolling ball with a ball in his hands and the rolling ball touches him in any manner.

A foul is called when a player holds a ball longer than 10 seconds without rolling at the opposing team. The ball must be immediately given to the opposing team. The bowling pins are placed anywhere in the team's area. Players may guard the pins, but must not touch them. When a pin is down, even if a member of the defending team knocked it over unintentionally, it is removed immediately from the game. The game is over when all pins on one side have been knocked down.

Dot Bridge (Cooperative Activity)

Formation: Groups of 5–6

Supplies: One rubber dot per player plus one additional dot

The challenge is for students to get from one side of the river (teaching area) to the other, but they can't touch the water (the floor). The only tools they have are their floating dots. If anyone touches the water, the entire team must start over

Teaching Tip: To add difficulty, place hazards (hoops, cones, etc.) that the students must avoid throughout the river to prevent the group from moving straight across the river. Also, add the rule that if at any time a dot is not being touched, it sinks and can no longer be used.

DPE Curriculum Guide – Lesson Plans
Softball Skills and Lead-up Activities (1)
Level III – Week 35

Objectives:
To throw and catch a softball
To hit a softball
To be able to field softball grounders
and fly balls
To know the basic rules of softball
To understand the roles of different
positions in softball

NASPE National Standards:
Introductory Activity: 1, 5
Fitness Activity: 1, 2, 4, 5
Lesson Focus: 2, 3, 5
Game: 2, 3, 5

Equipment Required:
Music, cones, and signs for Squad
Leader Exercises
Station 1: 2 batting tees, 4 balls, and 2
bats
Station 2: 4 balls
Station 3: 4 bases and 4 balls
Station 4: 4 balls and 2 bats

Instructional Activities	Teaching Hints

Introductory Activity — Personal Choice

Students select any type of activity they wish to use to warm up. They may use one they have previously learned in class, or they may create one of their own. Emphasis should be on a balanced approach that works all major muscle groups.

If desired, students can work with a partner and share ideas with each other for desired activities.

Fitness Development Activity — Squad Leader Exercises with Task Cards

Suggested exercises to be placed on task cards:

Sitting Stretch
Push-Up challenges
Body Circles
Jumping Jack variations
Crab Kick combinations
Abdominal challenges
Treadmills
Toe Touchers
Leg Extensions

The class is divided into groups of 4–5 students. Each group is given a task card that lists 8–10 exercises. One of the group members is leader and leads the group through an exercise. Each time an exercise is completed, the card is passed to a new leader.

Use alternating intervals of music to signal exercising (30 seconds) with silence (5–8 seconds) to indicate passing the card.

Lesson Focus — Softball Skills (1)

Skills
Practice the following skills:
1. Overhand Throw

In preparation for throwing, the child secures a firm grip on the ball, raises the throwing arm to shoulder height, and brings the elbow back. For the overhand throw, the hand with the ball is then brought back over the head so that it is well behind the shoulder at about shoulder height. The left side of the body is turned in the direction of the throw, and the left arm is raised in front of the body. The weight is on the back (right) foot, with the left foot advanced and the toe touching the ground. The arm comes forward with the elbow leading, and the ball is thrown with a downward snap of the wrist. The body weight is brought forward into the throw, shifting to the front foot. There should be good follow-through so that the palm of the throwing hand faces the ground at completion of the throw. The eyes should be on the target throughout, and the arm should be kept free and loose during the throw.

2. Pitching

Official rules call for the pitcher to have both feet in contact with the pitcher's rubber, but few elementary schools possess a rubber. Instead, the pitcher can stand with both feet about even, facing the batter, and holding the ball momentarily in front with both hands. The pitcher takes one hand from the ball, extends the right arm forward, and brings it back in a pendulum swing, positioning the ball well behind the body. A normal stride taken toward the batter with the left foot begins the throwing sequence for a right-handed pitcher. The arm is brought forward with an underhanded slingshot motion, and the weight is transferred to the leading foot. Only one step is permitted.

Whiffle balls and plastic bats are a much safer alternative for children this age. It is easier for them to swing plastic bats and the fear of getting hit by a softball will not be an issue.

Instructional cues for **throwing** are:
1. Place the throwing arm side of the body away from the target.
2. Step toward the target with the foot opposite the throwing hand.
3. Bend and raise the arm at the elbow. Lead with the elbow.

Instructional cues for **pitching** are:
1. Face the plate.
2. Keep your eyes on the target.
3. Swing the pitching arm backward and step forward.

3. Fielding Grounders

To field a grounder, the fielder should move as quickly as possible into the path of the ball and then move forward and play the ball on a good hop. The eyes must be kept on the ball, following it into the hands or glove. The feet are spread, the seat is kept down, and the hands are carried low and in front. The weight is on the balls of the feet or on the toes, and the knees are bent to lower the body. As the ball is caught, the fielder straightens up, takes a step in the direction of the throw, and makes the throw.

Instructional cues for **fielding** are:
1. Move into line with the path of the ball.
2. Give when catching the ball.
3. Use the glove to absorb the force of the ball.
4. For grounders, keep the head down and watch the ball move into the glove.

4. Batting (Right-Handed)

The batter stands with the left side of the body toward the pitcher. The feet are spread and the weight is on both feet. The body should be facing the plate. The bat is held with the trademark up, and the left hand grasps the bat lower than the right. The bat is held over the right shoulder, pointing both back and up. The elbows are away from the body. The swing begins with a hip roll and a short step forward in the direction of the pitcher. The bat is then swung level with the ground at the height of the pitch. The eyes are kept on the ball until it is hit. After the hit, there must be good follow-through.

Instructional cues for **batting** are:
1. Keep the hands together.
2. Swing the bat horizontally.
3. Swing through the ball.
4. Hold the bat off the shoulder.
5. Watch the ball hit the bat.

Station (Small-Group) Instruction

The teacher should instruct at a different station each day. Start at the station that demands the most instruction. Set up a system of rotation that assures all stations will be covered during the unit.

Station 1—Batting

Use a batting tee. For each station, two tees are needed, with a bat and at least two balls for each tee. Three to five children are assigned to each tee. There should be a batter, a catcher to handle incoming balls, and fielders. When only three children are in a unit, the catcher should be eliminated. Each batter is allowed a certain number of swings before rotating to the field. The catcher becomes the next batter, and a fielder moves up to catcher.

Hitters should avoid the following: lifting the front foot high off the ground, stepping back with the rear foot, or bending forward.

Station 2—Throwing and Catching

Work with a partner and practice some of the following throwing drills:
   a. Throw back and forth, practicing various throws.
   b. Gradually increase the distance of the throws.
   c. Focus on accuracy; if the throws are not caught, reduce the distance between players.

Stand about 7–10 yd apart when practicing throwing.

For youngsters who are afraid of the ball, use a whiffle ball.

Station 3—Pitching

Students find a partner and pitch and catch with each other. Set out a number of bases at each station so pitchers can pitch and catch using a base as a target (home plate).
   a. Pitch to another player over a plate.
   b. Call balls and strikes. One player is the pitcher, the second is the catcher, and the third is the umpire. A fourth player can be a stationary batter to provide a more realistic pitching target.

Face the batter, both feet on the rubber and the ball held in front with both hands. One step is allowed, and the ball must be delivered on that step.
Ball must be pitched underhanded.
No motion or fake toward the plate can be made without delivering the ball.

Station 4—Fielding

Players find a partner and practice throwing grounders and fly balls to each other.
   a. One partner throws a grounder or fly ball, the other partner fields the ball and throws it back to the other. Reverse roles.
   b. Do the same thing above except use a bat to hit the balls.

Show form for high and low catch.

Move into the path of the ball.

Softball Lead-up Activities

Scrub (Work-up)

Supplies: A softball, a bat
Skills: Most softball skills

The predominant feature of Scrub is the rotation of the players. The game is played with regular softball rules, with individuals more or less playing for themselves. There are at least two batters, generally three. A catcher, pitcher, and first-base player are essential. The remaining players assume the other positions. A batter who is out goes to a position in right field. All other players move up one position, with the catcher becoming the batter. The first-base player becomes the pitcher, the pitcher moves to catcher, and all others move up one place.

DPE Curriculum Guide – Lesson Plans
Softball Skills and Lead-up Activities (2)
Level III – Week 36

Objectives:
To throw and catch a softball
To hit a softball
To be able to field softball grounders
    and fly balls
To know the basic rules of softball
To understand the roles of different
    positions in softball

NASPE National Standards:
Introductory Activity: 1, 5
Fitness Activity: 1, 2, 4, 5, 6
Lesson Focus: 2, 3, 5
Game: 2, 3, 5

Equipment Required:
Music tape for Partner Fitness
    Challenges
Station 1: 1 bat and 4 balls
Station 2: 3 home plates and 3 balls
Station 3: 4 bases, balls, and bats
Station 4: 1 bat and 4 balls

Instructional Activities	Teaching Hints

Introductory Activity — Personal Choice

Students select any type of activity they wish to use to warm up. They may use one they have previously learned in class, or they may create one of their own. Emphasis should be on a balanced approach that works all major muscle groups.

If desired, students can work with a partner and share ideas for new activities.

Fitness Development Activity — Partner Fitness Challenges

Try to pair students with someone of similar ability and size. Emphasis should be placed on continuous movement and activity. The following are examples of partner activities that are both challenging and enjoyable.

Circle Five
Partner 1 stands stationary in the center of the circle with one palm up. Partner 2 runs in a circle around 1 and "gives a high five" when passing the upturned palm. The size of the circle is gradually increased. Reverse roles on signal.

Foot Tag
Partners stand facing each other. On signal, they try to touch each other's toes with their feet. Emphasize the importance of a touch, as contrasted to a stamp or kick.

Knee Tag
Partners stand facing each other. On signal, they try to tag the other person's knees. Each time a tag is made, a point is scored. Play for a designated amount of time.

Mini Merry-Go-Round
Partners face each other with the feet nearly touching and the hands grasped in a double wrist grip. Partners slowly lean backward while keeping the feet in place until the arms are straight. Spin around as quickly as possible. It is important that partners be of similar size.

Around and Under
One partner stands with the feet spread shoulder width apart and hands held overhead. The other partner goes between the standing partner's legs, stands up, and slaps the partner's hands. Continue the pattern for a designated time.

Partner challenges are fitness activities that can be used with intermediate-grade youngsters. They can be used to develop aerobic endurance, strength, and flexibility. Another advantage of partner challenges is that they can be performed indoors as a rainy-day activity.

Use 30-second intervals of music and silence to signal starting and stopping the partner fitness challenges. During the music interval, students perform the fitness challenges. During the silent intervals, they perform flexibility and strength development activities.

Lesson Focus — Softball Skills (2)

Skills
Review skills learned last week:
1. Overhand Throw
2. Pitching
3. Fielding Grounders
4. Batting
Introduce new skills:
Fielding Fly Balls
    There are two ways to catch a fly ball. For a low ball, the fielder keeps the fingers together and forms a basket with the hands. For a higher ball, the thumbs are together, and the ball is caught in front of the chin. The fielder should give with the hands, and care must be taken with a spinning ball to squeeze the hands sufficiently to stop the spinning. The eye is on the ball continually until it hits the glove or hands. The knees are flexed slightly when receiving and aid in giving

Whiffle balls and plastic bats are a much safer alternative for children this age. It is easier for them to swing plastic bats and the fear of getting hit by a softball will not be an issue.

Sure Stop for Outfield Balls
    To keep the ball from going through the hands and thus allowing extra bases, the outfielder can use the body as a barrier. The fielder turns half right and lowers one knee to the ground at the

when the ball is caught.

Station (Small-Group) Instruction
The teacher should instruct at a different station each day. Start at the station that demands the most instruction. Set up a system of rotation that assures all stations will be covered during the unit.

Station 1—Outfield Practice
One player in the group hits fly balls. The others field and practice using the sure stop when the ball is not caught on the fly. Rotate batters after eight fly balls have been hit.

Station 2—Pitching and Umpiring
Students find a partner and pitch and catch with each other. Set out a number of bases at each station so pitchers can pitch and catch using a base as a target (home plate).
1. Pitch to another player over a plate.
2. Call balls and strikes. One player is the pitcher, the second is the catcher, and the third is the umpire. A fourth player can be a stationary batter to provide a more realistic pitching target.

Station 3—Infield Practice
1. Throw around the bases clockwise and counterclockwise.
2. Throw grounders to infielders and make the play at first. After each play, throw around the infield.
3. If students have enough skill, bat the ball to the infielders in turn.

Station 4—Batting Practice
Each batter takes six swings and then rotates to the field. Catcher becomes batter and pitcher moves up to catcher.

point toward which the ball is traveling. The hands catch the rolling ball, but if it is missed, the body will generally stop the ball.

If youngsters are not able to hit the ball, they can catch and throw it to the fielders.

When umpiring, strikes are called by raising the right hand and balls require raising the left hand.

While having infield practice, one person at the station can run the bases and try to complete a circuit around the bases before the ball does.

Have more than one ball at the stations so the pitching can continue when a ball is hit or not caught.

Softball Lead-up Activities

Scrub (Work-up)
See the Lesson Plan, Softball Skills (Week 35) for a complete game description.

Slow-Pitch Softball
Supplies: A softball, a bat
Skills: Most softball skills

The major difference between regular softball and Slow-Pitch Softball is in the pitching, but there are other modifications to the game as well. With slower pitching, there is more hitting and thus more action on the bases and in the field. Outfielders are an important part of the game because many long drives are hit. Rule changes from the game of official softball are as follows.
1. The pitch must be a slow pitch. Any other pitch is illegal and is called a ball. The pitch must be slow, with an arc of 1 ft. It must not rise over 10 ft from the ground, however. Its legality depends on the umpire's call.
2. There are 10 players instead of 9. The extra one, called the roving fielder, plays in the outfield and handles line drives hit just over the infielders.
3. The batter must take a full swing at the ball and is out if he chops at the ball or bunts.
4. If a pitched ball hits the batter, she is not entitled to first base. The pitch is merely called a ball. Otherwise, balls and strikes are called as in softball.
5. The runner must hold base until the pitch has reached or passed home plate. No stealing is permitted.

Three-Team Softball
Supplies: A mask, a ball, a bat
Skills: All softball skills

Three-Team Softball works well with 12 players, a number considered too few to divide into two effective fielding teams. The players are instead divided into three teams. The rules of softball apply, with the following exceptions.
1. One team is at bat, one team covers the infield (including the catcher), and the third team provides the outfielders and the pitcher.
2. The team at bat must bat in a definite order. This means that because of the small number of batters on each side, instances can occur when the person due to bat is on base. To take a turn at bat, a player not on base must replace the runner.
3. After three outs, the teams rotate, with the outfield moving to the infield, the infield taking a turn at bat, and the batters going to the outfield.
4. An inning is over when all three teams have batted.
5. The pitcher should be limited to pitching one inning only. A player may repeat as pitcher only after all members of that team have had a chance to pitch.

DPE Curriculum Guide – Lesson Plans
Cross-Country Running and Walking Skills
Level III – Alternate Lesson Plan 1

Objectives:
To participate in cross-country activities
  as a participating team member
To show respect for peers regardless of
  individual differences in ability
To develop a personalized warm-up
  routine that enhances flexibility

NASPE National Standards:
Introductory Activity: 4, 5, 6
Fitness Activity: 4, 5, 6
Lesson Focus: 4, 5, 6
Game: 2, 3, 5, 6

Equipment Required:
Finish markers and team score cards
8–12 cones for cross-country "funnel"
Recreational and individual equipment
  as needed

Instructional Activities	Teaching Hints

Introductory Activity and Fitness Development Activity — Stretching

Combine the introductory and fitness activities during the track and field unit. This workout helps students learn to stretch and warm up for cross-country running. Warm-up before stretching.

Standing Hip Bend	30 seconds
Sitting Stretch	30 seconds
Partner Rowing	60 seconds
Bear Hug (do each leg)	40 seconds
Side Flex (do each leg)	40 seconds
Trunk Twister	30 seconds

Teaching Hints:
Keep stretching activities smooth and sustained. Stretches can be held for 6–10 seconds.

Allow students to lead each other in their warm-up routine. A goal should be for students to develop a personal warm-up routine they can use when they are away from school.

Youngsters should work independently during their warm-up. If they desire, they can work with a friend.

Lesson Focus — Cross-Country Running/Walking

Cross-country courses can be marked with a chalk line and cones so that runners follow the course as outlined. Checkpoints every 220 yd offer runners a convenient reference point so that they can gauge accurately how far they have run. Three courses of differing lengths and difficulty can be laid out. The beginning course can be 1 mile in length, the intermediate 1.25 miles, and the advanced 1.5 miles. Including sandy or hilly areas in the course increases the challenge. When students run cross-country, they can select the course that challenges them appropriately. **It is entirely appropriate to select a fast-paced walk if students judge themselves unable to run the entire distance.**

1. Discuss the sport of cross-country running and how it is scored.
    a. Seven members to a team.
    b. Lowest score wins.
    c. Total points for each team based on places finished in race.

2. Divide the class into equal teams by recording times for all members of the class regardless of whether they walked or ran. Create teams of equal ability by dividing students so that the total elapsed time (for all team members) is equal.

3. Depending on the age of youngsters, as well as their ability, teams can run different length courses. The following lengths are suggested:
    a. Beginning—1 mile
    b. Intermediate—1.25 miles
    c. Advanced—1.5 miles

4. Explain how to "warm down" after each course run.

Teaching Hints:
The attractiveness of cross-country competition lies in the fact that it is a team activity and all members of the team are crucial to its success. Youngsters should learn how to score a meet. Probably the easiest way to keep team scores is to assign seven (depending on class size) members to each team. Points are assigned to finishers based on their placement in the race. For example, the first-place runner receives 1 point, the tenth-place runner 10 points, and so on. The points for all team members are totaled, and the team with the lowest score is declared the winner.

A funnel made of cones at the finish line prevents tying times. As runners go through the funnel, the meet judges and helpers can hand each one a marker with the place of finish on it. This simplifies scoring at the end of the meet. Each team captain can total the scores and report the result.

Game Activity — Individual or Recreational Activities

When youngsters finish cross-country running, allow them the opportunity to participate in a choice of individual or recreational activities.

Objectives:
To understand the difference in racquet strokes between sports
To compete in the game of volley tennis

NASPE National Standards:
Introductory Activity:
Fitness Activity:
Lesson Focus: 2, 3, 5
Game: 2, 3, 5

Equipment Required:
One racquet and ball for each student
Volleyballs for volley tennis

Instructional Activities	Teaching Hints

Introductory Activity
Use the introductory activity from the lesson that was replaced.

Fitness Development Activity
Use the fitness activity from the lesson that was replaced.

Lesson Focus — Racquet Sport Skills

1. Discuss the proper method of holding the racquet using the forehand and backhand grips.
2. Air dribble the ball and try the following challenges:
   a. How many bounces without touching the floor?
   b. Bounce it as high as possible. Perform a heel click (or other stunt) while the ball is in the air.
   c. Kneel, sit, and lie down while air dribbling.
3. Dribble the ball on the floor with the racquet:
   a. Move in different directions—forward, backward, sideways.
   b. Move using different steps, such as skip, grapevine, and gallop.
   c. Move to a kneeling, sitting, and supine position while continuing the dribble. Return to a standing position.
4. Bounce the ball off the racquet and "catch" it with the racquet.
5. Place the ball on the floor:
   a. Scoop it up with the racquet.
   b. Roll the ball and scoop it up with the racquet.
   c. Start dribbling the ball without touching it with the hands.
6. Self-toss and hit to a fence, net, or tumbling mat. This drill should be used to practice the forehand and backhand. The ball should be dropped so it bounces to waist level.
7. Partner activities:
   a. One partner feeds the ball to the other, who returns the ball with a forehand or backhand stroke.
   b. Stroke the ball back and forth to each other with one or more bounces between contact.
   c. Self-toss and hit. Drop the ball and stroke it to a partner 20–30 ft away. Partner does the same thing to return the ball.
   d. Partner throw and hit. One partner throws the ball to the other, who returns the ball by stroking it with the racquet.
   e. Wall volley: If a wall is available, partners can volley against it.
8. Serving:
   a. Teach tennis serve without a racquet. Use a yarn ball and practice hitting it with the open hand. The serve is similar to the overhand throwing motion. The toss is a skill that will need to be mastered prior to learning the striking motion.
   b. Teach the racquetball serve in similar fashion. The hard, driving serve is done using a side-underhand throwing motion. The striking hand should be raised on the backswing. A small foam (Nerf) ball that bounces should be dropped to the floor and struck on the rebound.

The focus of this unit should be to give youngsters an introduction to tennis, badminton and racquetball. Give students two or three activities to practice so you have time to move and help youngsters. Alternate activities from each of the categories so students receive a variety of skills to practice.

Use instructional cues to improve technique:
a. Hold the wrist reasonably stiff.
b. Use a smooth arm action.
c. Stroke through the ball and follow through.
d. Watch the ball strike the paddle.

Proper grip must be emphasized, and seeing that children maintain this is a constant battle. The easiest method to teach the proper grip is to have the student hold the paddle perpendicular to the floor and shake hands with it. Practice in racquet work should move from individual to partner work as quickly as is feasible, because partner work is basic to racquet sports.

For the forehand stroke, the body is turned sideways; for a right-handed player, the left side points in the direction of the hit.

For the backhand stroke, the thumb is placed against the handle of the racquet for added support and force, and the body is turned sideways so the shoulder on the side of the racquet hand points in the direction of the stroke.

c. For a racquetball lob serve, the ball is bounced and hit with an underhand motion. The ball is hit high on the wall and bounces to the back wall.

d. The foam ball can be used for the badminton serve also. For this serve, the ball is dropped and hit with an underhand motion before it hits the floor.

e. Depending on facilities, racquets can be used after the basic motion has been learned.

During either type of stroke, a step is made with the foot that is forward with respect to the direction of the stroke.

Game Activity

Volley Tennis

Supplies: A volleyball

Skills: Most volleyball and tennis skills

The game can be played as a combination of volleyball and tennis. The net is put on the ground, as in tennis, and the ball is put into play with a serve. It may bounce once or can be passed directly to a teammate. The ball must be hit three times before going over the net. Spiking is common because of the low net. A point is scored when it cannot be returned over the net to the opposing team.

One-Wall Handball and Racquetball

Supplies: Racquetballs (or tennis balls) and racquets

Skills: Racquet skills

Two players find a wall and volley the ball back and forth off the wall. If desired, let players develop rules for the style of serve and out of bounds rules. The basic rule is that the ball can only bounce once on its return from the wall. When a player returns the ball to the wall, it cannot touch the floor before it hits the wall. Any of these rules can be modified by agreement of the players.

Objectives:
To understand the aerobic benefits of
rope jumping
To recognize that learning any skill
takes repetition and refinement

NASPE National Standards:
Introductory Activity:
Fitness Activity:
Lesson Focus: 1, 2, 3, 4, 5
Game: 1, 3, 5

Equipment Required:
One individual jump rope for each
student
Base and volleyball for game

Instructional Activities	Teaching Hints

Introductory Activity
Use the introductory activity from the lesson that was replaced.

Fitness Development Activity
Use the fitness activity from the lesson that was replaced.

Lesson Focus — Individual Rope-Jumping Skills

1. Introduce the two basic jump rhythms:
    a. Slow-time rhythm. In slow time rhythm, the performer jumps the rope and then takes a second jump while the rope is overhead. The jump while the rope is overhead is usually a small, light rebound jump. In slow time, the rope makes one full turn for each two jumps.
    b. Fast time rhythm. In fast time rhythm, the student jumps the rope with every jump. The rope makes one full turn for every jump.
2. Introduce some of the basic step variations. The basic steps can be done in slow or fast time.
    a. Side Swing. Swing the rope, held with both hands to one side of the body. Switch and swing the rope on the other side of the body.
    b. Double Side Swing and Jump. Swing the rope once on each side of the body. Follow the second swing with a jump over the rope. The sequence should be swing, swing, jump.
    c. Alternate-Foot Basic Step. In the Alternate-Foot Basic Step, as the rope passes under the feet, the weight is shifted alternately from one foot to the other, raising the non-support foot in a running position.
    d. Spread Legs Forward and Backward. For Spread Legs Forward and Backward, start in a stride position (as in the Rocker) with weight equally distributed on both feet. As the rope passes under the feet, jump into the air and reverse the position of the feet.
    e. Straddle Jump. Alternate a regular jump with a straddle jump. The straddle jump is performed with the feet spread to shoulder width.
    f. Cross Legs Sideward. In Cross Legs Sideward, as the rope passes under the feet, spread the legs in a straddle position (sideward) to take the rebound. As the rope passes under the feet on the next turn, jump into the air and cross the feet with the right foot forward. Then repeat with the left foot forward and continue this alternation.
    g. Toe-Touch Forward. To do the Toe-Touch Forward, swing the right foot forward as the rope passes under the feet and touch the right toes on the next count. Then alternate, landing on the right foot and touching the left toes forward.
    h. Toe-Touch Backward. The Toe-Touch Backward is similar to the Swing-Step Sideward, except that the toes of the free foot touch to the back at the end of the swing.
    i. Shuffle Step. The Shuffle Step involves pushing off with the right foot and sidestepping to the left as the rope passes under the feet. Land with the weight on the left foot and touch the right toes beside the left heel. Repeat the step in the opposite direction.

The length of the rope is dependent on the height of the jumper. It should be long enough so that the ends reach to the armpits or slightly higher when the child stands on its center. Grades 5 and 6 need a mixture of 7-, 8-, and 9-ft ropes. Ropes or handles can be color-coded for length.

Two types of ropes are available; the beaded (plastic segment) and the plastic (licorice) rope. The beaded ropes are heavier and seem easier to turn for beginning jumpers. The drawback to the beaded ropes is that they hurt when they hit another student. Also, if the segments are made round, the rope will roll easily on the floor and cause children to fall when they step on it. The plastic licorice ropes are lighter and give less wind resistance. For experienced jumpers more speed and control can be gained with this type of rope. An ideal situation would be to have a set of each type.

Posture is an important consideration in rope jumping. The body should be in good alignment, with the head up and the eyes looking straight ahead. The jump is made with the body in an erect position. A slight straightening of the knees provides the lift for the jump, which should be of minimal height (about 1 in.). The wrists supply the force to turn the rope, with the elbows kept close to the body and extended at a 90-degree angle. A pumping action and lifting of the arms is unnecessary. The landing should be made on the balls of the feet, with the knees bent slightly to cushion the shock.

3. Teach the Crossing Arms Step

Once the basic steps are mastered, crossing the arms while turning the rope provides an interesting variation. Crossing the arms during forward turning is easier than crossing behind the back during backward turning. During crossing, the hands exchange places. This means that for forward crossing, the elbows are close to each other. This is not possible during backward crossing. Crossing and uncrossing can be done at predetermined points after a stipulated number of turns. Crossing can be accomplished during any of the routines.

4. Teach Double Turning

The double turn of the rope is also interesting. The jumper does a few basic steps in preparation for the double turn. As the rope approaches the feet, the child gives an extremely hard flip of the rope from the wrists, jumps from 6 to 8 in. in height, and allows the rope to pass under the feet twice before landing. The jumper must bend forward at the waist somewhat, which increases the speed of the turn. A substantial challenge for advanced rope jumpers is to see how many consecutive double-turn jumps they can do.

5. Teach shifting from forward to backward jumping

To switch from forward to backward jumping without stopping the rope, any of the following techniques can be used.

    a. As the rope starts downward in forward jumping, rather than allowing it to pass under the feet, the performer swings both arms to the left (or right) and makes a half turn of the body in that direction (i.e., facing the rope). On the next downward swing, the jumper spreads the arms and starts turning in the opposite direction. This method also works for shifting from backward to forward jumping.

    b. When the rope is directly above the head, the performer extends both arms, causing the rope to hesitate momentarily, at the same time making a half-turn in either direction and continuing to skip with the rope turning in the opposite direction.

    c. From a crossed-arm position, as the rope is going above the performer's head, the jumper may uncross the arms and turn simultaneously. This starts the rope turning and the performer jumping in the opposite direction.

6. Teach Jumping with a Partner. One student turns and jumps the rope while her partner enters and jumps simultaneously. The following are some challenges partners can try:

    a. Run in and face partner, and both jump.

    b. Run in and turn back to partner, and both jump.

    c. Decide which steps are to be done; then run in and match steps.

    d. Repeat with the rope turning backward.

7. Teach side-by-side jumping. Partners clasp inside hands and turn the rope with outside hands.

    a. Face the same direction and turn the rope.

    b. Face opposite directions, clasp left hands, and turn the rope.

    c. Face opposite directions, clasp right hands, and turn the rope.

    d. Repeat routines with inside knees raised.

Usually, the feet, ankles, and legs are kept together, except when a specific step calls for a different position.

The rope should be held by the index finger and thumb on each side with the hands making a small circle. The elbows should be held near the sides to avoid making large arm circles with the rope.

Music can be added when jumpers have learned the first stages of jumping. Music provides a challenge for continued jumping.

To collect ropes at the completion of a rope-jumping activity, have two or three children act as monitors. They put both arms out to the front or to the side at shoulder level. The other children then drape the ropes over their arms. The monitors return the ropes to the correct storage area.

Instructional cues to use for improving jumping technique are:

a. Keep the arms at the side of the body while turning. (Many children lift the arms to shoulder level trying to move the rope overhead. This makes it impossible for the youngster to jump over the elevated rope.)

b. Turn the rope by making small circles with the wrists.

c. Jump on the balls of the feet.

d. Bend the knees slightly to absorb the force of the jump.

e. Make a small jump over the rope.

Partner jumping may require a slightly longer rope and partners of similar height.

Game Activity

Right Face, Left Face (Maze Tag)

Supplies: None

Skills: Running, dodging

Children stand in rows that are aligned both front to rear and side to side. Two runners and two chasers are chosen. Players all face the same way and join hands with the players on each side. The chasers try to tag the runners, who run between the rows with the restriction that they cannot break through or go under the arms. The teacher helps the runners by calling "Right face" or "Left face" at the proper time. On command, the children drop hands, face the new direction, and grasp hands with those who are then on each side, thus making new passages available. When the runner is caught or when children become tired, a new runner and chaser are chosen.

Variations:

    1. Directions (north, south, east, west) can be used instead of the facing commands.

    2. Streets and Alleys. The teacher calls, "Streets," and the children face in one direction. The call "Alleys" causes them to face at right angles.

3. The command "Air raid" can be given, and children drop to their knees and make themselves into small balls, tucking their heads and seats down. This allows unlimited movement by the taggers and runners.

One Base Tagball
Supplies: A base (or standard), a volleyball (8-in. foam ball for younger children)
Skills: Running, dodging, throwing

A home line is drawn at one end of the playing space. A base or standard is placed about 50 ft in front of the home line. Two teams are formed. One team is scattered around the fielding area, the boundaries of which are determined by the number of children. The other team is lined up in single file behind the home line. The object of the game is for the fielding team to tag the runners with the ball. Two runners at a time try to round the base and head back for the home line without being tagged. The game is continuous, meaning that as soon as a running team player is tagged or crosses the home line, another player starts immediately. The fielding team may run with the ball and pass it from player to player, trying to tag one of the runners. The running team scores a point each time a player runs successfully around the base and back to the home line.

At the start of the game, the running team has two players ready at the right side of the home line. The others on the team are in line, waiting for a turn. The teacher throws the ball anywhere in the field, and the first two runners start toward the base. They must run around the base from the right side. After all of the players have run, the teams exchange places. The team scoring the most points wins.

DPE Curriculum Guide – Lesson Plans
Fundamental Skills Using Climbing Ropes
Level III – Alternate Lesson Plan #4

Objectives:
To be able to recite safety rules for
rope climbing
To be able to hang on a climbing rope
for 5 seconds
To be able to hang, swing, or climb on
a climbing rope

NASPE National Standards:
Introductory Activity:
Fitness Activity:
Lesson Focus: 2, 3, 5
Game: 5, 6

Equipment Required:
Climbing Ropes
Tumbling mats placed under ropes
Benches or Jumping Boxes

Instructional Activities	Teaching Hints

Introductory Activity
Use the introductory activity from the lesson that was replaced.

Fitness Development Activity
Use the fitness activity from the lesson that was replaced.

Lesson Focus — Fundamental Skills using Climbing Ropes

Supported Pull-Ups
In supported Pull-Up activities, a part of the body remains in contact with the
floor.   The Pull-Up is hand-over-hand and the return is hand-under-hand.
1. Kneel directly under the rope. Pull up to the tiptoes and return to kneeling
position.
2. Start in a sitting position under the rope. Pull up; the legs are supported on the
heels. Return to sitting position.
3. Start in a standing position. Grasp the rope, rock back on the heels, and lower
the body to the floor. Keep a straight body. Return to standing position.

Hangs
In a hang, the body is pulled up in one motion and held up for a length of time (5,
10, or 20 seconds). Progression is important.
1. From a seated position, reach up as high as possible and pull the body from the
floor, except for the heels. Hold.
2. Same as the previous stunt but pull the body completely free of the floor. Hold.
3. From a standing position, jump up, grasp the rope, and hang. This should be a
Bent-Arm Hang with the hands about even with the mouth. Hold.
4. Repeat the previous stunt, but add leg movements—one or both knees up,
bicycling movement, Half Lever (one or both legs up, parallel to the floor), Full
Lever (feet up to the face).

Pull-Ups
In the Pull-Up, the body is raised and lowered repeatedly. The initial challenge
should be to accomplish one Pull-Up in the defined position. The number of
repetitions should be increased with care. All of the activities described for hangs
are adaptable to Pull-Ups. The chin should touch the hands on each Pull-Up.

Swinging and Jumping
For swinging and jumping, a bench, box, or stool can serve as a takeoff point. To
take off, the child reaches high and jumps to a bent-arm position. Landing should
be with bent knees.
1. Swing and jump. Add half turns and full turns.
2. Swing and return to the perch. Add single- and double-knee bends.
3. Jump for distance, over a high-jump bar or through a hoop.
4. Swing and pick up a bowling pin and return to the perch.
5. Carry objects (e.g., beanbags, balls, deck tennis rings). A partner, standing to

1. Mats should be placed under all ropes.

2. The hand-over-hand method should
be used for climbing and the hand-
under-hand method for descending.

3. Caution the children not to slide;
sliding can cause rope burns on the
hands and legs.

4. A climber who becomes tired should
stop and rest. Proper rest stops should be
taught as part of the climbing procedure.

5. Children also should be taught to
leave enough margin for a safe descent.
No children should go higher than their
strength allows.

6. Spotters should be used initially for
activities in which the body is inverted.

7. Rosin in powdered form and
magnesium chalk aid in gripping. It is
particularly important that they be used
when the rope becomes slippery.

8. Children swinging on the ropes
should be instructed to make sure that
other children are out of the way.

9. Marks to limit the climb can be put
on the rope with adhesive tape. A height
of 8–10 ft above the floor is reasonable
until a child demonstrates proficiency.

the side away from the takeoff bench, can put articles to be carried back on the takeoff perch by placing each article between the knees or feet.

6. Not using a takeoff device, run toward a swinging rope, grasp it, and gain momentum for swinging.

10. If the ceiling is higher than 15 or 16 ft, a bright piece of tape should be wrapped around the rope to limit climbing height.

Climbing the Rope

1. *Scissors Grip.* For the Scissors Grip, approach the rope and reach as high as possible, standing with the right leg forward of the left. Raise the back leg, bend at the knee, and place the rope inside the knee and outside the foot. Cross the forward leg over the back leg, and straighten the legs with the toes pointed down. This should give a secure hold. To climb using the Scissors Grip, raise the knees up close to the chest, the rope sliding between them, while supporting the body with the hand grip. Lock the rope between the legs and climb up, using the hand-over-hand method and stretching as high as the hands can reach. Bring the knees up to the chest and repeat the process.

2. *Leg-Around Rest.* Wrap the left leg completely around the rope, keeping the rope between the thighs. The bottom of the rope then crosses over the instep of the left foot from the outside. The right foot stands on the rope as it crosses over the instep, providing pressure to prevent slippage. To provide additional pressure, release the hands and wrap the arms around the rope, leaning away from the rope at the same time. To climb using the Leg-Around Rest, proceed as in climbing with the Scissors Grip, but loosen the grip each time and re-grip higher.

Descending the Rope

There are four methods to descend the rope. The only differences are in the use of the leg locks, as the hand-under-hand is used for all descents.

1. *Scissors Grip.* From an extended scissors grip position, lock the legs and lower the body with the hands until the knees are against the chest. Hold with the hands, and lower the legs to a new position.

2. *Leg-Around Rest.* From the leg-around rest position, lower the body until the knees are against the chest. Lift the top foot, and let the feet slide to a lower position. Secure with the top foot and repeat.

3. *Instep Squeeze.* Squeeze the rope between the insteps by keeping the heels together. Lower the body while the rope slides against the instep.

4. *Stirrup Descent.* Place the rope on the outside of the right foot and carry it over the instep of the left. Pressure from the left foot holds the position. To get into position, let the rope trail along the right leg, reach under, and hook it with the left instep. When the pressure from the left leg is reduced, the rope slides smoothly while the descent is made with the hands.

Stunts Using Two Ropes

Two ropes hanging close together are needed for the following activities.

Straight-Arm Hang. To do the Straight-Arm Hang, jump up, grasp one rope with each hand, and hang with the arms straight.

Bent-Arm Hang. Perform as for the Straight-Arm Hang, but bend the arms at the elbows.

Arm Hangs with Different Leg Positions

    a. Do single- and double-knee lifts.

    b. Do a Half Lever. Bring the legs up parallel to the floor and point the toes.

    c. Do a Full Lever. Bring the feet up to the face and keep the knees straight.

    d. Do a Bicycle. Pedal as on a bicycle.

Pull-Ups. The Pull-Up is the same as on a single rope, except that each hand grasps a rope.

Inverted Hangs.

    a. Hang with the feet wrapped around the ropes.

    b. Hang with the feet against the inside of the ropes.

    c. Hang with the toes pointed and the feet not touching the ropes

Skin the Cat. From a bent-arm position, kick the feet overhead and continue the roll until the feet touch the mat. Return to the starting position.

Moving Together (Cooperative Activity)
Formation: Groups of 4 students
Supplies: None

Groups of 4 students form teams on the sidelines of the teaching area. The objective is for the team to move to the other sideline with the following stipulations:

1. Six feet touching the floor and all team members touching an ankle.
2. Eight body parts (no heads) touching the ground at all times.
3. Half of the team at a high level and half the team at a low level.
4. Every foot touching one other foot.
5. Only four feet can touch the ground.
6. Four feet and one hand must be on the ground.
7. Move with the fewest number of feet as possible touching the floor.
8. Move with the most hands and fewest feet touching the floor.

Teaching Tips: Additional challenges can be made by providing the teams with different pieces of equipment to carry while attempting the challenges. To minimize competition provide each group with a list of challenges. Once they have completed one challenge, they choose their next challenge from the list. This provides continuous activity for all groups.

Who's Leading? (Cooperative Activity)
Formation: Entire class in a circle
Supplies: None

The entire class stands shoulder to shoulder in a circle. One student volunteers to go in the middle and cover her eyes. The teacher then selects a volunteer to lead the class in movements while remaining in the circle. This must be done quietly so the person in the middle does not know who the leader is. The teacher will need to provide the leader with examples of movements such as jogging or skipping in place, bicep curls, jumping jacks, etc. The leader will also be instructed to change activities every few seconds. The person in the middle then opens her eyes and watches the movements. She must stay in the middle but may scan the entire class in an effort to find the leader as he changes movements.

Teaching Tips: To add difficulty, encourage the leader to make small changes in movements. For example, start with normal jumping jacks and then move to skier jacks, and then to skiers with no arm movements and finally walking in place. Also, provide the guesser with the idea of watching one half of the circle. If the activity changes and they don't see anyone do it first, the leader is probably on the other half of the circle. Remind followers to not give the leader away by staring at her.

Appendix A: Equipment and Supplies for Physical Education

The following list identifies the equipment and supplies needed to teach a quality physical education program. The items are listed by priority in two categories—materials and supplies and capital outlay. Priority is based on cost, need, and versatility of the equipment. The first piece of equipment listed (playground balls) can be used to teach the most units making it the highest priority. The quantity of equipment is also listed to assure that the proper amount of equipment is ordered to facilitate a normal class size. Some of the equipment can be constructed (See Chapter 10 of *Dynamic Physical Education for Elementary School Children*, Seventeenth Edition) for specifications and construction tips.

The majority of listed equipment is available from **Gopher Sport, 220 24th Avenue NW, P.O. Box 998, Owatonna, MN 55060-0998, Phone: 1-800-533-0446 or www.gophersport.com**. The author has worked closely with this company in an attempt to assure that only quality equipment that is durable and reliable is shipped. Equipment is shipped quickly and is unconditionally guaranteed. If you are not satisfied with any Gopher purchase for any reason, at any time—contact Gopher and they will replace it, credit your account, or refund your money.

Priority	Material and Supplies	Quantity
1 (good)	8½" inflatable rubber playground balls	36
1 (better)	8" foam balls (can be substituted for playground balls)	36
1 (best)	8" polyurethane-coated medium bounce foam balls (a substitute for playground balls. They are much more durable and give a true bounce. They can be used for all types of sport activities.)	36
2	5" × 5" beanbags, assorted colors	72
3	Jump Ropes (plastic segments for beginners and speed ropes for experienced jumpers)	
	7 ft length	36
	8 ft length	36
	9 ft length	18
	10 ft length	12
	16 ft length (long-rope jumping)	12
4	Game Cones (12" bright orange vinyl)	20
5	Tambourine, single head double ring	1
6	Hoops (solid or segmented)	
	30" diameter	36
	36" diameter	36
7	Wands (36" length, ¾" diameter hardwood)	36
8	Junior Tennis Racquets	36
9	Coated Foam Tennis Balls	
10	Fleece Balls (3–4" diameter)	36
11	Floor Hockey Sticks and Pucks—36 of each	36
12	Whiffle Balls (use for throwing, hockey, softball, etc.)	36
13	Individual Mats (23" × 48" × ½")	36
14	Partner Tug-of-war Ropes (handles on both ends made with nylon webbing or garden hose and ¼" nylon rope)	18
15	Juggling Scarves	108
16	Beach Balls (18' to 20" diameter)	36
17	Soccer Balls (junior size or trainers)	18
18	Basketballs (junior size)	18
19	Footballs (junior size or foam rubber)	18
20	Volleyballs (lightweight trainer balls)	18
21	Softballs (whiffle or extra soft)	18
22	Softball Bats (plastic or aluminum)	3
23	Frisbees, 9" to 10" diameter	36
24	Tinikling poles and riding boards (2 per set)	9 sets
25	Magic Stretch Ropes	12
26	Cageball (24")	1
27	Pinnies (two colors—18 each)	36
28	Ball Bags (nylon see-through mesh)	12
29	Team Tug-of-War Rope (¾" × 50' nylon with sealed ends)	1
30	Scoops	36
31	Stopwatches (digital)	6
32	Batons (for track & field relays)	12

33	Scooter Boards, 12" with handles	18
34	Bowling Pins	24
35	Lummi Sticks	72

Priority	Capital Outlay Items	Quantity
1	Tumbling Mats (4' × 8' × 1⅜" thick; Velcro fasteners on all sides)	12
2	CD/Dual Cassette Tape Player	1
3	Parachute and Storage Bag (30' diameter)	1
4	Electric Ball Pump	1
5	Lockable Ball Carts	4
6	Balance-Beam/Benches (12' length)	6
7	Jumping Boxes (8" height)	6
8	Jumping Boxes (16" height)	6
9	Audiovisual Cart with Electrical Outlet (for tape player, etc.)	
10	Portable Game Standards (for volleyball nets, etc.)	4
11	25 lb Capacity Field Marker (for chalking lines)	1
12	Sit and Reach Box (measure flexibility)	4

Appendix B: Definitions of Academic Concepts

Academic Concept	Definition of Academic Concept	Academic Area
¼, ½, ¾, full turns	Turning the body or body parts a specified amount	Math
Accelerate/decelerate	Gradually move faster/slower	Language Arts
Action verbs	Words such as *skip, run, twist, leap, shake*	Language Arts
Addition	Finding the sum of two or more numbers combining a number of movements and actions	Math
Adjectives	A word that describes a noun or pronoun	Language Arts
Aerobic intensity	How hard the body is working to move such as brisk walking, jogging, and running	Science
Angles	Space formed by two lines such as right, 45 degrees, trajectory of release (throwing)	Math
Animal recognition	Identifying animals by name and movement, for example, bear walk, kangaroo jump, etc.	Science
Antonyms	Words that describe opposite movements	Language Arts
Area of a shape	Moving inside of and around the perimeter of a shape	Math
Balance	Maintaining a state of equilibrium while remaining stationary or moving	Science
Base of support	Generally, the placement of the feet to increase or decrease stability	Science
Beginning letter sounds	Used in games such as "ccrrrooowwwsss" in Crows and Cranes. Taught by identify letter sounds or making shapes with their body or a jump rope	Language Arts
Body part identification (anatomical terms)	Touching, leading with or moving a body part when asked. Identifying the body parts with the correct anatomical term	Science

Academic Concept	Definition of Academic Concept	Academic Area
Building sequences	Putting together a number of movements in proper sequence to perform a complex skill. Or, performing a number of movements in activities like rhythms.	Math
Categorization	Identifying how activities and movements are grouped by similar characteristics such as exercises and skills	Language Arts
Cause & effect	Explaining how one movement or force creates other movements. Understanding the effect of applying force to a piece of equipment.	Science
Center of an area	Knowing where the center of an area such as circle or rectangle is and being able to move there quickly	Math
Center of gravity	Estimating the point on one's body through which gravitational forces act. Knowing how lowering the center of gravity increases stability	Science
Choral response	Responding to questions verbally in a group setting	Music
Choral rhyming	Using chants in activities such as jump rope chants, simple games, or rhythmic activities	Language Arts
Circumference	Learning to move around the perimeter of a circle in clockwise or counterclockwise directions	Math
Coin value & recognition	Knowing the values of different coins and being able to add or subtract their values in a game setting	Math
Components of fitness	Knowing all the components of health related fitness (See Chapter 12 of *Dynamic Physical Education for Elementary School Children*)	Science
Contrasting terms	Similar to opposites; used to teach different movements such as move slowly—move quickly	Language Arts
Counting	Using counting sequences in activities such as jump rope chants	Math
Counting forward and backward	Used in many activities with an example being "Countdown"	Math
Counting steps (w/ pedometers)	Learning to use pedometers to count their steps. Also estimating the number of steps to complete an activity or cover a distance	Math
Cultural awareness	Understanding activities and customs of different cultures, for example, rhythmic activities	Social Studies

Academic Concept	Definition of Academic Concept	Academic Area
CW & CCW	Learning to move clockwise and counterclockwise in games and rhythmic activities	Science
Degrees 45°, 90°, 180°, 360°	Knowing the meaning of different degrees to stipulate a change of directions. Often used in Frisbee golf or orienteering.	Math
Diagonal	Slanting between opposite corners of an area	Math
Diameter	A straight line running from one side through the center of to the other side of a circle	Math
Directional cues	Specific words to help youngsters learn directions such as *forward*, *backward*, *left*, *right*, *north*, *south*	Geography
Directions (N/S/E/W)	Learning to identify the direction of movement in a variety of settings, i.e., gymnasium, field, or track	Geography
Dismounts	Getting off a piece of equipment such as balance beams or benches in a stipulated manner	Language Arts
Distance recognition	Estimating how far a projectile has been propelled or the distance between two points	Math
Division	Dividing into equal groups or splitting into smaller groups in games such as Chain Tag	Math
Dodging	Moving to avoid another person or projectile	Language Arts
Estimation	Estimate personal performance such as how fast can I run, how many times can I complete a task in a specified time	Math
Estimation of time	Estimating how long it will take to complete a task	Science
Flower recognition	Being able to identify different types of flowers in games such as Flowers and Wind	Science
Following a checklist	Used often in station teaching where a list of points to follow are listed on the station sign	Language Arts
Following a course or map	Learning to follow a map or sequence of directions to complete an activity such as Challenge Course or Orienteering	Geography
Fractions	Often used in directions such as a ½ turn	Math

Academic Concept	Definition of Academic Concept	Academic Area
Geometric shape recognition	Being able to recognize a number of shapers such as figure 8, rhombus, octagon, hexagon, circle, oval, spiral, star, semicircle	Math
Gravity (center of)	Understanding how the center of gravity impacts stability; often used in teaching stopping under control or moving on beams or benches	Science
Greater than & less than	Often used to teach students to form groups of "greater than ___ or less than___"	Math
Grouping	Used in many settings such as grouping students, like movements, skills, or equipment	Math
Health concepts	Teaching students a wide variety of health concepts such as relaxing, substance abuse, nutrition, and weight management	Science
Heartrate calculation	Learning to calculate heart rate using a 10-second count of pulse rate	Math
Height vs. distance	Understanding the relationship of leaping or jumping as high as possible versus jumping or leaping as far as possible	Math
High/medium/low	Being able to demonstrate movements that are performed at different levels	Language Arts
Horizontal & vertical	Moving in different planes and being able to identify such planes by name	Science
In front of/behind/beside	Moving in relationship to an object or another person	Language Arts
Intersecting lines	A set of two or more lines that have common points (intersections)	Math
Isometric exercises	Muscular contractions that are performed without movement	Science
Letter recognition	Being able to make or identify a variety of letters. Using the body or pieces of equipment to form different letter shapes	Language Arts
Level identification	Identifying the level that different movements are being performed	Math
Listening skills	Understanding the proper time to listen; being able to translate a verbal concept into a physical movement	Language Arts
Matching colors	Showing success in playing games that require color matching, such as Color Tag	Language Arts

Academic Concept	Definition of Academic Concept	Academic Area
Matching shapes	Being able to match or identify a shape	Math
Measurements (yards/feet/inches/mile)	Used in many lessons such as Track and Field	Math
Measuring time with a stopwatch	Used in cross country running and track and field	Math
Mental math problems	Used in many games and relays to identify players. For example, "all players with the number 2 + 5 are it."	Math
Midpoint	Finding the middle of the body, body part, area, or shape	Math
Missing numbers	Often used in introductory activities such as Magic Number Challenges. Students must identify the missing number in a sequence.	Math
Momentum	The motion of a projectile or person and its resistance to slowing down.	Science
Movement factors	Responding to movement factors such as high, low, zigzag, large, small, square, triangles, circles	Math
Multiplication	Adding a number to itself a certain number of times. Used in a variety of games and scoring	Math
Muscle identification	Know the basic names of large muscle groups in the body	Science
Number recognition	Being able to make or identify a variety of numbers. Using the body or pieces of equipment to form different numbers	Math
Number sequence	Performing numbers in different sequences, such as "perform 3 hops, 2 jumps, and 5 skips"	Math
Odds & evens	Used in games where odd or even numbered players are identified to move	Math
Offense and defense	Being able to explain when a person or team is on offense or defense	Language Arts
Opposites	See antonyms above	Language Arts
Opposition	Used in throwing skills; when throwing with the right hand, step forward with the left foot and vice versa	Science

Academic Concept	Definition of Academic Concept	Academic Area
Ordinal numbers	Numbers that identify order such as first and second, for example, used in squad leader warm-ups	Math
Over/under/around concepts	Moving in relationship to another student or students. Also used to learn to move in relationship to a piece of equipment or apparatus	Language Arts
Parallel lines	Two lines that never meet. Used in many games where there is a line of students lined up across from another line of students	Math
Patterning	Learning to perform a pattern of movements in a rhythmic manner, i.e., step-together-step-stamp!	Music
Percentages	A proportion of a larger set or group	Math
Perimeter	A boundary that encloses an area. Most often used to define an area they can move within	Math
Perpendicular lines	Lines that are at right angles to each other. Used to describe movement, such as "hang with your legs perpendicular to the climbing rope"	Math
Pivot	Keeping one foot fixed and moving around that foot such as a basketball pivot	Language Arts
Prediction	Guessing how many times or how far a physical movement can be performed, such as "how many times can you make the hoop spin?"	Science
Prime numbers	A number not divisible without a remainder	Math
Problem solving	Being able to solve a physical movement, i.e., "how many different ways can you move across the floor?"	Math
Quadrants	Usually used to divide the teaching area into 4 equal parts	Math
Radius	A straight line extending from the center of a circle to the edge of the circle	Math
Ratio	A proportional relationship between two different quantities. Often used when dividing the class or equipment into parts	Math
Reading instructional signs	Most often used in station teaching to explain tasks to be performed	Language Arts

Academic Concept	Definition of Academic Concept	Academic Area
Recognizing order of sequence	Often used in rhythms, skills, or fitness routines. Knowing in what order the activities should be performed	Math
Revolutions	Turning the body, body part, or piece of equipment a certain number of times	Science
Right & Left	Being able to identify right and left in relationship to oneself or others	Geography
Rotation	A turning motion related to projectiles or body movement. For example, ball rotation or rotating yourself around a piece of equipment. Also used in learning to rotate positions such as in volleyball	Math
Scoring	Knowing how to keep score in a variety of games	Math
Segments	Identifying different parts of a shape such as a circle or rectangle	Math
Sequencing patterns	Performing a series of similar movements. Often used in activities such as beanbags or juggling	Language Arts
Short/long side of a rectangle	Knowing which side of the rectangle is the long or short side	Math
Skip counting	Counting while skipping numbers, i.e., 2, 4, 6, 8 or 3, 6, 9, 12	Math
Slow & fast time	Most often used in rope jumping	Music
Small word recognition	Writing words with pieces of equipment such as jump ropes and being able to read the words of others	Language Arts
Sorting skills	Being able to separate equipment and skills by similarities such as red beanbags, yellow handled ropes	Language Arts
Spatial awareness	Being aware of movements that can be made in space	Science
Speed variations	Knowing all the words that identify speed, such as *fast*, *slow*, *accelerate*, and *decelerate*	Science
Steady beat	Learning to move in a rhythm that is even; often emphasized in European Running	Music

Academic Concept	Definition of Academic Concept	Academic Area
Steps per mile (w/ pedometer)	Being able to calculate how many steps equals a distance of one mile. (Stride length must be measured first)	Math
Subtraction	Deducting one number from another; often used to identify players by number such as all players with the number "6 minus 2."	Math
Syllables	A unit of spoken language; used in games such as Flowers and Wind	Language Arts
Synonyms	A word that means the same as another word	Language Arts
Target Heartrate	The pulse rate that needs to be reached to enter the "Training Zone"	Science
Time recognition	Knowing the time of day; for example, used in the game of Midnight	Science
Traffic Light Recognition	Knowing the colors of traffic lights and what they mean; can be used in game of Red Light–Green Light or to signal students to stop or move cautiously	Social Studies
Trajectory	The path a projectile makes through space; used to teach throwing for distance	Math
Tripod	A base of support using three body parts	Science
Unilateral movements	Movements performed on one side of the body only	Social Studies
Upper/lower	Understanding the relationship of upper and lower with relation to the body	Language Arts
Velocity/accuracy	Understanding how velocity often impacts the accuracy of a skill	Language Arts
Weather terminology	Understanding words that describe weather such as Thunderstorm, hurricane, or tornado. Used in games such as Aviator	Science
Wide/narrow	A relatively large distance (wide) between two points or relatively small distance (narrow) between two points. Most often used in base of support	Language Arts